MyWritingLab™ Online Course (access code required)
for *The Curious Writer, Fifth Edition* by Bruce Ballenger

MyWritingLab is an online homework, tutorial, and assessment program that provides engaging experiences for today's instructors and students.

Writing Help for Varying Skill Levels

For students who enter the course at widely varying skill levels, MyWritingLab provides unique, targeted remediation through personalized and adaptive instruction. Starting with a pre-assessment known as the Path Builder, MyWritingLab diagnoses students' strengths and weaknesses on prerequisite writing skills. The results of the pre-assessment inform each student's Learning Path, a personalized pathway for students to work on requisite skills through multimodal activities. In doing so, students feel supported and ready to succeed in class.

Respond to Student Writing with Targeted Feedback and Remediation

MyWritingLab unites instructor comments and feedback with targeted remediation via rich multimedia activities, allowing students to learn from and through their own writing.

- When giving feedback on student writing, instructors can add links to activities that address issues and strategies needed for review. Instructors may link to multimedia resources in Pearson Writer, which include curated content from Purdue OWL.
- In the Writing Assignments, students can use instructor-created peer review rubrics to evaluate and comment on other students' writing.
- Paper review by specialized tutors through Tutor Services is available, as is plagiarism detection through TurnItIn.

Learning Tools for Student Engagement

Learning Catalytics

Generate class discussion, guide lectures, and promote peer-to-peer learning with real-time analytics. MyLab and Mastering with eText now provides Learning Catalytics—an interactive student response tool that uses students' smartphones, tablets, or laptops to engage them in more sophisticated tasks and thinking.

MediaShare

MediaShare allows students to post multimodal assignments easily—whether they are audio, video, or visual compositions—for peer review and instructor feedback. In both face-to-face and online course settings, MediaShare saves instructors valuable time and enriches the student learning experience by enabling contextual feedback to be provided quickly and easily.

Direct Access to MyLab

Users can link from any Learning Management System (LMS) to Pearson's MyWritingLab. Access MyLab assignments, rosters, and resources, and synchronize MyLab grades with the LMS gradebook. New direct, single sign-on provides access to all the personalized learning MyLab resources that make studying more efficient and effective.

Proven Results

No matter how MyWritingLab is used, instructors have access to powerful gradebook reports. These reports provide visual analytics that give insight to course performance at the student, section, or even program level.

THE CURIOUS WRITER

WRITER

Fifth Edition

Bruce Ballenger

Boise State University

Boston   Columbus   Indianapolis   New York   San Francisco   Amsterdam
Cape Town   Dubai   London   Madrid   Milan   Munich   Paris   Montréal   Toronto   Delhi
Mexico City   São Paulo   Sydney   HongKong   Seoul   Singapore   Taipei   Tokyo

Vice President and Editor in Chief: Joseph Opiela
Program Manager: Eric Jorgensen
Senior Development Editor
  (Print Edition): Virginia L. Blanford
Senior Development Editor
  (Revel Edition): Marion B. Castellucci
Editorial Assistant: Emily Brower
Product Marketing Manager: Ali Arnold
Field Marketing Manager: Mark Robinson
Media Production Content Specialist:
  Laura Olsen

Media Producer: Marisa Massaro
Senior Media Producer: Tracy Cunningham
Project Manager: Rebecca Gilpin
Text Design, Project Coordination, and
  Electronic Page Makeup: Integra
Design Lead: Barbara Atkinson
Cover Designer: Jenny Willingham
Cover Illustrations: Infiniti
Senior Manufacturing Buyer: Roy L. Pickering, Jr.
Printer/Binder: RR Donnelley/Crawfordsville
Cover Printer: Lehigh-Phoenix Color/Hagerstown

Acknowledgments of third-party content appear on CR-1–CR-4, which constitute an extension of this copyright page.

PEARSON, ALWAYS LEARNING, and MYWRITINGLAB are exclusive trademarks owned by Pearson Education, Inc. or its affiliates in the United States and/or other countries.

Unless otherwise indicated herein, any third-party trademarks that may appear in this work are the property of their respective owners and any references to third-party trademarks, logos, or other trade dress are for demonstrative or descriptive purposes only. Such references are not intended to imply any sponsorship, endorsement, authorization, or promotion of Pearson's products by the owners of such marks, or any relationship between the owner and Pearson Education, Inc., or its affiliates, authors, licensees, or distributors.

Library of Congress Cataloging-in-Publication Data
Ballenger, Bruce P.
  The curious writer/Bruce Ballenger.
    pages cm
  Includes bibliographical references and index.
  ISBN 978-0-13-409002-3—ISBN 978-0-13-408038-3 (brief ed.)—ISBN 978-0-13-412070-6 (concise ed)
1. English language—Rhetoric—Handbooks, manuals, etc.   2. Interdisciplinary approach in education—Handbooks, manuals, etc.   3. Academic writing—Handbooks, manuals, etc.
I. Title.
  PE1408.B37 2017
  808'.042—dc23
                                                                        2015030685

2   16

Student Edition ISBN 13: 978-0-13-409002-3
Student Edition ISBN 10:   0-13-409002-0

A la Carte Edition ISBN 13: 978-0-13-412161-1
A la Carte Edition ISBN 10:   0-13-412161-9

PEARSON
www.pearsonhighered.com

Brief Contents

Part 1 THE SPIRIT OF INQUIRY   1

Chapter 1 **Writing as Inquiry   1**

Chapter 2 **Reading as Inquiry   36**

Part 2 INQUIRY PROJECTS   62

Chapter 3 **Writing a Personal Essay   62**

Chapter 4 **Writing a Profile   99**

Chapter 5 **Writing a Review   138**

Chapter 6 **Writing a Proposal   175**

Chapter 7 **Writing an Argument   211**

Chapter 8 **Writing an Analytical Essay   259**

Chapter 9 **Writing an Ethnographic Essay   298**

Part 3 INQUIRING DEEPER   341

Chapter 10 **Writing a Research Essay   341**

Chapter 11 **Research Techniques   382**

Chapter 12 **Using and Citing Sources   417**

Part 4 RE-INQUIRING   474

Chapter 13 **Re-Genre: Repurposing Your Writing for Multimedia Genres   474**

Chapter 14 **Revision Strategies   512**

APPENDIX A   The Writer's Workshop   552

APPENDIX B   The Writing Portfolio   562

APPENDIX C   The Annotated Bibliography   569

HANDBOOK   576

Index   I-1

v

Contents

Preface xxii

Acknowledgments xxx

Part 1 THE SPIRIT OF INQUIRY 1

Chapter 1 Writing as Inquiry 1

Motives for Writing 2

Beliefs About Writing and Writing Development 3

EXERCISE 1.1 This I Believe (and This I Don't) 3

ONE STUDENT'S RESPONSE Bernice's Journal 5

INQUIRING INTO THE DETAILS Journals 5

Unlearning Unhelpful Beliefs 6

The Beliefs of This Book 6

Allatonceness 6

Believing You Can Learn to Write Well 7

Habits of Mind 7

Starting with Questions, Not Answers 7

Making the Familiar Strange 8

Suspending Judgment 8

Being Willing to Write Badly 9

Searching for Surprise 9

EXERCISE 1.2 A Roomful of Details 10

ONE STUDENT'S RESPONSE Bernice's Journal 11

Writing Situations and Rhetorical Choices 12

A First Reflection on Your Writing Process 15

A Case Study 15

Thinking About Your Process 16

EXERCISE 1.3 Literacy Narrative Collage 16

EXERCISE 1.4 What Is Your Process? 17

Problem Solving in Your Writing Process 20

The Nature of the Writing Process 21

The Writing Process as Recursive and Flexible 22

A System for Using Writing to Think 22

INQUIRING INTO THE DETAILS Invention Strategies 23

EXERCISE 1.5 Two Kinds of Thinking 24

A Writing Process That Harnesses Two Currents of Thought 25

The Sea and the Mountain 26

Answering the *So What?* Question 27

A Writing Process Driven by Questions 28

A Strategy for Inquiry: Questioning, Generating, and Judging 30

EXERCISE 1.6 A Mini Inquiry Project: Cell Phone Culture 31

EXERCISE 1.7 Scenes of Writing 33

Using What You Have Learned 35

Chapter 2 Reading as Inquiry 36

Purposes for Academic Reading 37

EXERCISE 2.1 **Using the Four Purposes for Academic Reading** 39

Beliefs About Reading 40

EXERCISE 2.2 **A Reader's Memoir** 41

One Common Belief That Is an Obstacle 41

Reading Situations and Rhetorical Choices 42

Four Frames for Reading 43

Reading Scenarios 43

Scenario #1 43

Scenario #2 44

INQUIRING INTO THE DETAILS **Reading Perspectives** 45

EXERCISE 2.3 **Reading a Life** 45

A Process for Reading to Write 47

Questions for the Process of Reading to Write 47

What Do I Want to Know? 47

What Should I Read to Find Out? 48

What Do I Do with What I've Read? 48

Having a Dialogue with What You Read 49

INQUIRING INTO THE DETAILS **Reading the Visual** 50

EXERCISE 2.4 **Double-Entry Journaling with a Visual Text** 51

Techniques for Keeping a Double-Entry Journal 52

EXERCISE 2.5 **Reading Creatively, Reading Critically** 53

READING **Bruce Ballenger, "The Importance of Writing Badly"** 53

Alternatives to the Double-Entry Journal 56

Wrestling with Academic Discourse: Reading from the Outside In 57

Features of Academic Discourse 58

Using What You Have Learned 60

Part 2 INQUIRY PROJECTS 62

Chapter 3 Writing a Personal Essay 62

Writing About Experience and Observations 62

Motives for Writing a Personal Essay 64

The Personal Essay and Academic Writing 64

INQUIRING INTO THE DETAILS **The Power of Narrative Thinking** 65

Features of the Form 66

READINGS 69

PERSONAL ESSAY 1 **Laura Zazulak, "Every Morning for Five Years"** 69

Inquiring into the Essay 70

PERSONAL ESSAY 2 **Ginny Blanford, "The Dog That Made Us a Family"** 72

Inquiring into the Essay 73

SEEING THE FORM **Photo Essays** 74

THE WRITING PROCESS 75

Inquiry Project: **Writing a Personal Essay** 75

WRITING BEYOND THE
CLASSROOM   Essaying "This I
Believe"   76

What Are You Going to Write
About?   76

Opening Up   77

   Listing Prompts   78

   Fastwriting Prompts   78

   Visual Prompts   79

   Research Prompts   80

Narrowing Down   81

   What's Promising Material and
   What Isn't?   81

INQUIRING INTO THE DETAILS
Clustering or Mapping   81

   Questions About Purpose and
   Audience   82

Trying Out   82

   Questions for Reflection   83

Writing the Sketch   84

STUDENT SKETCH   Amanda
Stewart, "Earning a Sense of
Place"   85

Moving from Sketch to Draft   86

   Evaluating Your Own Sketch   86

   Reflecting on What You
   Learned   87

Developing   87

Drafting   88

   Methods of Development   88

   Using Evidence   89

INQUIRING INTO THE DETAILS   More
Than One Way to Tell a Story   89

Workshopping   90

   Questions for Readers   91

   Reflecting on the Workshop   91

Revising   91

Shaping   92

Polishing   93

STUDENT ESSAY   Seth Marlin,
"Smoke of Empire"   94

Evaluating the Essay   96

Using What You Have Learned   97

Chapter 4 Writing a Profile   99

Writing About People   99

Motives for Writing a Profile   100

The Profile and Academic Writing   101

Features of the Form   102

READINGS   104

PROFILE 1   Bruce Ballenger,
"Museum Missionary"   104

Inquiring into the Essay   106

PROFILE 2   Ian Frazier,
"Passengers"   107

Inquiring into the Essay   109

PROFILE 3   Amelia Pang, "The Life
of a Violin Prodigy from South
Bronx"   110

Inquiring into the Essay   113

SEEING THE FORM   "Sun Boy" by
William Soule   113

THE WRITING PROCESS   115

Inquiry Project: Writing a
Profile   115

Who Are You Going to Write
About?   116

Opening Up   116

   Listing Prompts   116

   Fastwriting Prompts   116

Visual Prompts   117
Research Prompts   117
ONE STUDENT'S RESPONSE   Bruce's Journal   118
Narrowing Down   118
What's Promising Material and What Isn't?   118
Questions About Audience and Purpose   119
Trying Out   119
Possible Frames   119
Questions for Reflection   120
Interviewing   120
Interview Approaches   120
Interview Techniques   120
WRITING BEYOND THE CLASSROOM   Digital Profiles   121
Making Contact   122
Conducting the Interview   123
INQUIRING INTO THE DETAILS   Recording Interviews   124
Listening and Watching   124
Flash Profile: Veterans History Projects   125
From Bullets to Bottles: The Two Wars of Dan Akee   126
Writing the Sketch   126
Moving from Sketch to Draft   127
Evaluating Your Sketch   127
Reflecting on What You've Learned   127
Developing   127
Research, Interviews, and Reinterviews   127
Establishing the Frame   128

Drafting   129
Methods of Development   129
Using Evidence   129
Workshopping   130
Reflecting on the Workshop   130
Revising   130
Shaping   131
Polishing   132
STUDENT ESSAY   Micaela Fisher, "Number 6 Orchard"   133
Evaluating the Essay   136
Using What You Have Learned   137

Chapter 5 Writing a Review   138

Writing That Evaluates   138
Motives for Writing a Review   139
The Review and Academic Writing   140
SEEING THE FORM   Choosing the Best Picture   140
Features of the Form   142

READINGS   144
FILM REVIEW   Roger Ebert, "A Christmas Story"   144
Inquiring into the Essay   147
REVIEW OF A METHOD   Carol E. Holstead, "The Benefits of No-Tech Note Taking"   148
Inquiring into the Essay   149
VIDEO GAME REVIEW   Seth Schiesel, "Grand Theft Auto Takes on New York"   151
Inquiring into the Essay   153

THE WRITING PROCESS   155

Inquiry Project: **Writing a Review Essay**   155

What Are You Going to Write About?   156

Opening Up   156

    Listing Prompts   156

    Fastwriting Prompts   156

    Visual Prompts   156

    Research Prompts   157

Narrowing Down   157

    What's Promising Material and What Isn't?   157

    Questions About Audience and Purpose   158

Trying Out   158

    Focusing the Category   158

    Fastwriting   159

    Web Research   160

    Interviews   160

    Experiencing Your Subject   160

Thinking About Criteria   160

    Refining Criteria for Better Evidence   160

    Considering Criteria and Rhetorical Context   161

Writing the Sketch   162

INQUIRING INTO THE DETAILS **Collaborating on Criteria**   163

STUDENT SKETCH **Laura Burns, "Recipe for a Great Film: Unlikeable People, Poor Choices, and Little Redemption"**   164

Moving from Sketch to Draft   164

    Evaluating Your Sketch   165

Reflecting on What You've Learned   165

Developing   165

    Talking It Through   165

    Re-Experience   166

    Interview   166

    Read   166

Drafting   167

    Finding an Opening   167

    Methods of Development   167

    Using Evidence   168

Workshopping   168

    Reflecting on the Draft   169

Revising   169

    Shaping   169

    Polishing   170

STUDENT ESSAY **Laura Burns, "How to Not Feel Good and Feel Good About It"**   172

Evaluating the Essay   173

Using What You Have Learned   174

Chapter 6 Writing a Proposal   175

Writing About Problems and Solutions   175

    Problems of Consequence   176

    Problems of Manageable Scale   177

Motives for Writing a Proposal   177

The Proposal and Academic Writing   178

INQUIRING INTO THE DETAILS **Writing a Research Proposal**   179

Features of the Form   179

READINGS 182

PROPOSAL 1 Buzz Bissinger, "Why College Football Should Be Banned" 182

Inquiring into the Essay 184

PROPOSAL 2 Robert F. Saltz, Ph. D., "Preventing Alcohol-Related Problems on College Campuses— Summary of the Final Report of the NIAAA Task Force on College Drinking" 185

Inquiring into the Essay 190

SEEING THE FORM A Problem in Pictures 191

THE WRITING PROCESS 193

Inquiry Project: **Writing a Proposal** 193

What Are You Going to Write About? 194

Opening Up 194

Listing Prompts 194

Fastwriting Prompts 195

Visual Prompts 195

Research Prompts 195

Narrowing Down 196

What's Promising Material and What Isn't? 196

Questions About Audience and Purpose 196

Trying Out 197

Researching to Answer the *So What*? Question 197

Giving Your Answer on a PowerPoint 198

Writing the Sketch 198

STUDENT SKETCH Jenna Appleman, "Loving and Hating Reality TV" 199

Moving from Sketch to Draft 200

Evaluating Your Own Sketch 200

Reflecting on What You Learned 200

Developing 201

Research 201

Focusing on the Justifications 202

Drafting 203

Methods of Development 203

Using Evidence 203

Workshopping 204

INQUIRING INTO THE DETAILS
Evidence—A Case Study 204

Reflecting on the Draft 205

Revising 205

Shaping 205

Polishing 206

STUDENT ESSAY Jenna Appleman, "Avoidable Accidents: How to Make Reality TV Safer" 207

Evaluating the Essay 209

Using What You Have Learned 210

Chapter 7 Writing an Argument 211

Writing to Persuade People 211

Motives for Writing an Argument 212

WRITING BEYOND THE CLASSROOM
Public Argument in a Digital Age 213

The Argument and Academic Writing 214

Features of the Form 215

What Is Argument?   216

Argument Has More Than Two Sides   217

Inquiry Arguments Begin with Exploration   218

What Do We Mean by Claims, Reasons, and Evidence?   219

Claims: What You Want People to Believe   219

Reasons: The "Because…" Behind the Claim   220

Evidence: Testing the Claim   220

SEEING THE FORM   The "Imagetext" as Argument   221

Analyzing What Makes a *Good* Argument   222

Classical Argument: Ethos, Pathos, Logos   222

Toulmin's Approach: What Do You Need to Believe Is True?   223

Rogers: Accurately Restating and Refusing Opposing Claims   224

EXERCISE 7.1   Argument as Therapy   225

ONE STUDENT'S RESPONSE   Rebecca's Journal   226

Avoiding Logical Fallacies   227

EXERCISE 7.2   Find the Fallacies   228

READINGS   229

FACTUAL ARGUMENT: IS IT TRUE THAT _____?   David Leonhardt, "Is College Worth It?"   229

Inquiring into the Essay   231

DEFINITION ARGUMENT: WHAT SHOULD WE CALL IT?   Khalid Sheikh Mohammed, "The Language of War Is Killing"   232

Inquiring into the Essay   233

CASUAL ARGUMENT: WHAT'S THE CAUSE?   Kevin Sabet, "Colorado Will Show Why Legalizing Marijauna Is a Mistake"   234

Inquiring into the Essay   236

THE WRITING PROCESS   237

Inquiry Project: **Writing an Argument**   237

What Are You Going to Write About?   237

Opening Up   238

Listing Prompts   238

ONE STUDENT'S RESPONSE   Rebecca's Journal   239

Fastwriting Prompts   239

Visual Prompts   240

Research Prompts   240

Narrowing Down   240

What's Promising Material and What Isn't?   240

Questions About Audience and Purpose   241

Trying Out   242

Kitchen Knives of Thought   242

Research Considerations   243

Interviews   243

Writing the Sketch   244

STUDENT SKETCH   Rebecca Thompson, "Twitter a Profound Thought?"   244

Moving from Sketch to Draft   245

Evaluating Your Own Sketch   245

Reflecting on What You've Learned   246

Developing   246
   Writing for Your Readers   246
   Researching the Argument   248
Drafting   249
   Designing Your Argument Rhetorically   249
   Methods of Development   249
   Using Evidence   250
INQUIRING INTO THE DETAILS   What Evidence Can Do   251
Workshopping   251
   Reflecting on the Draft   252
Revising   252
   Shaping   252
   Polishing   253
STUDENT ESSAY   Rebecca Thompson, "Social Networking Social Good?"   254
   Evaluating the Essay   257
Using What You Have Learned   257

Chapter 8 Writing an Analytical Essay   259
Writing to Interpret   259
Motives for Writing an Analytical Essay   260
The Analytical Essay and Academic Writing   260
EXERCISE 8.1   Interpeting an Image   262
Features of the Form   264

READINGS   267
LITERARY ANALYSIS   Bart Brinkman, "On 'The Shield That Came Back'"   268
Inquiring into the Poem   269

AD ANALYSIS   Alex Soojung-Kim Pang, "What Does Apple's 'Misunderstood' Advertisement Mean?"   270
Inquiring into the Ad   272
INQUIRING INTO THE DETAILS   Five Methods of Analysis   273
FILM ANALYSIS   Bryan Bishop, "'Why Won't You Die?' The Art of the Jump Scare"   274
Inquiring into the Essay   278
SEEING THE FORM   Brand as Visual Interpretation   278

THE WRITING PROCESS   280
Inquiry Project: Writing an Analytical Essay   280
What Are You Going to Write About?   281
Opening Up   281
   Listing Prompts   281
   Fastwriting Prompts   282
   Visual Prompts   282
   Research Prompts   282
INQUIRING INTO THE DETAILS   Common Literary Devices   283
Narrowing Down   284
   What's Promising Material and What Isn't?   284
   Questions About Audience and Purpose   286
Writing the Sketch   286
STUDENT SKETCH   Hailie Johnson-Waskow, "All About That Hate"   287
Moving from Sketch to Draft   288
   Evaluating Your Own Sketch   288

Reflecting on What You've Learned   288

Developing   288

Analysis   288

Research   289

Drafting   289

Methods of Development   289

Using Evidence   290

Workshopping   290

Reflecting on the Draft   291

Revising   291

Shaping   292

Polishing   292

STUDENT ESSAY   Hailie Johnson-Waskow, "All About That Hate: A Critical Analysis of 'All About That Bass'"   294

Evaluating the Essay   296

Using What You Have Learned   296

Chapter 9 Writing an Ethnographic Essay   298

Writing About Culture   298

Motives for Writing Ethnography   299

Ethnography and Academic Writing   299

Features of the Form   300

READINGS   303

ETHNOGRAPHIC ESSAY 1   Elizabeth Chiseri-Strater, "Anna as Reader: Intimacy and Response"   303

Inquiring into the Essay   305

ETHNOGRAPHIC ESSAY 2   Rebekah Nathan, "My Freshman Year: Worldliness and Worldview"   306

Inquiring into the Essay   309

SEEING THE FORM   German Cowboys   310

THE WRITING PROCESS   311

Inquiry Project: **Writing the Ethnographic Essay   311**

What Are You Going to Write About?   312

Opening Up   312

Listing Prompts   312

WRITING BEYOND THE CLASSROOM Commercial Ethnography   313

Fastwriting Prompts   314

Visual Prompts   314

Research Prompts   314

Narrowing Down   315

INQUIRING INTO THE DETAILS Researching Trends and Subcultures on the Web   315

What's Promising Material and What Isn't?   316

Questions About Audience and Purpose   316

Trying Out   317

INQUIRING INTO THE DETAILS Questions Ethnographers Ask   317

Taking Notes   318

INQUIRING INTO THE DETAILS Ethnography and Ethics   318

FIELD NOTES   Rita Guerra, "Field Notes on Friday Afternoon at Emerald Lanes"   319

Writing the Sketch   321

Moving from Sketch to Draft   322

Evaluating Your Own Sketch   322

Reflecting on What You've
Learned   322
Developing   322
Sources of Data   322
INQUIRING INTO THE DETAILS
Useful Library Databases for
Ethnography   324
Analyzing the Data   324
Drafting   325
Methods of Development   325
Using Evidence   326
Workshopping   326
Reflecting on the Draft   327
Revising   327
Shaping   327
Polishing   328
STUDENT ESSAY   **Kersti Harter,**
"Beyond 'Gaydar'"   330
Evaluating the Essay   339
Using What You Have Learned   340

Part 3 INQUIRING DEEPER   341

Chapter 10 Writing a Research Essay   341

Writing with Research   341
Research Essays, Research Papers,
and Research Reports   342
Motives for Writing a Research
Essay   343
The Research Essay and Academic
Writing   343
Features of the Form   344

READINGS: WHY
TATTOOS   347
EXERCISE 10.1   **Flash Research on**
Tattoos   347
EXCERPT 1: JOURNAL ARTICLE
Derek J. Roberts, "Secret Ink:
Tattoo's Place in Contemporary
American Culture"   349
EXCERPT 2: JOURNAL ARTICLE
Myrna L. Armstrong, Alden
E. Roberts, Jerome R. Koch, Jana
C. Sanders, Donna C. Owen,
and R. Rox Andreson, "Motivation
for Contemporary Tattoo
Removal"   350
EXCERPT 3: BOOK   **Miliann Kange**
and Katherine Jones, "Why Do
People Get Tattoos?"   351
EXCERPT 4: JOURNAL ARTICLE
Jenn Horne, David Knox,
Jane Zusman, and Marty
E. Zusman, "Tattoos and
Piercings: Attitudes, Behaviors,
and Interpretations of College
Students"   353

THE WRITING PROCESS   356
Inquiry Project: **Writing a**
Research Essay   356
What Are You Going to Write
About?   356
Opening Up   357
Listing Prompts   357
Fastwriting Prompts   357
Visual Prompts   358
Research Prompts   358

ONE STUDENT'S RESPONSE **Julian's Journal** 358

Narrowing Down 359

What's Promising Material and What Isn't? 360

Questions about Audience and Purpose 361

Trying Out 361

Refining the Question 361

Focus Like a Journalist 362

Writing a Proposal 362

SAMPLE RESEARCH PROPOSAL 363

Moving from Proposal to Draft 364

Evaluating Your Proposal 365

Reflecting on What You've Learned 365

Developing 365

INQUIRING INTO THE DETAILS **Scheduling Your Time** 366

Tools for Developing the Research Essay Draft 366

Drafting 367

Methods of Development 368

Using Evidence 370

Workshopping 371

Reflecting on the Draft 372

Revising 372

Shaping 372

Polishing 373

STUDENT ESSAY **Laura Burns, "The 'Unreal Dream': True Crime in the Justice System"** 374

Evaluating the Essay 380

Using What You Have Learned 380

Chapter 11 Research Techniques 382

Methods of Collecting 382

Research in the Electronic Age 383

Research Routines 383

Power Searching Using Google 385

INQUIRING INTO THE DETAILS **Google Tips and Tricks** 386

Google Scholar 387

Power Searching in the Library 388

Combining Terms Using Boolean Searching 388

Using Controlled Language Searches 389

Developing Working Knowledge 390

A Strategy for Developing Working Knowledge 391

Refine the Research Question 391

Developing Focused Knowledge 393

Library Research: A Strategy for Developing Focused Knowledge 393

Searching for Books 394

Searching for Periodicals and Newspapers 394

Web Research: A Strategy for Developing Focused Knowledge 396

Advanced Internet Research Techniques 396

Evaluating Library Sources 397

INQUIRING INTO THE DETAILS **The Working Bibliography** 398

Evaluating Web Sources 398

An Evaluation Checklist for Web Sources 400

Research with Living Sources: Interviews, Surveys, and Fieldwork   401

Interviews   401

Arranging Interviews   402

Conducting the Interview   403

Using the Interview in Your Writing   404

The Online Interview   405

Finding People Online   405

Contacting Someone for an Online Interview   405

Surveys   406

Defining a Survey's Goals and Audience   406

Two Types of Survey Questions   406

Crafting Survey Questions   407

INQUIRING INTO THE DETAILS **Types of Survey Questions   408**

Conducting a Survey: Paper or Electronic?   409

Testing the Survey   409

Finding the Target Audience   409

Using Survey Results in Your Writing   410

Fieldwork: Research on What You See and Hear   410

The Ethics of Fieldwork   411

Note-Taking Strategies   411

Using Field Research in Your Writing   412

Writing in the Middle: Note-Taking Techniques   412

Double-Entry Journal   413

Research Log   414

ONE STUDENT'S RESPONSE **Claude's Research Log   414**

Using What You Have Learned   416

Chapter 12 Using and Citing Sources   417

Controlling Information   417

Using and Synthesizing Sources   418

The Research Writer as Narrator   419

The Narrator as Synthesizer   420

The Note Taker's Triad: Summary, Paraphrase, and Quotation   421

Summarizing   421

Paraphrasing   422

Quoting   423

Citing Sources and Avoiding Plagiarism   424

Avoiding Plagiarism   425

INQUIRING INTO THE DETAILS **A Taxonomy of Copying   426**

EXERCISE 12.1 **The Accidental Plagiarist   427**

MLA Documentation Guidelines   429

INQUIRING INTO THE DETAILS **The Common Knowledge Exception   429**

Citing Sources   430

Where to Put Citations   430

INQUIRING INTO THE DETAILS **Citations That Go with the Flow   431**

When You Mention the Author's Name   432

When There Is No Author   432

Works by the Same Author   433

When One Source Quotes Another   434

Personal Interviews   434

Several Sources in a Single Citation   434

Sample Parenthetical References for Other Sources   435

Format **436**

    The Layout **436**

Preparing the Works Cited Page **440**

    Format **441**

    Citing Books **442**

    Sample Book Citations **443**

    Citing Periodicals **446**

    Sample Periodical Citations **448**

    Citing Online and Other Sources **451**

    A Sample Paper in MLA Style **454**

APA Documentation Guidelines **455**

    How the Essay Should Look **455**

    Page Format **455**

    Title Page **455**

    Abstract **455**

    Body of the Paper **457**

    References Page **458**

    Appendix **458**

    Notes **458**

    Tables and Figures **459**

    Language and Style **459**

    Citing Sources in Your Essay **459**

    When the Author Is Mentioned in the Text **459**

    When the Author Isn't Mentioned in the Text **460**

    When to Cite Page Numbers **460**

    A Single Work by Two or More Authors **460**

    A Work with No Author **460**

    Two or More Works by the Same Author **460**

    An Institutional Author **461**

    Multiple Works in the Same Parentheses **461**

    Interviews, E-Mail, and Letters **461**

    New Editions of Old Works **462**

    A Website **462**

Preparing the References List **462**

    Order of Sources **462**

    Order of Information **463**

    Sample References: Articles **465**

    Sample References: Books **466**

    Sample References: Other **470**

    A Sample Paper in APA Style **472**

Using What You Have Learned **473**

Part 4 RE-INQUIRING **474**

Chapter 13 Re-Genre: Repurposing Your Writing for Multimedia Genres 474

STUDENTS ON RE-GENRE **475**

What Writers Can Learn from Re-Genre: Knowledge Transfer **476**

Transfer from Blog Essay to Podcast: A Case Study **477**

Beyond Words: Communicating in Other Modes **478**

    The Problem of Definition **479**

STUDENTS ON RE-GENRE **480**

Re-Genre Is Deep Revision **481**

    Genre as a Way of Knowing and Seeing **481**

    Genre and Its Conventions **482**

STUDENTS ON RE-GENRE **482**

INQUIRING INTO THE DETAILS **Re-Genre and Re-Flect** **484**

Re-Genre: The Assignment **484**

    Planning the Re-Genre **485**

    Applying Rhetorical Goals **485**

INQUIRING INTO THE DETAILS **Levels of Content** 486

EXERCISE 13.1 **Re-Genre Pitch** 487

Eight Multimodal Genres 487

Slide Presentations 488

Infographic 490

Brochure 493

Conference Poster 494

Photographic Essay 496

Radio Essays or Podcasts 499

STUDENTS ON RE-GENRE 500

Web Page 501

Video PSA 503

Drafting Tools: Scripts, Storyboards, and Mock-Ups 504

Scripts 505

Storyboards 505

Mock-ups 507

EXERCISE 13.2 **Genre Analysis: Conventions and Best Practices** 508

ANALYZING YOUR EXAMPLES 508

INQUIRING INTO THE DETAILS **Citing Multimodal Content** 509

The Ethics of Borrowing 509

Creative Commons Licenses 509

Public Domain 510

Reflecting on Re-Genre 510

Using What You Have Learned 511

Chapter 14 Revision Strategies 512

Why Revise? 512

Divorcing the Draft 514

Strategies for Divorcing the Draft 515

Five Categories of Revision 516

Problems with Purpose 518

Revision Strategy 14.1: Dialogue with Dave 518

INQUIRING INTO THE DETAILS **Explore or Argue?** 519

Revision Strategy 14.2: What Do You Want to Know About What You Learned? 520

ONE STUDENT'S RESPONSE **Julia's Draft** 520

Revision Strategy 14.3: Finding the Focusing Question 521

Revision Strategy 14.4: What's the Relationship? 522

Problems with Meaning 523

Where Does Meaning Come From? 524

Methods for Discovering Your Thesis 525

Revision Strategy 14.5: Harvest Meanings in the Draft 525

Revision Strategy 14.6: Looping Toward a Thesis 525

Revision Strategy 14.7: Reclaiming Your Topic 526

Revision Strategy 14.8: The Believing Game 527

Methods for Refining Your Thesis 528

Revision Strategy 14.9: Questions as Knives 528

Revision Strategy 14.10: Qualifying Your Claim 529

Problems with Information 530

Revision Strategy 14.11: Explode a Moment 530

Revision Strategy 14.12: Beyond Examples 531

Revision Strategy 14.13: Research the Conversation   532

Revision Strategy 14.14: Backing Up Your Assumptions   533

Problems with Structure   534

Formal Academic Structures   535

Revision Strategy 14.15: Beginnings, Middles, Ends, and the Work They Do   536

Revision Strategy 14.16: Reorganizing Around Thesis and Support   536

Revision Strategy 14.17: Multiple Leads   538

INQUIRING INTO THE DETAILS Types of Leads   539

Revision Strategy 14.18: The Frankenstein Draft   540

Revision Strategy 14.19: Reverse Outline   541

Problems with Clarity and Style   542

Solving Problems of Clarity   543

Revision Strategy 14.20: The Three Most Important Sentences   543

The Very First Sentence   543

The Last Line of the First Paragraph   544

The Last Line of the Essay   544

Revision Strategy 14.21: Untangling Paragraphs   544

Revision Strategy 14.22: Cutting Clutter   546

INQUIRING INTO THE DETAILS Transition Flags   547

Revision Strategy 14.23: The Actor and the Action Next Door   548

Improving Style   549

Revision Strategy 14.24: Actors and Actions   549

Revision Strategy 14.25: Smoothing the Choppiness   550

Revision Strategy 14.26: Fresh Ways to Say Things   550

Using What You Have Learned   551

Appendix A The Writer's Workshop   552

Making the Most of Peer Review   552

Being Read   552

Divorcing the Draft   553

Instructive Talk   553

Models for Writing Workshops   554

Group Workshops   554

One-on-One Peer Review   555

The Writer's and Reader's Responsibilities   555

Useful Responses   556

Response Formats   556

The No-Response Workshop   556

The Initial-Response Workshop   557

The Narrative-of-Thought Workshop   557

The Instructive-Lines Workshop   557

The Purpose Workshop   558

The Graphing-Reader-Interest Workshop   558

The Sum-of-the-Parts Workshop   559

The Thesis Workshop   559

The Editing Workshop   560

Reflecting on the Workshop   560

Appendix B The Writing Portfolio 562

What Is a Portfolio? 562
Types of Portfolios 562
  Unevaluated Portfolios 563
  Evaluated Portfolios 563
Why Require a Portfolio? 564
Organizing Portfolios 565
Writing a Reflective Letter or Essay 566
Final Preparations 568

Appendix C The Annotated Bibliography 569

What Is an Annotated Bibliography? 569
  Indicative Bibliography 569
  Informative Bibliography 569
  Evaluative Bibliography 570
  Combination of Types 570
Writing an Annotated Bibliography 570
  Choose a Subject 570
  Gather Materials 570

Read Strategically 571
Length 571
Content 572
Sample Student Annotated Bibliography 572

HANDBOOK 576
1 Sentence Boundaries 578
2 Sentence Inconsistencies 586
3 Problems with Modification 591
4 Verbs 595
5 Pronouns 601
6 Style 606
7 Punctuation 610
8 Mechanics and Spelling 619
9 Review of Basic Grammar 628
10 Tips for ESL Writers 646

Credits CR-1
Index I-1

Preface

I have a friend, a painter, who teaches art at my university, and his introductory courses teach the subskills of painting, things like how to use a brush, mix paints, and understand color theory. Common sense suggests that such fundamentals are the starting place for any creative activity, including writing. But college writers walk into our classes with a lifetime of language use. They already know a lot about making meaning with words, more than they think they know. Yet there is much to teach, and perhaps the most powerful thing we can teach them is that writing isn't just for getting down what you know but for discovering what you think. I've learned to never underestimate the power of this discovery process, and that's why discovery is the beating heart of this book.

What's New in This Edition?

The fifth edition of *The Curious Writer* represents a substantial revision, including a new chapter on repurposing academic writing into contemporary genres like podcasts and infographics, and substantially revised chapters on argument and analytic writing. As always, I have also made revisions throughout with the overall aim of making the book more teachable and more reflective of the world in which today's students live. Here's what you will find:

- **A completely new chapter on repurposing ("re-genre-ing") writing (Ch. 13)** encourages students to transform academic writing into contemporary genres including blogs, audio and video podcasts, infographics, and more. In creating these transformations, students gain a deeper rhetorical knowledge of genre conventions, strengths, and limitations.
- **A thoroughly reorganized and revised chapter on argument (Ch. 7)** now offers clearer, more comprehensive guidance on what an argument is and how to write one—knowledge and skills that are at the center of almost all good writing.
- **A significantly revised chapter on critical analysis (Ch. 8)** widens its focus beyond literature to include images, objects, ads, and more—any "texts" in our lives that may have ambiguous meanings.
- **A significantly revised section on research** includes updated information about data searches, a new section on online interviews and surveys, and new student and professional essays, as well as expanded coverage of plagiarism and synthesizing sources.
- **New readings and illustrations throughout** offer fresh perspectives on current topics to engage students more effectively.

Inquiry in the Writing Classroom

Composition teachers often struggle to define what skills we can offer to students—beyond the acts of reading and writing—that they can export to their other classes and, later, into their lives. Often we vaguely refer to "critical thinking" skills. *The Curious Writer* suggests that what we can offer is the skill of *inquiring.* Most of us already teach inquiry, although we may not all realize it. For example, our writing classes invite students to be active participants in making knowledge in the classroom through peer review. When we ask students to fastwrite or brainstorm, we encourage them to suspend judgment and openly explore their feelings or ideas. And when we urge students to see a draft as a first look at a topic, and revision as a means of discovering what they may not have noticed before, we teach a process that makes discovery its purpose. Indeed, most composition classrooms create a "culture of inquirers."

For inquiry-based courses on any subject, I believe instructors should take five key actions:

1. **Create an atmosphere of mutual inquiry.** Students are used to seeing their teachers as experts who know everything. But in an inquiry-based classroom, instructors are learners too. They ask questions not because they already know the answers but because there might be answers they haven't considered.
2. **Emphasize questions before answers.** The idea that student writers should begin with an inflexible thesis or a firm position on a topic before engaging in the process of writing is anathema to inquiry-based learning. Questions, not preconceived answers, lead to new discoveries.
3. **Encourage a willingness to suspend judgment.** To suspend judgment demands that we trust that the process will lead us to new insights. This requires both faith in the process and the time to engage in it. The composition course, with its emphasis on process, is uniquely suited to nurture such faith.
4. **Introduce a strategy of inquiry.** Announcing that we're teaching an inquiry-based class is not enough. We have to introduce students to the strategy of inquiry we'll be using. In the sciences, the experimental method provides a foundation for investigations. What guidance will we give our students in the composition course?
5. **Present inquiry in a rhetorical context.** An essay, a research project, an experiment, any kind of investigation is always pursued with particular purposes and audiences in mind. In an inquiry-based class, the situation in which the inquiry project is taking place is always considered.

The Curious Writer is built on all of these elements. It features a strategy of inquiry that is genuinely multidisciplinary, borrowing from the sciences, the social sciences, and the humanities. Each assignment in Part 2, "Inquiry Projects," for example, leads students toward subjects that offer the most potential for learning. Rather than write about what they already know, students are encouraged to choose topics that they want to learn more about. In addition, the discussion questions that follow the student and professional essays do more than simply test students' comprehension or reduce the reading to a single theme. In many cases, these questions are open ended and can lead students in many directions. And throughout, I have tried to maintain a voice and persona that suggests I am working along with the students as a writer and a thinker—which is exactly the experience of mutual inquiry that I try to create in my classes. Finally, *The Curious Writer* is organized around a strategy of inquiry that is present in every assignment and nearly every exercise. I revisit the model "The Spirit of Inquiry," which is introduced in Part 1, in every subsequent chapter. This inquiry strategy is the thematic core of the book.

The Inquiry Strategy of *The Curious Writer*

A strategy of inquiry is simply a process of discovery. In the sciences, this process is systematic and often quite formal. The model I use in this book borrows from science in some ways through its insistence on continually looking closely at the "data" (sensory details, facts, evidence, textual passages, and so on) and using that data to shape or test the writer's ideas about a subject. But the heart of the model is the alternating movement between two modes of thinking—creative and critical—in a dialectical process. One way of describing this movement is as a shifting back and forth between suspending judgment and making judgments (see Figure A).

This inquiry strategy works with both reading and writing, but in Chapter 2, "Reading as Inquiry," I offer four categories of questions—those that explore, explain, evaluate, and reflect—that I think will help guide students in reading most texts more strategically. These types of questions will be most evident in the follow-up questions to the many readings throughout *The Curious Writer*.

Finally, a strategy of inquiry is useful only if it makes sense to students; I've tried very hard, particularly in the first section of the book, to make the model comprehensible.

How This Book Is Organized

The Curious Writer includes four parts. Because the inquiry-based approach is central to *The Curious Writer*, it's crucial for students to work through the first two chapters in Part 1, "The Spirit of Inquiry." Part 2—the largest—focuses on "inquiry projects." The range of assignments in this part should satisfy the needs of most composition instructors. If your university is lucky enough to have a two-semester sequence, *The Curious Writer* includes assignments suitable for both courses, including personal, argument, and research essays. (There is even enough here to allow the book's use in advanced composition courses.) Part 3 focuses

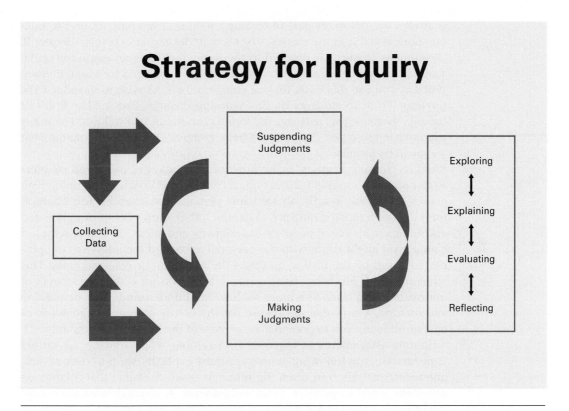

Strategy for Inquiry

Suspending Judgments

Exploring

Explaining

Evaluating

Reflecting

Collecting Data

Making Judgments

Figure A   In nearly every assignment in *The Curious Writer,* students will use this strategy of inquiry.

on research—the tools, strategies, and skills associated with academic research, including avoiding plagiarism and synthesizing and citing sources appropriately. Part 4 explores the critical process of revision, now with a new chapter about transforming writing into new, contemporary genres.

I organized the book to span, if necessary, a two-semester composition course, though it can easily be adapted for use in one semester. Typically, in a two-semester sequence the first course focuses on the writing process, exposition, critical analysis, writing to learn, and so on. The second semester often focuses on argument and research. A single-semester composition course combines all these areas. Fortunately, *The Curious Writer* is extremely flexible, with ample material to keep students busy for one or two semesters.

PART 1. While composition classes have—obviously—always focused on writing, in recent years, I've become interested in reading strategies, a topic that I never mentioned as a novice teacher. There was simply so much to say about the writing process that I didn't think reading was a topic that should get much airtime. Yet, as in writing, students bring many prior beliefs and assumptions about reading into our classrooms, and because reading is always an important part of teaching writing, I've come around to talking more about it in my classes. *The Curious Writer* reflects this. Chapter 2, "Reading as Inquiry," is devoted to the topic, including an emphasis on visual rhetoric that responds to our students' growing need for visual literacy. Whether you use this book for one course or two, it's wise to introduce *The Curious Writer* to students by first working through Part 1, "The Spirit of Inquiry," because this part lays the foundation for all that follows. The many exercises in these two chapters will help students experience firsthand what we mean by inquiry.

PART 2. "Inquiry Projects" is the heart of the book. I've organized chapters in an order that roughly follows typical composition courses, beginning with genres that draw heavily on students' personal experiences and observations and then moving outward to explore other sources of information and encounters with other people's experiences and ideas. In a one-semester course, you might begin with the personal essay and then move to the profile, followed by the review, and then the argument or research essay. This structure builds nicely by challenging students to work with more sources of information and leads to a more sophisticated understanding of persuasion and rhetoric. A two-semester course has the luxury of more assignments, of course, allowing you to potentially use most of the inquiry projects in Part 2.

Certain assignments go together. For example, while arguably all writing is persuasive, the following genres are most explicitly so: proposal, review, argument, analysis, and often the research essay. A course that focuses on argument might emphasize these assignments. A research-oriented course might exploit the book's wealth of material that has a strong emphasis on outside sources, including the proposal, review, argument, research essay, and ethnography sections. A single-semester composition course that covers critical thinking and writing as well as research and argument might move from personal essay to profile and then cover persuasion through the review or analytical essay, move on to the argument, and finish with the ethnographic and research essays.

Each inquiry, or genre, chapter is divided into three parts: an initial exploration of the genre and its rhetorical conventions and features; a selection of representative readings; and The Writing Process, a step-by-step guide to writing in that genre.

PART 3. The approach of *The Curious Writer* grows in part from my own scholarship on research writing, particularly the criticism that research is too often isolated in the writing course, which, understandably, leads students to get the idea that research is reserved for the research paper. This book makes research a part of every assignment, emphasizing that it is a useful source of information, not a separate genre. But research also receives special attention in Part 3, "Inquiring Deeper," where students are introduced not only to the research essay but also to research strategies and skills, including citing and synthesizing sources and avoiding plagiarism. I hope you will find that this part, particularly Chapter 11, "Research Techniques," is immediately relevant because students will be encouraged to consider research angles in every assignment they tackle. Consider assigning this chapter early in your course, particularly the sections on developing a working and focused knowledge of a subject.

- **PART 4.** Similarly, revision is an element of every assignment. That's hardly an innovative idea, but what is unusual about *The Curious Writer* is that the book devotes an entire part—Part 4, "Re-Inquiring"—to revision. Like the chapters on research, the chapters on revision are relevant to students from their very first assignment. Chapter 13, "Re-Genre" is a unique—and completely new—chapter that encourages students to consider how to transform classroom essays into contemporary genres like infographics, blogs, and video and audio podcasts. In exploring how to repurpose writing, students dive more deeply into the rhetorical strategies and tools associated with each genre. Finally, Chapter 14, "Revision Strategies," is a useful introduction to what it means to revise a piece of writing and features specific revision strategies that your students will use in every assignment. You might want to assign the first part of this chapter early on in your course.

This is the third textbook I've written with the "curious" moniker. Because all are inquiry based, the word is a natural choice. And although I'm very interested in encouraging my students to be curious researchers, readers, and writers, I also hope to remind my colleagues who use these books that we should be curious, too. We should model for our students our own passion for inquiring into the world. We should also celebrate what we can learn from our students, and not just about writing or the many topics they might choose to write about. Every time I walk into the writing classroom, I'm curious about what my students will teach me about myself. That's a lifetime inquiry project for all of us, as teachers and as people.

Using the Exercises

Learning follows experience, and the exercises in *The Curious Writer* are intended to help students make sense of the ideas in the text. I often plan the exercises as an in-class activity, and then assign the relevant reading to follow up that experience. Sometimes the discussion following these in-class exercises is so rich that some of the assigned reading becomes unnecessary. The students get the main idea without having to hear it again from the author. More often, though, the reading helps students deepen their understanding of what they've done and how they can apply it to their own work.

However, assigning all of the exercises isn't necessary. Don't mistake their abundance in the book as an indication that you must march your students in lockstep through every activity, or they won't learn what they need to. *The Curious Writer* is more flexible than that. Use the exercises and activities that seem to emphasize key points that you think are important. Skip those you don't have time for or that don't seem necessary. If you're like me, you also have a few rabbits of your own in your hat—exercises and activities that may work better with the text than the ones I suggest.

Other Features of *The Curious Writer*

A number of recurring features are designed to offer additional support to students. These include:

- **Learning Objectives and Using What You Have Learned.** Each chapter begins by establishing learning objectives, which are then revisited at the end of each chapter to reinforce the chapter's content. Notes throughout the chapter highlight where the objectives come into play.
- **Features of the Form.** These charts in each chapter of Part 2 summarize the particular features and conventions of the genre being explored.
- **Inquiring into the Details.** These boxed features dig deeper into specific, relevant topics.
- **Prose+.** This feature reflects the increasing importance of visual literacy by offering images for analysis.

Resources for Instructors and Students

The following resources are available to qualified adopters of Pearson English textbooks.

The Instructor's Resource Manual

ISBN 0-13-412158-9/978-0-13-412158-1
This manual, written by my colleague Michelle Payne, includes sample syllabi as well as a helpful introduction that offers general teaching strategies and ideas for teaching writing as a form of inquiry. It also provides a detailed overview of each chapter and its goals, ideas for discussion starters, handouts and overheads, and a large number of additional writing activities that teachers can use in their classrooms to supplement the textbook.

PowerPoint Presentation

A downloadable set of PowerPoint slides can be used by instructors who want to accompany chapter readings and discussions with presentable visuals. These slides, also designed by Michelle Payne, illustrate each learning objective and key idea in the text in visual form. Each slide includes instructors' notes.

MyWritingLab

MyWritingLab is an online practice, tutorial, and assessment program that provides engaging experiences for teaching and learning.

MyWritingLab includes most of the writing assignments from your accompanying textbook. Now, students can complete and submit assignments, and teachers can then track and respond to submissions easily—right in MyWritingLab—making the response process easier for the instructor and more engaging for the student.

In the Writing Assignments, students can use instructor-created peer review rubrics to evaluate and comment on other students' writing. When giving feedback on student writing, instructors can add links to activities that address issues and strategies needed for review. Instructors may link to multimedia resources in Pearson Writer, which include curated content from Purdue OWL. Paper review by specialized tutors through SmartThinking is available, as is plagiarism detection through TurnItIn.

Respond to Student Writing with Targeted Feedback and Remediation

MyWritingLab unites instructor comments and feedback with targeted remediation via rich multimedia activities, allowing students to learn from and through their own writing.

Writing Help for Varying Skill Levels

For students who enter the course at widely varying skill levels, MyWritingLab provides unique, targeted remediation through personalized and adaptive instruction. Starting with a pre-assessment known as the Path Builder, MyWritingLab diagnoses students' strengths and weaknesses on prerequisite writing skills. The results of the pre-assessment inform each student's Learning Path, a personalized pathway for students to work on requisite skills through multimodal activities. In doing so, students feel supported and ready to succeed in class.

Learning Tools for Student Engagement

Learning Catalytics. Generate class discussion, guide lectures, and promote peer-to-peer learning with real-time analytics. MyLab and Mastering with eText now provides Learning Catalytics—an interactive student response tool that uses students' smartphones, tablets, or laptops to engage them in more sophisticated tasks and thinking.

MediaShare. MediaShare allows students to post multimodal assignments easily—whether they are audio, video, or visual compositions—for peer review and instructor feedback. In both face-to-face and online course settings, MediaShare saves instructors valuable time and enriches the student learning experience by enabling contextual feedback to be provided quickly and easily.

Direct Access to MyLab. Users can link from any Learning Management System (LMS) to Pearson's MyWritingLab. Access MyLab assignments, rosters, and resources, and synchronize MyLab grades with the LMS gradebook. New direct, single sign-on provides access to all the personalized learning MyLab resources that make studying more efficient and effective.

Visit www.mywritinglab.com for more information

REVEL for *The Curious Writer,* 5/e by Bruce Ballenger

REVEL is designed for the way today's composition students read, think, and learn. In English, reading is never the endgame. Instead—whether in a textbook, an exemplar essay, or a source—it begins a conversation that plays out in writing. REVEL complements the written word with a variety of writing opportunities, brief assessments, model documents, and rich annotation tools to deepen students' understanding of their reading. By providing regular opportunities to write and new ways to interact with their reading, REVEL engages students and sets them up to be more successful readers and writers—in and out of class.

Video and Rich Multimedia Content. Videos, audio recordings, animations, and multimedia instruction encourage students to engage with the text in a more meaningful way.

Interactive Readings and Exercises. Students explore reading assignments through interactive texts. Robust annotation tools allow students to take notes, and low-stakes assessments and writing exercises enable students to engage meaningfully with the text outside of the classroom.

Integrated Writing Assignments. Minimal-stakes, low-stakes, and high-stakes writing tasks allow students multiple opportunities to interact with the ideas presented in the reading assignments, ensuring that they come to class better prepared.

Pearson eText

An interactive online version of *The Curious Writer* is available as an eText, which brings together the many resources of the MyLabs with the instructional content of this successful book to create an enhanced learning experience for students.

Acknowledgments

Making this book has been a team effort. From the first edition of *The Curious Writer*, I've been lucky to have an extraordinarily gifted group of Pearson people working with me, including Joe Opiela, who first encouraged me to write this book, and a remarkable team of development editors and production staff. In particular, I'd like to thank Ginny Blanford, whose editorial insight helped me enormously to rethink my work here, from tightening sentences to restructuring entire chapters. Her firm but always friendly guidance kept the project on track and kept me from panic. Dr. Michelle Payne, a colleague at Boise State and a longtime friend, has been involved in the development of this book since the beginning, reviewing chapters, writing instructor's manuals, and developing teaching materials. Michelle's help with the argument chapter in this edition was instrumental. And finally, for the last few editions, I've enlisted the help of my daughter Becca. I'm endlessly proud of her, which is as it should be.

My students are also key collaborators, though they often don't know it. For their assistance in the fifth edition, I'd like to thank Hailie Johnson-Waskow, Andrea Oyarzabal, Bernice Olivas, Seth Marlin, Amy Garrett, Amanda Stewart, Kersti Harter, Micaela Fisher and many others whose work may not appear here but who taught the teacher how to teach writing.

Reviewers of books like these can be crucial to their development. For the first four editions, I relied on feedback from the following folks:

Susan Achziger, Community College of Aurora; Jeffrey T. Andelora, Mesa Community College; Ken Autrey, Francis Marion University; Ellen Barker, Nicholls State University; Sandra Barnhill, South Plains College; Angela Cardinale Bartlett, Chaffey College; Melissa Batai, Triton College; Patrick Bizzaro, East Carolina University; Jennifer Black, McLennan Community College; Sara M. Blake, El Camino College; Pamela S. Bledsoe, Surry Community College; James C. Bower, Walla Walla Community College; Libby Bradford Roeger, Shawnee Community College; Mark Browning, Johnson County Community College; Shanti Bruce, Nova Southeastern University; Jo Ann Buck, Guilford Technical Community College; Carol Burnell, Clackamas Community College; Susan Butterworth, Salem State College; Sharon Buzzard, Quincy College; Maria A. Clayton, Middle Tennessee State University; Dr. Keith Coplin, Colby Community College; Donna Craine, Front Range Community College; Rachelle Darabi, Indiana University/Purdue University–Fort Wayne; Jason DePolo, North Carolina A&T State University; Brock Dethier, Utah State University; Rosemarie Dombrowski, Arizona State University (DPC); Virginia B. Earnest, Holmes Community College–Ridgeland; Terry Engebretsen, Idaho State University; John Christopher Ervin, University of South Dakota; Kevin Ferns, Woodland Community College; Greg Giberson, Salisbury University; Daniel Gonzalez, University of New Orleans; Gwendolyn N. Hale, Savannah State University; Michael Hammond, University of San Francisco; Shari Hammond, Southwest Virginia Community College; Vicki M. Hester, St. Mary's University; Nels P. Highberg, University of Hartford; Charlotte Hogg, Texas Christian University; Anneliese Homan, State Fair Community College; Shelly Horvath, University of Indianapolis; Dawn Hubbell-Staeble, Bowling Green State University; Chad Jorgensen, Metropolitan Community College; Lilia Joy, Henderson Community College; David C. Judkins, University of Houston; William Klein, University of Missouri–St. Louis; Robert Lamm, Arkansas State University; Mary C. Leahy, College of DuPage; Lynn Lewis, University of Oklahoma; Steve Luebke, University of Wisconsin–River Falls; Michael Lueker, Our Lady of the Lake University; Rosemary Mack, Baton Rouge Community College; Kara M. Manning, The University of Southern Mississippi; James C. McDonald, University of Louisiana–Lafeyette; Rhonda McDonnell, Arizona State University; Jacqueline L. McGrath, College of DuPage; Amanda McGuire Rzicznek, Bowling Green State University; James J. McKeown, Jr., McLennan Community College; Eileen Medeiros, Johnson & Wales University; Bryan Moore, Arkansas State University; John D. Moore, Eastern Illinois University; Margaret P. Morgan, University of North Carolina–Charlotte; Dr. Peter E. Morgan, University of West Georgia; Tom Moriarty, Salisbury University; Brigid Murphy, Pima Community College; Jason E. Murray, University of South

Dakota; Robin L. Murray, Eastern Illinois University; Amy Ratto Parks, University of Montana; Dorothy J. Patterson, Oakwood College; Susan Pesznecker, Clackamas Community College; Betty Porter, Indiana Wesleyan University; Steven R. Price, Mississippi College; Lynn Raymond, UNC Charlotte; Mark Reynolds, Jefferson Davis Community College; David H. Roberts, Samford University; Elaine J. Roberts, Judson College; Kristie Rowe, Wright State University; Kathleen J. Ryan, University of Montana; Teryl Sands, Arizona State University; Robert A. Schwegler, University of Rhode Island; Heath Scott, Thomas Nelson Community College; Bonita Selting, University of Central Arkansas; Mark A. Smith, Lock Haven University of Pennsylvania; Vicki Stieha, Northern Kentucky University; Elizabeth A. Stolarek, Ferris State University; Marian Thomas, Boise State University; Ruthe Thompson, Southwest Minnesota State University; Lisa Tyler, Sinclair Community College; Marjorie Van Cleef, Housatonic Community College; Worth H. Weller, Indiana University Purdue University–Fort Wayne; Ann R. Wolven, Lincoln Trail College; Richard T. Young, Blackburn College; and BJ Zamora, Cleveland Community College.

And for this fifth edition, reviewers include Susan Achziger, Community College of Aurora; Sarah Allen, University of Northern Colorado; Scott D. Banville, Nicholls State University; Lynn Chrenka, Ferris State University; Brianne M. DiBacco, University of Southern Indiana; Seán Henne, West Shore Community College; Rosemary Mack, Baton Rouge Community College; Amanda McGuire Rzicznek, Bowling Green State University; James J. McKeown, Jr., McLennan Community College; Eileen Medeiros, Johnson & Wales University; Steve Moore, Arizona Western College; Siskanna Naynaha, Lane Community College; and Ashley Bissette Sumerel, University of North Carolina at Wilmington.

Finally, I want to thank my daughters, Rebecca and Julia, who allow themselves to be characters in all of my books. They are both actors, and like good theater people, they are more than willing to play their parts in these texts, no matter what roles I assign. I'm especially grateful to Karen, my wife, who has endured multiple editions of these books and their hold on my attention, which has often come at her expense. She's the beacon I follow through this blizzard of words, always guiding me home.

BRUCE BALLENGER

1

Writing as Inquiry

Learning Objectives

In this chapter, you'll learn to

1.1   Reflect on and revise your beliefs about yourself as a writer.

1.2   Understand what kinds of questions will sustain inquiry into any subject.

1.3   Practice a method of writing and thinking that will help you generate ideas.

1.4   Apply rhetorical knowledge to make choices in specific writing situations.

Yesterday in class, Tina wrote an essay about whether adultery is forgivable. She isn't married but has good friends who are, a couple she said everyone thought had the "perfect" marriage. The woman's husband, apparently, had an affair. Tina, who is in a pretty tight relationship with her boyfriend, has strong feelings about cheating on a partner. It ticks her off. "If it happened to me," she wrote, "I would have dumped him." Tina's essay could easily have become a rant about infidelity—a blunt, perhaps shrill argument about adultery's immorality or the depravity of two-timing men. It wasn't. Instead, she wondered about the relationship between friendship and love in marriage. She wondered about what kind of communication between spouses might short-circuit cheating. She wondered how attitudes towards sex differ between men and women. Many of these questions were explored by Michel de Montaigne, a sixteenth-century writer we were studying in that class, and Tina began to wrap his thinking around hers as she struggled to make sense of how she felt about what happened to her friends.

Tina was engaged in an act of inquiry.

Her motive was to *find out* what she thought rather than prove what she already knew. And writing was the way Tina chose to think it through.

Many of us admit that we really don't like to write, particularly when forced to do it. Or we clearly prefer certain kinds of writing and dislike others: "I just like to write funny stories," or "I like writing for myself and not for other people," or "I hate writing research papers." I can understand this, because for years I felt much the same way. I saw virtually no similarities between a note to a friend and the paper I wrote for my philosophy class in college. Words had power in one context but seemed flimsy and vacant in another. One kind of writing was fairly easy; the other was like sweating blood. How could my experiences as a writer be so fundamentally different? In other words, what's the secret of writing well in a range of writing contexts *and* enjoying it more in all contexts? Here's what I had to learn:

1. You don't have to know what you think before you're ready to write. Writing can be a way of *discovering* what you think.

2. A key to writing well is understanding the *process* of doing it.

They're not particularly novel ideas, but both were a revelation to me when I finally figured them out late in my career as a student, and they changed for good the way I wrote. These two insights—that writing is a means of discovery and that reflecting on how we write can help us write—are guiding principles of this book. I won't guarantee that after they read *The Curious Writer*, haters of writing will come to love it or that lovers of writing won't find writing to be hard work. But I hope that by the end of the book, you'll experience the pleasure of discovery in different writing situations, and that you'll understand your writing process well enough to adapt it to the demands of whatever situation you encounter.

Motives for Writing

Why write? To start, I'd propose two motives, one obvious and the other less so:

1. To share ideas or information—*to communicate*.

2. To think—*to discover*.

These two motives for writing—to *communicate* with others and to *discover* what the writer thinks and feels—are equally important. And both may ultimately relate to what I call our *spirit of inquiry*, which is born of our deeper sense of wonder and curiosity or even confusion and doubt, our desire to touch other people, our urge to solve problems. The spirit of inquiry is a kind of perspective toward the world that invites questions, accepts uncertainty, and makes each of us feel some responsibility for what we say. This inquiring spirit should be familiar to you. It's the feeling you had when you discovered that the sun and a simple magnifying glass could be used to burn a hole in an oak leaf. It's wondering what a teacher meant when he said that World War II was a "good" war and Vietnam was a "bad" war. It's the questions that haunted you yesterday as you listened to a good friend describe her struggles with anorexia. The inquiring spirit even drives your quest to find a smartphone, an effort that inspires you to read about the technology and visit the *Consumer Reports* website at consumerreports.org. Inquiry was Tina's motive when she decided to turn her academic essay on adultery away from a shrill argument based on what she already believed into a more thoughtful exploration of why people cheat.

Beliefs About Writing and Writing Development

Most of us have been taught about writing since the first grade. We usually enter college with beliefs not only about what makes a good paper and what "rules" of writing to follow, but also about how we can develop as writers. As I mentioned earlier, I've learned a lot about writing since my first years in college, and a big part of that learning involved unraveling some of my prior beliefs about writing. In fact, I'd say that my development as a writer initially had more to do with *unlearning* some of what I already knew than it did with discovering new ways to write. But you have to make your beliefs explicit if you're going to make decisions about which are helpful and which aren't. So take a moment to find out what your beliefs are and to think about whether they actually make sense.

1.1
Reflect on and revise your beliefs about yourself as a writer.

Exercise 1.1

This I Believe (and This I Don't)

STEP ONE: From the following list, identify the one belief about writing that you agree with most strongly and the one that you're convinced isn't true.

1. Writing proficiency begins with learning the basics and then building on them, working from words to sentences to paragraphs to compositions.

2. The best way to develop as a writer is to imitate the writing of the people you want to write like.

3. People are born writers like people are born good at math. Either you can do it or you can't.

4. The best way to develop as a writer is to develop good reading skills.

5. Practice is the key to a writer's development. The more a writer writes, the more he or she will improve.

6. Developing writers need to learn the modes of writing (argument, exposition, description, narration) and the genres (essays, research papers, position papers, and so on).

7. Developing writers should start with simple writing tasks, such as telling stories, and move to harder writing tasks, such as writing a research paper.

8. The most important thing that influences a writer's growth is believing that he or she can improve.

9. The key to becoming a better writer is finding your voice.

STEP TWO: Look over the following journal prompts (for more on journals, see the "Inquiring into the Details: Journals" box). Then spend five minutes writing in your journal about *why* you agree with the one belief and disagree with the other. This is an open-ended "fastwrite." You should write fast and without stopping, letting your thoughts flow in whatever direction they go. In your fastwrite, you can respond to any or all of the prompts to whatever extent you want.

Rules for Fastwriting

1. There are no rules.
2. Don't try to write badly, but give yourself permission to do so.
3. To the extent you can, think through writing rather than before it.
4. Keep your pen moving.
5. If you run out of things to say, write about how weird it is to run out of things to say until new thoughts arrive.
6. Silence your internal critic to suspend judgment.
7. Don't censor yourself.

Journal Prompts

- *What* do you mean, exactly, when you say you agree or disagree with the belief? Can you explain more fully why you think the belief is true or false?

- *When* did you start agreeing or disagreeing with the belief? Can you remember a particular moment or experience as a student learning to write that this agreement or disagreement connects to?

- *Who* was most influential in convincing you of the truth or falsity of the belief?

One Student's Response

Bernice's Journal

EXERCISE 1.1
STEP TWO

I used to be a firm believer in the idea of born writers—it was a genetic thing. People were gifted with the gold pen genes, or they weren't. Writing as a process involved a muse, inspiration, and luck. Things uncontrollable by the writer. Then I started writing, mostly for my 101 class, and I started to feel powerful when I put words on paper. In control. The idea of my voice, my words, just being on the page and other people reading it and maybe liking it was a rush. I was always the girl who specialized in the art of being unnoticed, unseen, blending in. My Comp 101 prof. liked my writing and pushed me really hard to work on my basics, to think about my process, to prewrite and revise. I started to see a clear distinction between how to write and what to write. How is all mixed up with the process, with discipline, with practice and perseverance.... The how isn't something you are born with; it's something you develop, something you practice, a skill you hone.... Becoming a good writer takes learning how to write, figuring out a process that works for you, and then letting your voice be heard on the page.

Inquiring into the Details

Journals

Here are five things that make a journal especially useful for writers:

- *Feel comfortable writing badly.* Whether print or digital, the journal must be a place where you're able to largely ignore your internal critic.

- *Use it throughout the writing process.* Journals can be indispensable for invention whenever you need more information, not just at the beginning. They can also be a place where you talk to yourself about how to solve a writing problem.

- *Write both specifically and abstractly.* Sometimes you'll be trying to be as concrete as possible, generating details, collecting facts, exploring particular experiences. Other times, use the journal to think in more-abstract language, thinking through ideas, reflecting on process, analyzing claims.

- *Don't make any rules about your journal.* These rules usually begin with a thought like "I'll only write in my journal when...." Write in your journal whenever you find it useful, and in any way that you find useful, especially if it keeps you writing.

- *Experiment.* Your journal will be different from my journal, which will be different from the journal of the woman sitting next to you in class. The only way to make a journal genuinely useful is to keep trying ways to make it useful.

Unlearning Unhelpful Beliefs

You won't be surprised when I say that I have a lot of theories about writing development; after all, I'm supposedly the expert. But we are *all* writing theorists, with beliefs that grow out of our successes and failures as people who write. Because you don't think much about them, these beliefs often shape your response to writing instruction without your even knowing it. For example, I've had a number of students who believe that people are born writers. This belief, of course, would make any kind of writing class a waste of time, because writing ability would be a matter of genetics.

A much more common belief is that learning to write is a process of building on basics, beginning with words and then working up to sentences, paragraphs, and perhaps whole compositions. This belief was very common when I was taught writing. I remember slogging my way through Warriner's *English Grammar and Composition* in the seventh and eighth grades, dutifully working through chapter after chapter.

Today, along with a lot of experts on writing instruction, I don't think that this foundational approach to writing development is very effective. While I can still diagram a sentence, for example, that's never a skill I call on when I'm composing. And yet building on the basics seems like common sense, doesn't it? This brings up an important point: Unlearning involves rejecting common sense *if* it conflicts with what actually works. Throughout this book, I hope you'll constantly test your beliefs about writing against the experiences you're having with it. Pay attention to what seems to work for you and what doesn't. Mostly, I'd like you at least initially to play what one writing instructor calls the *believing game*. Ask yourself, *What will I gain as a writer if I try believing this is true?* For example, even if you've believed for much of your life that you should never write anything in school that doesn't follow an outline, you might discover that abandoning this "rule" sometimes helps you to use writing to *discover* what you think.

> Unlearning involves rejecting common sense if it conflicts with what actually works.

The Beliefs of This Book

Allatonceness. One of the metaphors I very much like about writing development is offered by writing theorist Ann E. Berthoff. She said learning to write is like learning to ride a bike. You don't start by practicing handlebar skills, move on to pedaling practice, and then finally learn balancing techniques. You get on the bike and fall off, get up, and try again, doing all of those separate things at once. At some point, you don't fall and you pedal off down the street. Berthoff said writing is a process that involves allatonceness (all-at-once-ness), and it's simply not helpful to try to practice the subskills separately. This book shares the belief in the allatonceness of writing development.

Believing You Can Learn to Write Well. Various other beliefs about writing development—the importance of critical thinking, the connection between reading and writing, the power of voice and fluency, and the need to listen to voices other than your own—also help to guide this book. One belief, though, undergirds them all: *The most important thing that influences a writer's growth is believing that he or she can learn to write well.* Faith in your ability to become a better writer is key. From it grows the motivation to learn how to write well.

Faith isn't easy to come by. I didn't have it as a writer through most of my school career, because I assumed that being placed in the English class for underachievers meant that writing was simply another thing, like track and math, that I was mediocre at. For a long time, I was a captive to this attitude. But then, in college I wrote a paper I cared about; writing started to matter, because I discovered something I really wanted to say and say well. This was the beginning of my belief in myself—and of my becoming a better writer. Belief requires motivation, and one powerful motivator is to approach a writing assignment as an opportunity to learn something—that is, to approach it with what I have called the spirit of inquiry.

Habits of Mind

When I first started teaching writing, I noticed a strange thing in my classes. What students learned about writing through the early assignments in the class didn't seem to transfer to later assignments, particularly research papers. What was I doing wrong? I wondered. Among other things, what I'd failed to make clear to my students was that certain "habits of mind" (or *dispositions*, as one writer terms them) could be consistently useful to them, in writing papers in my course and in any course involving academic inquiry—habits related to seeing writing as a process of discovery. We'll look at several closely related habits here; later in this chapter, you'll see how they play a role in the writing process.

Starting with Questions, Not Answers

A lot of people think that writing is about recording what you already know, which accounts for those who choose familiar topics to write on when given the choice. "I think I'll write about _____," the thinking goes, "because I know that topic really well and already have an idea what I can say." Writers who write about what they know usually start with answers rather than questions. In some writing situations this makes a lot of sense, because you're being asked specifically to prove that you know something. I'm thinking of an essay exam, for instance.

1.2
Understand what kinds of questions will sustain inquiry into any subject.

But more often, writing in a university is about inquiry, not reporting information. It's about discovery. It's about finding the questions that ultimately lead to interesting answers.

Making the Familiar Strange. Starting with questions rather than answers changes everything. *It means finding new ways to see what you've seen before.* Take this for example:

What is it? An iPhone, of course. Not much more to say, right? But imagine that your purpose isn't to simply provide the quickest answer possible to the simple factual question *What is it?* Consider instead starting with questions that might inspire you to think about the iPhone in ways you haven't before; for example,

- *What does it mean* that iPhone owners spend twice as much time playing games as other smartphone users?
- *What should be done* about the environmental impacts of iPhone production in China?

Both these questions lead you to potentially new information and new ways of seeing that familiar phone in your pocket. They promise that you'll discover something you didn't know before.

Questions open up the inquiry process, while quick answers close it down. When you discover what you think, you don't cook up a thesis before you start—you discover the thesis as you explore. But to work, the inquiry process demands something of us that most of us aren't used to: suspending judgment.

Suspending Judgment

We jerk our knee when physicians tap the patellar tendon. If everything is working, we do it reflexively. We're often just as reflexive in our responses to the world:

- "What do you think of American politicians?"

  "They're all corrupt."
- "Is it possible to reconcile economic growth with the preservation of natural resources?"

  "No."
- "Isn't this an interesting stone?"

  "It's just a rock."

We make these judgments out of habit. But this habit is in fact a way of seeing, based on this premise: Some things are really pretty simple, more or less black-and-white, good or bad, boring or interesting. Academic inquiry works from another, very different premise: The world is really a wonderfully complex place, and *if we look closely and long enough*, and ask the right questions, we are likely to be surprised at what we see. A condition of inquiry is that you *don't* rush to judgment; you tolerate uncertainty while you explore your subject. Academic inquiry requires that you see your preconceptions as hypotheses that can be tested, not established truths. It is, in short, associated with a habit of *suspending* judgment.

> It's okay to write badly. Resist the tendency to judge too soon and too harshly.

Being Willing to Write Badly

In a writing course such as this one, the challenge of suspending judgment begins with how you approach your own writing. What's one of the most common problems I see in student writers? Poor grammar? Lack of organization? A missing thesis? Nope. *It's the tendency to judge too soon and too harshly.* A great majority of my students—including really smart, capable writers—have powerful internal critics, or, as the novelist Gail Godwin once called them, "Watchers at the Gates." This is the voice you may hear when you're starting to write a paper, the one that has you crossing out that first sentence or that first paragraph over and over until you "get it perfect."

The only way to overcome this problem is to suspend judgment. In doing so, you essentially tell your Watcher this: *It's okay to write badly.* Godwin once suggested that writers confront their internal critics by writing them a letter.

Dear Watcher,

Ever since the eighth grade, when I had Mrs. O'Neal for English, I've been seeing red. This is the color of every correction and every comment ("awk") you've made in the margins on my school writing. Now, years later, I just imagine you, ready to pick away at my prose every time I sit down to write. This time will be different. . . .

It might help to write your internal critic a letter like this. Rein in that self-critical part of yourself, and you'll find that writing can be a tool for *invention*—a way to generate material—and that you can *think through writing* rather than waiting around for the thoughts to come. You need your internal critic. But you need it to work with you, not against you. Later in this chapter, I'll show you how to accomplish this.

1.3
Practice a method of writing and thinking that will help you generate ideas.

Searching for Surprise

Starting with questions, making the familiar strange, suspending judgment, and writing badly—all are related to searching for surprise. In fact, one of the key benefits of writing badly is *surprise*. This was a revelation for me. I was convinced that you never pick up the pen unless you know what you want to say. Once I realized I could write badly and use writing not to *record* what I already knew, but to *discover* what I thought, this way of writing promised a feast of surprises that made me hunger to put words on the page. If you're skeptical that your own writing can surprise you, try the following exercise.

Conditions That Make "Bad" Writing Possible

1. Willingness to suspend judgment
2. Ability to write fast enough to outrun your internal critic
3. Belief that confusion, uncertainty, and ambiguity help thought rather than hinder it
4. Interest in writing about "risky" subjects, or those about which you don't know what you want to say until you say it

---

Exercise 1.2

A Roomful of Details

STEP ONE: Spend ten minutes brainstorming a list of details based on the following prompt. Write down whatever comes into your mind, no matter how silly. Be specific and don't censor yourself.

> Try to remember a room you spent a lot of time in as a child. It may be your bedroom in the back of your house or apartment, or the kitchen where your grandmother made thick, red pasta sauce or latkes. Put yourself back in that room. Now look around you. What do you see? What do you hear? What do you smell?

Brainstorming

- Anything goes.
- Don't censor yourself.
- Write everything down.
- Be playful but stay focused.

STEP TWO: Examine your list. If things went well, you will have a fairly long list of details. As you review the list, identify the one detail that surprises you the most, a detail that seems somehow to carry an unexpected charge. This might be something that seems connected to a feeling or a story. You might be drawn to a detail that confuses you a little. Whatever its particular appeal, circle it.

STEP THREE: Use the circled detail as a prompt for a seven-minute fastwrite. Begin by focusing on the detail: What does it make you think of? And then what? And then? Alternatively, begin by simply describing the detail more fully: What does it look like? Where did it come from? What stories are attached to it? How does it make you feel? Avoid writing in generalities. Write about specifics—that is, particular times, places, moments, and people. Write fast, and chase after the words to see where they want to go. Give yourself permission to write badly.

You may experience at least three kinds of surprise after completing a fast-writing exercise such as the one above:

1. Surprise about *how much* writing you did in such a short time
2. Surprise about discovering a topic you didn't expect to find
3. Surprise about discovering a *new way of understanding or seeing a familiar topic*

One Student's Response

Bernice's Journal

EXERCISE 1.2
STEP THREE

DETAIL: STAINLESS STEEL COUNTERS

When I was five or six my father and I made cookies for the first time. I don't remember what prompted him to bake cookies, he liked to cook but he didn't read very well so he didn't like to use cook books. I remember sitting on the cold stainless steel, the big red and white cook book splayed over my lap. I was reading it out loud to my dad. The kitchen was warm but everything gleamed; it was industrial and functional. It was the only room in our house that still looked like it belonged to the "Old Pioneer School." My dad and uncles had renovated every other room into bedrooms, playrooms, family rooms. The place was huge but cozy, it was home. I remember reading off ingredients until I got to the sugar. It called for 3/4 cup and I didn't understand the fraction. I thought it meant three or four cups. We poured so much sugar into the bowl. The cookies were terrible. Hard and glassy, too sweet and brittle. It wasn't until years later that I understood that my dad didn't understand the measurement either. He was persistent though. We pulled down every cook book in the house until we found one that described the measuring cups and what they meant. We started all over and our

> second batch was perfect. My dad is one of the smartest people I know, inventive, imaginative but he only has a rudimentary education. He can read and write enough to get by, he's gifted with numbers, but I can't help looking back and wondering what he could have been, what he could have done for the world if just one person had taken him by the hand and showed him what he showed me. If just one person had told him not to give up, to keep trying, that in the end it will be worth all the work, I wonder who he could have been if one person had seen his curiosity and imagination and fostered it instead of seeing his muscles and capable hands and putting him to work. If just one person had told him that his mind was the greatest tool he possessed. If just one person baked cookies with him.

The kind of surprises you encounter doing this sort of writing may not always be profound. They may not even provide you with obvious essay topics. With any luck, though, by hunting for surprises in your own work, you will begin to experience the pleasure of writing *to learn*. That's no small thing, particularly if you've always believed that writers should have it all figured out before they pick up the pen.

Writing Situations and Rhetorical Choices

1.4

Apply rhetorical knowledge to make choices in specific writing situations.

The following isn't good writing, is it?

> im happy to be back w/u guys it was a too long of a weekend- dancing friday then? u hailey and i runnin tomorrow- sounds fun 2 me

Actually, the answer is, of course, that it depends.

Writing occurs in a writing situation, and different writing situations are associated with different types of writing and forms of communication—different genres and media. Think of how many writing situations we encounter these days and how many types of writing we do. For example, besides writing part of this textbook chapter, I wrote e-mails to an editor and a student, freewrote in my journal, drafted some text for a web page, sent a text to my daughter, and posted a comment on Facebook.

In each case, the writing situation demanded something different from me. In each, however, I had to make appropriate *rhetorical* choices—choices related to the following four considerations:

- **Purpose for writing:** What is the text trying to do?
- **Audience:** For whom is it intended?
- **Subject:** What is it about?
- **Genre/Medium:** What type of writing—what form of communication—would work best in view of my purpose, audience, and subject? What are its strengths and limitations, and what are its conventions?

That is, to write effectively, I had to think about why I was writing, to whom I was writing, what I was writing about, and what type of text I was writing. The effectiveness of my writing depended on my making appropriate choices in light of these considerations. And the rhetorical choices that we make in a writing situation are wide ranging; they include not only big choices (What's the best genre for accomplishing my purpose with this audience?), but also many smaller choices (Is it okay to say "ur" instead of "you're"?).

Now let's go back to the text message, written by my daughter to a friend.

Rhetorical Consideration	The Text Message
Purpose	Expressive and informational purposes: to reinforce intimacy; to plan
Audience	A close friend, with considerable shared knowledge
Subject	Personal details related to knowledge of a shared experience
Genre/Medium	Text message; limited to 160 characters, with a shorthand shared by users

Based on this analysis, my daughter's text message is clearly good writing after all. It uses the conventions of the genre/medium to fulfill its purpose—reinforce intimacy and make a Friday-night plan—for the audience the writer had in mind. My daughter used her *rhetorical knowledge* to make choices that resulted in an effective piece of writing. Of course, she would think it is weird to call her understanding of how to write a text message "rhetorical knowledge." But that's exactly what it is. She just doesn't think about it that way.

But what happens when you *do* think about it?

1. You become more skillful at composing in writing situations with which you are familiar.
2. You can learn to master unfamiliar writing situations much more quickly.

You have more rhetorical knowledge than you think. After all, you've been writing and speaking all your life. But when you start becoming aware of this knowledge, it becomes more powerful, and you become a better writer. Throughout *The Curious Writer*, I'll encourage you to think rhetorically.

In the next years of college, you'll be encountering unfamiliar writing situations, so learning to reflect on how each involves *rhetorical choices* will make you a much better communicator. (By the way, we also use this rhetorical knowledge to analyze how well someone else communicates, which is the focus of Chapter 2.) Learning to write well, then, isn't simply learning how to craft transitions, organize information, and follow grammatical "rules"—it's also learning to recognize that each writing situation asks you for something different. For example, in college writing situations, the basic rhetorical considerations, as in Figure 1.1, "Thinking rhetorically," may be expanded with questions such as these:

- What is the purpose of the assignment? To interpret or analyze? Synthesize or summarize? Argue or explore?
- What is the subject, and what does that imply about my approach? Are there certain ways of writing about topics in history, psychology, or literature that differ from writing about topics in biology, social science, or business?
- Am I writing for an expert audience or a general audience? For my instructor or my peers?
- What is the form or genre for this assignment, and what are its conventions? What kind of evidence should I use? How is it organized?

You won't always have control over all of these choices. In college, you'll get writing assignments that may supply you with a purpose: "Write an essay that compares the energy efficiency of solar panels with that of a conventional coal power plant." Sometimes the form isn't up to you: "Write a five-page argument paper." But even when you have such constraints, you still have a lot of rhetorical choices to make—things like: "Should I use the first person? What evidence do I need, and where should it come from?"

Each genre and medium imposes its own conditions on the writer. For example, my daughter's text message can't be more than 160 characters, and that

Purpose
What is it
trying to do?

Audience
For whom is
it intended?

Subject
What is it
about?

Genre/Medium
What are the
conventions?

Figure 1.1 Thinking rhetorically. Rhetorical choices involve four considerations: purpose, subject, audience, and genre/medium. Each consideration is associated with questions. For genre/medium, these include conditions and conventions regarding what you can say and especially how you say it. While all considerations have always been important in rhetorical thinking, genre and medium are especially critical to consider now that you may have alternatives to writing traditional term papers, including PowerPoints, podcasts, video, visuals, and a host of other multimodal approaches.

limitation inspired, among other things, a shorthand for composing that uses characters sparingly. Considering genre and medium is especially important now that the forms of communication have expanded radically, even in academia. You may write not just a term paper. You might do a PowerPoint, make a poster, build a web page, collaborate on a wiki, or produce a podcast.

Thinking about rhetorical contexts increases the chance that you'll make good choices when you solve problems as a writer, particularly in revision. Much like riding Berthoff's bike, in composing, writers usually think about purpose, audience, subject, and genre/medium all at once, drawing on their experience with similar writing situations.

A First Reflection on Your Writing Process

There is a process for doing almost anything—fixing a broken washing machine, learning how to play tennis, studying for the SAT, and, of course, writing. Why, then, do some English teachers seem to make such a big deal out of reflecting on your writing process? Here's why:

- First, the process of writing, like any process that we do frequently, is not something that we think about.

- As a consequence, when we write, we tend to focus just on *what* and not on *how*, just on the product and not on the process. And then, when problems arise, we don't see many options for solving them—we get stuck and we get frustrated.

- If, however, we start to pay attention to how we write in a variety of situations, two things happen: We become aware of our old habits that don't always help and may actually hinder our success with writing. Second—and this is most important—we begin to understand that there are actually *choices* we can make when problems arise, and we become aware of what some of those choices are.

- In short, *the more we understand the writing process, the more control we get over it*. Getting control of the process means the product gets better.[1]

A Case Study

Here's an example of what I mean. Chauntain summarized her process this way: "Do one and be done." She always wrote her essays at the last minute and only wrote a single draft. She approached nearly every writing assignment the same way: Start with a thesis, and then develop five topic sentences that support the thesis, with three supporting details under each. This structure was a container

---

[1]There is considerable research in learning theory that confirms these conclusions; in particular, so-called metacognitive thinking—the awareness of how you do things—increases the transfer of relevant knowledge from one situation to another. In other words, what you learn about how to do something in one situation gets more easily activated in another situation.

into which she poured all her prose. Chauntain deliberated over every sentence, trying to make each one perfect, and as a result, she spent considerable time staring off into space searching for the right word or phrase. It was agony. The papers were almost always dull—she thought so too—and just as often she struggled to reach the required page length. Chauntain had no idea of any other way to write a school essay. As a matter of fact, she thought it was really the *only* way. So when she got an assignment in her economics class to write an essay in which she was to use economic principles to analyze a question that arose from a personal observation, Chauntain was bewildered. How should she start? Could she rely on her old standby structure—thesis, topic sentences, supporting details? She felt stuck.

Because she failed to see that she had choices related to both process and this particular writing situation, she also had no clue what those choices were. That's why we study process. It helps us solve problems such as these. And it must begin with a self-study of your own habits as a writer, identifying not just how you tend to do things, but the patterns of problems that might arise when you do them.

Thinking About Your Process

You will reflect on your writing and reading processes again and again throughout this book, so that by the end you may be able to tell the story of your processes and how you are changing them to produce better writing more efficiently. The reflective letter in your portfolio (see Appendix A) might be where you finally share that story in full. Now is a good time to begin telling yourself that story.

What do you remember about your own journey as a writer both inside and outside of school? One of my earliest, most pleasant memories of writing is listening to the sound of the clacking of my father's old Royal typewriter in the room down the hall as I was going to sleep. I imagine him there now, in the small study that we called the "blue room," enveloped in a cloud of pipe smoke. It is likely that he was writing advertising copy back then, or perhaps a script for a commercial in which my mother, an actress, would appear. I loved the idea of writing then. The steady hammering of typewriter keys sounded effortless yet at the same time solid, significant. This all changed, I think, in the eighth grade when it seemed that writing was much more about following rules than tapping along to a lively dance of words.

Spend some time telling your own story about how your relationship to writing evolved.

When you get a writing assignment, your habit may be to compose carefully. This assignment, in contrast, is all about invention—about generating ideas.

Exercise 1.3

Literacy Narrative Collage

In your journal, create a collage of moments, memories, and reflections related to your experience with writing. *For each prompt, write fast for about four minutes. Keep your pen or fingers on the keyboard moving, and give yourself permission to write badly*. After you've responded to one prompt, skip a line and move on to the next one. Set aside about twenty minutes for this generating activity.

1. What is your earliest memory of writing? Tell the story.

2. We usually divide our experiences as writers into private writing and school writing, or writing we do by choice and writing we are required to do for a grade. Let's focus on school writing. Tell the story of a teacher, a class, an essay, an exam, or a moment that you consider a *turning point* in your understanding of yourself as a writer or your understanding of school writing.

3. Writing is part of the fabric of everyday life in the United States, and this is truer than ever with Internet communication. Describe the roles that writing plays in a typical day for you. How have these daily roles of writing changed in your lifetime so far?

4. What is the most successful (or least successful) thing you've ever written in or out of school? Tell the story.

Congratulations. You've made a mess. But I hope this collage of your experiences as a writer is an interesting mess, one that brought some little surprises. As you look at these four fragments of fastwriting, you might begin to sense a pattern. Is there a certain idea about yourself as a writer that seems to emerge in these various contexts? It's more likely that one, or perhaps two, of the prompts really took off for you, presenting trails you'd like to continue following. Or maybe nothing happened. For now, set your journal aside. You may return to this material if your instructor invites you to draft a longer narrative about your writing experiences, or you might find a place for some of this writing in your portfolio.

Now that you've spent some time telling a story of your background as a writer, use the following survey to pin down some of your habits and experiences related to school writing. The questions in the survey can help you develop a profile of your writing process and help you identify problems you might want to address by altering your process.

Exercise 1.4

What Is Your Process?

STEP ONE: Complete the Self-Evaluation Survey.

Self-Evaluation Survey

1. When you're given a school writing assignment, do you wait until the last minute to finish it?

    Always————Often————Sometimes————Rarely————Never

2. How often have you had the experience of learning something you didn't expect through writing about it?

    Very often———Fairly often———Sometimes———Rarely———Never

3. Do you generally plan out what you're going to write before you write it?

    Always———Often———Sometimes———Rarely———Never

4. *Prewriting* describes activities that some writers engage in before they begin a first draft. Prewriting might include such invention activities as freewriting or fastwriting, making lists, brainstorming or mapping, collecting information, browsing the web, talking to someone about the essay topic, reading up on it, or jotting down ideas in a notebook or journal. How much prewriting do you tend to do for the following types of assignments? Circle the appropriate answer.

    ■ A personal narrative:

    A great deal———Some———Very little———None———Haven't
    written one

    ■ A critical essay about a short story, novel, or poem:

    A great deal———Some———Very little———None———Haven't
    written one

    ■ A research paper:

    A great deal———Some———Very little———None———Haven't
    written one

    ■ An essay exam:

    A great deal———Some———Very little———None———Haven't
    written one

5. At what point(s) in writing an academic paper do you often find yourself getting stuck? Check all that apply.

    ❑ Getting started

    ❑ In the middle

    ❑ Finishing

    ❑ I never/rarely get stuck (go on to question 9)

    ❑ Other: _____

6. If you usually have problems getting started on a paper, which of the following do you often find hardest to do? Check all that apply. (If you don't have trouble getting started, go on to question 7.)

    ❑ Deciding on a topic

    ❑ Writing an introduction

    ❑ Finding the time to begin

    ❑ Figuring out exactly what I'm supposed to do for the assignment

    ❑ Finding a purpose or focus for the paper

❑ Finding the right tone

❑ Other: _____

7. If you usually get stuck in the middle of a paper, which of the following cause(s) the most problems? Check all that apply. (If writing the middle of a paper isn't a problem for you, go on to question 8.)

❑ Keeping focused on the topic

❑ Finding enough information to meet page-length requirements

❑ Following my plan for how I want to write the paper

❑ Bringing in other research or points of view

❑ Organizing all my information

❑ Trying to avoid plagiarism

❑ Worrying about whether the paper meets the requirements of the assignment

❑ Worrying that the paper just isn't any good

❑ Messing with citations

❑ Other: _____

8. If you have difficulty finishing a paper, which of the following difficulties is/are typical for you? Check all that apply. (If finishing isn't a problem for you, go on to question 9.)

❑ Composing a last paragraph or conclusion

❑ Worrying that the paper doesn't meet the requirements of the assignment

❑ Worrying that the paper just isn't any good

❑ Trying to keep focused on the main idea or thesis

❑ Trying to avoid repeating myself

❑ Realizing I don't have enough information

❑ Dealing with the bibliography or citations

❑ Other: _____

9. Rank the following list of approaches to revision so that it reflects the strategies you use *most often to least often* when rewriting academic papers. Rank the items 1–6, with the strategy you use most often as a 1 and the strategy you use least often as a 6.

_____ I just tidy things up—editing sentences, checking spelling, looking for grammatical errors, fixing formatting, and performing other proofreading activities.

_____ I look for ways to reorganize existing information in the draft to make it more effective.

_____ I try to fill holes by adding more information.

_____ I do more research.

_____ I change the focus or even the main idea, rewriting sections, adding or removing information, and changing the order of things.

_____ I rarely do any revision.

10. Finally, do you tend to impose a lot of conditions on when, where, or how you think you write most effectively? (For example, do you need a certain pen, do you always have to write on a computer, do you need to be in certain kinds of places, must it be quiet or noisy, do you write best under pressure?) Or can you write under a range of circumstances, with few or no conditions? Circle one.

Lots of conditions———Some———A few———No conditions

If you impose conditions on when, where, or how you write, list some of those conditions here:

1.

2.

3.

STEP TWO: In small groups, discuss the results of the survey. Begin by picking someone to tally the answers to each question. Post these on the board, a large sheet of paper, or a spreadsheet, so they can then be added up for the class. Analyze the results for your group. In particular, discuss the following questions:

- Are there patterns in the responses? Do most group members seem to answer certain questions in similar or different ways? Are there interesting contradictions?
- Based on these results, what "typical" habits or challenges do writers in your class seem to share?
- What struck you most?

Problem Solving in Your Writing Process

If you took the survey, you probably uncovered some problems with your writing process. The great news for those of us who struggle with certain aspects of writing—and who doesn't?—is that you can do something about it. As you identify the obstacles to doing better work, you can change the way you approach writing tasks. For instance, consider some of the more common problems students struggle with and some ideas about how *The Curious Writer* can help you with them.

Writing Problem	Possible Cause	A Solution
Consistently writes short. Often can't meet page requirements for assignments.	Writer works from scarcity. Begins the draft with too little information on the topic.	Focus on invention. Generate more material *before* you begin the draft, through research, fastwriting, etc. (see "Inquiring into the Details: Invention Strategies" in this chapter).
Dislikes revision, especially if it involves more than "tidying" things up.	Writer spends a great deal of time writing the first draft and trying to make it "perfect." Gets over-committed to the initial approach to the topic.	Write a fast draft and then do deeper revision. Attack the draft physically (see Revision Strategy 14.18 in Chapter 14).
Writer's block.	Internal critic is too harsh too early in the writing process. Often involves anxiety about audience.	Find a place where you can write badly without it feeling like a performance. A journal or notebook often works (see "Inquiring into the Details: Journals" in this chapter).
Dislikes open-ended assignments. Would rather be told what to write about.	Writer may be unused to valuing own thinking. Little experience with assignments in which writer must discover own purpose.	Use your own curiosity and questions to drive the process. Craft questions that are useful guides for exploration and promise discovery and learning (see "Starting with Questions, Not Answers" in this chapter).
Struggles with focus. Able to write a lot but can't seem to stay on topic.	Writer doesn't exploit key opportunities to look at writing critically, to evaluate and judge what she has generated.	Effectively combine invention with evaluation, generating with judging, by using a process that makes room for both as you write (see "The Nature of the Writing Process" below).

The Nature of the Writing Process

Earlier you saw Chauntain's writing process. Here was my writing process when I was in school:

1. Get the assignment. Find out when it is due and how long it is supposed to be.
2. Wait until the night before it is due and get started.
3. Stare off into space.
4. Eat ice cream.

5. Write a sketchy outline.

6. Write a sentence; then cross it out.

7. Stare off into space.

8. Write another sentence, and then squeeze out a few more.

9. Think about Lori Jo Flink, and then stare off into space.

10. Write a paragraph. Feel relief and disgust.

Suspending judgment feels freer, exploratory…. Making judgments shifts the writer into an analytical mode.

I would get the work done eventually, but the process was agonizing and the product mediocre. What did I conclude from this back then? That I wasn't good at writing, which was no big surprise because I pretty much hated it. Something happened to me to change that view, of course, because you hold my book in your hands. I came to understand the problems in my writing process: I viewed writing as a straight march forward from beginning to end, one where I had to wait for something to come into my head and then try to get it down. At all costs, I avoided things like new ideas or other ways of seeing a topic—anything that might get in the way of the drive to the conclusion. If I thought about anything, it was trying to find the "perfect" way of saying things or worrying about whether I was faithfully following a certain structure. I rarely learned anything from my writing. I certainly never expected I should.

The Writing Process as Recursive and Flexible

But this straight march isn't the way experienced writers work at all. The writing process isn't a linear trajectory, but a looping, recursive process—one that encourages *thinking*, not simply recording the thoughts that you already have. Writing doesn't involve a series of steps that you must follow in every situation; on the contrary:

- The writing process is *recursive*, a much messier zigzag between collecting information and focusing on it, exploring things and thinking about them, writing and rewriting, reviewing and rearranging, and so on. For example, invention strategies are useful at many points in the writing process.

- The process is *flexible* and always influenced by the writing situation. For instance, experienced writers have a keen sense of audience, and they use this to cue their choices about a change in tone or whether an example might help clarify a point. These are exactly the kinds of adjustments you make in social situations all the time.

A System for Using Writing to Think

What do I mean when I say the writing process encourages thinking? Usually, when we imagine someone who is "deep in thought," we see him staring off into space with a furrowed brow, chin nested in one hand. He is not writing. He may be

Inquiring into the Details

Invention Strategies

Invention is a term from rhetoric that means the act of generating ideas. While we typically think of *rhetoric* as something vaguely dishonest and often associated with politics, it's actually a several-thousand-year-old body of knowledge about speaking and writing well. Invention is a key element in rhetoric. It can occur at any time during the writing process, not just at the beginning in the "prewriting" stage. Some useful invention strategies include:

■ *Fastwriting:* The emphasis is on speed, not correctness. Don't compose, don't think about what you want to say before you say it. Instead, let the writing lead, helping you discover what you think.

■ *Listing:* Fast lists can help you generate lots of information quickly. They are often in code, with words and phrases that have meaning only for you. Let your lists grow in waves—think of two or three items and then pause until the next few items rush in.

■ *Clustering:* This nonlinear method of generating information, also called *mapping*, relies on *webs* and often free association of ideas or information. Begin with a core word, phrase, or concept at the center of a page, and build branches off it. Follow each branch until it dies out, return to the core, and build another. (For an example, see p. 80.)

■ *Questioning:* Questions are to ideas what knives are to onions. They help you cut through to the less obvious insights and perspectives, revealing layers of possible meanings, interpretations, and ways of understanding. Asking questions complicates things but rewards you with new discoveries.

■ *Conversing:* Conversing is fastwriting with the mouth. When we talk, especially to someone we trust, we work out what we think and feel about things. We listen to what we say, but we also invite a response, which leads us to new insights.

■ *Researching:* This is a kind of conversation, too. We listen and respond to other voices that have said something, or will say something if asked, about topics that interest us. Reading and interviewing are not simply things you do when you write a research paper, but activities you use whenever you have questions you can't answer on your own.

■ *Observing:* When we look closely at anything, we see what we didn't notice at first. Careful observation of people, objects, experiments, images, and so on generates specific information that leads to informed judgments.

thinking about what he's *going* to write, but in the meantime the cursor is parked on the computer screen or the pen rests on the desk. Thinking like this is good—I do it all the time. But imagine if you also make thought external by following your thinking on paper or screen and not just in your head. Here is some of what happens:

- You have a record of what you've thought that you can return to again and again.

- As you *see* what you've just said, you discover something else to say.

- Because the process of thinking through writing is slower than thinking in your head, you think differently.

- Because externalizing thought takes mental effort, you are more immersed in thought, creating what one theorist called a state of "flow."

As I've already mentioned, thinking through writing is most productive when you suspend judgment, reining in your internal critic. You may actually do some pretty good thinking with some pretty bad writing.

Using writing as a way of thinking is even more powerful if there is a *system* for doing it that reliably produces insight. One method, which we could call a *dialectical system*, exploits two different kinds of thinking—one creative and the other critical, one wide open and the other more closed. So far in this chapter, we've focused on the creative side, the generating activities I've called "writing badly" that restrain your internal critic. But you need that critical side. You need it to make sense of things, to evaluate what's significant and what's not, to help you figure out what you might be trying to say. If you use both kinds of thinking, "dialectically" moving back and forth from one to the other, then you're using a method that is at the heart of the process you'll use throughout *The Curious Writer*.[2] Try the next exercise to see how this might work for you.

Exercise 1.5

Two Kinds of Thinking

Let's return to the subject you began writing about in Exercise 1.3—your experiences as a writer—but focus on something that was probably part of your response to the third prompt in that exercise: your experience with writing technology.

Using Creative Thinking

STEP ONE: What are your earliest memories of using a computer for writing? In your journal or on the computer, begin by telling the story and then let the writing lead from there. Keep your pen or the cursor moving, and allow yourself to write badly.

---

[2] For Greek philosophers such as Plato, dialectic was a way of arriving at truth through back-and-forth conversation between two people who were open to changing their minds. Similarly, the process of writing and thinking I propose here is a back and forth between two parts of yourself—each receptive to the other—in an effort to discover your own "truths," ideas, and insights.

STEP TWO: Brainstorm a list of words or phrases that you associate with the word *literate* or *literacy*.

Reread what you just wrote in steps 1 and 2, underlining things that surprise you or that seem significant or interesting to you. Skip a line and move on to step 3.

Using Critical Thinking

STEP THREE: Choose one of the following sentence frames as a starting point. Complete the sentence and then develop it as a paragraph. This time, compose each sentence while thinking about what you want to say before you say it and trying to say it as well as you can.

> What I understand now about my experiences with writing on computers that I didn't understand when I started out is _____.
>
> When they think about writing with computers, most people think _____, but my experience was _____.
>
> The most important thing I had to discover before I considered myself "computer literate" was _____.

Reflecting

If you're like most people, then the parts of this exercise where you creatively generated material felt different than the part where you judged as you wrote. But *how* were they different? How would you distinguish between the experiences of generating and judging? Talk about this or write about it in your journal.

A Writing Process That Harnesses Two Currents of Thought

The two parts of Exercise 1.5 involving creative and critical thinking were designed to show you the difference between the two and also to simulate the shift between them, the shift from suspending judgments to making judgments—something I referred to as "dialectical" thinking. In the first two steps, you spent some time fastwriting without much critical interference, trying to generate some information from your own experience. In the third step, which began with "seed" sentences that forced you into a more reflective, analytical mode, you were encouraged to look for patterns of meaning in what you generated.

As you probably noticed, these two distinct ways of thinking each have advantages for the writer:

- *Suspending judgment* feels freer, is exploratory, and may spark emotion.
- *Making judgments* shifts the writer into an analytical mode, one that might lower the temperature, allowing writers to see their initial explorations with less feeling and more understanding.

Thus, creative thinking creates the conditions for discovery—new insights or ways of seeing—while critical thinking helps writers refine their discoveries and focus on the most significant of them.

The Sea and the Mountain. Here's another way to conceptualize creative and critical thinking (see Figure 1.2):

- When you write creatively, you plunge into the sea of information. You don't swim in one direction, but eagerly explore in all directions, including the depths.

- When you write critically, you emerge from the water to find a vantage point—a mountain—from which to see where you've swum. From the mountain (which occasionally erupts and belches forth two words: "So What?"), you are able to see patterns that aren't visible from the water. You are able to make judgments about what you encountered there: What's significant? What isn't? Why?

The key is not to stay on the mountain. Instead, you take the patterns you saw and the judgments you made and plunge back into the sea, this time with a stronger

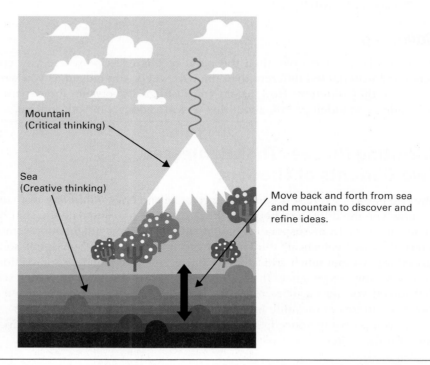

Mountain
(Critical thinking)

Sea
(Creative thinking)

Move back and forth from sea and mountain to discover and refine ideas.

Figure 1.2   Generating insight using critical and creative thinking. Thinking to inquire is like the movement back and forth from the sea of information to the mountain of reflection. In one you explore, and on the other you evaluate. Insight develops when you continually move back and forth; as you refine your ideas, when in the sea, you swim in ever smaller circles with a stronger sense of purpose.

sense of purpose. You're clearer about what you want to know and where you need to swim to find it. This back and forth between mountain and sea continues until you've discovered what you want to say. In fact, you made just this sort of movement in Exercise 1.2 and then in Exercise 1.5 when you moved from generating to judging. It is a process of induction and deduction, working upwards from specifics to infer ideas, and then taking those ideas and testing them against specifics.

Figure 1.3 lists yet other ways in which you can visualize the movement between creative and critical thinking. In narrative writing, for instance, creative thinking helps you generate information about *what happened*, while critical thinking may lead you to insights about *what happens*. Likewise, in research writing, investigators often move back and forth between their *observations of* things and their *ideas about* them.

As you work through the book, you'll find it easier to shift between contrasting modes of thought—from collecting to focusing, from generating to judging, from showing to telling, from exploring to reflecting, from believing to doubting, from playing to evaluating. In short, you'll become better able to balance creative and critical thinking. You'll know when it's useful to open up the process of thinking to explore and when it's necessary to work at making sense of what you've discovered.

Answering the *So What?* Question. An important function on the critical thinking side is to make sure you can answer the one question you must answer when writing for an audience:

So what?

Creative Thinking	⟷	Critical Thinking
Fastwriting	⟷	Composing
Showing	⟷	Telling
Specifics	⟷	Generalities
Collecting	⟷	Focusing
Observations of	⟷	Ideas about
What happened	⟷	What happens
Generating	⟷	Criticizing
Exploring	⟷	Reflecting
Seeing	⟷	Interpreting
Evaluating	⟷	Generating

Figure 1.3   Alternating currents of thought. When writers alternate between creative and critical thinking, they move back and forth between two opposing modes of thought—the creative and the critical. One seems playful and the other judgmental; one feels open ended and the other more closed. Activities such as fastwriting and brainstorming promote one mode of thought, and careful composing and reflection promote the other.

So what? can be a pretty harsh question, and I find that some students tend to ask it too soon in the writing process, before they've fully explored their topic. A danger is that this can lead to frustration. You may, for example, have found yourself high and dry if you've tried to reflect on possible meanings of a moment you've written about for only eight minutes. Another danger is that the writer is tempted to seize on the first convenient idea or thesis that comes along. This abruptly ends the process of inquiry before the writer has had a chance to explore.

When you can't come up with an answer to the *So what?* question, the solution is usually to generate more information.

A Writing Process Driven by Questions

The inquiry approach is grounded in the idea that the writing process depends, more than anything else, on finding good questions to address.

I recently visited teachers in Laredo, Texas, and I told them that with a good question, even the most boring topic can become interesting. I would prove it, I said, and picked up a lemon that was sitting on a table and asked everyone, in turn, to ask a question about the lemon or about lemons. Twenty minutes later, we had generated sixty questions. In the process, we began to wonder how the scent of lemons came to be associated with cleanliness, why lemons appeared so often in wartime British literature, why the lime and not the lemon is celebrated in local Hispanic culture. We wondered a lot of interesting things that we never expected to wonder about, because a lemon is ordinary. Questions can make the familiar world we inhabit yield to wonder.

The point is this: *There are no boring topics—just wrong questions.*

But what are *good* inquiry questions? Obviously, for a question to be good, you have to be interested in it. Furthermore, others must also have a stake in the answer, because you'll be sharing what you learn.

Usually, when we investigate something we don't know much about, we start by asking informational questions. Say you're interested in the Disney Corporation's sustainability projects. You first need to know what those are. You might search online and read about Disney's commitment to recycling or to energy efficiency. This is basic background information—facts about what has already been said about a topic. But in college writing, you're usually not writing a report or a summary of what's known about a topic. Just explaining what Disney is doing to reduce emissions isn't enough. You have to *do* something with that information. This involves that critical mind that we talked about earlier, one that asks you to make judgments.

Different types of questions lead to different kinds of judgments. And it's landing on the appropriate type of question for your project that will launch you into meaningful inquiry. These question types include the following:

- *Value questions:* Is it good or bad? Useful or useless?

- *Relationship questions:* Are they similar or dissimilar? Is there a cause and effect? What's the connection?

- *Policy questions:* What should be done?
- *Interpretation questions:* What might it mean?
- *Hypothesis questions:* What is the best explanation?
- *Claim questions:* Are the assertions valid? What is most persuasive?

You can apply these kinds of questions to nearly any topic, depending on what interests you about it. For example, in Figure 1.4 I tried to imagine how someone exploring Disney's sustainability programs might use each of these question types. With a little factual background, it isn't hard to start framing possible inquiry questions that can really steer your project in different—and possibly interesting—directions.

A good question not only lights your way into a subject, but may also illuminate what form you could use to share your discoveries. Certain kinds of writing—reviews, critical essays, personal essays, and so on—are often associated with certain types of questions, as you can see in Figure 1.4. In Part 2 of *The Curious Writer*, which features a range of inquiry projects from the personal essay to the research essay, you'll see how certain questions naturally guide you towards certain kinds of writing.

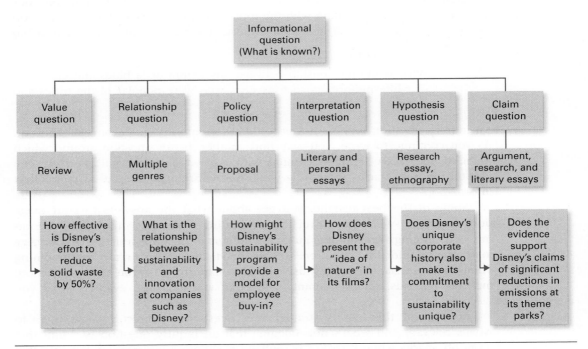

Figure 1.4 Categories of inquiry questions. The inquiry process often begins with informational questions: What is already known about this? As writers learn more about their topics, they refine their questions so that they are more likely to lead to analysis or argument rather than mere report. Some of these questions are associated with certain kinds of writing that are covered in this book.

A Strategy for Inquiry: Questioning, Generating, and Judging

If you combine the power of good questions with the back-and-forth process of writing creatively and critically, you have a strategy of inquiry that you can use for every assignment in this book. The key is to alternately generate—topics, ideas, questions—and judge. Typically, you begin exploring a subject, sometimes generating some initial thoughts through fastwriting, listing, or other invention methods. But like landscape shots in photography, subjects cover a huge amount of ground. You need to narrow your subject and eventually arrive at a yet narrower topic, or some *part* of the landscape to look at more closely. As an example, take popular music. That's a huge subject. But as you write and read about it a little, you may begin to see that you're most interested in the blues, and especially in its influence on American popular music. This last might seem promising as a general topic.

With a tentative topic in hand, you then need to search for a few inquiry questions about your topic that both interest you and will sustain your project. These are the questions that will help you focus your topic, that will guide your research, and that may eventually become the heart of an essay draft on your topic. For example, beginning with the topic of the influence of the blues on pop music, you might arrive at an inquiry question something like this relationship question:

> What is the relationship between Mississippi delta blues and the music of white performers such as Elvis who were popular in the fifties and sixties?

An inquiry question may be no more than a temporary guide on your journey. As you continue to write, you may find another, better question around which to build your project. But beginning with a good question will get and keep you on the right track—something you'll find enormously helpful as you collect information.

Some of the best insights you get about what the answers to your questions might be will come from the alternating currents of thought—generating and judging, suspending judgment and making judgments—that energize your writing and thinking processes. In practical terms, this means combining open-ended methods, such as fastwriting, to explore what you think with more focused methods, such as summarizing, that will help you evaluate what you discover.

Most of all, this inquiry strategy uses questions to direct your attention to what's relevant and what's not. Imagine that an inquiry question is a flint that gives off sparks when it strikes potentially meaningful information, whether that information comes from personal experiences or research. These sparks are the things that will light your way to discoveries about your topic. In Part 2 of this book, you'll be led through this process in the last part of each chapter, as you *open up* your thinking about topics (generate), *narrow down* those topics through focused questioning (judge), *try out* various approaches (generate), *think about* criteria (judge)—and finally, develop, draft, and revise your writing.

The inquiry strategy I'm proposing should work with nearly any topic. Let's try one in Exercise 1.6.

Exercise 1.6

A Mini Inquiry Project: Cell Phone Culture

The alternating currents of thought—generating and judging, exploring and evaluating, opening up and focusing, mountain and sea—can be put to work in any situation where you want to figure out what you think. Writing is a key part of the system. In this exercise, I'll guide you to think one way and then another. Later, you may find you do this on your own without thinking about it. But for now, let me guide you.

More than 90 percent of us now have cell phones, and according to one study, about a third of people aged eighteen to twenty-nine say that they "couldn't live without" them. Cell phones make us feel safer, and of course they're an enormous convenience. But they've also introduced new annoyances into modern life, like the "halfalogue," the distracting experience of being subjected to one half of a stranger's conversation with someone on their cell phone. It's a technology that is fundamentally changing our culture—our sense of community and connection, our identities, the way we spend our time. But how? Try exploring that question for yourself, to see if you can discover what *you* find interesting about the topic.

Invention: Generating

STEP ONE: Let's first take a dip in the sea of information. Recent research on "cell phone addiction" suggests that, as with Internet addiction, "overuse" of the technology can result in anxiety, depression, irritability, and antisocial behavior. This research also suggests that college students are particularly vulnerable to cell phone addiction. One survey to determine whether someone is cell phone addicted asks some of the following questions:

- Do you feel preoccupied about possible calls or messages on your mobile phone, and do you think about it when your cell is off?
- How often do you anticipate your next use of the cell phone?
- How often do you become angry and/or start to shout if someone interrupts you when you're talking on a cell phone?
- Do you use a cell to escape from your problems?

Start by exploring your reaction to this list in a fastwrite in your journal, print or digital. Write for at least three minutes, but write longer if you can. What do you make of the whole idea of "cell phone addiction"? What does this make you think about? And then what? And then?

Judging

STEP TWO: Reread your fastwrite, underlining anything that you find interesting, surprising, or possibly significant. Pay particular attention to anything that might have surprised you. Then thoughtfully finish the following sentence.

One interesting question that this raises for me is: _____ ?

Generating

STEP THREE: Focus on the question you came up with in step 2. Return to the sea and write about specific *observations, stories, people, situations, or scenes* that come to mind when you consider the question you posed. Don't hesitate to explore other questions as they arise as well. Let the writing lead. Write fast for *at least* another three minutes without stopping.

Judging

STEP FOUR: Review what you just wrote, thoughtfully complete the following sentence, and then follow that first sentence for as long as you can compose here, thinking about what you're going to say before you say it, rather than fastwriting.

So far, one thing I seem to be saying is that we. . . .

Finding a Question

STEP FIVE: You haven't generated much writing on cell phone culture yet, but if you've written for ten minutes or so, you should have enough information to take a stab at writing a tentative inquiry question. Using the question categories in Figure 1.4, try to draft a question about cell phones, cell phone culture, cell phone addiction, or any other topic suggested by your writing. Remember, the question should be one of the following:

- A value question: Is it any good?
- A policy question: What should be done?
- A hypothesis question: What is the best explanation?
- A relationship question: What is the relationship between _____ and _____?
- An interpretation question: What might it mean?
- A claim question: What does the evidence seem to support?

Reflecting on the Process

STEP SIX: In your journal, or on an online discussion board, answer the following questions about what you've just drafted.

1. What, if anything, do I understand now that I didn't before?
2. What most surprised me?
3. What's the most important thing I take from this?

Reflective Inquiry About Your Writing

I should be a really good guitar player. I've played since I was eleven. I'm okay. But among my other problems was a lousy sense of rhythm—at least until recently, when I began playing with my friend Richard, who can play skillfully in all the ways I can't. How did I solve the rhythm problem by playing with Richard? What exactly did I learn to do that helped me adjust my strum so I could provide passably good backup to Richard's leads?

To get better at a process, we need to ask questions about it. And to answer these questions, we have to have three things:

1. Some knowledge of how the process is done or how it might be done
2. The language to define the problem
3. Some ideas about possible solutions

Since the beginning of this chapter, I've argued that taking the time to reflect on your knowledge and think about writing, and paying attention to how you use this knowledge and thinking as you write, is well worth the effort. It will speed up your learning, help you to adapt more easily to a range of writing situations, and make writing less frustrating when things go wrong. Experts call this "reflective inquiry," and they observe that experienced professionals in many fields often do this kind of thinking. In a way, reflective inquiry is thinking *about* thinking. It isn't easy. But it is also one of the most important ways in which we *transfer* what we know from one situation to another. Reflective thinking is key to making the most of your learning in this writing course.

You've tried your hand at reflective inquiry in several exercises so far, including the previous one on "cell phone culture." Let's get a little more practice with it before we move on.

Exercise 1.7

Scenes of Writing

Think about the writing and thinking you've done about yourself as a writer in this chapter. Review your notes from all of the exercises you tried that asked you to reflect on that (Exercise 1.1, your beliefs about writing; Exercise 1.3, your literacy collage; and Exercise 1.4, the survey on your writing process). Now imagine the kind of writer *you would like to be.*

Scene 1

A month ago, you got a writing assignment in your philosophy course: a twelve-page paper that explores some aspect of Plato's dialogues. It's the night before the paper is due. Describe the scene. What are you doing? Where? What's happening? What are you thinking? If you can, make use of the various types of writing that can convey scene: setting, action, description, narration, dialogue.

Scene 2

Rewrite scene 1. This time, script it as you *wish* it would look.

Finally, imagine that each scene is the opening of a film. What would they be titled?

Reflective Inquiry

Think about the terms we've used in this chapter to talk about the writing process—terms such as these:

- *Prewriting*
- *Revision*
- *Focusing*
- *Critical and creative thinking*
- *Invention*
- *Reflection*
- *Exploration*
- *Inquiry questions*
- *Habits of mind*
- *Suspending judgment*
- *Genre*
- *Alternating currents of thought*
- *Writing situation*
- *Rhetorical choices*

Draft a 200- to 250-word essay or discussion-board post about your own writing process—past, present, or future—that uses as much of the terminology of the writing process as you find relevant and useful to your essay or post.

Using What You Have Learned

Remember the learning goals at the beginning of the chapter?

1. **Reflect on and revise your beliefs about yourself as a writer.** In this chapter, you started to tell yourself the story of yourself as a writer. Like any good story, you tell it for a reason: What does it tell you about the kind of writer you think you've been? Is that the writer who will work for you now as you deal with a wider range of writing situations in college and out of college? The great thing is that if your beliefs about yourself are holding you back, you can change them. And you will as you work your way through this book. Reflect continuously on what you do as a writer that works for you (and on what you do that doesn't). This isn't just an academic exercise; it is knowledge that you can put to work to help solve your writing problems.

2. **Understand what kinds of questions will sustain inquiry into any subject.** Academic inquiry is driven by questions that will keep you thinking. But what kinds of questions will sustain your investigation of a subject over time? In this chapter, you learned how you can start with an informational question—What is known about a topic?—and refine that into a question that will help you discover what you want to say. You'll see later how these questions often lead to certain kinds of writing. The ability to understand what kinds of questions will guide your writing and thinking is something that you can draw on in nearly every college class.

3. **Practice a method of writing and thinking that will help you generate ideas.** Throughout *The Curious Writer*, you'll use the technique you were introduced to here: using your creative mind to explore and generate material, and using your critical mind to narrow down and evaluate what you've generated. As you get more practice with this method, you'll find that you may not even think about it but instead shift naturally from withholding judgment to making judgments. If this works for you, you'll find that it's a powerful way to use writing to discover what you think in nearly any writing situation.

4. **Apply rhetorical knowledge to make choices in specific writing situations.** In this book, *rhetoric* is never a bad word. You learned here that the term doesn't describe someone who blows smoke in an attempt to deceive, but rather represents a way of thinking about how to communicate effectively. Rhetoric is a system for analyzing writing situations by looking at purpose, audience, and genre, so that you can see more clearly what your choices are when you're composing any kind of text. You already have considerable rhetorical understanding. Anyone with any skill in social situations does. But as you become more conscious of rhetorical analysis, you'll discover how fundamental it is to speaking and writing well.

2

Reading as Inquiry

Learning Objectives

In this chapter, you'll learn to

2.1 Apply reading purposes relevant to reading in college.

2.2 Examine your existing beliefs about reading and how they might be obstacles to reading effectively.

2.3 Recognize reading situations and the choices about approaches to reading that they imply.

2.4 Understand the special demands of reading to write, and practice doing it.

2.5 Understand some conventions of academic writing and recognize them in texts.

You've been reading all of your life. Why read a chapter on the subject, especially in a book about writing? Well, I'm going to argue that reading in college is different from much of the reading you've done in school up until now. To start with, the *kinds* of reading, or *genres*, you'll encounter will range widely from poems to journal articles with dense academic prose. You'll also be reading subjects about which you may have very little prior knowledge. It's hard to overstate what a difference lacking knowledge about a subject makes in your ability to understand what you read and use what you read in your writing. When readers know a lot about a subject, they have mental categories and hierarchies for that subject—slots into which the new information they read is organized—which makes it easier for them to retrieve and use the information later in their writing. In contrast, when readers don't know much about the subject of their reading—and that's often the case in undergraduate inquiry-based projects—they don't know what to make of what they're reading. We can picture their mental process as a scrambled struggle to simply understand the text. Going on to actually *use* the information in their writing will be an entirely different, and much bigger, problem. You've probably experienced these situations, and they don't feel good. You're bored or frustrated with what you're reading. You can't focus. All you want to do is watch *Keeping Up with the Kardashians* on TV, and you actually hate that program.

An obvious solution to this problem is to develop some knowledge about a topic so you can read with more understanding. But there are other strategies, too, that can help you read—and use—difficult texts in unfamiliar genres, and I'll introduce you to them in this chapter. They include the following:

- *Be clear about your goals in reading a text.*

- *Use questions to drive the process.* In reading to inquire there are four types of questions that can direct your attention as you read: exploring, explaining, evaluating, and reflecting questions.

- *See a text in its rhetorical context.* In other words, you can work more effectively with any kind of reading if you can see the kind of work its author *intended* it to do.

- *Understand that reading is a process.* The more you reflect on how you do it, including in different situations, the more control you gain over the process.

- *Write as you read.* You can apply creative and critical thinking to generating insights about texts, too, through tools such as a double-entry journal (described further on in this chapter).

- *Understand the features of academic discourse.* Knowing what to look out for will help you understand what you're reading.

Purposes for Academic Reading

Why read? We pick up a book for pleasure, read a news website for information, and so on. But I'd like to be more specific. What are the purposes for reading in college? First imagine some typical contexts for academic reading. You might, for example,

2.1

Apply reading purposes relevant to reading in college.

- Read a textbook to acquire knowledge about a subject. You may be required to demonstrate what you've learned on a test or in a paper.

- Read a textbook (such as this one) that is a guide to a process. You use it to help you *do* something—write, perform an experiment, design a website.

- Read a journal article or short story closely, to analyze the arguments of the article or interpret the meaning of the story.
- Read material you have found online, to see how you might use the information in your own writing or to prepare a presentation.

Reading with the spirit of inquiry turns books, essays, and articles into one side of a dialogue that you're having with an author.

Each of these reading situations involves multiple purposes, and in each case one or two purposes are especially important. Although reading is a cognitively complex thing, I'd propose that the purposes of academic reading boil down to four—to *explore, explain, evaluate*, and *reflect*.

Imagine that each purpose involves asking a text different kinds of questions. We don't typically start reading with questions in mind. I know when I was an undergraduate, the question I usually had when I was reading a textbook (aside from "When will I be done so I can go play the guitar?") was "Will this be on the test?" On my really deep thinking days, I might read an assigned article in, say, my environmental studies class and wonder, "Do I agree or disagree with this?" These are reasonable questions. But they aren't very good guides for reading well. The research on reading says that the best readers have conscious goals when they read. These goals can be expressed as questions. Here, then, are some general questions that can express the different purposes. Notice that you can ask these questions about both the text and parts of the text.

Purpose	Some Examples of Readers' Questions
Explore	What could I learn from this? What does this make me think?
Explain	What do I understand this to be saying?
Evaluate	Is this persuasive? How do I interpret this?
Reflect	How is this put together? What do I notice about how I'm thinking about this?

Each of these questions will lead you to read the same text in a different way. In using the purposes and questions, keep in mind that we often have more than one main purpose for reading a text. For example, when we read a biology textbook to learn about cell structure for a test in two weeks, we will read it to explore *and* explain. When we have to analyze a website as a source for an academic paper, we have to make a judgment about whether it has persuasive content (evaluate) *and* think about how it's designed to be persuasive (reflect).

But to demonstrate how each of these purposes might change the way you read a text, we'll try to apply each of them separately in the following exercise.

Exercise 2.1

Using the Four Purposes for Academic Reading

Every year, the *Chronicle of Higher Education* publishes data about last year's college undergraduates. Here's a table (Figure 2.1) from that report that describes students' employment levels outside of school. Read the table using the four purposes for reading—exploring, explaining, evaluating, and reflecting—one at a time.

Explore

STEP ONE: First just figure out what you make of this information. Data tell stories. What are some of the stories the data in this table seem to be telling? Make a list of these in your journal. Some inferences are probably obvious. For example, part-time students clearly work more than full-time students. No surprise there. Work towards teasing out some of the less obvious implications, especially those that you find surprising. When you're done, look at your list of inferences. What questions do they raise? For example, private college students who are full-time clearly work less than full-time students enrolled in public schools. And yet, if they attend part-time, students enrolled at private colleges work *far more than* part-time students at public institutions. Why? What might explain this?

Percentage of college students age 16 to 24 who were employed, by hours worked per week, October 2009				
	Full-time students		Part-time students	
	Worked 20 or more hours	Worked less than 20 hours	Worked 20 or more hours	Worked less than 20 hours
All undergraduates	23%	16%	62%	11%
Female	25%	18%	64%	12%
Male	21%	13%	59%	10%
Hispanic	27%	10%	60%	12%
White	24%	19%	63%	13%
Black	20%	9%	64%	n/a
Asian	12%*	9%	n/a	n/a
By type of institution attended:				
Public 2-year	28%	16%	59%	11%
Public 4-year	24%	15%	63%	13%
Private 4-year	13%	20%	80%	n/a
* Large margin of error				
Note: The designation "n/a" means no figures were provided because statistical standards were not met. For that reason, no figures were provided for American Indians or Pacific Islanders.				
				Source: Census Bureau

Figure 2.1   Employment patterns for college undergraduates

Explain

STEP TWO: Turn your list from step 1 into a fat paragraph that summarizes what you think are the story lines in this table. What are the things it seems to be saying?

Evaluate

STEP THREE: Based on your reading of the data in the table, make a one-sentence assertion about what you think is *the most significant finding*. Write this down in your journal.

Reflect

STEP FOUR: Statistical tables are inevitably selective on what data they include. They also group information into categories that make the data easier to understand but may obscure important results. In this table, students' employment was categorized into students who work more than twenty hours and students who work less than twenty hours. Does this seem sensible to you? Make a case for or against using that distinction.

In class, or on the online discussion board, talk about your experience with reading for each of these four purposes.

- Which step of the exercise was hardest for you?
- With which of these purposes do you typically read texts in school? Which are new to you?
- How did each reading purpose change the focus of your reading?

We always have a purpose for reading something, but we rarely think much about it. In this section, I've tried to convince you that you'll read much more skillfully and efficiently—particularly in college—when you do consider *why* you're reading something. The advantages of this awareness are huge: You'll know what to look for in a text that's relevant to the task. You'll know what questions to ask yourself to evaluate what you're reading. And you'll know what you might use from a text in your own writing. There's another thing that will help, too. Reading, like writing, is something you've done much of your life, and you've developed habits and beliefs that govern how you approach reading. These can help you or they can hurt you. But you can't determine that until you know what they are.

2.2

Examine your existing beliefs about reading and how they might be obstacles to reading effectively.

Beliefs About Reading

You have theories about reading much like you have theories about writing—including beliefs about what makes a "good" reader and about yourself as a reader. They're not beliefs you're aware of, probably, but they profoundly affect how you read everything you read. Through an exercise that gets you thinking a little about your own literacy history, let's start to tease some of these beliefs out into the open so you can get a look at them.

Exercise 2.2

A Reader's Memoir

Generating

STEP ONE: There is considerable evidence that attitudes about reading are heavily influenced by how reading is viewed at home. Were there books around when you were growing up? Did your parents encourage you to read? Did they read? Fastwrite for five minutes about your memories of reading as a child in your home. Describe what you remember, and try to be as specific as possible.

Judging

STEP TWO: Speculate about the beliefs these early experiences with reading might have encouraged. In your journal, compose an answer to this inquiry question: *What is the relationship between my early reading experiences at home and my current beliefs about reading?*

Generating

STEP THREE: Now think about your reading experiences in school up until now. Fastwrite for five minutes, telling stories about your experiences with particular books or teachers, especially those that might have influenced the way you think of reading and of yourself as a reader.

Judging

STEP FOUR: As before, try to summarize how these experiences in school might have influenced how you view yourself as a reader now. Answer this question: *What is the relationship between my experiences reading in school and my current beliefs about reading and myself as a reader?*

One Common Belief That Is an Obstacle

I hope that Exercise 2.2 revealed some of the beliefs that shape how you feel about reading. When I wrote about my memories of reading at home, I realized that I had been lucky to grow up in a family that celebrated reading but that I had preferred to "read" television instead of a book. I can see now how this made me a reluctant reader who lacked confidence in his reading ability. When I wrote about my memories of academic reading, I immediately remembered—with revulsion—tanking on the reading portion of the SAT, and I realized that for years I'd thought the only purpose of reading in school is to say back what it said in a test or a paper.

My belief about school reading is a common one, and for good reason. Most reading instruction seems to focus on comprehension—you know, the SAT- or ACT-inspired kind of situation in which you are asked to read something and then

Only by understanding how we read in certain situations can we acquire more control over what we get out of the reading experience.

explain what it means. This often becomes an exercise in recall and vocabulary, an analytical challenge in only the most general way. Essentially, you train yourself to distinguish between specifics and generalities and to loosely follow the author's reasoning. In English classes, sometimes we are asked to perform a similar exercise with stories or poems—what is the theme, or what does it mean?

Instruction and assignments such as these encourage students to see reading as an archaeological expedition where they must dig for hidden meaning. The "right" answers to the questions are in the text, like a buried bone; you just have to find them. The trouble with this approach is the belief that it tends to foster, which is that *all meaning resides in the text and the reader's job is merely to find it.* This belief limits the reader's interaction with the text. If meaning is fixed within the text, embedded like a bone in antediluvian mud, then all the reader has to do is dig. Digging isn't a bad thing, but reading can be so much more than laboring at the shovel and sifting through dirt.

Reading Situations and Rhetorical Choices

2.3
Recognize reading situations and the choices about approaches to reading that they imply.

This chapter began with a list of typical reading situations you might encounter as an undergraduate. You read a textbook to acquire information for a test. You mine an article for material to put in a paper or analyze a short story to interpret its theme, and so on. In each of these situations, you're going to make choices about *how* you read that text. Usually, these choices are governed by habit. This is the way you *always* read a textbook or a short story.

I'm going to try to convince you to make these choices differently. First, they should be conscious choices. For example, earlier we talked about purpose-directed reading. To read by asking questions based on your purpose is to make conscious choices.

Recall from Chapter 1 that to write effectively in a writing situation, you need to make appropriate rhetorical choices and that one of the considerations these are based on is your writing purpose. Similarly, in a reading situation, to read effectively you make choices based in part on your reading purpose.

When you're reading for a writing assignment, your purpose for reading basically has already been determined. For example, you might get an assignment like this in an English class:

   ▪ *Closely read and **explicate** the poem by Mary Oliver.*

Or perhaps you get an assignment like this in a marketing class:

   ▪ *Find and read company websites for mission statements and **explain** how companies distinguish between goals and objectives.*

In each of these situations, what you need to do is to start by *reading the assignment rhetorically,* to make sure you understand your purpose for reading. The main clue is usually the verb: *explicate, explain, argue, summarize, interpret, analyze*, and so on. These verbs tell you what you are supposed to do with what you read.

Frequently, however, you will have much less direction than this on what to do with your reading. Sometimes reading is just a part of a larger project, presentation, or paper, and *you* have to figure out what to do with every text you encounter. In these cases, you will need to figure out your purpose along with three other considerations that affect the choices you make about how to read something. These considerations, which I'll call *frames for reading*, are similar to those that come into play in rhetorical choices for writing.

Four Frames for Reading

- **Your purpose:** Why are you reading this text? (To explore, explain, evaluate, and/or reflect?)
- **Your knowledge of the genre/medium:** What do you know about this kind of text, and what do you therefore expect? What is it trying to do, and for whom was it likely written?
- **Your knowledge of the subject:** What do you already know about the subject of the reading? What biases might you have about it?
- **Self-perception:** How good do you think you are at reading a text in this genre and on this subject?

These considerations inevitably affect our reading. For example, a few years ago, when I was a novice at the shorthand of text messaging, I was painfully aware that I lacked genre knowledge. What do those abbreviations mean? When one of my daughters sent me a message, my first concern was decoding some of it. As I gained familiarity with the form, the problem of genre knowledge faded and I could focus more immediately on *why* they were telling me what they were telling me. They were asking for money? They wanted me to back off on the boyfriend? Experienced readers are aware of these frames and deliberately look at a text through them in order to make their reading more efficient.

Reading Scenarios

Consider a couple of scenarios involving academic reading and how an experienced writer might apply the four frames for reading.

Scenario #1. You're assigned two chapters in your college physics textbook for an exam. You don't know physics, much less college physics. Based on your feelings about reading textbooks and your inexperience with the subject, you're not feeling good about the time you'll spend reading for the assignment.

Faced with this situation, an experienced reader might apply the four frames as follows:

1. *Purpose.* I'm reading this to be able to explain what I know on an exam. I'd better pay attention to key concepts and terms when I read it and make sure

I can explain them to myself. I think I'll write a summary in my notebook of the key ideas—and a running list of terms and definitions—as I read. This is gonna slow me up but in the end will be worth it.

2. *Genre/medium knowledge.* I know that textbooks for intro courses are intended for readers with low subject knowledge, but even so, it might be a struggle for me to understand and remember terms. Textbooks usually have clues about what's important—I'll pay particular attention to terms that are emphasized by length of treatment and visual cues such as italics and headings.

3. *Subject knowledge.* I don't know much about physics, so I can't skip around when I read this. I'll need to work through the text from the beginning and not move on to a new section until I think I understand the current one.

4. *Self-perception.* I stink at science and don't much like reading textbooks. Because I know I'm going to get frustrated, I'll allow some extra time to get through this—maybe reading over a few days rather than in one sitting.

Scenario #2. You're writing a research essay for your composition class on the impact of climate change in Australia, a place that one observer noted is a kind of "miner's canary" on the issue—in other words, likely to be among the first to experience problems and provide a warning sign for what is to come in the rest of the world. The question you're asking is whether chronic water shortages in the Outback are really climate related. Along with other material, you've found a great article in *Rolling Stone Magazine* that seems really on topic.

Here's how an experienced reader might approach reading the article:

1. *Purpose.* No one is telling me why I should read this article. I've got to figure that out. The *Rolling Stone* piece might be the most strongly stated thing I've read so far that argues that climate change is responsible for Australia's environmental problems. I'm going to read it to find some of those passages. Maybe I can use them in my paper. I'm also going to pay particular attention to the evidence provided on water shortages.

2. *Genre/medium knowledge.* This is *Rolling Stone*, not an academic article. It won't provide the quality of evidence that a journal article would. I also know that because of the magazine's youthful audience and its focus on popular music, *Rolling Stone* might be prone to overstating things a bit for dramatic effect. I'm going to read a little more critically.

3. *Subject knowledge.* I know a fair amount about the climate-change issue, and because I feel really strongly about it, I'm going to try to read this article critically, as a doubter more than a believer (see "Inquiring into the Details: Reading Perspectives"). What is the writer ignoring? Does he address counterarguments?

4. *Self-perception.* This article should be easy for me to read and understand.

Inquiring into the Details

Reading Perspectives

One of the best ways to read strategically is to consciously *shift* our perspective while we read. Like changing lenses on a camera or changing the angle, distance, or time of day to photograph something, this shift in reading perspective illuminates different aspects of a text. Here are some of the perspectives you might take:

- **Believing:** What the author says is probably true. Which ideas can I relate to? What information should I use? What seems especially sound about the argument?

- **Doubting:** What are the text's weaknesses? What ideas don't jibe with my own experience? What are the gaps in the information or the argument? What isn't believable about this?

- **Updating:** What does this add to what I already know about the subject?

- **Hunting and gathering:** What can I collect from the text that I might be able to use?

- **Interpreting:** What might be the meaning of this?

- **Pleasure seeking:** I just want to enjoy the text and be entertained by it.

- **Connecting:** How does this information relate to my own experiences? What is its relationship to other things I've read? Does it verify, extend, or contradict what other authors have said?

- **Reflecting:** How was this written? What makes it particularly effective or ineffective?

- **Resisting:** This doesn't interest me. Why do I have to read it? Isn't *Survivor* on television right now?

Exercise 2.3

Reading a Life

Here's a scenario for you to consider, one that involves reading a different kind of text—a photograph. I'd like you to apply the four frames for reading to this photograph, much the way I applied them in the previous two scenarios.

First, some background. One of the many ways we all make inferences about other people is by paying attention to the details of their lives. What things do they value? What is their behavior in significant social situations? What groups do they belong to? While we may do this informally all the time, academics and writers do it, too—for example, when they study members of social or cultural groups or when they plan to write a profile of someone. One academic version of this is called *ethnography*, something you may learn about in Chapter 9. It relies on very close observations of people in the places that their groups typically inhabit. Photographs can be an important source of data for such inquiries.

The photograph above, "Ruth's Vanity (on the day she died)," potentially tells us a lot about who Ruth Smith was, through the things on her vanity and on the dresser that is visible in the mirror above the vanity. I'd like you to think about how to read this photograph by applying the four frames for reading: purpose, genre/medium knowledge, subject knowledge, and self-perception. Explain, as I did in the previous scenarios, how each frame might influence *how* you read this photograph: Number each frame, and then write a brief paragraph explaining how the frame influences how you read the photograph to make inferences about Mrs. Smith. Your instructor may ask you to do this in your journal, submit it as a short response, or post it to the online discussion board.

Reading situations, like writing situations, can really differ, and each asks something different from you. There is no one "right" way to read well, or to write well, in most situations. Instead, there are choices. These choices are rhetorical; in every reading situation, you need to think about your purpose in reading the text, about the text itself—its subject, its genre/medium, and the author's likely purpose and audience—and about your self-perception in relation to the text's subject and genre/medium. You need to think about what these frames together imply about how you *might* approach the text. It's not a science. There's no formula to follow. Mostly, you simply want to be a *flexible* reader and writer, one who can read a situation well enough to make decisions about how to approach it. This becomes possible when you pay attention to your process.

A Process for Reading to Write

The process of reading to write is going to be different from, say, that of reading for pleasure. For example, lately I'm reading books about rafting the Colorado River. My motives are both learning and pleasure, but I really don't plan on writing anything about rafting, so I'm not as active a reader as I am when I'm reading something for, say, an essay I'm writing or a book I'm researching. I spend considerably less time taking notes, marking passages, mining the bibliography, and doing other things like that. I'm less worried about *what I can do* with what I'm reading.

2.4
Understand the special demands of reading to write, and practice doing it.

Not long ago, I was working on an essay in which I was exploring why certain landscapes—usually the ones we know best from our childhoods—often get under our skins even if we no longer live in those places. My reading for this project led me to all kinds of sources—articles in anthropology, history, and literary works. This reading was enjoyable, but it was also work. In the back of my mind, I was always asking, *Does this relate to the questions I'm interested in?* It was a reading process that was much more directed by my purposes—by my desire to use what I was reading in my own writing.

Questions for the Process of Reading to Write

So far we've explored the various ways we might approach academic reading situations in general. We've explored questions like these: What are typical situations? How might reading frames such as purpose or genre knowledge influence what we do? Now let's look specifically at processes for those reading situations—typical in college—in which you have to write about what you read, especially when this involves inquiry into a topic.

What Do I Want to Know? Inquiry is driven by questions, not answers. What do you want to know? In Chapter 1 (see "A Writing Process Driven by Questions" on pp. 29–30), I explained that inquiry into most topics about which you know little often begins with informational questions: What is known about the impact

Figure 2.2   Reading to write is one of the most goal-oriented types of reading. First, you are guided by your research question: What do you want to know? If you know this, you know what to look for and how to use it in your own work.

of climate change in the Australian Outback? Why are reality shows so popular? In the beginning of an inquiry project, this larger goal—to develop some background knowledge—provides some guidance for how you should read, but the reins will be pretty loose. You're likely to wander around a lot. That's okay as a start, but the reading and writing processes need the discipline of good questions that will keep you focused.

Consider some writing I did about theories of dog training. This writing actually originated with the behavior of our golden retriever: Ada was being bad—jumping on people, barking, and generally being a pest. Ada's behavior inspired some research on websites, in books, and even in academic articles. At first, I just wanted to know what the schools of thought were on getting Ada in line—a question of fact. Before long, I knew enough to come up with much better questions, more specific and more directive, which changed not only what I was reading, but also how I read it. From the question "What are theories of dog training?" I ended up asking, "What is the relationship between the use of shock collars and dog aggression and submission?"

Obviously, the second question is a much better guide to what to read and what to ignore. That one step of focusing the reading process on a narrower question, taken at an appropriate point, can then make a huge difference in the efficiency of the process.

What Should I Read to Find Out?

Should I buy a new iPhone? Who cares? Well, I care. But because this is a question in which only I have a stake, I'm likely to read all kinds of things to help me answer the question. I won't be picky. But suppose my question were less personal and more academic, or less concerned with just me and instead addressed to a larger audience—for example, "Do people's emotional attachments to their iPhones have any of the qualities of clinical addiction?" With this question, I'll be a lot more picky about what I read. I'll look in the usual places—some quality websites—but I'll also check out some books on addictive behavior and search scholarly articles, probably in psychology, to see if anyone has studied users' emotional bonds to their cell phones.

In other words, *what* you read (the kinds of texts you focus on) is determined not just by the question you're asking but the context in which you're asking it—the rhetorical choices related to your writing: Who are you writing for and why? What kinds of information will that audience find most persuasive? Are there certain kinds of evidence they would expect you to offer?

What Do I Do with What I've Read?

There are lots of reading situations in which this question is answered by someone else:

> *Based on your reading about painters in the Italian Renaissance, explain in 250 words how an artist such as Caravaggio chose his subject matter.*

In this case, you know why you're reading and what you need to do with what you've read—explain a particular point. But in many reading situations, especially those that are inquiry based, you'll have considerable freedom to determine not only your own purposes for your reading, but also, more specifically, how you might use some of it in your paper or presentation. For example, are you reading a book chapter to find an explanation for a particular idea? Are you analyzing a statistical table to find evidence that supports a point you're trying to make?

In either type of reading situation, to actually do something with what you've read, you first have to know what you think about what you've read. How can you possibly make a decision about whether to quote an author or summarize someone's ideas or select this fact or another if you don't know what *you* make of what the text is saying? If you don't know much about the Italian Renaissance, let alone Caravaggio, then at the very least you'll need to try to *understand* as much as you can from your reading about both.

We've already talked about how reading isn't a monologue. "Blah, blah, blah," says a text, and you mindlessly write, "The text says, 'Blah, blah, blah.'" That's a monologue, not a conversation. You're not talking with—or back to—what you're reading; you're parroting what you've read. In the next section, I'll propose a method for encouraging conversations with what you read that will help you to discover what you think.

Having a Dialogue with What You Read

A typical process for reading to write:

1. Google some keywords on a topic.
2. Go to the first link that seems promising and click on it.
3. If the site seems relevant, read it once quickly online. Bookmark or print.
4. Go read something else and repeat the process.
5. Hope that you'll remember what you've read when you have to write on the topic.

Another standard version of the process:

1. Get a reading assignment.
2. Read it once, maybe twice. Highlight a few things.
3. Compose something quickly about what you've read for the assignment, looking for slots to insert what you highlighted.

These are passive readings. While they're fine for some reading tasks, they don't work well when you have to write or talk about what you read in a paper or for a presentation.

Imagine an alternative scenario: An assigned reading, a book, or an article is open in front of you, but so is your notebook. Your pen is poised to mark up the text—underlining, making marginal notes, adding question marks next to confusing passages and checkmarks next to those you think are important. When you're finished with your first reading, you go back and focus on what you marked. On the left-hand page of your notebook, you write down quoted passages that seem important; you jot down some facts that struck you. You might add a summary of a key idea or paraphrase the author's assertions. Then, on the right-hand page of your notebook, you fastwrite for five minutes, thinking about what you just read, looking at the notes you collected on the opposing page to spur you along.

What I'm proposing, quite simply, is that you write while you read. But I'm also suggesting a method for doing this writing that some call a "double-entry notebook" or "dialogue journal." If you're using a notebook, you use the left-hand page to collect important ideas, facts, quotations, or arguments from what you've read, and then you use the right-hand page to think about them through writing. You

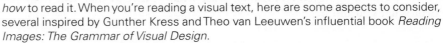

Inquiring into the Details

Reading the Visual

As you know by now, it helps enormously when reading a new text to have some knowledge of *how* to read it. When you're reading a visual text, here are some aspects to consider, several inspired by Gunther Kress and Theo van Leeuwen's influential book *Reading Images: The Grammar of Visual Design*.

- *Framing:* As in writing, what the photographer, advertiser, painter, or designer chooses to include in an image and what she chooses to leave out profoundly affect the story, idea, or feeling that an image communicates. Framing might also establish a viewer's distance from the action. An up-close-and-personal image suggests intimacy, while a long shot has the opposite effect.

- *Angle:* A front-on view of a subject creates a different effect than looking up, or down, at it.

- *Relationships:* One of the most important of these is the relationship between you and the image itself. Is the subject of an image looking directly at the viewer or looking away? In the first case, the subject seems to make some kind of demand, and in the second, the subject perhaps makes an invitation to simply be an onlooker.

- *Color:* Designers know that color affects mood. Not surprisingly, for example, red is a color that communicates feelings of passion and energy. White suggests "purity" and innocence. Yellow is sunny and joyous. For further analysis on color and emotion in visuals, search the web on the subject.

- *Arrangement:* In writing, we give certain information emphasis by where we place it in a sentence, in a paragraph, or in the composition as a whole. Visual information also uses the physical arrangement of objects for emphasis, making some things larger or smaller, in the foreground or background, to one side or the other. Kress and van Leeuwen, for example, suggest we perceive the left side of an image as information that is a "given," things that viewers readily accept, while the right side is perceived as "new," information that viewers aren't familiar with. Thus, the right side becomes a key feature for communicating a message.

- *Light:* What is most illuminated and what is in shadows—and everything in between—also influences what is emphasized and what is not. But because light is something we strongly associate with time and place, it also has an emotional impact.

can use this method with any kind of text, including visual texts. See how the double-entry journal technique works for you to analyze an image. (You can find some ideas about analyzing images in "Inquiring into the Details: Reading the Visual.")

Exercise 2.4

Double-Entry Journaling with a Visual Text

Advertisements make arguments. They are carefully designed to combine text and images to persuade a particular audience to *do* something: buy a product, join an organization, vote for a referendum, make a donation. You know this, of course. But most of us are generally unaware of the methods of visual arguments. We don't think much about how they use visual language to direct our gaze and touch our emotions (see "Inquiring into the Details: Reading the Visual" for more on how visual texts are designed to persuade). To read an advertisement with these things in mind involves *rhetorical analysis*. Up until now, we've looked at analyzing the rhetorical situations we find ourselves in as readers. Now we'll turn our attention to analyzing texts. What is the intended audience of an ad? What are the appeals designed specifically for that audience? How does the ad use emotion? How was it composed to emphasize certain ideas or feelings?

In Chapter 7, on writing arguments, we'll look at this kind of rhetorical analysis more closely, but for now, select an advertisement from a magazine, or focus on a screen ad on your computer. Try to find one with lots going on visually. Take a close look. Then practice using the double-entry journal technique to analyze the ad's visual argument.

STEP ONE: Here are the questions for reading your ad:

- What specifically are the appeals in the advertisement, and to whom are they directed?

- What specific evidence in the ad would you point to as examples of those appeals?

- Do you think they are persuasive for the intended audience? Why or why not?

Following the instructions below, use two blank opposing pages in your journal to explore these questions.

STEP TWO: On the left-hand page, collect some information from the ad. Make a list of everything you look at in the ad, *in the order you look at it*. What do you see first? Then what? Then what? Be as specific as you can. When you've got a satisfactory list, circle those items that you think are particularly effective.

STEP THREE: On the right-hand page, explore your thinking about what you've collected. Begin a fastwrite by explaining to yourself what you notice about the *order* of the details you noticed in the ad. How did the ad direct your gaze?

Then explore the items you circled on the other side of the page. Why were they effective. For whom? What kind of audience response might they get? How would these visual arguments convince a person to buy what is advertised?

STEP FOUR: Go back to the questions in step 1. How would you answer them?

STEP FIVE: Reflect in writing, in class, or on your class's online discussion board about your experience using the double-entry journal to analyze your ad.

- What worked? What didn't?
- How might you apply the double-entry journal to other reading situations?
- What did the method encourage you to do in the exercise that you don't usually do when you read?

Techniques for Keeping a Double-Entry Journal. You're going to discover ways to make a reading journal work best for you. But if the journal is going to help you have *conversations* with what you read, there are some essential elements.

1. **Focus on what the author or text actually says.** That's the beauty of the left-facing page of a double-entry journal. Because it contains passages, facts, ideas, and claims from your reading, you're working with what the text said, not with what you vaguely remember that it said.

2. **Try to suspend judgment.** When we feel strongly about what we're reading, it's human nature to decide right away whether we agree or disagree with an author or come to a quick conclusion about what a text says and what it means. But you can use writing—and especially the open-ended, exploratory process of fastwriting—to really think things through before you come to conclusions.

3. **Use questions.** Sometimes, as in Exercise 2.4, the questions are provided to direct your reading. More often, you read to discover the questions that interest you about a topic. These will fuel bursts of writing that lead you towards having something to say about what you read.

4. **Read to write and write to read.** This is fundamental. No matter what technique you use to include what you read in your writing, you should always write *as you read* and, if possible, immediately after.

The double-entry journal method I'm proposing here typically involves a notebook and a pen, but if you prefer to work on a tablet or laptop, you can accomplish much the same thing with a two-column Word or Pages document. If you use a notebook, imagine that the spiral binding that divides opposing pages is a kind of table. On the left sits a text and an author; on the right sits you. You're having a conversation across that imaginary table. What do you talk about?

First, you have to try to understand what a text is saying. That's what the left-hand page is for—to try to collect information and ideas from what you're reading that you think are central to understanding the reading. On the right-hand page of your journal, you respond to, think and ask questions about, and explore what you've collected on the opposite page.

Exercise 2.5

Reading Creatively, Reading Critically

Now that you've seen how the double-entry journal can help you analyze an image, let's try it with a more familiar kind of text. I published the essay "The Importance of Writing Badly" some years ago, but I think it still expresses several of the main ideas behind this book. I'd like you to read the piece critically, though, using the double-entry journal method I just described.

As before, you'll use opposing pages of your journal.

STEP ONE: Read the essay once through, marking it up. (Make a copy if you don't want to write in your book.) Read it a second time and, on the left-hand page of your notebook, carefully *copy* lines or passages from the essay that

- Connected with your own experience and observations
- Raised questions for you
- Puzzled you
- Seemed to be key points
- Evoked disagreement or agreement or made you think differently
- Were surprising or unexpected

The Importance of Writing Badly
Bruce Ballenger

I was grading papers in the waiting room of my doctor's office the other day, and he said, "It must be pretty eye-opening reading that stuff. Can you believe those students had four years of high school and still can't write?" 1

I've heard that before. I hear it almost every time I tell a stranger that I teach writing at a university. 2

I also hear it from colleagues brandishing red pens who hover over their students' papers like Huey helicopters waiting to flush the enemy from the tall grass, waiting for a comma splice or a vague pronoun reference or a misspelled word to break cover. 3

And I heard it this morning from the commentator on my public radio station who publishes snickering books about how students abuse the sacred language. 4

I have another problem: getting my students to write badly. 5

6   Most of us have lurking in our past some high priest of good grammar whose angry scribbling occupied the margins of our papers. Mine was Mrs. O'Neill, an eighth-grade teacher with a good heart but no patience for the bad sentence. Her favorite comment on my writing was "awk," which now sounds to me like the grunt of a large bird, but back then meant "awkward." She didn't think much of my sentences.

7   I find some people who reminisce fondly about their own Mrs. O'Neill, usually an English teacher who terrorized them into worshipping the error-free sentence. In some cases that terror paid off when it was finally transformed into an appreciation for the music a well-made sentence can make.

8   But it didn't work that way with me. I was driven into silence, losing faith that I could ever pick up the pen without breaking the rules or drawing another "awk" from a doubting reader. For years I wrote only when forced to, and when I did it was never good enough.

9   Many of my students come to me similarly voiceless, dreading the first writing assignment because they mistakenly believe that how they say it matters more than discovering what they have to say.

10   The night before the essay is due they pace their rooms like expectant fathers, waiting to deliver the perfect beginning. They wait and they wait and they wait. It's no wonder the waiting often turns to hating what they have written when they finally get it down. Many pledge to steer clear of English classes, or any class that demands much writing.

11   My doctor would say my students' failure to make words march down the page with military precision is another example of a failed education system. The criticism sometimes takes on political overtones. On my campus, for example, the right-wing student newspaper demanded that an entire semester of Freshman English be devoted to teaching students the rules of punctuation.

12   There is, I think, a hint of elitism among those who are so quick to decry the sorry state of the sentence in the hands of student writers. A colleague of mine, an Ivy League graduate, is among the self-appointed grammar police, complaining often about the dumb mistakes his students make in their papers. I don't remember him ever talking about what his students are trying to say in those papers. I have a feeling he's really not that interested.

13   Concise, clear writing matters, of course, and I have a responsibility to demand it from students. But first I am far more interested in encouraging thinking than error-free sentences. That's where bad writing comes in.

14   When I give my students permission to write badly, to suspend their compulsive need to find the "perfect way of saying it," often something miraculous happens: Words that used to trickle forth come gushing to the page. The students quickly find their voices again, and even more important, they are surprised by what they have to say. They can worry later about fixing awkward sentences. First, they need to make a mess.

15   It's harder to write badly than you might think. Haunted by their Mrs. O'Neill, some students can't overlook the sloppiness of their sentences or their lack of

eloquence, and quickly stall out and stop writing. When the writing stops, so does the thinking.

The greatest reward in allowing students to write badly is that they learn that language can lead them to meaning, that words can be a means for finding out what they didn't know they knew. It usually happens when the words rush to the page, however awkwardly.

16

I don't mean to excuse bad grammar. But I cringe at conservative educational reformers who believe writing instruction should return to primarily teaching how to punctuate a sentence and use *Roget's Thesaurus*. If policing student papers for mistakes means alienating young writers from the language we expect them to master, then the exercise is self-defeating.

17

It is more important to allow students to first experience how language can be a vehicle for discovering how they see the world. And what matters in this journey—at least initially—is not what kind of car you're driving, but where you end up.

18

Page #	Notes from Reading	Exploratory Response
	<ul><li>Direct quotations</li><li>Summaries of key ideas</li><li>Paraphrases of assertions, claims</li><li>Facts, specific observations, data</li><li>Premises and reasons</li><li>Interesting examples or case studies</li></ul>	<ul><li>Focused fastwrite on material in left-hand column or page.</li><li>What's relevant to the question?</li><li>What questions does it raise?</li><li>What do I think and feel about this?</li><li>How does it change the way I think about the subject?</li><li>What surprised me?</li><li>What's the most important thing I take away from the reading?</li><li>How does it connect to what I've heard, seen, or read before?</li></ul>

Figure 2.3 An approach to keeping a double-entry journal. Note that you should keep track of page numbers (if any) in the reading from which you collected information and put them in the left-hand column or page. Particularly when doing research, you should begin by jotting down key bibliographic information about each source.

STEP TWO: Now use the right-hand page of your notebook to think further about what you wrote down on the left-hand page. Use the questions in Figure 2.3 as prompts for a focused fastwrite. Write for five or six minutes without stopping.

STEP THREE: Reread what you've written. Again, on the right-hand page of your notebook, write your half of the following imaginary dialogue with someone who is asking you about the idea of "bad writing."

> Q: I don't understand how bad writing can help anyone write better. Can you explain it to me?
>
> A:
>
> Q: Okay, but is it an idea that makes sense to you?
>
> A:
>
> Q: What exactly (i.e., quotation) does Ballenger say that makes you feel that way?
>
> A:

STEP FOUR: Finish the exercise by reflecting in your journal for five minutes on what, if anything, you noticed about using the double-entry journal to have a "conversation" with a text. In particular:

- How did it change the way you usually read an article such as this one?
- How might you adapt it for other situations in which you have to read to write?
- What worked well? What didn't?
- Do you think the method encouraged you to think more deeply about what you read?

Alternatives to the Double-entry Journal. Though the double-entry journal nicely structures your thinking about what you read between collecting and evaluating, generating and judging, it's hardly the only method for writing as you read. Here are some other approaches you can try:

1. **Three-Act Notes.** This is a simple but effective way of thinking about what you just read. Immediately after you finish the text, set it aside and fastwrite for as long as you can, exploring your response. Act 1: In your notebook or in Word, begin with this seed sentence: *The thing that strikes me most about this is ...* and follow it from there, writing as fast as you can. Act 2: Return to the reading. Review your underlinings and reread what you thought were interesting passages, tables, or data. Jot down a bulleted list of key concepts, facts, statistics, or claims that you harvest from this review. Act 3: End with another fastwrite—*second thoughts*—in which you focus on one or more of the bulleted items. Explore what you find significant, interesting, or relevant.

2. **After-words.** At a minimum, spend a few minutes immediately after you finish reading something by beginning with a summary: *What I understand this to be saying is....* Get this down first, and then fastwrite your thoughts about the argument, key concept, or significant findings you highlighted in your summary. How does it change the way you think about the topic? How does it connect with other things you've read? What do you find surprising?

Wrestling with Academic Discourse: Reading from the Outside In

The one thing that most influences your ability to understand and use what you read is prior knowledge. If you're reading about an unfamiliar topic—say, the biology of the Palouse worm, a creepy, disturbingly large creature that lives deep underground in northern Idaho—then you will have to work harder than if you read about a familiar topic. In college, unfortunately, much of what you read will be about subjects that are new to you. This means, quite simply, that you may struggle. You'll get frustrated. In your worst moments, you might want to throw an assigned reading out the window. I did that once.

But here's the good news: The more you learn about a topic, the more competent you'll feel. And it isn't just topic knowledge that will make you feel this way. It's also learning to understand the *discourse* of a particular discipline. You learn how to read, for instance, the discourse of biologists who write about worms, or the discourse social workers use to write to each other about poverty. There are all kinds of *discourse communities*, or groups of people who share certain ways of thinking, asking questions, and communicating—not just scholarly ones. Electricians share certain ways of communicating with each other. So do surfers.

It might seem that reading specialized discourses such as these is just about deciphering jargon. It's actually about much more than that. Academic discourse, for example, includes not just the language insiders use, but also

- The kinds of questions participants typically ask that guide research in the field
- Preferred methods for answering questions
- The kinds of evidence a discourse community considers persuasive
- Conventions for reporting discoveries

Even a couple of sentences on the same topic—the appeal and the effects of watching reality television—can yield some hints about how discourses differ.

EXAMPLE 1

There has been a considerable interest in how real reality television shows are as well as how such programming creates and reinforces gender and racial stereotypes (Cavender and Bond-Maupin 1993; Eschhotz et al. 2002; Estep and Macdonald 1983; Oliver 1994; Prosise and Johnson 2004).[1]

---

[1]Monk-Turner, Elizabeth, Homer Martinez, Jason Holbrook, and Nathan Harvey. 2007. "Are Reality TV Crime Shows Continuing to Perpetuate Crime Myths?" *The Internet Journal of Criminology* (n.d.). Web. Retrieved 1 Sept. 2011.

EXAMPLE 2

Reality TV: An Insider's Guide to TV's Hottest Market[2]

For all of Reality's faults, I still liken critics who blanketly bash it while favoring sit-coms and dramas to wine snobs who can't just enjoy an orange soda now and then.

The first example is from an academic journal and the second from a popular book. It isn't hard to draw some contrasts between them. Imagine that you are asked, based on just these two sentences, to infer a list of "rules" (or conventions) for academic writing. What would they be? For example, what would you say about the kinds of evidence that seem necessary in academic writing and the preferred methods of answering questions? What would you infer about the conventions for reporting discoveries?

What you're doing here with just a couple sentences is the kind of rhetorical analysis that will help you understand how to read—and later, how to write—in discourses that may not be familiar to you. Let's look at academic discourses specifically to see what features they might share.

Features of Academic Discourse

2.5

Understand some conventions of academic writing and recognize them in texts.

There isn't a single academic discourse. There are *discourses*. Academic discourse varies from discipline to discipline. Why? Though all academic disciplines—from those in the humanities to those in the natural sciences—are dedicated to creating new knowledge, they each look at different aspects of the world. Some, say, look at language. Others observe natural phenomena. A few, like math, work with often highly abstract concepts or ideas. Because the materials for discovery differ, the methods of discovery do, too. These differences naturally lead to unique ways of describing things and reporting them. Before long, you have different discourse communities.

Despite all these differences, it is possible to make some observations about academic discourse that apply across discourse communities. As you become more experienced reading texts in various fields, you will begin to recognize some of these basic patterns, and this will help immensely with your academic reading.

1. **Billboards.** Academic writers announce, usually somewhere near the beginning of an article, what they are going to do.
2. **Reviews.** Like the first example about reality shows, academic texts often include a review of what others have already said on a topic. This is also near the beginning.

---

[2]Devold, Troy. 2011. *Reality TV: An Insider's Guide to TV's Hottest Market*. Studio City, CA: Michael Weise Productions, 22. Print.

3. **Hedges.** Contrary to the popular assumption that academic texts usually deal in certainty, much academic writing qualifies assertions. They signal caution by using words such as *appear to be, tend*, or *suggest*.

4. **Signposts.** Most academic subjects are complicated neighborhoods, and scholarly writing offers plenty of explicit direction about deviations in an argument (e.g., *however*), presentation of reasons (e.g., *because*), and evidence (e.g., *for example*).

5. **Questions.** Academic writing is about inquiry and discovery, and these arise from questions to explore or problems to solve. Identifying the question or the problem that an academic article proposes to address is key to understanding what it's about; knowing the question driving the research also makes the path authors took to a study's conclusions much more obvious.

These five conventions are some handholds that you can seize as you wrestle your way through much academic discourse. Figure 2.4 may also help you understand how scholarly articles typically organize their content.

I distinctly remember the first time I had to read articles in biology, my undergraduate major. I was lost. I felt stupid. And I vowed to avoid scholarly books and articles if at all possible. In the Internet age, this kind of avoidance can seem even more possible. But the truth is that, even if it's more possible, it's not a good idea. Popular writing on the web can help you to develop a working knowledge of your topic—and this will help you begin to understand the scholarship—but it is the academic sources that will always lead you to the deepest, richest understandings of the things that interest you. Now is the time to learn how to break

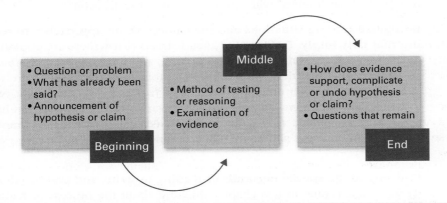

Figure 2.4 How academic articles are organized. Scholarly articles have a beginning, middle, and end, like stories do. Beginnings "billboard" the research question and review the literature. In the middle, writers tell what happened in their own investigation of the question, and in the end, they analyze the significance of what they've found.

through the initial reaction to academic prose—"This is so boring!"—and enter the messy, exciting marketplace where knowledge is made. That, after all, is the business of the university, and, as a curious writer and reader, you're invited to become a part of it.

Using What You Have Learned

Reflect on the learning goals introduced at the beginning of the chapter.

1. **Examine your existing beliefs about reading and how they might be obstacles to reading effectively.** You began to explore this when you wrote about your past experiences with texts, beginning with the attitudes about reading that you inherited from home and school. As you become a more experienced reader in college, your beliefs about your own competence should *evolve* along with your understanding of how different kinds of texts work. In the days ahead, think about this. Are you thinking about reading any differently than when you began the course?

2. **Apply reading purposes relevant to reading in college.** In other classes, you'll be asked to do a lot of reading. Often enough, you'll know why you're doing it: You have to memorize information from a textbook for a test. You've got to summarize findings from a research article. On the other hand, your purpose for much of the reading you do will be decided by you. You're researching a paper or a presentation, for instance, and you collect all kinds of texts. How do you want to *use* them? To explore, explain, evaluate, or reflect? What "frames" will you use to make that decision?

3. **Recognize reading situations and the choices about approaches to reading that they imply.** In Chapter 1, you learned that writers are guided by their rhetorical awareness. Why am I writing, and for whom? Are there certain kinds of writing that will work best in this situation? Readers are rhetorically aware, too, in much the same way. Just as there is no "right" way to write in all situations, there is no "right" way to read whenever you have a reading assignment. Hopefully, you will see that each situation implies certain choices. Think about what they are and you'll read much more strategically.

4. **Understand the special demands of reading to write, and practice doing it.** We've spent time in this chapter thinking about the process of reading in a very particular situation: when you have to write about what you read. This is active reading, and the best way to jumpstart your engagement with a text is *to write* while you read and after. Always have a pen in your hand. We think in dialogue with a text. It is from this conversation that we collaborate

with a text to discover our own ideas about something. Throughout *The Curious Writer*, I'll encourage you to keep up this dialogue, using some form of the double-entry journal and through questions.

5.   **Understand some conventions of academic writing and recognize them in texts.** In this chapter, you learned about *academic discourse,* a weighty-sounding term that describes the range of conventions that scholarly communities use to ask questions, choose methods, and report on discoveries. Whatever major you end up in, you'll be required to learn some of the conventions of academic discourse in your field. Don't let anyone tell you that academic discourse is just one thing—it varies from scholarly community to scholarly community—but we have explored general features of much academic writing, features such as how many scholarly articles are organized. I hope that the practice you've had here of looking for some of these conventions makes you alert to them as you continue to take courses in other fields. It's invaluable rhetorical knowledge that will help you immensely as you write papers for other classes.

3
Writing a Personal Essay

Learning Objectives

In this chapter, you'll learn to

3.1 Use personal experiences and observations to drive inquiry.
3.2 Apply the exploratory thinking of personal essays to academic writing.
3.3 Identify the characteristics of personal essays in different forms.
3.4 Use invention strategies to discover and develop a personal essay topic.
3.5 Apply revision strategies that are effective for shaping narratives.

Writing About Experience and Observations

Most us were taught and still believe that we need to know what we are going to write about before we actually pick up the pen or sit in front of the computer. My student Lynn was typical.

"I think I'll write about my experience organizing the street fair," she told me the other day. "That would be a good topic for a personal essay, right?"

"Do you think so?" I said.

"Well, yes, because I already know a lot about it. I'll have a lot to write about."

"Okay, but is there anything about this experience that you want to understand better?" I said. "Anything about it that makes you curious?"

"Curious? It was just a street fair," she said.

"Sure, but is there something about what happened that makes you want to look at the experience again? Is there a chance that you might learn something about yourself, or about street fairs, or about the community, or about people, or…?"

Lynn was probably sorry she asked. What I should have said was much more to the point: The best personal essay topics are those that raise questions you may not know the answers to. They are head-scratching topics, experiences that you look back at and say to yourself, "What was *that* about?" They are likely not experiences you have already figured out, or that you choose simply because you know them well. The best topics ask to be written about because they make you wonder *Why did I do that? What does that mean? Why did that happen? How did I really feel? What do I really think?*

Like all other forms of inquiry, the personal essay is driven by questions, but more than any other form, it is a vehicle for writers to work through their thinking and feeling on a subject, directly in front of their readers. The drama of the personal essay is watching a writer *coming to know.*

As a form, the *personal* essay places the writer at center stage. This doesn't mean that once she's there, her responsibility is to pour out her secrets, share her pain, or confess her sins. Some essays do have these confessional qualities, but more often they do not. Yet a personal essayist, no matter the subject of the essay, is still *exposed*. There is no hiding behind the pronoun *one*, as in "one might think" or "one often feels," no lurking in the shadows of the passive voice: "An argument will be made that.…" The personal essay is first-person territory.

> The personal essay is a vehicle for writers to work through their thinking and feeling on a subject, directly in front of their readers.

In this sense, the personal essay is much like a photographic self-portrait. Like a picture, a good personal essay tells the truth, or it tells *a* truth about the writer/subject, and it often captures the writer at a particular moment in time. This explains why the experience of taking a self-portrait, or of confronting an old picture of oneself taken by someone else, can create the same feeling of exposure that writing a personal essay often creates.

But it does more. When we gaze at ourselves in a photograph, we often see it as yanked from a larger story about ourselves, a story that threads its way through our lives and gives us ideas about who we were and who we are. This is what the personal essay demands of us: We must somehow present ourselves truthfully and measure our past against our present. In other words, when we hold a photograph of ourselves, we know more than the person we see there knew, and as writers of the personal essay, we must share that knowledge and understanding with readers.

Though the personal essay may be an exploration of a past experience, it needn't always be about memories. A personal essay can instead focus on some aspect of writers' present lives, just as long as it raises questions that interest them. Just last week, for example, my students spent two days at the local zoo, taking notes on what they saw there, and from this came personal essays about feeling caged, the hunger for eye contact with wild things, and the irony of a bald eagle, our national symbol, missing its right wing.

Motives for Writing a Personal Essay

3.1
Use personal experiences and observations to drive inquiry.

Essai was a term coined by the sixteenth-century French nobleman Michel de Montaigne, a man who endured plague epidemics, the bloody civil war between French Catholics and Protestants, and his own bouts of ill health. His tumultuous and uncertain times, when old social orders and intellectual traditions were under assault, proved to be ideal ferment for the essay. The French verb *essayer* means "to attempt" or "to try," and the essay became an opportunity for Montaigne to work out his thoughts about war, the education of children, the evils of doctors, and the importance of pleasure. The personal essay tradition inspired by Montaigne is probably unlike what you are familiar with from high school. The high school essay is often formulaic—a five-paragraph theme or thesis-example paper—while the personal essay is an open-ended form that allows for uncertainty and inconclusiveness. It is more about *the process of coming to know* than presenting *what* you know. The personal essay attempts *to find out* rather than *to prove*.

It is an ideal form of inquiry if your purpose is exploratory and if you're particularly interested in working out the possible relationships between your subject and yourself. Because the personal essay is openly subjective, the writer can't hide. The intruding *I* confronts the writer with the same questions over and over again: *Why does this matter to me? What do I make of it? How does this change the way I think of myself and the way I see the world?* Because of this, one of the principal dangers of the personal essay is that it can become narcissistic; it can go on and on about what the writer thinks and feels, and the reader can be left with that nagging question—*So what?* The personal essayist must always find some way to hitch the particulars of his or her experience to something larger—an idea, a theme, or even a feeling that readers might share.

On the other hand, one of the prime rhetorical advantages of the personal essay is its subjectivity. Because it is written with openness and honesty, the essay can be a very intimate form, inviting the reader to share in the writer's often concealed world. The *ethos* of personal essayists, or their credibility, revolves around the sense that they are ordinary people writing about ordinary things. In the personal essay, we often get to see the face sweating under the mask.

3.2
Apply the exploratory thinking of personal essays to academic writing.

The Personal Essay and Academic Writing

In some ways, the personal essay might seem like a dramatic departure from the kind of academic writing you may have done in other classes. Explicitly subjective and sometimes tentative in its conclusions, the personal essay is a relatively open form that is not predictably structured like much academic writing. Additionally, the tone of the personal essay is conversational, even intimate, rather than impersonal and removed. So, if your sociology or economics professor will never ask for a personal essay, why bother to write one in your writing class?

It's a fair question. While the pleasures of personal essay writing can be reason alone to write these essays, there are also other important reasons related to your academic work. Writing a personal essay will encourage you to:

- *Emphasize invention.* More than any other writing assignment, the personal essay encourages writers to suspend judgment. Since essayists' motives are to find out what they didn't know they knew, the form makes exploration the main engine of inquiry. This places emphasis on invention—techniques like fastwriting or research that *generate* information and ideas—a process you can use (and will throughout *The Curious Writer*) in any assignment.

- *Practice dialectical thinking.* The personal essay is *inductive* like scientific thinking; it looks closely at the data of experience and attempts to infer from that information theories about the way things are, and then returns to the experience with new understanding.

- *Expose the drama of coming to know.* The essay emphasizes the *process* of learning about yourself and your subject, exposing your reasoning and the ways you use knowledge to get at the truth of things. Reflecting on these components can tell you a lot about how you think.

- *Establish your role as narrator.* We tend to think of narrators as a literary device, or something that is only relevant when writing in the first person. But you narrate all of your writing, from the least formal personal responses to the most formal academic essays. You are always the guiding hand, leading readers through the material. Writing personal essays makes that role visible, of course, and it's a powerful experience for those who aren't used to feeling present in their writing. This presence is something you can carry into all the writing you do, even when you don't use first person.

Inquiring into the Details

The Power of Narrative Thinking

In a classic study of the culture of the Kpelle tribe in Liberia, anthropologists presented tribal members with twenty items—garden and kitchen tools, fruits and vegetables, clothing, etc.—and asked them to organize the items in a way that made "sense." What the Kpelle did surprised the anthropologists. Instead of putting the items in conceptual categories—garden tools in one category, food in another—the Kpelle put them in functional ones. The potato and knife were paired because "you take the knife and cut the potato."

In the West, we are mostly trained as school writers to use the kind of categorical, conceptual thinking that leads us quite naturally to write that way, too. When we write

(continued)

Inquiring into the Details (*continued*)

thesis-driven essays, for example, we organize the writing hierarchically, starting with a main idea and subordinating everything that comes after it. One theorist called this "paradigmatic" thinking. Personal essays call on a different kind of thinking, the kind that the Kpelle tribesmen used, and a key part of this thinking is looking for relationships—particularly causal ones—between things that are seen in a particular context. It's the kind of thinking that is behind storytelling. We want to make sense of an experience by finding reasons that might help explain it, and we do this not by trying to organize information into conceptual categories but by examining the particulars of the experience.

   What's powerful about this kind of narrative thinking is that instead of stripping away context so that it's easier to manage abstract ideas, narrative thinking makes the evidence found in particular times and places central to understanding. While academia seems to emphasize paradigmatic thinking, narrative thinking is a part of some disciplines like anthropology, teacher education, and nursing, all communities of practice that are vitally interested in trying to interpret what happens to particular groups of people in specific contexts. The personal essay is an instrument to engage in this kind of narrative thought.

Features of the Form

3.3
Identify the characteristics of personal essays in different forms.

Feature	Conventions of the Personal Essay
Inquiry questions	What does it mean to me? What do I understand about this now that I didn't then?
Motives	Self-discovery is often the motive behind writing a personal essay—the essay is in first person, and the essayist is center stage.
Subject matter	Essayists often write about quite ordinary things; they find drama in everyday life, past or present. Personal essays can be about taking a walk, breaking up on Facebook, the housefly on your beer glass. In some ways, the real subject of a personal essay is the writer herself and how she makes sense of her world.
Structure	Essays often tell stories, but, unlike some fiction, they both show *and* tell, using both narrative and exposition, sometimes alternating between the two.
	When about the past, there are two narrators in the essay—the "then-narrator" and the "now-narrator." One describes what happened and the other describes what the narrator makes *now* of what happened.
	The thesis may come near the end rather than at the beginning. And the essay isn't necessarily chronological.

Feature	Conventions of the Personal Essay
Sources of information	Like any essay, the personal essay might use all four sources of information—memory, observation, reading, and interview. But it is likely to lean most heavily on memory and observation.
Language	Personal essays work in two registers—the more general language of reflection and the very specific details of experience and observation. This specific language is often sensory: What did it look like exactly? What did you hear? How did it feel?

Prose+

Josh Neufeld's "A Matter of Perspective" is a kind of personal essay. The theme—the idea that we all have moments in our lives when we feel "very, very small"—speaks not only to Josh's experience, but to our own. A graphic essay such as this one exploits image and text in combination, amplifying the power of each.

READINGS

▶ **Personal Essay 1**

Try this exercise: Think about things, ordinary objects, that you have held onto all these years because you simply can't throw them away. They *mean* something to you. They are reminders of another time, or a turning point in your life, or a particular moment of joy, or sadness, or perhaps fear. Consider a few of mine: a green plaster Buddha, handmade; a glow-in-the-dark crucifix; an old pair of 7 × 50 Nikon binoculars; a 1969 Martin D 28 guitar; a brown-handled flathead screwdriver with a touch of red nail polish on the handle; a homemade lamp made from a wooden wallpaper roller; a red dog collar. While they are meaningless to you, to me each of these objects carries a charge; they remind me of a story, a moment, a feeling. The personal essay makes space for writers to explore the meanings of such ordinary things.

Taking Things Seriously: 75 Objects with Unexpected Meanings, the book from which the following short essay was taken, is a gallery of objects—a bottle of dirt, a Velveeta Cheese box, a bear lamp, a pair of shells, and more—that are displayed along with the meditations on their significance by the writers who have carefully kept the objects as reminders on a shelf, in a closet, by their beside. Laura Zazulak's short essay focuses on a doll that she snatched from a neighbor's trash can. Just telling a story about what happened is not enough in a personal essay. The essay must have something to say to someone else. As you read Zazulak's brief piece, consider what that something might be.

Every Morning for Five Years
Laura Zazulak

Every morning for five years, I was not so welcomingly greeted by my middle-aged, developmentally disabled neighbor across the street. Scotty never smiled and seemed to hate everyone. He never left the perimeter of his mother's lawn and apparently didn't know how to do anything but rake, shovel, take out the trash, and yell in a high-pitched voice. I'd pull out of my driveway and see him there, wearing a neon orange hunting cap, raking absolutely nothing at the same spot that he'd raked the day before. I'd think to myself, "Don't make eye contact!" But I always did. He'd stare at me and neither of us would blink.   1

Near the end of my fifth year on the street, Scotty stopped coming out of his house. At first, I was thankful. But as time passed, I began to worry. Then one Saturday morning in the middle of January I noticed that his window was wide open. Later that day, a police car showed up. Maybe Scotty and his mother got into one of their   2

(continued)

(continued)

screaming matches again? Then a funeral-home van pulled up and they brought out Scotty's body. Although it came as a surprise to me to discover that he knew how miserable his life was, he had killed himself.

3   The next day Scotty's uncle came over and began furiously carting things off to the dump. He left behind a garbage can in the driveway piled with all of Scotty's earthly possessions. I noticed two little pink feet sticking up into the air.

4   After dark, I crept across the street to the garbage can, armed with a travel-sized bottle of hand sanitizer. I looked left, then right. I dashed forward, tugged at the feet, and then ran as fast as I could back into my own backyard with my prize. Only then did I look at what I'd rescued. I would like you to meet Mabel.

Inquiring into the Essay

Throughout *The Curious Writer*, I'll invite you to respond to readings using questions related to the four motives for reading discussed in Chapter 2. The following questions, therefore, encourage you to explore (*What do I think about this?*), explain (*What do I understand that this is saying?*), evaluate (*What's my judgment about this?*), and reflect to discover (*How does this work?* or *How am I thinking about it?*) and shape what you think about the reading. In Chapter 2, I encouraged you to write while you read and after. Try that now using the double-entry journal technique introduced in Chapter 2 (see pp. 52–54). As soon as you finish your first reading of "Every Morning for Five Years," open up your journal and on the right-hand page, fastwrite your response to the explore and explain questions above. Write for at least three minutes. Then go back to Zazulak's essay and on the left-hand page, jot down sentences or passages from it that you think are important to your understanding of it. Build your responses to the questions that follow from these first thoughts about what you just read.

1. **Explore.** All of the essays in the book *Taking Things Seriously*, including Zazulak's, have this to say: It is remarkable how much meaning we can invest in the ordinary when we take the time to notice it. This is an idea you can explore on your own. Brainstorm a list of objects that might have "unexpected significance" to you. Choose one and fastwrite about it for four minutes. Then skip a line, choose another, and write for another four minutes. If this is interesting to you, repeat this process over a few days and create a collage of brief stories that four or five objects inspired. Are there any themes that seem to run through all of them? Do they speak to each other in any way?

2. **Explain.** Explain how the photograph and the essay work together to create meanings that might not be apparent if we had either one without the other.

3. **Evaluate.** Personal essays like "Every Morning for Five Years" *imply* their meaning rather than state it explicitly. In that way, an essay like this one is more like a short story. Make an argument for your own understanding of the meaning of Zazulak's essay, and use passages from the piece to support your claim.

4. **Reflect.** One of the features of the personal essay is two narrators: the "now-narrator" and the "then-narrator." One looks back on an experience from the present, applying knowledge that the "then-narrator" did not have. From this comes fresh insight. But these two narrators aren't always obvious. Can you see them in this essay?

▶ Personal Essay 2

One of the ways that personal essays differ from the thesis-proof structure of much school writing is that they are *end-weighted*—the full meaning of the essay emerges later in the work. The conventional academic essay is *front-weighted*, with the thesis often parked in the first paragraph or two. You can see that end-weighted structure in Ginny Blanford's lovely personal essay about an adopted daughter, a survivalist dog, and a moment when the recognition of loss led towards the light. This is how personal essays work—the writer wonders about something she's experienced and uses the writing to arrive at some new understanding, an understanding that wasn't apparent when the experience happened. It is a process that begins with questions, not answers, and often starts with a gut feeling that there is some meaning there, just out of reach. We write personal essays to find that meaning.

The Dog That Made Us a Family
By Ginny Blanford

1   We inherited my daughter Liana when she was not quite 5. She had been adopted from China by my closest friend of 30 years, Linda, a single 51-year-old woman, tiny and fragile-looking but full of steel. Linda had a history of various illnesses, and my husband later told me that when she walked happily off the plane on Christmas Day in 1994, with her round, worried-looking Chinese baby wrapped in bright red and clutching a teddy bear, he had a premonition that we would eventually raise this child. Three years later, my best friend died—complications from Crohn's disease—and Liana came home with us. I was 55, a fulltime textbook editor with two almost-grown daughters. My husband, an English professor, was 48. I was looking forward to a few years of empty nesting and then some grandchildren. Starting over with a feisty kindergartner was, to be candid, not in my plans.

2   Shortly after she came to us, Liana began asking for a dog. She had been passed from family to family during her mother's six-month illness, indulged by people who wanted to make her happy. She was not used to hearing the word "no." I love dogs—I had grown up with a beautiful collie named Sunbeam—but I already had one unexpected new responsibility and I didn't want another. Initially our apartment was our excuse: too little space. But four years later we moved to a house, and we could no longer resist Liana's pleas. So off we went to an animal shelter.

3   Molly was a regal chow mix, chestnut red with a feathery tail that wagged all the time. She was gentle but energetic. As long as Liana and my husband, John, promised to do the walking, I decided I could handle having a dog. So we brought Molly home. Twenty-four hours later I opened the front door, and a red streak pushed by me— Molly, bolting out the door, through a neighbor's yard, into a nearby woods. Liana ran after her, screaming, and John headed out, too, into the dark, drizzling rain, frequently catching sight of the dog and then losing the trail.

4   Liana came back into the house, sat on her new dog's bed and cried. In her four years with us, she had hardly ever cried. And she had hardly ever mentioned her adoptive mother, my best friend. I almost resented that she seemed to have moved past grief without a second thought. But now she sobbed. She howled. Her thick black hair stuck to her cheeks, wet with tears. She wrapped her arms around herself, then around me, squeezing hard. She cried for three hours—until well after John returned. "She's gone," Liana moaned. "My dog is gone. My mother is dead. I loved my dog. Why did my mother die?"

5   She hadn't moved past grief, it turned out. She had just buried it, deep beyond reach, until now.

6   For John, finding Liana's dog became a mission. Luckily, we had taken some cellphone photos of Molly during her few hours with us, and we sent them out to all the shelters in the area. After three weeks I gave up. But then we got a call. A woman had spotted a dog matching Molly's picture 15 miles away, in the woods near her home—

across two highways, two rivers and I-95. As John often points out, Molly could have easily made it back to the shelter she'd left if she'd only had an E-ZPass.

Despite repeated sightings, Molly somehow stayed out of reach. For two more months our dog lived in the woods. The wonderful woman who'd noticed Molly left scraps on her back porch and enlisted the neighborhood kids to report sightings. The food would be gone every morning, but the red dog eluded them all. Finally John hired a team of animal facilitators—they used to be called dogcatchers—and they set out a cage. For another week Molly ignored it until they changed the bait, at John's suggestion, from tuna to steak. Then she walked in, and she came home.

For five years now, Molly has slept with Liana every night. When Liana is away, her dog paces. Molly's tail still wags, but she is 7 now, a little slower and much less rambunctious. Liana, a tiny beauty of 15 with fashionably black nails and a loyal circle of ebullient friends, has moved on to "Twilight" and the Jonas Brothers. She still loves dogs, but she'd prefer the Paris Hilton model—a yappy little dog that she can dress up and put on like a pair of rhinestone earrings. Sometimes it seems as though Liana hardly remembers when her dog ran away and she hollered for her dead mother. But John and I remember, because that was the moment that Liana and our lost friend and our lost dog all came together, and we became a family.

Inquiring into the Essay

In the last chapter I argued that writing about what you read right after you read it is the best way to both understand and analyze the text. Use these questions for some writing in your journal about "The Dog That Made Us a Family."

1. **Explore.** The last time that I cried deeply—the chest-rattling, breath-choking kind of crying—was when my dog Stella died suddenly and unexpectedly from post-surgical complications. I sensed then, as Blanford does in this essay, that those tears were not just about a dog. Fastwrite about your own experience of losing a pet, or losing something or someone dear to you, exploring the event and your reaction. Ask yourself, too, whether your feelings of loss might have been amplified by other things going on in your life at the time. What were those other things?

2. **Explain.** The narrative begins with an adopted child, and then continues with the adoption of a dog, who runs away soon after. The child, who lost her first mother, grieves for both lost dog and lost mother. The narrator's husband, after much effort, finds the dog, who is reunited with the child and her family. This is the situation. But what is the *story*? What is this narrative really about?

3. **Evaluate.** Because the motive behind personal essays is to find out, rather than to prove, we don't often see them as making an argument. But if you were to read "The Dog That Made Us a Family" as an essay trying to make

a claim about how families work, or what the best ways to deal with loss might be, or whatever else, what would that claim be?

4. **Reflect.** While there's no formula for structuring a personal essay, one thing you often see is the movement between the "now-narrator" (the writer looking back from the present) and the "then-narrator" (the writer who is telling what happened). See if you can identify the movement between these two narrators in the essay. Where do you see it?

Seeing the Form

Photo Essays

Rebecca Benedict, a student in my first-year writing class last semester, wrote a personal essay about her trip with her family to visit the beaches of Normandy a few years ago. The trip was a moving experience, as it often is for visitors whether they are relatives of the combatants or not. When I asked her to "re-genre" her written essay (see Chapter 13), she decided to create a photographic essay, one that juxtaposes images of her trip with archival images of the battle. She then added text (and a musical soundtrack) to the slides. Here's the PowerPoint slide that opens her photo essay.

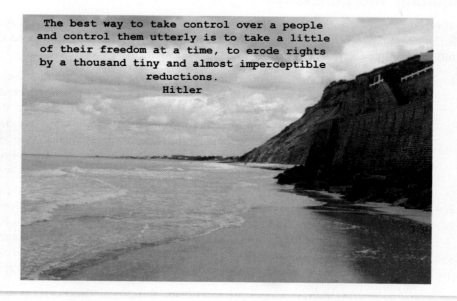

The best way to take control over a people and control them utterly is to take a little of their freedom at a time, to erode rights by a thousand tiny and almost imperceptible reductions.
Hitler

THE WRITING PROCESS

Inquiry Project   **Writing a Personal Essay**

Inquiry questions: What does it mean to me? What do I understand about this now that I didn't understand then?

Here are some approaches to writing a personal essay as an inquiry project—a traditional essay and some multimodal methods. Your instructor will give you further guidance on the details of the assignment.

Write a personal essay on a topic that you find confusing or that raises interesting questions for you. Topics need not be personal, but they should arise from your own experiences and observations. The essay should offer a central insight about what you've come to understand about yourself and/or the topic. In other words, you will "essay" into a part of your life, past or present, exploring the significance of some memories, experiences, or observations. Your motive is personal discovery—reaching that new insight.

Your essay should do all the following (see also the Features of the Form box earlier in this chapter on p. 66 for typical features of the personal essay):

■ Do more than tell a story. There must be a *purpose* behind telling the story that speaks in some way to someone else. It should, ultimately, answer the *So what?* question.

■ Include some reflection to explain or speculate about what you understand *now* about something that you didn't understand *then*. Your essay should have both a then-narrator and a now-narrator, one narrator who remembers what happened and one narrator who views what happened with the understanding you have now.

■ Be richly detailed. Seize opportunities to *show* what you mean rather than simply explain it.

Prose+

In the Seeing the Form box on page 74, I showed you how one of my students took a written personal essay and made a photographic essay from it using PowerPoint. There are all sorts of possibilities for creating a personal essay that go beyond the usual written text by exploiting images, sound, and even video. You can find lots of ideas for doing so in Chapter 13, "Re-Genre." In addition, you might consider experimenting with the online version of the personal essay genre: the blog.

Study the genre first by reading some online blogs, and then model yours after your favorites. You can publish your essay on the web using Blogger, Wordpress, or other blogging software.

Finally, consider writing a personal essay modeled after "Every Morning for Five Years" (pp. 69–70). Begin with a digital photograph of an object that is meaningful to you, and then explore its significance.

Writing Beyond the Classroom

Essaying "This I Believe"

The essay genre, which has been around for about five hundred years, is a vibrant and increasingly common form of writing on the radio and for online audio. Why? One reason might be that the intimacy of the essay—the sense of a writer speaking directly to a reader without the masks we often wear when we write—seems particularly the voice of writing embodied in speech. Certainly, the ease with which we can "publish" essays as podcasts accounts for the explosion of online essayists.

This I Believe, a program heard on public radio (thisibelieve.org), is typical of radio programs that actively seek to broadcast student essays (which are subsequently published as podcasts). The program was begun in the 1950s by famed journalist Edward R. Murrow, who invited radio listeners and public figures to submit very brief (350- to 500-word) essays that stated some core belief that guided their "daily lives." As revived by the nonprofit organization This I Believe, the program is enormously popular and features work from people in all walks of life, including college students who may have written a "This I Believe" essay in their writing courses.

The program's website offers this advice to essayists:

1. Find a way to succinctly and clearly state your belief.
2. If possible, anchor it to stories.
3. Write in your own voice.
4. "Be positive," and avoid lecturing the listener.

What Are You Going to Write About?

3.4
Use invention strategies to discover and develop a personal essay topic.

With the personal essay, nearly anything goes. Essayists write about everything from their struggles with eating disorders, adjusting to life after military service, or dealing with the loss of a sibling to what we typically consider utterly commonplace things: a walk, negotiating the use of an armrest with a fellow airplane passenger, a fondness for weird hats. Whatever you write about, what matters most is that you've chosen the topic because you aren't quite sure what you want to think about it. Write about what confuses you, what puzzles you, or what raises itchy questions.

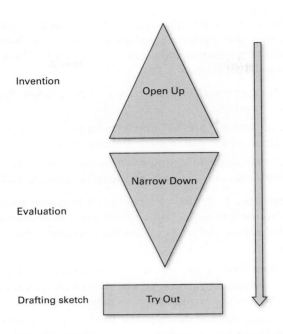

Figure 3.1 To discover a personal essay topic, we'll follow a pattern that will be repeated in every assignment chapter. It emphasizes "invention", or spending some time first simply exploring possibilities through writing, brainstorming, and visualizing. From there, you'll narrow down the material, focusing on the most promising material for a first draft, or "sketch".

The process for discovering a topic (see Figure 3.1) begins simply with what I call opening up, or generating lots of material. Open the warehouse of memory and walk around, or open your eyes and look around you *now*. Just collect some things, without judging their value for this project.

Opening Up

Even if you've already got an idea for a personal essay topic, spend some time exploring the possibilities before you make a commitment. It doesn't really take much time, and there's a decent chance you'll discover a great topic for your essay that you never would have thought of otherwise.

The journal prompts that follow will get you going. What you're after is to stumble on an interesting topic. Actually, it's more like stumbling through the *door* to an interesting topic—a door that gives you a look at what you might fruitfully explore with more-focused writing. Try several prompts, looking for a topic that might, after some writing, raise questions such as these:

- *Am I uncertain about what this might mean?*
- *Is this topic more complicated than it seemed at first?*
- *Might I understand these events differently now than I did then?*

Listing Prompts. Lists can be rich sources of topic ideas. Let them grow freely, and when you're ready, use a list item as the focus of another list or an episode of fastwriting. The following prompts should get you started thinking about both your experiences and your observations.

1. Make a list of experiences or places that you can't forget. Reach into all parts and times of your life.

2. Make a list of "turning points," moments in your life in which you sensed that things changed for you in some fundamental way.

3. Make quick lists from the following prompts: toys from childhood, regrets, firsts (kisses, disappointments, losses of innocence, memories, relationships, etc.).

Fastwriting Prompts. Early on, fastwriting can help you settle on a narrower topic, *if* you allow yourself to write "badly." Then use a more-focused fastwrite, trying to generate information and ideas within the loose boundaries of your chosen topic.

1. Choose an item from a list you've created to use as a prompt. Just start fastwriting about the item; perhaps start with a story, a scene, a situation, a description. Follow the writing to see where it leads.

2. Most of us quietly harbor dreams—we hope to be a professional dancer, a good parent, an activist, a marketing executive, an Olympic luger, or a novelist. Begin a fastwrite in which you explore your dreams. When the writing

When they work, writing prompts open a door to promising topics. More-focused writing later will help you to explore what's beyond the door and generate the information that may lead to a sketch or draft.

stalls, ask yourself questions: *Where did this dream come from? Do I still believe in it? In what moments did it seem within reach? In what moments did it fade?* Plunge into those moments.

3. What was the most confusing time in your life? Choose a moment or scene that stands out in your memory of that time, and, writing in the present tense, describe what you see, hear, and do. After five minutes, skip a line and choose another moment. Then another. Make a collage.

4. Begin with this prompt: "You know that feeling when...." For example, you know that feeling when you wake up after something terrible happened the day before, and for a minute you forget, and the world feels fresh and new but then it hits you that, no, the world is not right? Come up with your own "you know that feeling" statement, and then tell yourself the story.

Visual Prompts. Images trigger ideas, and so can more-visual ways of thinking. Let's try both. Boxes, lines, arrows, charts, and even sketches can help us see more of the landscape of a subject, especially connections between fragments of information that aren't as obvious in prose. The clustering or mapping method is useful to many writers early in the writing process as they try to discover a topic. (See the "Inquiring into the Details" box later in this chapter on p. 81 for more details on how to create a cluster.) Figure 3.2 shows my cluster from the first prompt listed here.

1. What objects would you most regret losing in a house fire? Choose a most-treasured object as the core for a cluster. Build a web of associations from it, returning to the object in the core whenever a strand dies out.

2. Find a photograph from your past, perhaps like the one from mine that opens this chapter. Fastwrite about what you see in the picture, what you don't see, and a story that it inspires.

3. Draw a long line on a piece of paper in your journal. This is your life. Divide the line into segments that seem to describe what feels like distinct times in your life. These don't have to correspond to familiar age categories such as adolescence or childhood; they could correspond to periods in your life that you associate with a place, a relationship, a dilemma, a job, a personal challenge, and so on. In any case, make the segments chronological. Examine your timeline, and, as a fastwrite prompt, put two of these periods in your life together. Explore what they had in common, particularly how the earlier period might have shaped the later one.

4. Get on Google Earth. Find the town or city where you were born or lived as a young child. Zoom in on your neighborhood. Fastwrite about what this makes you remember. Alternatively, find the house you live in now. Using the "street view" feature, "walk" down the street, stopping at the homes of interesting neighbors that you know or have observed. With the image on the screen, fastwrite in your journal, telling yourself stories about the people in your neighborhood.

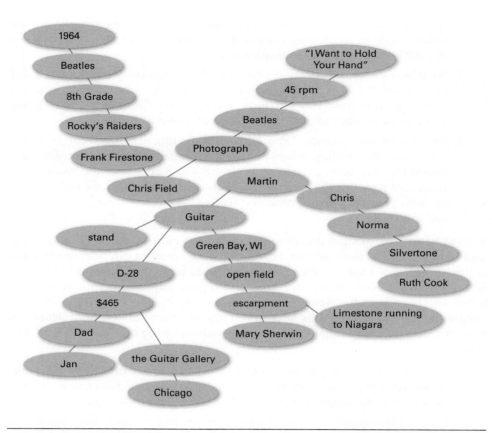

Figure 3.2 A cluster built around the one object I would most regret losing in a house fire: my Martin guitar

Research Prompts. Things we hear, see, or read can be powerful prompts for personal essays. It's tempting to believe that personal essays are always about the past, but just as often essayists are firmly rooted in the present, commenting and pondering on the confusions of contemporary life. In that sense, personal essayists are researchers, always on the lookout for material. Train your eye with one or more of the following prompts.

1. Put this at the top of a journal page: "Things People Do." Now go outside and find a place to observe people. Write down a list of everything you see people doing. Choose one action you find interesting and fastwrite about it. Is it weird? Why?

2. Look up the definition of "infatuation." Write it down at the top of a journal page, and then write for five minutes about your experience and observations of infatuations with people, things, places, ideas.

Narrowing Down

Okay, you've generated some "bad" writing about your experiences and observations. Can any of it be shaped into a personal essay? Are there any clues about a topic you could develop with more-focused fastwriting? These are particularly tough questions when writing a personal essay, because most of us are inclined to think that the only one who could possibly care about what happened to us or what we observe is ourselves (or maybe Mom).

Don't make the mistake of judging the material too soon or too harshly. Personal essayists write successfully about any topic—often including quite ordinary things—so don't give up on a promising topic this early in the game. But first, how do you decide what's promising?

What's Promising Material and What Isn't? The signs of a promising personal essay topic include the following:

- **Abundance.** What subject generated the most writing? Do you sense that there is much more to write about?

Inquiring into the Details

Clustering or Mapping

A method of visual thinking and invention, clustering (or mapping), is a refreshing alternative to the linear quality of most fastwriting. It thrives on bursts of branches inspired by an idea, detail, feeling, word, or phrase at the center of the cluster.

    Clusters are in code. If you look at Figure 3.2, my cluster on the word *guitar*, the items in the cluster won't say to you what they say to me, because I'm familiar with their meanings and you, of course, can't be. For me, each strand suggests a story, an idea, or a feeling that I might explore. In this same way, any cluster you make will be in a code that only you fully understand.

    How do you cluster?

1. Begin with a blank page in your journal. Choose a core word, phrase, name, idea, detail, or question; write it in the middle of the page and circle it.
2. Relax and focus on the core word or phrase, and when you feel moved to do so, build a strand of associations from the core, circling and connecting each item. Write other details, names, dates, place names, phrases, and so on—whatever comes to mind.
3. When a strand dies out, return to the core and begin another. Keep clustering until the page looks like a web of associations. Doodle, darkening lines and circles, if that helps you relax and focus.
4. When you feel the urge to write, stop clustering and use one of the strands as a prompt for journal work.

- **Surprise.** Did you see or say something you didn't expect about a topic?
- **Confusion.** What subject raises questions you're not sure you can answer easily?

In the personal essay, this last item—confusion and uncertainty—may yield the most-fertile topics. All of the questions listed at the beginning of the "Opening Up" section are related in some way to a feeling that some experience or observation— even if it's familiar to you—has yet to yield all of its possible meanings.

Questions About Purpose and Audience. Who cares about my middling career as a high school cross-country runner? Who cares that I grew to love that gritty neighborhood in Hartford? Who cares that I find high school reunions weird? When we write about ourselves, we can't help but wonder why anyone, other than ourselves, *would* care. Maybe they won't. But if you discover something about your life that helps you to understand it better—even in a small way—you will begin to find an audience. After all, we are interested in understanding our own, often ordinary lives, and perhaps we can learn something from you.

To find an audience for a personal essay, you have to discover something to say about your experiences and observations that speaks to others—a larger theme that comments on what your story might mean. People don't read personal essays for "morals" about life, but for insights that arise from the recognition that what happened to you might be a category of experience you share with others. An essay about the death of your father could offer insights about how we adapt to loss. An essay about going to the zoo might say something about how zoos trigger our desire for connection to animals. Can you see that in both of these examples, there is a shift from "I" to "we," and from "me" to "us"? This shift signals the necessary change from your observations of something to your ideas about it, from your memory of what happened to your insight about what happens, from the sea of experience to the mountain of reflection. This is the change that readers of personal essays are looking for.

Trying Out

A few years ago, shortly after attending my fortieth high school reunion, I began working on a personal essay about my experiences attending these affairs. As I generated "bad writing" on the subject of high school reunions, I kept returning to the same question: If I find these reunions generally weird and unsatisfying, why do I keep going? Using this inquiry question, I tried out my topic with the focused fastwrite that follows:

> *Last fall, I went to my 40th high school reunion...I had been to the 10th and the 20th, both of which required travel, once from the East coast and once from the West. I have no idea why I went to the effort...I didn't like high school...and I don't have many friends left in the Chicago suburb where I grew up. Why does anyone go to a high school reunion? I wonder if I've gone because...like it or not...high school is part of the narrative of our growing up that is at once mysterious and utterly*

familiar. I can remember everything . . . my failure to make the swim team that my brother was a star on . . . breaking the mercury barometer in physics class with my elbow while cleaning chalk erasers at the window . . . the sexual thrill of sitting on a bench next to Suzie Durment at a football game and feeling her thigh press close to mine. And yet I can't explain so much of high school . . . It just doesn't make sense. Why would I run cross country for four years and absolutely hate every minute of it? . . . How could I so thoroughly mishandle the kindness and affection of Jan Dawe, my first serious girlfriend? . . . And why all those years did I still pine for Lori Jo Flink, a girl from the 7th grade? . . . I guess that's one reason I go to my high school reunion . . . To enjoy the melancholy of seeing Lori Jo again and to relish the bittersweet taste of rejection. . . . She always comes . . . Yet when I did see her this time it wasn't the same. We had a very brief conversation . . . "I looked you up on the Internet," she said, and was promptly swept to the dance floor by Larry Piacenza . . . She looked me up on the Internet . . . This should have given me a thrill but it didn't . . . Why not? . . . These days I've been stripping the siding off so many old narratives about myself, stories that I've mistaken for walls that bear weight . . . Perhaps I tossed Lori Jo on that pile of discarded lumber . . . along with the desire to attend another high school reunion. As I'm counting the gifts of middle age, I gladly add this one.

What I hope you notice in my focused writing on reunions is how I keep using questions to tease out meaning, starting with a question I'd never really asked myself before: Why do I go to high school reunions? Why would anyone? These inquiry questions pulled me out of the sea of experience and onto the mountain of reflection (highlighted passages), where I begin to see a possible answer: I go to reunions to revive old stories about myself that may no longer matter. In the personal essay, judging involves *reflection*. What do we make of what happened then that we didn't quite see until now? What might our observations of the world around us now *say* about that past world and, maybe more important, about ourselves?

Questions for Reflection. In Chapter 1, I talked about thinking with writing as a movement back and forth between the creative and critical minds. In a way, personal essays and other narrative genres make this movement of the mind visible. For example, in Ginny Blanford's essay on p. 72, "The Dog That Made Us a Family," if you look closely you'll see the subtle movement from telling the story to reflecting on its meaning, culminating with this line: *She hadn't moved past grief, it turned out. She had just buried it, deep beyond reach, until now.* This is the "now-narrator," the writer who has the benefit of time and experience since something happened, attempting to make sense of it as she looks back. The "then-narrator" is in charge of telling what happened; the "now-narrator" takes a stab at saying *what happens*, what it might mean.

Now that you've tried out your topic, put yourself in the now-narrator's perspective, answering questions such as these:

- What do you understand now about this topic that you didn't fully understand when you began writing about it? Start some writing with this phrase: "As I look back on this now, I realize that. . . ."

- What seems to be the most important thing you're trying to say so far?

- How has your thinking changed about your topic? Finish this seed sentence as many times as you can in your notebook: *Once I thought* _____, *and now I think* _____.

Writing the Sketch

Throughout *The Curious Writer*, I'll encourage you to write what I call "sketches." As the name implies, this is a first look at something roughly drawn. It is a pretty rough draft of your piece, perhaps no more than about 300–400 words, with a tentative title. Though it may be sketchy, your sketch should be reader-based prose. You want someone else to understand what it's about. Don't assume others know what you know. When you need to, explain things.

A sketch is a good starting point for a personal essay in any mode. If you're working on a radio essay, for example, the sketch will be much the same as one that you write for a conventional essay. It's simply a very early script.

Choose your most promising material, and tell the story. If it's drawn from memory, incorporate both what happened then and what you make of it now. If it's built on observations, make sure they are detailed, anchored to particular times and places, and in some way significant.

You may or may not answer the "So what?" question in your sketch, though you should try. Don't muscle the material too much to conform to what you already think; let the writing help you figure out what you think.

To summarize, then, in a sketch try to do the following:

- Have a tentative title.
- Keep it relatively short.
- Write it fast.
- Don't muscle it to conform to a preconceived idea.
- Write to be read, with an audience in mind.
- Make it specific instead of general.

▶ Student Sketch

Amanda Stewart's sketch, "Earning a Sense of Place," faintly bears the outlines of what might be a great personal essay. When they succeed, sketches are suggestive; it is what they're not quite saying that yields promise. On the surface, "Earning a Sense of Place" could seem simply a piece about Amanda's passion for skiing. So what? And yet, there are lines here that point to larger ideas and unanswered questions. For example, Amanda writes that the "mental reel" of her swishing down a mountain on skis is "the image that sustains me when things are hard, and when I want to stop doing what is right and start doing what is easy." Why is it that such a mental image can be sustaining in hard times? How well does this mental image work? The end of the sketch is even more suggestive. This really might be a piece about trying to find a "sense of place" that doesn't rely on such images; in a sense, the sketch seems to be trying to say that joy on the mountain isn't enough.

The pleasure of writing and reading a sketch is in looking for what it might teach you, learning what you didn't know you knew.

I've highlighted portions of the text to illustrate a revision exercise that follows Amanda's essay.

Earning a Sense of Place
Amanda Stewart

The strings to my earflaps stream behind me, mixing with my hair as a rooster-tail flowing behind my neck. Little ice crystals cling to the bottom of my braid and sparkle in the sunlight. The pompom on top of my hat bobs up and down as I arc out, turning cleanly across the snow. I suck in the air, biting with cold as it hits my hot lungs, and breathe deep as I push down the run. 1

This is what I see when I picture who I want to be. It's the image that sustains me when things are hard, and when I want to stop doing what is right and start doing what is easy. I have made so many terrible decisions in the past that I know how far astray they lead me; I don't want that. I want the girl in the mental reel in her quilted magenta jacket and huge smile. She's what I grasp at when I need help getting through the day. 2

She's an amalgam of moments from the past mixed with my hopes for the future. I love to ski, and have since my parents strapped little plastic skis onto my galoshes when I was a year and a half old. From that day I flopped around our snow-covered yard, I've been in love with skiing. It's the only time I feel truly comfortable. Day to day I often feel so awkward. I wonder if my hair is right, or if my clothes fit. Last night, my roommate had a boy over, and as he sat on the couch talking to me, all I felt was discomfort and awkwardness. I didn't know what to say, felt judged, felt out of place. I never feel that way on skis. Even floundering in heavy, deep snow, or after a fall that has packed my goggles with snow and ripped the mittens off my hands I know exactly what to do. I'm a snow mermaid, only comfortable in my medium. I often wish I could trade in my walking legs for something like a tail that is more truly me. 3

My dad's coffee cup at home says, "I only work so I can ski," and for him, it's true. Sometimes I feel like I only push through my daily life so I can get to the next mountain and zip up my pants and go. I don't want to live like that though: it's too much time looking forward to something, and not enough looking at what I'm living in. I need to appreciate my life as it is, snowy cold or sunny warm. That sense of place I have on skis can probably be earned here on the flat expanses of campus just as easily as I got it pushing myself down the bunny slopes so long ago. I just have to earn it. 4

Moving from Sketch to Draft

Here's the journey with the assignment you've taken so far:

1. You've generated some "bad writing," openly exploring possibilities for personal essay topics while suspending judgment.

2. You landed on a tentative topic.

3. You tried out this topic through more writing, some of it still "bad."

4. Your critical mind took over as you began to judge what you have so far. What questions does this material raise for you? What might it *mean*? With judgment comes a growing concern for audience. Why would they care about this?

5. You tried out the topic in a sketch. It's written with an audience in mind.

At the heart of the process I'm describing is a movement from "writer-based" to "reader-based" prose. This movement occurs with any type of writing, but it's particularly tricky with the personal essay. When you're writing about yourself, there is always this: *Who cares?*

The movement from sketch to draft must address this question. But how?

Evaluating Your Own Sketch. One way to assess whether your sketch might be meaningful to someone other than you is to look for the balance between narrative and reflection, or the then-narrator and the now-narrator. Try this:

- Take two highlighters, each a different color.

- Go through your sketch from beginning to end, using one color to highlight text that's storytelling, what happened or what you saw (the then-narrator), and then use the other color to highlight text that is explanatory, more-general commentary about what happened or what you saw (the now-narrator). What's the pattern of color?

There are several possibilities here:

1. **One color dominates.** Your sketch is mostly narrative or mostly summary, all then-narrator or all now-narrator. A personal essay that is mostly narrative usually fails to address the "So what?" question. It seems to tell a story without a purpose. On the other hand, a personal essay that is all explanation fails to engage readers in the writer's *experiences*. It's all telling and no showing. Personal essays must both show *and* tell.

2. **One color dominates except at the end.** Typically, there is all narrative until the very end, when the writer briefly reflects, much like the formula for a fable, with its moral at the end. This can seem predictable to readers. But you can work with it in revision by taking the reflection at the end and using it to reconceive the essay *from the very beginning*. Can you take the ending and use its insight to organize your thinking in a revision?

3. **The colors alternate.** Sometimes this is the most interesting type of personal essay, because the two narrators are in genuine collaboration, trying to figure out what happened and what it *means*.

In my markup of Amanda's sketch (p. 85), you can see how there is some shifting in the pattern of color. But exposition dominates. Her revision might need more story, more *showing* readers what happened that has made her think the things she now thinks.

If our personal experiences and observations are to mean anything to someone else, then they must, at the very least, both show and tell. They should, through details, descriptions, and scenes, invite an audience into the sea of our experiences. But they must also be clear about the *reason* behind the invitation—about what we have come to understand and want our audience to understand. In revising your sketch, focus on these two concerns above all.

Reflecting on What You Learned. In Chapter 1, I introduced the dialectical method of thinking through writing that moves back and forth between creative thinking and critical thinking, generating and judging. Highlighting the two narrators in your sketch is a way to actually see yourself thinking that way *in your own writing*—or not, depending on the patterns of color you see. Make a journal entry about this. In your sketch, which of the two narrators is more active, and why do you think that's so? In a revision of this sketch, how might you address any imbalance between the two? Where could the now-narrator tell more, or where could the then-narrator show more?

Developing

In the last section, you focused on using a sketch to identify the *purposes* of telling someone else about your memories, experiences, or observations. For example, in the sample sketch, Amanda seems to be telling us about her love for skiing because that love suggests a longing that most of us feel: to transfer the confidence we feel in one part of our lives to every other part. The key to developing your draft is to arrive at a fuller understanding of what your purpose is in telling your own stories *and then to rebuild your essay around that insight from the beginning*.

In other words, as you begin your revision, focus on exploring the answer to these questions:

- What might this essay be saying, not only about me, but more generally about people who find themselves in similar situations? Sometimes the best way to get at this insight is through a pronoun shift: Instead of "What does my story tell *me*?", consider "What might it be trying to tell *us*—people who might have experienced something similar?" In other words, shift from "I" to "we." What do *we* seem to do or say in the situations you're writing about?
- What questions does the essay raise that might be interesting, not only to me, but also to others who do not know me?

Fastwrite in your journal about these questions for as long as you can. One word of caution, though, and I can't stress it enough: YOU DO NOT NEED TO BE PROFOUND. Most of us aren't philosophers or really deep thinkers. We are ordinary people who are just trying to make sense of our lives and work towards those little insights that make us understand things a little better.

As you get a grip on the purpose behind your essay, you can focus your efforts on developing those parts of the narrative that are relevant. What scenes, anecdotes, details, observations, facts, stories, and so on might focus your attention—and later your readers' attention—on what you're trying to say about the topic?

To do so, try some of the following strategies:

- *Explode a moment.* Choose a scene or moment in the story or stories you're telling that seems particularly important to the meaning of the essay. Reenter that moment and fastwrite for a full seven minutes, using all your senses and as much detail as you can muster.

- *Rewrite the lead.* Think about where you might begin that would best dramatize the question, dilemma, problem, or idea that you're exploring. Find a scene, description, fact, profile, or event that points the beginning of the essay towards your purpose in telling the story.

- *Research.* Yes, research can be a great source of information for narrative essays, too. Say you're writing about your observations of pacing animals in the zoo. Is there scholarship on boredom in captive animals? (I can answer that—yep.)

- *Generate.* Cluster the idea or question you're exploring to discover other personal stories or details that might expand the ways you're looking at things. Brainstorm lists of details to flesh out scenes. Fastwrite about the question driving your essay, telling yourself the story of what you initially thought and what you think now about the question. Build those insights into the draft.

Drafting

As you begin drafting, consider the pieces that come together to make a strong personal essay:

1. *Question.* While personal essays might lead to a thesis, they always begin with a question—something that the writer is trying to understand by exploring certain experiences and observations. When you draft you have a tentative idea of what this question is.

2. *Lead.* Find a way to begin your essay that dramatizes that question or highlights the dilemma you're exploring. This gives your essay a sense of purpose from the start.

3. *Now- and Then-Narrator.* Most personal essays move back and forth throughout between what happened (then-narrator) and what the writer is starting to understand about its meaning (now-narrator).

4. *End-Weight.* Unlike conventional thesis-proof essays, personal essays are end-weighted. They accumulate meaning throughout, often culminating in the major point of insight. This insight is neither profound nor extremely general, but some understanding that you've worked hard to come to as you consider the question that arises from certain experiences you've had.

Methods of Development. Narrative is an especially useful method of development for personal essays. How might you use it to develop your subject?

Narrative   Narrative can work in a personal essay in at least three ways. You can use it to:

1. Tell an extended story of what happened.

2. Tell one or more anecdotes, or brief stories, that somehow address the question behind your interest in the topic.

3. Tell the story of your thinking as you've come to understand something you didn't understand before.

Often, a single essay uses narrative in all three types of ways.

Consider beginning your draft with the anecdote or the part of the story you want to tell that best frames the question, dilemma, or idea that is the focus of your essay (see "Inquiring into the Details: More Than One Way to Tell a Story"). If you're writing about the needless destruction of a childhood haunt by developers, then consider opening with the way the place looked *after* the bulldozers were done with it—description related to the end of your narrative.

Time in writing is nothing like real time. You can ignore chronology, if doing so serves your purpose. You can write pages about something that happened in seven minutes or cover twenty years in a paragraph. The key is to tell your story or stories in ways that emphasize what's important.

Using Evidence. How do you make your essay convincing, and even moving, to an audience? It's all in the details. Like most stories, the personal essay thrives on particularity: What exactly did it look like? What exactly did she say? What exactly did it sound and smell like at that moment? Evidence that gives a personal essay authority consists of details that make a reader believe the writer can be trusted to observe keenly and to remember accurately. Both the professional essays in this chapter are rich in detail. There is the neighbor with the "neon orange hunting cap" who rakes the same spot every day in Laura Zazulak's "Every Morning for Five Years," and the description of the teenage Liana "with fashionably black nails and a loyal circle of ebullient friends" in Ginny Blanford's "The Dog That Made Us a Family." This focus on the particular—what it exactly looked like, smelled like, felt like, sounded like—makes an essay come alive for both writer and reader.

As you draft your essay, remember the subtle power of details. Tell, but always show, too.

Inquiring into the Details

More Than One Way to Tell a Story

This is my daughter Julia telling a story:

"And she was like...."
"And then I was like...."
"And then she was like...."

(continued)

Inquiring into the Details (*continued*)

When we think about organizing experiences—something that personal essays try to do—we immediately think of narrative, and then, naturally, we think of the most common narrative structure: chronology. This is Julia's method of oral story-telling, as it is for most of us.

Yet in essay writing, strict chronology—this happened and then this and then this—may not be the best way to tell a story. Once locked into a strictly chrono-logical narrative, you may feel compelled to tell the *whole* story. While chronological storytelling might be a good way to remember what happened as you explore your experiences in your journal or in early drafts, what you need to do in your essay is to tell those *parts* of the story (or stories) that are relevant to the question you're exploring or the thing you're trying to say.

Structure in the personal essay, as in all writing, must be a servant to purpose. Simply put, purpose is how you might answer a potential reader who wants to know this: *So what?* Why should I read this? Organize a narrative essay with the *So what?* question in mind. That may mean that you start a narrative essay in the part of the story that illuminates the question you're exploring, the idea you're trying to under-stand. Typically, this won't be the beginning of the story ("The alarm clock went off at 6 am, and I was groggy from sleep"); it may be the middle or even the end.

The most important part of organizing a personal narrative is not how you tell what happened. It is what you *now* think about the significance of what happened. It is this shift from past to present—from what you remember and what you under-stand about it now that you didn't then—that is the most important structure of all.

Workshopping

If your draft is subject to peer review, see Chapter 14 for details on how to orga-nize workshop groups and decide on how your group can help you. To help you decide, use the guidance starting on p. 554 in Appendix A about workshopping. Each workshop type is described more fully in that section.

Sharing a personal essay with peers might present some special challenges. After all, in this kind of essay, you're really putting yourself out there. You're hon-estly talking about yourself, and about *your* experiences and observations. If your essay is a podcast or radio piece, you'll be sharing not only your writing but also your voice, and my students tell me that in a spoken essay, it's nearly impossible to lie. It's a kind of writing that, as E. B. White once said, should not indulge "in deceit or in concealment," for the writer "will be found out in no time."

Under these circumstances, it's hard not to feel at least a little vulnerable when sharing a personal essay. (If this is a real source of anxiety, talk to your instructor.) But you will find that exactly *because* the personal essay is personal, your peers will be enthusiastic readers of your work. The key is to channel that enthusiasm towards a response that will help you revise.

At this stage in writing the personal essay—the first full draft—what you may need most are responses that address the issues you've worked on most in your sketch: Does the draft clearly answer the "So what?" question (purpose)? Is it clear what one main thing the essay is trying to say (meaning)? All other revision concerns are subordinate to these questions. Why? Because without a clear purpose and clear sense, it's impossible to make any judgments about content.

Annie Dillard, a writer of many nonfiction books and essays, once said that she believed that the biggest challenge in writing comes down to this basic question: *What to put in and what to leave out.* In a personal essay such as the one you're working on, you might conclude that the answer to the question is equally basic (simple): You tell the "whole" story. Yet the truth is that you never do, even in telling a story to friends. We shape and shade a story depending on our motive for telling it. The same is true in prose. Your purpose and what you are trying to say are the two things that determine what belongs in a story and what doesn't. So this is where you should begin.

Questions for Readers. The following box, which focuses on these two key concerns, can help you to guide your peers' response to your first draft.

Questions for Peer Reviewers	
1. Purpose	What would you say this essay is about? Do you have a clear sense of *why* I'm writing about this topic?
2. Meaning	Most essays need to say one fricking thing (S.O.F.T.). What would you say is the point of this draft? What is the main thing I seem to be saying about this topic?

Reflecting on the Workshop. After the workshop session, do a follow-up entry in your notebook that explores these questions:

- What main impression did you take away from the conversation about your draft?
- What do you think worked in the draft?
- What do you think needs work?
- What was/were your favorite sentence or passages in the draft? Why?

Revising

Revision is a continual process—not a last step. You've been revising—"reseeing" your subject—from the first messy fastwriting in your journal. But the things that get your attention vary depending on where you are in the writing process. With your draft in hand, revision becomes your focus through what I'll call "shaping and tightening your draft."

Chapter 14 contains strategies that can help you revise any inquiry project, and the "Guidelines: Revising Your Work" box later in this chapter can help you locate these strategies. There are also certain things to think about that are especially useful for shaping a personal essay.

3.5
Apply revision strategies that are effective for shaping narratives.

Shaping. In your draft, you made a tentative commitment to your topic, hoping that you could shape it into something that might have meaning for someone other than you. Fundamentally, you've been trying to figure out *what you're trying to say* and then rebuild your essay so that what you're trying to say is both clear and convincing. You might also want your personal essay to be moving.

Shaping focuses on larger concerns first: purpose and meaning—the very largest concerns, which you've looked at if you workshopped your draft—and the next-to-largest concerns of information and organization. It starts with knowing what your essay is about—your inquiry question and maybe your theme—and then revising to make every element of the draft focused on that question or idea.

What to Cut and What to Add   Ryan wrote a personal essay about the epic battles he had with his brother growing up. He realized as he wrote it that, while they didn't exactly hate each other, they certainly behaved like they did back then. The purpose of Ryan's essay was to explore a question: *Why were these sibling rivalries so intense, and how do they shape the brothers' relationship today?* As he reflects on what he wrote and understands what he wants to convey, Ryan can make the decisions that Dillard says revision demands: what to cut and what to add. Ryan will cut the part that focuses on his father, because it does little to help readers see the brothers' rivalry. He will add more about the chess game in which they finally came to blows. A key to revising a personal essay, then, is this:

Given my essay's purpose and meaning, what should I cut and what should I add?

- What information—scenes, descriptions, observations, explanations—is no longer relevant to the purpose and meaning?
- What information is missing that should be added to help readers understand and, in a small way, experience, so that they will appreciate my point?

The Question of Time   Revising a narrative essay also involves the question of time. Consider this in two ways:

1. Where will the information to develop your story come from—from the past or from the present? The then-narrator is master of the past: What happened? And then what? The now-narrator is charged with commenting from the present: What do I make of what happened from where I sit now? Personal essays that tell stories need information from both past and present.

2. How does time organize the information in the draft? Do you tell your story chronologically? Is that the best way to structure the essay? What might happen, for example, if you begin in the middle of the story, or even at the end? Will that better dramatize the question or dilemma that you're exploring?

Research   I'm not talking about extensive research, but about quick searches for background information, relevant facts, and maybe even something on what other writers or experts have said. Here's an example. I was writing an essay in which I recalled a total solar eclipse that happened in August 1964. Did it really? A quick web search confirmed it, but I also got information about exactly how long it lasted, and this information helped strengthen the scene I was writing. Say you're writing an essay about iPhone infatuation. Why not look up a definition of "infatuation" and then do some quick research on how students use their iPhones in a typical day?

Other Questions for Revision   Make sure you address the following questions as you revise:

- Does the draft begin in a way that gives your readers a sense of where the essay is going? Is your purpose clear? (This is especially important for podcast essays.)

- Is there too much explaining? Narrative essays are usually built on the backbone of story—anecdote, scene, and description. This is how we help the audience appreciate, in some small way, the experiences that have inspired the insights we want to share. Personal essays *do* need to tell, but they must also *show*.

- By the end of your essay, will the reader appreciate the significance of the story you're telling? Have you said what you need to say about how, though it's your own experience, the meaning you discover might apply to others as well?

Polishing.   When you are satisfied with the shape of your draft, focus on paragraphs, sentences, and words. Are your paragraphs coherent? How do you manage transitions? Are your sentences fluent and concise? Are there any errors in spelling or syntax? The section of Chapter 14 called "Problems with Clarity and Style" can help you focus on these issues.

Before you finish your draft, work through the following checklist:

- ✓ Every paragraph is about one thing.
- ✓ The transitions between paragraphs aren't abrupt.
- ✓ The length of sentences varies in each paragraph.
- ✓ Each sentence is concise. There are no unnecessary words or phrases.
- ✓ You've checked grammar, particularly for verb agreement, run-on sentences, unclear pronouns, and misused words (*there/their, where/were*, and so on).
- ✓ You've run your spellchecker and proofed your paper for misspelled words.

Chapter 14 has strategies to help you solve all kinds of revision problems, large and small. Use the following "Guidelines: Revising Your Work" to know where to look in that chapter to both shape and polish your draft.

Guidelines: Revising Your Work

A first effort is almost never a best effort. To make sure your essay is really your best work, check out Chapter 14 for help with these questions:

- What is my paper really about? (See p. 518.)

- What am I really trying to say? (See p. 523.)

- Do I have enough convincing evidence? (See p. 530.)

- Does this paper move logically and smoothly from paragraph to paragraph? (See p. 534.)

- Are the sentences and paragraphs in this paper too choppy or hard to follow? (See p. 542.)

▶ Student Essay

Military veterans often bring their rich, complicated experiences into my writing classes, and because what they've seen and done often raises questions they can't easily answer, they learn to love the personal essay. Seth Marlin served in Iraq. In the essay "Smoke of Empire," he recalls that during his first night in the country, there was a stench he didn't recognize. It turns out this stench was the smell of things—often perfectly good things—burning. The refuse of war. This memory inspires a meditation on war, waste, and empire.

The piece was written for the radio, and Seth produced an audio essay using Audacity software that blended his vocal reading of "Smoke of Empire" with music that gave the essay even more power. As you read Seth's essay, keep in mind that he wrote it with the idea that his audience would hear it a single time. Consider as you read it how that changed his approach to the writing. You can also listen to the essay at bruceballenger.com.

Smoke of Empire
Seth Marlin

1   When I was in Iraq, we used to have this rotating detail. Call it *"Hajji*-watch." Bring in local guys, pay them ten bucks to move sandbags, haul trash. Post a couple soldiers with rifles in case anyone gets froggy. Locals try to sell you stuff, turn them down. They ask for soap, shampoo, toothpaste, say you don't have any. That's the order they drill into you: *Do Not Buy, Sell, or Give Items to Local Nationals.*

Locals were poor. Dirt poor. Steal the gloves out of your pocket if they thought they'd get some use. Who could blame them? One guy I saw stole a bedroll once; another, maybe fifteen, jacked a soccer-ball, said it was for his little brother. Our squad-leader said it was contraband, said the ball would be waiting for him when he came back next week, soon as he got a memorandum from the base-commander.   2

That kid never got his ball, you kidding me? Lot of poor guys with families; that line stretched two miles up the road back into town. He'd have been lucky to get in at all. I doubt he ever got that ball back; most likely, it just went to the burn-pit.   3

* * *

Fun fact: Wars generate waste. The Department of Defense estimates that its wars each generate ten pounds of garbage per service member per day. At over 150,000 service members deployed, that's a lot of trash. Unfortunately, the locals tend not to cotton to your leaving messes all over their soil; thus, in the name of diplomacy, the invaders have to clean up after themselves. On places like Joint Base Balad, all that refuse goes to one place: the burn-pit.   4

Picture a base, fifteen miles across, set in a swath of palm-dotted farmland. Now picture on part of that a landscape of hills, valleys, and craters—all of it garbage, all bigger than a dozen football fields. Now picture that on fire. Through the haze, you might see the figures who manage all that incoming drek—orange-turbaned Sikhs wearing blue jumpsuits, some of them wearing goggles and surgical masks if they're lucky. These pits are typically run by private contractors; OSHA guidelines mean little to nothing here. Your tax dollars at work.   5

My first night in Iraq, I remember looking west from my trailer and being surprised to see a sunset of blazing orange. It was at least two hours after dusk, and the stars were out, at least a couple anyway. Then I realized that *that wasn't sunlight I was seeing*—that it was *flames*. Those weren't clouds I was seeing, but rather smoke. I didn't know what all that was yet, only that it took up half the northern sky. But oh, I learned. The first thing I learned about was the smell, like burning oak-leaves mixed with scorched plastic and warping aluminum. Wood, fabric, paper, metal—if it burned, they burnt it. If not, they threw something on it until it did. On a clear day it threw smoke a half-mile high; on the cold days during the rainy season, October through March, the flames got tamped down by the constant downpour. Made the world smell like a half-smoked cigarette, all wet soot and chemicals. Made you gag passing through it on your way to the motor pool. During the summer months the ashes blew into the town just north of us, a little two-rut burg called Yethrib. Turned the air gray, sent hot embers raining down on the farmers' fields. Sitting in a tower on a weeklong rotation of guard-duty, I remember watching one day as some hundred-odd acres of sunflower, sorghum, and lentils went up in flames. An entire season's crops destroyed, in a part of the country where the median income was two dollars a day.   6

* * *

I remember convoying home from bridge-sites late at night; I used to peer over the steering-wheel and look for the banded floodlights, the blood-red haze of smoke. Waste   7

(continued)

(continued)

never sleeps. On a bulletin-board in my platoon's Ops office, I remember they'd posted a memo signed by two Air-Force lieutenants-colonel. The memo cited the effects of long-term exposure to the smoke, expressed outrage at the lack of incinerators, ordered the memo posted in every company headquarters, every permanent file of every soldier in service on that base. I'm sure that memo's still in my record somewhere; then again, the VA does have a tendency to lose things.

8   I saw a lot of strange, scary, moving things during my time deployed. Sunrises over the Tigris, Sumerian ruins, farmers praying in their fields at dawn. But the image that sticks with me is the burn-pit. Why? Maybe because the sight of all that waste, made tangible, left some mark on me, like tracking mud on floors as a guest, uninvited. War is consumption, I've realized. Conspicuous consumption. It's embarrassing, really: this is the democracy we bring to a foreign nation, consumption and waste. Look at all we've got. Fast-food, electronics, medicine. You can't have any, and we're going to burn it all right in front of you.

9   You know, the last night I was writing this I pulled up Google Earth, pinned down where I was posted. Our old motor-pool was taken down, bulldozed over; our old living-areas and trailers had been carted away. Even the burn-pit was silent, but it still sits there, like a grease-stain you can see from the air. Big sign in English: "NO DUMPING," it says, while behind it sits a mountain of blackened, twisted steel. The Balad pit may sit quiet now, but I'll bet even money those fires are still going elsewhere.

10   All day. Every day. The smoke of consumption, of Empire.

Evaluating the Essay

Discuss or write about your response to Seth Marlin's essay, using some or all of the following questions.

1. What do you understand this essay to be saying about war, empire, and waste? Where does it say it most clearly or memorably?
2. Throughout this chapter, I've promoted the idea that personal essays have two narrators—the now-narrator and the then-narrator. Are they both present in "Smoke of Empire"? Where?
3. What is the main thing you might take away from reading this piece and apply when you write or revise your own personal essay?
4. This piece was written to be heard rather than read, and the writer assumed that it would be heard only once. Imagine this rhetorical situation: You're in the car listening to the radio while driving to campus and you hear Seth reading "Smoke of Empire." Because he's not in the car with you, you don't have to be polite. You don't even know him. You can change the station if what you hear doesn't interest you. What special demands does this situation make on *how* a personal essay is written? How might it affect the writing and organization of a piece?

Using What You Have Learned

Let's revisit the list of things at the beginning of this chapter that I hoped you'd learn.

1. **Use personal experiences and observations to drive inquiry.** Even before you read this chapter, you'd told stories about yourself—we all do all the time—but it rarely occurs to us that these stories can be a source of insight even in some academic situations. The questions that drive our inquiry into how we understand our lives are no less important than the questions that inspire us to explore other subjects. In fact, Montaigne, the first essayist, believed that self-knowledge is the most important knowing of all.

2. **Apply the exploratory thinking of personal essays to academic writing.** Next time you get a writing assignment in another class, start the work by "essaying" the topic—by developing a quick list of questions and responding to them. One great template for exploring almost any topic is a relationship question: What is the relationship between _____ and _____? For example, "What is the relationship between tutoring programs for college athletes and academic success?" Rather than trying to come up with a quick answer, spend some time fastwriting to find out what *you* think based on what you've read, heard, experienced, or observed. What you discover might lead to a thesis later.

3. **Identify the characteristics of personal essays in different forms.** Personal essays lend themselves to different forms, and if you know what a personal essay looks like, you can write yours in one of these different forms. Some of the most vibrant examples of the genre are podcasts, radio essays, and photographic essays. With the availability of free software for digitally recording your voice, publishing an essay online is easier than ever. The blog is also an extremely popular form of the personal essay. Though these media can work with almost any form of writing, they seem to lend themselves especially to autobiographical work. There's something about hearing the writer's voice in a podcast or the easy intimacy of the blog that encourages personal essays.

4. **Use invention strategies to discover and develop a personal essay topic.** When I suggest using invention strategies, I mean this in two ways. First, you can use techniques such as fastwriting and clustering to discover a topic for personal writing. But perhaps more important, you can use such invention techniques to generate *insight*—not just an idea about something to write about, but discoveries about what you think about that topic.

5. **Apply revision strategies that are effective for shaping narratives.** The story—whether it's a recollection of what happened or our experience observing what is happening—is one of the most basic ways we all organize information: This happened, and then this, and then this....Yet chronologically isn't always the best way to organize information from experience in writing, and, more important, story isn't just about what happened. It's also a "narrative of thought," or the story of what we now make of what happened. Even if you never write another personal essay, you can use narrative to tell the story of what you first thought about a subject and what you came to understand.

4

Writing a Profile

Learning Objectives

In this chapter, you'll learn to

4.1 Use a profile of a person as a way to focus on an idea, a personality trait, a particular category of people, or a situation.

4.2 Identify some of the academic applications of profiles.

4.3 Identify the characteristics of profiles in different forms.

4.4 Use invention strategies, including interviews, to discover and develop a profile of someone.

4.5 Apply revision strategies that are effective for shaping profiles.

Writing About People

Researching a book on the culture of the New England lobster-fishing industry, I wandered into the lighthouse keeper's house in Pemaquid Point, Maine. The lighthouse, built in 1827, was automated—like all but one lighthouse on the East Coast—but the empty keeper's house had been turned into a tiny fishing museum. I found my way there one late spring day, stepped inside, and was greeted by Abby Boynton, sitting on a folding chair, working on needlepoint. I had come to look at historical objects related to lobster fishing, but instead I encountered Abby, an elderly widow whose husband, a local lobsterman, had died of cancer several years before.

I liked Abby immediately, and as she led me to the back of the museum to show me a picture book that documented a few days of her husband's work at the traps offshore from New Harbor, Maine, I began to think that she was opening a door to a topic I hadn't considered: What is it like to live with a man who makes his living hauling lobster traps? I had researched the science, gone out in boats, and interviewed lobstermen. But what about their wives (or, in rare cases, husbands), who, as Abby told me that day, are charged with "keeping dinner warm" while waiting? And what about that waiting? What is it like?

These are the seeds of a profile. You meet someone interesting, and you're drawn to that person's unique story, and at the same time you sense that he or she might also stand in for a larger idea or group: What does it mean to wait every day for a boat to come in? Who are these people who do the waiting?

There may be no better way of dramatizing the impact of a problem or the significance of an idea than showing how it presents itself in the life of one person.

This accidental interview with the lobsterman's wife led to a brief vignette, much like the one you'll read later in this chapter of a man who owns a lobster museum. Had I developed the vignette further, I would have talked to Abby Boynton again. I might have included statistics about the divorce rate among Maine fishing families, or information about the economic pressures on families during a bad fishing season—all the factors that might easily make it hard for a marriage to survive. The result would have been a profile that put a face on the idea that lobster fishing is difficult, but for many a good life.

Motives for Writing a Profile

4.1
Use a profile of a person as a way to focus on an idea, a personality trait, a particular category of people, or a situation.

E. B. White, author of the children's classics *Charlotte's Web* and *Stuart Little* and many essays for the *New Yorker* magazine, once offered this advice: "If you want to write about mankind, write about a man." The profile is the form that accomplishes this most directly. Through Abby Boynton we can see something about other lobstermen's wives and families—and about human beings in general. There may be no better way of dramatizing the impact of a problem, the importance of a question, or the significance of an idea than showing how it presents itself in the life of one person.

Although when we think of profiles we often think of the celebrity profile—a form we see in slick magazines such as *People*, on websites such as TMZ, and in segments on *Entertainment Tonight*—profiles of "ordinary" people like Mrs. Boynton are more relevant and revealing to most of us. They are lives we recognize—lives that are no less complex and interesting than those of the rich and famous. In fact, we may even write profiles as part of preserving our family history (see "Writing Beyond the Classroom: Digital Profiles" later in this chapter on pages 121–123).

The most important motive behind composing a profile—whether it's a conventional written essay, a photo essay, or any other mode—is that the subject is *interesting*. What makes someone interesting? That's pretty subjective, of course. But generally, interesting people can stand in for larger groups to which they belong—lobstering families, fast-order chefs, nannies, international students, world-class bicyclists—and have stories to tell about their experiences. As an inquiry project, a profile is driven by a question: If I look closely at this one person, might I gain insight about *people*, and particularly about people like him or her?

The Profile and Academic Writing

The profile is closely related to the case study, a common academic form, especially in the social sciences. The case study, like the profile, takes a close look at the life of a person who is interesting and in some way representative of a group, in order to arrive at a fuller picture of that group. For example, suppose you're interested in examining the progress of your university's commitment to ethnic and racial diversity, a principle the administration has publicly embraced. One way to approach the topic is through a profile or case study of an international student. What has been her experience on campus? Which campus programs have proved useful? What programs are needed? The voice of your profile subject and the details of her experience would help dramatize an otherwise abstract policy debate, and the story she tells could offer a foundation from which to explore the issue.

4.2
Identify some of the academic applications of profiles.

The profile relies on interviews and observation, particularly those revealing details that say something about the character or feelings of the person profiled.

Profiles might also be an element of an ethnography, a method used in anthropology and other academic disciplines (see Chapter 9). Through fieldwork, ethnographers attempt to document the customs, rituals, and behaviors of cultural groups in the locations where members live, work, or play. This often involves interviewing and describing individuals. For example, an ethnographer interested in the superhero phenomenon (regular people who dress up in costumes and actually try to fight crime) might describe the interactions of budding superheroes in online discussion boards and profile a particularly interesting participant.

More than any other form of inquiry, the profile relies on interviews. This is not only for information, so that the voice of the writer's subject can come through, but also for observation, because the right details can say a lot about the character or feelings of the person profiled. The way one man stands with his feet apart and arms folded on his chest to emphasize his biceps can show his arrogance, the way a woman carefully knots the scarf around her neck can show her fastidiousness, and so on. Interview skills are a key method of collecting information in communications and the social sciences, and writers who want to practice these skills will find the profile a useful challenge.

Features of the Form

Feature	Conventions of the Profile
Inquiry questions	Does this one person's story tell us anything about the perspectives of others who belong to a group and about people in general? What does this person's story say about social situations, trends, or problems?
Motives	Profiles put a "face" on groups and on issues, problems, or questions, and in doing so, dramatize them. Whether they're anecdotes or case studies in a larger work or fully developed portraits of someone, profiles are in the service of ideas. They aren't simply objective pictures of someone, but an effort to *use* a portrait to say something.
Subject matter	You can profile anyone, of course, but not everyone makes a good profile. The best profile subjects are both unique *and* typical. Their very individual attitudes and experiences might set them apart, but they also stand in as representative of others. They are also accessible, willing, and interesting to talk to.
Structure	*Why this person?* Profiles must start by answering that question—or providing a strong hint. From there, a profile might be structured as a story (e.g., a day in the life, significant events, the story of the interview). Anecdote is a building block of a profile. Other typical elements are background (subject's name, place, reputation, social relationships), quotations or dialogue, scenes, description of the subject, and commentary from the writer. Point of view is a key decision. Will the writer be part of the story or stay in the background?
Sources of information	The profile depends most on interview and observation. The more you can talk to your profile subject, the better; and if you can see your subject in action, then you have the material for a scene, an element that brings a profile to life. You might also interview people who know your profile subject, to get a fuller picture of who he or she is. Information might also come from research—taped interviews, archived articles, letters, e-mails.
Language	Scene, anecdote, and description—all key to "seeing" a person—require writing with sensory detail. This language is very specific and often exact. What *exactly* did she look like? What did she say? Background information is similarly concrete: date of birth, age, hometown, job, favorite books.

Prose+

The radio essay has been around for a long time, but the National Public Radio Program *This American Life*, hosted by Ira Glass (pictured above), has inspired millions of listeners along with quite a few writers who see the power of audio storytelling. *This American Life* specializes in the audio profile. These pieces often weave interview clips of a subject with music and voice narration to tell a story about often regular people. My own students have experimented with audio profiles of all kinds of people: interesting relatives, people with careers the students want to pursue, amazing teachers they had. Now that smartphones are quite capable recording devices, audio profiles are easier to do. For more details on how to create an audio essay, see pp. 477–478 in Chapter 13.

READINGS

▶ Profile 1

While working on my book about lobster fishing in New England, I happened into the Mt. Desert Oceanarium, a museum dedicated to protecting Maine's coastal environment. The founder and director was an energetic former Episcopal priest named David Mills. When he discovered I am a writer, David volunteered to be my guide, introducing me to local fishermen and showing me around town. Within minutes of meeting him, I knew I wanted to write about David Mills, though I had no idea what I might want to say about him. It turned out that my profile, "Museum Missionary," says as much about the interviewer as about his subject.

If the writer doesn't step into a profile directly by offering commentary or appearing in scenes, profiles can appear to be completely objective and readers' gaze will remain focused on the profile subject. But sometimes the writer enters the frame, and inescapably his or her presence in the picture—asking questions, offering comments, and sharing observations—shifts the focus. Profiles such as these—and "Museum Missionary" is one of them—read in some ways like a personal essay. There's nothing wrong with this *if* the writer doesn't crowd out the profile subject, who is usually the person readers most want to learn about.

I'm happy to report that David Mills is still director of the Mt. Desert Oceanarium in Maine, and he's still wowing visitors with frightfully large lobsters, the fodder for delicious nightmares.

Museum Missionary

Bruce Ballenger

1   David Mills, surrounded by children, held a small lobster aloft and asked if anyone wanted to touch it. Index fingers sprouted everywhere. "Just don't knock him," he said. "We don't want to give him a headache." I stood at the back of the Lobster Room, an exhibit area in the Mount Desert Oceanarium, and watched while Mills instructed children and their parents in the ways of the lobster and the lobsterman. Twenty of us were there, crowded into that little room, and though I had been to such talks before, I was enchanted.

2   Mills reached into the Touch Tank and pulled out a berried female lobster, carrying a mass of eggs under her tail. The kids gasped. "There's a passage in the Bible where the Lord said to be fruitful and multiply. This lobster sure be fruitful," he said. The adults laughed.

3   "How many of you have ever eaten an eight- to twelve-pound lobster?" No one raised their hands. "Well, that's good. When I do find people who have I ask them whether they'll ever eat another, and nine times out of ten they say they won't have

a second one. They just don't taste very good." Mills went on to argue the merits of Maine's maximum-size law, the only lobstering state that has one, which prohibits taking lobsters larger than five inches in carapace length.

"There are two reasons not to buy big lobsters," he said. "They make more babies, and they don't taste good."   4

Mills, a former Episcopal priest, found a new ministry in 1972 when he started the Mount Desert Oceanarium: preaching to kids and their parents about marine life off the northern New England coast and the need to protect it. "We'd been coming up here on vacation, and my wife has some family in Bangor. We love scuba diving and developed an interest in oceanography. I had hoped my kids would take it up. But if you've done any counseling, you learn that sometimes the desires you have for your kids are really your own."   5

"I had been an inner-city pastor," he continued. "I marched in Selma, that sort of thing, but didn't really change any lives. I was one of the ministers who didn't really know the Lord. When I prayed I did all the talking. But one day the Lord said go to Maine and start that museum."   6

Sixteen years ago, Mills and his wife heeded that call and moved into an old waterfront building in Southwest Harbor that once served as a chandlery for schooners. It was heavily timbered, able to stand up to twenty tons of seawater aquaria and to tourist foot traffic. Contributions from local fishermen soon filled his saltwater tanks with the local marine life. Despite the years he's put into the Oceanarium, David Mills still zips around the place with missionary zeal, pointing out the holes in the floor where rigging rope was once sold, explaining the eyes on a sea scallop, examining a strange-looking starfish. But he seems most taken by lobsters.   7

On one wall of the Lobster Room hang the wooden pot buoys used by four generations of the Spurlings, a local lobstering family. Mills handed me a Maine Lobsterman's Association hat and told me he'd take me down to the wharf to talk to Ted Spurling.   8

We found him in a back room of the Southwest Lobster Company, standing near bait barrels that bulged with salted herring and mackerel, talking to several other fishermen. Ted Spurling is a small man, with a reserve that seemed to deepen every time I lifted my note pad. "Don't know that there's much I can tell you," he said quietly, when David Mills introduced us. We talked awkwardly for a time, while David rushed about trying to find more people for me to interview, and I realized then how odd it must seem to a man like Ted Spurling that I should be writing about how he makes a living.   9

"I felt kind of bad for Ted," David told me in the car later. "It's hard to have someone firing questions at you."   10

"What should I have done differently?" I asked.   11

"Well, I think it's better to just go with the flow."   12

I knew he was right, and it reminded me once again how difficult it is for someone "from away" to easily walk into a lobsterman's life and expect to understand much about it. I wonder if in some ways the working fishermen are as much victims of the   13

(continued)

(*continued*)

public passion for lobsters as they are beneficiaries. Those of us who don't work the water sentimentalize their lives, or at least have a nosy curiosity about it. Hangerson at the waterfront wharves often find lobstermen sullen, partly because they have work to do.

14   "You know, years ago a fisherman was classed with those people who used to go around and clean outhouses," seventy-year-old lobsterman Willie Morrison told me one evening, as we sat talking on his front porch in Rye, New Hampshire. "As a matter of fact, when someone would ask what your father does, you'd say he was a farmer. You'd never say he was a fisherman. After World War II, all of a sudden for crying out loud, the lobsterman was something special. People were constantly coming up to you and asking all sorts of questions. It was a pain."

15   Some lobstermen like Morrison find all the attention a bother. Others may even find it a bit alienating, especially when the popular notion of what their lives are like is often so much at variance with its realities. It is a feeling they may share with cowboys and writers and actors—anyone whose livelihood is the subject of popular myth.

16   I didn't ask Ted Spurling about this feeling. I was too busy taking notes, thinking up questions, trying to pry my way into the secrets of his work. I was so eager to find insights about the lobstermen's culture that I had stopped really listening to this quiet man, who happened to be a lobsterman.

17   Years ago, David Mills had learned something about listening, and it led him to open a museum. In his own kind way, he passed the advice on to me.

Inquiring into the Essay

1. **Explore.** In your journal, brainstorm a list of people you've known whom you can't forget. Let this list grow in waves for about four minutes. Choose one person you'd like to focus on. Put his or her name in the center of a blank journal page and quickly build a cluster (see page 81 in Chapter 3 for more on this technique), building branches outward from the name, listing moments, words, other names, dates, places, things, and other details you associate with the person you chose. When a branch dies out, start another. Each branch is a potential beginning to a profile on your subject. Draft a lead paragraph for a possible profile that, like "Museum Missionary," begins with a scene.

2. **Explain.** Explain the ways in which "Museum Missionary" exemplifies the profile essay as it's described in the "Features of the Form" box (p. 102).

3. **Evaluate.** Like most other types of essays, a profile is organized around one main thing the writer is trying to say. In a sense, a profile is making an argument—you need to see this person *this* way—and offering evidence to convince you that the profile's perspective is believable. I was trying to argue in "Museum Missionary" that David Mills is a person who found an

unusual channel for his religious faith: in praise of lobsters and lobstering. Evaluate the evidence in the profile that you think supports this thesis. What do you think is the *best* evidence? Does this evidence indicate anything about the types of evidence that are most persuasive in a profile? Explain what you think "Museum Missionary" is trying to say. Where does it say it most clearly, at least for you?

4. **Reflect.** If you want to write about somebody else, one of the decisions you've got to make is whether to talk about yourself. What kind of presence, if any, will you have in your essay? Will you mention that you're asking questions? Will you comment on the answers? Or will you stay out of it completely, working behind the scenes? In "Museum Missionary," I decide to step in. Reflect on what this adds to—and takes away from—this profile and any profile.

▶ **Profile 2**

The memory of 9/11 is seared into the brains of most Americans, and perhaps New Yorkers most of all. Many were eyewitnesses, and too many suffered the loss of people they knew or loved. But with the passing of time, at least for those of us not directly touched by the tragedy, the memory loses some of its edge. Ian Frazier's profile of Salvatore Siano, a retired New Jersey bus driver, demonstrates E. B. White's dictum that if you want to write about humankind, you should write about a person. This is the power of the profile—to put a face on something that is abstract and to show, through one person, why that something matters. In "Passengers," written on the tenth anniversary of 9/11, Frazier finds in Siano a way of writing about 9/11 that transforms it from a public tragedy into a personal loss. His profile helps us recalibrate our response to the attack, looking beyond the public symbols and the speeches to see, once again, the many ways 9/11 continues to affect people's lives.

Passengers
Ian Frazier

Before Salvatore Siano, known as Sal, retired, last December, he had driven a bus for the DeCamp bus company, of Montclair, New Jersey, for forty-two years. DeCamp has eight or ten routes, but Sal mostly drove the No. 66 and the No. 33, which wind among West Caldwell and Bloomfield and Clifton and Nutley before joining Route 3 and heading for the Lincoln Tunnel. Unlike some bus drivers and former bus drivers, Sal himself is not buslike but slim and quick, with light-gray hair and eyebrows, and a thin, mobile face. In a region where the most efficient way to commute is by train, the bus can be

1

(continued)

(continued)

cozier, more personal. When he drove, Sal reconfigured his bus as his living room, lining the dashboard with toy ducks, chatting over his shoulder with passengers, and sometimes keeping snowballs handy to throw at policemen through the open door. He used to caution children, "I am not a role model!" His travel-guide monologues upon arrival at the Port Authority Bus Terminal—"Welcome to sunny Aruba! Don't forget your sunblock! Cha-cha-cha!"—won him minor fame.

2   On the morning of September 11, 2001, Sal was driving a No. 66 bus that began its run at eight-twenty-five. As he headed for the city on Route 3, he saw the smoke rising from downtown. By the time he reached the tunnel, it had been closed, and Sal had received a call from another driver telling him about the first plane. Wedged in heavy traffic, Sal managed to back the bus onto an entrance ramp, turn around, and retrace his route, dropping the passengers at their stops and returning their tickets or cash fares along the way. Six hundred and seventy-nine New Jerseyans, many from towns that Sal drove through, died in the attacks. Afterward, Sal stopped joking around on the bus. When asked why, he grew sad and dispirited, and said that he was too emotionally caught up in the tragedy. Eventually, he began to joke again.

3   Among his passengers, Sal had many fans. Once, when he pulled up to the Bellevue Plaza stop, in Upper Montclair—this was years ago, before September 11th—he saw such a crowd that he thought he would have to order another bus. But then everyone yelled, "Surprise!" They had been waiting there to give him a party. He had great affection for his riders, and considered ninety-nine percent of them to be wonderful people. He never asked anyone's name or occupation, but he learned a lot about his regulars anyway. He believed that he had a skill for picking out the ones who would succeed and, as an example, cites a boy named John Miller, then a Montclair high-school student, who became a well-known journalist and one of the only Americans to interview Osama bin Laden.

4   Sal lives by himself in a garden apartment in Clifton. In his retirement, he sometimes works for an auto shop, driving to pick up parts. Afternoons, he goes to Brookdale Park, in Montclair, and spends a couple of hours playing tennis or reading the newspapers. Recently, one of his fan-passengers—who can recall many drab morning walks that were improved by the sight of Sal waving to him from the driver's seat of a passing No. 66—stopped by the park to say hello. Sal was sitting in his car, taking shelter from the rain. A gloomy, apocalyptic quality of the light, maybe caused by the approaching hurricane, led to thoughts about the upcoming anniversary of September 11th. Sal said, "The other day, I was remembering this one passenger from Upper Montclair who always got on at the Norwood Avenue stop, by the public library. After the attacks, I read in the paper—someone must have told me his name—that this man had passed away. He was such a pleasant human being. A man about my height, wore glasses. I had seen him just the week before. The obituary in the *Times* said this man volunteered to work in homeless shelters, and sometimes slept in them to experience what they were like." (Here Sal began to cry.) "When I read that, I knew that my instincts about him had been right. I remember him whenever I go by Norwood and the library."

The passenger's name was Howard L. Kestenbaum. Along with the names of   5
nearly three thousand other people who died that day, his is inscribed on a granite
wall at the edge of the memorial garden in Eagle Rock Reservation, a county park in
nearby West Orange, at the top of a ridge with a clear view of lower Manhattan. "He
had a wife and daughter, and they are special people, too," Sal continued. "I still see
them around Montclair on a regular basis. Whenever I do, I embrace them and give
them a kiss on the cheek."

Inquiring into the Essay

1. **Explore.** In "Passengers," Frazier writes that Salvatore Siano, "unlike some
    bus drivers and former bus drivers," is "not buslike but slim and quick, with
    light-gray hair and eyebrows, and a thin, mobile face." A physical descrip-
    tion of the person you're writing about is often an element of a profile, and
    it's hard to compose. Practice it by writing a one-sentence description of
    three people you know (or can see): parent, sibling, spouse, friend, class-
    mate. What distinguishes a good physical description from one that's not so
    good?

2. **Explain.** "Passengers" exemplifies the idea that showing readers a problem
    through the experiences of one person affected by that problem is more
    powerful than just generally explaining the problem. If you think there's
    truth to this, can you explain why it might be so? How is Salvatore's unique
    experience (after all, we're not bus drivers and likely don't live in New Jer-
    sey) a better way of understanding the 9/11 attack than explanations about
    its effects on people?

3. **Evaluate.** Compare and contrast the different choices the writers of "Museum
    Missionary" (pp. 104–106) and "Passengers" made about their own presence
    in their essays. One is part of the narrative, and the other stays out of it.
    It's hard to say which is the better approach in a profile, but what might be
    some factors that influence this decision? How will you decide in the profile
    you will write?

4. **Reflect.** What are the ethics of writing about someone else? After all, a
    profile essay isn't fiction; you're not inventing a character, you're making a
    character out of a real person. What ethical obligations, if any, do you have
    to the person you profile?

▶ Profile 3

There's an appealing simplicity to this online profile of Jafari Sampson, a young
violinist from the South Bronx. It opens, as profiles often do, with a scene that
shows the subject in action; here, we drop in on Sampson playing violin in Grand

Central Terminal, deftly inventing his own composition. From there, we learn the young musician's background and discovery of his passion for violin. Notice how the writer, Amelia Pang, always keeps Sampson at the center of her profile, never explicitly stepping in to interpret or comment; her views are implied through her choice and arrangement of material. As you read the essay, consider what you believe is the theme of the profile, the idea about Sampson that Pang most wants to communicate.

The Life of a Violin Prodigy from South Bronx

Amelia Pang

1   Sitting in front of a subway station column, his fingers dance across the strings of his umber violin. Nearby, construction workers unreel yellow caution tape, as sounds of rolling suitcases fill the hollow halls of Grand Central Terminal. But Jafari Sampson, a 19-year-old prodigy, hears silence amid the clamor.

2   "Silence gives me inspiration," he said.

3   Sampson has always been good at finding silence. He spent most of his childhood in a quiet room with his violin, hearing different meanings of motifs as they repeat.

4   He grew up in the South Bronx, a place not renowned for its output of classical musicians. But when someone is born with a gift, it doesn't matter where he is born.

Sampson not only has perfect pitch, but his ears can recognize which major a knock on a wall falls under.   5

He is currently studying at the Berklee College of Music in Boston, a school whose alumni have won a total of 231 Grammy Awards since it was founded in 1945.   6

For the past two years, whenever Sampson returns to New York during the holidays, he plays in the corridor between the shuttle and the No. 6 train platforms at Grand Central. He said it helps him with stage fright. But one can't tell if he has any.   7

There is a richness in his sound that cannot be acquired from hard work alone.   8

In the station, he plays melodies that smoothly transition into a series of compelling movements. The piece is not composed by Beethoven, Sarasate, or John Williams. Sampson improvises, making the notes up as he goes along. He said perhaps he will call it the "Subway Song."   9

Sampson is a musical genius who dreams of being a composer one day. He began learning the violin at age 12—a somewhat late age for a prodigy. Most have already been accepted into a conservatory by then.   10

It takes a lot to guide a late-discovered prodigy to a level that Sampson is at today. But he comes from a family with a history of endurance and a vision that sees beyond the veneer of physical realities.   11

Opportune Futures, Not Dour Pasts

A childhood in South Bronx did not yield many dulcet times.   12

"In the Bronx, you have to be strong and hold your own ground," Sampson said. "Otherwise you could end up in the wrong hands."   13

Sampson would arrive at school and find his classmates with new wounds, fresh from violent encounters from the night before. The school he attended allowed children to stay overnight if they felt it was too dangerous to walk home.   14

But during tough times, his grandfather was always a purveyor of wisdom.   15

His grandfather, Dr. Shellie Sampson Jr., is a reverend with a doctorate in Urban Education and Psychology, and has a number of other doctoral degrees as well.   16

Sampson said that although memories of segregation and church burnings probably remain in the recesses of his grandfather's mind, he did not hear much about that part of his grandfather's personal history. Instead, the focus has always been on the future and on the opportunities that Sampson has access to today.   17

For high school, Sampson went to the Putney School, an independent boarding high school in Vermont. It was there that he began to take group violin lessons.   18

Sampson said the first note he ever played sounded like a screaming cat. At the time, he thought he might not play again. But his teacher soon recognized he was developing at an unusual pace; he was a fecund player, a marvel.   19

"My teacher told me I needed to pursue this now, and follow it for the rest of my life," he said.   20

(continued)

(continued)

21   Although his family is not musically inclined, his parents are elementary and middle school teachers in the Bronx who value hard work and the pursuit of one's passion.

22   "They're passionate about their work too, that's probably where I get it from," Sampson said. They have pushed him to practice several hours everyday.

23   "It turned out I enjoyed it, I enjoyed playing for hours and hours," Sampson recalls.

24   Sampson remembers the first performance he attended at the New York Philharmonic, not long after learning the violin. They performed Vivaldi's "Four Seasons"; Sampson's favorite is "Summer."

25   After the show he got an autograph from the conductor, Lorin Maazel. He peered up at the ivory-haired conductor with soft eyes, at that moment he realized that he wanted to be a professional violinist and that he could be one.

26   And so he goes on practicing and practicing, missing movies, games, and outings with friends. But what he gains is indelible.

27   His handwork has paid off at the Berklee School of Music where he met Alicia Keys, Victor Wooten, and even had a lengthy Skype call with Don Hahn, the producer of "The Lion King."

28   "[Hahn] inspired me so much. ... I felt that I could one day be where he was," Sampson said. "There's nothing to be afraid of because if it's what you love, people will help you." Sampson wants to compose for Disney films one day.

29   "Had I not worked so hard, I wouldn't have met these people," he said.

Life Lessons From Music

30   What Sampson learns from music lessons, he applies to more than his performance.

31   "Life makes sense if you think about it," he said. "You can eat an elephant one bite at a time. Everything is simple if you take it at face value."

32   "You're not going to learn a piece all in one day, you break it up section by section, phrase by phrase, and note by note," he said. "That's how it is in life too."

33   His teachers often tell him to play louder, which Sampson interprets as a lesson for his demeanor as well.

34   "I used to be always nervous that my ideas were never enough for people," he said. "To really get respect from other people is something I had to overcome and learn. I had to learn how to speak up."

35   But to speak or play pompously is not the way to be heard either in his view.

36   "The ego is what takes away the blessing and inspirations," Sampson said. "Before you played out of love, but when people get worshiped they forget what it's about."

37   He recalls when he was discovered for his talent there were moments he thought it felt good to be better than other people.

38   "As soon as I had those thoughts, I stopped being able to express myself, to play the way that I did before," he said. "It happened almost immediately."

He says when he becomes a famous composer one day, he will make sure not to   39
become egotistical. In essence, he will remain the same quiet boy who listens to the
beauty of silences.

"My grandfather always told me that anything is possible if there is a purpose   40
behind it," Sampson said. "I think my purpose is to share what I love, my music, with
the world."

Inquiring into the Essay

1. **Explore.** Jafari Sampson says that "the ego is what takes away the blessing
   and inspirations," noting that until he could let go of the idea that his talent
   made him "better" than others, he couldn't play the violin well. Explore this
   idea. Have you ever been talented in something and found that your ego got
   in the way? Or perhaps you've never felt very talented in anything. Why is
   that? Fastwrite about this for as long as you can.

2. **Explain.** One of the themes that surfaces early in the essay is the idea of
   "finding silences," and how they inspire Sampson. Can you explain why,
   exactly, silence is a source of inspiration?

3. **Evaluate.** The essay is framed, to some extent, around a familiar story: Dis-
   advantaged person transcends his circumstances to find unexpected success.
   Do you think the essay itself transcends the standard "bootstrap" clichés?
   Does it take the old story and make it new in some interesting ways?

4. **Reflect.** One academic version of the profile is a case study—a close look
   at a person (or groups of people) in a particular context (time and place).
   The assumption is that describing people in context will reveal things that
   describing people out of context generally will not. The downside is that in
   the former case, the "data" aren't easily generalizable. What do you think
   about this? What does writing (mostly narrative forms) that foregrounds context provide to readers that other writing (thesis-driven essays) does not?

Seeing the Form

"Sun Boy" by William Soule

Visual anthropology uses images as a way to study culture. Photographs such as
this one, a portrait of a Kiowa man taken by the well-known Plains photographer
William Soule, would presumably be a great subject for study of the tribe in the late
1800s. But can a photographic profile be trusted as historical evidence? We like to
imagine that photographs are documentary, objective reports of reality. But pictures
are taken by photographers, who are influenced by their own sense of what's real.
Culture also profoundly influences beliefs, and when this photograph was taken,

(continued)

Seeing the Form (*continued*)

attitudes about Native American people among whites included the idea that they were "noble savages," or simply "savages." Portraits of Indian women often presented them as "maidens" or Indian "princesses." With these cultural biases in mind, how would you critically "read" this profile of Sun? What does doing so tell you about critically reading all kinds of profiles?

THE WRITING PROCESS

Inquiry Project   **Writing a Profile**

Inquiry questions: Does this one person's story tell us anything about the perspectives of others who belong to the group the person belongs to and about people in general? What does this person's story say about social situations, trends, or problems?

Write a profile of someone who strikes you as interesting. Consider four possible "frames" for your inquiry into this person: group, ideas about, event, or quality (see the "Possible Frames" subsection later in this chapter on pp. 119–120).

Your essay should do all of the following (see also the "Features of the Form" box earlier in this chapter on p. 102 for typical features of the profile essay):

- Use one of the four frames to focus your profile.
- Be organized around a theme. What one main thing are you trying to say about or through your profile subject?
- Include several revealing anecdotes about your profile subject.
- Include a physical description of the person you're writing about.
- Incorporate the voice of your subject through interesting and revealing quotes.

Prose+

- Add images to your profile essay by taking photographs of your subject or incorporating relevant images that your subject provides. Alternatively, consider a photographic essay of your subject. This might be a collage of photographs of the person, organized around some theme.
- Audio archives abound online that provide great material for profiles of people who were involved in historical events like World War II and 9/11. For example, the Library of Congress's Veterans History Project (http://www.loc.gov/vets/) is a remarkable archive of voices, videos, photographs, and documents of veterans who served in America's major conflicts, from World War I through the recent conflicts in the Middle East. For an example of how material from the site might be used, see the "Flash Profile" later in this chapter on page 126.

Who Are You Going to Write About?

One of the great profile writers, John McPhee, wrote recently that promising subjects for profiles "are everywhere. They just go by in a ceaseless stream." But McPhee also observed that the great majority of people he chooses to write about are those who know something about a topic he has long been interested in. Begin there. What have you wondered about for a while, and is there a person who might teach you more about that topic?

A challenge with any writing project in college is time. This is especially true for assignments, such as this one, that depend on someone besides you. Therefore, you'll want to choose someone to write about who is accessible, willing, and with whom you might spend some time.

In the three sections that follow—"Opening Up," "Narrowing Down," and "Trying Out"—you can use writing to help you get ideas about who you might profile. You'll use a series of prompts to generate a range of possibilities, which you'll then narrow down to a possible profile subject. Next, you'll try out this subject, in your journal or on your computer, and judge what you have.

Opening Up

4.4
Use invention strategies, including interviews, to discover and develop a profile of someone.

As McPhee suggests, subjects for profiles are "everywhere." Let's start by looking everywhere for possibilities. Remember that you're not after a celebrity profile; it is far more likely that you want to discover someone who seems pretty ordinary but who might put a face on an idea, an important event, a category of people, or a personality trait.

Listing Prompts. Quick lists are great triggers for ideas. Try these:

1. To select a topic for which you'd like to find someone to profile, generate each of these lists in thirty seconds.

   ▪ List types of people—categories such as "musicians," "teachers," "church leaders," "college athletes," or "car mechanics"—that interest you or with whom you have had contact.
   ▪ List local issues, controversies, or problems that you have an opinion on.
   ▪ List jobs that interest you.
2. Spend two minutes making a fast list of people you think of when asked this question: *Who have you known who you can't forget?*

Fastwriting Prompts. Fastwriting is a great way to loosen up your creative side and at the same time generate raw material. Here are a few prompts to get you writing:

1. Choose someone you know who you might want to profile. Use the "seed sentences" below to launch two separate fastwrites on your subject, each lasting at least three minutes.

- *When I first think of _____, I think of _____.*
- *The one word I would use to describe _____ would be _____.*
- *_____ had an unusual habit.*
- *Typically, _____ would _____.*
- *_____ is best known for _____.*
- *The one thing that most people fail to notice about _____ is _____.*
- *When I first met _____, I noticed _____.*
- *_____ always says, "_____."*

2. Think about three people you've observed or spent time with who do something that you admire. Maybe they're a dancer, police officer, a fly fisher, and a great chef. Start with one of these people and fastwrite for about four minutes, describing this person and what happened the last time you saw him or her. For this exercise, focus on description. Write as if you are behind a camera, describing in words what you see. Skip a line and do the same thing for each of the two others. Which of these snapshots seems most compelling to you?

Visual Prompts. Visual prompts can be images or they can be visual methods of thinking, such as clusters, charts, drawings, and diagrams.

1. Put the name of a possible profile subject in the center of a cluster. Build a web of associations for five minutes, and then begin fastwriting when you feel the urge.

2. Go through your digital photographs for ideas about profile subjects; this might be especially useful for reminding yourself of family and friends who might be good subjects.

Research Prompts. It is impossible to write a profile without conducting research of some sort, if not in the library or online, then in the field with one's subject. Doing some research up front, then, can be a useful way to find a subject to write about.

1. Return to the list of local issues you generated in the "Listing Prompts" subsection. Choose an issue in the community or on campus. Check the community and campus newspapers to discover who has been active as an advocate on the issue, or who has been impacted by it. Is any one person suitable for a profile?

2. Discuss your topic with your friends or people in your class. Who do they know who would be good as a profile subject?

3. If you have a career interest, a profile of a working member of the profession can be compelling. Call or e-mail the state professional association for suggestions about how to find an interview subject, or ask friends and family for suggestions.

4. Search online for audio archives and transcripts such as the Library of Congress Veterans History Project or interviews with people who witnessed or survived the 9/11 attacks.

One Student's Response

Bruce's Journal

RESEARCH ON LIST OF ISSUES

Issue	Interview Subjects
Recall	Margaret the storekeeper, Mayor Coles
Owyhee's wilderness	Congressperson, Simpson, Pat Ford
Migrant workers	Miguel Gomez, Rep. Bieter
Foothills preservation	Jack Coulter, Mayor, Nancy Maynard

Narrowing Down

You've got several ideas for profile subjects. How do you narrow them down to one?

What's Promising Material and What Isn't? Consider the following criteria:

- **Assignment.** Which subjects best fit the requirements of the assignment?
- **Accessibility.** The greatest subject in the world is no good to you if he is inaccessible.
- **Unfamiliarity.** A stranger is often a better choice of subject than a family member or friend. The challenges of setting up an interview with a stranger might seem a little daunting. However, you are more likely to learn something interesting from a stranger; you are far less likely to have a preconceived idea about your subject, so your profile is more likely to be based on the ideas you *discover*; and you'll learn more about the interviewing process—not only about gathering and recording information, but also about collaboration and organization.
- **Background.** Writers often look for information that may already exist: perhaps an article or two, a diary, a cigar box full of old pictures. Might you have access to such information on a possible subject?
- **Typicality.** Is the subject representative in some way of an aspect of a topic you'd like to investigate?
- **Extremity.** On the other hand, you may look for a subject who represents not the norm in a category of experience, but an extreme.
- **Spontaneity.** Less-experienced subjects, the kind you are most likely to profile, often have appeal because they aren't practiced at talking about themselves. There can be a freshness and even naïveté about what they say and how they say it that make a profile particularly compelling.
- **Quotability.** Sometimes you simply can't know how quotable a subject might be until the interview. But if your subject speaks in an interesting way, you may have a great profile subject.

◾ **Willingness.** This shouldn't be a problem. A few people may resist being interviewed, but most people love to talk about themselves. An interview gives a subject a willing listener; how often do we enjoy the undivided attention of someone who is vitally interested in what we have to say about ourselves?

Questions About Audience and Purpose. I'll admit that I read celebrity profiles in *People* in the waiting room at my doctor's office. The appeal of the celebrity profile to many of us is hard to explain (that would be a good essay topic, in fact), but because you're likely to be writing about someone who is not famous at all, you've got a rhetorical challenge. Why would anyone be interested in your profile of your neighbor who invents things in her garage? They won't be unless the purpose of your profile is clear. The possible "frames" discussed in the next section can help you to discover this purpose.

> The profile can, like good fiction, provide insight into the complexities of the human mind and soul.

The readers of profiles also respond to stories. So anecdotes are important, and when you interview, a key question will be *Can you tell me the story behind that?*

If you're ready to choose a tentative profile subject, try it out using some of the following strategies.

Trying Out

Like any inquiry project, a profile is an attempt to find patterns in the information you collect. The more data you have to work with, the easier it will be for you to see these patterns. This means making sure your interviews are long enough to give you enough data. It also means having a sense, before your interviews, of what patterns you might look for.

Possible Frames. One way to think about patterns to look for is to see this search in terms of looking for a suitable frame for your portrait. Each frame represents a different purpose for a profile:

◾ **Group.** Sometimes we can understand a little about a group of people by examining one person who belongs to that group. One nurse is, in some ways, like other nurses. A woman who stayed home in rural Illinois while her husband fought in the war stands in for military spouses whose partners are overseas.

◾ **Ideas about.** Profiles can also be in the service of ideas about something. Subjects might exemplify something you want to say about an issue, a problem, a place. The frame for your profile of a cowboy can be the idea that the mythology of the American West is still strong.

◾ **Event.** Your subject might have been a participant in a public event—national or even international (9/11, the invasion of Iraq), or just local (the founding of a homeless shelter). These events become the frame for your profile.

- **Quality.** In each of these first three frames, the profile makes a point about something more general than the subject. But your frame can also be your dominant impression of your subject. What strikes you most about your subject's personality? Perhaps your subject is intensely competitive, or painfully shy. Maybe he or she is a dreamer or a bully. This possible frame probably won't occur to you until you interview your subject.

Questions for Reflection. We see people and we see through them. A guy on the street in layered clothing and a wool hat pulled over his ears pushes a shopping cart full of stuff. We see him as we drive by, but we also see the problem of homelessness. We can only know if the man is homeless if we ask him, of course, which is why the profile, like many other forms of writing, requires evidence. But here's the problem: Do our assumptions about someone—the judgments we make in the absence of evidence—trip us up even as we're talking with a profile subject? How do you deal with those assumptions so that you are seeing someone on her own terms, at least as much as is humanly possible? Reflect on your own assumptions about the person you've tentatively chosen to write about.

Interviewing

You're ready to start talking with an interview subject. How should you approach that encounter? That doesn't seem like a complicated question. You arrange a time and place to talk, collect as much material as you can, and go write your profile. But should you talk to him more than once? Should you talk to people who know him? Should you spend *time* with your subject, watching him do what he does?

Interview Approaches. For his more lengthy profiles of an environmentalist, a birch-bark canoe maker, a long-distance truck driver, and many others, John McPhee describes his method as something like the process represented in Figure 4.1[1]:

At the center are interviews with the subject of the profile, the person that McPhee will talk to the most. The surrounding circles represent interviews with *people who know* the subject. Obviously, this is a much more time-consuming approach. But what an extraordinarily rich portrait it leads to! Alternatively, your profile might be based on a much more limited model: interviewing only the person you're going to write about. Experienced interviewers will tell you that a single conversation with your subject is usually not enough. The first interview gives you the seeds of the story, and subsequent interviews allow you to harvest the material you need to make the story work. Which approach you're going to take is the first decision you need to make about interviewing once you've chosen your subject.

Interview Techniques. His interview subjects sometimes see John McPhee as "thick-witted." At times McPhee seems to ask the same questions over and over, and he frequently seems to possess only the most basic information about his subjects.

---

[1]McPhee, John. "Progression." *The New Yorker* (Nov. 14, 2011): 36–42.

Figure 4.1 John McPhee's process

According to William Howarth, when McPhee "conducts an interview he tries to be as blank as his notebook pages, totally devoid of preconceptions." McPhee's theory is that unless his interview subjects "feel superior or equal to their interviewer," they won't talk freely or at length. McPhee never uses a tape recorder, but jots down spare notes in a notebook; these are the telling details and facts that reveal his subjects' character.

You can find more information about interviewing techniques in Chapter 11, "Research with Living Sources," but the tips here should help you start developing a plan for your interviews.

Writing Beyond the Classroom

Digital Profiles

Susan was a graduate student of mine who was working on a memoir about growing up on a farm in the desolate desert country of southern Idaho. Though her plan was to publish her book, Susan's project is typical of the kind of family history projects that have inspired millions to unravel genealogies, interview aging grandparents, and revisit the places where family roots run deep.

Interviews with living family members can yield compelling profiles, and the family members become characters in a longer story we discover about ourselves. For example, Susan's Uncle Al, her father's brother, was not only an invaluable source of information, but he also became a memorable presence in her story, with a richer portrait than any photograph or painting could have offered.

(continued)

Writing Beyond the Classroom (*continued*)

There are many genealogical resources online (just try Googling "researching family history"), but the audio recordings you make of your family members are profiles that wouldn't otherwise exist. Making these recordings is easier than ever. Digital recording is easily edited on your computer using free audio editing software such as Audacity (see Chapter 13, "Re-genre," for more on using this program). You can trim and move audio clips from your interview into a more coherent profile, and even add voiceovers or music. Your audio files can be easily converted to MP3 format, which can be played on MP3 players and computers and sent to your relatives in Kansas. These family profiles can also be combined with visuals using a program such as Microsoft's Photo Story, another free download, and this program can help you tell an even more powerful story about someone who matters in your family.

Microsoft Photo Story, a free download, can be used to tell a story with photos.

Making Contact. Asking a family member or friend to be an interview subject is easy, but how do you ask a stranger? You start by introducing yourself and straightforwardly describing the profile assignment, including your belief that the subject would be a great focus for your piece. You must be prepared to answer the almost inevitable follow-up question: "Well, gee, I'm flattered. But what is it about me that you find interesting?" Here's where McPhee's elementary knowledge is crucial: Although you need to know only a very little about your interview subject, you must know enough to be able to say, for instance, that you're aware of his role in a bit of history or his involvement in a local issue, or recognize him as being knowledgeable about a topic you find of interest.

What you want from this initial contact is *time*. The conventional interview—when you sit across from your informant asking questions and writing down answers—can be very useful, but it may be more productive if you can spend time *doing* something with your profile subject that relates to the reason you've chosen him or her. For example, if you are profiling a conservative activist, spend an hour watching him work the telephone, lining up people for a meeting at city hall. Your interview with a homeless woman could take place during lunch at the local shelter. *Seeing* your subject in a meaningful situation, which is what academic ethnographers do, can generate far more information than the conventional interview. Give some thought to what the best situations might be.

What do you do if your subject doesn't want to be interviewed? In that unlikely event, you're permitted to ask why. If your reassurances aren't sufficient to change the person's mind, then you need to find another subject.

Conducting the Interview. Should you prepare questions? Sure, but be prepared to ignore them. Interviews rarely go as planned, and if they do, they are often disappointing. An interview is a *conversation*, and these are best when they head in unexpected directions.

Certain generic questions can reveal things about a subject's character. These are *open-ended questions* that often lead in surprising and interesting directions. As I said before, one of the most important questions you can ask prompts a subject to tell a story: *What happened?... And then what happened?* Other questions that often yield useful information include the following:

- In all your experience with _____, what has most surprised you?
- What has been the most difficult aspect of your work?
- If you had the chance to change something about how you approached _____, what would it be?
- Can you remember a significant moment in your work on _____? Is there an experience with _____ that stands out in your mind?
- What do you think is the most common misconception about _____? Why?
- What are significant trends in _____?
- Who or what has most influenced you? Who are your heroes?
- If you had to summarize the most important thing you've learned about _____, what would you say? What is the most important thing that people should know or understand?

Inquiring into the Details

Recording Interviews

Some tips on recording your interviews digitally:

- **You can use your smartphone.** Nearly all current smartphones are capable of recording audio and uploading the files to a computer. Some smartphones produce surprisingly high-quality recordings.

- **You can record phone conversations.** A $20 adapter allows you to record phone conversations, but legally you may need to ask your subject's permission. Covert recordings are very uncool. You can also use Skype to record phone conversations.

- **You can use software to transcribe recordings.** Several free programs like Audacity are available online that will help you control the playback speed so you can more easily type what you're hearing and will allow you to label and reorganize interview clips.

- **Take notes.** A combination of old (well, really old) technology, such as handwritten notes, with new technology, such as digital recording, makes it more likely that your interview will yield the best material. Your notes—even if sketchy—provide an outline of what you've recorded and help you to find that great quote or essential piece of information more easily.

Note taking during an interview is a challenge. I'd recommend digitally recording your interviews as well as taking notes. For more information on how to combine the two, see the box above. Your notes should include any facts, details, phrases, mannerisms, or even personal reactions you have during the interview.

While my students have used the double-entry journal effectively as a note-taking format for profiles, putting the observed information and quotations on the left page and personal responses on the right, I'm keen on a pocket-sized memo book. It's unobtrusive, easy to carry, and forces you to be spare. I especially like the ease with which I can take the memo book out and put it away, at times using it to signal to my subject that I'm more—or less—interested in something he's saying.

Listening and Watching. The art of interviewing relies, more than anything else, on the craft of listening. Few of us are good listeners, which is why profile writing can be so hard. First you must control your anxiety about getting things down, asking the next question, and making your subject relaxed.

When is a conversation good? When it generates the kind of information that will help you write the profile, including the following:

- **Stories.** Interesting anecdotes help you build a narrative backbone.

- **Memorable quotations.** A typical interview produces only a handful of these, so don't desperately write down everything a subject says. Using a digital recorder helps moderate the anxiety that you'll miss something, allowing you to concentrate on writing down nicely put or distinctive quotes, particularly those that reveal something about your subject's character.

- **Background information.** This can be related in the form of stories, but might also be basic but essential information such as your subject's age, place of birth, and history of involvement in relevant jobs or issues.

- **Feeling.** A good conversation is an honest one in which the subject is willing to let the mask slip to reveal the face sweating underneath. Be alert to those moments of feeling when your subject seems to be revealing herself— what *really* matters to her, what might be hard, where she finds joy.

▶ Flash Profile: Veterans History Project

As practice for your profile (or as a substitute assignment), consider crafting a brief or "flash" profile of someone from archival sources. I mentioned the Veterans History Project (www.loc.gov/vets/) earlier in the chapter, and this is a rich online site with primary materials on our nation's (and other countries') veterans. There are thousands of audio and video interviews, transcripts, photos, and sometimes even letters from former soldiers who served in World War II, Korea, Vietnam, and more recent conflicts in the Middle East and from their families. You will encounter stories there from veterans who survived some of the great battles of these wars, as well as stories of people who provided essential support to American combatants. With work, this kind of material—what scholars call "primary sources"—can be shaped into a compelling anecdote that is the kernel of a profile. The following flash profile of Dan Akee, a Marine and Navajo "code talker" who fought at Iwo Jima in World War II, demonstrates what might be done with what you find at the Veterans History Project website. Notice how this flash profile, while brief, has a beginning, middle, and end.

From Bullets to Bottles: The Two Wars of Dan Akee

1   Dan Akee remembers stepping over the bodies, so numerous and so randomly scattered that they seemed like "trash." After the third day, it broke him. "I was getting tired of all the battles I went through," Akee said. "I was scared." By the time the five Marines and one Navy corpsman raised the flag on Mt. Suribachi in the famous photograph, Iwo Jima was littered with the dead, and Akee was not among them. One reason, perhaps, is that when he went crazy after hours of Japanese shelling, Akee did not run out of his foxhole. He imagined it. "I felt like I was running. We should go, that's on my mind. But somehow I left there. I was out of my mind. Before I left … the foxhole, I sat down, and I said 'God help me. I'm too young to die.'"

2   A lot of people did die on Iwo Jima. Of the 18,000 Japanese soldiers who occupied the island when the Marines landed, only 216 were captured. Akee's Marines suffered, too. Seven thousand were killed and there were over 20,000 casualties. But sometimes the dying is slow, and comes from a bottle not a bullet, and when Dan Akee, a Navajo, returned from the war, the nightmares began. After he was discharged, Akee enrolled in college through the GI Bill. "That year in school, I started having nightmares," he said. "Every night I was having a nightmare." They were so bad that Akee returned to his home in Arizona, but the nightmares about the war never ceased. "One day in July I had a vision. It was a lady that came up against me with a blank face, so that's when I fainted and I was unconscious for a long time." The tribe attempted traditional ceremonies to vanquish Akee's demons, but none worked, so the survivor of Iwo Jima turned to drink. "Sometimes, I starting thinking, what's the use? Nobody is going to help me. The only way I kept myself awake at night was some kind of drink, beer or wine."

3   After some time living on the streets of Flagstaff, begging for quarters, Akee's war on alcohol began when he walked into a doctor's office, and the physician told him that he had liver disease, and if Akee kept on drinking he was going to die. "So I started walking to the door, and (the doctor) called me back…. That was the time I found out this doctor was a Christian man." Forty-five minutes later, Akee went to where he was living and "destroyed" all his booze and the cigarettes, went to church and later became a minister. In the end, Akee survived both wars. Both brought him to his knees. But courage and faith led him out of a foxhole on the beaches of Iwo Jima and, a few years later, away from the lonely back alleys of Flagstaff. No flags were raised to commemorate Akee's successful battle with alcohol. But you can hear in his voice that it might have been the sweetest victory of all.

Writing the Sketch

Your sketch is a kind of "flash profile" like the one on Dan Akee. Like that piece, it should have the following qualities:

- At least two potentially revealing anecdotes about your profile subject
- At least two strong quotations from your subject.
- A title.
- A beginning, middle, and end.
- Information from any relevant background research on your profile subject or the events he or she was involved in.

Moving from Sketch to Draft

In its roughest form, a profile sketch might look something like this:

1. Here's who I'm writing about.
2. Here's something she did.
3. And here's something she said.
4. And here's something else she did.
5. And another thing she said.
6. Here's why I'm writing about this person, or what I'm trying to say about her.

This isn't a bad start. But your goal in revising your sketch into a draft is to find the "frame"—the idea, event, group, or dominant impression related to your subject—and rebuild the draft around it *from the beginning*. If this frame isn't apparent to you at this point, it's probably because you don't have enough material yet.

Evaluating Your Sketch. To see if you've got a possible frame for your profile, ask yourself these questions:

1. **Frame.** What exactly am I trying to show—or might I show in the next draft—about my subject's connection to an idea, an event, or a group? Or is the sketch focusing on a quality of my subject—a personality trait or belief?
2. **Theme.** If someone were to ask this question—"What do you want readers of your profile to understand most about your subject?"—what would I say?
3. **Information.** If I've tentatively decided on the frame and theme for the profile, what questions should I ask in my next interview to develop the frame and theme further?

Reflecting on What You've Learned. Before you begin composing the next draft, make a journal entry that explores your thinking about the sketch and everything you heard. Begin an entry with the prompt *Based on what I've learned so far about my profile subject, the main thing I seem to be trying to show is* _____.

Developing

Like most writing projects, developing your profile involves research: conducting more interviews and collecting relevant secondary sources (articles about your subject, information from their web pages, background research on a relevant event, etc.).

Research, Interviews, and Reinterviews. Now that you're closing in on a frame for your profile, you can focus on getting the information you need to develop the portrait you hinted at in your sketch. Interview your profile subject again. In addition, you might consider ways to gather other sources of information:

- Interview people who know your profile subject (the John McPhee approach mentioned earlier).

- Do background research on your profile subject. Find out more about what she does or where she does it. Find out how she fits into a larger context. If you're writing about a nurse-midwife, find out how many are working in the state and what their licensing requirements are.

- If your subject is a public figure, do library or web research for background information.

- Research the idea, issue, or event, if any, that provides the context for your profile. This is especially useful for profile frames that focus on events and ideas.

The quotes and information you gather can be used in your profile, usually with attribution.

Establishing the Frame. Your opening paragraph or two—often called "leads" in journalism—should help readers understand the frame (or purpose) you're planning to build your subject around. For example, look at the following "lead" from "Museum Missionary," one of the readings earlier in the chapter:

> *David Mills, surrounded by children, held a small lobster aloft and asked if anyone wanted to touch it. . . . I stood at the back of the Lobster Room, an exhibit area in the Mount Desert Oceanarium, and watched while Mills instructed children and their parents in the ways of the lobster and the lobsterman. . . . Mills reached into the Touch Tank and pulled out a berried female lobster, carrying a mass of eggs under her tail. . . . "There's a passage in the Bible where the Lord said to be fruitful and multiply. This lobster sure be fruitful," he said.* ("Museum Missionary")

A lead establishes, usually within a couple of paragraphs in a short essay, the frame the writer is taking on the profile subject. For example, the opening above establishes the quality of David Mills that will be the focus of the profile: He is a man who brings missionary zeal to the wonders of the lowly lobster.

Revise your sketch so that the frame you're tentatively using becomes clear within the first two paragraphs. Use the title, too, to help with this (e.g., the title of the profile of David Mills is "Museum Missionary"). Try either or both of these revision techniques to clarify the frame:

- **Title tsunami.** In your notebook, spend two minutes brainstorming as many titles as you can for your profile. Play with descriptive titles, one-word titles, titles from great quotations. Try multiple variations of the same title. Make a long list and don't censor yourself, riding each wave of ideas until it dies. Choose a title for your draft that points to the frame you want to use.

- **Multiple leads.** Instead of writing just one opening, write three, starting the draft in three different places, with three different anecdotes, scenes, or descriptions. Choose the one that points the draft in the way you want it to go. (See Chapter 14, Revision Strategy 14.17, "Multiple Leads.")

Drafting

You've collected more information and thought about possible openings for your draft that establish in the very beginning why you're writing the profile. Why this person? Of the many things one might say about someone, what is the one thing you want to say about your subject? Choose a lead that establishes the frame for your subject (quality, idea about, event, or group), and follow it and see where it goes. Remember as you draft your profile that you want to present the person you're writing about in a way that makes him or her memorable to readers. Think about which of the following methods of developing the material might help you make the person memorable.

Keep in mind, too, that as your subject is likely a stranger to your readers, you must introduce him or her in writing: name, age, physical description, relevant background (e.g., birthplace, job, quirks). And, especially if you're putting yourself into the profile, make sure that the voice of your subject is an integral part of the profile.

Methods of Development. You can pursue various strategies to structure your profile.

Narrative.   The profile form often relies on narrative. Most commonly, a piece uses narrative to tell the story of the writer's encounter with his or her subject. For example, the profile of David Mills (see pp. 104–106) is organized around the writer's visit one day to Mills's Mount Desert Oceanarium. The account includes the writer's reactions to what the subject was saying and doing. Often, profile writers make this kind of narrative a first-person account—my day with my subject. Another way to use narrative is evident in the flash profile of Dan Akee, the Navajo veteran of Iwo Jima (page 126). There the essay is built on a succession of anecdotes—little stories about the subject—that are selected to tell a particular and revealing story. In that essay, the writer avoids using the first person to keep the focus on the subject.

Known to Unknown.   If your profile subject is a public figure and your motive is to reveal a less well-known aspect of your subject's life or work, beginning the essay with information that first seems to confirm public perceptions but then promises to challenge those perceptions—in other words, moving from what's known to what's less known—can be an effective way to structure the profile. This method of development is quite common in celebrity profiles.

Using Evidence. The most authoritative information in a profile is the voice of your subject. It is also the information that will be most heavily scrutinized by the subject herself: "Did I really say that?" Readers of the profile often believe that the subject's voice is the most authentic information because it is less mediated by the writer, an assumption that isn't always accurate. After all, unless quotations were recorded, interviewers must rely on their note-taking skill. Even with a recorded transcription, writers commonly tidy up bad grammar and remove irrelevant utterances such as "uh" and "um."

Profile writers must also establish their authority by giving readers a sense that they are keen and careful observers; they do this by carefully using not just quotation, but also detail, description, and research.

Workshopping

If your draft is subject to peer review (see Appendix A for details on how to organize workshop groups), think carefully about the kinds of responses you need from readers at this point in the process. In a workshop of a profile essay, you're introducing your peers to a stranger. You have to give them some reasons to be interested in the person you're profiling, and particularly in an audio profile, those reasons need to be obvious right away.

One of the essential issues of revision seems simple: what to put in and what to take out. But how do you decide? There's an equally simple answer: You must know your purpose and what you're trying to say. That knowledge guides the saw and the shovel; it helps you decide what to cut away, what new information to dig for, and where that information might be added. You can talk about a lot of things in a workshop, but you should always begin with purpose and meaning.

Reflecting on the Workshop. After your workshop, annotate your draft with ideas about how you might revise it based on peer comments. You can do this by hand or by using the "review" feature of your word processing program. Your instructor may ask you to hand this reflection in.

Questions for Peer Reviewers	
1. Purpose	What seems to be the "frame" for this profile: quality, event, idea, or group? Why does the writer seem to think this person is interesting? When in the draft do you know that? Is it early enough?
2. Meaning	What's the S.O.F.T.?
	■ If the profile is focused on a quality of its subject, what is that quality?
	■ If the profile is using its subject to say something about an idea, what's the idea?
	■ If it's focused on how the subject represents a larger group, what is it saying about that group?
	■ If the profile is using its subject to illuminate a public event, what is it saying about that event?

4.5

Apply revision strategies that are effective for shaping profiles.

Revising

Revision is a continual process, not a last step. You've been revising—"reseeing" your subject—from the first messy fastwriting in your journal. But the things that get your attention vary depending on where you are in the writing process. With your draft in hand, revision becomes your focus through what I'll call shaping and tightening your draft.

Chapter 14 contains strategies that can help you revise any inquiry project, and the "Guidelines: Revising Your Work" in this chapter on page 133 can help you locate these strategies. There are also certain things to think about that are especially useful for shaping a profile essay.

Shaping. If you wrote a sketch and a draft of your profile, you're essentially working on the third draft. If all is going well, you've clarified the purpose and meaning of the piece. Now you want to redesign it around both purpose and meaning.

Analyzing the Information.   After purpose and meaning, shaping focuses on information and organization. It involves, among other things, arranging and rearranging information so that it is organized around the main idea, question, or theme. One way to think about the structure of your profile is to see the information you've collected as being in categories. In a profile, these categories typically include the following:

Anecdote	Background	Description
Scene	Dialogue/Quote	Commentary

When shaping a profile, you'll be working with information that falls into categories such as these and that you'll have to arrange in an effective order. There is no formula for this. But consider the readings earlier in the chapter. For example, "Museum Missionary" (pp. 104–106) is organized something like this:

Scene	• David Mills regaling children with a "fruitful" lobster
Background	• Personal background and information about founding the museum
Scene	• Conversation with Ted Spurling on waterfront
Dialogue	• Discussion with David Mills in car
Quote	• Comment by Willie Morrison, New Hampshire lobsterman
Comment	• A lesson about listening

This essay uses information categories typical of a profile. Like many profiles, it begins with a scene that helps to dramatically establish the focus of the piece. Remember that whatever information category you choose to open your profile, your opening needs to help readers understand why you're writing about your subject.

One way to play around with the structure of your profile is to use the "Frankenstein Draft" (Revision Strategy 14.18 in Chapter 14). Cut up your draft with scissors into pieces that fall into the categories mentioned here—anecdote, scene, background, etc.—and then play with the order. Worry about transitions later.

Other Questions for Revision.   Profiles typically have some of the following problems, most of which can be addressed by selecting appropriate revision strategies, or by repeating some of the steps presented earlier in this chapter.

- The frame for the profile needs refining or clarifying.
- There isn't enough material for the frame to work. Do you need to do another interview?
- The profile subject is obscured by the writer's intrusions into the text, or by too much telling and not enough showing. Perhaps add more scenes, anecdotes, or descriptions?

Polishing.   Shaping focuses on things such as purpose, meaning, and design. No less important is looking more closely at paragraphs, sentences, and words. Are your paragraphs coherent? How do you manage transitions? Are your sentences fluent and concise? Are there any errors in spelling or syntax? The section of Chapter 14 called "Problems with Clarity and Style" (p. 542) can help you focus on these issues.

Before you finish your draft, work through the following checklist:

- ✓ Every paragraph is about one thing.
- ✓ The transitions between paragraphs aren't abrupt.
- ✓ The lengths of sentences vary in each paragraph.
- ✓ Each sentence is concise. There are no unnecessary words or phrases.
- ✓ You've checked grammar, particularly verb agreement, run-on sentences, unclear pronouns, and misused words (*there/their*, *where/were*, and so on).
- ✓ You've run your spellchecker and proofed your paper for misspelled words.

Chapter 14 has strategies to help you solve all kinds of revision problems, large and small. Use the "Guidelines: Revising Your Work" below to know where to look in that chapter to both shape and tighten your draft.

Guidelines: Revising Your Work

A first effort is almost never a best effort. To make sure your essay is really your best work, check out Chapter 14 for help with these questions:

- What is my paper really about? (See p. 518.)

- What am I really trying to say? (See p. 523.)

- Do I have enough convincing evidence? (See p. 530.)

- Does this paper move logically and smoothly from paragraph to paragraph? (See p. 534.)

- Are the sentences and paragraphs in this paper too choppy or hard to follow? (See p. 542.)

▶ Student Essay

Micaela Fisher took the city bus one day—the Number 6 Orchard—and she encountered a bus driver much like the one profiled earlier in Ian Frazier's "Passengers"— a man who endears himself to commuters through his large heart and quirky character. To write her profile of Oscar, Micaela rode the bus with him again and took copious notes that allowed her to write the profile through one extended scene. It's beautifully written. But it's also a wonderful example of how a profile can use a subject to express an idea about other things. In this case, Micaela comes to understand how Oscar's tale of a California man who lost millions—as unbelievable as it seemed—is just another of the many stories we all tell, large and small, that melt away every hour, immediately after they are told by one stranger to another. Does this make them any less important?

Number 6 Orchard

Micaela Fisher

The You-Are-Here arrow my bike is leaning against points at "Zone 1."   1

    "Is there a bus coming shortly?" asks a kid in a black coat.   2

    "I don't know," I say. "I would like to know, too." My hands are numb and there are what the   3
weatherman called "trace amounts of snow" in the air, though none adhered to any surface.

(continued)

(continued)

The bus does come. Number 6 Orchard; maybe it will take me to climates where the trees have green leaves and ripening fruit.

4   A young man waves to the bus driver from outside, and then he veers toward the bus and boards. "I'm back," he says. The bus driver doesn't quite remember him.

5   "It's been a while," the young man says helpfully. The bus driver asks, "What's your name again?" and the young man says, "Oh, it doesn't matter. Names don't matter." The bus driver nods. "Oh, you're back," he says.

6   The bus heaves out into traffic, like an iceberg calving and rolling toward 16th, toward Main. The two well-dressed ladies say, "You'll tell us where to get off close to the hotel, won't you?" The bus driver says, "Yeah, sure, sure, like I said." He tells them, as the brakes creak, "Now. And then walk over the bridge, and your hotel is right there." A woman with grey hair blown back like a cartoon character tells them, "Just walk over the bridge, and you'll be right there." They thank her, and the bus driver. The river under the bridge has glassy edges of ice, like my bus window has icy edges around its glass.

7   We turn left onto Orchard Street, no apples or peaches or cherries to be seen. A young man in a green hoodie and glasses gets on. He says, "Cesar, man, it's been a long time."

8   "Yeah, a long time," says the bus driver. The young man stands on the white line, the line that passengers are prohibited from crossing while the bus is in motion. He looks polite, well raised. Cesar asks, "Still reading the Bible?"

9   "Yeah, yeah, all the time," the green hoodied kid says. Cesar says, "That's what your mom tell me."

10   "Yeah, my mom," the young man says. "She's still working at Micron, she's in a different department now."

11   "And she like it? She's less stressful now?"

12   "I do think she likes it. She seems a lot less stressed." Neither says anything more, and after a couple of minutes, Cesar hands the kid a card. "This is my phone number," he says. "Call me." The young man in the green hoodie nods, and as he is sliding the card into his billfold, his cell phone rings. "Speaking of which," he says, and then answers the phone.

13   "Hello, Mama," he says. He explains that since Dick's car broke down, he just caught the bus. "Oh, I'll make it work, Mama," he says, "I'll make it work if I have to ride the bus the entire way out there. Don't start getting stressed. You have a good night. I love you." He pulls the yellow cable, Cesar stops the bus, and the young man says goodbye to Cesar and steps past the white line and into the thin winter air.

14   We turn right onto Curtis Road.

15   A woman carrying three grocery bags boards, calling, "Hi, Cesar!" as she slides her electronic bus pass through the ticket counter. A block later a young man climbs on and sits across from the woman. He has on a blue and orange BSU t-shirt and a blue and orange BSU jacket. He is edgy and glances around as he eats from his blue bag of chips, but he doesn't look at the woman with the grocery bags when she says, "Hi, John. How are you?" He simply answers too loudly, "Fine."

16   "Well, that's better than not fine," she says, "right?"

17   "True," the young man says too loudly.

"Cesar, dear," the woman calls a few minutes later, "can you let me off at the daycare?"   18

"I need off at the Seven-Eleven," the blue and orange man says quickly, and then he says   19
it again more loudly, "I need off at the Seven-Eleven." The woman says, "He'll take you up to
the church, John," but John gets upset and says, "I don't get off at Overland anymore. I don't
get off at Overland anymore!"

"Why don't you?" asks Cesar from up front.   20

"Because I got chased by a dog last Thursday," John says, and adds loudly, "I don't like   21
this bus change." But he gets off at the 7-11. The bus lurches three rights and then a left that
puts us back on Curtis.

I've been the only passenger for several blocks before the bus driver's curiosity gets the   22
better of him. "Have you take the wrong bus?" his mouth in the mirror asks.

"No, I'm just riding around today," I say. "I've never taken the bus before. I would like to   23
get to know the routes."

"How do you get around usually then?" he asks. I say I ride my bike usually, I live in the   24
north end. "Number Fourteen," he says nodding. "Hyde Park." I understand and nod too.

"Have you been driving buses for a while?" I ask the bus driver.   25

"Thirteen years," he says.   26

I say, "Do you get bored riding in circles?"   27

"Sometimes yes, sometimes I do," the bus driver says. "Before, I have a job driving in   28
California. And before that, I was accountant. And this job is so much better, has so much more
interest."

We are on the I-184 ramp, above the city. White mountains form in M's of landscape on the   29
driver's side, far enough away that I can't make out the buses of skiers rounding switchbacks
and more switchbacks to the top. My snowboarding class starts in a few weeks.

"Do you go to school?" the bus driver asks me.   30

"Yeah," I say. "BSU. I'm studying English. Writing."   31

"You write books?" he asks, more attentive now.   32

"Maybe someday," I say smiling to the mirror. He says, "I am looking for a person who   33
write—I know someone who say I can write a story of his life, but I need a person who is really
a writer." I say, Oh, and he continues with the life story, glancing back and forth between the
road and the mirror.

"I worked in California for a man who have millions," he says. "The man he has a son, and   34
the son was airline pilot, made a lot of money. One day the son had an accident, he crashed
and was in coma for three years."

"Three years," I say. "And he woke up?"   35

"Yes, for three years he was in coma, and one day, he wake up, he just wake up from his   36
coma. But while he was in coma, his mother, who is millionaire too, she took all the money
from the insurance, I think was twenty-three million or something. A lot of money, she took
it and spend it on houses, and traveling, and everything she want. She has three houses. And
when the young man wake up, she bought him YMCA pass and bus pass, you know, little things.
Well, there was this teacher, too, and the teacher had a problem with her legs, she couldn't
walk from the time she was girl in school and other children in class take her wheelchair. Well,

(continued)

(continued)

she want to grow up and be a teacher, and so she is teacher now in a wheelchair. And she goes to this YMCA every day to do exercises for her legs, and here comes this young man. They liked each other, and the man tell his mother, 'I want to get married to this teacher.' His mother say, 'You can't get married,' because, you know, he have lost, he has some problem with his mental, and his mind is not like it used to be. Well, they get married anyway. And they take his mom to court for all the money she steal from him, and they in fact win. And you know they have this little girl now? I saw them last week when I was in California, I was in Costco with my brother and hear, 'Cesar!' and there that young man is pushing the teacher in a wheelchair, and she have this little girl on her lap. And you know, it's beautiful this marriage, because what the girl can't do because she can't walk—and they spend a lot of money for doctors, because they have a lot of money now—the man, he can do that for her. And what the man can't do because his mind is not so strong, the teacher, she do that for him, because she is real smart woman. And I tell them, 'I want to make a book and a movie of your life, and I will give you half the money,' and he tell me, 'Cesar, you take this paper that say you can write all my life, and don't you worry about the money, because I have all the money I need right now.' And so I am looking for a writer."

37   The bus driver gets up and walks over so that he is standing in front of me. I have been in [a] coma listening. The story is amazing, I tell him. I say three years in a coma, and I shake my head. I tell him good luck, that is definitely a story worth writing. I gather my hat and gloves and backpack and step off the bus to unhook my bike for a cold ride home.

38   A week later I sit at home and type phrases into a search engine: "three years in a coma," "plane crash," "california," "son of a millionaire." I stop soon with nothing found; there's no way. Names matter in search engines.

39   It is not my story to write, and likely it won't ever be written. Most bus drivers never produce art the size of books or screenplays, though they may dream of it when the interest of all-day one-hour circles lags, though they may tell every passenger on the bus those dreams. And the passengers have their own stories, and together with the bus driver they create even more—scenes and conversations forgotten even as they form. Tiny moments like snowflakes that melt as soon as they touch a surface. It's no great loss most of the time. No one cares whether young men without names chat with bus drivers they call Cesar; no one would remember what is said or unsaid. And if someone cared, who could write the stories of a day, of a single hour? Even the most beautiful stories melt as soon as they are spoken, from thin air returning to thin air.

Evaluating the Essay

1. In your own words, what do you understand "Number 6 Orchard" to be saying in the last paragraph?
2. Analyze how Micaela uses the categories of information typical of a profile: anecdote, scene, description, background, and comment.
3. What is one thing that you might take away from this reading and apply to your own writing?

Using What You Have Learned

Let's revisit the list of things at the beginning of this chapter that I hoped you'd learn about this form of writing.

1. **Use a profile of a person as a way to focus on an idea, a personality trait, a particular category of people, or a situation.** Think of any problem that you really care about—the degradation of the oceans, tax policies, the treatment of wild horses—and you can probably think of a way to put a "face" on that problem to make it compelling for someone else. The power of the profile is that it not only appeals to our interest in the lives of other people, but it makes their situations more compelling, too. In future writing projects, think about when a profile—or simply an anecdote about someone—can help you make a case that a problem needs attention.

2. **Identify some of the academic applications of profiles.** Profiles can be entertaining, but they can also be serious academic work. The case study is a version of the profile that is qualitative research—looking closely at an individual in a social setting to study his or her circumstances. This use of observational skills—sometimes called "deep description"—is invaluable in fieldwork in a range of disciplines.

3. **Identify the characteristics of profiles in different forms.** Now when you think of a profile, you might think of a portrait of someone that is drawn not only from interviews but also from archival research. You might also imagine a profile that combines images and texts or even uses images alone in a revealing sequence.

4. **Use invention strategies, including interviews, to discover and develop a profile of someone.** You can apply some of the techniques for generating ideas about profile subjects to any project that might benefit from a case study, anecdote, or individual example. In particular, use the idea of frame to brainstorm: Might a portrait of someone help reveal aspects of a situation, an idea, a quality, or a social type?

5. **Apply revision strategies that are effective for shaping profiles.** Revision of a profile builds on your rewriting skills by encouraging you to organize several stories around a main idea and to use these stories to say something about someone. This revision requires that you manipulate more kinds of information, too, and because much of it comes from observation and interview—and not out of your head—you confront a fundamental problem of rewriting: the need to write from abundance. You also have to be able to throw stuff away.

Writing a Review

Learning Objectives

In this chapter, you'll learn to

5.1 Use reasons and evidence to support a judgment about something's value.

5.2 Identify the criteria behind a judgment and determine their relevance.

5.3 Identify the characteristics of different forms of the review, including academic applications.

5.4 Use invention and focusing strategies to discover and develop a review essay.

5.5 Apply revision strategies that are effective for shaping reviews.

Writing That Evaluates

Both of my daughters excelled in modern dance, something I knew virtually nothing about. I would go to their performances, the proud dad, and afterwards I'd say, "Oh, that was beautiful. Wasn't that beautiful?" Naturally, this is the proper sentiment for a dad to express. But I also really meant it. Modern dance *can* be extraordinarily beautiful. However, when pressed about exactly why a performance moved me so, I was at a loss for words. I simply didn't know enough about modern dance to have any idea what the *reasons* were behind my judgment. I just knew what I felt.

Not knowing much about certain things rarely stops us from offering our evaluations of those things. We usually just follow our biases and gut feelings. The problem is that this "rationale" is rarely *persuasive*. People hear me gush about a modern dance performance, and in the absence of thoughtful reasons for my evaluation, they think I'm just a proud dad. I want to be both—a proud dad *and* a thoughtful critic. When I offer an evaluation of something, I want people to believe it, and this requires persuasive reasoning. In this chapter, we'll look at five elements of persuasive evaluations:

1. *Judgment(s).* Something is good or bad, useful or not useful, relevant or not relevant, convincing or not convincing, worth doing or not worth doing—or perhaps somewhere in between.

2. *Reasons.* We have reasons for deciding whether something is good or bad or somewhere in between and for all our other judgments. Our reasons usually are based on our criteria and evidence.

3. *Criteria.* These form the basis for deciding whether something is good or bad, useful or not useful, and so on. Our criteria are often implicit and may even be subconscious. The more we know about something—cars, movies, or whatever—the more elaborate and sophisticated our criteria become.

4. *Evidence.* The evidence (specific details, observations, or facts about the thing itself) in support of our reasons is what makes our judgment—and evaluation—persuasive.

5. *Stake.* Someone has a stake in our evaluation when he or she cares about the quality of the thing we're evaluating.

Forming a judgment is the easy part, particularly when it's driven by feeling. There's usually some initial reason, too. "This toaster sucks because it burns my toast every morning." The implied criterion here is pretty straightforward as well: "Good" toasters don't burn the toast. This reasoning is sound, more or less, but there's one big problem: Who really cares about your toaster besides you? However, when an evaluation is an argument (and not just your personal opinion), then you must make others realize that they have a stake in your judgments. Lots of people have toasters. They just don't have *your* toaster. In order to make an argument, then, you have to have something to say about *toasters*: This brand is better than that brand, for example. Similarly, when I praise a particular modern dance performance, no one but my friends and family will care about my judgment if it's just about my daughters. I have to discover criteria about the features of superb modern dance *performances*, criteria that others who care about dance might buy.

Motives for Writing a Review

Once you start thinking about evaluative writing, you'll find it everywhere—the book reviews in the Sunday *Times*, the music reviews in *Spin*, the analysis of websites on Web Sites That Suck. It's probably the most common form of workplace writing, too, for everything from assessing the performance of an employee to evaluating a plan to preserve historic buildings. One motive for reviews is to help people make informed decisions.

5.1
Use reasons and evidence to support a judgment about something's value.

   The review is a genre of persuasive writing. In a way, it's an aggressive writing form: *You should see this thing the way I see it.* In some cases, the stakes can be high.

5.2
Identify the criteria behind a judgment and determine their relevance.

The fate of a Broadway show may be in the hands of the theater critic at the *New York Times*. The success of a tech product launch might depend on its reception by the reviewer in *Wired*. Enrollments at a university may be affected by its ranking in the "best" college list of *US News and World Report*. Critics can be arbiters of taste and quality, which is a powerful (and sometimes intoxicating) motive for some.

Evaluative writing is an enormously practical form, relevant in all sorts of situations in and out of school.

For the rest of us, the stakes in writing a review may not be quite as high, but there are many occasions in which our judgments can make a significant difference. Your boss hands you a marketing plan and asks you to evaluate it. Followers of your cooking blog want to know your take on the best kitchen knife. You're writing a letter to the editor on the redesign of a neighborhood park. These are everyday—and fairly common—occasions for the review, and you will want to do it well.

The Review and Academic Writing

We don't usually think of the review as an academic form, although you may be asked to review a film you're shown in an English class or perhaps a performance in a theater class. But reviews are a form of evaluative writing that is among the most common types of writing in all kinds of college classrooms. Here are some examples:

- In English, you might do a rhetorical evaluation of a document, a film, or a story.
- Courses in music, theater, and dance might include a review of performances.
- Courses in art history or photography might call for you to review one or more artworks (see the box "Seeing the Form: Choosing the Best Picture").
- In science and social science classes, you may evaluate the methodology of studies.
- Business writing often involves reviewing proposals or marketing plans.
- Philosophers make arguments, but they also evaluate whether others' arguments are effective.
- In composition, you'll review the writing of your peers.

Seeing the Form

Choosing the Best Picture

When documentary photographer Dorothea Lange encountered Florence Thompson and her family camped by a frozen pea field, she took multiple pictures. One—and only one—of them became famous. Titled "Migrant Mother," it is considered an indelible image of the Depression. If you were charged with evaluating the five shots that Lange took of Thompson and her family, seen here, which would you choose as the best shot? What reasons would you have for making this judgment?

Seeing the Form (*continued*)

Five photographs Dorothea Lange took of Florence Thompson and her family.

5.3

Identify the characteristics of different forms of the review, including academic applications.

Features of the Form

Feature	Conventions of the Review Essay
Inquiry questions	How good is it? What is its value?
Motives	Your basic motive is to make a judgment about something that you may or may not be familiar with, and then, using reasonable criteria and evidence, convince others that your judgment is sensible.
Subject matter	Reviews aren't just about books, films, and performances. Nearly anything is fair game: consumer products, web pages, cars, apps, policies, restaurants, ski areas, college dorms, vacation destinations, and so on. The key is that you evaluate something that interests you and that also might interest someone else.
Structure	Many reviews have the following elements: • *Description.* What does it look like? What are some other key characteristics? • *Back story.* What is the background? What do readers need to know about if they don't know as much as you do? • *Judgments.* What do you think? These judgments don't have to lead to some grand thesis—it was good or bad—but can be a series of assessments given over the course of the review. • *Reasons, evidence.* What are the reasons behind your judgments? And what evidence do you have to support these reasons? • *Criteria.* What is the basis for your reasons? Criteria may be stated explicitly or implied. • *Relevant comparisons.* What category does it belong to? What else is it like, and why is it better or worse?
Sources of information	The raw material of any review is specific evidence drawn from your experience and research on the subject. What specifically influenced your judgment? What did you see? What did you hear? How did it work? What did they say? What were the results? What are the facts? How does it compare? Many review topics (e.g., film, plays, cars, clothes, books) will be most informed by your direct experience with your subject. But research can help any review. You can read about it or ask people what they think of it.

Feature	Conventions of the Review Essay
Language	The review can be tricky, especially if you're an expert on the thing you're reviewing. Be careful of "insider" language—terms, definitions, and so on that people unfamiliar with your topic may not understand. Frequently, the "voice" of the reviewer, especially a particular way of saying things, is especially strong. For example, think about successful music or movie reviewers. Often, the persona they project through their writing voice is part of their appeal: sometimes cranky or even snarky, sometimes humorous, frequently clever.

Prose+: Beyond Words

In four frames, cartoonist Tatsuya Ishida offers her review of the book *Fifty Shades of Grey*, a hugely successful erotic novel and now a motion picture.

READINGS

▶ Film Review

One hallmark of a great film is one's willingness to see it again and again, with each viewing yielding some new pleasure. However, holiday films seem like a special category. We see them every year at least in part because of ritual; we watch a certain movie at Christmastime because we always watch that movie at Christmastime. For a lot of people, *A Christmas Story* (1983) is one of those cinematic rituals. The film tells the story of Ralphie, who more than anything wants a Daisy Red Ryder BB gun for Christmas. Unfortunately, everyone in Ralphie's universe is convinced that if he possesses such a weapon, he will surely "shoot his eye out."

What distinguishes *A Christmas Story* from other popular holiday films, according to the late movie critic Roger Ebert, is that the film possesses "many small but perfect moments" that remind us of "a world that no longer quite exists in America." In other words, this isn't simply a great Christmas film. It's a great film by any measure.

Roger Ebert was perhaps the dean of American movie critics. He was a long-time columnist for the *Chicago Sun-Times*, and his website remains a popular resource for all things related to film.

A Christmas Story
Roger Ebert

1   One of the details that "A Christmas Story" gets right is the threat of having your mouth washed out with Lifebuoy soap. Not any soap. Lifebuoy. Never Ivory or Palmolive. Lifebuoy, which apparently contained an ingredient able to nullify bad language. The only other soap ever mentioned for this task was Lava, but that was the nuclear weapon of mouth-washing soaps, so powerful it was used for words we still didn't even know.

2   There are many small but perfect moments in "A Christmas Story," and one of the best comes after the Lifebuoy is finally removed from Ralphie's mouth and he is sent off to bed. His mother studies the bar, thinks for a moment, and then sticks it in her own mouth, just to see what it tastes like. Moments like that are why some people watch "A Christmas Story" every holiday season. There is a real knowledge of human nature beneath the comedy.

3   The movie is based on the memoirs of Jean Shepherd, the humorist whose radio programs and books remembered growing up in Indiana in the 1940s. It is Shepherd's voice on the soundtrack, remembering one Christmas season in particular, and the young hero's passionate desire to get a Daisy Red Ryder 200-shot Carbine Action BB Gun for Christmas—the one with the compass in the stock, "as cool and deadly a piece of weaponry as I had ever laid eyes on."

In a memorable scene from *A Christmas Story,* Ralphie observes firsthand what happens when a warm tongue meets cold metal.

I owned such a weapon. I recall everything about it at this moment with a tactile memory so vivid I could have just put it down to write these words. How you stuffed newspapers into the carton it came in to use it for target practice. How the BBs came in a cardboard tube with a slide-off top. How they rattled when you poured them into the gun. And of course how everybody warned that you would shoot your eye out.

Ralphie's life is made a misery by that danger. He finds that nobody in northern Indiana (not his mother, not his teacher, not even Santa Claus) is able to even *think* about a BB gun without using the words "shoot your eye out." At one point in the movie, in a revenge daydream, he knocks on his parents' door with dark glasses, a blind man's cane and a beggar's tin cup. They are shocked, and ask him tearfully what caused his blindness, and he replies coolly, "Soap poisoning."

The movie is not only about Christmas and BB guns, but also about childhood, and one detail after another rings true. The school bully, who, when he runs out of victims, beats up on his own loyal sidekick. The little brother who has outgrown his snowsuit, which is so tight that he walks around looking like the Michelin man; when he falls down he can't get up. The aunt who always thinks Ralphie is a 4-year-old girl, and sends him a pink bunny suit. Other problems of life belong to that long-ago age

4

5

6

(continued)

(*continued*)

and not this one: clinkers in the basement coal furnace, for example, or the blowout of a tire. Everybody knows what a flat tire is, but many now alive have never experienced a genuine, terrifying loud instantaneous ***blowout.***

7   "A Christmas Story" was released in the Christmas season of 1983, and did modest business at first (people don't often go to movies with specific holiday themes). It got warm reviews and two Genie Awards (the Canadian Oscars) for Bob Clark's direction and for the screenplay. And then it moved onto home video and has been a stealth hit season after season, finding a loyal audience. "Bams," for example, one of the critics at the hip Three Black Chicks movie review Web site, confesses she loves it: "How does one describe, in short form, the smiles and shrieks of laughter one has experienced over more than 15 years of seeing the same great movie over and over, without sounding like a babbling, fanboyish fool who talks too much?"

8   The movie is set in Indiana but was filmed mostly around Toronto, with some downtown shots from Cleveland, by Clark, whose other big hits were "Porky's" and "Baby Geniuses." It is pitch-perfect, telling the story through the enthusiastic and single-minded vision of its hero Ralphie, and finding in young Peter Billingsley a sly combination of innocence and calculation.

9   Ralphie's parents, Mr. and Mrs. Parker, are played by Darren McGavin and Melinda Dillon, and they exude warmth, zest and love: They are about the nicest parents I can remember in a non-smarmy movie. Notice the scene where Mrs. Parker gets her younger son, Randy, to eat his food by pretending he is "mommy's little piggie." Watch the delight in their laughter together. And the enthusiasm with which the Old Man (as he is always called) attacks the (unseen) basement furnace, battles with the evil neighbor dogs and promises to change a tire in "four minutes flat—time me!" And the lovely closing moment as the parents tenderly put their arms around each other on Christmas night.

10   Some of the movie's sequences stand as classic. The whole business, for example, of the Old Man winning the "major award" of a garish lamp in the shape of a woman's leg (watch Mrs. Parker hiding her giggles in the background as he tries to glue it together after it is "accidentally" broken). Or the visit by Ralphie and Randy to a department store Santa Claus, whose helpers spin the terrified kids around to bang them down on Santa's lap, and afterward kick them down a slide to floor level. Or the sequence where a kid is not merely dared but Triple-Dog-Dared to stick his tongue onto a frozen lamp post, and the fire department has to be called. And the deep disillusionment with which Ralphie finally gets his Little Orphan Annie Secret Decoder Ring in the mail, and Annie's secret message turns out to be nothing but a crummy commercial.

11   There is also the matter of Scut Farcas (Zack Ward), the bully, who Ralphie assures us has yellow eyes. Every school has a kid like this, who picks on smaller kids but is a coward at heart. He makes Ralphie's life a misery. How Farcus gets his comeuppance makes for a deeply satisfying scene, and notice the perfect tact with which Ralphie's

mom handles the situation. (Do you agree with me that Dad already knows the whole story when he sits down at the kitchen table?)

In a poignant way, "A Christmas Story" records a world that no longer quite exists in America. Kids are no longer left unattended in the line for Santa. The innocence of kids' radio programs has been replaced by slick, ironic children's programming on TV. The new Daisy BB guns have a muzzle velocity higher than that of some police revolvers, and are not to be sold to anyone under 16. Nobody knows who Red Ryder was, let alone that his sidekick was Little Beaver.   12

So much has been forgotten. There is a moment when the Old Man needs an answer for the contest he is entering. The theme of the contest is "Characters in American Literature," and the question is: "What was the name of the Lone Ranger's nephew's horse?"   13

Victor, of course. Everybody knows that.   14

Inquiring into the Essay

1. **Explore.** Think about the holiday film that you'd like to see every year. Fast-write for five minutes about the film and your memories of watching it. After the fastwrite, answer this question: What makes this a "good" film? Or think about some other film that you'd like to see every year and do the fastwrite and answer the question.

2. **Explain.** Underline or highlight sentences or passages in which Ebert is telling readers how and why *A Christmas Story* is a great movie. Then summarize in your own words what Ebert is saying about the film, incorporating several words or phrases from the material you underlined or highlighted.

3. **Evaluate.** Ebert uses various kinds of evidence to support his judgment that this is a great movie because of its "small but perfect moments" that get all the details of childhood in America right. He uses personal evidence, evidence from others, and of course lots of evidence from the movie. Find examples of these different kinds of evidence, and assess how effective they are in supporting the reasons Ebert gives for his judgment of the movie.

4. **Reflect.** In evaluative writing, judgments can be as small as brief comments or as big as thesis statements. Is there a thesis statement somewhere in Ebert's review of *A Christmas Story*? If so, where is it? If not, is the lack of a thesis statement a problem? Does every piece of persuasive writing need a thesis?

▶ **Review of a Method**

One of the most basic moves in a review is comparison. How does one thing stack up against another, similar thing? In the essay that follows, a college professor wonders what's better, notes taken on a computer or by hand? You might be surprised at her conclusion.

The Benefits of No-Tech Note Taking
Carol E. Holstead

1   The moment of truth for me came in the spring 2013 semester. I looked out at my visual-communication class and saw a group of six students transfixed by the blue glow of a video on one of their computers, and decided I was done allowing laptops in my large lecture class. "Done" might be putting it mildly. Although I am an engaging lecturer, I could not compete with Facebook and YouTube, and I was tired of trying.

2   The next semester I told students they would have to take notes on paper. Period.

3   I knew that eliminating laptops in my classroom would reduce distractions. Research has shown that when students use their laptops to "multitask" during class, they don't retain as much of the lecture. But I also had a theory, based on my college experience from the dark ages—the 70s, aka, before PowerPoint—that students would process lectures more effectively if they took notes on paper. When students took notes on laptops they barely looked up from their computers, so intent were they on transcribing every word I said. Back in my day, if a professor's lectures were reasonably well organized, I could take notes in outline format. I had to listen for the key points and subpoints.

4   Some of the students I teach are journalism majors. For them, taking notes by hand is an enormously helpful skill since journalists often have no choice but to take notes on paper. You can tape an interview, but transcribing tapes is inefficient when you're on deadline, and you're not going to pull out a laptop in somebody's office or in the middle of a protest and start typing. Now, if you're interviewing people over the phone, you might type as they talk, but if you try typing every single word your interview subjects say, you end up not really listening to them.

5   In laying down my no-tech note-taking decree, I explained that it would help students engage in the lectures and also pay off later in their careers. I use PowerPoint in my visual-communication course but only to outline the lecture and show examples of designs. I told students they would need to listen to what I said about each slide and selectively write down the important points. I said I believed they would remember more of my lectures by taking notes on paper.

6   It turned out my theory was right and now is supported by research. A study published last year in ***Psychological Science*** showed that students who write out

notes longhand remember conceptual information better than those who take notes on a computer. "Whereas taking more notes can be beneficial," the article's abstract reported, "laptop note takers' tendency to transcribe lectures verbatim rather than processing information and reframing it in their own words is detrimental to learning."

The researchers, Pam Mueller and Daniel Oppenheimer, wanted to learn if students could recall more factual and conceptual information from notes taken longhand or from those typed on a laptop. Mueller and Oppenheimer did a series of studies using 327 students on three campuses. They gave some students laptops and others pens and paper. The students watched TED talks and were told to take notes as they normally would in class.   7

In one study, students were tested 30 minutes after the lecture. In another they were tested a week later and allowed to study for 10 minutes beforehand. The students were asked questions about facts ("What is the purpose of adding calcium propionate to bread?") and concepts ("If a person's epiglottis was not working properly, what would be likely to happen?").   8

Students tested right after a lecture tended to answer factual questions equally well regardless of how they took notes, but students who handwrote their notes did consistently better on conceptual questions. What's more, when students were tested again a week later, the longhand note takers performed consistently better on both factual and conceptual questions.   9

The researchers found that students who used laptops were inclined to try to take notes verbatim—even when they were told not to. The longhand note takers took selective, organized notes because they couldn't write fast enough to get everything down. As a result, they processed lectures more deeply, which allowed them to retain more information and even understand it better.   10

After my first semester without laptops, I gave my students a questionnaire to find out how they felt about taking notes longhand. My survey was of course unscientific. Still, I was heartened by the results: Roughly 86 percent of the 95 students who responded said they felt they paid the same or better attention in the class without a laptop in front of them. About 52 percent said they paid more attention. A third of the class said they always took notes longhand, which surprised me.   11

When I asked the open-ended question "Did you take notes differently because you had to write them down? If so, how?" I got a variety of responses ranging from "Yes! I couldn't get everything down! I can't write as fast as I can type!" to "I learn from writing things down, so it helped me a lot."   12

Their answers reinforced the note-taking study. The students who tried to transcribe my lectures, even without a laptop, hated taking notes longhand. The students who figured out how to take selective notes liked it.   13

Interestingly, test scores in my visual-communication course have gone up since I gave laptops the boot a year ago. Now I coach students on how to take notes longhand to help those who have not used that muscle much, because I am convinced that while laptops have a lot of good uses in the classroom, note taking is not one of them.   14

Inquiring into the Essay

1. **Explore.** Like a lot of research, this review of note-taking methods begins with a hunch: Carol Holstead remembers taking notes longhand in school when she was a college student, and she suspects that method is superior to taking notes on laptops. Think about a hunch you have about why one thing is better than another. For example, why is a PC better than a Mac, a real book better than an e-book, etc. Fastwrite about it, exploring why you think you're right.

2. **Explain.** What are the reasons that Holstead gives for her claim "that while laptops have a lot of good uses in the classroom, note taking is not one of them"? Draft a summary of her argument in a brief paragraph.

3. **Evaluate.** Holstead notes that after she banned laptops from her class, and encouraged longhand note taking on her lectures, grades in the course went up. Does this seem like a reasonable correlation? Do you have any questions about the methods used in the research cited in the essay?

4. **Reflect.** The review is a type of argument. At the heart of argument is a claim (e.g., "Longhand notes are better than those written on laptops"), reasons, and evidence. All of those elements are at work in this essay. But where? Using three different colored highlighters, identify each of the three elements. Then look at the pattern of color. What do you notice? What does that pattern imply about how arguments are structured?

▶ Video Game Review

The video gaming industry hauls in something like $10 billion a year, so it's no surprise that more writers than ever are penning reviews of the latest releases. These reviews, if they're any good, balance technical information about the game with attention to the experience of playing it. It is a well-described gaming experience, not arcane detail, that will appeal to most readers. That's why Seth Schiesel's review of "Grand Theft Auto IV," a hugely popular video game released in 2008, is such a great example of how to write a review that might make even non–video game players interested in giving it a try.

Even when he doesn't make them explicit, the criteria Schiesel uses to determine the qualities of a good game aren't hard to find. One criterion he clearly uses is what we often look for in film and literature: "fully realized characters." When you think about it, this is a pretty extraordinary accomplishment in a video game. After all, characters in a game such as "Grand Theft Auto IV" must consistently service the action, making things (usually violent things) happen, and this wouldn't seem to provide the time or the situations to develop character. But according to Schiesel, protagonist Niko Bellic is "one of the most fully realized characters video games have yet produced."

Seth Schiesel sidesteps the ethics of producing games such as "Grand Theft Auto IV," which makes efficient killing a key to advancement. But this is a review, not a public argument on the virtues of gaming, and his readers likely aren't interested in such ethical questions. They just want to know whether the game is any good. As you read "Grand Theft Auto Takes on New York," consider what exactly Schiesel sees as being a good video game. On what other criteria does he base his judgment?

Grand Theft Auto Takes on New York
Seth Schiesel

I was rolling through the neon deluge of a place very like Times Square the other night in my Landstalker sport utility vehicle, listening to David Bowie's "Fascination" on the radio. The glittery urban landscape was almost enough to make me forget about the warehouse of cocaine dealers I was headed uptown to rip off. 1

Soon I would get bored, though, and carjack a luxury sedan. I'd meet my Rasta buddy Little Jacob, then check out a late show by Ricky Gervais at a comedy club around the corner. Afterward I'd head north to confront the dealers, at least if I could elude the cops. I heard their sirens before I saw them and peeled out, tires squealing. 2

It was just another night on the streets of Liberty City, the exhilarating, lusciously dystopian rendition of New York City in 2008 that propels Grand Theft Auto IV, the ambitious new video game to be released on Tuesday for the Xbox 360 and PlayStation 3 systems. 3

Published by Rockstar Games, Grand Theft Auto IV is a violent, intelligent, profane, endearing, obnoxious, sly, richly textured and thoroughly compelling work of cultural satire disguised as fun. It calls to mind a rollicking R-rated version of Mad magazine featuring Dave Chappelle and Quentin Tarantino, and sets a new standard for what is possible in interactive arts. It is by far the best game of the series, which made its debut in 1997 and has since sold more than 70 million copies. Grand Theft Auto IV will retail for $60. 4

Niko Bellic is the player-controlled protagonist this time, and he is one of the most fully realized characters video games have yet produced. A veteran of the Balkan wars and a former human trafficker in the Adriatic, he arrives in Liberty City's rendition of Brighton Beach at the start of the game to move in with his affable if naïve cousin Roman. Niko expects to find fortune and, just maybe, track down someone who betrayed him long ago. Over the course of the story line he discovers that revenge is not always what one expects. 5

Besides the nuanced Niko the game is populated by a winsome procession of grifters, hustlers, drug peddlers and other gloriously unrepentant lowlifes, each a caricature less politically correct than the last. 6

(continued)

(*continued*)

7   Hardly a demographic escapes skewering. In addition to various Italian and Irish crime families, there are venal Russian gangsters, black crack slingers, argyle-sporting Jamaican potheads, Puerto Rican hoodlums, a corrupt police commissioner, a steroid-addled Brooklyn knucklehead named Brucie Kibbutz and a former Eastern European soldier who has become a twee Upper West Side metrosexual.

8   Breathing life into Niko and the other characters is a pungent script by Dan Houser and Rupert Humphries that reveals a mastery of street patois to rival Elmore Leonard's. The point of the main plot is to guide Niko through the city's criminal underworld. Gang leaders and thugs set missions for him to complete, and his success moves the story along toward a conclusion that seems as dark as its beginning. But the real star of the game is the city itself. It looks like New York. It sounds like New York. It feels like New York. Liberty City has been so meticulously created it almost even smells like New York. From Brooklyn (called Broker), through Queens (Dukes), the Bronx (Bohan), Manhattan (Algonquin) and an urban slice of New Jersey (Alderney), the game's streets and alleys ooze a stylized yet unmistakable authenticity. (Staten Island is left out however.)

9   The game does not try to represent anything close to every street in the city, but the overall proportions, textures, geography, sights and sounds are spot-on. The major landmarks are present, often rendered in surprising detail, from the Cyclone at Coney Island to the Domino Sugar factory and Grand Army Plaza in Brooklyn and on up through the detritus of the 1964–65 World's Fair in Queens. Central Park, the Empire State Building, various museums, the Statue of Liberty and Times Square are all present and accounted for. There is no Yankee Stadium, but there is a professional baseball team known, with the deliciousness typical of the game's winks and nods, as the Swingers.

10   At least as impressive as the city's virtual topography is the range of the game's audio and music production, delivered through an entire dial's worth of radio stations available in almost any of the dozens of different cars, trucks and motorcycles a player can steal. From the jazz channel (billed as "music from when America was cool") through the salsa, alt-rock, jazz, metal and multiple reggae and hip-hop stations, Lazlow Jones, Ivan Pavlovich and the rest of Rockstar's audio team demonstrate a musical erudition beyond anything heard before in a video game. The biggest problem with the game's extensive subway system is that there's no music underground. (Too bad there are no iPods to nab.)

11   The game's roster of radio hosts runs from Karl Lagerfeld to Iggy Pop and DJ Green Lantern. It is not faint praise to point out that at times, simply driving around the city listening to the radio—seguing from "Moanin'" by Art Blakey and the Jazz Messengers to the Isley Brothers' "Footsteps in the Dark" to "The Crack House" by Fat Joe featuring Lil Wayne—can be as enjoyable as anything the game has to offer.

Grand Theft Auto IV is such a simultaneously adoring and insightful take on modern America that it almost had to come from somewhere else. The game's main production studio is in Edinburgh, and Rockstar's leaders, the brothers Dan and Sam Houser, are British expatriates who moved to New York to indulge their fascination with urban American culture. Their success places them firmly among the distinguished cast of Britons from Mick Jagger and Keith Richards through Tina Brown who have flourished by identifying key elements of American culture, repackaging them for mass consumption and selling them back at a markup.   12

It all adds up to a new level of depth for an interactive entertainment experience. I've spent almost 60 hours practically sequestered in a (real world) Manhattan hotel room in recent weeks playing through Grand Theft Auto IV's main story line and the game still says I have found only 64 percent of its content. I won't ever reach 100 percent, not least because I won't hunt down all 200 of the target pigeons (known as flying rats here) that the designers have hidden around the city.   13

But like millions of other players I will happily spend untold hours cruising Liberty City's bridges and byways, hitting the clubs, grooving to the radio and running from the cops. Even when the real New York City is right outside.   14

Inquiring into the Essay

1. **Explore**. This review doesn't address the ethical questions raised by a game that celebrates "gloriously unrepentant lowlifes" including potheads, gangsters, and "crack slingers." "Grand Theft Auto IV" may be no worse than other violent video games, and unless you've played it, criticism or praise of this particular game is unfair. But in a four-minute fastwrite, explore your own feelings about violent video games. In his review, Schiesel argues that "Grand Theft Auto IV" is "cultural satire." Would that make a difference? Can games such as this one serve a larger, even useful purpose?

2. **Explain**. In your own words, state what Seth Schiesel seems to see as the qualities of a good video game.

3. **Evaluate**. How rhetorically effective is this review for different readers? Assess what parts would work—or wouldn't—for the following categories of readers:
   a. People who have never played a video game in their lives but might consider it.
   b. People who are avid and experienced gamers.
   c. People who, when asked, usually consider playing video games "a waste of time."

4. **Reflect.** Video game reviews are but one type of a growing number of review subgenres, which include reviews of movies, books, blogs, websites, best and worst dressed, and so on. Consider the subgenres of reviews you read or might read. What exactly would you be looking for in a "good" review?

THE WRITING PROCESS

Inquiry Project **Writing a Review Essay**

Inquiry questions: How good is it? What is its value?

Write a review essay on any subject—a performance, a book, a website, a consumer product, a film, whatever. Just make sure your review has the following qualities (see also the "Features of the Form" box on pages 142–143 for typical features of the review essay):

■ The essay is focused on a specific example of a larger category. (For instance, the film *Maltese Falcon* is an example of forties film noir, *The Curious Writer* is an example of a composition textbook, and Lady Gaga's song "Born This Way" is an example of politically themed contemporary rock music.)

■ The writer's judgments are clearly stated and are supported with reasons and evidence.

■ The evaluation seems balanced and fair. The criteria for judging the value of the subject seem sound.

Prose+

Write and publish your review for an online audience. There are review sites for nearly anything, from the very focused (e.g., birding binoculars) to the quite broad (music, film, TV, *and* video games). For example,

■ For a book review, consider publishing on the Amazon or Barnes & Noble site, or on a site such as Goodreads or LibraryThing.

■ For music, check out the website Music-Critic.

■ For music, movies, TV, apps, or video games, look to sites such as Metacritic.

■ For consumer products, there is Eopinions.

Turn your review into a video project. If you're writing about a consumer product, for example, demonstrate in a short film how it works and how it could work better. (There are a gazillion examples of this on YouTube.) If you're reviewing a movie or television show, put together a short film that incorporates clips, if available online, with your voiceover commentary. Make sure you allow time to learn how to use the basics of your video-editing software.

Add images to your essay. You might, for example, take a series of photographs to demonstrate how something works or to highlight its key features. See Chapter 13 for more ideas and guidance on how to turn your review into a multimodal project.

What Are You Going to Write About?

5.4

Use invention and focusing strategies to discover and develop a review essay.

Imagine all the things about which you might ask, "How good is it?" From smartphones to theater performances, movies to college websites, books to dog-training programs—the possibilities are endless. You don't have to start with an opinion about your review subject—and it's better if you don't—but it should be something that interests you.

Get started thinking about what you're going to write about by opening up the possibilities with the following prompts, most of which involve generating ideas. Later, you'll narrow things down to a promising topic and try it out.

Opening Up

Suspend judgment to explore a range of possible review essay topics.

Listing Prompts. Lists can be rich sources of triggering topics. Let them grow freely, and when you're ready, use a list item as the focus of another list or an episode of fastwriting. The following prompts should get you started.

1. Fold a piece a paper into four equal columns. You'll be making four different brainstormed lists. In the first column, write, "Things I Want." Spend two minutes making a quick list of everything you wish you had but don't: a new computer, a classical guitar, a decent boyfriend, and so on.

2. In the next column, write, "The Jury Is Still Out." In this column, make a fast list of things in your life that so far are hard to judge: the quality of the school you attend, this textbook, your opinion about the films you saw last month, how well Susie cuts your hair, and so on.

3. In the third column, write, "My Media." Devote a fast list to particular films, TV shows, books, websites, or musicians you like or dislike; jot down whatever you watch, listen to, or read regularly.

4. Finally, make a list of "Things of Questionable Quality." Try to be specific.

Fastwriting Prompts. Remember, fastwriting is a great way to stimulate creative thinking. Turn off your critical side and let yourself write "badly."

1. Choose an item from any of the four preceding lists as a prompt for a seven-minute fastwrite. Explore your experience with the subject, or how your opinions about it have evolved.

2. Begin with the following prompt, and follow it for five minutes in a fastwrite: *Among the things I have a hard time judging is* _____. If the writing stalls, shift subjects by writing, *And another thing I can't judge is* _____.

Visual Prompts. Sometimes the best way to generate material is to see what we think represented in something other than sentences. Boxes, lines, webs, clusters, arrows, charts, and even sketches can help us see more of the landscape of a subject, especially connections that aren't as obvious in prose.

1. On a blank page in your journal, cluster the name of an artist, musician, film, book, author, performance, band, building, academic course or major, restaurant, university bookstore, tablet, computer, food store, or pizza joint. Cluster the name of anything about which you have some sort of feeling, positive or negative. Build a web of associations: feelings, details, observations, names, moments, facts, opinions, and so on. Look for a single strand in your essay that might be the beginning of a review.

2. Draw a sketch of what you think is an *ideal version* of something you need or use often: a computer, a classroom, a telephone, a wallet or handbag, and so on. If you could design such a thing, what would it look like? Use this as a way of evaluating what is currently available and how it might be improved.

Research Prompts. Explore what other critics are saying, look around, or collaborate.

1. Do an Internet or library search for reviews on one of your favorite films, books, sports teams, artists, and so on. Do you agree with the evaluations? If not, consider writing a review of your own that challenges the critics.

2. Take a walk. As you wander on and off campus, look for things to evaluate—downtown architecture, local parks, paintings in the art museum, neighborhoods, coffee shops. You'll be amazed at how much is begging for a thoughtful judgment.

3. Here's an entertaining generating activity: Plan a weekend of movie watching with a few friends. Ask each of them to suggest two or three favorite films, and then obtain a slew of them. When you're thoroughly spent watching the films, discuss which one might be the most interesting to review.

Narrowing Down

Now that you've opened up possibilities for review topics, there are choices to make. Which do you want to write about?

What's Promising Material and What Isn't? My favorite coffee shop in my hometown of Boise, Idaho, is a place called the Flying M. It's a funky place with an odd assortment of furniture: overstuffed couches, worn armchairs, and wobbly tables. On the walls, there's work from local artists, mostly unknowns with talent and unusual taste. There are other coffee places in town, including the ubiquitous Starbucks and another, more local chain called Moxie Java. I don't find much difference in the coffee at any of these places, and they're all rather pleasant. What makes me prefer the Flying M?

I've never really thought about it. That's one of the reasons I liked the idea of reviewing my favorite local coffeehouse when "the Flying M" appeared on one of my lists. The best inquiry-based projects begin when you're not quite sure what you think and want to explore a topic to find out.

- *Is there anything in your lists and fastwrites that you might have an initial judgment about but really haven't considered fully?*

- *As you consider potential subjects for your review, do some clearly suggest the possibility of comparison with other, similar things in that category?*

- *Do any of your potential subjects suggest the possibility of conducting prima-ry research, or research that might involve direct observation?* Can you listen to the music, attend the performance, read the novel, examine the building, visit the website, look at the painting?

- *Does a topic lend itself to demonstration through visuals or video?* Can you download clips, film a demonstration, take pictures, create an info-graphic?

- *Does someone have a stake in your evaluation of the thing?* Are more people than just you interested in your judgments about its value?

Questions About Audience and Purpose. When people read reviews, they either are actively *seeking information* (they are considering buying the tablet or attending the dance performance) or are *looking for reinforcement* (reasons why what they've already decided to do makes sense). I bought a Ford Escape recently, and now I read every review I see on the car, hoping to feel good about my decision. These two audiences have very different dispositions. The information-seekers are more critical readers than those who seek reinforcement. But what they both share is a stake in the topic under review. They're *interested*. As you consider a review topic, ask yourself whether it's easy to imagine an audience who would care, one way or another, about a judgment about the usefulness or value of the thing you might review.

Trying Out

Let's work with your tentative topic, doing some more-focused work, culminating in a sketch, or a first try at writing it up for an audience.

Focusing the Category. First, let's try focusing your topic in the context of a category. Can you see how your topic fits into broader and narrower categories? An inverted pyramid, as shown in Figure 5.1, is a nice model for this.

Suppose you love the 1940s film classic *The Maltese Falcon*, and you'd like to explore why it's so good. You can evaluate the film as an example of movies gen-erally, but that makes little sense because the category's too broad. However, sup-pose you list progressively narrower subcategories of film to which *The Maltese Falcon* might belong. You might end up evaluating the film as an example of 1940s film noir. Why is this narrowed focus useful?

1. *It gives you a way of seeing appropriate comparisons*. You're comparing *The Maltese Falcon* not to all Hollywood movies—there are, after all, so many different kinds—but to other 1940s Hollywood crime films that belong to the film noir genre.

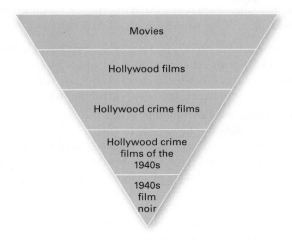

Figure 5.1 An inverted triangle model for focusing a topic

2. *It helps you focus on appropriate criteria.* Just as it would be weird to compare *The Maltese Falcon* with *A Christmas Story* because they are such different types of films, it would be hard to arrive at criteria for such an evaluation. What makes a 1940s crime film "good" will be very different from what makes a family comedy "good."

Try creating an inverted pyramid on your subject, looking for a category that is narrow enough to make comparisons and criteria appropriate.

Fastwriting. Through a focused fastwrite, explore your initial feelings and experiences, if any, about your subject. Use one of the following prompts to launch this exploration. If the writing stalls, try another prompt to keep you going for five to seven minutes.

- *Write about your first experience with your subject.* This might be, for example, the first time you visited the restaurant, or heard the performer, or saw the photographs. Focus on scenes, moments, situations, and people.

- *Write about what you think are important qualities of your subject.* Ideally, this would be what the thing should be able to do well or what effects it should have on people who use it or see it.

- *Write about how the thing makes you feel.* Explore not just your initial good, bad, or mixed feelings about your subject, but also the place from where those feelings arose. Why do you feel anything at all about this thing?

- *Compare the thing you're evaluating with something that's similar.*

Web Research. Try some web searches, gathering as much relevant background information as you can.

- *Search for information on product websites or web pages devoted specifically to your subject.* If your review is on Ford's new electric car, visit the company's website to find out what you can about the vehicle. Visit Green Day's home page or fan site for your review of the band's latest CD.

- *Search for existing reviews or other evaluations on your subject.* One way to do this is to Google the keyword "review" or "reviews" (or "how to evaluate") along with your subject. For example, "laptop reviews" will produce dozens of sites that rank and evaluate the machines. Similarly, there are countless reviews on the web of specific performers, performances, CDs, consumer products, and so on.

Interviews. If possible, interview people about what they think. You may do this formally by developing a survey (see pages 406–410), or informally by simply asking people what they like or dislike about the thing you're evaluating. Also consider whether you might interview someone who's an expert on your subject. For example, if you're evaluating a website, ask people in the technical communications program what they think about it, or what criteria they might use if they were reviewing something similar.

Experiencing Your Subject. This may be the most useful activity of all. Visit the coffeehouse, examine the website, listen to the music, attend the performance, read the book, view the painting, visit the building, look at the architecture, watch the movie. As you do this, gather your impressions and collect information. Take notes. Take pictures. Shoot video.

Thinking About Criteria

You hate something. You love something. You have mixed feelings about it. All of these judgments arise from your criteria, your assumptions about the qualities that make such a thing good. And thinking about your criteria can help you know what to look for.

Refining Criteria for Better Evidence. Consider a process of evaluation something like the one in Figure 5.2.

You see a website and think, "This is really ugly." You look more closely and conclude, "I think there's too much text." You could stop there, of course, but you want to provide a more thorough evaluation. A natural next step, then, would be to consider the criterion behind your reason and judgment. You could simply say, "Good websites don't use too much text," but that doesn't advance your evaluation any further because the criterion is too general and vague. After a little research into what this criterion's really about, you arrive at this: "Good sites break text into readable chunks." Sites that don't have readable chunks give the visual appearance

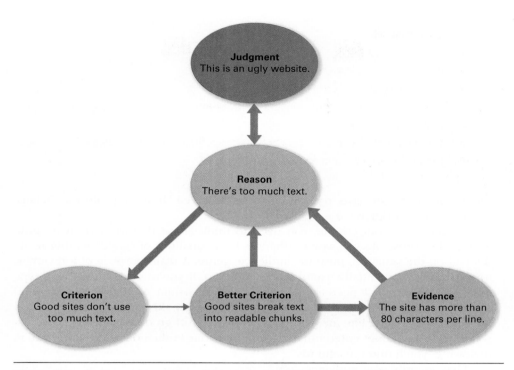

Figure 5.2   A process for refining criteria and using criteria to generate better evidence

of too much text. What's a "readable chunk"? Turns out it is around 80 characters per line. Now you can take another look at your ugly website with a criterion that really helps you support your judgment with better evidence.

This implies a couple things about good criteria in evaluation:

1. The more specific your criterion for evaluation, the better.
2. Identifying criteria is a powerful tool for finding better evidence to support your judgment.

The more you know about something, the more specific your criteria are likely to be. For example, I asked my daughter Becca what criteria she would use to judge a modern dance performance (see the box). I'm unschooled in dance, so I don't understand all of her criteria, but I'm certain I could use some of them the next time I see a modern dance performance, to evaluate what I see.

Considering Criteria and Rhetorical Context. We often don't think about our criteria and whether they're valid; we treat them as self-evident and may assume that our audience would agree with them. But careful reviewers at the very least *consider* the criteria that shape their reactions and decide whether they're fair and sensible. (If you're finding your criteria hard to tease out, or want to know what

> **Becca's Criteria**
>
> A good modern dance performance has...
>
> 1. Interesting features—props, comedy, or music
> 2. Something improvised
> 3. Visible expressions of the dancers' enjoyment
> 4. Interesting variation
> 5. Good balance in choreography between repetition and randomness
> 6. Beginning, middle, and end seamlessly joined

criteria others might have, try getting some help; see "Inquiring into the Details: Collaborating on Criteria.")

In thinking about criteria, you need to think about rhetorical context: audience and purpose. As you saw in Chapter 1, the qualities of "good" writing really depend on the situation: purpose, audience, genre. A main purpose of a review is to give readers potentially useful information. So, if you're evaluating a new type of downhill skis, you'll need to think about skis for whom. An advanced skier fond of deep powder will have different expectations of her skis' performance than will an intermediate skier like me, who falls on his face off groomed runs. For this reason, in thinking about criteria that might guide your evaluation of the thing you're reviewing, you'll find it useful to

First, identify your audience:

- *Who will be using the thing (going to the performance, etc.)?*

Then, take another look at your criteria:

- *Are the criteria that you are thinking in terms of appropriate for your audience?*

Writing the Sketch

A sketch, as the name implies, is a kind of verbal drawing of your topic—an early draft—to see if you should develop it further. Even when you write a sketch with readers in mind, it is hardly polished. You are "essaying" the topic to try it out, and you may not know yet what you think or what you want to say. Your review sketch, however, should include the following:

- A tentative title.
- An effort to help readers understand why they might have a stake in the thing you're evaluating. What's significant about this particular CD, book, performance, place, or product?
- A tentative answer to the inquiry question "How good is it?"
- A few convincing reasons for your judgment that are tied to specific evidence from the thing itself.

Inquiring into the Details

Collaborating on Criteria

What makes it "good"? Being clear on your criteria can help you discover what you think and, once you discover that, it can help you explain your reasons. Asking others for their opinions can also help. Consider the following strategy:

1. Write the category of the thing you're reviewing—a modern dance performance, coffeehouses, a hip-hop CD, a science fiction novel, or whatever—on the top of a piece of newsprint or paper.
2. Post your newsprint on the wall of your classroom.
3. For twenty minutes, rotate around the room to each newsprint, trying to answer the following question about the category listed there: *In your judgment, what makes a particularly good* _____ (dance performance, coffeehouse,...)?
4. Briefly list your criteria for judging each category on the newsprint, or elaborate on criteria that are already there. In other words, in your mind, what makes a good _____?
5. If you don't know that much about the category, make a reasonable guess about a basis for judging it.

▶ Student Sketch

Here are some common criteria for a good film:

1. There is someone in the film who we come to like, despite that person's flaws.
2. Characters change. They learn from mistakes.
3. The story ends with some resolution of the conflict.

According to Laura Burns, whose sketch of the Charlize Theron film *Young Adult* follows, that movie doesn't meet any of the three criteria. And yet, she argues, *Young Adult* is a great film. Obviously, Laura is saying that the criteria most of us assume must be met for a film to be good in fact don't have to be met. Because she challenges our assumptions, Laura needs to be particularly persuasive in her review. How persuasive is she in this first attempt?

Recipe for a Great Film: Unlikeable People, Poor Choices, and Little Redemption

Laura Burns

1   Charlize Theron is arguably the most traditionally beautiful woman in film. High, smooth cheekbones, long, thin legs, a delicate nose set at the center of a perfectly proportioned face. This considered, it's remarkable how ugly she can get.

2   *Young Adult* is a movie about unlikeable people making poor life choices which they don't learn from. Theron plays Mavis Gary, an ex-prom queen from Mercury, Minnesota, making her living as a ghostwriter of a teen series in what the Mercurians call the "Mini-apple." From the first sequence of the film, we can tell that Mavis is a mess. She gets wasted, slumps around her apartment in sweats, and guzzles Diet Coke in a way that almost gave me heartburn. Upon receiving a birth announcement email from her now-married ex-prom king, the aptly named Buddy (Patrick Wilson), Mavis decides to pop an old mixtape into her dirty Mini Cooper and win him back.

3   This is, essentially, the entire plot of *Young Adult*. Mavis' trip back to Mercury is a kind of *anti*-hero's journey. On her first night in town, getting wasted in a local dive, she meets her "guide," Matt (the wonderful Patton Oswalt), a former classmate who remains crippled from an assault during high school. Through the course of the film, as she reunites with her parents (Jill Eikenberry & Richard Bekins), insinuates herself into Buddy and his wife Beth's (Elizabeth Reaser) lives, and gets plastered on Matt's home-brewed bourbon, rather than moving towards revelation, Mavis seems to retreat further and further into her past.

4   Unlike *Juno*, writer Diablo Cody's most well-known film, *Young Adult* rejects preciousness in favor of obscenity. It's difficult to make a film about terrible people enjoyable, but Cody injects just enough silliness to keep us from feeling too badly. Director Jason Reitman rightly focuses on Mavis, and both Theron and Oswalt are brave enough to let us into their characters' grossness and un-likeability. Smartly, Cody refuses to manufacture empathy for her characters, leaving us to boldly accept the ugliness of these people fully.

5   I don't doubt that *Young Adult* will displease many movie-goers who are used to redemptive stories and characters who are "good at heart." Cody refuses to indulge that expectation. When Mavis dresses to go out (which is often), Theron's extraordinary beauty is obvious. Yet we're never allowed to shake that Mavis is truly ugly at her core—an effective subversion of expectation that is the exemplar of this memorable performance. This isn't a feel-good film, and thank goodness. If Cody and Reitman had tried, I think we might leave the theater feeling worse.

Moving from Sketch to Draft

A sketch is an audition. It's a brief performance for an audience that may or may not work out well. In a review, what do you look for in your own performance? To start with, you've got to still care about your topic, of course. This should be a topic you still want to write about. But what else?

Evaluating Your Sketch. Start with a summary of what you think the sketch is saying by finishing the following sentence.

Because of __(reason 1)__ and __(reason 2)__, I think that __(thing you're evaluating)__ is __(judgment of value)__, and the strongest evidence for this is _____ and _____.

Example: Because of its unusually hefty neck and its thick, solid rosewood body, the Martin 0-28VS acoustic guitar has a bright sound that belies its small size, and the strongest evidence for this is how great it sounds with light fingerpicking and its long sustains.

If you can finish the sentence to your satisfaction, your audition was successful. You know, more or less, where you might be going. (Don't be surprised if you change your mind as you revise.) However, you might have encountered some problems. Maybe you haven't yet arrived at a judgment. Or perhaps you can't come up with two compelling reasons for the judgment you do have. In any case, here are the things you should focus on as you develop your review:

- *Clarify your judgment.* What is the one thing you're trying to say (S.O.F.T.) about the thing you're reviewing?
- *Explain your reasons.* What is behind your evaluation? And are the criteria that these reasons are based on sensible?
- *Provide the back story.* What is it, where did it come from, how does it compare, why is it important, what is the history?
- *Gather evidence.* How will you prove that your reasons are persuasive? What specifically can you point to?

Reflecting on What You've Learned. To get some perspective on what you've learned so far about the thing you're reviewing, fastwrite in your journal or on the computer using the following prompt:

When I first started exploring this, I thought _____, and now I'm beginning to think _____.

Developing

Before you revise your sketch into a draft, generate more material through writing and research. This is almost always necessary.

Talking It Through. Generate more material by having a conversation with me about your topic. Imagine I'm sitting across the table from you, asking you the following questions about the thing you're reviewing. Respond in your journal to each question, in order, fastwriting a response for at least a few minutes. If the writing takes off in response to any one question, run with it. The order of the questions may prove to be a useful organizing principle for your draft, so write as much as you can in this exercise.

Bruce	You
To start with, why are you reviewing this? To whom might it matter and under what circumstances?	
Can you describe it? What does it look like? What is the story behind it? Would you compare it to anything else I might know about?	
Okay, so what do you most want me to know about it? What is it you're saying, exactly?	
Interesting. Why do you say this?	
Surely not everyone thinks this. What do people who disagree with you say? How would you respond to them?	

Consider the following research strategies for developing your draft.

Re-Experience. Probably the single most useful thing you can do to prepare for the next draft is to collect more observations of your subject. Why? You're much more focused now on what you think, what criteria most influence that judgment, and what particular evidence you were lacking in the sketch that will make your review more convincing. You might also consider documenting your research not only with notes but multimedia as well. Could you take pictures to demonstrate a feature or show how the thing you're reviewing is used? Might you include screenshots of the relevant websites? Download images of the thing being used?

Interview. If you haven't already done so, collect the comments, opinions, and observations of others about the subject of your review. If you reviewed a concert or other event, find others to interview who also attended. If you reviewed a film, get some friends to watch the movie with you and jot down their reactions afterward. If it would be helpful to collect data on how people feel, consider designing a brief survey.

Also consider interviewing someone who is an expert on the thing you're reviewing.

Read. Go to the library and go online and search for information about your subject. Try finding:

- *Information about how it's made or designed.*
- *Other reviews on your topic.*
- *Information on relevant people, companies, traditions, local developments— any background that will help readers see the thing you're reviewing in a larger context.*

Drafting

When you've got enough information, start your draft, beginning at the beginning.

Finding an Opening. Here's how Carol Holstead's comparison of class note taking on paper versus on computers begins (see earlier in this chapter on pp. 148–149):

> The moment of truth for me came in the spring 2013 semester. I looked out at my visual-communication class and saw a group of six students transfixed by the blue glow of a video on one of their computers, and decided I was done allowing laptops in my large lecture class. "Done" might be putting it mildly. Although I am an engaging lecturer, I could not compete with Facebook and YouTube, and I was tired of trying.
>
> The next semester I told students they would have to take notes on paper. Period.

There's no thesis in this introduction (that will come later), but it clearly establishes the dilemma the essay proposes to explore: Was it a good idea to force students to close their laptops and take notes by hand? But this beginning does more than billboard the essay's purpose. It also

1. Raises questions the reader might want to learn the answers to.
2. Creates a relationship between reader and writer.
3. Gets right to the subject without unnecessary scaffolding.

Here are some other approaches to creating a strong lead for a review:

- Begin with a common misconception about your subject and promise to challenge it.
- Begin with an anecdote that reveals what you like or dislike.
- Help readers realize the relevance of your subject by showing how it's used, what it says, or why it's needed in a familiar situation.
- Provide interesting background that your readers may not know.

Methods of Development. What are some ways to organize your review?

Narrative. If you're reviewing a performance or any other kind of experience that has a discrete beginning and end, then telling a story about what you saw, felt, and thought is a natural move. Another way to use narrative is to tell the story of your thinking about your subject—an approach that lends itself to a delayed-thesis essay, where your judgment comes late in the review.

Comparison/Contrast. Comparison with other items in the same category—say, other science fiction films, electric cars, or laptops—is a common and useful element in reviews. If comparison is especially important to your review, you might structure your essay around it.

Question to Answer. One of the most straightforward methods of structuring a review is to simply begin by raising the question *What makes _____ good?* This way, you make your criteria for evaluation explicit. From there, the next move is obvious: How well does the thing you're evaluating measure up?

Using Evidence. As you compose your draft, keep in mind that the most important evidence in a review is probably your own observations of the thing. These should be specific, and most likely they will draw on *primary research* you conducted by attending the concert, listening to the CD, or visiting the coffeehouse. As illustrated in Figure 5.2, thinking about your criteria can be a tool for finding strong evidence. You may also use evidence from secondary sources: For example, what did another critic say or observe?

Workshopping

If your draft is subject to peer review, see Appendix A for details on how to organize workshop groups and decide on how your group can help you. To help you decide, use the guidance, starting on p. 554, in Appendix A. Each workshop type is described more fully in that section.

When you workshop a review, you're sharing your evaluation of something your peers may have no experience with. Maybe they've never seen the movie, tried the coffee, visited the restaurant, or listened to the music. This has rhetorical implications you should consider as you prepare to discuss your draft:

1. *Context.* Do you provide enough background on the thing you're evaluating: what it is, how it works, why it's significant, what it does, etc.?

2. *Comparisons.* Even if none of your readers have, say, ridden the road bike you're reviewing, most have ridden a bicycle of some kind. Did you establish common ground with readers by exploiting any overlaps between their experience and your review topic?

3. *Definitions.* You can't assume that your peers are familiar with insider jargon. Did you define terms and explain features and so on that readers may not understand?

In workshopping the first draft of your review, your initial focus should be on what peers make of the purpose and meaning of your essay. Above all else, knowing what you're trying to do and say in an essay will help you decide what to cut and what to add in revision. It's the most powerful knowledge you can have for rewriting. This box can help you frame the questions for your workshop group.

Questions for Peer Reviewers	
1. Purpose	Why is this being reviewed? Who has a stake in whether it's good or not?
2. Meaning	In your own words, what exactly is my judgment? In your words, what are my main reasons for this judgment? Are they persuasive? Why or why not?

If you're reviewing something that your peers may be familiar with—and perhaps have strong feelings about—you might consider a workshop for your draft that encourages participants to debate your conclusions, both supporting your judgments and challenging them (see box).

Option for Review Essay Workshop

1. Divide each workshop group into two teams—believers and doubters.

2. Believers are responsible for presenting to doubters why the writer's review is convincing and fair.

3. Doubters challenge the writer's judgments and respond to the believers' claims.

4. The writer observes this conversation without participating.

5. After five minutes, believers and doubters drop their roles and discuss suggestions for revision with the writer.

Reflecting on the Draft. Immediately after your workshop session, fastwrite in your journal (paper or computer) on what you learned about writing an effective review *from reading your peers' drafts.* How might you apply these things to your revision?

Revising

Revision is a continual process—not a last step. You've been revising—"reseeing" your subject—from the first messy fastwriting in your journal. But the things that get your attention vary depending on where you are in the writing process. With your draft in hand, revision becomes your focus through what I'll call "shaping and tightening your draft."

5.5

Apply revision strategies that are effective for shaping reviews.

Chapter 14 contains strategies that can help you revise any inquiry project, and the "Guidelines: Revising Your Work" in this chapter on page 171 can help you locate these strategies. There are also certain things to think about that are especially useful for shaping a review essay.

Shaping. You've clarified the purpose and meaning of the piece. Now you want to redesign it around both purpose and meaning.

Analyzing the Information.   Shaping involves, among other things, arranging and rearranging information so that it is more effectively organized around your main idea. One way to think about the structure of your review is to look at its information in terms of the elements that reviews typically include:

The Basics (Description, Back Story) What is it? How does it work? What's the story? Who is it for?	**Judgments** How good is it? What works and what doesn't? How could it be better?
Criteria What makes things like this good? What is the standard?	**Reasons, Evidence** Why is it good/not good? What's an example? What was observed? How does it compare? What do other reviewers say?

By analyzing your draft in this way, you can look at whether you've included enough information for each element. While there's no formula for ordering this information, consider the structure of your draft rhetorically. If your audience is familiar with the item you're reviewing, then "the basics" need less emphasis; obviously, the opposite is true if your audience has little knowledge of the item. In either case, the basics are usually presented early in the draft. Similarly, audiences who are familiar with your topic (e.g., they've seen the movie or used the device) may already share your assumptions about your criteria. In that case, you can spend less time explaining them. Others who are unfamiliar with your topic need to learn the criteria you're using, so give them more emphasis. Judgments can appear anywhere in the draft, not just as a thesis in your first paragraph.

To imagine organizing strategies, you can try the "Frankenstein Draft" (Revision Strategy 14.18 in Chapter 14): Cut up your draft with scissors into the different elements mentioned here, and then play with the order. What seems to be most effective? Worry about transitions later.

Other Questions for Revision.   Because a review's a form of argument, start by asking yourself, "Is my evaluation clear, and will it be persuasive to readers?" For example, here's a paragraph from Jesse's review of the film *Crank*:

> *Crank* (2006), written and directed by Mark Neveldin and Brian Taylor, is a fast-paced, dark, action comedy. This is not your typical "good guy saves the day" action film though. With a lot of profanity, wild antics and defiance of the law, it is very edgy. It really reminds me of a Grand Theft Auto Vice City. The star of the show even steals a cop's motorcycle and rides it around the city recklessly. But don't be quick to judge this film only by its novel gamer appeal. This movie also had good theatrical performances.

Jesse's evaluation is clear: The film *Crank* is good. And he explains why: strong performances and an "edgy" feel similar to that of the video game "Grand Theft Auto." One way to "resee" an evaluation is to plunge under its surface to see the criteria and assumptions underneath. Jesse works from an assumption that a film that has the feel and look of a familiar video game is a good film. But why? To make his evaluation more compelling to readers, when Jesse revises, he should probably explain that assumption.

Consider starting your rewrite by thinking about the criteria and assumptions behind the judgments you make. Which need to be explicitly addressed because an audience might not agree with them?

Polishing. Shaping focuses on things such as purpose, meaning, and overall design and structure. No less important is polishing—looking more closely at paragraphs, sentences, and words. Are your paragraphs coherent? How do you manage transitions? Are your sentences fluent and concise? Are there any errors in spelling or syntax? The section of Chapter 14 called "Problems with Clarity and Style" on page 542 can help you focus on these issues.

Before you finish your draft, work through the following checklist:

✓ Every paragraph is about one thing.

✓ The transitions between paragraphs aren't abrupt.

✓ The lengths of sentences vary in each paragraph.

✓ Each sentence is concise. There are no unnecessary words and phrases.

✓ You've checked grammar, particularly verb agreement, run-on sentences, unclear pronouns, and misused words (*there/their, where/were,* and so on).

✓ You've run your spellchecker and proofed your paper for misspelled words.

Chapter 14 has strategies to help you solve all kinds of revision problems, large and small. Use the "Guidelines: Revising Your Work" below to know where to look in that chapter to both shape and tighten your draft.

Guidelines: Revising Your Work

A first effort is almost never a best effort. To make sure your essay is really your best work, check out Chapter 14 for help with these questions:

- What is my paper really about? (See p. 518.)

- What am I really trying to say? (See p. 523.)

- Do I have enough convincing evidence? (See p. 530.)

- Does this paper move logically and smoothly from paragraph to paragraph? (See p. 534.)

- Are the sentences and paragraphs in this paper too choppy or hard to follow? (See p. 542.)

▶ Student Essay

Earlier in the chapter, you saw Laura Burns's sketch, a review of the Charlize Theron film *Young Adult*. Here you can see Laura's next draft. Her positive evaluation of the film is nicely captured by the title she chose and the punchy prose that follows it. Like a lot of reviews, "How Not to Feel Good and Feel Good About It" depends on a strong writing voice, and Laura's celebration of "unlikeable people making poor life choices from which they don't learn a thing" is easy to read, even if you don't agree with it. She's added images, too, which makes the essay easy on the eyes.

How to Not Feel Good and Feel Good About It

A Review of *Young Adult*

Laura Burns

1   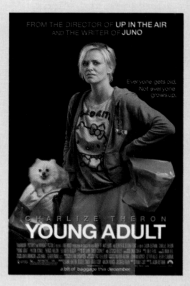 Charlize Theron is certainly one of the most beautiful women in film. High, smooth cheekbones, long, thin legs, and a delicate nose set at the center of a perfectly proportioned face. This considered, it's remarkable how ugly she can get.

2   *Young Adult* is a movie about unlikeable people making poor life choices from which they don't learn a thing. Theron plays Mavis Gary, an ex-prom queen from Mercury, Minnesota, making her living in the "Miniapple" (as the Mercurians call Minneapolis) as the ghostwriter of a formerly popular teen book series. From the first sequence of the film, we can tell that Mavis is a mess. She gets wasted, slumps around her apartment in sweats, and guzzles Diet Coke in a way that almost gave me heartburn. Upon receiving a birth announcement email from her now-married ex-prom king beau, the aptly named Buddy (the similarly beautiful Patrick Wilson), Mavis decides to pop an old mix tape into her dirty Mini Cooper and go home to Mercury to win him back.

3   This is, essentially, the entire plot of *Young Adult*. Mavis' trip back to Mercury is a kind of *anti-hero's* journey. On her first night in town, getting wasted in a local dive, she meets her guide, Matt (the wonderful Patton Oswalt), a former classmate who remains crippled from a high school assault by jocks who mistakenly thought he was gay. Through the course of the film, as she reunites with her parents (Jill Eikenberry & Richard Bekins), insinuates herself into the lives of Buddy and his wife Beth (Elizabeth Reaser), and gets plastered on Matt's home-brewed bourbon, rather than moving towards revelation, Mavis seems to retreat further and further into her past.

4   Unlike writer Diablo Cody's most well-known and Oscar-winning screenplay *Juno, Young Adult* rejects preciousness in favor of obscenity. It's difficult to make a film about terrible people enjoyable, but Cody injects just enough silliness to keep us from feeling too badly. Director Jason Reitman (who also paired with Cody on *Juno*) wisely keeps us focused on Mavis through every moment, from the night out to the morning after, and both Theron and Oswalt are brave enough to let us into their characters' grimy inner selves. Smartly, Cody refuses to manufacture empathy for her characters, leaving us to boldly accept the ugliness of these people fully.

(continued)

I don't doubt that *Young Adult* will displease many movie-goers who are used to redemptive stories and characters who, as *Salon* put it are "good at heart." Cody refuses to indulge that expectation. When Mavis dresses to go out and drink (which is often), Theron's extraordinary physical beauty is obvious. Yet we're never allowed to shake that Mavis is truly ugly at her core— an effective subversion of expectation that is the reason this memorable performance works. This isn't a feel-good film, and thank goodness. If Cody and Reitman had tried, I think we might leave the theater feeling worse.

5

Young Adult is writer Diablo Cody's most mature work yet.

Evaluating the Essay

1. As I've already mentioned, reviews often thrive on the persona—and the voice—of the reviewer. I think Laura has a strong persona in this review. The question is, how is persona communicated in a piece such as this one? What exactly would you point to in her review that reflects an individual voice and character?

2. Describe the structure of Laura's review. Diagram it using the elements of a review: description, back story, judgment, reasons, evidence, and criteria.

Using What You Have Learned

Let's revisit the list from the beginning of this chapter of things I hoped you'd learn about this form of writing.

1. **Use reasons and evidence to support a judgment about something's value.** Even if you never write another review (although I'm guessing you probably will because evaluative writing is so common), this chapter has introduced you to the basics of argument. In the next two chapters, you'll see how judgments (or claims), reasons, and evidence figure into all kinds of persuasive writing. Of course, it's not news that judgments are supported by reasons and evidence, but now you can think about these things more systematically and, as a result, have tools to analyze not only your own arguments but the arguments of others.

2. **Identify the criteria behind a judgment and determine their relevance.** In a review, we make assumptions about what makes something "good," and these assumptions are often unexamined. In Chapter 7, "Writing an Argument," you'll see that assumptions can make or break an argument. Knowing to look for assumptions will give you a strong footing when analyzing any argument.

3. **Identify the characteristics of different forms of the review, including academic applications.** Reviews aren't written about just books and films. They are a method of evaluating virtually anything. Whenever you are asked to evaluate something—a professor, a proposal, a methodology, even an argument—you can apply the skills you practiced here.

4. **Use invention and focusing strategies to discover and develop a review essay.** One of the biggest challenges in academic writing (and much other writing) is focusing your topic. In this chapter, you practiced a skill you can apply in nearly any paper you write: how to see your topic *in context*, recognizing its place in an ever-larger scheme of things (remember the inverted pyramid?). Use this skill to imagine how any topic can be divided and subdivided to find a frame that is appropriate for your purpose.

5. **Apply revision strategies that are effective for shaping reviews.** In Chapter 4, you applied revision strategies that helped you build an essay around an idea by seeing it through a person. In this chapter, you did something similar, except instead of a profile, you wrote about a thing. What's different, however, is that your review used a wider range of evidence, and this required you to cast a wider net for information as you revised. This is a skill that you'll build on in the next assignments, as you write more and more using outside sources.

6

Writing a Proposal

Learning Objectives

In this chapter, you'll learn to

6.1 Describe a problem of consequence, framing it narrowly enough to explore convincing solutions.

6.2 Identify the wide range of rhetorical situations that might call for a proposal argument.

6.3 Argue effectively for both the seriousness of the problem and the proposed solutions, using strong evidence.

6.4 Use appropriate invention strategies to discover and develop a proposal topic.

6.5 Apply revision strategies that are effective for a proposal.

Writing About Problems and Solutions

Several students sit around the table in my office. We're talking about problems each of us would love to solve. "I've got a short story due at three this afternoon and I've only written three pages," says Lana. Everyone nods sympathetically. "I'd really like to feel better about work," confides Amy, who works as a chef at a local restaurant. "Most days I just don't want to go." Margaret is a history major, familiar with the making and unmaking of nations and other grand narratives of colonialism, war, and social change. Her problem, however, is a bit more local. "I can't get my boyfriend to clean up the apartment," she says.

"What about you?" they ask me.

"The problem I most want to solve today is how to avoid getting scalded in the shower when someone in my house flushes the toilet," I say, getting into the spirit of things.

This conversation had not gone quite the way I expected. I know these students are socially engaged, politically aware, and academically gifted people. When I asked about problems that need solutions, I expected that they might mention local issues such as housing developments that threaten the foothills, the difficulty that nontraditional students have adjusting to the university, or budget cuts that threaten the availability of courses next semester. If they had been thinking on a larger scale—say, nationally or even internationally—perhaps the conversation would have turned to the federal deficit or the conflict in Darfur. Of course, I hadn't asked them to suggest social or economic problems. I had simply asked them what problems most vexed them at the moment.

I should not have been surprised that these problems involved boredom with work, too little time, and a messy boyfriend. These problems are quite real, and they demand attention, *now*. One was easy to solve. Lana would carve out extra time in the afternoon to finish her story—"I already know what I need to do," she said. But Amy and Margaret saw their respective problems—disenchantment with work and a boyfriend who's a slob—not so much as problems to solve as realities they had to live with. In fact, all the students admitted that they rarely look at the world from the perspective of problem solving—the perspective that's at the heart of a proposal.

"What if you did?" I asked.

"Then I guess I'd ask myself if there was an opportunity to learn something," said Amy.

Problems of Consequence

6.1

Describe a problem of consequence, framing it narrowly enough to explore convincing solutions.

While not all problems are equally solvable, the process of seeking and proposing solutions can be rewarding if you see, as Amy did, the opportunity to learn. There's another motivation, too: If the problem is shared by others, whatever you discover may interest them. Part of the challenge is recognizing problems *of consequence*. What makes a problem consequential?

1. It potentially affects a number of people.
2. There may be multiple solutions and people disagree about which is best.

> While not all problems are equally solvable, the process of seeking and proposing solutions can be rewarding if you see it as an opportunity to learn.

My problem with getting scalded in the shower if somebody flushes a toilet is clearly not consequential; all I need to do is go to Ace Hardware and buy a device for the showerhead. But what about Margaret's problem with her boyfriend? Is that a problem of consequence? Undoubtedly there are lots of people with messy mates, the solution is not at all obvious (just ask Margaret), and there are likely multiple ways of dealing with the problem.

If a problem is consequential, it's likely that someone has said something about it. Like many other forms of inquiry, problem solving usually requires some research. An important consideration, then, is whether others have said something about the problem that might help us think about the best ways to solve it. On a quick search of the web and several library databases, Margaret found some material that she thought could serve as background for an essay that looks at the problem of a messy mate and proposes some solutions. While Margaret may not succeed in getting her boyfriend to pick up his socks, she will probably learn a few things about how to deal with the problem.

Problems of Manageable Scale

You can't write about solving the problem of radical Islam in five pages. But you probably can write about the potential of reconciliation projects between Sunni and Shiite Muslims in Iraq. Basically, you can't write in five or even twenty pages about how to solve a big problem—there's just too much territory to cover—so an early step in this process is to keep shaving away at your topic until it's a manageable size. You might start by thinking about your topic this way:

- Who's involved? Who are the key actors?
- Why is this a problem? What are some of the causes?
- Where is this a problem? Are there specific places that dramatize either the problem or the solution?
- What are some of the solutions people have already proposed?

Use each of these questions on a subject as you might use a knife to carve a block of wood. The shavings offer potentially workable *pieces* of a larger problem that you can write about. For example, you might localize the problem, or focus on just one of the key actors or proposed solutions.

In other words, when you are choosing a problem to explore in a proposal, the *manageable scale* of the problem is as important as its consequentiality.

Motives for Writing a Proposal

Quite simply, people write proposals to try to argue convincingly to others that a problem is worth tackling and a proposed solution is a good way to tackle it. Your motives for writing a proposal will probably include the following:

- *You care about the problem.* Whether it's something in your personal life (avoiding procrastination, having a more obedient dog, or finding a way to use less water in the garden) or a public issue (protecting bicyclists from traffic, increasing neighborhood police protection, or battling adolescent obesity), you should feel that the problem deserves your attention.

- *You hope to change something.* Writing a proposal is a way of overcoming powerlessness. Maybe you feel helpless about the daily deluge of scammers and junk messages in your e-mail. You can just complain about it. I do. But you can also research a proposal that might help you—and the many others affected by the problem—to avoid the Nigerian scammers who want to "give" you $8.5 million if you just send them a copy of your passport and $1,750.

- *You hope to learn something.* A proposal is like all other inquiry projects: You choose a topic because you're motivated to discover things you don't know. This motive alone isn't sufficient, of course. Others must be affected by the problem and have a stake in considering your solution. But if the problem is sufficiently complex and the solutions varied enough, then you stand to learn a lot.

> Writing a proposal is a way of overcoming powerlessness.

The Proposal and Academic Writing

Numerous academic situations call for proposal writing and, more generally, writing to solve problems. Here are some such situations you might come across in classes you take:

- The case-study approach, popular in business, medicine, and some social sciences, is essentially the presentation of a real-world problem for you to solve.

- Problem-based learning is an approach to inquiry common in the sciences that begins with a messy problem and involves learners in coming up with tentative solutions.

6.2
Identify the wide range of rhetorical situations that might call for a proposal argument.

- In some classes, you'll be asked to write proposals. For example, political science courses may include an assignment to write a policy proposal or an essay that looks at a specific public policy problem—say, the organization of the city government or the state's role in wolf management (a big issue here in Idaho)—and suggests some possible solutions. In a marketing class, you might be asked to draft a proposal for dealing with a particular management problem.

Academics in many disciplines write research proposals. These identify a question and then propose a plan for studying it (see "Inquiring into the Details: Writing a Research Proposal"). The research question may relate to a problem (air pollution inversions in the valley, energy inefficiencies in buildings, and so on) or simply to a topic that could be useful to study (use of iPads in the classroom or the effects of birth order). To get grants for their research, academics usually need to submit proposals.

Inquiring into the Details

Writing a Research Proposal

A research proposal is a kind of action plan that explains your research question, what you expect might be the answer, how your investigation will contribute to what has already been said on the topic, and how you will proceed.

While the format varies, most research proposals aim to persuade readers that (1) the project is reasonable given the investigator's time and resources, (2) the research question or problem is significant, and (3) the researcher has a good plan for getting the job done.

The following elements are typically included in a research proposal:

- *Title:* Short and descriptive.

- *Abstract:* A brief statement of what you intend to do, including your research question and hypothesis, if you've got one.

- *Background or context:* Why is the project worth doing? What problem does it solve, or how does it advance our understanding of the subject? This key section establishes where your question fits into the ongoing conversation about your topic in your class, in the academic literature, or both. You also want to demonstrate that you've done your homework—you've got a handle on the relevant literature on your topic and understand how you might build on it.

- *Methodology or research design:* How will you try to answer your research question? How will you limit your focus? What information will you need to gather, and how will you gather it?

- *Results:* This isn't a common section of proposals in the humanities, but it certainly is in the sciences. How will you analyze the data you collect?

- *References or works cited:* Almost all research proposals, because they review relevant literature, include a bibliography. Sometimes you may be asked to annotate it (see Appendix B, "The Annotated Bibliography").

Because the research proposal is a persuasive document, craft it to keep your reader engaged: Find a good balance between generalities and detail, avoid jargon, and demonstrate your curiosity and eagerness to pursue your question.

Features of the Form

Feature	Conventions of the Proposal
Inquiry questions	What is the problem? What should be done?
Motives	You hope to change a problem related to something that matters to you and others, and there is the potential that you will learn something about the problem and possible solutions.

Feature	Conventions of the Proposal
Subject matter	Proposals suggest a best plan of action on any problem of consequence. Proposals could address large problems (the homeless problem in town) or small ones (a boyfriend who doesn't take dirty dishes seriously), as long as others have a stake in solving the problem. Research proposals suggest a plan for studying a problem or other issue.
Structure	Proposals typically address both the problem and the solution, in that order, but may emphasize one or the other. When an audience largely agrees that the problem is significant, a proposal might focus on the solution. When there is disagreement about the significance of the problem, a proposal might focus on why the problem needs attention. Other elements of a proposal include: • *Causes and effects.* These can help establish why the problem needs attention and why the proposed solution will deal with the problem. • *Justifications.* Typically proposals that argue for certain solutions over others offer clear reasons why the proposed solutions are the best ones. • *Evidence.* Evidence from research and experience makes a case for the problem and for the solutions. • *Other perspectives.* If you're writing about a problem of consequence, then other people have said something about it and probably have proposed various solutions. • *Visual rhetoric.* Often, problems and/or solutions can be illustrated with pictures, tables, and graphs; headings and bulleted lists can also be useful.
Sources of information	Writers who have experience with a problem should tap that experience in a proposal. However, if they're not experts, then personal experience alone may not be persuasive evidence. Proposals usually depend on information from research—reading or interviews—on what people who *are* experts on the problem say about it.
Language	Proposals are a form of argument. As with other arguments, the language you use depends largely on the rhetorical situation. Formal proposals intended for an expert audience, such as research or marketing proposals, take a formal tone. Others—for example, a proposal that's a letter to the editor or a blog entry—are much more casual and even personal.

Prose+

The nonprofit group Bluewater Baltimore, formed to prevent pollution in the city's watershed, adopts a "holistic" solution to the problem, one that combines local activism, stream monitoring, and advocacy. That's a pretty abstract idea, until it's captured in a "How We Work" graphic, which you can see below. One way to read this image is as a story, something that seems especially relevant to proposals, since like proposals narrative is about causes and effects. Try analyzing the image as a story: What is the significant event? Who are the characters? How is the rising action and resolution visually represented? How is the image organized in relation to time?

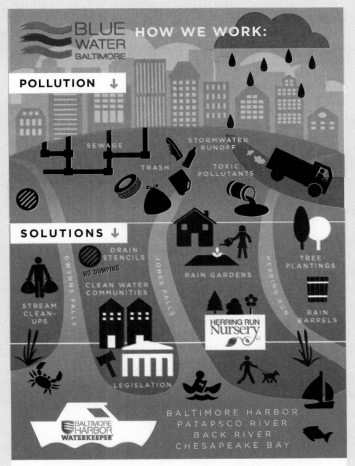

Courtesy of Blue Water Baltimore. WWW.BLUEWATERBALTIMORE.COM.

READINGS

▶ Proposal 1

I teach at a university with a football team that is frequently ranked in the top twenty-five nationally. Our stadium's blue turf is more famous than any one of our academic programs, prompting the university's marketing folks to coin the slogan "Beyond the Blue." In other words, we just want you to know that there is actually teaching and research going on here, not just football. And yet, the games are fun, and the athletic program is the strongest link the university has to the community. The sale of sports paraphernalia—hats, t-shirts, bobble-heads, and dog collars emblazoned with the school colors—funds student scholarships. Is college football really a problem? Buzz Bissinger thinks so. He notes that these are often hugely expensive programs that hemorrhage money in a time of endless tuition hikes. The solution: Ban college football.

Why College Football Should Be Banned

Buzz Bissinger

1 In more than 20 years I've spent studying the issue, I have yet to hear a convincing argument that college football has anything do with what is presumably the primary purpose of higher education: academics.

2 That's because college football has no academic purpose. Which is why it needs to be banned. A radical solution, yes. But necessary in today's times.

3 Football only provides the thickest layer of distraction in an atmosphere in which colleges and universities these days are all about distraction, nursing an obsession with the social well-being of students as opposed to the obsession that they are there for the vital and single purpose of learning as much as they can to compete in the brutal realities of the global economy.

4 Who truly benefits from college football? Alumni who absurdly judge the quality of their alma mater based on the quality of the football team. Coaches such as Nick Saban of the University of Alabama and Bob Stoops of the University of Oklahoma who make obscene millions. The players themselves don't benefit, exploited by a system in which they don't receive a dime of compensation. The average student doesn't benefit, particularly when football programs remain sacrosanct while tuition costs show no signs of abating as many governors are slashing budgets to the bone.

5 If the vast majority of major college football programs made money, the argument to ban football might be a more precarious one. But too many of them don't—to the detriment of academic budgets at all too many schools. According to the NCAA, 43 percent of the 120 schools in the Football Bowl Subdivision lost money on their

programs. This is the tier of schools that includes such examples as that great titan of football excellence, the University of Alabama at Birmingham Blazers, who went 3-and-9 last season. The athletic department in 2008–2009 took in over $13 million in university funds and student fees, largely because the football program cost so much, *The Wall Street Journal* reported. New Mexico State University's athletic department needed a 70% subsidy in 2009–2010, largely because Aggie football hasn't gotten to a bowl game in 51 years. Outside of Las Cruces, where New Mexico State is located, how many people even know that the school has a football program? None, except maybe for some savvy contestants on "Jeopardy." What purpose does it serve on a university campus? None.

The most recent example is the University of Maryland. The president there, Wallace D. Loh, late last year announced that eight varsity programs would be cut in order to produce a leaner athletic budget, a kindly way of saying that the school would rather save struggling football and basketball programs than keep varsity sports such as track and swimming, in which the vast majority of participants graduate.   6

Part of the Maryland football problem: a $50.8 million modernization of its stadium in which too many luxury suites remain unsold. Another problem: The school reportedly paid $2 million to buy out head coach Ralph Friedgen at the end of the 2010 season, even though he led his team to a 9-and-4 season and was named Atlantic Coast Conference Coach of the Year. Then, the school reportedly spent another $2 million to hire Randy Edsall from the University of Connecticut, who promptly produced a record of 2-and-10 last season.   7

In an interview with the *Baltimore Sun* in March, Mr. Loh said that the athletic department was covering deficits, in large part caused by attendance drops in football and basketball, by drawing upon reserves that eventually dwindled to zero. Hence cutting the eight sports.   8

This is just the tip of the iceberg. There are the medical dangers of football in general caused by head trauma over repetitive hits. There is the false concept of the football student-athlete that the NCAA endlessly tries to sell, when any major college player will tell you that the demands of the game, a year-round commitment, makes the student half of the equation secondary and superfluous. There are the scandals that have beset programs in the desperate pursuit of winning—the University of Southern California, Ohio State University, University of Miami, and Penn State University among others.   9

I can't help but wonder how a student at the University of Oregon will cope when in-state tuition has recently gone up by 9% and the state legislature passed an 11% decrease in funding to the Oregon system overall for 2011 and 2012. Yet thanks to the largess of Nike founder Phil Knight, an academic center costing $41.7 million, twice as expensive in square footage as the toniest condos in Portland, has been built for the University of Oregon football team.   10

Always important to feed those Ducks.   11

(continued)

(*continued*)

12   I actually like football a great deal. I am not some anti-sports prude. It has a place in our society, but not on college campuses. If you want to establish a minor league system that the National Football League pays for—which they should, given that they are the greatest beneficiaries of college football—that is fine.

13   Call me the Grinch. But I would much prefer students going to college to learn and be prepared for the rigors of the new economic order, rather than dumping fees on them to subsidize football programs that, far from enhancing the academic mission instead make a mockery of it.

Inquiring into the Essay

1. **Explore.** Here's a sampling of assertions from Bissinger's essay:

    - "College football has no academic purpose."
    - The beneficiaries of college football aren't the students, the athletes, or the school but coaches who pull in salaries in the millions.
    - The vast sums invested in coaches, stadiums, and training facilities often end up being a drain on universities' budgets. This is especially objectionable in an age of tuition increases.

    Choose one of these assertions (or another from the essay you'd like to write about) and fastwrite for five minutes, exploring your own thinking about the claim. If you can, write about what you observe on your own campus.

2. **Explain.** Follow up on your fastwrite in the last step by composing a summary of your own thinking about Bissinger's proposal to ban college football.

3. **Evaluate.** One of Bissinger's key claims is that college football programs often lose big money, and as evidence he cites the NCAA, which reported that 43 percent of the schools in the Football Bowl Subdivision were in the red. Using your own research, evaluate that claim.

4. **Reflect.** A proposal is an argument: There is a problem, here are some solutions, and this is evidence that makes these solutions credible. It's never that simple, of course. For one thing, you have to secure audience agreement that there is a problem in the first place, and if your audience agrees, then there are many possible solutions. Why yours? Finally, some evidence is better than other evidence, and there is the issue of what you *don't* say. Is there a counterargument? Is there inconvenient evidence you ignore? With all this in mind, how would you evaluate Bissinger's proposal that college football should be banned?

▶ Proposal 2

Okay, so this isn't the most scintillating reading, but the topic is certainly relevant to anyone in college, and it's a useful model of the basic elements of many proposals. The problem, of course, is obvious to anyone who has hung around young people clutching red plastic cups: the epidemic of alcohol abuse on college campuses. What might be done? The National Institute on Alcohol Abuse and Alcoholism, drawing on a range of studies, offers a series of recommendations, but first, the author establishes the significance of the problem with a bulleted list of fairly startling facts about college drinking. The recommendations follow, listed in order of relevance to the problem *and* strength of the support from various studies. When writing a proposal, it's easy to think that you're charged with coming up with the *one* best solution. This proposal takes another approach, offering a range of recommendations, but grading each in terms of its potential effectiveness.

Preventing Alcohol-Related Problems on College Campuses—Summary of the Final Report of the NIAAA Task Force on College Drinking

Robert F. Saltz, Ph.D.

College administrators and their prevention staff face numerous challenges when attempting to reduce the prevalence and severity of alcohol consumption and alcohol-related harm on their campuses. For example, drinking, and particularly binge drinking have been shown to be pervasive and persistent behaviors among college students (Wechsler et al. 2000). In addition, until a few years ago research assessing the effectiveness of various prevention approaches in the college setting was scarce, making it difficult to identify effective measures. In recent years, however, several studies have looked more closely at approaches to preventing college drinking. For example, Dowdall and Wechsler (2002), Borsari and Carey (2001), Perkins (2002*a*), and Berkowitz (2004) reviewed or analyzed prevention approaches among college populations. Another important contribution was the final report from the National Institute on Alcohol Abuse and Alcoholism (NIAAA) Task Force on College Drinking (NIAAA 2002), which reviewed epidemiological and intervention research on college drinking and issued recommendations for prevention strategies. This article describes the motivation for focusing on college student drinking and summarizes the Task Force's findings and recommendations.

Why Target College Student Drinking?

Given the all-too-common reports in the press of occasional tragic deaths and of mass celebrations or riots among college students that are accompanied by alcohol consumption, the answer to this question may seem obvious. But these singular events do

(continued)

(continued)

not accurately reflect the actual prevalence of death and injury associated with alcohol use among college students. Based on epidemiological data from a variety of sources, Hingson and colleagues (2002) generated the following estimates of the consequences of college student drinking:

- More than 1,400 college students die annually in alcohol-related events, primarily traffic crashes.
- More than 2 million college students (of a total of 8 million) occasionally drive under the influence of alcohol, and more than 3 million students ride with a drinking driver.
- More than 500,000 students annually suffer unintentional injury under the influence of alcohol.
- More than 600,000 students annually are hit or assaulted by another student who has been drinking.

3   In addition to these acute consequences of drinking, evidence suggests that alcohol consumption can lead to longer term cognitive impairment (Spear 2002; White 2003).

4   The college environment itself (specifically, such factors as peer influence and alcohol availability) may contribute to college students' risk of alcohol-related harm. O'Malley and Johnston (2002) found that although college-bound high school students drink less than their peers, their alcohol consumption surpasses that of their noncollege peers during the college years, only to decrease again after they finish college. In light of these observations, drinking among college students deserves special attention.

The NIAAA Task Force on College Drinking

5   The NIAAA Task Force on College Drinking commissioned several review papers on various aspects of drinking among college students (e.g., drinking patterns and consequences of alcohol consumption). (These reviews are available at www.collegedrinkingprevention.gov.) With respect to prevention research, however, the Task Force found that studies evaluating prevention approaches focused mostly on interventions aimed at individual student drinkers rather than on interventions aimed at entire college populations (i.e., universal interventions).

6   The Task Force's findings regarding the efficacy of individual-level interventions have been reviewed and summarized by Larimer and Cronce (2002), who distinguish between educational or awareness programs, cognitive-behavioral interventions, and motivational enhancement techniques. With one or two exceptions, this review found little evidence to support the effectiveness of purely educational or awareness programs. Newer approaches combining provision of information with other components, such as motivational enhancement, await evaluation and may be found to be more successful.

7   Cognitive-behavioral skills training programs attempt to teach skills relevant to moderating alcohol consumption, including those specific to drinking (e.g., monitor-

ing one's consumption or gauging one's blood alcohol levels) and more general life skills, such as stress management. These programs also can include components such as clarification of values, information, and/or education.

One cognitive-behavioral approach focuses on identifying students' expectancies regarding alcohol's effects, because studies have shown that a substantial portion of alcohol's effects is attributable to such expectancies rather than to alcohol's physiological effects.[*] Research indicates that focusing on expectancies impacts the drinking behavior of students, particularly males.   8

Larimer and Cronce (2002) concluded that the most promising interventions incorporate several components, such as training in drinking skills and life skills, self-monitoring, and challenges to students' expectancies.   9

Brief interventions—which include alcohol information, skills training, and personalized, nonjudgmental feedback to enhance motivation to change—can be effective in both individual and group formats.   10

NIAAA Task Force Recommendations

The NIAAA Task Force summarized its findings and recommendations in a comprehensive report (NIAAA 2002). At the time the report was written, the interventions described above represented nearly all that had been rigorously evaluated with college students. However, the Task Force expanded the scope of the recommendations by including universal prevention efforts that had been evaluated in other community settings and could reasonably be extended to college settings as well as those already adopted by some colleges without being formally tested. The recommendations were organized in four "tiers" based on both the interventions' relevance to college student drinking and the degree to which they are supported by empirical evidence. Although this classification is not universally accepted and may have to be modified in response to more recent research, it can help college administrators and researchers to choose the most promising approaches.   11

Tier 1   Based on the findings described in the previous section, the Tier 1 category included strategies that show evidence of effectiveness with college students, including: 12

- Combinations of cognitive-behavioral skills training with norms clarification and motivational enhancement interventions.
- Brief motivational enhancement interventions.
- Interventions challenging alcohol expectancies.

---

[*] "Alcohol expectancies" is a term often used in scholarship focused on problem drinking. It essentially means the set of beliefs someone has about alcohol's effects. For example, drinkers with social anxiety might believe that drinking with people will make it easier to be around them.

(continued)

(continued)

13 ***Tier 2***   This category includes strategies that research shows have been successful with general populations and could be applied to college settings, including efforts either to restrict the availability of alcohol or to create an environment supportive of such restrictions. These universal strategies are critical because alcohol-related harm to society can be attributed not only to the heaviest drinkers but also to the large numbers of light and moderate drinkers (Gruenewald et al. 2003). Tier 2 strategies could include approaches involving minimal legal drinking age (MLDA) laws (e.g., increased enforcement of MLDA laws) and other alcohol-related criminal and administrative measures such as:

- Implementation, increased publicity, and enforcement of laws to prevent alcohol-impaired driving.
- Restrictions on alcohol retail outlet density.
- Increased prices and excise taxes on alcoholic beverages.
- Responsible beverage service policies in social and commercial settings.
- Campus and community coalitions of all major stakeholders to implement these strategies effectively.

14   The Tier 2 interventions have not been evaluated on college campuses, at least in part because such measures are challenging to implement and studies are difficult to design. Efficacious community-level prevention interventions, such as the Massachusetts Saving Lives program (Hingson et al. 1996), Communities Mobilizing for Change on Alcohol (Wagenaar et al. 2000), and the Community Trials Project (Holder et al. 2000), however, can guide future college-based efforts.

15 ***Tier 3***   Tier 3 consists of strategies with logical and theoretical promise that require more comprehensive evaluation. These strategies could prove effective in future studies, and some already are highly regarded by prevention program professionals and college administrators. The Task Force Report suggested the following Tier 3 strategies:

- Marketing campaigns to correct student misperceptions of peer alcohol use, sometimes called "social norms marketing" or normative education (see Perkins 2002*b*). (This strategy already is widely used; evaluation reports will be available in the near future.)
- Consistent enforcement of campus alcohol policies.
- Provision of safe rides for students who drink too much to drive.
- Regulation of happy hour promotions.
- Information for new students and their parents about alcohol use and campus policies.
- Other strategies to address high-risk drinking, such as offering alcohol-free residence halls and social activities or scheduling classes on Fridays to reduce Thursday night parties.

16 ***Tier 4***   Tier 4 strategies include those with "evidence of ineffectiveness," such as simple educational or awareness programs used alone, without any other strategies or

components. The Task Force warned against the use of breathalyzers to give students information about their level of impairment, because this approach has produced negative results (i.e., students have used the information as a challenge to reach higher levels of intoxication).

Future Research and Applications

Although the NIAAA Task Force and others have identified some strategies to prevent college drinking, more research and evaluation are needed to identify more effective approaches for college administrators to add to their repertoire. Additional research needs to focus on how to implement successful universal campus or community interventions. Although researchers have achieved some successes in implementation (at least, judging from the positive examples of Tier 2 strategies), many of these interventions have not been subject to systematic research. Few researchers are developing measures of organizational or community "readiness" based on an underlying theory or hypothesis about what facilitates implementation (see Oetting et al. 1995). Nevertheless, developing general models of organizational or community change that are applicable to alcohol prevention is critically important to the design of reliable strategies that will keep college students safe from harm.

17

References

Berkowitz, A.D. *The Social Norms Approach: Theory, Research, and Annotated Bibliography.* Department of Education, Higher Education Center for Alcohol and Other Drug Abuse and Violence Prevention, 2004. Available online at: www.edc.org/hec/socialnorms/theory.html.

Borsari, B., and Carey, K. Peer influences on college drinking: A review of the research. *Journal of Substance Abuse* 13:391–424, 2001. PMID: 11775073

Dowdall, G.W., and Wechsler, H. Studying college alcohol use: Widening the lens, sharpening the focus. *Journal of Studies on Alcohol* (Suppl. 14):14–22, 2002. PMID: 12022719

Gruenewald, P.J.; Johnson, F.W.; Light, J.M.; et al. Understanding college drinking: Assessing dose response from survey self-reports. *Journal of Studies on Alcohol* 64:500–514, 2003. PMID: 12921192

Hingson, R.; McGovern, T.; Howland, J.; et al. Reducing alcohol-impaired driving in Massachusetts: The Saving Lives Program. *American Journal of Public Health* 86:791–797, 1996. PMID: 8659651

Hingson, R.; Heeren, T.; Zakocs, R.; et al. Magnitude of alcohol-related morbidity, mortality, and alcohol dependence among U.S. college students age 18–24. *Journal of Studies on Alcohol* 63:136–144, 2002. PMID: 12033690

Holder, H.D.; Gruenewald, P.J.; Ponicki, W.R.; et al. Effect of community-based interventions on high-risk drinking and alcohol-related injuries. *JAMA: Journal of the American Medical Association* 284:2341–2347, 2000. PMID: 11066184

(continued)

(continued)

Harimer, M., and Cronce, J. Identification, prevention and treatment: A review of in-dividual-focused strategies to reduce problematic alcohol consumption by col-lege students. *Journal of Studies on Alcohol* (Suppl. 14):148–163, 2002. PMID: 12022721

National Institute on Alcohol Abuse and Alcoholism (NIAAA). *A Call to Action: Chang-ing the Culture of Drinking at U.S. Colleges. Final Report of the Task Force on Col-lege Drinking.* NIH Pub. No. 02–5010. Rockville, MD: NIAAA, 2002.

O'Malley, P.M., and Johnston, L.D. Epidemiology of alcohol and other drug use among American college students. *Journal of Studies on Alcohol* (Suppl. 14):S23–S39, 2002. PMID: 12022728

Oetting, E.R.; Donnermeyer, J.F.; Plested, B.A.; et al. Assessing community readiness for prevention. *International Journal of the Addictions* 30:659–683, 1995. PMID: 7657396

Perkins, H.W. Surveying the damage: A review of research on consequences of alcohol misuse in college populations. *Journal of Studies on Alcohol* (Suppl. 14):91–100, 2002*a*. PMID: 12022733

Perkins, H.W. Social norms and the prevention of alcohol misuse in collegiate contexts. *Journal of Studies on Alcohol* (Suppl. 14):164–172, 2002*b*.PMID: 12022722

Spear, L.P. Adolescent brain and the college drinker: Biological basis of propensity to use and misuse alcohol. *Journal of Studies on Alcohol* (Suppl. 14):71–81, 2002. PMID: 12022731

Wagenaar, A.C.; Murray, D.M.; Gehan, J.P.; et al. Communities Mobilizing for Change on Alcohol: Outcomes from a randomized community trial. *Journal of Studies on Alcohol* 61:85–94, 2000. PMID: 10627101

Wechsler, H.; Lee, J.E.; Kuo, M.; and Lee, H. College binge drinking in the 1990s: A continuing problem. Results of the Harvard School of Public Health 1999 Col-lege Alcohol Study. *Journal of American College Health* 48:199–210, 2000. PMID: 10778020

White, A. Substance use and adolescent brain development: An overview of recent findings with a focus on alcohol. *Youth Studies Australia* 22:39–45, 2003.

Inquiring into the Essay

1. **Explore.** You've been on campus long enough to know that college stu-dents drink, and some drink excessively. Fastwrite about what you've seen, heard, or experienced, perhaps starting with one of your first encounters with the drinking scene at your school. Do you think this is an issue, and if so, what do you think should be done about it?

2. **Explain.** What is your takeaway from reading this report? Summarize what you believe to be the central argument. When doing so, try to use some of terms from the article, explaining them in a way that a nonexpert would understand them.

3. **Evaluate.** The report claims that "educational or awareness programs" directed at students have little effect on alcohol abuse. Do you agree or disagree? Why? Which of the recommendations here make the most sense to you?

4. **Reflect.** Like a lot of academic writing, this article uses terms that insiders in the area of scholarship wouldn't need defined: "alcohol expectancies" and " cognitive-behavioral approaches." The rest of us, who aren't experts, can feel befuddled when reading writing like this. Certainly you have had the experience of reading in a genre, like this one, that is unfamiliar to you, in a discourse that makes you feel like an outsider. How do you deal with this, especially when you need to read and try to understand it? What are your reading strategies?

Seeing the Form

A Problem in Pictures

When members of the San Francisco Bicycle Coalition (SFBC) wanted to dramatize the problem of insufficient space for bikes on a city commuter train, they did it with pictures. It was a powerfully simple idea. They took shots of three morning trains, each overloaded with bicycles and nearly empty of passengers. The contrast is obvious. And so is the solution to the problem: Add more space for bicycles on trains. A few months later, transit authorities did just that.

No Space for Bikes:
A photo study of trains bumping cyclists out of SF.

1: Train 134: Sept 22 9:07 AM   2: Train 134: Sept 22 9:07 AM

Seeing the Form (*continued*)

3: Train 230: Sept 24 8:53 AM

4: Train 230: Sept 24 8:53 AM

5: Train 332: Sept 30 8:56 AM

6: Train 332: Sept 30 8:56 AM

Submitted to JBP Oct 2
by Benjamin Damm

THE WRITING PROCESS

6.3
Argue effec-
tively for both
the seriousness
of the problem
and the proposed
solutions, using
strong evidence.

Inquiry Project **Writing a Proposal**

Inquiry questions: What is the problem? What should be done?

Write a proposal to help resolve a problem that you care about. Make sure your proposal does the following (see also the "Features of the Form" box on pp. 179–180 for typical features of proposals):

- Addresses a problem that is of consequence and of a manageable scale, including the problem's causes and effects.
- Provides evidence for the seriousness of the problem and for ways to solve it, justifying these solutions over alternative solutions. You can draw on your experience but should also use outside sources.
- Is appropriate in both form and content to your purpose and audience.
- Includes graphics if relevant.

Prose+

You can find additional ideas about multimodal approaches to your assignment as well as tips on how to understand the basics of mocking up and designing some of the following projects in Chapter 13, "Re-Genre."

Design a web page (see pp. 501–503) for your proposal that has the following features:

- Links to relevant sites that provide additional evidence or information on the problem and/or solution.
- At least one image or graphic.
- A boxed feature with additional information, suggestions, helpful summaries, key ideas, etc.

Turn your proposal into a radio documentary (see pp. 499–501). Rewrite the proposal around interview clips with people who are affected by the problem or who are trying to solve it. Tell a story.

Alternatively, use the San Francisco Bicycle Coalition's visual proposal (pp. 496–499) as inspiration and present your problem "in pictures." Consider, for example, producing a conference poster (see pp. 494–496).

What Are You Going to Write About?

The explosion of "how-to" and "self-help" books and articles is evidence of the popularity of writing that attempts to solve problems.

Perhaps you already have a topic in mind for your proposal. But if you don't, or you want to explore some other possibilities, begin by generating a list of problems you'd like to solve. Don't worry too much about whether they're problems of consequence or about whether you have solutions to the problems. Try some of the generating exercises that follow.

Opening Up

6.4

Use appropriate invention strategies to discover and develop a proposal topic.

Play with some ideas about subjects for the proposal assignment. Remember not to judge the material at this stage.

Listing Prompts. Lists can be rich sources of triggering topics. Let them grow freely, and when you're ready, use a list item as the focus of another list or an episode of fastwriting.

Open a Word document and make the following table (or jot down these headings in your journal). At the risk of totally ruining your day, brainstorm four lists of problems that you think need to be solved in four arenas: international, national, local, and personal. Jot down anything that comes to mind.

World problems
National problems
Local problems
Personal problems

Fastwriting Prompts. Write fast without stopping, and don't think too much about what you're going to say before you say it. Allow yourself to write "badly."

1. Pick any item from the preceding lists as a launching place for a five-minute fastwrite. Explore some of the following questions:

   ◼ When did I first notice that this is a problem? What, if any, is my experience with it?
   ◼ What's the worst part about it?
   ◼ What might be some of its causes?
   ◼ What moment, situation, or scene is most typical of this problem? Describe it as if you're experiencing it by writing in the present tense.
   ◼ How does this problem make me feel?
   ◼ What people do I associate with it?

2. Depending on how familiar you are with a problem that interests you, do a five-minute focused fastwrite that explores solutions, beginning with the sentence *I think one of the ways to deal with* _____ *is* _____. Follow that sentence as long as you can. When the writing stalls, use the following prompt: *Another possible solution to the problem of* _____ *might be* _____.

Visual Prompts. Only a few problems have a single root cause. Use the template in Figure 6.1 to begin thinking about some of the possible causes of a problem. Describe the problem in the middle circle and then build arrows to as many explanations of possible causes as come to mind.

Research Prompts. Reading, observing, and talking to people can be great ways to discover a proposal topic. The following research prompts can help you along.

1. Interview your classmates about what they think are the biggest problems facing them as students. Interview student or faculty leaders or administrators about what they think are the biggest problems facing the university community. Do the same with community leaders.

2. Design an informal survey targeted to a particular group that you're interested in—students, student-athletes, local businesspeople, sports fans, migrant workers, and so on. This group may or may not be one to which you belong. Discover what they believe are the most serious problems they face.

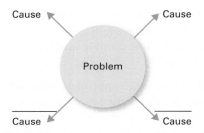

Figure 6.1 Exploring the possible causes of a problem

3. Become a student of a local newspaper. In particular, pay attention to the letters to the editor and the local community pages. What seems to be a recurrent problem that gets people's attention? Clip articles, letters, or editorials that address the problem.

4. Google the following phrase: "solution to the problem of." Scan the results for topic ideas.

Narrowing Down

Feeling a little overwhelmed? Seeing problems everywhere? It can be wearing to focus on what's wrong with your life, your university, and your community. But remember that your ultimate goal is to write a proposal that suggests ways these problems might be resolved. You may have already explored some of these solutions, but if you haven't, don't worry—you'll get the chance later. Begin by scrutinizing the material you generated for possible topics.

What's Promising Material and What Isn't?   We've talked about some initial judgments you can make. Now look at the material you generated in the fastwrites, lists, research, or clusters, and ask yourself which of the problems listed do you care about the most, or which are you most interested in? Once you've selected some tentative topics for your proposal, narrow them down using the following questions:

- *Does someone aside from you have a stake in finding a solution? Is there an identifiable audience for proposals about solutions?*
- *Is the problem a manageable one?*
- *Have other people said something about the problem and possible solutions?*
- *Which subject offers you the most opportunity for learning?*

Questions About Audience and Purpose.   This assignment asks you to craft a proposal appropriate to your audience and purpose. When you have identified an audience for your proposal, consider what exactly might be your purpose with respect to that audience. Do you want to:

- *Inform* them about the problem and explore possible solutions?
- *Advocate* certain solutions as the best ways to solve the problem?
- *Inform and advocate*, dramatizing the problem because your audience may not fully appreciate and understand it, and then persuading them to support the solutions you favor?

These purposes will shape your approach. And which purpose you choose will depend partly on how your audience already thinks and feels about the problem you're tackling and the solutions you offer. Use the chart in Figure 6.2.

Although it might be premature to decide on the *form* your proposal will take, sometimes an awareness of purpose and audience will suggest an appropriate

Awareness of the problem	If low, increase emphasis on dramatizing the problem.	If high, emphasize proposed solutions.
Initial disposition toward proposed solution	If favorably disposed, emphasize action that needs to be taken to implement solution. Emphasize *pathos* over *logos*.	If unfavorably disposed, offer balanced treatment of possible solutions before stating yours. Emphasize *logos* over *pathos*.
Attitude toward speaker	If positive, emphasize stronger action to solve the problem.	If negative, emphasize the views or experience speaker *does* share with audience.

Figure 6.2   Audience analysis chart. As with other forms of argument, the persuasiveness of a proposal depends on a rhetorical understanding of your audience. This is discussed in more detail in Chapter 7, where I introduce the rhetorical triangle, as well as *ethos, pathos*, and *logos* (see pp. 222–223 for a discussion of those terms). See if you can do a rhetorical analysis on your proposal, and use what you discover to revise your essay.

form. Ask yourself this question: Given the problem I'm writing about, which audiences are (1) most affected by it and (2) most likely to contribute to the solution? Next, think about how to best reach one or both of those audiences. For example, suppose that Cheryl's purpose is to advocate for a new nontraditional-student center on campus and her audience is school administrators. Her best approach for getting her message across might be to write her proposal in the form of a letter to the university's president.

Trying Out

Got a topic you want to try? Good. Let's do some focused work on that topic to generate some more material on it. Unless you've got a lot of personal experience with the problem you're considering writing about (and probably even if you do), you need to develop a working knowledge of the topic through some quick research.

Researching to Answer the *So What?* Question. To start with, you need to be able to establish that the problem you're interested in is significant. To do that, you'll need to answer a skeptic's question: *Okay, so what's the big deal about this?* That will be the focus of your initial research.

Using Google, Google Scholar, or library databases, find at least three sources online that show the significance of the problem you're interested in writing about. These sources may

a. Provide statistics or facts that suggest the seriousness of the problem.
b. Relate a story, case study, or anecdote about people who are affected by the problem.
c. Visually illustrate the effects of the problem.
d. Offer assertions by experts who are concerned with the problem.

Giving Your Answer on a PowerPoint. Using what you've learned, prepare a single PowerPoint slide that you would use to answer the question "So what's the big deal about this?" Figure 6.3 is a slide that one of my students, Andrea, developed to dramatize the problem of disappearing honeybees. While it isn't a very effective PowerPoint slide—there's too much text, for one thing—it's a really useful summary of the problem.

Use the material you generate from this exercise to help establish the significance of the problem in your sketch.

Writing the Sketch

Try out a tentative proposal topic by writing a sketch, a relatively brief early draft written with an audience in mind. Your sketch should:

- Have a tentative title.
- Use appropriate evidence (personal experience, facts, statistics, etc.) to dramatize the problem.
- Identify one or more causes of the problem and offer some tentative solutions for addressing those causes.
- Be written with an appropriate audience and purpose in mind.

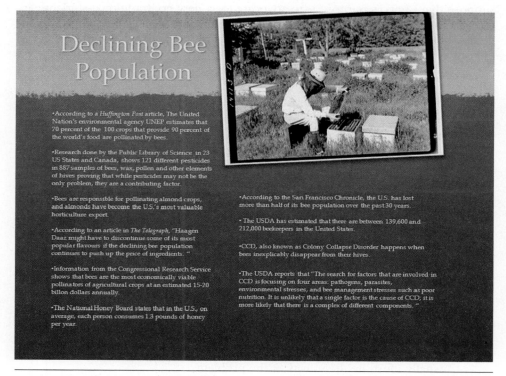

Figure 6.3 Develop a single PowerPoint slide like this one on the crash of bee populations to establish the significance of the problem you're writing about.

You might also develop this sketch in a form that you think would be particularly effective given your purpose and audience. Your sketch might be an essay or a letter, a PowerPoint, a podcast, a web page, or the text of a brochure or ad.

▶ Student Sketch

Loving and Hating Reality TV
Jenna Appleman

When I moved into my own apartment without TV or cable, I assumed I'd be watching much less television. My TV consumption had never been a problem—I'd watch *Law & Order* and HBO when I was home, but didn't follow very much else. I prided myself on watching intelligent television, avoiding the low-culture reality series with a sneer. But in the silence of a studio apartment in the busiest semester of my college career, I needed a way to fill the space and blow off some steam. That's when I started watching reality TV. 1

There are TV channels dedicated exclusively to reality programming. Bravo houses the various *Real Housewives* series (my gateway), as well as their many spinoffs, E! plays the various Kardashian series, and reality competition shows like *The Biggest Loser* and *The Bachelor* rake in thousands of viewers on primetime. Certainly such success is indicative of something, and there are those who would disagree with my assumptions, but I stand by my initial negative cast on the cultural saturation of reality TV. 2

Reality television is (theoretically) unscripted and unacted, removing thousands of paying jobs for writers and actors from the market. I also sense that such excessive exposure can be exploitative. One show I have guiltily watched on Lifetime called *Dance Moms* follows a team of very young competitive dancers, between the ages of 7 and 14. Surely having their emotional breakdowns and embarrassing parents on camera at that young age isn't helping their development. 3

And yet, I watch it. Frequently. But in public, I pretend I don't know the names of the Kardashians and roll my eyes wildly at front page news about the Housewives. For better or worse, I have grown accustomed to the comfort of curling up in bed with my cat and watching a marathon of *Millionaire Matchmaker* after an exhausting day. I watched an episode of *The Bachelor* while I was drafting this proposal, just to have some noise in the background to help me think. I want to hate it, but there's a lot about it I love. 4

I don't propose that we change the burgeoning culture of reality television entirely. That's far from realistic, and I have a feeling eventually this too will cycle out of popularity. But I do feel that I need to find a way to reconcile how I feel about reality TV with my penchant for it. The first step, I recognize, is admitting that I have a problem. 5

I don't propose that I stop watching reality television. But I do think it's important to clarify *why* I do—if it's to help me focus on schoolwork, that's a benefit. If I find it calming after a long day, that's okay too. But if I start watching because I simply *must* find out what's happening in these people's lives, if I begin to really stake weight in it, that's when I need a 6

(continued)

(*continued*)

reality check. If I can accept the reasons why, then I can start feeling less guilty about it. I also think I should make a point to also watch other television; the normal kind that employs actors and writers. It would also be good to try to utilize my gym membership and watch these "guilty pleasures" on the cardio machines' TVs while I'm actually doing something physical. I should also recognize the shows that I find particularly exploitative, and avoid them, or at least view them with an intelligent, critical eye in order to form an opinion.

Moving from Sketch to Draft

Return to the inquiry questions behind a proposal: *What is the problem? What should be done about it?* How well does your sketch answer those questions? Is the problem clear, and would a skeptical reader be convinced that it is serious enough to address? Based on what you know now, do the solutions make sense? Explore these considerations in the next section.

Evaluating Your Own Sketch. Proposal sketches, no matter what their form, usually need work in the following areas:

- *Refining the problem.* It's too big and needs to be more focused.
- *Insufficient evidence.* More research is required to establish the seriousness of the problem, identify key causes, and/or support proposed solutions.

For example, Jenna's sketch argued that people watch too much TV. Okay, but might that assertion be easier to write about if it were less general? Which people, exactly, watch too much TV? What do they watch too much of? Violent programs? Advertising? Reality TV? What is "too much"? And finally, what are the consequences of watching that much? All of these questions require research. Jenna might discover that the effects of TV watching are especially problematic for a certain age group, or that certain kinds of advertising—say, snack food commercials aimed at children—are particularly troublesome. So Jenna can refine his problem from "People watch too much TV" to something more focused like "Television commercials for high-calorie snack foods contribute to childhood obesity." Now, that's much easier to work with! Jenna's much clearer about the problem and its consequences, and can now focus his research.

See if you can refine the problem statement in your sketch in similar ways. "Wh" questions (who, which, what, where, when, why) can help you pare down a big problem to something more manageable. Use the example in Figure 6.4 as a guide, applying the "Wh" questions to the problem you discussed in your sketch. Then restate the problem as Jenna did, so that it's more specific.

Reflecting on What You Learned. The thing I like about sketches is that they are very early drafts—attempts, really—at trying out a topic without a huge investment of time. At least they're not supposed to be huge investments of time. But pretty often I have students who approach nearly every writing assignment as if it

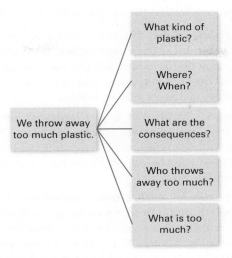

Figure 6.4   Using "Wh" questions to pare down a problem

requires "perfection" or who have such harsh internal critics that writing is always kind of painful and slow. For these students, sketches are no different. What about you? Do a journal entry in which you fastwrite for a few minutes about your experience writing this sketch. In particular, was it hard for you to accept that your sketch didn't meet your usual standards for writing something to hand in? What are your "usual standards," and do they get in the way of drafting and revising?

Developing

If you refined the problem you're exploring, stating it more clearly and concretely, then you've made it much easier to develop your draft. Developing your draft is a process that will require research.

Research. But what kind of research will you need to do? What are you looking for? The table below shows some key elements of proposals and questions to think about for each. Consider these questions as guides for your research.

Element	Questions for Research
Problem	What's the evidence that it's serious? Who does it affect and under what circumstances?
Effects and causes	What will happen if nothing is done? Why is it happening? Why does this matter?
Solutions	What should be done? How do these proposals address key causes and effects?

Where should you look to find the evidence to answer these questions?

- *Exploit local publications.* If you've chosen a topic of local interest, then sources such as the local daily newspaper, government reports, and university policies may be important sources for your proposal. Some of these sources, such as local newspapers and government documents, may be available in online databases at your library.

- *Interview experts.* In Chapter 4, you practiced interview skills. Here's a chance to put them to use again. One of the most efficient ways to collect information for your revision is to talk to people who have knowledge about the problem. These may be experts who have researched the problem or people who are affected by it.

- *Search for experiences with similar solutions elsewhere.* If your proposal calls for an education program on binge drinking, what other universities might have tried such a program? What were their experiences? Search for information using keywords that describe the problem you're writing about ("binge drinking"), and try adding a phrase that describes the solution ("binge drinking education programs"). Also check library databases that might lead you to articles in newspapers, magazines, and journals on the problem and its solutions.

A word of advice about solutions: Researching and thinking about solutions can be a bit like following a horse race: You might favor one solution until another one suddenly races up from behind as you learn more. In an inquiry project, that's normal. Make sure that the solutions you end up writing about are consistent with your own experience and with your values about the best ways to solve problems.

Focusing on the Justifications. In my part of the country, everyone has an opinion about wolves. Many people hate them. Wolf packs were reestablished in the West under the Endangered Species Act, and in recent decades wolves have extended their range well beyond the national parks and into ranching and agricultural areas. The problem is that some wolves kill livestock. What does one do with a wolf pack that won't stop killing sheep? Some popular solutions include: (1) Nothing—they were here first; (2) capture them and relocate them away from populated areas; (3) kill them.

Each of these solutions has problems of its own—and advocates and critics who will energetically argue over them. If you're working on an essay that focuses on a problem that affects people (and isn't that the definition of a problem?), then you will discover controversies over what to do about it. One thing your draft should not do is pretend that these controversies don't exist. On the contrary, your draft should not only justify the solutions you prefer, but also identify the solutions you've rejected and show why your solutions are better.

You've done some research on the problem and solutions. Develop your draft by focusing on the justifications for your solutions:

- Why are they the best solutions?
- How do they effectively address the causes and effects of the problem?

- What is evidence that they will work?
- What might critics say? Why are they wrong?

These *justifications* for your solutions will be a key part of your draft.

Drafting

As you think about how to organize your draft, consider some of the suggestions below.

Methods of Development. As mentioned earlier in the chapter, a proposal often moves from problem to solution, and some proposals, like the research proposal, need to follow a specific form. But if the form of your proposal has not been specified, you can organize it in a number of ways. One way to think about how to organize your draft is to imagine the questions typical readers of a proposal, or a problem-solution paper, might ask and the order in which they might ask them:

- What's the big deal?
- Who says it's a big deal besides you?
- What's at stake?
- What causes the problem? What are its effects?
- What solutions have other people proposed? Are they justified?
- Which solution do you prefer? How do you justify it?
- What are the potential problems with the solution you like?
- Why do you still like it?
- If we do this, is everything going to be okay? Is there anything you're asking us to do?

You might play with the order in which you deal with these questions in your draft, but you will likely have to address all of them somewhere.

Using Evidence. You will answer the preceding questions with evidence that you've gathered from research (reading, interviewing, observing) and experience. Like much else, the evidence you use depends on your intended audience. In other words, choosing the strongest evidence in a proposal is an exercise in audience analysis:

- How much does your audience know about the problem?
- Is your audience likely to favor your idea, oppose it, or have no opinion?
- What kind of evidence is most likely to convince your audience?

The *amount* of evidence you need to provide depends on whether your audience is likely to be predisposed to agree or disagree with the solutions you propose. Obviously, if readers will need convincing, you will need to offer more justification. The *types* of evidence you provide depend on your assessment of what your audience will be most likely to believe. The "Inquiring into the Details: Evidence—A Case Study" box gives you a chance to think about audience in choosing among types of evidence. As you compose your draft, consider who your readers will be and the kinds of evidence they will find most persuasive.

Workshopping

If your draft is subject to peer review, see Appendix A for details on how to organize workshop groups and decide on how your group can help you. To help you decide, use the guidance, starting on p. 554, in Appendix A. Each workshop type is described more fully in that section.

Because a proposal is a form of argument, your workshop is a chance to test its persuasiveness with readers. One key thing to consider before the session is how much your peers already know regarding the problem you're writing about. The less they know, the more work your draft needs to do in these areas:

1. Convince readers of the seriousness of the problem.

2. Provide a context for the problem: who's involved, who's affected, what's been tried, how long it's been going on, what will happen if nothing is done.

Inquiring into the Details

Evidence—A Case Study

Suppose a proposal argues that the university needs an alternative or independent film series. The proposal, in the form of a memo, is written to the Student Activities Board, a group of students who decide how to spend student fee money collected at registration. Which of the following types of evidence used to justify such a film series might be *most* persuasive to that audience?

1. The writer's personal enjoyment of foreign films.
2. A petition signed by 100 people who support the idea.
3. A quotation from Woody Allen about the educational and cultural virtues of independent films.
4. Information about the success of the independent film theater in town.
5. A quote from an English professor supporting the idea.
6. An estimate showing that the cost of renting five independent films is half the cost of renting the same number of Hollywood films.
7. A survey of 200 students that indicates 60 percent support the idea.
8. Data on good attendance at a similar series at another, larger university.

Do a quick audience analysis for your proposal topic. Who has the most at stake in solving the problem, and who can influence the solution? Then make a list of the types of evidence that would be most convincing to this audience.

Questions for Peer Reviewers	
1. Purpose	After reading the draft, what do you think is at stake? If nothing is done to solve the problem, what might be the consequences?
2. Meaning	In your own words, how does the essay answer the inquiry question *What should be done?* Play the doubting game for a moment: What potential problems do you see with the solution I'm proposing?

3. Persuade peers that your proposal is fair and reasonable. That means not only providing convincing evidence to support your solution, but also considering the arguments of critics of your approach.

In addition to these concerns, when you workshop the first draft of your proposal, you should focus on what peers make of the purpose and meaning of your essay, using their responses to guide your revision. The "Questions for Peer Reviewers" box can help you frame these questions for your workshop group.

Reflecting on the Draft. Following your workshop, make an entry in your journal that follows these prompts:

- If I were going to write this over again, the one thing I think I'd do would be....
- The most important thing I've learned so far about writing a proposal....
- The most difficult part of the process for me has been....
- The biggest question I have about the draft is....

Revising

Revision is a continual process—not a last step. You've been revising—"reseeing" your subject—from the first messy fastwriting in your journal. But the things that get your attention vary depending on where you are in the writing process. With your draft in hand, revision becomes your focus through what I'll call "shaping and tightening your draft."

6.5
Apply revision strategies that are effective for a proposal.

Chapter 14 contains strategies that can help you revise any inquiry project, and the "Guidelines: Revising Your Work" in this chapter on page 207 can help you locate these strategies. There are also certain things to think about that are especially useful for shaping a proposal.

Shaping. Shaping involves, among other things, arranging and rearranging information so that it is organized around the main idea or question.

Analyzing the Information One way to think about the structure of your proposal is to see the information you've collected as being in categories. In a proposal, remember that these categories typically include the categories shown in Figure 6.5.

This isn't a recipe for organizing your draft, but a way to look at whether you've included enough information in each category. One way to play around with the structure of your proposal is to use the "Frankenstein Draft" (Revision

Problem	Causes and Effects	Solutions and Justifications
What is it? Why is it important? What is at stake? Who's involved?	What causes it? What's the impact? What will happen? Why does it happen?	What should be done? Why is this the best solution?

Evidence	Other Perspectives
What are the facts? What do experts say? What are your experiences and observations?	What is the controversy? What do others propose? Who has a different perspective?

Figure 6.5 Structuring your review

Strategy 14.18 in Chapter 14). Cut up your draft with scissors into pieces that fall into the categories mentioned here—problem, solution, evidence, and so on—and then play with the order. Worry about transitions later.

Other Questions for Revision Proposal drafts also have some fairly typical weaknesses at this stage in the process, most of which can be addressed by repeating some of the steps in this chapter or selecting appropriate revision strategies in Chapter 14. Here are some questions to consider as you decide which of these strategies might be most helpful.

✓ Have you done enough to dramatize the problem if you're writing for an audience that may not be aware of it? Should you do more to establish how your readers have a stake in solving the problem?
✓ How well have you justified your solutions? Is there enough evidence? Is it appropriate evidence for your audience?
✓ Have you overemphasized one solution at the expense of the others? Would your proposal be more balanced and persuasive if you considered alternative solutions, even if you ultimately reject them?

Polishing. Shaping focuses on things such as purpose, meaning, and design. No less important is looking more closely at paragraphs, sentences, and words. Are your paragraphs coherent? How do you manage transitions? Are your sentences fluent and concise? Are there any errors in spelling or syntax? The section of Chapter 14 called "Problems with Clarity and Style" on page 542 can help you focus on these issues.

Before you finish your draft, work through the following checklist:

✓ Every paragraph is about one thing.
✓ The transitions between paragraphs aren't abrupt.
✓ The lengths of sentences vary in each paragraph.
✓ Each sentence is concise. There are no unnecessary words or phrases.
✓ You've checked grammar, particularly verb agreement, run-on sentences, unclear pronouns, and misused words (*there/their, where/were,* and so on).
✓ You've run your spellchecker and proofed your paper for misspelled words.

Chapter 14 has strategies to help you solve all kinds of revision problems, large and small. Use the "Guidelines: Revising Your Work" below to know where to look in that chapter to both shape and tighten your draft.

Guidelines: Revising Your Work

A first effort is almost never a best effort. To make sure your essay is really your best work, check out Chapter 14 for help with these questions:

- What is my paper really about? (See p. 518.)

- What am I really trying to say? (See p. 523.)

- Do I have enough convincing evidence? (See p. 530.)

- Does this paper move logically and smoothly from paragraph to paragraph? (See p. 534.)

- Are the sentences and paragraphs in this paper too choppy or hard to follow? (See p. 542.)

▶ Student Essay

Jenna watches reality TV and feels guilty about it. But that's not the problem that interests her. She can see the appeal of programs such as *American Idol*, and she'd like to continue to watch them from time to time, but she would really like to watch reality shows that follow an ethical code of conduct. Jenna proposes that reality TV producers agree to a code that would minimize the emotional and physical injuries inflicted on participants, which she thinks is a problem on many of the shows.

Avoidable Accidents: How to Make Reality TV Safer

Jenna Appleman

When I moved into my own apartment without TV or cable, I assumed I'd be watching much less television. My TV consumption had never been a problem—I'd watch *Law & Order* and HBO when I was home, but didn't follow very much else. I prided myself on watching intelligent television, avoiding the low-culture reality series with a sneer. But in the silence of a studio

(continued)

(continued)

apartment in the busiest semester of my college career, I needed a way to fill the space and blow off some steam. That's when I started watching reality TV.

2   There are TV channels dedicated exclusively to reality programming. Bravo houses the various *Real Housewives* series (my gateway), as well as their many spinoffs; E! plays the various Kardashian series; there are kid-centered shows like *Toddlers and Tiaras* on TLC and *Dance Moms* on Lifetime; and reality competition shows like *The Biggest Loser* and *The Bachelor* rake in thousands of viewers on prime time. Reality TV dominates American programming.

3   How dominant is it? According to the Nielson ratings for the week I'm writing this, seven of the top ten shows on cable were reality programs. *Jersey Shore* and *Pawn Stars* were one and two ("Top Tens"). On TV, *American Idol* is a perennial viewer favorite, often the most-watched program.

4   Yet my instinctive guilt about watching these shows is indicative of a pressing problem. "People are attracted to reality television because they know it has real consequences," said reality blurred editor Andy Dehnart. "You get the sense this is a real human being who could be hurt or injured" (Dehnart). And in August 2011, Russell Armstrong, the husband of Beverly Hills *Real Housewives'* Taylor Armstrong, committed suicide. While A[r]mstrong's suicide is an extreme example, injuries on reality TV programs are rampant. A brawl on *Survivor* in 2010 resulted in a dislocated shoulder and broken toe. In 2011, an athlete on the reality show *Jump City* fell doing a stunt and shattered his wrist. Injuries on shows like *So You Think You Can Dance* are common.

5   Not only are contestants injured but viewers "inspired" by the programs are also at risk. Recently, for example, the American Medical Association warned that viewers of the TV show *Extreme Makeover,* now off the air, might have had a distorted understanding of the risk of plastic surgery: "Heavily edited and selected scenes from reality TV have lulled the public into thinking there are no real risks or complications in these procedures. It's easy for viewers to forget that these are real people, who face the real risks—not just the benefits—of surgery" (216). All of this is a brash reminder that reality television is just that—*real*.

6   "These shows are Roman coliseums that we visit virtually," writes Matt Seitz of Salon. "Participants in contact sports have corner men and doctors on hand to nurse their wounds, and determine if they are fit enough to step in the ring in the first place." So, too, then, should the participants of reality television shows.

7   To lower the risks to participants and viewers of watching reality TV, I propose the following:

1. Possible candidates for a reality television show should be pre-screened, to ensure that they are fit emotionally and physically to withstand the rigors of a reality set.
2. Candidates with substance abuse, physical abuse, self-destructive behaviors, among others, would not be permitted to participate on the show *unless* they are provided with the following:
   a. Active counseling throughout the filming process
   b. Guaranteed after-care once filming ceases
   For example, *Hoarders* on A&E provides healthcare services during and after filming to the subjects it follows.
3. *All* participants should be provided with free after-care and counseling once filming wraps, for at least three months.
4. All participants should have immediate and total access to medical care, with the show absorbing all medical costs incurred during filming.

5. No footage of participants under the influence of alcohol should be used *if* the alcohol had been provided by producers.
6. Only non-incidental footage of minors should be used.
7. If a show focuses on minors (such as *Toddlers and Tiaras* and *Dance Moms*), counselors with training in adolescent and child psychology should be present during *all filming* and available to children before and after the conclusion of filming.
8. All participant contracts should be public.

An ethical code like this would admittedly be hard to implement and impossible to require. Further, as NPR's Linda Holmes writes, "there is . . . no solution for people who want to watch *The Real Housewives Of Beverly Hills* without guilt . . . you have to live with the fact that it exploits emotionally charged situations" (Holmes). Nonetheless, having an adoptable ethical code for reality television producers, and public knowledge of which shows abide by the code, would at least put a modicum of power back in the hands of the viewer. We would be given the ability to make informed choices about which programs we choose to watch—"to shop for ethical television the same way [we] might shop for ethically produced goods of any other kind, and to provide the financial incentives [for producers]," as Holmes says.

I will probably never stop feeling guilty for watching reality television, particularly the more exploitative shows. However, if I were given the option to watch reality programs that I could feel comfortable indulging in, knowing that there were an ethical code in place, I would like to think I'd choose those shows. Such a code wouldn't cure the problem, but at least it would empower viewers and encourage them to support less destructive programming.

Works Cited

D'Amico, Richard. "Plastic Surgery Is Real, Not Reality TV." *Virtual Mentor: American Medical Association Journal of Ethics* 9.3 (March 2007): 2150-218. Print.

Dehnart, Andy. "Real Housewives Cast Member Russell Killed Himself." *Reality Blurred*. 16 Aug. 2011. Web. 20 Feb. 2012.

Holmes, Linda. "Ethical 'Reality': A Proposed Code for Producers to Live By." *NPR*. 31 August 2011. Web. 11 Nov. 2011.

Seitz, Matt Zoller. "Reality TV: A Blood Sport That Must Change." *Salon*. 18 August 2011. Web. 20 Jan. 2012.

"Top Tens and Trends." *The Nielson Co.* 20 Feb. 2012. Web. 20 Feb. 2012.

Evaluating the Essay

1. A key part of a persuasive proposal is establishing the seriousness of the problem. Are you convinced that reality stars are at risk on these programs? If not, what would you suggest about strengthening that part of the essay?

2. Suppose Jenna were considering incorporating visuals—images, video, graphics, and tables—into the essay. What visuals would you suggest?

3. What's your evaluation of the solution that she proposes? Is it convincing? Why or why not?

Using What You Have Learned

Let's revisit the list from the beginning of this chapter of things I hoped you'd learn about this form of writing.

1. **Describe a problem of consequence, framing it narrowly enough to explore convincing solutions.** It's hard to overstate the importance of this skill, not just for proposal writing, but also for most writing tasks. A fundamental problem with early drafts in any genre is that they're not focused enough; the writer takes a landscape shot when she needs to take a close-up. This is especially true with research-based writing such as proposals, where you're dealing with a lot of information. See if you can apply some of the things you learned here to, for example, a research essay.

2. **Identify the wide range of rhetorical situations that might call for a proposal argument.** There are all kinds of proposals—marketing proposals, business plans, grant proposals, policy proposals, and so on—but they are all in the service of the same question: What should be done? As you write for other college classes, you will probably have assignments that aren't called proposals but essentially ask you to answer this question.

3. **Argue effectively for both the seriousness of the problem and the proposed solutions, using strong evidence.** If you wrote a review for the previous chapter, then you already have some practice with making arguments, because evaluation is a form of argument. In this chapter, you built on those skills. Among other things, the proposal relies more heavily on research than does the review, and in subsequent assignments you'll be drawing on what you learned here, especially your understanding of what is appropriate evidence to support a claim.

4. **Use appropriate invention strategies to discover and develop a proposal topic.** The invention techniques themselves don't vary much from assignment to assignment. You've gotten considerable practice with fastwriting, clustering, listing, and so on. But with each assignment, you've cast a wider net for information. The proposal, for example, asks you to generate considerably more information from outside sources than, say, the profile or personal essay do. Invention isn't just trying to get what's already in your head out on paper or screen. Invention also includes using techniques for *finding* information and thinking about what you make of it. This skill will become increasingly important in later assignments.

5. **Apply revision strategies that are effective for a proposal.** As we move towards increasingly argumentative forms of writing, revision is increasingly focused on considering how a skeptical audience might respond to what you say. In this chapter, you've spent time considering not only how to convince someone that a problem you care about is something he or she should care about, too, but also crafting proposals that are persuasive. Reviews, proposals, public arguments, and research essays are among the most reader-based forms, and it becomes even more important in revising these forms to imagine readers who may not think much like you do.

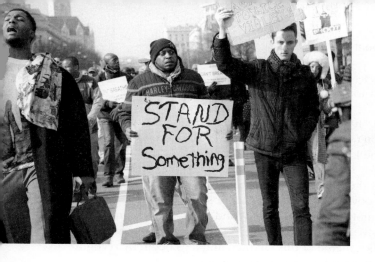

7

Writing an Argument

Learning Objectives

In this chapter, you'll learn to

7.1 Understand the connection between inquiry and persuasion, and apply inquiry strategies for exploring and developing an argument topic.

7.2 Distinguish between causal, factual, and definitional arguments, and develop an essay that uses one of those three approaches to persuasion.

7.3 Identify the key elements of argument—reasons, claims, and evidence—and apply them in both reading and writing.

7.4 Develop a question that is focused enough to lead to a strong claim and convincing evidence.

7.5 Use audience analysis and logical methods to help guide revision of an argument.

Writing to Persuade People

When you teach, it pays to check your assumptions at the door. This semester, Hailie, a student in my first-year writing class, was a member of the debate team. Successful debaters are typically deeply committed to going all in on the proposition they're supporting—doubt and uncertainty don't win points in these contests. Inquiry-based investigations, as you know by now, begin with questions, not answers, and at least initially, welcome complexity and even uncertainty. You write about a topic not because you know what you think but because you want to find out what you think. I thought Hailie would struggle with this ("Just give me a side to argue!"), and that she would see little connection between inquiry and argument.

I was wrong.

"How do you decide on a topic that you want to argue?" I asked her one day in conference.

"It interests me," she said. "It's something I want to learn about."

"But don't you quickly jump over the exploration phase and rush to some kind of judgment about what you think?" I said.

"Um, no, not really. I always explore the topic first," she said. "That's the most interesting part."

It was obvious to me that Hailie saw no conflict between the initial motive of inquiry—to find out—and the motive of argument—to prove. Cementing the connection between the two is a major theme of this chapter, and let's begin by recognizing that all persuasion begins with inquiry.

> Persuasive essays such as the op-ed are a great way to participate in public debates that affect your campus and community, and even your nation.

Motives for Writing an Argument

Obviously, we use persuasion all the time to try to get others to see things our way. Today, my wife, Karen, and I politely argued about what movie to see tonight. But that's not the kind of argument that I'm talking about here because, really, *who cares* (other than Karen and me) what movie we choose tonight? Instead, I'm talking about arguments in which people *have some kind of stake*. In inquiry-based argument, that's where inquiry first finds a home: in a community that seeks answers but that can't agree on which answer is best.[1] The investigator may belong to that community or not (you don't have to be a college football player to be interested in whether amateurism is corrupted by money), but either way, as Hailie knows, the inquiry begins with an exploration into what that community cares about, what it already believes, and what others have to say about issues of common concern.

While a writer may have feelings, one way or another, about what the community *should* think, it would be irresponsible not to inquire first into the debate, and this is often wonderfully complicated. So the formula for argument is **not** this:

> *Pick an issue + take a side + line up evidence*
> *that supports that side.*

The formula for inquiry-driven argument is more like this:

> *Identify communities with a stake in the question + explore what*
> *those communities believe + craft a case, supported by evidence,*
> *for the best answer.*

---

[1]This focus on community as the basis for identifying what is worth arguing draws from rhetoric expert Sharon Crowley, and especially her work on argumentative writing, as well as pedagogies developed by composition scholar Michelle Payne.

Writing Beyond the Classroom

Public Argument in a Digital Age

An argument with Northwest Airlines over whether they owe you a lunch voucher after your flight was cancelled is typical of everyday uses of persuasion. But arguing well—and ethically—is an important civic duty in a democratic society. A few thousand years ago, the Greeks and Romans created schools of rhetoric where people could learn the art of speaking persuasively in public settings.

These days, probably more than ever, argument is a vibrant part of civic life in the United States, particularly on the Internet. Here are a few of the many genres of public argument available to you for persuading people to think or do something you consider important:

- ■ *Op-ed essays:* These essays, ubiquitous in newspapers, remain among the most common brief argumentative essays for a general audience.
- ■ *Letters to the editor:* Like op-ed essays, these appear in print or online publications; they're often a response to a previous contribution.
- ■ *Blogs:* One of the newest forms of public argument is the blog. Hosted by such online sites as Wordpress or Google's "Blogger," the so-called blogosphere has grown so explosively that no one really knows how big it is.
- ■ *Photo essay:* Over one hundred years ago, Jacob Riis used photographs of immigrants' squalid conditions in New York City tenements to incite a public outcry—and policy change—on how we treat the poor.
- ■ *YouTube:* It's not just a forum for videos of weird cat tricks.
- ■ *PowerPoint:* Former vice president Al Gore's slide presentation "An Inconvenient Truth" made the point that there really can be power in PowerPoint.

For example, college students (a community) are plagued by loan debt. There's considerable debate about whether, at certain income levels, this debt should be forgiven or reduced (answers). After investigating this issue, what do you believe is the best approach, and why? Many athletes and fans of the Olympics (several communities) are concerned about the impact of corporate sponsorship on the Games' guiding principles. Some think this sponsorship is an inevitable part of the modern Olympics, while others think there should be some restrictive sponsorship policies (answers), and still others believe that the Games should return to its simple roots, without all the fanfare. What is the answer that will best address these communities' concerns, and why? The central motive for argument, then, is not simply to offer evidence to support your point of view but to first investigate a wide range of ideas to determine what might be best for the communities with a stake in the debate.

We argue not to *win* but to *learn*. This is a distinction that philosopher Daniel Cohen believes is subverted by the most common way we tend to think about argument—that it is a war. Arguments *can* involve conflict, but they are rarely combat—despite the frequent use of war metaphors such as "finding ammunition" or "attacking a position." Far more often, the motives for arguing are more benign, including learning something (even if we "lose") and actually feeling good about it.

The Argument and Academic Writing

Proposals, reviews, and analytical essays (discussed in the next chapter) are all types of arguments you might write in college. What distinguishes them from the argumentative essay you will write here? One difference is the kind of questions (and the claims that arise from them) that each genre typically emphasizes. For example, a proposal (Chapter 6) asks policy questions—what should be done? A review (Chapter 5) asks an evaluative question—how good is it? Argumentative essays like the one you will write tend to focus on three kinds of questions:

- What's the cause? (e.g., Deforestation of the Amazon has led to the decimation of native cultures.)
- What's true? (e.g., The evidence suggests voter ID legislation suppresses the African-American vote.)
- What is it and how should it be classified? (e.g., Russia's behavior in Ukraine re-creates its Cold War foreign policy.)

These three types of questions are relevant to all kinds of writing assignments you'll encounter in your college classes, including things like position papers, opinion pieces, persuasive essays, and cause-effect essays. If you can learn to identify the kind of question a writing assignment involves, you will know the genre of argument your instructor expects and the type of claims that arise from it.

In general, academics value argument not because they're argumentative (though some are), but because it's the way that they "make knowledge," which is the central business of the university. Scholarly communities make discoveries through contesting what was once assumed to be true. Reasoned argument supported by research is the engine behind academic inquiry.

Fundamental to academic argument is an idea that isn't always obvious to newcomers to college: "Facts" can be contested. While it often seems that the facts we take for granted are immutable truths—as enduring as the granite peaks I can see through my office window—things often aren't immutable at all. Our knowledge of things—how the planet was formed, the best ways to save endangered species, the meaning of a classic novel, how to avoid athletic injuries—is entirely made up of ideas that are *contested*. And the primary tool for shaping and even changing what we know is argument.

Features of the Form

Feature	Conventions of the Argument Essay
Inquiry questions	What is true? What's the cause? How should it be defined and classified?
Motives	We hope to convince others to think as we do. Sometimes, however, we first need to convince ourselves, and argument is an invitation to *explore* as well as to persuade. A fundamental motive is discovery.
Subject matter	Any topic is fair game, but one thing is essential: Others must have a stake in the issue. An audience should be persuaded that whatever claim you're making matters.
Structure	Like any form of writing, the design of arguments depends on the situation. However, outlines for arguments developed by rhetoricians share some of these features: • Background on the issue, especially what people seem to agree on. What's the controversy as most people understand it? • The inquiry question. • Claims and supporting reasons and evidence. • Acknowledgement of counterarguments and analysis of their significance. • Closing that refines the claim, summarizes it, or returns to the beginning to affirm how the argument addresses the issue.
Sources of information	Experts on your topic, sources of reliable data on your topic, your experiences and observations, and the stories of others can all potentially be evidence for your argument.
Language	Who is the audience? Arguments for expert audiences are often formal. Arguments for the general public are much less formal, with relatively relaxed rules of evidence and casual language. The balance of appeals should be appropriate to the audience.

Prose+

Editorial cartoons such as this one are a popular form of argument, and one reason they're effective is a quality that comics share: By simplifying things, they amplify those things. Cartoonist Joe Heller notes that when we render something more abstractly—in this case, taking a coal mine and superimposing a graveyard and smoke—the details that were eliminated make the details that remain more apparent. Cartoons that make an argument, however, also have features typical of any argument: a claim (often implied) and reasons. The cartoon strip here, for example, combines drawings with very few words to make a pretty unambiguous claim: Wind power is preferable to nuclear, oil, and coal energy. The reason offered? The problems associated with wind power are relatively benign.

What Is Argument?

We've already distinguished an argumentative essay from a proposal and a review. Each works from a different inquiry question and claim. But let's bore more deeply into the question of what we mean by argument, starting first with another popular misconception.

Argument Has More Than Two Sides

TV talk shows stage "discussions" between proponents of diametrically opposed positions. Academic debating teams pit those for and those against. We are nurtured on language such as *win or lose, right and wrong,* and *either . . . or.* It's tempting to see the world this way, as neatly divided into truth and falsehood, light and dark. Reducing issues to two sides simplifies the choices. But one of the things that literature—and all art—teaches us is the delightful and nagging complexity of things. Huck Finn is a racist, and in *Huckleberry Finn* there's plenty of evidence in his treatment of Jim that confirms this. Yet there are moments in the novel when we see a transcendent humanity in Huck, and we can see that he may be a racist, *but. . . .* It is this qualification—this modest word *but*—that trips us up in our apparent certainty. Rather than *either . . . or,* can it be *both . . . and?* Instead of two sides to every issue, might there be thirteen?

Here's an example:

One side: General education requirements are a waste of time because they are often irrelevant to the students' major goal in getting a college education— getting a good job.

The other side: General education requirements are invaluable because they prepare students to be enlightened citizens, more fully prepared to participate in democratic culture.

It's easy to imagine a debate between people who hold these positions, and it wouldn't be uninteresting. But it *would* be misleading to suggest that these are the only two possible positions on general education requirements in American universities.

One of the reasons why people are drawn to arguing is that it can be a method of discovery, and one of the most useful discoveries is that of a side to the story that doesn't fall neatly into the usual opposed positions. The route to these discoveries is twofold: *initially withholding judgment* and *asking questions.*

For instance,

What might be goals of a university education other than helping students get a good job and making them enlightened citizens?

Is it possible that a university can do both?

Are general education courses the only route to enlightenment?

Are there certain situations in which the vocational motives of students are inappropriate?

Are there certain contexts—say, certain students at particular schools at a particular point in their education—when general education requirements should be waived or modified?

As often happens with two-sided arguments, all of these questions, and others, tend to unravel the two sides of the argument and expose them for what they are: *starting points* for an inquiry, in this case, into the question *What good are general education requirements?*

Inquiry Arguments Begin with Exploration

7.1

Understand the connection between inquiry and persuasion, and apply inquiry strategies for exploring and developing an argument topic.

Oh, how tempting it is to simply build an argument from what you already think! It seems so much more efficient, allowing you to leap over the messy, exploratory part of the process and get right to the point—you know, the point that you started with, the one you just *know* is true. But this shortcut comes with a serious cost: You'll learn less. Inquiry is about discovery, and as you know, this means beginning with questions, not answers, and taking the time to listen to what others have said about your topic.

So you begin with a question—"What good are general education requirements?"—and before you make any claims about it, you do some research on who has a stake in the answer to the question (see Figure 7.1).

You don't have an argument until you identify the areas of disagreement. The discovery phase of an inquiry-based argument explores the range of existing beliefs among communities with a stake in your question. For the question about the effectiveness of general education requirements, several stakeholders are obvious, none more so than students. Educators also have an investment in the

Figure 7.1 Stakeholder analysis

question. Parents of college students are probably less apparent stakeholders, but many feel strongly that their children not "waste" time with "unnecessary" courses. And finally, do people who hire college graduates care whether potential employees have taken courses in a range of subjects?

You still don't really have an argument to make yet. That will emerge when you find the points of disagreement among stakeholders. One way to do that is to work through a series of questions:

1. *Do the stakeholders agree on the facts?* (e.g., Is it true that most college students would prefer not to take general education courses?) If it isn't true, then perhaps there's a factual argument you might make.

2. *Do they agree on what key terms mean?* (e.g., Is there confusion about what is meant by "general education"?) If there isn't confusion, should you make a definitional claim?

3. *Do they agree on the causes?* (e.g., General education makes students "well-rounded" citizens.) Is there a causal argument lurking here?

Once you've identified which one of the three types of argument you might want to make, then comes the hunt for a claim that you can get behind.

What Do We Mean by Claims, Reasons, and Evidence?

Claims: What You Want People to Believe

"I have a headache" is simply a statement, and not a claim, because no one is likely to disagree with it. "Headaches can be caused by secondhand smoke" is a statement that is also a claim (a causal one) because reasonable people might agree or disagree with it. Exploration into your topic will help you identify the areas of disagreement, and from one of these areas you can work towards discovering a particular kind of claim, which is linked, of course, to what kind of question you're posing: factual, definitional, or causal.

7.2 Distinguish between causal, factual, and definitional arguments, and develop an essay that uses one of those three approaches to persuasion.

- *Factual claims.* One of the most controversial debates these days is a factual one: Do humans cause global warming? What does the evidence suggest is true? It isn't hard to see plenty of examples of factual arguments. Here in the Pacific Northwest, for example, some people can't agree whether removing dams is the best way to help endangered salmon, or if the state government would be a better manager than the feds of public lands.

- *Causal claims.* Closely related to factual claims, causal claims address a disagreement about why something is happening, or what caused it. Following the midterm elections in 2014, there were plenty of causal arguments about why the Democrats did so poorly and the Republicans did so well.

■ ***Definitional claims.*** Is gay marriage an equal-rights issue or a moral one? Is a corporation a "person"? What does it mean to be a "feminist"? Does talking on your cell phone in a nice restaurant constitute rude behavior? All of these questions try to pin down the meanings and classifications of things that a dictionary can't help with.

Reasons: The "Because..." Behind the Claim

I asked my first-year students what they thought of general education, or "core," classes at our university. It provoked a lively debate. Here's what one of them said:

> I am all for the rant about higher education costing a fortune. The core classes are a joke, to be quite honest. Who hasn't had math, science, and history in high school?

7.3

Identify the key elements of argument— reasons, claims, and evidence— and apply them in both reading and writing.

This student makes the definitional claim that "core classes are a joke." She gives a reason: Students have already studied math, science, and history in high school. This is the "because" behind her claim. But notice that behind this reason there's an unstated assumption: Math, science, and history classes in high school are equivalent to university core classes in these subjects. Is this true? It may be. But it's certainly debatable, and because this assumption is never addressed, the claim that core classes are a joke is built on a pretty weak foundation.

Reasons—either stated or implied—hold up your claim. Your claim is *what* you believe is true, and your reasons are *why* you believe it is true. A claim and a reason can be linked with the word "because." So, stating its assumption explicitly as part of the reason, we could restate the claim and reason above as "Core classes are a joke *because* their content is similar to what most students learn in high school."

Evidence: Testing the Claim

The phrase "building an argument" implies that it's a construction job that is merely about assembling the parts—claim, reasons, evidence—according to some preconceived plan concocted by a mastermind who has it pretty much figured out. But an inquiry-based argument is actually nothing like that. It's when writers start looking at evidence that the building is most likely to crumble because evidence is the element of argument that is most likely to shatter assumptions. But you should let evidence mess things up.

Examining evidence is a *test* of a claim; evidence is just as likely to revise what you think as it is to confirm it ... *if you let it*. That's the hard part: allowing information to change your mind. For one thing, it's inconvenient. But it's also essential because the motive of argument is to learn something. This learning begins by seeing the landscape of a controversy when figuring out what kind of argument you want to make, and continues by looking at evidence that challenges what you already think.

Look at the best evidence you can find, which will likely come from the following sources:

- Expert testimony (statements by authorities on the topic)
- Reliable data (facts from credible sources)

Seeing the Form

The "Imagetext" as Argument

While model Kate Moss is likely disturbed by the appropriation of her image by advocates in the pro-anorexia ("pro-ana") movement, Moss's picture—along with those of other celebrities such as Calista Flockhart, Mary-Kate Olsen, and Keira Knightley—appear as "thinspiration" on websites that argue that eating disorders are a "lifestyle choice," not a disease. Some of these images (though not this one) are digitally altered to make the models seem even thinner than they really are. In an article on the "imagetexts" used by these controversial websites, Robin Jensen notes that in their new context, pictures like this one of Kate Moss are in effect given a "frame" quite different from the one originally intended. In this way, the meaning of the picture is manipulated to make an argument that serves the purpose of the pro-ana movement. In a sense, this is like quoting someone out of context, and raises a similar ethical question: Is it fair?

Kate Moss in ultra-thin pose.

- Observation and personal experience (what you see and what has happened to you)
- Stories, case studies, anecdotes (the narratives of others that help you dramatize an issue or support a point)

Keep in mind that the kind of evidence that is persuasive will depend on the disposition of your audience—readers who are skeptical about your claim will be harder to convince—and also on the discourse community you're writing in. Obviously, appropriate evidence in a biology article will be different from appropriate evidence in a philosophy article. For the purposes of this assignment, you're probably writing for peers (or a general audience) and, generally speaking, as you move from an expert audience to one that is less so, the rules of evidence get looser.

Analyzing What Makes a *Good* Argument

The simplest method of making an argument is perfected in the third grade: You're wrong and I'm right. So there. Aristotle had problems with this, as does everyone else who lines up behind reason and civility. However, there is considerably less agreement about what actually makes an argument effective. Let's look at three ideas about this: classical argument and two more-contemporary approaches—Toulmin and Rogerian arguments.

Classical Argument: Ethos, Pathos, Logos

Plato thought that we arrive at Truth through dialogue—a back and forth between two parties who are interested in discovering what it all means. Aristotle thought Truth-finding is the business of science. But he also argued that there is a real need for people to sort out disagreements, and that a method exists for doing this. Aristotle's ideas about argument proved durable, and so when we talk about argument, we often focus on how we can use ethos (the appeal of the writer's or speaker's credibility), pathos (the appeal to emotion), and logos (the appeal to reason) to try to persuade a receptive audience. (See Figure 7.2 for a representation of the balance among these appeals.) Aristotle also proposed a structure for how to make a persuasive argument, and it includes a lot of the things we usually associate with persuasive writing:

- **Introduction:** Dramatize the issue to engage reader interest, identify common ground between writer and audience, and lay out the claim (ethos and pathos).
- **Narration:** Provide the background so that readers know what's at stake (logos).
- **Confirmation:** Return to your claim and offer persuasive evidence (usually examples) to support that it's the best answer (logos).

Disposition of Audience	*Ethos*	*Pathos*	*Logos*
Resistant	Most important	Less important	Most important
Neutral	Important	Important	Important
Receptive	Less important	Most important	Less important

Figure 7.2   Audience and the balance of ethos, logos, and pathos

- **Refutation and concession:** Refrain from pretending that your answer is the only one or that it can't be critiqued. What are some of the opposing views (logos)?
- **Conclusion:** Reach back into the essay to reaffirm why your claim is best. Leave a strong impression (ethos and pathos).

While classical argument remains a go-to method, it has drawbacks. For one thing, it can seem formulaic—a dutiful march through a series of logical steps that can seem predictable. It's also easy to imagine that the classical method is less suited to inquiry-based arguments. Will writers be tempted to lock down their thinking, sidestepping complexity and uncertainty, in their determination to prove a point to an already receptive audience?

Toulmin's Approach: What Do You Need to Believe Is True?

Stephen Toulmin, an English philosopher, was interested in practical argument. He worried that classical approaches rely too much on formal logic divorced from real-world situations. What may be most powerful about the Toulmin method is that it offers not *an approach to composing* an argument but *a method of analyzing* an argument—one you've drafted or one you've been asked to read.

For our purposes, we'll simplify the Toulmin approach a bit. First, he suggested that arguments about any subject include:

- claims
- evidence
- warrants
- backing

In an argument, the *claims* are supported by *grounds* (reasons) or *evidence* (examples, observations, statistics, etc.). The most significant aspect of Toulmin's approach is the idea that claims and evidence are linked together by *warrants*— or assumptions about the way things are. If the claim *Michelle must have a lot of*

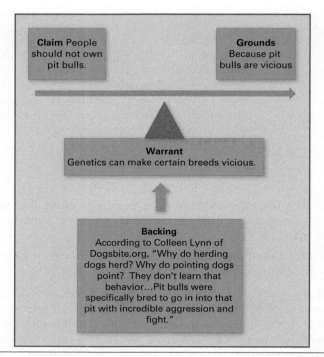

Figure 7.3 The relationship among claims, grounds, warrants, and backing

money is based on the evidence of the half-dozen credit cards in her purse, the person making the claim assumes there's a correlation between the number of credit cards one has and wealth. That's a warrant. To believe the claim based on this evidence, you would have to also believe the assumption. Essentially, then, a warrant is the answer to the question *What do you need to believe is true in order to accept the validity of a claim based on grounds or evidence?*

For example, what do I have to believe is true to accept the claim that people shouldn't own pit bulls on the grounds that they are a vicious breed (see Figure 7.3 above)? I'd have to believe that viciousness is a genetic trait that all dogs of a certain breed share. That's a warrant (there are probably more). If I were going to make the case against pit bulls, I think I'd feel obligated to find some evidence that backs that warrant.

Rogers: Accurately Restating and Refuting Opposing Claims

The Rogerian approach is especially appealing for inquiry arguments because it accommodates the complex issues of stakeholders whose positions are less clear. It's also a method of argument that encourages writers to bend over backwards to understand what those stakeholders believe, especially those with whom writers might disagree.

How might you analyze this letter writer's argument?

Dear Editor,

As part of my required humanities class, I was forced to see the art exhibit "Home of the Brave" at the university gallery. As a combat veteran, what I saw there deeply offended me. I saw so-called "art" that showed great American military leaders such as General Petraeus with skulls superimposed on their faces, and a photo of a man with an American flag wrapped around his head and lashed with a plastic tie at his neck. It's popular to say these days that we should support the troops. Apparently, a group of artists who haven't defended our freedom feel free to use that freedom to be unpatriotic. I wonder if they would feel differently if they had to pay the real cost for freedom of speech.

Most arguments like this don't provoke an analytical response at first. We react emotionally: "This guy is so full of it!" or perhaps, "It's about time someone spoke up about the cost of freedom!" This letter, like many that raise controversial issues, triggers a whole set of deeply held beliefs about things such as patriotism, freedom of speech, and the purpose of art. These are things that *should* provoke discussion—and that inevitably trigger feelings. But without involving the head as well as the heart, it's impossible to have a civil discussion—one that will lead to new understanding. We need to understand not only what we ourselves believe, but also what the other guy believes. To see how this might work, try Exercise 7.1, based on some of American psychologist Carl Rogers' ideas about argument.

Exercise 7.1

Argument as Therapy

Carl Rogers was a therapist and one of the most famous experts on argument theory. Not surprisingly, he thought that when people feel really, really strongly about something, reason just doesn't work well. Instead, he believed, a prerequisite to entering into an argument with someone else about a value-laden topic is to first listen and "say back" what you understand him or her to be saying. Let's do that here.

STEP ONE: Summarize what you understand to be the letter writer's basic argument. What claim is he making, and what seem to be the (implied) reasons behind it? You might use this as a template for your summary:

> *Because of* _____ *and* _____, *the letter writer argues that* _____.

STEP TWO: Now fastwrite for a few minutes in your notebook, exploring your own take on the validity of the claim and the reasons.

STEP THREE: Finally, write a brief analysis of the argument that includes the following:

1. Begin with your understanding of the letter writer's argument and include something about the circumstances that might lead someone to make such claims.
2. Analyze the soundness of the reasons behind the argument. Do you agree or disagree with them? Is there a different way of thinking about them?
3. State your own position (e.g., What would you say about the relationship between art and politics?), including the reasons behind it.

Of all the models for argument discussed here, Rogerian may be most suited to inquiry arguments because it seems to invite complexity. Consider the structure of a typical Rogerian argument:

- What's the issue (history, context, stakeholders, etc.)?

- What are the perspectives on the issue? What are the perspectives of those with whom I don't agree?

- What is sensible about my opponents' views?

One Student's Response

Rebecca's Journal

EXERCISE 7.1

The letter writer, a combat veteran, found himself "deeply offended" by a collection of artwork in his university's gallery called "Home of the Brave." The writer is incensed that the artists are using their freedom of speech—a freedom which the letter writer feels he has defended in war—to present "unpatriotic" images. Had these artists experienced combat firsthand, the writer claims, they might be less inclined to create these images.

In fact, it is partly the letter writer's experience of combat himself that has led to this intense reaction. The process of going to war is traumatic and singular—one a person can't understand unless they've experienced it first-hand. However, the artwork in the exhibition is not claiming to understand war from the perspective of a soldier, but rather to explore the issues from the artists' unique viewpoint in a creative way. The letter writer's argument that the artists might feel differently if they had been in combat is accurate—surely they would. However, such an argument doesn't invalidate the right of American citizens to express themselves and their diverse opinions through words and images.

I think this discussion is an important one, although I wish the letter writer had used it to spark debate. The vast disparity of experience in artist and audience is what makes art so valuable, encouraging reactions, discussions, and perhaps new understanding. I disagree with the letter writer that the artwork is unpatriotic—in fact, I think the artistic expression of a unique viewpoint is one of the greatest uses of freedom of speech. I also think that the artists could have something valuable to learn from the letter writer as a combat veteran, and I think such a meeting of opposing minds is one of the greatest reactions to art there is.

- What is my view?
- What are the reasons and evidence that supports it?
- How might my ideas *complement* the ideas of others in addressing the issue?

As you can see, this method of argument takes a *both/and* view rather than an *either/or* view, and as a result it's more likely that writers of Rogerian arguments will accept complexity rather than suppress it.

Avoiding Logical Fallacies

An important way to evaluate the soundness of an argument is to examine its logic and, in particular, look for so-called logical fallacies that may lead writers' reasoning astray. Aristotle was one of the first to point out many of these, and a quick search on the web using the term "logical fallacies" will reveal dozens and dozens of them that plague public argument. Many have indecipherable Latin names, testifying to their ancient origins.

Here are ten of the most common logical fallacies. They cover about 90 percent of the ways in which writers stumble when making an argument.

1. *Hasty generalization:* We're naturally judgmental creatures. For example, we frequently make a judgment about someone after just meeting him or her. Or we conclude that a class is useless after attending a single session. These are generalizations based on insufficient evidence. Hasty generalizations *might* be true—the class might turn out to be useless—but you should always be wary of making them.

2. *Ad hominem:* When arguments turn into shouting matches, they almost inevitably get personal. Shifting away from the substance of an argument to attack the person making it, either subtly or explicitly, is another common logical fallacy. It's also, at times, hard to resist.

3. *Appeal to authority:* We all know that finding support for a claim from an expert is a smart move in most arguments. But sometimes it's a faulty move because the authority we cite isn't really an expert on the subject. A more common fallacy, however, is when we cite an expert to support a claim without acknowledging that many other experts disagree on the point.

4. *Straw man:* One of the sneakiest ways to sidetrack reason in an argument is to misrepresent or ignore the actual position of an opponent. Unfortunately, the "straw man" fallacy thrives in many political debates: "I can't support this proposal for universal health care," says politician A. "It's clear that politician A doesn't really take the problem of American health care seriously," says politician B. Huh?

5. *False analogy:* Analogies can be powerful comparisons in argument. But they can also lead us astray when the analogy simply doesn't hold. Are A and B *really* similar situations? For example, when a critic of higher education argues that a public university is like a business and should be run like one, are the two really analogous? Fundamentally, one is nonprofit and the

other is designed to make money. Is this really a useful comparison?

6. ***Post hoc or false cause:*** Just because one thing follows another thing doesn't necessarily mean one *causes* the other. It might be coincidence, or the cause might be something else entirely. For example, if you're really keen on arguing that losing the football coach was the cause of the team's losing record, you might link the two. And it's possible that they are linked, but it's also just as possible that the injury to the quarterback was one of the real reasons for the losing record.

7. ***Appeal to popularity:*** In a country obsessed with polls and rankings, it's not hard to understand the appeal of reasoning that argues that because something is popular, it must be good or true. Advertisers are particularly fond of this fallacy, arguing that because their brand is most popular, it must be the best. In fact, the brand might not be the best at all. The majority's opinion can be wrong.

8. ***Slippery slope:*** I love the name of this one because it so aptly describes what can happen when reasoning loses its footing. You might start out reasonably enough, arguing, for example, that a gun control law restricts the rights of some citizens to have access to certain weapons, but pretty soon you start sliding toward conclusions that simply don't follow, such as that a gun control law is the beginning of the end of gun ownership in the country. Now, you might really believe this is true, but logic isn't the route to prove the truth of your view.

9. ***Either/or fallacy:*** In a black-and-white world, something is right or wrong, true or false, good or bad. But ours is a colorful world with many shades. For instance, while it might be emotionally satisfying to say that opponents of the war in Afghanistan must not support the troops there, it is also possible that the war's opponents are against the war *because* they're concerned about the lives of American servicepeople. Rather than *either/or*, it might be *both/and*. We see this fallacy often in arguments that suggest that there are only two choices and that each is opposite to the other.

10. ***Begging the question:*** This one is also called *circular reasoning*, because it assumes the truth of the arguer's conclusion without bothering to prove it. An obvious example of this would be to say that a law protecting people from Internet spam is good because it's a law, and laws should be obeyed. But why is it a good law?

Exercise 7.2

Find the Fallacies

Identifying common logical fallacies in other people's arguments can provide explanations for that gut feeling you have that something just isn't right with certain claims. In other words, fallacies can be a powerful analytical tool. Use the section on ten logical fallacies above to analyze the argument by Khalid Sheikh Mohammed in "The Language of War Is Killing" later in this chapter on page 232.

READINGS

▶ # Factual Argument: Is it true that ___?

We all have that moment in a conversation when we begin with, "Is it true that ___?" Sometimes the question is fun and frivolous: Is it true that your heart stops when you sneeze? (I believed this in the eighth grade.) Is it true that no two snowflakes are alike? But when there are people who have a stake in the answer to the question, then you have a factual argument. For example, climate change and whether it is influenced by human activity is the factual controversy of the day. Another controversy is one that matters a lot to anyone who is facing the prospect of student debt and rising college tuition costs: Does it pay to go to college? In the essay that follows, David Leonhardt has an answer to that question.

Is College Worth It?
David Leonhardt

Some newly minted college graduates struggle to find work. Others accept jobs for which they feel overqualified. Student debt, meanwhile, has topped $1 trillion.

It's enough to create a <u>wave of questions</u> about whether a college education is still worth it.

A new set of income statistics answers those questions quite clearly: Yes, college is worth it, and it's not even close. For all the struggles that many young college graduates face, a four-year degree has probably never been more valuable.

The pay gap between college graduates and everyone else reached a record high last year, according to the new data, which is based on an analysis of Labor Department statistics by the Economic Policy Institute in Washington. Americans with four-year college degrees made 98 percent more an hour on average in 2013 than people without a degree. That's up from 89 percent five years earlier, 85 percent a decade earlier and 64 percent in the early 1980s.

There is nothing inevitable about this trend. If there were more college graduates than the economy needed, the pay gap would shrink. The gap's recent growth is especially notable because it has come after a <u>rise</u> in the number of college graduates, partly because many people went back to school during the Great Recession. That the pay gap has nonetheless continued growing means that we're still not producing enough of them.

"We have too few college graduates," says <u>David Autor</u>, an M.I.T. economist, who was not involved in the Economic Policy Institute's analysis. "We also have too few people who are prepared for college."

It's important to emphasize these shortfalls because public discussion today— for which we in the news media deserve some responsibility—often focuses on the

(continued)

(*continued*)

undeniable fact that a bachelor's degree does not guarantee success. But of course it doesn't. Nothing guarantees success, especially after 15 years of <u>disappointing economic growth</u> and <u>rising inequality</u>.

8   When experts and journalists spend so much time talking about the limitations of education, they almost certainly are discouraging some teenagers from going to college and some adults from going back to earn degrees. (Those same experts and journalists are sending their own children to college and often obsessing over which one.) The decision not to attend college for fear that it's a bad deal is among the most <u>economically irrational</u> decisions anybody could make in 2014.

9   The much-discussed cost of college doesn't change this fact. According to a <u>paper</u> by Mr. Autor published Thursday in the journal Science, the true cost of a college degree is about ***negative*** $500,000. That's right: Over the long run, college is cheaper than free. Not going to college will cost you about half a million dollars.

10   Mr. Autor's paper—building on <u>work by</u> the economists Christopher Avery and Sarah Turner—arrives at that figure first by calculating the very real cost of tuition and fees. This amount is then subtracted from the lifetime gap between the earnings of college graduates and high school graduates. After adjusting for inflation and the time value of money, the net cost of college is negative $500,000, roughly double what it was three decades ago.

11   This calculation is necessarily imprecise, because it can't control for any pre-existing differences between college graduates and nongraduates—differences that would exist regardless of schooling. Yet <u>other research</u>, comparing otherwise similar people who did and did not graduate from college, has also found that education brings a <u>huge return</u>.

12   In a similar vein, the new Economic Policy Institute numbers show that the benefits of college don't go just to graduates of elite colleges, who typically go on to earn graduate degrees. The wage gap between people with only a bachelor's degree and people without such a degree has also kept rising.

13   Tellingly, though, the wage premium for people who have attended college without earning a bachelor's degree—a group that includes community-college graduates—has not been rising. The big economic returns go to people with four-year degrees. Those returns underscore the importance of efforts to reduce the college dropout rate, such as those at the University of Texas, which Paul Tough described in a recent Times Magazine <u>article</u>.

14   But what about all those alarming stories you hear about indebted, jobless college graduates?

15   The anecdotes may be real, yet the conventional wisdom often <u>exaggerates the problem</u>. Among four-year college graduates who took out loans, <u>average debt</u> is about $25,000, a sum that is a tiny fraction of the economic benefits of college. (My own student debt, as it happens, was almost identical to this figure, in

inflation-adjusted terms.) And the unemployment rate in April for people between 25 and 34 years old with a bachelor's degree was a mere 3 percent.

I find the data from the Economic Policy Institute especially telling because the institute—a left-leaning research group—makes a point of arguing that education is not the solution to all of the economy's problems. That is important, too. College graduates, like almost everyone else, are suffering from the economy's weak growth and from the disproportionate share of this growth flowing to the very richest households. 16

The average hourly wage for college graduates has risen only 1 percent over the last decade, to about $32.60. The pay gap has grown mostly because the average wage for everyone else has fallen—5 percent, to about $16.50. "To me, the picture is people in almost every kind of job not being able to see their wages grow," Lawrence Mishel, the institute's president, told me. "Wage growth essentially stopped in 2002." 17

From the country's perspective, education can be only part of the solution to our economic problems. We also need to find other means for lifting living standards—not to mention ways to provide good jobs for people without college degrees. 18

But from almost any individual's perspective, college is a no-brainer. It's the most reliable ticket to the middle class and beyond. Those who question the value of college tend to be those with the luxury of knowing their own children will be able to attend it. 19

Not so many decades ago, high school was considered the frontier of education. Some people even argued that it was a waste to encourage Americans from humble backgrounds to spend four years of life attending high school. Today, obviously, the notion that everyone should attend 13 years of school is indisputable. 20

But there is nothing magical about 13 years of education. As the economy becomes more technologically complex, the amount of education that people need will rise. At some point, 15 years or 17 years of education will make more sense as a universal goal. 21

That point, in fact, has already arrived. 22

http://p.nytimes.com/email/re?location=InCMR7g4BCKC2wiZPkcVUuK0r2vZpJSA&user_id=e6280687a88fcb1239d67a2d4c34f938&email_type=eta&task_id=1415995277422344&regi_id=0 23

Inquiring into the Essay

1. **Explore.** You've made the decision to go to college. But did you have any doubts? Spend four or five minutes fastwriting your response to that question.

2. **Explain.** Here's the common perception: College graduates these days have a really hard time finding a job. Here's Leonhardt's claim: "But from almost any individual's perspective, college is a no-brainer." Can you explain what Leonhardt says in his essay that reconciles what seem like two contradictory perspectives?

3. **Evaluate.** Using Toulmin's argument model (see page 223) to analyze "Is College Worth It?" For example, Leonhardt argues that excessive talk about the "limitations of education" discourages some students from enrolling, which he calls "among the most economically irrational decisions anybody could make...." That's a claim. The grounds to make that claim is that despite high tuition and debt, college graduates still make significantly more money than people with only a high school education. What are the assumptions that make the grounds persuasive support for the claim? In other words, what do you have to believe is true about what is meant, say, about the "limitations of education"?

4. **Reflect.** Think about what evidence is most persuasive in a factual argument (see pages 220–221 for types of evidence). Think about what evidence is most persuasive in an evaluation argument like a review. Are they different? Why?

▶ Definition Argument: What should we call it?

Because the sanctioned mass killing that we call war is so horrific, so counter to our moral instincts, we traumatize the language we use to talk about it, too. We have to define war in a way that makes "sense," that makes it less horrific. It's hard to imagine that one of the chief planners of the September 11, 2001, attacks on New York and Washington, DC, might invoke George Washington as his hero. In the excerpt that follows, Khalid Sheikh Mohammed, a commander for al Qaeda who has been in custody since 2003, argues that, like Washington, Islamic extremists are just fighting for their independence. The language of war, says Mohammed, is universal, and that language is killing.

This partial transcript of Mohammed discussing his role in the 9/11 attacks, the murder of journalist Daniel Pearl, and the hotel bombings in Bali was released by the U.S. Department of Defense and later appeared in *Harper's Magazine.*

The Language of War Is Killing
Khalid Sheikh Mohammed

1   I'm not making myself a hero when I said I was responsible for this or that. You know very well there is a language for any war. If America wants to invade Iraq, they will not send Saddam roses or kisses. They send bombardment. I admit I'm America's enemy. For sure, I'm America's enemy. So when we make war against America, we are like jackals fighting in the night. We consider George Washington a hero. Muslims, many of them, believe Osama bin Laden is doing the same thing. He is just fighting. He needs his independence. Many Muslims think that, not only me. They have been oppressed

by America. So when we say we are enemy combatants, that's right, we are. But I'm asking you to be fair with many detainees who are not enemy combatants. Because many of them have been unjustly arrested. You know very well, for any country waging war against their enemy, the language of the war is killing. If man and woman are together as a marriage, the others are kids, children. But if you and me, two nations, are together in war, the others are victims. This is the way of the language. You know forty million people were killed in World War I. Many people are oppressed. Because there is war, for sure, there will be victims. I'm not happy that three thousand have been killed in America. I feel sorry even. Islam never gives me the green light to kill people. Killing, in Christianity, Judaism, and Islam, is prohibited. But there are exceptions to the rule. When you are killing people in Iraq, you say, We have to do it. We don't like Saddam. But this is the way to deal with Saddam. Same language you use I use. When you are invading two thirds of Mexico, you call your war "manifest destiny." It's up to you to call it what you want. But the other side is calling you oppressors. If now we were living in the Revolutionary War, George Washington would be arrested by Britain. For sure, they would consider him an enemy combatant. But in America they consider him a hero. In any revolutionary war one side will be either George Washington or Britain. So we considered American Army bases in Saudi Arabia, Kuwait, Qatar, and Bahrain. This is a kind of invasion, but I'm not here to convince you. I don't have to say that I'm not your enemy. This is why the language of any war in the world is killing. The language of war is victims. I don't like to kill people. I feel very sorry kids were killed in 9/11. What will I do? I want to make a great awakening in America to stop foreign policy in our land. I know Americans have been torturing us since the seventies. I know they are talking about human rights. And I know it is against the American Constitution, against American laws. But they said, Every law has exceptions. This is your bad luck—you've been part of the exception to our laws. So, for me, I have patience. The Americans have human rights, but enemy combatant is a flexible word. What is an enemy combatant in my language? The Ten Commandments are shared between all of us. We are all serving one God. But we also share the language of War. War started when Cain killed Abel. It's never gonna stop killing people. America starts the Revolutionary War, and then the Mexican, then the Spanish, then World War I, World War II. You read the history. This is life. You have to kill.

Inquiring into the Essay

1. **Explore.** Does Mohammed have a point when he compares Islamic extremists who fight for "freedom" to American revolutionaries such as George Washington, who fought for independence? Fastwrite on this question in your journal for five minutes, exploring what you think. When you're done, skip a line and compose a one-sentence answer to this question: *What surprised you most about what you said in your fastwrite?*

2. **Explain.** Are there examples of the logical fallacy of false analogy? Find one and explain why it's false.

3. **Evaluate.** Use the model of classical argument (see page 222) to analyze Mohammed's argument. In particular, evaluate how he uses ethos, pathos, and logos to address an audience that is quite likely to be resistant to his appeal.

4. **Reflect.** The September 11 attacks have, understandably, made many Americans very emotional about terrorism and terrorists. What did you notice about your emotional reaction to Mohammed's argument in "The Language of War Is Killing"? Did you find it difficult to read the transcript analytically, as the previous questions asked you to do?

▶ Causal Argument: What's the Cause?

A few weeks ago, my neighbor state of Oregon joined Colorado and Washington in legalizing recreational marijuana. Leading up to all of these votes was a fury of causal arguments offered by both sides of the debate, all addressing the question "What's going to happen if we do this?" Naturally, in those few states that have made the move, the argument has changed to "What *has* happened here since legalization?" The jury, as they say, is out; it's still fairly early in this social experiment. But in Colorado, where implementation of the laws first started, this new debate is building.

Kevin Sabet, writing in the newspaper *The Washington Times*, weighed in fairly early, within a month of implementation of the law, on the effects of legalization in Colorado, arguing that "legalization's worst enemy is itself." He then goes on to detail what he believes will be the negative effects. It's interesting to consider these early predictions now that we're getting some data on the effects of Colorado's law. Does this new information confirm, complicate, or challenge Sabet's claims? Read the essay, do some Googling, and see what you think. Sabet is a former White House drug policy adviser.

Colorado Will Show Why Legalizing Marijuana Is a Mistake
Kevin Sabet

1   On Jan. 1, Colorado made history as the first jurisdiction in the modern era to license the retail sales of marijuana.

2   To be sure, there were no bloody fistfights among people waiting in line and, as far as we know, no burglaries or robberies. Legalization advocates cheered.

3   While it is true that most people who use marijuana won't become addicted to heroin or otherwise hurt society as a result, Colorado's experiment with legal pot can be called anything but successful.

4   What didn't make the news were some troubling developments.

Multimillion-dollar private investing groups have emerged and are poised to become, in their words, "Big Marijuana"; added to a list of dozens of other children, a 2-year-old girl ingested a marijuana cookie and had to receive immediate medical attention; a popular website boldly discussed safe routes for smugglers to bring marijuana into neighboring states; and a marijuana-store owner proudly proclaimed that Colorado would soon be the destination of choice for 18- to 21-year-olds, even though for them marijuana is still supposed to be illegal.   5

Popular columnists spanning the ideological spectrum, in The New York Times, The Washington Post and Newsweek/Daily Beast, soon expressed their disapproval of such policies as contributing to the dumbing down of America.   6

Colorado's experience, ironically, might eventually teach us that legalization's worst enemy is itself.   7

This raises the question: Why do we have to experience a tragedy before knowing where to go next?   8

Sadly, the marijuana conversation is one mired with myths. Many Americans do not think that marijuana can be addictive, despite scientific evidence to the contrary.   9

Many would be surprised to learn that the American Medical Association (AMA) has come out strongly against the legal sales of marijuana, citing public health concerns. In fact, the AMA's opinion is consistent with most major medical associations, including the American Academy of Pediatrics and American Society of Addiction Medicine.   10

Because today's marijuana is at least five to six times stronger than the marijuana smoked by most of today's parents, we are often shocked to hear that, according to the National Institutes of Health, one in six 16-year-olds who try marijuana will become addicted to it; marijuana intoxication doubles the risk of a car crash; heavy marijuana use has been significantly linked to an 8-point reduction in IQ; and that marijuana use is strongly connected to mental illness.   11

Constantly downplaying the risks of marijuana, its advocates have promised reductions in crime, flowing tax revenue and little in the way of negative effects on youth. We shouldn't hold our breath, though.   12

We can expect criminal organizations to adapt to legal prices, sell to people outside the legal market (e.g., kids) and continue to profit from other, much larger revenue sources, such as human trafficking and other drugs.   13

We can expect the social costs ensuing from increased marijuana use to greatly outweigh any tax revenue—witness the fact that tobacco and alcohol cost society $10 for every $1 gained in taxes.   14

Probably worst of all, we can expect our teens to be bombarded with promotional messages from a new marijuana industry seeking lifelong customers.   15

In light of the currently skewed discourse on marijuana, these are difficult facts to digest. In one fell swoop, we have been promised great things with legalization. However, we can expect to be let down.   16

Voters in other states should watch Colorado closely and engage in a deep conversation about where they want this country to go. Buyer, beware.   17

http://www.washingtontimes.com/news/2014/jan/17/sabet-marijuana-legalizations-worst-enemy/?page=all   18

Inquiring into the Essay

1. **Explore.** In a fastwrite, explore your reaction to this statement: "Fairness dictates that policymakers either need to play nanny and ban everything that's bad for us—from sugar-laden soda to fat-filled fast food—or they need to allow Americans to make adult decisions about what they want to put in their bodies. Making cigarettes, beer, and whiskey legal, while banning joints and hash brownies, unfairly favors the makers of certain harmful products."[2]

2. **Explain.** Using the Rogerian approach discussed earlier (pp. 224–225), "say back" what you understand to be Sabet's argument. Summarize his argument, including his main claim (or S.O.FT.) and some of the reasons he offers to support it.

3. **Evaluate.** This article was written within a few weeks of the implementation of Colorado's marijuana law. Do some research on whether the reasons Sabet offers to support his claims are backed by the most recent evidence on the law's effects. How would you evaluate his argument based on what you discovered?

4. **Reflect.** What would you say is your feeling about the question of legalization of recreational marijuana at this moment—oppose, neutral/not sure, supportive? How do you suppose your view influenced your reading of the essay compared to the reading by someone with a different view? What does this imply about how an audience's disposition towards an issue might affect how you make an argument?

---

[2]Shane, Scott. "Why Colorado and Washington Were Wise to Legalize Pot." *Entrepreneur*. Entrepreneur.com, 20 January 2014. Web. 20 November 2014.

THE WRITING PROCESS

Inquiry Project **Writing an Argument**

Inquiry questions: What is true? What should it be called? What is the cause?

Write an essay in which you make a factual, causal, or definitional claim about an issue or controversy that interests you. You are writing for an audience of nonexperts. Make sure your essay includes the following:

- *Claims* that are supported by clear reasons.
- *Relevant evidence* from your research, observations, and personal experience to support your claims and reasons.
- A strong sense of *what is at stake* for your readers. Why should they care as much as you do about the issue?
- At least some attention to *counterarguments*. What are other ways of looking at the issue, and why did you reject them?

Prose+

After writing a draft, also consider a re-genre of your essay (see Chapter 13) and the many ways to re-genre your essay that exploit visual, audio, or gestural modes along with writing. To start thinking about this, consider which of these three rhetorical goals might apply to your topic if you repurpose it from a written text to a multimodal composition:

- To dramatize a problem or idea for certain audiences. To encourage certain audiences *to feel something*.
- To change behavior. To encourage certain audiences *to do something*.
- To inform a particular audience about an aspect of a topic *in a timely way*. When and where might the information be most persuasive or most relevant?

What Are You Going to Write About?

Gun control, abortion rights, and other hot-button public controversies often make the list of banned topics for student essays. This is not because they aren't important public debates. Instead, the problem is much more that the writer has likely already made up his or her mind and sees the chance to ascend a soapbox.

Now, I have my own favorite soapboxes; people with strong convictions do. But as you think about subjects for your essay, consider that the soapbox may not be the best vantage point for practicing inquiry. If you've already made up your mind,

The best argument essays make a clear claim, but they do it by bowing respectfully to the complexity of the subject, examining it from a variety of perspectives, not just two opposing poles.

will you be open to discovery? If you just want to line up ducks—assembling evidence to support an unwavering belief—will you be encouraged to think deeply or differently? Will you be inclined to filter the voices you hear rather than consider a range of points of view?

The best persuasive essays often emerge from the kind of open-ended inquiry that you might have used for writing the personal essay. What do you want to understand better? What issue or question makes you wonder? What controversies are you and your friends talking about? Be alert to possible subjects that you might write about *not* because you already know what you think, but because you want to find out what you think. Or consider a subject that you might have feelings about but feel uninformed on, lacking the knowledge to know exactly what you think.

Opening Up

Play around with some ideas first by using some of the following triggers for thinking-through-writing in your journal. Suspend judgment. Don't reject anything. Explore. Remember that your goal is to come up with a factual, causal, or definitional argument, so always be on the lookout for those types of arguments as you generate ideas.

Listing Prompts. Lists can be rich sources of triggering topics. Let them grow freely, and when you're ready, use a list item as the focus of another list or an episode of fastwriting. The following prompts should get you started.

1. In your journal, make a quick list of issues that have provoked disagreements between groups of people in your hometown or local community. What about on campus?

2. Think about these important areas of your life: school, family, work, hobbies, relationships. Title columns with each of these words in your journal or on your computer, and then make a fast list of whatever comes to mind when you think of controversial issues in each category. (See "One Student's Response: Rebecca's Journal.")

3. Try brainstorming lists from the inquiry questions. Quickly complete the following seed sentences. See if you can generate five of each.
   - I wonder if _____ causes _____?
   - I wonder how people define _____?
   - Is it true that _____?

4. Jot down a list of the classes you're taking this semester. Then make a quick list of topics that prompt disagreements among people in the fields that you're studying. For example, in your political science class, did you learn that there are debates about the usefulness of the Electoral College? In your biology class, have you discussed global warming? In your women's studies class, did you read about Title IX and how it affects female athletes?

One Student's Response

Rebecca's Journal

LISTS OF POSSIBLE ARGUMENT TOPICS

1. **Issues:** Gay marriage, rent control, cat calling on the street (or in restaurant jobs!), cleanliness, encouraging diversity vs. affirmative action, underage drinking, abortion rights
2. **School:** funding for the arts
3. **Family:** retirement/money issues, distance between family members, aging
4. **Work:** survival job vs. dream job, bad economy
5. **Hobbies:** too much work, NYC too expensive
6. **Relationships:** too much work, how to meet people?
7. **Cultural trends:** Twitter/Facebook/Tumblr/other social media, going to movies, drinking/clubbing, gossip

Fastwriting Prompts. Remember, fastwriting is a great way to stimulate creative thinking. Turn off your critical side and let yourself write "badly." Don't worry too much about what you're going to say before you say it. Write fast, letting language lead for a change.

1. Search online for the *Harper's Index*, a monthly list of interesting statistics that often tell a story about the way things were, are, or will become.

   Here are a few examples:

   > Percentage of all Americans who consider themselves part of the top 1 percent of U.S. earners: 13
   > Percentage of Hispanic Americans who do: 28
   > Percentage of 27- to 45-year-old women who have at least four sexual fantasies per week: 35
   > Percentage of 18- to 26-year-old women who do: 27

   Fastwrite about one of these facts. In your fastwrite, explore the following questions:
   - Is this surprising?
   - Does this fact seem true? If so, what would explain it? If not, what makes me skeptical?
   - What is my personal experience with this? Does it remind me of any stories, people, situations?
   - What might be the cause?

2. Use something from your lists in the preceding section for a focused fastwrite.

3. In a seven-minute fastwrite, explore the differences between your beliefs and the beliefs of your parents. Tell yourself the story of how your own

beliefs about some question evolved, perhaps moving away from your parents' positions. Can you imagine the argument you might make to help them understand your point of view?

Visual Prompts. Think about words whose meanings are contested or raise questions for you. For example: feminism, attractiveness, intelligence, manhood, redneck. In your journal, choose one of these words as a nucleus for a cluster. Then build branches, free-associating names of people, ideas about, personal observations, common definitions, memories, facts, places, questions, and so on.

Let your cluster grow as many branches as possible; when one dies out, start another. Are you growing an idea about a definition argument?

Research Prompts. By definition, argument essays deal with subjects in which people beyond the writer have a stake. And one of the best ways to collect ideas about such issues is to do a little quick and dirty research. Try some of the following research prompts:

1. Read the letters to the editor in your local paper a few days in a row. What issues have people riled up locally? Is there one that you find particularly interesting?

2. Do a Google search for terms or phrases on an issue that interests you, such as "global warming Greenland glaciers" or "pro-anorexia websites." Did you find any results that make you curious or make you feel something about the issue, one way or another?

3. Your Facebook friends may list groups that support or oppose social causes. Browse some of them to see if one inspires an argument topic.

Narrowing Down

7.4
Develop a question that is focused enough to lead to a strong claim and convincing evidence.

Remember that the task here is to discover a topic that might inspire one of these three types of arguments: *factual, causal,* or *definitional.*

What's Promising Material and What Isn't? First, you must be interested in the topic, even if you know little about it. Also consider some of the following as you make your choice:

- *Evidence.* Do you think you'll be able to find facts, statistics, comments from experts, or stories about people affected by the issue?

- *Disagreement.* A topic lends itself to argumentative writing if it leads to disagreement among reasonable people.

- *Inquiry.* Do you already have strong feelings about what you think about a topic? If so, using another topic will provide more opportunities for learning and discovery.

To help narrow down towards an essay topic that might lead to the *type* of argument we're focusing on here, review the ideas you generated and consider which of the following observations seem relevant to the potential topics you have so far.

Argument Type	Initial Observations on a Topic
Factual	No one seems to agree on the facts!
Causal	It seems like there is a cause/effect relationship that might explain the problem.
Definitional	Different people seem to call this issue, problem, or phenomenon really different things.

Questions About Audience and Purpose. In the beginning of the chapter, I emphasized that we make public arguments only about issues in which certain people have a stake. Who are those people? What audiences might care that the issue is addressed? To whom does it matter? For each potential topic, map out potential stakeholders in a mind map like the one in Figure 7.4. If you can, break

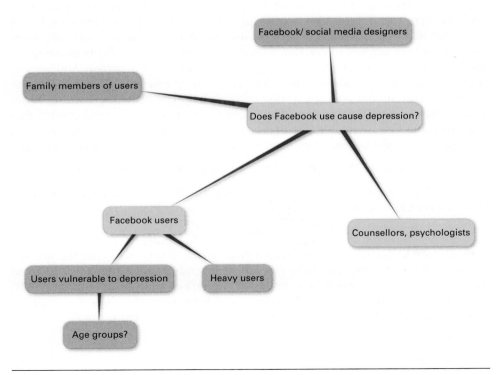

Figure 7.4   Audience analysis

each audience down further, identifying more specific groups of stakeholders in each target audience.

Looking at your mind map, identify which of these audiences has the most at stake in the answer to the question you're posing. In Figure 7.4, a causal argument that asks, "Does Facebook use cause depression?", it isn't hard to see that Facebook users are the most important stakeholders. Is this group likely to have existing attitudes about the answer to the question you're asking? What are those attitudes? Are there secondary audiences, perhaps those not directly affected by the issue but who can influence the solution to the problem? For example, certainly psychologists who treat adolescent depression would be keenly interested in the answer to the question about Facebook's relationship to depression. They're also a group in a position to do something about it.

Keeping all of this in mind, can you imagine at this point the audience you are most interested in reaching in your argument? What might be your purpose in doing so?

Trying Out

Okay, you've got a tentative topic and inquiry question for your argument essay: *Does Facebook use cause depression?* At this point, you're thinking that your claim might be that, yes, it does. This isn't a bad start. But your opening question is still pretty broad. What *aspects* of Facebook use might you focus on? After all, users have all kinds of ways of interacting with the site. The question also begs the question of which users you might be talking about. Certainly not everyone. And are you talking about certain kinds of depression? Like a lot of research-based projects, the argument essay should pose a question that will help you make the decision about what information to look for and what to ignore. It should be focused enough that you can wade into a creek rather than a raging river of information. If you think your question might be too general, try the following activity to cut it down to size.

Kitchen Knives of Thought. Try the following steps in your journal:

STEP ONE: Write your tentative argument question at the top of a page of your notebook, and circle or underline every general or vague term.

Does (Facebook) use cause (depression?)

STEP TWO: "Wh" questions (who, what, which, when, where, why) are the kitchen knives of thought. They can help you cut abstractions and generalities down to size. For each circled word in your inquiry question, find an appropriate "Wh" question that might help you make your research question more specific. Then jot down a quick list of ideas to answer the question you pose. For example,

1. *What* **kinds** of Facebook use?
   - Number of friends
   - Online interactions—rejection, being blocked, etc.
   - Authoring or reacting to certain posts on emotional state

2. *Which* **users**?
    - Adolescent
    - Heavy users
    - Users with existing emotional problems
3. *What* **kinds** of depression?
    - Major, possibly leading to treatment or hospitalization
    - Minor, affecting self-esteem
    - Suicidal

STEP THREE: Restate your inquiry question, making it more specific and focused.

> Do social interactions on Facebook cause major depression
> among heavy users?

Research Considerations. While writing this argument essay does involve some research, it isn't exactly a research paper. A research paper is a much more extended treatment of a topic that relies on more-detailed and scholarly information than is usually needed for an argument essay. In addition to the research strategies in this section, in Chapter 11 you'll find more information that might be helpful, including information on conducting effective Internet searches, evaluating the sources you find, and using library resources.

To develop a working knowledge of the topic for your argument essay, focus your research on the following:

1. *The back story:* What is the history of the controversy? (When did it begin, who was involved, how was the issue addressed, and what were the problems?)
2. *Popular assumptions:* What do most people currently believe is true about the issue?
3. *The evidence:* Which particular people have said which particular things that seem to support your claim or provide backing for your assumptions?
4. *Opposing arguments:* Who offers a counterargument that you might need to consider?

Chapter 10 offers a wide range of research strategies for finding information online and in the library.

Interviews. While both the web and the university library are great sources of information on your topic, often the best way to learn about it—and get some good quotes for your essay—is to find someone to talk to. Your reading will probably give you the best clues about who to contact. Who is often quoted in news stories? Who has been writing or blogging about the issue? You might also be able to find someone on your own campus. If you're writing, say, about measures that attempt to protect students from date rape on your campus, someone in the criminal justice department or in Student Affairs can tell you more about the issue in a few minutes than you might learn in a couple hours online.

Writing the Sketch

Now draft an exploratory sketch with the following elements:

- It has a tentative title.
- It raises a causal, definitional, or factual question.
- It presents and analyzes several contrasting points of view on the question.
- It offers a tentative answer to the question that includes a few reasons that support the claim, as well as supporting evidence: an anecdote or story, a personal observation, data, an analogy, a case study, expert testimony, other relevant quotations from people involved, a precedent.
- It includes a Works Cited or References page listing the sources used.

▶ Student Sketch

Rebecca Thompson takes up a causal question: Do social media (things meant to connect us) actually undermine communication between users? At this point, she's inclined to argue that social media like Twitter enhance communication, but she concedes that there are many critics who believe that sites such as Facebook do harm by undermining our social relationships rather than enhancing them, as Rebecca starts to argue here. Her sketch is the seed of an argument: There's a claim, reasons that support it, evidence, and consideration of another point of view. We'll see later in the chapter how the argument develops from here.

Twitter a Profound Thought?

Rebecca Thompson

1   Facebook Chat. iPhone texting. Checking in on FourSquare. Twitter hashtags. Tumblr blogging. These days, there's no limit to the ways we can talk to each other. Suddenly, talking and listening is much more complicated. But is this a good thing?

2   I use social media regularly. I use my email, Facebook, Twitter, and iPhone in all areas of my life, from connecting with high school friends now scattered across the country, to networking and advertising projects I'm involved in, to keeping updated on news stories. When Hurricane Irene struck the East Coast, I was out of town. I kept tabs on my friends via Facebook, and followed the news stories by following the hashtag #HurricaneIrene on Twitter. It was a relief to be connected, even from far away. "At its core, it is about connections and community," said Mailet Lopez, the founder of the networking site I Had Cancer, to *Forbes* magazine. "Social networking provides an opportunity beyond physical support networks and online forums . . . because with a social network, people can connect based on whatever criteria they want, regardless of location."

3   Yet detractors argue that social media does the opposite of what Lopez claims—it encourages *disconnectivity*. By focusing more on the kind of communication based around gadgets and the internet, critics argue that social media deconstructs traditional methods of conversation and undermines interpersonal relationships. "Technology is threatening to dominate our lives

and make us less human," writes Paul Harris, referencing Sherry Tunkle's book *Alone Together.* "Under the illusion of allowing us to communicate better, it is actually isolating us from real human interactions in a cyber-reality that is a poor imitation of the real world."

While there is certainly truth to this claim, I argue that social media sites have the potential, if used to their best advantage, to facilitate communication and networking. Because I can respond to emails and texts on the go, I can plan ahead. I can keep in touch with my friends studying abroad when phones aren't an option. I get lost a *lot* less. Even the Pope has spoken of the benefits of the internet, social networking, and media. "Search engines and social networks have become the starting point of communication for many people who are seeking advice, ideas, information and answers," he said. "In our time, the internet is becoming ever more a forum for questions and answers...In concise phrases, often no longer than a verse from the Bible, profound thoughts can be communicated." 4

Works Cited

Harris, Paul. "Social networking under fresh attack as tide of cyber-skepticism sweeps US." *The Guardian.* 22 January 2011. Web. 10 February 2012.

John, Tracey. "New social network connects cancer survivors, patients, and supporters." *Forbes.* 25 August 2011. Web. 12 February 2012.

Shariatmadari, David. "Pope Benedict praises Twitter-like forms of communication." *The Guardian.* 24 January 2012. Web. 12 February 2012.

Moving from Sketch to Draft

A successful sketch points the way to the next draft. But how can you get your sketch to point the way, particularly for an essay that makes an argument? One of the most useful things you can ask yourself about your sketch is this: *What is the balance between explaining what I think and presenting evidence to support it?* If your sketch is mostly what writing expert Ken Macrorie once called "explainery," then the most important thing you might do is refocus on research. Gather more information on your topic. Test your ideas against your current opinions.

Evaluating Your Own Sketch. There are some other, more specific ways of evaluating your sketch. For example, answering these questions should give you some guidance:

- **Is the question you started with narrow enough?** Does it use specific terms rather than general terms ("society," "people," etc.)? When you did some research, were you either overwhelmed with information or unsure of where to look? If you conclude that your question still isn't focused enough, try "Kitchen Knives of Thought," earlier in this chapter.

- **Does the sketch point to a S.O.F.T.?** What seems to be the main claim you're making based on the evidence you've gathered so far?

- **Is that claim linked to one or more reasons?** Remember that claims are built on reasons (e.g., Twitter played a key factor in the success of Egypt's "Arab spring" *because* the regime couldn't control it.).

Reflecting on What You've Learned. Based on your experience so far with developing an argument essay, make an entry in your journal that explores the following questions:

- What's the difference between a fact and an opinion? Between a claim and an opinion?

- Consider what you've always thought about making arguments. How has that changed since you started working on this project?

Developing

7.5

Use audience analysis and logical methods to help guide revision of an argument.

Writing for Your Readers. You've read and written about an issue you care about. Now for the really hard part: getting out of your own head and into the heads of your potential readers, who may not care as much about your issue as you do. One way to do this is to imagine what someone in your target audience might say to you if you were telling him or her about the topic. Figure 7.5 suggests just such a conversation in three parts:

- **Backstory.** What does someone who is familiar or unfamiliar with the issue need to know to appreciate that he or she has a stake in it?

- **Concessions, Qualifications, and Complications.** People disagree. Questions have many possible answers. What have other people said?

- **Reason-Evidence Loop.** At the heart of your argument is circling this loop enough times to convince your questioner to believe your claim. (See Figure 7.5.)

This is not necessarily a scheme for structuring your essay—just for identifying the key parts of an argument that make it persuasive to readers. Which of these parts are underdeveloped or even missing from your sketch?

Another element of argument is the way the writer comes across to readers—his or her ethos. In the writing you've done so far on your topic, how do you think you might come off to an audience? Is your tone appealing, or might it be slightly off-putting? Do you successfully establish your authority to speak on this issue, or is the persona you project in the sketch somewhat unconvincing, perhaps too emotional or not fair enough?

As we develop convictions about an issue, one of the hardest things to manage in early argument drafts is creating a persuasive persona (ethos). Another is finding ways to establish connections with our audience; this does not merely involve connecting writer and readers, but also includes creating some common ground between readers and *the topic*. There are many ways to do this, including the following:

1. Connecting your readers' prior beliefs or values with your position on the topic.

2. Establishing that readers have a *stake*, perhaps even a personal one, in how the question you've raised is answered; this may be self-interest, but it may also be emotional (remember the advertiser's strategy).

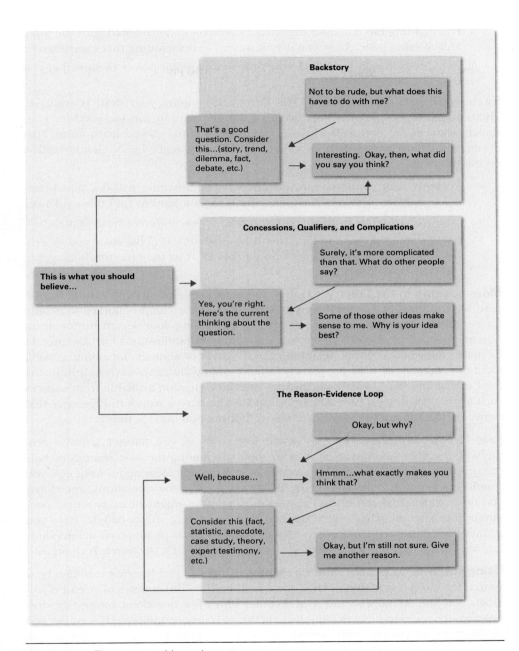

Figure 7.5 The reason-evidence loop

3. Highlighting the common experiences readers may have had with the topic and offering your claim as a useful way of understanding that experience.

4. Being reasonable. Do you devote time to looking at points of view that you may not share?

Researching the Argument. The key to developing your draft is research. Though you might be able to use some of the information you gathered for your sketch, chances are that your focus or claims are shifting as you learn more. That means going back to the research well. In particular, you need enough information on the following:

- Evidence that supports your claims. Not just anything will do. Which evidence is most *persuasive*? You may have to look hard to find this evidence.

- Counterarguments from sources that take a view different from yours.

- Background information that establishes the *context* of the issue you're writing about. What's the debate? Who's involved? How long has this been going on? Why does it matter?

More Looking in the Library.   One of the most useful things you can do to prepare for the draft is to spend forty-five minutes at the campus library searching for new information on your topic. Consider expanding your search from current newspapers and periodicals to books or government publications (see Chapter 11 for more information about searching for all kinds of sources, including government documents). In addition, you can refer to online almanacs such as Infoplease, the CIA's online World Factbook, and statistical information available from sources such as the U.S. Census Bureau's American Fact Finder—a wonderful resource that draws on the Bureau's massive database of information on U.S. trends.

Face-to-Face Interviewing.   Try some interviews if you haven't already. People who are somehow involved in your topic are among the best sources of new information and lively material. An interview can provide ideas about what else you should read or who else you might talk to, as well as the quotations, anecdotes, and case studies that can make the next draft of your argument essay much more interesting. After all, what makes an issue matter is how it affects people. Have you sufficiently dramatized those effects? For more information on face-to-face interviewing, see Chapter 4, "Writing a Profile," as well as Chapter 11, "Research Techniques."

Using the Web to Obtain Interviews and Quotes.   The Internet can also be a source for interview material. Look for e-mail links to the authors of useful documents you find on the web and write to them with a few questions. Interest groups, newsgroups, or electronic mailing lists on the web can also provide the voices and perspectives of people with something to say on your topic. Remember to ask permission to quote them if you decide to use something of theirs in your draft. For leads on finding web discussion groups on your topic, visit Google Groups or Yahoo Groups, which allow you to search for online discussion groups on virtually any topic, or Catalist, the official catalog of electronic mailing lists, which has a database of about 15,000 discussion groups.

Finding Images. When appropriate, look for images to dramatize your claims or your evidence. Images are easy to find using search engines such as Google Image Search. But any images you use must be specifically relevant to your argument. If you do use online images in your essay, make sure to give the source credit in the text and the bibliography.

Drafting

Designing Your Argument Rhetorically. The argument essay is one of those forms of writing that are plagued by organizing formulas. The claim must go in the first paragraph. The reasons behind the claims should be topic sentences, followed by evidence. The conclusion should restate the claim. But take a look at any published arguments, and you'll see how far this formula is from the way arguments are actually written.

On the other hand, arguments do typically have the features that we've discussed: a question, a claim that addresses it, reasons, evidence, counterclaims. Just don't ever imagine that you should march through these features in some strict order. You need to decide the design of your argument. And what will help you most in doing this is thinking about audience, especially:

This rhetorical awareness of your audience has implications for what information you include—and especially what you emphasize—in your draft:

- **Prior knowledge.** If your audience knows little about your topic, then you'll spend more time with background and context than you might if they largely understand the issue.

- **Receptivity.** Audiences that are already inclined to strongly agree are less critical. They probably need less evidence to be convinced of your position than neutral readers do. A resistant audience is the toughest sell: Strong evidence, and lots of it, are key.

- **Stake.** Neutral audiences—the kind you're most likely to encounter—have little awareness that your topic matters to them. You have to make it matter, and make it matter quickly.

Methods of Development. Earlier in this chapter, we explored three models for argument: classical, Toulmin, and Rogerian. Each of these is typically associated with certain ways of structuring an argument (for structures of classical and Rogerian arguments, see pages 222 and 226). While there is no formula for organizing an argument, there are some ways of developing parts—and sometimes all—of your essay.

Narrative. Telling a story is an underrated way of developing an argument. Can you imagine a way to present your topic in an extended story, perhaps by focusing on the experience of a particular person or group of people, in a particular place, at a particular time? Obviously, the story must somehow be logically linked to your claim.

There are other ways to use narrative, too. Anecdotes, or brief stories that illustrate an idea or a problem, are frequently used in argument essays. One effective way to begin your essay might be to tell a story that highlights the problem you're writing about or the question you're posing.

Question to Answer. Almost all writing is an attempt to answer a question. In the personal essay and other open forms of inquiry, the writer may never arrive at a definite answer, but an argument essay usually offers an answer. An obvious method of development, therefore, is to begin your essay by raising the question and end it by offering your answer.

Are there several key questions around which you might organize your draft, leading to your central claim at the end?

Problem to Solution. This variation on the question-to-answer structure can be particularly useful if you're writing on a topic readers may know very little about. In such cases, you might need to spend as much time establishing what exactly the problem is—explaining what makes it a problem and why the reader should care about it—as you do offering your particular solution.

Effect to Cause or Cause to Effect. At the heart of some arguments is the *relationship* between causes and effects; often what is at issue is pinpointing such a relationship. Once a relationship is pinpointed, solutions can be offered. Sadly, we know the effects of terrorism, but what are its causes? If you were to argue, as some do, that Islamic radicalism arose in response to U.S. policies in the Middle East, including its policies toward Israel and the Palestinians, then you would be arguing from effect to cause. As the solution, you might go on to propose a shift in foreign policy. Some arguments can be organized simply around an examination of causes and effects.

Combining Approaches. As you think about how you might organize your first draft, you don't necessarily have to choose among these various methods of development. In fact, most often they work well together.

Using Evidence. All writing relies on evidence—that is, on specific information that has some relationship to the general ideas expressed. For some of these relationships, see "Inquiring into the Details: What Evidence Can Do." Although all these relationships are possible in an argumentative essay, especially common is the use of evidence to support ideas that the writer wants the reader to believe.

What Evidence Can Do

Usually we think of using evidence only to support an idea or claim we're making. But evidence can be used in other ways, too. For example, it can do the following:

- ■ *refute* or challenge a claim with which you disagree
- ■ *show* that a seemingly simple assertion, problem, or idea is actually complex
- ■ *complicate* or even contradict an earlier point you've made
- ■ *contrast* two or more ways of seeing the same thing
- ■ *test* an idea, hypothesis, or theory

What *kind* of evidence to include is a rhetorical issue. To whom are you writing, and what kind of evidence will they be most likely to believe?

Generally speaking, the narrower and more specialized the audience, the more particular they will be about the types of evidence they'll find convincing. As you continue on in your chosen major, you'll find that the types of evidence that help you make a persuasive argument will be more and more prescribed by the field. In the natural sciences, the results of quantitative studies count more than case studies; in the humanities, primary texts count more than secondary ones.

The important thing for this argument essay, which you're writing for a more general audience, is that you attempt to *vary* your evidence. For example, rather than relying exclusively on anecdotes, include some quotes from an expert as well.

Workshopping

If your draft is subject to peer review, see Appendix A for details on how to organize workshop groups and decide on how your group can help you. To help you decide, use the guidance, starting on p. 554, in Appendix A. Each workshop type is described more fully in that section.

Workshops on argument drafts can be lively affairs. People have opinions, and other people may disagree with those opinions. Facts can be contested with counterfacts. As you prepare to share your draft, I'd encourage you to ask peers to speak to two separate issues:

1. Do you agree with my argument? What are your feelings about it?
2. No matter what your disposition is toward the argument in my draft, can you help me make it better?

Both discussions are important. But it may be hard to get to the second discussion if your workshop group is consumed by a debate over the issue itself.

As always, focus your peer review on the central concerns of a first draft: purpose and meaning. You can use the following box.

Questions for Peer Reviewers	
Purpose	What is the question driving my argument? At what point in the draft do you first understand the question? Is that early enough?
Meaning	Do you understand the claim I'm making? Are the reasons I'm taking this position clear? Which do you find most convincing? Least convincing? What questions do you have that I haven't answered?

Reflecting on the Draft. After having spent time choosing an argument topic and developing and drafting your argument, what do you now understand about making effective arguments that you didn't when you started? If you were to make a single PowerPoint slide explaining that, what would it say?

Revising

Revision is a continual process—not a last step. You've been revising—"reseeing" your subject—from the first messy fastwriting in your journal. But the things that get your attention vary depending on where you are in the writing process. With your draft in hand, revision becomes your focus through what I'll call "shaping and tightening your draft."

Chapter 14 contains strategies that can help you revise any inquiry project, and the "Guidelines: Revising Your Work" in this chapter on page 253 can help you locate these strategies. There are also certain things to think about that are especially useful for shaping an argument.

Shaping. In your draft, you made a tentative commitment to your topic, hoping that you could shape it into something that might have meaning for someone other than you. Fundamentally, you've been trying to figure out *what you're trying to say* and then rebuild your essay so that it is both clear and convincing. In an argument essay, you also want it to be convincing.

Shaping focuses first on the largest concerns of purpose and meaning—which you've already looked at if you workshopped your draft—and on the next-to-largest concerns of information and organization. It starts with knowing what your essay is about—your inquiry question and maybe your claim—and then revising to make every element of the draft focused on that question or assertion.

This chapter includes some useful tools that should help you shape the next draft, and in particular examine your reasoning strategies.

1. **Toulmin and Rogers.** A helpful technique for revising the first draft of your argument essay is to use a method of analyzing argumentative reasoning, such as Toulminian or Rogerian logic (see pages 223–224). Toulmin logic is particularly powerful for detecting the warrants or assumptions that might be lurking behind your reasons and claims. Are these assumptions valid? Should they be addressed in the revision?

2. **Logical fallacies.** Did you get yourself on any slippery slopes or beg a question? Find out by looking at the "Avoiding Logical Fallacies" section earlier in this chapter.

3. **Rhetorical analysis.** We've talked about Aristotle's elements of persuasion: ethos, pathos, and logos. Is there an effective emphasis on each of these in your draft, and have you used them in proportions appropriate for your topic and audience?

Polishing. When you are satisfied with the shape of your draft, focus on paragraphs, sentences, and words. Are your paragraphs coherent? How do you manage transitions? Are your sentences fluent and concise? Are there any errors in spelling or syntax? The section of Chapter 14 called "Problems with Clarity and Style" can help you focus on these issues.

Guidelines: Revising Your Work

A first effort is almost never a best effort. To make sure your essay is really your best work, check out Chapter 14 for help with these questions:

- What is my paper really about? (See p. 518.)

- What am I really trying to say? (See p. 523.)

- Do I have enough convincing evidence? (See p. 530.)

- Does this paper move logically and smoothly from paragraph to paragraph? (See p. 534.)

- Are the sentences and paragraphs in this paper too choppy or hard to follow? (See p. 542.)

▶ Student Essay

One of the things I really like about Rebecca Thompson's causal argument "Social Networking Social Good?" is that even though she's a fan of social networking, she readily concedes that there are downsides to it. Rebecca could have quickly nodded to critics of her position in a sentence or two. But instead she explores the case against social media in some detail, quoting extensively from people who worry that social media undermine conversations and personal relationships. Rebecca agrees with some of this. But she argues that, overall, media such as Facebook and Twitter have made her life better. Acknowledging opposing viewpoints is an important move in argumentative essays. But writers of these essays rarely take these viewpoints seriously. Because Rebecca recognizes the complexity of her topic, and tries to deal with it in her essay, the claim she makes seems more persuasive.

Social Networking Social Good?

Rebecca Thompson

1   Facebook Chat. iPhone texting. Checking in on FourSquare. Twitter hashtags. Tumblr blogging. OkCupid matchmaking. These days, there's no limit to the ways we can talk to each other. Suddenly, the basic human foundation of communication—talking and listening—has become much more complicated. It's incontrovertible that our society has changed in response to technological and media advancements. The day-to-day functions of our lives are different than they were even five years ago. We read differently (on Kindle or Nook), we watch differently (on Netflix, Hulu, or OnDemand), we hear differently (earbuds and surround sound), we even learn differently (smart boards, smart phones, Google). Despite the major advancements in rapid response, worldwide networking, as well as major shifts in the arts and sciences, many are concerned that there are major downfalls to the way that we, as a society, have begun to use social networking and media devices. Yet overall the explosion of social networking has provided unforeseen benefits, too. We can now find comfort in the company of strangers, erase the distance between far-flung friends, and most important, participate in conversations that spread new knowledge.

2   I use social media, like e-mail, Facebook, Twitter, and Wordpress, in all areas of my life, from connecting with high school friends now scattered across the country, to networking and advertising projects I'm involved in, to keeping updated on news stories. When Hurricane Irene struck the East Coast, I was out of town. I kept tabs on my friends via Facebook, and followed the news stories by following the hashtag #HurricaneIrene on Twitter. It was a relief to be connected, even from far away. Similarly, following the devastating tornado in Missouri in May 2011, so-called "small-media efforts" (such as Facebook, local radio, and Twitter) were the ones that led most mainstream media to the scene. Facebook groups formed instantaneously and expanded exponentially, featuring posts from families searching for survivors as well as complete strangers offering prayers and support. As one poster wrote, "On one hand, my heart is just aching for your loss and devastation . . . [O]n the other hand, seeing everyone pulling together reminds me how resilient the human spirit is" (Mustich).

3   In instances of catastrophe like Hurricane Irene and the tornados in the Midwest, social networking is put to effective use in networking relief efforts, gathering and spreading crucial information, and sharing messages of support. Few would argue the positive effects of these technological advances. However, social media also functions on a more personal level, connecting people on a one-on-one basis, often inviting them into the most clandestine parts of their lives. "At its core, it is about connections and community," said Mailet Lopez, the founder of the networking site I Had Cancer, to *Forbes* magazine. "Social networking provides an opportunity beyond physical support networks and online forums . . . because with a social network, people can connect based on whatever criteria they want, regardless of location" (John).

4   Thousands of anonymous viewers can read about the inner workings of thousands of other social media users, following their Twitter, subscribing to their blogs, mapping their location on FourSquare. This is a new phenomenon, thanks to the rapid developments in speed and

accessibility in the technology, and is often cited as a cause of heightened disconnectivity and impersonality in human relationships. For some, though, social networking's seemingly impersonal associations actually provide great personal comfort. During the time her husband suffered from debilitating cancer and treatment, writer Lee Ann Cox chronicled her struggles on Twitter, her own "defiant cry to be seen, to testify, bearing witness to suffering in 140 characters or less." Cox tweeted about the mundane, the terror, and the absurdities of handling her husband's condition, and though she had followers, the simple act of tweeting in and of itself was her therapy. "Maybe I did get something I needed from Twitter," she writes. "With no one's permission, I gave myself a voice...I needed to say these things and imagine some heart in the Twittersphere absorbing my crazed reality" (Cox).

Social media critics see the downside of Cox's experience, arguing that rather than encouraging communication and interpersonal relationships, it diminishes them. These critics worry that social media deconstructs traditional methods of conversation and undermines interpersonal relationships. I have certainly sat in a room with four of my friends, all of us checking our iPhones and laptops, barely speaking. I've had more communication with some people on Facebook than I have with them in real life. I'm sure that the authors of certain blogs I follow have more "blog friends" than real friends. Certainly, this kind of distance makes communication easier. If there's an awkward pause in a conversation, pull out your phone. If you're too shy to actually talk to a boy you're interested in, poke him on Facebook. The risk that online conversations might impoverish actual conversations is real. However, as Susan Greenfield, director of the Royal Institution of Great Britain, put it

5

> Real conversation in real time may eventually give way to these sanitized and easier screen dialogues, in much the same way as killing, skinning and butchering an animal to eat has been replaced by the convenience of packages of meat on the supermarket shelf. Perhaps future generations will recoil with similar horror at the messiness, unpredictability and immediate personal involvement of a three-dimensional, real-time interaction (qtd. in Mackey).

Greenfield's gruesome image exemplifies the lowered stakes of communication, and therefore, repercussions, online. In 2011, the *Oxford English Dictionary* put the term "cyberbullying" into its lexicons. With increasing anonymity, access to personal information, and expanded public forums, social media has opened the door to new forms of cruelty—and not just for kids. Take the Dharun Ravi case. He used his webcam to tape his college roommate Tyler Clementi in a homosexual encounter with another student, and then shared it online with his friends. Clementi subsequently committed suicide. The case is unusual because it was based primarily on records of online interaction. Both the prosecution and defense used mountains of electronic evidence, including numerous tweets (some of which were tampered with), Facebook posts (including Clementi's final status update), text messages, screenshots, e-mails, and web chats. The sheer volume of evidence on social networking tools is beyond the scope of any other major bullying case in recent history. In many ways, this is a boon to the judicial process, as records of the students' online interactions are prime evidence for both the prosecution and defense.

6

(continued)

(continued)

On the other hand, it is disturbing to note how the deteriorated relationship between these two boys "played out on social media with curiously few face-to-face exchanges" (Clayton).

7   Ravi's ability to quickly disperse the contraband video highlights is another inherent problem in social media. In mere seconds, an online post can be captured, saved, reposted, and shared. While a great boon for marketing and the quick dissemination of crucial information (such as in the case of a major natural disaster or a political event), there exists no system to judge the veracity and reliability of viral posts. The most viral video of all time is a 30-minute documentary made by the organization Invisible Children about Ugandan leader Joseph Kony, which received over 100 million hits in under a week when it was first posted in March 2012. However, after that first week had passed and certain critics began to look deeper, deep flaws in the message of the video emerged. "To call [Kony2012's] campaign a misrepresentation is an understatement," writes Angelo Izama, quoted in Time's "Global Spin" blog (Tharoor). The organization itself, Invisible Children, is under fire for its practices as an NGO. Most concerning to critics, though, is the extreme simplification and digestibility of the message itself. In this telling, to simply "know" about Kony . . . would be enough to bring him down," writes Ishaan Tharoor in "Global Spin." "That quest takes place in a world of moral simplicity, of good and evil, of innocence and horror . . . justice is about much more than manhunts and viral video crusades" (Tharoor).

8   I recall seeing the Kony post on Facebook, and watched a few minutes before closing it down. I almost reposted, but then figured I should perhaps watch the whole 30 minutes before showing my support to my friends and followers. Upon reading the criticism of the documentary, now nearly as viral as the video itself, it seems to me that knowledge has been disseminated, albeit in a non-traditional way. Social networking allows for great diversity of opinion, and also opens the door to conversation. "Knowledge consists of a network of people and ideas that are not totally in sync, that are diverse, that disagree," states David Weinberger in an interview with Salon's Thomas Rogers. "Books generally have value because they encapsulate some topic and provide you with everything you know, because when you're reading it you cannot easily leap out of the book to get to the next book. The Web only has value because it contains difference" (Rogers).

9   Weinberger elucidates precisely the problems with, and the importance of, social media and the way knowledge is shared. It has inherently changed our tools of communication and of functioning in modern society—we can't go back now. "Ask anybody who is in any of the traditional knowledge fields," states Weinberger.

> She or he will very likely tell you that the Internet has made them smarter. They couldn't do their work without it; they're doing it better than ever before, they know more; they can find more; they can run down dead ends faster than ever before . . . Now we have a medium that is as broad as our curiosity (qtd. in Rogers).

10   I agree that social networking tools have the potential, if used to their best advantage, to facilitate communication, networking, and the spread of knowledge. It's made functioning on a day-to-day basis much easier. Because I can respond to emails and texts on the go, I can plan ahead. I can keep in touch with my friends studying abroad when phones aren't an option. I get lost a lot less. Even the Pope has spoken of the benefits of the Internet, social networking, and media. "Search engines and social networks have become the starting point of

communication for many people who are seeking advice, ideas, information and answers," he said. "In our time, the Internet is becoming ever more a forum for questions and answers... In concise phrases, often no longer than a verse from the Bible, profound thoughts can be communicated" (Shariatmadari).

Works Cited

Clayton, Mark. "Rutgers Spycam Case: Why It's Not Open and Shut." *Christian Science Monitor*. Christian Science Monitor, 22 Feb. 2012. Web. 15 Mar. 2012.

Cox, Lee Ann. "Losing My Husband, 140 Characters at a Time." *Salon*. 24 Jan. 2012. Web. 12 Mar. 2012.

Harris, Paul. "Social Networking Under Fresh Attack as Tide of Cyber-skepticism Sweeps US." *The Guardian*. The Guardian, 22 Jan. 2011. Web. 10 Feb. 2012.

John, Tracey. "New Social Network Connects Cancer Survivors, Patients, and Supporters." *Forbes*. Forbes, 25 Aug. 2011. Web. 12 Feb. 2012.

Mackey, Robert. "Is Social Networking Killing You?" The Lede Blog: *New York Times*. New York Times, 24 Feb. 2009. Web. 12 Mar. 2012.

Mustich, Emma. "Joplin rescue efforts HQ: Facebook." *Salon*. 23 May 2011. Web. 18 Mar. 2012.

Rogers, Thomas. "Are We on Information Overload?" *Salon*. 1 Jan. 2012. Web. 14 Mar. 2012.

Shariatmadari, David. "Pope Benedict Praises Twitter-like Forms of Communication." *The Guardian*. The Guardian, 24 Jan. 2012. Web. 12 Feb. 2012.

Tharoor, Ishaan. "Why You Should Feel Awkward About the 'Kony2012' Video." *Time*. Time, 8 Mar. 2012. Web. 14 Mar. 2012.

Evaluating the Essay

1. Rebecca claims that, overall, social media offer "comfort," eliminate "the distance between far-flung friends," and contribute to the creation of "new knowledge." Do you agree?

2. Use the rhetorical concepts of ethos, pathos, and logos to analyze the effectiveness of the essay. If the claim is that social networking, despite its potential shortcomings, is beneficial, what are the reasons Rebecca uses to support the claim? Which do you find most convincing? Least convincing?

Using What You Have Learned

Let's return to the learning objectives I outlined in the beginning of the chapter.

1. **Understand the connection between inquiry and persuasion, and apply inquiry strategies for exploring and developing an argument topic.** Argumentative writing is one of those forms that, at first, seem to have little to do with exploration: The point is to prove, not to find out. However, in this chapter I've emphasized that the object of argument is not winning but learning—discovery

remains the heart of the process. When you receive assignments that ask you to make an argument, consider writing about topics about which you may not already have a strong opinion, and use the writing process—especially at the invention stage—to discover what you think. A practical advantage of this is that you can write about nearly anything if it interests you.

2. **Distinguish between causal, factual, and definitional arguments, and develop an essay that uses one of those three approaches to persuasion.** In the two preceding chapters—on review and proposal assignments—you began your study of argument. Reviews begin with questions of value, and proposals begin with questions of policy—what should be done? Now you've got three more ways of identifying argument types: causal, factual, and definitional. When other writing situations call for argument or persuasion, return to your understanding of these argument types. What type does this writing task require? Once you know that, you'll also know the type of question that will drive your essay and what your argument will need to prove.

3. **Identify the key elements of argument—reasons, claims, and evidence—and apply them in both reading and writing.** The next time you listen to a friend argue that Boise State's football team isn't a BCS-worthy team, or that general education classes are a waste of time, or that the foreign aid budget is bankrupting the country, you'll have some tools with which to respond. Making and recognizing a claim in an argument isn't hard. But most of us aren't so good at crafting reasons for what we believe and using evidence to make those reasons persuasive. You will find this understanding powerful, not just in school, where you make arguments all the time, but in life, too, where we also make arguments all the time.

4. **Develop a question that is focused enough to lead to a strong claim and convincing evidence.** This is a consistent theme in *The Curious Writer*. Inquiry begins with questions. But not just any questions. They must be questions that are sufficiently focused, and that help you to know more explicitly what you need to know. Here you've learned three more *types* of inquiry questions that lead arguments, and also used new strategies for refining your inquiry question. This is knowledge that is essential in any research-based project, as you'll see if you tackle the ethnography and research essays later in the book.

5. **Use audience analysis and logical methods to help guide revision of an argument.** We began the study of argument essays by establishing that the reason to engage in argument in the first place is to serve the needs of stakeholders, people who have something to lose if the issue isn't addressed. Audience analysis *begins* the process of developing an argument. Who cares? Why do they care? What do they currently think? Understanding what others, especially stakeholders, believe is (to borrow from Rogers) an act of empathy, of listening. This is an essential part of civil discourse as well as a key part of making a persuasive argument. The techniques you practiced here for identifying stakeholders and analyzing audiences should prove useful whenever you want to convince others.

8

Writing an Analytical Essay

Learning Objectives

In this chapter, you'll learn to

8.1 Apply the methods of analysis to a subject whose meanings aren't apparent.

8.2 Use evidence from primary sources to argue effectively for a convincing interpretation.

8.3 Use appropriate invention strategies to discover a topic for an analytical essay.

8.4 Apply revision strategies that are effective for the analytical essay.

Writing to Interpret

On the top of a bookcase in my campus office, there's a plastic leg from a mannequin, and on its pointed foot are spurs. My students, at least the ones who notice it, think this is weird, and a few of them ask, "Hey, what's with the leg?" In other words, they are asking, "What does that mean?" Think how often we ask that question when we encounter something whose meanings aren't immediately apparent. On the other hand, consider how much more often we see things whose meanings are settled for us. The stop sign on the exit from the parking lot outside my office doesn't have ambiguous meanings at all. It tells me to stop, and I stop. No analysis needed.

We make the move to interpret things like a mannequin's leg in a professor's office—and not the stop sign outside it—because one has ambiguous meanings and the other does not. If you think about it, there is no

259

shortage of things in everyday life with ambiguous meanings: tattooed eyeballs, Facebook profile pictures, Lady Gaga, advertisements for men's cologne, the zombie craze, retro eyewear, the Honey Boo Boo reality TV show, misogynistic rap lyrics, the evolution of the Apple logo, motorcycle riders, a Langston Hughes poem. When we write to interpret, the challenge is to try to untangle the meanings of things like these, not to find *the* explanation but to offer a convincing argument for a few possible meanings. This is an analytical act that is central to academic study and is also something—in a less systemized fashion—that human beings do every day. In this chapter, we'll explore some of these analytical methods.

Motives for Writing an Analytical Essay

8.1

Apply the methods of analysis to a subject whose meanings aren't apparent.

Fortunately, traffic signs have fairly settled meanings for most American drivers, at least until they start driving in another country. It's hard to think of an interpretive activity with higher stakes, something I discovered recently upon encountering my first Scottish traffic circle. Social situations and observations, while less risky, involve interpreting meanings that help us make our way in the world. Last week, Sean wrote an essay that examined the complicated gender dynamics of whether a man opens a door for a woman. Consumer culture offers endless opportunities for interpretation. Analyzing advertising is a popular classroom activity, but beyond that, it is interesting to interpret the meanings behind changes in fashion, or the evolution of brands like Apple's iconic apple image. Entertainment media—film, TV, YouTube, etc.—are ripe for interpretation. How might we interpret the meaning of Bart Simpson's ragged haircut or the pleasures of watching zombies being dismembered in shows like *The Walking Dead*? Whether the stakes are high (the meaning of gender to transgender people filling out college applications) or relatively low (the meaning of landscape in Leslie Silko's novel *Ceremony*), interpretation is one of the most important ways we make judgments about what we see and what those things might mean. Interpreting things thoughtfully has the potential to make a real difference in our lives. As I write this, controversy over a grand jury's failure to indict an officer who killed a black teenager in Ferguson, Missouri, has raised, among other things, interesting questions about the militarization of the police. How are we to interpret the symbolism of police officers riding in Mine Resistant Ambush Protected vehicles (MRAPs) rather than Ford police cruisers? Depending on how you see it, this choice of vehicle is reassuring or disturbing. Figuring out how you sort out the meanings of things like this is an act of interpretation.

To fully appreciate what authors are saying or what effects they're trying to create in an essay, poem, or story, you often need to look closely, and in doing so, you see beyond the obvious.

The Analytical Essay and Academic Writing

No term is used more often than "critical thinking" to describe the goals of a college education. This term means a lot of things, of course, but it certainly involves what Gregory Fraser and Chad Davidson call an "analytical frame of mind." This is the kind of thinking that you'll use whenever you take a class that asks you to interpret something: In art, you might interpret a medieval painting; in English, a story by Alice Walker; in sociology, the indoctrination rituals of street gangs; in nursing, the meaning of certain kinds of informal talk among nurses about doctors; and in biology, data on the flight patterns of bees. All of these disciplines have their own theories that determine analytical methods, of course. A scientist might use statistical theories to interpret data. An anthropologist might use theories related to cultural ecology. A literary critic might use feminist theory. For many of these disciplines, no matter what theories inform it, critical analysis is in the service of an argument that answers the question *What might it mean?*

But what method of analysis might you use here? When we analyze a picture, a poem, a fashion trend, an advertisement, or a representation of an animated character on TV, we're doing *qualitative* analysis. We examine things that aren't easily measured. There are lots of methods for doing qualitative analysis, but they all typically involve two general moves, which you can imagine are like analyzing a metaphorical iceberg:

1. Looking closely at the thing (text, image, trend, brand, character, etc.) you're trying to interpret. What does it look like, how often do you see it, where do you see it?

2. Looking underneath the thing at what isn't readily seen—what is it trying to sell, what is its context, what larger ideas does it seem to promote?

Seeing what's in front of you

- **Frequency:** How often do you see it?
- **Comparison:** What is it like and unlike?
- **Location:** Where do you see it?
- **Relations:** What is its relationship to other parts?

Looking at what's underneath

- **Context:** Historical, social, genre.
- **Convention:** What are the usual meanings assigned to this?
- **Ideology:** What are the ideas this seems to be promoting?

If you're analyzing a short story, what's visible are the words in front of you. What images recur in the text? How is this character unlike that character? How does one scene in the story connect with another scene? The work of analysis always begins with the tip of the iceberg, the part above water. But it's underneath, the less visible ideas and meanings, that can give what you see above water more meaning. When analyzing a short story, we might first ask *when* was this story written—in what historical period—and *how* might this period influence what the story is trying to do? Is the story trying to challenge certain commonly held ideas about, say, family, or nature, or race?

Try applying this two-part method of analysis to the following Depression-era photograph.

Exercise 8.1

Interpreting an Image

Lewis Hines, a documentary photographer who was best known for his crusading work against child labor in the early twentieth century, in 1920 took the photograph on page 263, which is titled "Power House Mechanic Working on a Steam Pump." Keeping in mind the historical context of the image—the nation was in a titanic shift from a primarily rural economy to an industrial one—as well as Hines's interest in using photography as a form of social commentary, what would be your analysis of this image? Account for both what you actually see in the photograph—significant details in the image—and the less apparent, "submerged" meanings that you think are in it. The "Inquiring into the Details: Five Methods of Analysis feature on page 273 will also help you analyze various elements of the composition of the photo.

Generate

8.2

Use evidence from primary sources to argue effectively for a convincing interpretation.

Analytical essays are built around a main idea, claim, or interpretation you are making about a text.

STEP ONE: In your notebook, begin with a narrative-of-thought fastwrite: *The first thing I notice in the picture is…. And then I notice… And then… And then….* When the writing stalls, return again to look at the image.

Judge

STEP TWO: Review your fastwrite, looking at things you noticed in the picture that strike you—perhaps in conjunction with other details there—as potentially significant, that might hint at what the photograph is suggesting about industrialization, workers, work, masculinity, and so on.

STEP THREE: Compose a four- to six-sentence caption for the photograph that captures your interpretation. Make sure that you link that interpretation to specific evidence in the photograph.

Features of the Form

Feature	Conventions of the Analytical Essay
Inquiry question	What might it mean?
Motives	We turn to forms such as the analytical essay whenever the meaning of something is unsettled. This analysis requires that we examine it more closely to identify patterns, and then find convincing reasons about why those patterns are significant to understanding the meaning of the thing.
Subject matter	While analytical essays are a common assignment in English, focusing on literary texts, they also might explore film, art, popular culture, social behaviors, or any other subject matter whose meanings are unsettled.
Structure	There are three elements in most analytical essays: 1. Identifying *specific* features of the object being analyzed (e.g., characters in a story, elements of an image, etc.) that raise a question about meaning. 2. Exploring how those features are the tip of the iceberg of less apparent and larger themes or ideas. 3. Finding reasons, drawn from evidence in the object itself, to support this interpretation.
Sources of information	This depends on what's being analyzed. An interpretation of a story, for example, would draw evidence from the story itself: lines, passages, scenes, characters. Analytical essays, at least initially, are written *inductively*, through close analysis and observation of the object of study. This yields specific information that influences any interpretation. In addition, analytical essays might include information from other critics or analysts who have contributed to the conversation about possible interpretations.
Language	The tone of an analytical essay, as for most essays, depends on the audience. Formal essays, the kind assigned in literature classes, rarely use the first person, focusing readers' attention on the argument, not the writer. Less-formal response essays might use much more casual language.

PROSE+

In Chapter 13, you might explore how to take a writing assignment and "repurpose" it into another genre for another audience. It's a move that involves, among other things, an act of interpretation, an effort to analyze what's significant in the original text that might be communicated well in another genre. Design student Motoko Ishii "re-genred" the lyrics of a Radiohead song, "Last Flowers," into wall art using ribbon. It's visually arresting, as you can see. Ishii's design, with its black-and-white tones and cascading ribbons bleeding from the lyrics, points to an interpretation of "Last Flowers" that is somber, almost desperate, and implies that "relief, relief, relief, relief" is even less likely as the song goes on and the lyrics are obscured by more and more ribbon. In an artist's statement, Ishii writes that this was a semester-long project, and that a key moment was the transition from "working with paper to working with ribbon, which I decided to try out just by how the music felt to me—a process very much like dancing to music."

Lyrics to "Last Flowers" by Radiohead

Appliances have gone berserk
I cannot keep up
Treading on people's toes
Snot-nosed little punk

And I can't face the evening straight
And you can't offer me escape
Houses move and houses speak
If you take me there you'll get relief
Relief, relief, relief, relief...

And if I'm gonna talk
I just wanna talk
Please don't interrupt
Just sit back and listen

Cause I can't face the evening straight
And you can't offer me escape
Houses move and houses speak
If you take me there you'll get relief
relief, relief, relief, relief...

It's too much
Too bright
Too powerful

Too much
Too bright

READINGS

▶ Literary Analysis

"There are a lot of hidden meanings in poems." I suppose there is some truth to this characterization of poetry—poems can certainly have ambiguous meanings—but the implication is that poets stealthily scatter these "hidden meanings" for readers to find, that these are already cast with a certain significance, and that the job of readers is to hunt the meanings down and report what they find, hoping they get the meanings "right."

Thankfully, poetry (and, for that matter, all other literary texts) is a lot more interesting than this. Yes, meaning is waiting to be found. But readers aren't miners, they're meaning-makers. We each bring our own histories and perceptions to our encounters with literature, and we have access to tools (like literary theories or analytic methods) that help make some of the less visible patterns emerge. Bart Brinkman's brief analysis of the N. Scott Momaday poem "The Shield That Came Back" is a nice example of how this meaning-making works. Momaday, a Kiowa, is one of our greatest Native American writers, and this poem, drawing on myth, history, and allegory, is typical of much of his work.

The Shield That Came Back

N. Scott Momaday

Turning Around tested his son Yellow Grass. "You must kill   1
thirty scissortails and make me a fan of their feathers."
"Must I make the whole fan?" asked Yellow Grass. "Must I do
the beadwork too?" Yellow Grass had never made a fan.
"Yes. You must do the beadwork too—blue and black and
white and orange."
"Those are the colors of your shield," said Yellow Grass.
Yellow Grass fretted over the making of his father's fan, but
when at last it was finished it was a fine, beautiful thing, the
feathers tightly bunched and closely matched, their sheen like a
rainbow—yet they could be spread wide as a disc, like a shield.
And the handle was beaded tightly. The blue and black and white
and orange beads glittered in every light. And there was a long
bunch of doeskin fringes at the handle[']s end.
When Turning Around saw the fan he said nothing, but he was
full of pride and admiration. Then he went off on a raiding
expedition to the Pueblo country, and there he was killed. After

(continued)

(*continued*)

that, Yellow grass went among the Pueblos and redeemed his father's shield. But the fan could not be found.

When he was an old man Yellow Grass said to his grandson Handsome Horse, "You see, the shield was more powerful than the fan, for the shield came back and the fan did not. Some things, if they are very powerful, come back. Remember that. For us, in this camp, that is how to think of the world."

On "The Shield That Came Back"
Bart Brinkman

1   N. Scott Momaday's "The Shield that Came Back," from the poetry sequence, "In the Presence of the Sun: A Gathering of Shields[,]" takes as one of its central metaphors the Plains Indian warrior shield. Made from the thick chest skin of a male buffalo, the warrior shield is painted with talismanic—often animal—symbols, such as birds and deer. It was commonly believed that the design on the shield, rather than the shield itself, would protect the warrior. In making the shield a prominent metaphor in his poem, Momaday places "The Shield that Came Back" within a long Indian tradition, drawing on one of its most important cultural markers. But the shield is also suggestive of Western tradition. The shield has been a prominent Western image at least as far back as the depiction of Achilles' shield in the Iliad and has resonated through much of the literature of the West. In suggesting both Indian and Western traditions, the shield as central metaphor and Momaday's poem in general signals its need, and the need of the Modern American Indian, to negotiate both of these traditions.

2   For a poem ostensibly about a shield, however, there is a disproportionate emphasis on a fan. It is, in fact, one of the jobs of the poem to work out the identification between the fan and the shield. The poem opens with Turning Around's instructions to his son Yellow Grass that, "'You must kill/thirty scissortails and make me a fan of their feathers.'" The fan that Yellow Grass is to make—which will require a great amount of skill and effort both in hunting the scissortails and weaving together their feathers—will resemble his father's shield. As Yellow Grass tells Turning Around, of the blue and black and white and orange beadwork, "'Those are the colors of your shield.'" And the "tightly bunched and closely matched" feathers of the fan "could be spread wide [as] a disc, like a shield." In its shape and color, the fan is patterned after the shield, just as the son is patterned after the father.

3   After Turning Around is killed on a raiding expedition to the Pueblo country, Yellow Grass retrieves his father's shield "[b]ut the fan could not be found." The poem does not reveal what happened to the fan, whether it was lost, stolen, or kept close

to the father, but much later, when Yellow Grass was an old man, he told the story of the shield to his grandson Handsome Horse, with the explanation "'You see, the shield was more powerful than the fan, for the shield came back and the fan did not. Some things,/ if they are very powerful, come back. Remember that. For us, in/ this camp, that is how to think of the world." The moral to Yellow Grass's story is that tradition is powerful and will come back to protect them. It is important for his grandson to remember that "in this camp" as they struggle through a marginalized existence encapsulated by Western tradition.

But the poem offers a means of resisting Yellow Grass's moral. The fan can be seen as not only an excellent imitation of the shield, but as its successor, an object in its own right and one that is lauded by the father. Although the shield returns, it is no longer necessary because Turning Around is now dead. But the fan, as a successor to the shield, is lost in the world, just as Yellow Grass as successor to his father is also lost. The son cannot be protected by his father's shield, but must recover his own fan just as his camp cannot be protected by tradition but must identify with it to make something new. The poem (which is itself not unlike the fan in its imitation and transformation of the past) suggests that, rather than looking back to traditional ways to be saved, one must use traditional ways to look forward. This is the way that the modern American Indian can survive in the face of Western tradition and begin to draw that tradition into its own.

4

Inquiring into the Poem

1. **Explore.** This will be most useful *before* you read Brinkman's interpretation of the Momaday poem: On the left page of your notebook, jot down at least five lines or passages that you believe were key to your understanding of the poem. These may include details that seem important, names, or moments in the narrative. On the right page, do a narrative-of-thought fastwrite about what you first noticed, and then what, and then…. Whenever the writing stalls, look left at a detail or passage you collected and fastwrite about why you found it interesting or significant.

2. **Explain.** Brinkman writes, "The poem … suggests that, rather than looking back to traditional ways to be saved, one must use traditional ways to look forward." Explain what you understand this to mean.

3. **Evaluate.** Do some quick online research on the significance of the warrior shield in Native American cultures. Use what you learn to evaluate Brinkman's claims about the significance of the shield.

4. **Reflect.** When you studied poetry in high school, you developed certain routines for writing analytical papers. What were they? Was your experience analyzing Momaday's poem different from what you're used to doing when you're asked to interpret poetry?

▶ Ad Analysis

Students of marketing often worship at the altar of Apple, whose "brand strategy" has helped make it the "world's most valuable company," according to *Forbes* magazine. Its advertising successes make Apple's promotion campaigns the subject of intense interest among people who analyze marketing. Even those of us who don't share that interest may own at least one Apple product, and it's interesting to consider what sold us on an "i" device or, perhaps more important, what keeps us going back for more. Analysts often point to "Apple's emotional branding"—how its marketing (like most advertising) is heavy on pathos, making us *feel* part of the "Apple experience." The company's television advertising is an important part of this effort, and in December 2013 Apple released its "Misunderstood" ad. Critics were divided on the commercial's effectiveness. In the blog essay that follows, Alex Soojung-Kim Pang, an expert on the social implications of new technologies, analyzes "Misunderstood" and finds himself at odds with its critics. See the ad for yourself on YouTube, and then consider Pang's argument.

What Does Apple's "Misunderstood" Advertisement Mean?

Alex Soojung-Kim Pang

1   "In its latest ad, with an 'if you can't beat em, join 'em' message, Apple isn't carving aspirational ground, it's caving to people's vices," Jennifer Rooney <u>declares</u>. She's talking about "Misunderstood," the Apple Christmas commercial that's become a kind of Rorschach test: Everyone seems to find their own moral from it. (You can find the 2013 ad on YouTube).

2   It focuses on a teenage boy who's going with his family to the grandparents' house (they live just outside Thornton Wildertown, near Walden Pond, by the looks of things) for Christmas.

3   Families gather, cousins go skating, snowmen are built, the tree is decorated, dinner made—and the teen seems focused on his phone. Then, on Christmas Day, he plays the video he's been shooting. He hasn't been disengaged; he's been watching the whole time. You can even watch "Harris Family Holiday" (hereafter "HFH") for yourself.

4   Some people quite like it: The Verge, for example, <u>thought it was charming</u>; *Entertainment Weekly* called it a "<u>merry little cry</u>." Emma Mustich describes it as a "<u>completely beautiful surprise</u>." Rooney's objection is that "while he was creating, he

wasn't really living the day, he was a mere voyeur during it." That "life is better through video. Don't live life, tape it." Gizmodo <u>saw it as fundamentally antisocial, too</u>. "He's not letting anything come between him and his iPhone, not even the memories he cares enough about to record," Brian Barrett writes. "He's experiencing the holidays at an anthropological remove." (By the way, when did "anthropological" become an epithet? Aren't anthropologists some of the most astute observers around? Isn't this like as insulting as calling an athlete "ninja-like"?)

5   But I'm not so sure.

6   I saw the exact opposite of an equally controversial advertisement: the <u>Facebook Home</u> ad, in which a young woman escapes the droning tedium of Thanksgiving with her family by vicariously enjoying the lives of her much cooler, kite-surfing, nightclubbing friends.

7   "Misunderstood," in contrast, doesn't celebrate technology's ability to let us escape from boring family events. It shows how we might use it to participate.

8   Maybe I've watched too many Akira Kurosawa movies, and so I assume that complicated backstories can be revealed in just a few seconds (watch *Seven Samurai* to see how he was the master of revealing a whole village's life histories in an amazingly sparse manner). But while I'm sure the Apple ad wizards want us to assume that the teen could be any kid with an iPhone, the ad raised all kinds of questions for me. What if the kid is <u>on the autism spectrum</u>, or extremely shy (notice he never speaks, and rarely makes eye contact)? What if he's an exchange student? Thirty years earlier, would he have done the same thing with a Betamax camcorder (you can imag[in]e Spielberg at a family gathering acting like this)?

9   This last came to mind because "HFH" is actually *really good*. It's not just the work of a teen playing around: It's the work of someone who spends plenty of time watching people, and who had a <u>good eye</u> for the little scenes and artifacts and vignettes that capture a mood *and* will hold a viewer's attention. In other words, it's not the equivalent of <u>two minutes of selfies</u>. (And indeed people have argued about whether <u>photography</u> makes you more engaged with the world, or creates a distance from it.)

10   In other words, I see this kid and I don't see an ordinary tech-absorbed slacker. I come away with the sense that there's a backstory here, which makes me less willing to project my own anxieties about kids today with their damn smartphones onto it.

11   Further, as Jason <u>Morehead observes</u> in Patheos, "I'm not so sure that someone making a video like this teen's is quite as detached" as critics think. The video backs this up. It has tons of action shots: Clearly the kid is sledding with his cousins, watching the little ones, noticing little moments of affection and goofiness—he's not always off to the side, and he's certainly *not* staying inside, blasting the latest from Norwegian death metal rappers Maülhammer and playing *GTA V* while everyone else is out being

(continued)

(continued)

human. In this respect, the ad cheats a little—you have to see "HFH" to realize that the original commercial has obscured his participation.

12   Finally, I sympathized with the kid because I do something like this myself. At events at <u>my kids' school</u>, I often bring my good camera and take lots of pictures. Of course I help put up tents or serve soup or what have you—I sign up for real jobs—but at some point I usually grab the XE-1 and go wandering.

13   People by now either appreciate it or put up with it. It means that we have a far better record of school events than we used to. I like providing for the collective memory: Lots of the pictures are now in school publications, brochures, fundraising letters, and so on.

14   But it also gives me an excuse to both wander around and watch people, while also providing a little buffer from socializing *too much*.

15   In a school full of business development and VC parents who never really turn it off, being able to take pictures lets me be involved and useful on my terms.

16   Maybe I don't wonder about the "Misunderstood" teen's backstory that much, after all.

Inquiring into the Ad

1. **Explore.** Watch Apple's "Misunderstood" commercial on YouTube. Critics of the ad claim it exemplifies one of the worst things about technology like smartphones: It isolates us from others. Apple implicitly addresses this concern in the ad. Explore your own experience with this isolation, and the extent to which the commercial speaks to that experience. Do you buy what Apple is selling? What is it selling (beyond iPhones)?

2. **Explain.** Video, like writing, has a grammar. There are certain conventions—use of camera angles, framing, integration of music, cuts from scene to scene, use of lighting, and so on—that are intended to have certain effects on the viewer. Based on your own experience as a viewer of video and film, how are some of these conventions handled in the Apple ad? Which do you find particularly effective?

3. **Evaluate.** Here's what we see on the surface of the ad: An American family of multiple generations gathers on a snowy day for Christmas in a suburban home. An apparently distracted teenager appears to be a marginal participant, spending most of his time staring at his iPhone. But then he surprises everyone with a touching video he made of the family's time together. What's under the surface of this ad? In particular, *what ideas does it seem to be selling* about technology, about families and family relationships, about an American holiday like Christmas?

4. **Reflect.** Suppose your instructor asked you to analyze the Apple ad using one or more of the approaches to analysis in the "Inquiring into the Details: Five Methods of Analysis." Which method do you think might yield the most interesting results?

Inquiring into the Details

Five Methods of Analysis

We casually interpret the meanings of things all the time, especially in social situations: "That guy is always wearing a long black trench coat. He must be some kind of trench coat mafia loner dude." We observe and quickly interpret, and then the analysis is over. However, thoughtful analysis—in an effort to arrive at a more considered judgment about something—looks more methodically at how we interpret something, and most importantly *why* we interpret something the way we do. Frequently, the object of analysis is not just social behavior but texts, and I mean "texts" in the broadest sense as anything that can be "read": writing, transcripts, TV commercials, film, advertisements, etc.

As you can imagine, there are a range of methods for doing this analysis. Below are five common approaches used in a range of disciplines. You can learn more about each method by searching online. You might consider using one or more of these methods in your own analysis.

Method	Approach	Examples
Content Analysis	Counts the frequency of content in a text (certain words, phrases, ideas, themes, images, references, information types, comments, categories, etc.) and infers what they might mean. What does the text actually contain?	Recurring images in student anxiety dreams, violent images in "Grand Theft Auto," use of personal anecdote in *The Curious Writer*.
Rhetorical Analysis	Examines the effectiveness of ethos, pathos, and logos in a particular communication situation. How does the text work? What makes it persuasive? Also involves analyzing purpose, audience, and genre to investigate how they influence a text's composition.	Persuasiveness of ads for men's cologne, analysis of Dr. King's "I Have a Dream" speech, effectiveness of a website on academic honesty.
Semiotic Analysis	Identifies "signs" (in texts and social situations) that are assigned certain implied social meanings in particular contexts. What does it mean? What ideas is it selling? Who will benefit?	Significance of wearing baseball caps with stickers, the evolution of the Apple logo, the cultural meaning of Bart Simpson's haircut, analysis of ads for Mercedes-Benz automobiles.

(continued)

Inquiring into the Details (*continued*)

Method	Approach	Examples
Critical Analysis	Identifies patterns in a text that, when seen in relationship to each other, imply certain themes or ideas. Applying a context (historical, theoretical, traditional) can help tease out these patterns.	Feminist analysis of female characters in "Tomb Raider," light and dark motifs in Hawthorne's *Scarlet Letter*.
Genre Analysis	Analyzes the "family resemblances" that constitute genre. These might include certain conventions, structures, discourses, and rhetorical assumptions.	The convention of the "jump scare" in horror movies (see the essay by Bryan Bishop). Analysis of introductions to academic articles in criminal justice.

▶ Film Analysis

If you've ever watched a horror movie, you've been victim to a "jump scare," though you probably didn't know what it is called. The evil one is dead and gone, and all seems well again, until suddenly a withered hand is thrust upward from the fresh grave and grabs an ankle, and the musical soundtrack crescendos. The jump scare is a *convention* of the horror genre, a technique that is used again and again. Genre analysis often examines these conventions, describing how they work and why. "Why Won't You Die?!" is exactly this kind of analysis, exploring how jump scares work (and why they don't when they don't) and why the technique seems to be making a comeback in the horror genre.

"Why Won't You Die?!" The Art of the Jump Scare
Bryan Bishop

1   *An alarm clock glows in the darkness: 3:18AM. All is silent... until a low, steady creak groans through the house.*

2   *A young woman turns on the bedside lamp, squinting across the room. Shadows gather around vague outlines of furniture. Nothing moves. Then, voices. Murmuring. Somewhere down the hall.*

She pads into the living room on bare feet. The television must have been left on, 3
but there's a problem with the signal. The picture flickers, briefly coalescing around the
shape of a shadowy figure, only to break apart into digital noise.

Moving closer, she reaches out towards the TV. With every step, the image becomes 4
clearer; it's almost as if the figure can see her…

CLICK! She turns the television off. Exhales. 5

That's when a pair of hands shoot out from the screen, wrapping around 6
her face.

The audience screams. 7

If you've ever watched a horror film, you've seen a jump scare. It's that moment when 8
a character thinks they're safe, only to have a demon appear suddenly behind them.
The final coda when it feels like the movie's wrapping up—but the killer comes back
for one last jump. A mix of tension, cinematic sleight-of-hand, and score, it's one of
the most basic building blocks of horror movies, and it excels at one thing: catching
the audience off guard, and jolting the hell out of them.

'80s slasher films drove the jump scare into the ground, and the technique eventu- 9
ally became a cliché in its own right—with moviegoers often watching *for* the surprise
rather than being shocked themselves. In the last few years, however, we've seen the
technique make a comeback with audiences. Movies like the *Paranormal Activity*
series, which rely almost exclusively on the jolt of the jump scare, have pulled in
impressive grosses and spawned multiple sequels.

How do these scares work, and what's behind the recent uptick in audience inter- 10
est? Lock your doors and turn off the lights; let's go check out that noise in the basement and find out.

"What makes a jump scare work is classic misdirection." C. Robert Cargill is one of 11
the screenwriters of this year's *Sinister*, and a film critic who's written for *Ain't It Cool
News* and *Film.com*. "A good jump scare is a magic trick," he says. "It's 'I'm going to get
you to look over here while I'm doing this,' and then out of nowhere—bam!—something's going to get you."

In fact, a well-done jump scare breaks down the same way Michael Caine describes 12
illusions in *The Prestige*, with three distinct steps. First there's the pledge: a character is
introduced into a situation where danger is present. They hear a rattling in the kitchen,
or voices when they're home alone. Then comes the turn, where the character finds
a reasonable explanation, or the immediate threat is somehow removed. Everything
seems alright, and the audience lets its guard down. That's when the filmmakers
execute the prestige, hitting an unsuspecting audience with the actual scare—usually
accompanied by a shrieking music cue or sound effect.

Film history is littered with them (see some of our favorites below), but one only 13
needs to look at the original *A Nightmare On Elm Street* for a textbook example. Tina
wanders through her nightmare, stalked by … *something*. Just when her fear builds to
a crescendo, however, the danger dissipates. The noises stop—she thinks she's going
to be okay. We relax. And that's when Krueger strikes.

(*continued*)

(*continued*)

14   While we may associate the technique with modern horror movies, it's actually been with us almost as long as genre films themselves. Director Jacques Tourneur used it 70 years ago in *Cat People*, using the arrival of a bus to craft a scare that still plays today. Other filmmakers tried their own riffs in subsequent decades. Showman William Castle even brought the jump scare into the real world in 1959 with *The Tingler*, rigging seats in theaters to vibrate during a key sequence in the movie.

15   Alfred Hitchcock, however, put it front and center with *Psycho*. In the film's climax, Vera Miles searches for Mrs. Bates, knowing that she has mere moments before Norman discovers she's poking around his house. In the basement she finds the old woman sitting in a chair, seemingly ending the nightmare once and for all. But when Miles spins her around, she discovers something horrific—that nobody was expecting back in 1960.

16   The jump scare hit a wall in the '80s. At first slasher films used it to great effect; the original *Friday the 13th* features what could be considered the definitive "killer returns" scare, when a young Jason emerges from the lake to attack the heroine. As knock-offs rolled out, however, the technique became less and less of a surprise, and was soon as rote and obvious as the now-parodied genre conventions themselves.

17   It wasn't that the horror movies of the era were bad as a whole—though to be fair, for every *Evil Dead II* there's also a *Silent Night, Deadly Night Part II*. Instead, it was a matter of repeating the same gags in movies that weren't actually frightening anymore.

18   If you look at the best horror films, Cargill says, "the common thread is almost all of them have amazing characters." From the original *The Texas Chainsaw Massacre* to *Poltergeist*, the characters pull the audience in, and the more you care, the more anxious you'll be that something bad's going to happen to them. Many horror flicks of the '80s stepped off that path, instead presenting a parade of lookalike characters that not only weren't developed, but could be straight-up obnoxious. "When you put five kids out in the woods and they're all douchebags, you don't care that they're getting killed," he says. "In fact you kind of enjoy it, it's kind of cathartic. It becomes more comedy than it is tragedy." The result were movies that were more like gory rollercoaster rides rather than something that would keep audiences up at night.

19   Compounding the problem was a general lack of inventiveness with the scares themselves. Instead of setting the audiences up with clever misdirection, some filmmakers would try to cheat the system, relying on just the third element of the jump scare formula—having a cat randomly leap on-screen with an accompanying music hit, for example. As horror entered its self-reflective phase in the 1990s, movies like *Scream* called out the clichés directly. While that twist may have imbued them with new short-term life, it also pulled back the curtain, making them even less effective in the long run. Worst of all was the constant recycling of some gags, none of which has received more screen time than the dusty "mirror scare." That particular trick, where a character closes a medicine cabinet or mirrored door to reveal a monster just behind them, is so played out it's become a meme unto itself. When a movie trick gets its own supercut, it's not surprising—or scaring—anyone.

20   That's not to say the basic principles behind the jump scare aren't sound, however. The key is in the execution, and as a result filmmakers today have to be just as

cognizant of audience expectations as they do of any other element. "When we sat down to write the script," Cargill says of *Sinister*, "the first thing I did is I composed a list of all the tropes and clichés that appear in all the mainstream horror movies that people are tired of." The audience's built-in scare awareness can even be used to a movie's advantage. In *Sinister*, Cargill says, they at times used tropes to suggest the film was going in one direction—only to hit viewers from a different angle altogether.

With such incredible longevity—the jump scare has appeared in everything from *Jaws* to *Seven*—it's clear audiences appreciate a well-tuned jump. Mary Beth Oliver, Professor and Co-Director of the Media Effects Research Laboratory at Penn State University's College of Communications, thinks the reasons behind it are twofold. "I do believe that there's a tendency for some people to simply enjoy the actual adrenaline rush of the scare itself right then and there," she says, comparing it to a ride. On the other hand, she suggests, being scared heightens the physiological state of the audience—intensifying emotions they feel during the movie, and making any dramatic payoffs at the end that much more satisfying. In that sense, being scared may actually make the story in a horror movie stronger. 21

That notion of catharsis is also in play when it comes to the found footage set-up of the *Paranormal Activity* series. The conceit is as straightforward as it was back in *The Blair Witch Project*: bad things happened to some people with cameras, and here's what they recorded. In found footage movies, however, there's often little emphasis on character or traditional dramatic narrative. The *PA* movies are basically made up of creepy vignettes, which use the jump scare formula for almost every interesting beat. One might think that such an exercise would fall flat, but they've been enormously successful thus far. 22

The key may be the found footage approach itself. "Some research," Oliver says, "has wrestled with the idea that we tend to find fascination in things that are violent and frightening when we feel threatened ourselves." By playing off our lack of privacy in a world of Facebook oversharing and YouTube videos, the films may be appealing to underlying fears without the audience even realizing it. 23

Cargill sees the aesthetic intensifying scares by placing the movies in a world audiences are familiar with—and where they could be the victims. "I think the reason why they work right now is because audiences feel like they're watching something genuine," he says. "And it allows that audience to put themselves in the mindset that what they're watching could actually happen." 24

There's also an inherent tension in the format itself. Let's face it; you buy your ticket knowing terrible things are going to happen to these people, you just don't know *when*. Without a traditional story to guide your expectations, it becomes a voyeuristic waiting game. When you're anticipating a scare around every corner, even the slightest movement in the background is enough to ratchet up the tension. 25

Of course, *Paranormal Activity* didn't invent the idea of found footage; it's been percolating in the horror world since 1980's *Cannibal Holocaust*, with recent standouts like the Spanish film *REC* breaking through to broader audiences. The *PA* franchise has gotten Hollywood's attention, however, cementing the approach as a viable subgenre—and bringing its own set of tropes and audience expectations to the table. 26

Inquiring into the Essay

1. **Explore.** To go to a horror movie is to *expect* to be scared, writes Bishop. Why in the world would we choose to be scared? There is scholarship that suggests certain personality types are drawn to the horror genre. Are horror lovers more—or less—empathetic? Other research explains attraction to horror as "sensation-seeking" behavior, and there's particular pleasure in seeing bad things resolved at the end of the movie. Explore your own ideas about the appeal (or repulsion) of the horror genre. Think about your own reactions and those of people that you know. What do you think about why some people might choose to be scared?

2. **Explain.** The "key" to a good jump scare, Bishop notes, is in the "execution." What does he believe are the elements of a properly executed jump scare? Why is the convention now more popular?

3. **Evaluate.** How would you evaluate the organization of this essay? Go through it, paragraph by paragraph, and make a note of what each one seems to be saying or doing. Map the basic pieces of Bishop's argument. Can you imagine another way it might have been organized?

4. **Reflect.** Many of us don't hesitate to throw around the word "genre" from time to time, especially when we're talking about film. But how exactly do we distinguish one genre from another? For example, what's the difference between the horror film genre and the action film genre? What are the types of conventions or rhetorical features you might look for in making the distinction?

Seeing the Form

Brand as Visual Interpretation

I've been around Boise State University for long enough to see the evolution of its "brand," an effort that includes the logo. There's nothing unique about this. Universities, like companies, invest considerable time and money thinking about how they want to market themselves to students, donors, athletic recruits, alumni, and others. When I started teaching here twenty years ago, the Boise State logo looked like this:

Seeing the Form (*continued*)

Now, with a little help from Nike, with which the school has an affiliation, the logo looks like this:

BOISE STATE UNIVERSITY

The "B" logo, according to the university president, "represents our personality traits of being determined, strong, innovative, and community based." It's fair to assume that the graphic designers were given the charge to somehow *visually interpret* those ideas in the logo, carefully choosing things like typography, size, color, spacing, visual lines, and all the other elements that go into graphic design. It's a "B" but it's so much more than a "B." At least that's the idea.

THE WRITING PROCESS

Inquiry Project: Writing an Analytical Essay

Inquiry Question: What might it mean?

Write an analytical essay about something that is open to interpretation. By now you know there is a world of possibilities for this. You might analyze literary works, films or television programs, advertisements, video games, speeches, fashion trends, photographs, brands, etc. Whatever you choose as an object for analysis must be *suggestive*: that is, there must be meanings that are not obvious. The ad might explicitly be selling luxury cars, but it's also selling some ideas about wealth or privilege. The poem might seem to be about the "road not taken," but this isn't necessarily what we usually think the poem means. The Apple vs. PC commercial is obviously trying to promote Macs, but it also draws on certain cultural ideas about "hipness." The local newspaper's coverage of football injuries seems balanced, but a content analysis suggests it isn't. In general, your analytical essay should do the following three things:

1. Describe the object of your analysis and then identify the patterns, elements, passages, references, or features that interest you.
2. Examine how these elements are connected to certain larger themes, ideas, ideologies, representations, historical contexts, or traditions.
3. Finally, argue for a particular interpretation, a particular answer to the question: What might this mean?

Prose+

- Consider producing an infographic to represent your interpretation. This genre is particularly useful for analyses that involve the frequency of certain elements or that might involve other statistical patterns.
- Build a web page around an analytical essay focused on a literary text, embedding video or audio of interviews with the author of the work and links to the works of other critics who comment on it. You might also add images, including those that you think echo the interpretation you're arguing for. Other features might include a bibliography with links to the sources you used, a list of other works by the author or artist, a sidebar that highlights an important passage, etc.
- Develop a PowerPoint or Pages presentation for your analytical essay, or as a supplement to it. This would be especially effective if you're analyzing a visual work, because you can include close-ups of significant features that are key to your interpretation. But a slide presentation can be effective for conventional literary analysis, too. Consider developing slides that provide background on the work, a statement of your thesis, and key passages or quotes from criticism that you're using as evidence.

What Are You Going to Write About?

When generating ideas for subjects, you can start big (deductively) with large themes about society that interest you and work down to find specific examples of things that might help you explore those themes. Or you might start small (inductively) with a particular film, poem, advertisement, or other object that you find interesting because it has unsettled meanings. We'll work both ways in the exercises that follow.

In the conversation between what a text says and what it might be saying, you discover fresh understandings of what you read.

Opening Up

Listing Prompts.

1. Let's start small by brainstorming specific things that might invite interpretation.

Cultural trends	Great songs	Favorite movies	Favorite books, stories, essays	Memorable pictures, paintings, images

   In each column, generate a fast list of things that come to mind. What cultural trends do you find hard to explain, what songs do you find strangely moving, what films or TV shows capture your interest? Are there books you love, paintings or photographs you remember?

2. Now let's go big, and generate three different lists of ideas about society that you think are important. In your journal, make a fast list of values, beliefs, or ideas that you think are *endangered* (e.g., public education, respect for elders, race relations, etc.). Then make a list of things that come to mind under the heading "This I Believe." Make another list under the heading "This I Used to Believe." We'll work with these lists in the subsection "Visual Prompts."

8.3

Use appropriate invention strategies to discover a topic for an analytical essay.

Fastwriting Prompts. Remember, fastwriting is a great way to stimulate creative thinking. Turn off your critical side and let yourself write "badly."

1. Choose one of the items in a column from step 1 of the "Listing Prompts" subsection to write about. If possible, re-experience the thing you'd like to interpret: Reread the poem, skim the stories, watch the film, listen to the song, study the ad. When you're finished, write a narrative-of-thought fastwrite: *When I first watched/read/observed this, I thought…. And then I thought… And then….* If you get some traction on some idea in this fastwrite, focus on that.

2. Choose an idea, value, or belief from your lists in step 2 of the listing subsection. Write fast about the idea, using this phrase as an opening prompt: *The best example of why I think this is important is….*

Visual Prompts. Visual thinking might help you play with ideas about how to analyze the work you're studying. Try these prompts to explore your response to a literary work:

1. Return to the fastwriting activities you tried earlier, and focus on the ideas, values, themes, and beliefs you generated in step 2. Make one of these the center of a cluster. Now build branches, identifying any times, places, people, and things you associate with that idea or value. Grow branches in your cluster that make what you're thinking more concrete (and less abstract).

2. Make a visual map of a story, if that's what your potential topic is about. Begin by placing at the center of a blank page a brief description of what you believe is the most significant moment in the story. This might be a turning point, or the point of highest tension, or perhaps the moment when the main character achieves his or her desires and dreams. Consider that moment the destination of the story. Now map out events or details in the narrative that threaten to lead the protagonist away from that destination and those that appear to lead the protagonist toward it.

Research Prompts. Analysis often involves working with primary sources: the poem, novel, essay, photograph, or painting. Sometimes, especially if the work isn't a text, you have to observe the object, performance, or behavior. If you're considering a subject like these for your analytical essay, then you need to go out and look. This fieldwork might include

1. Attending a performance (e.g., watching the modern dance, going to see the drama, etc.)

2. Observing a behavior (e.g., observing how people behave in a certain social situation)

3. Going to a museum (e.g., browsing paintings)

4. Seeing the films or shows (e.g., an evening watching zombie films)

On the other hand, if you're considering analyzing a literary text, you can research your favorite authors' work online, but you can also research top-ten lists of short stories, poems, and essays. There are annual "Best of" collections published every year in your university library.

Inquiring into the Details

Common Literary Devices

Many key concepts provide useful frameworks for analyzing literature. The key is to see the following ideas as an angle for viewing an essay, story, or poem much as you might approach a subject from different camera angles. Each provides a different way of seeing the same thing. In addition, each becomes a platform from which to pose a question about a text.

- *Plot and significant event:* Plot is what happens in a story and what moves it forward. One way of thinking about plot is to consider this: What are the key moments that propel the story forward? Why do you consider them key? How do they add tension to the story? In an essay, these moments often give rise to the question the writer is exploring. In short stories, there is often a significant event that happens inside or outside of the story, and the entire narrative and its characters act or think in response to that event.

- *Characters:* Imagine a still pond upon which small paper boats float. Someone throws a rock—big or small—into the pond, and the ripples extend outward, moving the boats this way and that. Depending on the size of the ripples, some of the boats may list or capsize, sinking slowly. Characters in a short story are like those boats, responding in some way to something that happened, some significant event that is revealed or implied. They move almost imperceptibly, or quite noticeably, or even violently. Is there logic to their responses? How exactly are the characters changed? How do they relate to each other?

- *Setting:* Where a story takes place can matter a lot or a little, but it always matters. Why? Because where a story takes place signals things about characters and who they are. A story set in rural Wyoming suggests a certain austere ranching culture in which the characters operate. Even if they're not ranchers, they must somehow deal with that culture. Similarly, a story set in Chicago's predominantly black South Side introduces a set of constraints within which characters must operate. In some cases, setting might even become a kind of character.

- *Point of view:* In nonfiction essays, point of view is usually straightforward—we assume the narrator is the author. But in fiction, it's much more complicated; in fact, *how* a story is told—from what perspective—is a crucial aesthetic decision. Telling a story from the first-person point of view in the present tense gives the story a sense of immediacy—the feeling that it's happening *now*—but at the same time limits our understanding of the other characters, because we can't get into their heads. So-called omniscient narrators can introduce a feeling of distance from the action, but they are also gratifyingly godlike because they can see everything, hovering above all the action and even entering characters' minds at will. Why might an author have chosen a particular point of view? Is the narrator trustworthy? What might be his or her biases, and how might they affect the telling?

(continued)

Inquiring into the Details (*continued*)

- ***Theme:*** One way to understand a story or essay is to consider that everything—character, point of view, and setting—contributes to a central meaning. In a good story, everything is there for a purpose—to say something to the reader about what it means to be human. In essays, this theme may be explicit, because essays both show *and* tell. Short stories, and especially poems, are often short on explanation of theme, operating with more ambiguity. The writer hopes the reader can *infer* certain ideas or feelings by paying close attention to what he or she *shows* the reader. To get at the theme, begin with the simple question *So what?* Why is the author telling this story or sharing this experience? What significance are we supposed to attach to it?

- ***Image:*** Stories and poems ask us to see. When I read them, I imagine that their writers take my face in their hands and gently—or sometimes brutally—direct my gaze. What are they insisting that I look at, and how do they want me to see it? Images that recur may also be significant.

Narrowing Down

Now that you've opened up possibilities for analysis topics, there are choices to make. Which do you want to write about? First thing, naturally, is that you should pursue a subject that interests you. But also consider the following:

1. Returning to the iceberg metaphor that opened this chapter, might your potential subject have both obvious, visible meanings as well as less obvious, more submerged meanings?

2. Is the object of your analysis specific enough? If you started with a larger theme about society, did you manage to anchor it to *particular representations of that theme*? In other words, if you are interested in representations of manhood, how might manhood be implicated in the evolution of the action figure (doll?) GI Joe?

What's Promising Material and What Isn't? Try out a possible topic for your analytical essay by doing some more-focused writing and by thinking about it. First, generate some thinking-through-writing.

- **First thoughts?** Interpretation is inspired by this question: *What might it mean?* And that's not a bad question to start with. Spend some time rereading, observing, or studying the work you've tentatively chosen, and if you're using a double-entry journal, collect notes (e.g., key passages, lists of observations, descriptions, etc.) on the left-facing page of your journal. Then, on the right, fastwrite for as long as you can, exploring and speculating about possible interpretations. When the writing stalls, pick up on something in your notes on the left page. This writing should be very open ended; you don't need to come to conclusions yet.

Now judge what you've generated:

- Can you refine your question? Analysis asks that you look closely at something and discover connections between it and the world of ideas. Imagine, for example, a bottomless bucket full of ideas about how people act and think in the world. Undoubtedly, there are ideas in that bucket that help to describe some of the implied meanings in the object of your analysis. You just have to figure out what those ideas are.

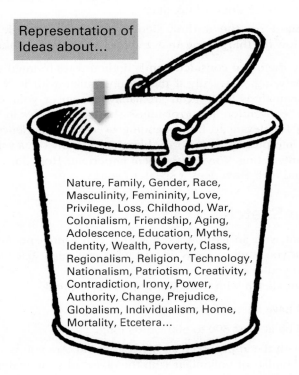

Representation of Ideas about...

Nature, Family, Gender, Race, Masculinity, Femininity, Love, Privilege, Loss, Childhood, War, Colonialism, Friendship, Aging, Adolescence, Education, Myths, Identity, Wealth, Poverty, Class, Regionalism, Religion, Technology, Nationalism, Patriotism, Creativity, Contradiction, Irony, Power, Authority, Change, Prejudice, Globalism, Individualism, Home, Mortality, Etcetera...

Try to tease out some of these connections by completing this sentence as many times as you can, each time focusing on some different aspect or element of the thing you're analyzing:

> The (name an aspect or element of your subject) ___ seems to be representing certain ideas about ___.

For example,

> The slow, shuffling gait of zombies in shows like The Walking Dead seems to be representing certain ideas about human vulnerability—civilization is threatened by the apocalypse but it will come at us slowly and relentlessly.

Consider doing some online research to generate ideas to help complete these interpretive statements.

Questions About Audience and Purpose. One basic rhetorical question is this: Is your audience familiar with the work you're interpreting? If not, should you provide background so that they share enough knowledge of it to appreciate your analysis? This might include things like

- **Background on the work.** When was it published or created? How was it received? What was it compared to?
- **Summary or description.** What is the basic plot? What happens? What does it say? What does it look like?
- **Background on the author.** Significance in literary, design, or artistic circles? How the thing being analyzed fits into the body of the author's work?

Another key rhetorical consideration is finding ways to interest readers in the work you're analyzing, especially if they're unfamiliar with it. Why should they care about your analysis of N. Scott Momaday's poem or your interpretation of the "jump scare" convention in horror films? Think about ways in which the thing you're studying is relevant to understanding everyday experience. That's not so hard with your interpretations of horror films, since many of us watch them. But a poem? Make it interesting. Why is this poem important? How does it speak to how we might live and feel? How does it speak to you?

Writing the Sketch

We'll begin again with an early draft, a sketch that represents an initial attempt to discover what you want to focus on and what you might have to say about the work (or works) you've chosen.

Develop your sketch with the following things in mind:

- It should have a tentative title.
- It should be at least 500 to 600 words long.
- Write it with the appropriate audience in mind. Are you writing for readers who are familiar or unfamiliar with the object of your analysis?
- It should both describe a few key elements of the thing you're analyzing and offer some tentative interpretations of what those elements mean.

▶ Student Sketch

Hailie, a student in my first-year writing course last semester, brings her university debate skills to her analysis of the Meghan Trainor song "All About That Bass," a tune that is ostensibly a celebration of female body types that don't conform to a skinny ideal. However, in writing her sketch, Hailie discovers that she's troubled by the lyrics, and begins to build an argument that suggests that Trainor's good intentions go awry.

All About That Hate

By Hailie Johnson-Waskow

Meghan Trainor's breakout hit *All About That Bass* is a spirited attempt to create an anthem for women that society has deemed 'overweight'. However, Trainor's song falls desperately short of achieving the message of equality and acceptance that it was initially tasked with. In a feigned attempt at feminism Trainor has created a false dichotomy with her song; pitting the 'skinny girls' against the 'big girls.' This leads to her promotion of a culture that uses criticism to find self-solace. 1

The central message of the song is seen strongly in the chorus, and, not surprisingly, the opening line when Trainor claims she is "... all 'bout that bass, no treble." Trainor told Billboard magazine in December 2012, "You know how the bass guitar in a song is like its 'thickness,' the 'bottom'? I kind of related a body to that." This analysis alone seems to create the separation between thick and thin. The phrase 'all about that' encourages the acceptance of one body type while actively discouraging another. Trainor attempts to make larger bodies acceptable by pushing the small into the 'no treble' category. Further, it is interesting to note that the bass and treble are both music scores. The bass are round and thick while the treble clefs are tall and skinny. This symbolism is made by no coincidence and further enforces the skinny/fat dichotomy. Because she is ''bout' larger body types but says 'no' to other types she creates two separate groups. She argues that you must be part of one of these groups, you are either larger or smaller, and indicates that those who are smaller are lesser. The symbolism of the bass and treble create the basis for Trainor's work. 2

Immediately following the chorus, which opens the song with the repeated line "I'm all 'bout that bass, 'bout that bass, no treble," Trainor begins her first verse by proclaiming "Yeah it's pretty clear, I ain't no size two." This only further entrenches the idea that smaller women, specifically the particularly small at a size two, are unacceptable. This line is followed by the statement "But I can shake it, shake it like I'm supposed to do." By implying that women who are smaller cannot do what society expects of them, Trainor bluntly states that smaller women are inadequate. This idea of inadequacy and unacceptability is discussed further when Trainor states "I'm bringing booty back/Go ahead and tell them skinny b****** that." By explicitly calling smaller women an obscenity associated with rudeness, hostility, etc. Trainor places women who do not resemble herself into a specific category. This category seems to be marked by inferiority. She seems to continue her message of negativity toward women who are smaller than herself. 3

Although Trainor claims that she initially set out to create a song that encouraged the acceptance of all women, she has created a song that perpetuates bullying in order to achieve happiness. Trainor encourages the acceptance of larger bod[y] types but she is only able to do this by bringing down those who are not like herself. Thus, "All About That Bass" should be critically analyzed to ensure that those looking for happiness never bring others down to achieve it. 4

Moving from Sketch to Draft

How well does your sketch lead you to assertions about the meaning of the thing you're analyzing? Does it have a clear focus?

Evaluating Your Own Sketch. Among the key concerns in evaluating this early draft of your analytical essay is whether you've discovered a workable focus and whether you're beginning to get some clear idea of what you're trying to say. One of the best things you can do at this point is to use your sketch to craft a tentative thesis *or* the question that will be the focus of the next draft.

- **Thesis.** On the back of your sketch, in a sentence or two (but no more), state the main thing you're trying to communicate in answer to the question *What does it mean?*
- **Inquiry question.** Compose a question that reflects what you want to focus on in your interpretation. A relationship? The significance of certain recurring elements? An analysis based on a certain context—when the work was written or a tradition or theory?

Reflecting on What You've Learned. At the beginning of this chapter, I talked about some of the basic elements of analysis (see p. 261) and said that a close examination of *evidence* leads to inferences about what the evidence might mean. This in turn leads to an *interpretation* that you think makes sense, and, drawing on the evidence, an *argument* that convinces someone else of the soundness of your interpretation. How well did you incorporate those three elements into your sketch? What needs more development in the next draft? What do these elements tell you about the act of interpretation? Does the analytical essay encourage a kind of thinking that can be distinguished from the thinking encouraged by other forms of writing?

Developing

To develop your sketch into a draft, work on two fronts:

1. Closer analysis of the primary work or phenomenon
2. Research in secondary sources on the context of the thing you're writing about: what other critics say, theories that guide the analysis, relevant background on the work or situation

Analysis. Interpretation is an inductive process. By looking closely at the specifics, you develop ideas about patterns in the work that might be significant. If you're studying a text, for example, then your analysis must be grounded in what exactly you see in the poem, story, or essay. In literary analysis, you might focus on common devices such as setting and characters (see "Inquiring into the Details: Common Literary Devices" earlier in this chapter on p. 283). What exactly is the setting? What exactly do the characters say and when do they say it? What you look at will depend, of course, on your thesis or inquiry question. This evidence is the foundation of any analytical essay, because it helps writers discover the reasons that support a particular interpretation.

Research. Any significant work of art—a painting or novel or a cultural artifact such as reality TV or Facebook profile pictures—exists in context. These contexts include:

- **Historical.** When was it created? Is it part of a tradition? In what ways does the work or performance reflect the politics and culture of its time?
- **Biographical.** Who created the work? What does its author say about it or about his or her aesthetic intentions?
- **Critical.** What do other critics who have studied the work or phenomenon say about it?
- **Methodological.** Look at the five approaches to analysis in the "Inquiring into the Details: Five Methods of Analysis" feature earlier in this chapter on page 273. Is one of these methods relevant to your project? If so, do some further research online about the basics of the relevant method so that you can apply it to your project.

Drafting

Because an analytical essay is an argument, your draft needs to make an argument. If you're writing a formal analytical paper, then your thesis—the interpretation that is at the heart of your argument—should be stated explicitly pretty early in your paper. In a less formal analytical essay (see "Why Won't You Die?!" earlier in the chapter), the thesis isn't necessarily a fixture of the introduction. You might instead work your way to it, like the unraveling of a ball of string. The question that is driving your essay, however, should be clear in the beginning (e.g., What does the popularity of zombies in American film say about us?).

Methods of Development. Like most writing, there is no formula for structuring your analytical essay, but if you're writing for an audience that is relatively unfamiliar with your subject, you should probably assume that your draft needs to answer a series of questions in roughly the following order:

- What do you find particularly interesting in the work or phenomenon that inspired your analysis? (Show something specific.)
- What's the question that interests you? (Make sure your thesis answers that question.)
- Can you summarize or describe what you're analyzing?
- What have other critics or experts said about it? (Include interpretations that differ from yours.)
- What's a reason behind your interpretation? What's the evidence that led you to see it?
- What's another reason? And the evidence?
- Can you tell me again what your close analysis or observation helped you to see about the meaning of the work or phenomenon?

Here are some of the other ways you might organize your analytical essay:

Narrative. An entirely different approach is to use your question as the starting point for a story you tell about how you arrived at an answer. This approach is more essayistic in the sense that it provides the story of *how* you came to know rather than reports *what* you think. A narrative essay might also involve relevant autobiographical details that influenced your analysis. For example, what feelings or experiences did you *bring* to the reading of the text?

Question to Answer. Because the assignment is designed around a question you're trying to answer about the topic, the question-to-answer approach is an obvious choice. Consider spending the first part of your essay highlighting the question you're interested in. The key is to convince readers that yours is a question worth asking, and that the answer might be interesting to discover.

Compare and Contrast. Analytical essays often benefit from this method of development. The approach might be to compare and contrast certain elements within the work. In a story there might be several characters, symbols or metaphors, plot developments, and so on—or you might compare the work to others by the same or even different authors. Note that these comparisons have to be relevant to the question you're asking.

Combining Approaches. Frequently, an analytical essay uses several or even all of the methods of development mentioned here: question to answer, comparison and contrast, and narrative. Consider how you might put them all to work, especially in certain sections of your draft.

Using Evidence. You need to consider two main kinds of evidence in an analytical essay: evidence that comes from so-called *primary* sources—especially the work itself, but also letters or memoirs by the author; and evidence that comes from *secondary* sources—books, articles, and essays by critics who are writing about the work or author. Primary sources are generally more important. In more-personal literary responses, however, your personal associations, anecdotes, stories, or feelings may be used as evidence, if they're relevant to the question you're posing.

Workshopping

If your draft is subject to peer review, see Appendix A for details on how to organize workshop groups and decide on how your group can help you. As you now know, an analytical essay argues for a particular interpretation of a text or phenomenon. As you prepare to share your draft, you'll want to look for some of these weak links in your argument; consider asking peer reviewers whether you've avoided them:

- **Insufficient evidence.** Remember that this is a form of writing that works mostly with *primary sources*—the short story, the film(s), the ad, the first-hand observations, etc. Most of the information in your essay should be your close examination of the primary sources you're focusing on.

- ■ **Broad focus.** Even lengthy analytical essays should look only at the *particular aspects* of the primary source that most contributed to the writer's interpretation.

- ■ **General interpretation.** After all your analysis, you're not going to write something like "zombies are everywhere in film and are an interesting cultural phenomenon" as your thesis. That might be a setup for your thesis, which must be an interpretation with a much sharper edge: *The rise of the zombie in American film is testimony to the growing cultural nightmare that there are no safe places anymore, especially with the spread of nuclear weapons.*

In addition to these concerns, when you workshop the first draft of your analytical essay, you should focus first on what peers make of the purpose and meaning of your essay, both of which guide your revision. The following box can help you frame these questions for your workshop group.

Questions for Peer Reviewers	
1. Purpose	After reading the draft, can you explain back to me why I think the topic I chose to analyze is significant? Do I convince you that it might be significant to you, too?
2. Meaning	In your own words, how does the essay answer the inquiry question *What does it mean?* What evidence do you find most convincing in support of this interpretation? Least convincing?

Reflecting on the Draft. Take a look at the draft before you and circle the passage that you think is the best in the essay so far. Now circle the passage that you think is weakest.

In your notebook, fastwrite for five minutes about both passages. What seems to be working in the better passage? What problems do you notice about the weaker one? Does either one address the question you're writing about? If so, how? If not, how might it? When you compare the two passages, what do you notice about the differences? How might you make the weaker passage more like the stronger one? How might you make the rest of the essay stronger?

Revising

Revision is a continual process—not a last step. You've been revising—"reseeing" your subject—from the first messy fastwriting in your journal. But the things that get your attention vary depending on where you are in the writing process. With your draft in hand, revision becomes your focus through what I'll call "shaping and tightening your draft."

Chapter 14 contains strategies that can help you revise any inquiry project, and the "Guidelines: Revising Your Work" in this chapter on page 293 can help you locate these strategies. There are also certain things to think about that are especially useful for shaping an analytical essay.

8.4

Apply revision strategies that are effective for the analytical essay.

Shaping. When we shape a draft, the focus is on design—the order of information, the chain of reasoning, the coherence of paragraphs, and the paragraphs' contributions to the whole composition. In an analytical essay, some of the basic units of reasoning are the moments of analysis in your essay, or those places where you actually work with a primary source to tease out its implications.

Here's an example from an analytical essay I once wrote on how American Indian writers seem to use memory in their fiction, poetry, and nonfiction. My focus here was on Sherman Alexie's work, and his character Thomas-Builds-the-Fire, who appears in several of the writer's stories.

Interpretation

Evidence

> I think that the implications of this—that tribal memory and personal memory merge—are profound. Perhaps that's why nobody wants to listen to the stories of Thomas Builds-the-Fire in Spokane/Coeur d'Alène writer Sherman Alexie's recent works, *Reservation Blues* and *Tonto and the Lone Ranger Fistfight in Heaven.* Thomas, whose stories came to him before he "had the words to speak" (*Reservation* 73), tells stories that many of the Indians on the Spokane reservation refuse to hear, "stealth stories" that work their way into dreams and into "clothes like sand, [that] gave you itches that could not be scratched" (15). I wonder if the antipathy to Thomas's stories is really resistance to the hegemonic power of someone else's story to structure and contain individual experience and memory. Is that why Victor and Junior, two Spokanes who are adrift, unable to find the symmetry between personal past, history, and legend that Momaday discovers in *Rainy Mountain,* "tried to beat those stories out of Thomas, tied him down and taped his mouth shut" (*Reservation* 15).

Notice how the analysis here is *layered.* An interpretation is introduced and then explicated with evidence, which then leads to an elaboration of the initial interpretation and ends with some supporting evidence.

Examine your own paragraphs in a similar way. Take a highlighter and use two different colors, one for interpretation (assertion) and the other for evidence. Look to see if your analysis is layered—working back and forth from your ideas about a work or phenomenon and the evidence from the text or your observations—and if not, revise to encourage that quality in the paragraphs or passages of your draft.

Polishing. Shaping focuses on things such as purpose, meaning, and design. No less important is looking more closely at paragraphs, sentences, and words. Are your paragraphs coherent? How do you manage transitions? Are your sentences fluent and concise? Are there any errors in spelling or syntax? Chapter 14 can help you focus on these issues.

Before you finish your draft, work through the following checklist:

✓ Every paragraph is about one thing.
✓ The transitions between paragraphs aren't abrupt.
✓ The lengths of sentences vary in each paragraph.
✓ Each sentence is concise. There are no unnecessary words or phrases.
✓ You've checked grammar, particularly verb agreement, run-on sentences, unclear pronouns, and misused words (*there/their, where/were*, and so on).
✓ You've run your spellchecker and proofed your paper for misspelled words.

Chapter 14 is a buffet of revision strategies that will help you solve all kinds of revision problems, large and small. Use the "Guidelines: Revising Your Work" below to know where to look in that chapter to both shape and tighten your draft.

Guidelines: Revising Your Work

A first effort is almost never a best effort. To make sure your essay is really your best work, check out Chapter 14 for help with these questions:

- What is my paper really about? (See p. 518.)

- What am I really trying to say? (See p. 523.)

- Do I have enough convincing evidence? (See p. 530.)

- Does this paper move logically and smoothly from paragraph to paragraph? (See p. 534.)

- Are the sentences and paragraphs in this paper too choppy or hard to follow? (See p. 542.)

▶ Student Essay

To fully appreciate Hailie's sketch about the Meghan Trainor song "All About That Bass," (see page 294), I watched the music video on YouTube, something I recommend before you read the revision of the piece below. Here, Hailie's analysis is richer and more fully developed. Like any strong analysis, the essay looks more closely at the visible elements of her study object—in this case, the lyrics of the Trainor song—and then teases out a network of implications that aren't readily apparent.

All About That Hate: A Critical Analysis of "All About That Bass"

By Hailie Johnson-Waskow

1   Meghan Trainor's breakout hit *All About That Bass* is a spirited attempt to create an anthem for women that society has deemed 'overweight.' However, Trainor's song falls desperately short of achieving the message of equality and acceptance that the artist initially intended. In a feigned attempt at feminism Trainor has created a false dichotomy with her song; pitting the "skinny girls" against the "big girls" which promotes the solace of one group at the expense of another. She then encourages male approval as the only way of measuring self-worth. Overall, Trainor's piece will never have the ability to be a song that all may use as an anthem for body acceptance.

2   When one initially listens to Trainor's song, the first thing noticed is that it does not sound much like the other popular songs of its time. "All About That Bass" has a very '50s/'60s doo-wop feel. Watching the music video cements the idea that this was an intentional move on the artist's part. The music video for the song features the artists in scenes you would expect from the '50s/'60s and wearing clothing that would also seem to reflect this time period. Specifically, the use of pastel colors throughout the video indicates that Trainor uses this time period to symbolize antiquated notions, specifically that larger girls are not attractive. She does this very purposefully to create humor in the idea that larger girls are unacceptable in society. She effectively shows that this prejudice toward larger women is out of date and that society must move forward. This creates the message that, in the 21st century, it is necessary to accept women of larger body types. However, another listen to Trainor's lyrics shows that she does not effectively argue for the acceptance of larger body types.

3   The central message of the song is seen strongly in the chorus, and, not surprisingly, the opening line when Trainor claims she is "... all 'bout that bass, no treble." Trainor told Billboard magazine in December 2012, "You know how the bass guitar in a song is like its 'thickness,' the 'bottom'? I kind of related a body to that." This analysis alone seems to create the separation between thick and thin. The phrase 'all 'bout that' encourages the acceptance of one body type while 'no treble' actively discourages another. Further, it is interesting to note that the bass and treble are both music notation. The bass are round and thick while the treble clefs are tall and skinny. This symbolism is no coincidence and further enforces the skinny/fat dichotomy. Because she is ''bout' larger body types but says 'no' to other types she creates two separate groups. She argues that you must be part of one of these groups, you are either larger or smaller, and indicates that those who are smaller are lesser, a theme Trainor develops in the rest of her song.

4   Immediately following the chorus, which opens the song with the repeated line "I'm all 'bout that bass, 'bout that bass, no treble," Trainor begins her first verse by proclaiming "Yeah it's pretty clear, I ain't no size two." This only further entrenches the idea that smaller women, specifically the particularly small at a size two, are unacceptable. This line is followed by the statement "But I can shake it, shake it like I'm supposed to do." By implying that women who

are smaller cannot do what society expects of them, Trainor bluntly states that smaller women are inadequate. This idea of inadequacy and unacceptability is discussed further when Trainor states "I'm bringing booty back/Go ahead and tell them skinny b****** that." By explicitly calling smaller women an obscenity, Trainor marks women who do not resemble her as inferior. She seems to continue her message of negativity toward women who are smaller than her.

But Trainor does not stop at critiquing smaller women. In both verses of her song she sings, "You know I won't be no stick-figure, silicone Barbie doll." This "stick-figure, silicone Barbie doll" symbolizes another category of women she has create[d]; women who participate in plastic surgery of any type. She signals this with the use of the word 'silicone' which is what many assume is used in most of these procedures. She implies that these women are fake or not authentic by calling them Barbies, reducing them to no better than plastic dolls. This association with a doll further indicates that Trainor believes women who use plastic surgery to be idiotic, or empty-minded like a doll. By associating this "Barbie doll" with the derogatory "stick-figure" she also argues that those who are smaller can only get that way through plastic surgery rather than exercise or a healthy diet.

However, one of the largest ways that she hopes to achieve acceptance is arguably even more flawed. There are several lines in this song including "But I can shake it, shake it like I'm supposed to do/'Cause I got that boom boom that all the boys chase" and "Boys they like a little more booty to hold at night" implying that self-acceptance comes only through male approval. The first example uses the phrase "shake it like I'm supposed to do" [and] displays subservience to men in order to feel good about oneself. It also argues that a woman is 'supposed to do' certain things for a man that make women slaves to male approval. This line enforces the patriarchy that modern feminism has made great strides to eliminate. The next example "Boys they like a little more booty to hold at night" also perpetuates the idea of male superiority. It takes a shot where many women find trouble already: their sexuality. Trainor suggests that a woman may only feel attractive when she has the 'right amount of booty to hold at night.' This leaves women struggling to find acceptance and relying on whether or not a man finds them sexually attractive. Essentially, it leaves a woman's confidence up to a man, which only supports the ridiculous notion that men are superior to women.

The other problem with these lines is one that is especially troubling in a song that encourages acceptance: Lyrics that encourage women to find acceptance through men are incredibly heteronormative and sexist. The ideas presented in this song make the assumption that all listeners are heterosexual women. If a listener is a homosexual woman she quickly learns that she will never achieve body acceptance because she does not have any desire to be with a man. This further pushes listeners of this type into the periphery simply because they do not fit Trainor's mold. This assumption also hurts any male listeners. Trainor makes the assumption that only women struggle with body acceptance but that could not be further from the truth. While many will argue that wom[e]n's struggle with body acceptance is more difficult, it is important to remember that any struggle is important to consider. Instead the male listener is completely ignored in this message of acceptance and, instead, told he should be telling women whether or not their bodies are fit for society. The narrowness of Trainor's message of equality in body types undermines its goals.

(continued)

(continued)

8   With lines like "Every inch of you is perfect from the bottom to the top" it is clear that Trainor had the chance to achieve greatness but never was able to do so. Trainor should have created an anthem for all body types; of any gender and any sexuality. Instead she created a disappointing, dangerous song. Although Trainor claims that she initially set out to create a song that encouraged the acceptance of all women, she has created a song that perpetuates criticism in order to achieve happiness. Trainor encourages the acceptance of larger bod[y] types but she is only able to do this by bringing down those who are not like herself. Furthermore, the only way that those of her body type are able to achieve happiness is through the approval of men. This song then pushes numerous people to the periphery by insisting that they fit into what Trainor considers acceptable. "All About That Bass" is never able to achieve a message of true body acceptance.

Evaluating the Essay

1.   Hailie's argument is clear: "All About That Bass" masquerades as liberation but ultimately just cooks up another variety of discrimination. After reading her essay and watching the video, what is your analysis?

2.   Compare the sketch with this revision. What moves does Hailie make in the second draft of the essay, and do they make it more persuasive?

Using What You Have Learned

1.   **Apply the methods of analysis to a subject whose meanings aren't apparent.** If you're not an English major, why should you learn to write an analytical essay? I hope the answer is obvious by now. The act of interpretation is a fundamental part of making sense of the world; it's also an essential academic skill. In the future, you'll be asked to interpret data, field observations, historical narratives, case studies, and many other primary sources. Interpretation is a method of thought you can't practice enough.

2.   **Use evidence from primary sources to argue effectively for a convincing interpretation.** The last three chapters—the proposal, the argument, and now the analytical essay—are all persuasive forms of writing. In some ways, you build arguments in all three forms in very similar ways. But with an analytical essay, you've composed an argument that works with a particular kind of evidence: primary sources. This is a more scholarly approach to argument that builds on the foundations of persuasive writing you've developed in previous chapters.

3.   **Use appropriate invention strategies to discover a topic for an analytical essay.** Though research has been part of the invention toolbox since the

first assignment chapter on the personal essay, it has become increasingly important as we move towards writing on subjects outside our experience and knowledge. Because it relies on close reading and observation, the analytical essay is mostly research. By now it should be apparent that research (reading, interviewing, observing) *is* an invention strategy—a source of discovery—not just a move to build support for what you already know. This becomes even more obvious if you write a research paper or ethnography in later chapters.

4. **Apply revision strategies that are effective for the analytical essay.** Research is, of course, not only an invention strategy but a revision strategy, especially with a form such as the analytical essay. When we "do research," particularly on the web, it often seems haphazard—looking here and there unsystematically, hoping to stumble into something usable. In the final two chapters, I hope you see that revising with research is, well, strategic. There are certain *categories* of information that you should look for. For example, in this chapter we talked about researching in terms of context: historical, biographical, critical, and methodological. Various forms of writing—and types of inquiry questions—give you guidance about types of information to research as you draft and revise. Look at your future research-based assignments rhetorically: What are the features of this kind of writing, and are there recognizable categories of information that are typically present?

9

Writing an Ethnographic Essay

Learning Objectives

In this chapter, you'll learn to

9.1 Understand the idea of culture as a "web," and apply techniques of field research to describe it.

9.2 Use appropriate features of an ethnographic essay in a project that interprets how a social group sees itself and its world.

9.3 Use relevant methods of invention to identify a local culture to study.

9.4 Analyze and interpret qualitative information.

9.5 Apply revision strategies that are effective for an ethnographic essay.

Writing About Culture

My daughter used to hate spiders. In fact, she was so repulsed by them that she refused to utter the word, calling them "s-words" whenever she spotted one of the bugs. In sadistic moments, I wanted to explain to her that there are invisible webs everywhere and that we walk into them all the time. In fact, we may spin a few threads ourselves occasionally. Like the spiders in our basement, subcultures abound right under our very noses. We just have to learn to see the webs they weave.

The "web of culture" is a good metaphor because, like spider webs, the many cultures and subcultures we encounter in our everyday lives are often difficult to detect. These webs are also something in which we are all enmeshed, whether we know it or not. To some extent they limit our movements, shape our beliefs, and determine our traditions.

Ethnography is a method of inquiry into culture that exposes cultural webs much the way the morning dew exposes the intricacies of a spider web in your backyard. In this chapter, you'll practice this approach to research and learn some ways that you can apply ethnographic techniques to all kinds of research projects. The real value of trying ethnography isn't that you'll be writing lots of ethnographies in other classes. Instead, writing an ethnographic essay will expand your research skills by bringing them out of the library and into the field. That "field" might be the park where skateboarders gather, a hall where World War II veterans meet, a mall where fifteen-year-olds congregate, or the fields where migrant workers toil. You might even wander online, where electronic subcultures abound. You'll learn to be a more careful observer. And ethnography will also raise interesting questions about whether all research can be objective.

Motives for Writing Ethnography

Ethnography may be new to you, but you've almost certainly enjoyed its non-academic versions. Magazine articles on other cultures in *National Geographic* and *Discover* have some elements of ethnography, and arguably so do some of the reality TV shows. In a way, *Jersey Shore* had elements of ethnography in its implicit insistence that "Guidos" and "Guidettes" represent a certain type of Italian American youth culture that really exists. Programs such as *Jersey Shore* or *Orange County Housewives* invite us into cultural worlds that we may not be familiar with or recognize. I think that's one reason they're popular. Reality TV may be staged, overdramatized, and sometimes jaw-droppingly stupid, but in their own ways these programs do some of the things that ethnography does: show us types of people in the social setting they live in, doing what they do to find meaning in their lives. There are also traces of ethnographic methods in some photographic essays, movies, podcasts, and documentaries; whenever people go into the field with cameras, microphones, or pens to document a culture—including those in their own communities—they're doing ethnographic work.

Of course, the world is not a laboratory. You can't control the many variables that influence what people say and what they do. But that's the point. From the outset, ethnography concedes that social communities are complicated. Fieldwork will never be able to completely untangle them. But it can unknot a few strands. Ethnographers try to do this while acknowledging their own biases. Like much "qualitative" research, ethnography is subjective, but in many ways this adds to the richness of the results. We get a truer look at the chemistry between the observer and the observed, something that is always present in research with human subjects but frequently hidden behind the veil of "objectivity."

Ethnography and Academic Writing

Interest in academic ethnography has boomed in recent years, something you'll probably discover if you take an anthropology course. But you may also encounter ethnographic ways of seeing—or interest in the ways social groups behave

9.1
Understand the idea of culture as a "web," and apply techniques of field research to describe it.

More than in other forms of inquiry, ethnographers must spend time in the field simply watching and taking notes.

and believe—in sociology, English, and even the visual arts, where something called "visual ethnography" might be practiced in formal or informal ways. Some researchers are using both film and still photography to capture a subculture in action, something you might consider doing as you work on your own ethnographic project.

Increasingly, ethnography is going online to study online cultures such as YouTube or using the web to report findings in multimedia formats. Studying social communities on the web is a relatively new form of ethnography, and it often has very practical implications. For example, marketing specialists who study how consumers behave when shopping for a product online can harvest invaluable data that help sell things. To refine a website's features, usability experts want to know how people interact with the site. Sociologists might use online ethnography to study gay culture and other groups that in certain countries may be hard to reach otherwise.

As I mentioned earlier, ethnography is what scholars call *qualitative* research. Instead of experimental data, ethnographers analyze case studies, artifacts (objects that are meaningful to a particular group), and especially the firsthand observations they've collected in field notes. Quantitative research often isn't the best way to study people, because variables are hard to control and we're really complicated subjects to study. But qualitative research such as ethnography is well suited to providing a picture of social communities; it may lack the authority of quantitative methods, but it provides a much richer picture.

In this chapter, you won't be tackling a formal ethnographic project. Save that for your anthropology class. Instead, you'll attempt to create an ethnographic *essay* or project that uses some of the basic methods of that kind of research, including:

- Field (or online) observations
- Interviews
- Photographs, video, audio recordings
- Collection and study of artifacts
- Background research on the culture you're studying

9.2

Use appropriate features of an ethnographic essay in a project that interprets how a social group sees itself and its world.

Features of the Form

Feature	Conventions of the Ethnographic Essay
Inquiry question	How do the people in a social group or culture see themselves and their world?
Motives	We put people in categories all the time: This person is a "geek," or that person is a "skater." But is there actually evidence that justifies a social category, a culture with which certain people identify? The only way to find out is to observe, interview, and describe members of these groups. What do they say and do? What things do they value?

Feature	Conventions of the Ethnographic Essay
	How do they see each other? The motives for doing this might include practical purposes: • Discovering the best ways to understand and communicate with a particular audience. • Proposing policies that incorporate how affected people see the problems. • Improving products and services targeted to certain groups. Or more academic purposes: • Developing an informed understanding of cultural groups and the theories that explain their beliefs and behaviors.
Subject matter	We all belong to subcultures that we don't recognize we belong to—or perhaps refuse to acknowledge. But ethnography tends to focus on people who, at least when pressed, freely identify with a specific group. Cultures for study can be as remote as a Pacific island or as close as the researcher's neighborhood. Student projects have described skateboarders, international students, quilters, truck drivers, thirteen-year-old cheerleaders, football fans, and birdwatchers. Whatever the cultural group you choose, what's key is that you *study it in its local setting*.
Structure	Projects that use ethnographic methods often tell a story. For this project, consider using one or more of the following structures: • A typical day: What does it look like for group members? • Collage: a series of richly described scenes • Narrative: the story of your understanding of the culture from your research
Sources of information	Above all, evidence is gleaned from field research. Sources of information include: • Field observations • Interviews • Artifacts • Images, recordings, video • Research, including statistics and background information on the group

(continued)

Feature	Conventions of the Ethnographic Essay
Language	Because the researcher is inevitably a part of the research, ethnography is often openly subjective. Researchers may use the first person and, in their role as narrators of their findings, write up their work in something like a literary style—scenes, descriptions, dialogue, and so on. Imagine for this project that your audience is nonexpert; they're not anthropologists or authorities on the culture you're studying. The language you use may be informal, speculative, and personal.

Prose+

While visual ethnography as an academic field is relatively new, filmmakers and photographers have long been interested in documenting cultures. Films such as *Nanook of the North* (1922), an early documentary about the Inuit people in the Arctic, is one famous example. Today, visual methods—especially photographs—are often a part of more conventional studies, but the wide availability of digital video, audio, and images has made visual ethnography an important subdiscipline. For example, here's the opening photograph from an ethnography of undergraduate gamers, all of whom worked in a 1927 mansion owned by the nearby university.[1] The house was dedicated to "immersive learning." This photograph, and many others, were used to document the "lived experience" of the young gamers in an attempt to capture what it means to "do" game design.

[1]McNely, Brian, Gestwicki, Paul, Gelms, Bridget, and Ann Burke. "Spaces and Surfaces of Invention: A Visual Ethnography of Game Development." *Enculturation: A Journal of Rhetoric, Writing, and Culture 15*. 28 Feb. 2013. Web. 29 March 2015.

READINGS

▶ Ethnographic Essay 1

One of the social groups that you likely know pretty well is one you've probably experienced in this class: the small discussion group. Sometimes these churn along successfully—everybody participates, no one dominates, and the conversation is really interesting. Sometimes small groups run aground immediately. Unraveling the mysteries of how class discussion groups work—or don't—is a great focus for an ethnography, and in the excerpt that follows, we look into the social interactions of one such group in an English class. This is taken from a larger ethnographic study called *Academic Literacies: The Public and Private Discourse of University Students*, by my friend and colleague Elizabeth Chiseri-Strater. She follows Anna, an art and dance student at the University of New Hampshire, from class to class, exploring how Anna experiences writing, reading, and thinking in each one. In this excerpt, Elizabeth observes Anna in her English class—a course called Introduction to Prose Writing—and listens in as Anna participates with other students in a small group discussing several readings. In some ethnographies, researchers find a theoretical "frame" for understanding what they're seeing. These frames might include theories about how power works in organizations, or about how people communicate, or about gender relations. In this case, Elizabeth draws on some ideas about how women and men talk to each other as a way to understand what she sees one day in Anna's English class.

Anna as Reader: Intimacy and Response
Elizabeth Chiseri-Strater

Anna's conversation in small reading groups reveals an even more intimate style than in the whole-class discussions. In these small peer groups, narrative, spontaneous talk dominates. In many of the reading-group transcripts for this class, the reading serves primarily as a stimulus for students to reread their own lives, rather than as a context devoted solely to deconstruction of the author's intentions. 1

The following reading-group episode I call "The Banking Concept of Love" because it reveals some of [the] students' culturally acquired attitudes about love, particularly Nick's concept of love as an "investment." In the transcript as a whole, Anna has a difficult time wresting the conversational floor from Nick and Carlos[,] who take over at many points, leaving Anna and Mary as spectators in the friendly male wrangle. For women, gaining access to the dominant discourse is often problematic, particularly in public settings. In the entire transcript from which this excerpt is taken, Nick has ninety-five conversational turns to Anna's twenty-five, so that she claims the floor 76 percent less of the time than he does. These small reading groups offer women an opportunity to work within a communal circle that is familiar and appropriate for 2

(continued)

(*continued*)

members who belong to what anthropologists Edwin Ardner and Shirley Ardner[1] and, later, feminist literary critic Elaine Showalter (1981) call the muted discourse group. The muted group belongs to, but is not always allowed full participation in the talk of, the dominant group. Ardner developed this idea to describe research claims he felt were being made about particular cultures or tribes based only on interviews with the men. Women, he said, were left out of the generation of meaning within these groups. Showalter, picking up on his metaphor, applies it to women and speech: "Thus muted groups must mediate their beliefs through the allowable forms of dominant structures. Another way of putting this would be to say that all language is the language of the dominant order, and women, if they speak at all, must speak through it" (1981, 200).

3   In the following frame we see that Anna *does* manage to bring in some personal responses to the group talk about Carver's story "What We Talk About When We Talk About Love." Nick is the designated leader of this group of Anna, Carlos, and Mary because he has selected the story for the group to discuss.

ANNA: That's a point in the essay too. People have a need for love.

MARY: Different kinds of love.

NICK: When you invest in a relationship, you invest a part of yourself so you necessarily are giving part of yourself up. You become half a person.

CARLOS: Do you think people can have a relationship without giving themselves up?

ANNA: I think you are fooling yourself if you're in a relationship and don't put anything in.

NICK: Yes. You're not committed.

MARY: You have to give up certain beliefs, certain prejudices. I know—my boyfriend—I've always been the type of person who says no drugs, no this, no that. He smokes pot. I say, "You shouldn't be doing that; it's wrong." He says, "I know it's wrong."

ANNA: If you can accept that, that's good.

MARY: You have to accept it—you give up a lot of your own moral values, not necessarily giving them up but accepting the ones that you know are wrong. Not that you are going to go out and do them but accepting the fact that you can't always change them.

ANNA: Someone I know, someone who's married and his wife doesn't let him smoke in the house, and when he's at work, he smokes like a madman. His wife, if she smells beer on his breath, makes him sleep on the couch. It's ridiculous stuff. She's not accepting him as a whole person.

MARY: If you love someone you have to accept them the way they are because you can't change them. You're not really loving them.

NICK: You also need their *investment.* You [need] to know that they're committed. You need to know that they have *taken a piece of themselves and given it to you.*

---

[1]The Ardners' anthropological work is cited in the Introduction to *Language, Gender, and Professional Writing: Theoretical Approaches and Guidelines for Nonsexist Usage*, edited by F.W. Frank and P. Treichler (19).

While the women in this group explore the interpersonal aspects of forming a relation-   4
ship—of accepting new values, of welcoming the whole person—the males (mainly
represented by Nick here) discuss commitment as an object—an emotional investment, as an actual piece of the self. From this short snip of conversation we learn that
in intimate relationships, Nick draws boundaries: half of me for you and half for me.
And Nick expects his part back.

Anna later reflects on this group discussion in her journal, which represents an   5
ongoing dialogue since she knows that Donna will respond. Donna underlines the
following parts of Anna's entry as being interesting:

> Then he [Nick] went on to say that after he had broken up with his girlfriend, he was
> left with this refound half and didn't know what to do with it. Instead of putting it into
> another relationship, he had to sort through it. But I'm finding that *I gave or put more*
> *than half of myself into a relationship* and I need some of it back for me to become
> complete.

Anna's entry indicates that while women place fewer boundaries on relationships, they   6
also make a larger capital investment ("more than half of myself"). Anna uses her journal to work out personal responses to ideas and readings that have been discussed in
small peer groups. In her last journal entry for Prose Writing, Anna returns to the issue
of love and relationships, showing that she is very much tuned into these concerns.
She writes: "I think about love, I know I spend an incredible amount of time trying to
figure out my love, his different channels, and where I can find myself in relation to
these channels."

Reference

Showalter, E. 1981. Feminist criticism in the wilderness. In *Critical inquiry*, Winter:
179–205.

Inquiring into the Essay

1. **Explore.** The focus of this excerpt is gender relations in small groups—how
   men and women interact with each other in class. You no doubt have some
   experience with this. One theory is that there is a "dominant group" and this
   group determines not only who participates but also how things are talked
   about. Fastwrite about this idea. Do you have experience with this kind of
   thing, and does it reflect gender difference, as this excerpt suggests? Tell the
   story of your experience with a successful or unsuccessful class discussion
   group. What does your experience tell you about the theory?

2. **Explain.** Explain in your own words the concept of "muted discourse."

3. **Evaluate.** The excerpt includes a transcript of the group talking about
   Raymond Carver's story "What We Talk About When We Talk About Love."

Chiseri-Strater's interpretation of this discussion is that the women "explore the interpersonal aspects of forming a relationship," while the men talk about "commitment as an object" that is divided up between partners. Do you read the discussion differently? If so, how?

4. **Reflect.** Theory is a lens that helps you to see, but its optics can also be limiting. Where do you see these trade-offs in the excerpt?

▶ Ethnographic Essay 2

A few years ago, an anthropology professor in her fifties decided to move into the freshman dorm at her university. She registered as a freshman with an undeclared major and spent an academic year doing exactly what other freshmen did: attending parties, going to classes, making new friends. But she was also quietly collecting data on her experience for an ethnography about student life that was then published as a book, *My Freshman Year.*

The professor, Cathy Small, assumed a pseudonym for her project, Rebekah Nathan, and managed to conduct her research without arousing the suspicion of fellow freshmen at the school, Northern Arizona University. Her research was based not only on extensive observations, but also on a number of interviews with fellow students, including international students who attended the school. In the excerpt that follows, Small reports on how students from England, Germany, France, Japan, Malaysia, Mexico, India, China, and the United Arab Emirates (UAE) viewed an American college and its students. It isn't often that we can see ourselves as these students see us, and the portrait is revealing.

My Freshman Year: Worldliness and Worldview
Rebekah Nathan

1   The single biggest complaint international students lodged about U.S. students was, to put it bluntly, our ignorance. As informants described it, by "ignorance" they meant the misinformation and lack of information that Americans have both about other countries and about themselves. Although most international students noted how little other students asked them about their countries, almost all students had received questions that they found startling: "Is Japan in China?" "Do you have a hole for a bathroom?" "Is it North Korea or South Korea that has a dictator?" "Where exactly is India?" "Do you still ride elephants?" "Do they dub American TV programs into British?"

2   These are just a few of the questions American students actually asked of international students. While they no doubt came from the less sophisticated among their classmates, it was clear that international students across the board felt that most Americans—even their own friends—are woefully ignorant of the world scene. It is

instructive to hear how students from diverse countries discuss their perceptions of American students' views of themselves and the world.

JAPAN: Really, they don't know very much about other countries, but maybe it's just because a country like Japan is so far away. Japanese probably don't know about the Middle East. Sometimes, students keep asking about ninjas.

UAE: American students are nice, but they need to stop being so ignorant about other countries and other cultures. Americans need to look at the world around them, and even the cultures around them in their own country.

MEXICO: The U.S. is not the center of the world. [Americans] don't know anything about other countries. Many of them don't have an interest in learning about other cultures. The only things students ever ask me about in my culture is food.

CHINA: Americans know very little about China or its culture. Most people think China is still very poor and very communist-controlled, with no freedom. There is a very anticommunist feeling, and people know little about today's China, which is quite changing and different. New Zealanders know much more about China—perhaps it's their proximity. I think that older people here have more of a sense of history, and that history, about the wars, about the cold war, makes them understand more about the world. Younger people seem to have no sense of history.

ENGLAND: People here know surprisingly little about England, and they assume a lot of things, some true, some not. People's impressions of me when I say I'm from England is that I might drink tea off a silver tray, and maybe live in a castle, and use a red telephone box. That's the honest truth. The questions that I've been asked are unbelievable.

MALAYSIA: I tell people that I am Muslim, and they take for granted that I'm an Arab. How can they not realize that not all Muslims are Arabs when they have many Muslims here who are American?

GERMANY: American students are much more ignorant of other countries and cultures. I suppose it's because it's so big, and knowing about California for you is like us knowing about France. It's a neighbor. The U.S. is less dependent on other cultures, and maybe that's why they need to know less. Still, Americans come across as not interested in other cultures, like they don't really care about other countries. So they think things like Swedish people are only blonds.

INDIA: Somebody asked me if we still ride on elephants. That really bothered me. If I say I'm Indian, they ask which reservation? I say I'm from Bombay. "Where is Bombay?" Some people don't even know where India is. A friend of mine and I tried to make these Americans see what it was like and we asked them where they're from. They said California. And we said, Where was that?

FRANCE: People here don't know where anything is. For World War II, the teacher had to bring in a map to show where Germany and England are—it was incredible! I read

(continued)

(*continued*)

somewhere a little research that said only 15 to 20 percent of Americans between the ages eighteen to twenty-five could point out Iraq on a map. The country will go to war, but it doesn't know where the country is!

3   Despite the critical consensus in these comments, it would be unfair of me to represent international student perspectives as roundly negative. In general, students from outside the United States warmly appreciated the American educational system as well as the spirit of the American college student. The criticisms that they did have, though, were pointed and focused. Taken together, they amounted to nothing less than a theory of the relationship among ignorance, intolerance, and ethnocentrism in this country, one that international eyes saw bordering on profound self-delusion. When I asked the linked questions, "What would you want American students to see about themselves?" and "What advice would you give them?" one German student stated succinctly what many students communicated to me at greater length: "Americans seem to think they have the perfect place to live, the best country, the best city. I hear that all the time. I used to think you just got that from politicians, but now I see it's from regular people too. The patriotism thing here really bothers me."

4   It is sobering to hear these words from a German student, whose country's historical experience in the 1930s and 1940s taught him the dangers of hypernationalism. To his fellow U.S. students he offered this recommendation: "I'd give them advice to live elsewhere. They should recognize that the way of living in the U.S. is fine, but it isn't necessarily the best way for everyone. I don't like to evaluate, and I'd like that applied to me. Be more informed. Information leads to tolerance."

5   It bothered a Chinese student who read in an article that American students don't want to study a foreign language because they believe that the world language will be English. "I think they need to learn about the world, to learn a foreign language," he urged. It bothered a British student, who lamented how much of world music American students seem to miss. "Everything here [on his corridor] is either black gangster rap or punk rock, and that's basically it. They don't want to hear other music—contemporary music from around the world."

6   The connection between lack of information and intolerance translated occasionally into personal stories of frustration, hitting home in the lives of some students. "I wish they [his hall mates] were accepting of more different music," said an Indian student. "I play my own music. I play it loud just like they do—Arabic and Punjabi and other stuff—and they complain to the RAs. But it's my right to play that too. Why don't they understand that?"

7   "They don't accept other cultures," speculated one Japanese student.

Once I was eating the food I had made—Japanese noodles—and we Japanese eat noodles with a noise. Somebody else in the kitchen area looked at me funny. She asked, "Why are you making so much noise?" I told her that's the way Japanese eat their noodles, and I can see by her face that she is disapproving. It hurt me to see that. Some Americans don't care about other worlds.

One key toward creating a more positive cycle of information, self-awareness, and   8
tolerance was for many the university and university education itself. Learn a foreign
language and study overseas, many recommended for individual students. Use your
education to expand your purview beyond your own country. For the university, other
students recommended a greater emphasis on self-awareness, including a more critical
eye directed to our own institutions and history.

For one Chinese student, the need to be more reflective about the media repre-   9
sentation of news and issues was critical: "Media coverage has a very great influence
here. In China, it has less influence because everyone knows it's propaganda. Here
it is not seen that way because there is a free press. But it's curious." In American
newspaper articles and TV news, "the individual facts are true often, but the whole is
not sometimes. I can see how Americans need to question the way stories are being
represented to them."

A French student beseeched us to examine our own educational system: 10

> Americans teach like the only important thing is America. There is no required his-
> tory course in college. The history course I took on Western civ. at AnyU was middle-
> school level, and it was very biased. I mean they taught how, in World War II, America
> saved France and saved the world, how they were so great. The courses don't consider
> what Americans have done wrong. All the current events here is news about America
> and what America is doing. If it's about another country, it's about what America is do-
> ing there. There's nothing about other countries and their histories and problems. [In
> France] we had lots of history and geography courses, starting very young. I learned
> about France, but then we had to take a course in U.S. industrialization, in China,
> Russia, Japan, too. We got the history and geography of the world, so we could see
> how France now fits into the bigger picture.

For the international students I interviewed, American college culture is a world   11
of engagement, choice, individualism, and independence, but it is also one of cross-
cultural ignorance and self-delusion that cries out for remediation. It was a Somali
student who summed up all of their hopes for "America": "You have so much here,
and so many opportunities. I wish America would ask more what this country can do
to make the world a better place."

Inquiring into the Essay

1.   **Explore.** International students, according to Nathan's research, feel that
     many American college students are "ignorant" about the world, even eth-
     nocentric, often feeling as if the United States is the only place worth living
     in. This sometimes translates into a kind of supernationalism or patriotism
     that further feeds Americans' isolation from other cultures. This is a strong
     assertion. Fastwrite for seven minutes about whether you believe this asser-
     tion is true, turning your writing whenever you can to your own personal
     experiences with other cultures on and off campus.

2. **Explain.** Would-be members of a culture learn what it is they need to do to join and, later, how they should behave to maintain their status. These international students are obviously confused about what it takes to belong to American student culture. Explain how they've got it wrong, and how they've got it right.

3. **Evaluate.** Ethnography and most other qualitative research attempt to infer from the few what might be true of the many. Evaluate the generalizability of the data reported here about international students and how they view us. Do you find Nathan's findings plausible? Why or why not?

4. **Reflect.** Reflect on the methodology of this ethnography. Imagine, for example, that you were one of the students who lived on the same dorm floor as Rebekah Nathan. How would you have responded to her presence? How reliable do you think were the data she collected?

Seeing the Form

German Cowboys

Photographer Eric O'Connell has been visually documenting the dress and lifestyles of a group of former East Germans, some of whom have embraced the American cowboy. O'Connell notes that "emerging from Communist rule, their self-determination found new identity with the spirit of the Wild West." This picture is one of a series O'Connell shot of these Germans, who live near the Czech border. O'Connell is a professional photographer enrolled in the University of Southern California's graduate program in visual anthropology. Read ethnographically, images such as this one are rich sources of "data."

THE WRITING PROCESS

Inquiry Project **Writing the Ethnographic Essay**

Inquiry Question: How do the people in a culture see themselves and their world?

Write an essay that uses field research and reading as the basis for an interpretation of how a subculture sees itself and others. This necessarily will be a limited picture, so it should focus on some aspect of the culture that emerges from your observations.

The essay should also have the following qualities:

- Be narrowly focused. You can't cover much in a relatively brief essay, so find some aspects of the study subject to focus on.
- Be organized around some thesis or interpretation of how this culture sees things. For example, how does the culture view authority figures, or what constitutes a leader in the group? (See the "Inquiring into the Details: Questions Ethnographers Ask" box later in this chapter on page 317.)
- Offer a rationale for why this group constitutes a distinct culture.
- Provide enough evidence from your field observations to make your interpretations and commentary convincing.

Prose+

- The digital camera is a great tool for ethnography. Focus your fieldwork on collecting as many images as you can of your study subjects doing things that are meaningful for that group (e.g., athletes putting on gear to play, quilters at work on a coverlet, etc.). Incorporate these images into your essay or make them the centerpiece of your analysis of the culture. Describe in detail what you see in the images and how they're relevant to your inquiry question.

- One approach to ethnography is to present a "day in the life" of a subject, trying to capture some of the ordinary rituals, habits, customs, conversations, and activities of someone who might be representative of the larger social group. This one-day snapshot can certainly be done in words alone, but it also lends itself to multimedia approaches—particularly audio and video. Imagine, for example, following your subject around one day with a digital recorder, collecting conversations and sounds that you'll later edit into an audio documentary. Audio clips would be surrounded by your narration, explaining the significance of what listeners hear.

- Another exciting development in the last decade is "hypermedia ethnography," or projects that combine images, videos, audio, and graphics in web pages rich with hyperlinks among the materials. Can you imagine creating a web page for your project that both helps you think about the connections among your findings and helps viewers to see those connections?

To learn more about some of these multimodal genres along with production tips on things like web pages, audio essays, and other genres, refer to Chapter 13.

What Are You Going to Write About?

9.3

Use relevant methods of invention to identify a local culture to study.

Possible subjects for your ethnography are all around you. We are all enmeshed—or wish to be—within intricate webs of cultures. Might your professional interests be relevant to this project? Say you want to be a police officer; might it be enlightening to hang out with a few officers to find out what that life is like? If you're a student at an urban campus, then the possibilities are nearly limitless, but even if you attend a rural university, you can still find a culture to study on your own campus. However, there are two conditions that you should keep in mind when deciding on a group to study:

1. Do members of the group identify with it? Is it a social group with some cohesion?

2. Is it accessible? Will you be able to talk to and describe group members in the field in the coming few weeks?

Opening Up

Begin exploring possible subjects for an ethnography by generating material in your notebook. This should be an open-ended process, a chance to use your creative side without worrying too much about making sense or trying to prejudge the value of the writing or the subjects you generate. In a sense, this is an invitation to play around.

Listing Prompts. Lists can be rich sources of triggering topics. Let them grow freely, and when you're ready, use a list item as the focus of another list or an episode of fastwriting. The following prompts should get you started.

1. In class or in your journal, create a four-column table, labeling the first column Trends, the second Hobbies, the third Community Groups, and the fourth Campus Groups (see the following example). Brainstorm a list of *cultural trends* that are a visible part of American culture. Write the name of each trend under the first column in the table. Create a similar list for popular hobbies (it's okay to repeat items in different columns), and write the name of each hobby in the second column. Finally, brainstorm a list of identifiable social groups in the community and on campus—fraternities, truck drivers, Goths, and so on. Write these, respectively, in the third and fourth columns of your table.

Writing Beyond the Classroom

Commercial Ethnography

Ethnography isn't just for academics. Increasingly, businesses are using the method to analyze consumer behavior, and they are finding that ethnography is often better than the usual surveys, questionnaires, and focus groups. Why? Because the information researchers get from observing people where they work and live is a more accurate measure of what people think. Even more important, because ethnographers are interested in watching how people behave and not just in surveying people's attitudes, they get a much more realistic picture than other researchers about what people are willing to actually *do*. Using video, photographs, audio, interviews, and observation, commercial application of ethnography gives designers and marketers a glimpse into cultural norms or can reveal some of the ways a product may—or may not—fit into our ordinary lives.

Trends	Hobbies	Community Groups	Campus Groups
Snowboarding	Fly fishing	Kiwanis	Fraternities
Blogging (participating in web logs)	Ballroom dancing	Pentecostal church	Black student alliance
	Computer games	Gospel singers	Graduate students
Atkins/South Beach/low-carb diet craze	Autograph collecting	Truck drivers	
Reality TV programming			

2. Create a new three-column table, labeling the first column Artifacts, the second Language, and the third Rituals. Now choose one of the trends, hobbies, community groups, or campus groups from your first table, and under the first column of the new table, list all of the artifacts—tools, equipment, devices, clothing—that you can think of that people typically use when they participate in the activity/group you have selected. In the second column, list the language—special terms, jargon, and other words or phrases—that group members regularly use. In the third column, list the rituals—habits, patterns of behavior, or traditions—that are typical of the activity/group. Creating the new table will help you expose some of the threads of a particular activity's or group's culture. Objects that group members typically use, their ways of speaking, and the traditions and rituals that govern their behavior are three key elements you need to consider when writing an ethnographic essay. The accompanying table identifies some of the artifacts, language, and rituals of fly fishing.

Fly Fishing

Artifacts	Language	Rituals
Fly rod (not "pole")	"Working water"	Keeping physical distance from other fly fishers
Artificial fly	"Skunked"	Catch and release of fish
Vest	"Meat fisherman"	Winter fly tying

Fastwriting Prompts. Choose an item from one of your lists as a fastwrite prompt. Write quickly, exploring each of the following questions:

1. What are your own experiences and observations with this trend, hobby, or group?

2. What are your presuppositions, biases, or assumptions about this trend, hobby, or group? What do you assume about the kind of people who participate in it, for example, and what might their motives be for belonging?

3. Based on what you know now, what things—or artifacts—seem particularly important to participants?

4. What questions do you have about why this trend exists, or why people participate in the group or hobby?

Visual Prompts. Sometimes the best way to generate material is to see what we think represented in something other than sentences.

1. If you like to take photographs, go through your collection looking for suggestive pictures you've captured of subcultures. Perhaps you took pictures of an on-campus or community event, or you have some shots of people back home who represent certain social groups.

2. Take a word or phrase from the table you created for the first question in the "Listing Prompts" subsection and use it as a nucleus word for a cluster on a blank page of your journal. When you cluster a hobby, cultural trend, or community or campus group, build associations using the five W's: *What, When, Where, Who,* and *Why. Where* do participants of this hobby, group, or trend gather, and *when? Who* are the kinds of people who belong? *What* are their activities and rituals? *Why* do people belong?

Research Prompts. Research can be helpful even this early in the process. New or more-detailed information might trigger ideas about possible topics for your paper that you otherwise would never have considered. At this stage, your research will be open ended and not particularly methodical. Just enjoy poking around.

1. In the United States, there's a magazine for nearly every subculture. Go online and survey the hobby and special-interest magazines. The web also has

useful sites with links to resources on American subcultures or information on cultural trends (see "Inquiring into the Details: Researching Trends and Subcultures on the Web"). Do any of these interest you?

2. There are a number of historical archives online that provide primary materials such as interview transcripts, letters and photographs, video interviews, and sound files of people who belong to identifiable groups: former slaves, 9/11 survivors, World War II veterans, Depression-era farmers, etc. Start with the digital collections at the Library of Congress. Is there enough data there for an essay?

3. One quick way to gain entry to a culture you don't belong to is to find someone in your class who is a member of that culture. Stay alert to what others in class say about their own identifications with certain social groups, and interview anyone who belongs to a culture that interests you.

Narrowing Down

The generating process may produce the messy, incoherent writing that would earn you bad grades in most classes. Its virtue, however, should be obvious by now: "Bad" writing gives a writer material to work with. And while it's always better to work from abundance rather than scarcity, this material still must be judged, shaped, and evaluated.

Inquiring into the Details

Researching Trends and Subcultures on the Web

If you're browsing for ideas about a topic, or researching the cultural group you've chosen to investigate, a number of sites on the Internet can help.

- **The Pew Internet and American Life Project** features up-to-date information on trends in Internet use. http://www.pewinternet.org

- **The Census Bureau** publishes online data on trends in education, families, health, population, economic development, and much more. Some of these data will help you to identify particular groups of people in the U.S. that are affected by these trends. http://www.census.gov

- **The Gallup Poll** website features recent survey results on social trends. http://www.gallup.com

- **The Google Directory** also lists subcultures, with links to resources on the web.

- **Wikipedia,** the "free encyclopedia," isn't necessarily a good source for academic writing, but it is the "largest reference site on the Web." Its list of subcultures is impressive. http://en.wikipedia.org/wiki/Category:Subcultures

What's Promising Material and What Isn't?   Earlier, I mentioned two conditions that are key: Your study subject is a cohesive cultural group and is accessible to you in the next few weeks for field observations. There's another key issue to consider now, too: Should this be a group to which you belong? Ethnographic methods ask that writers be *participant-observers*. As the term implies, you're not just watching, but also are involved in some way in the activities of the group you're studying (with their permission). Participation is easy if you're an insider, and you're likely to get considerable access, which is no small thing, given that you'll be doing this project relatively quickly. On the other hand, being an outsider makes you a better observer. Because of your unfamiliarity with your study subjects, you're likely to notice things an insider would miss, and you'll also be freer from bias. Weigh the advantages and disadvantages before you decide.

Finally, consider how much data you'll be able to gather.

- Does the cultural group you want to study meet regularly?
- Is there any background research on the group in the library or online that might provide additional information?
- Will there be any privacy issues? For example, do members of the group engage in activities (legal or otherwise) that would make them reluctant to talk to you?

9.4
Analyze and
interpret
qualitative
information.

Questions About Audience and Purpose.   No matter how fascinated you are by the people who do medieval battle reenactments at the park, you still have to have something *to say* about that subculture to readers who may not share your fascination. Most academic ethnographies are written to fellow experts. Researchers, to some extent, assume prior knowledge and interest in their subjects. However, you're writing an ethnographic *essay*—a much shorter, less extensively researched work. It's okay to imagine an audience that knows something about your subject (after all, most of us are aware of many social groups), but make sure your essay helps readers to see what perhaps they've seen before but in a way they hadn't previously seen it. Good essays make the familiar strange. And good ethnographies don't simply describe—they *analyze* and *argue*.

How do you do this?

1. *Look hard and look closely.* If you're going to see anything new, you have to have as much data as you can. That means doing as much fieldwork as you can.
2. *Focus on what is less obvious.* If you're going to surprise your audience, you need to surprise yourself. What are you noticing about those battle reenactors that you never noticed before?
3. *Find the question.* What aspect of your culture are you most interested in exploring?
4. *Discover one main thing you're trying to say.* You can't know what this is until you've done a lot of fieldwork and some reading. But in the final draft,

the main idea you're trying to get across about the group you observed should be clear.

5. *Tell stories, provide profiles, use dialogue, incorporate abundant description.* To bring the culture you studied to life for readers, try to employ some of the literary techniques you know from good storytelling.

Trying Out

Prepare to do fieldwork by confirming the best places to conduct observations of the culture in which you're interested. Sometimes that's easy to figure out: Snowboarders hang out at the lodge, surfers at the beach, fraternity brothers at the fraternity house, homeless men at the shelter. But there will also be less-obvious gathering places, locations you may only learn of through interviews with group members. Are there other locations where group members gather to socialize, plan activities, celebrate successes, or learn from each other?

Writing ethnographically requires that you expand your repertoire of research to include interviews and fieldwork.

Inquiring into the Details

Questions Ethnographers Ask

When you study a social group, whether it's skateboarders or opera singers, there are certain basic things you want to find out about how that group operates. For example,

- How do group members view outsiders?
- What motivates members to belong?
- What artifacts are present, how are they typically used, and what significance is attached to them?
- What is the nature of gender relations in the group?
- Where does the group gather and why?
- What is the group's social hierarchy, and how is it organized and maintained?
- What's the relationship between this local culture and the larger culture with which it identifies?
- Does this group seem to define itself *in opposition to* other groups, and if so, why?
- What are the culture's most symbolic or significant rituals? Why is meaning assigned to them?
- Is there an initiation of some kind?

If the sites you want to visit aren't public, you may need permission to conduct your observation. In addition, make sure you plan for your own safety. While it's unlikely that you'll study a city gang or a gun-toting right-wing militia or some similar group that can be dangerous to outsiders, make sure that you will be safe wherever you go. Bring a friend with you; tell others where you'll be and for how long.

Taking Notes. The most important source of information for your essay will be the observation notes you take in the field. You practiced note taking during the profile assignment, but the notes for the ethnography project will involve more observation. In the initial stages, focus on your first impressions of the group you're studying. Jot down everything, including:

- Conversations, both formal and informal. What do people say, where do they say it, and who does the talking?
- Topics or issues that arise that might merit follow-up interviews.
- Things that members of the group often talk about, or things they say that surprise you.
- Detailed descriptions of activities, especially those that happen regularly or that have particular significance for the group you're studying.

Inquiring into the Details

Ethnography and Ethics

Unlike most other undergraduate research projects, an ethnography involves working with human subjects. As you might imagine, this raises some ethical issues. How open should you be with your research subjects about your project? Do you need their permission to chronicle what they say and do? What responsibility do you have to protect your subjects' identities?

For faculty who do research with people, a university review board charged with protecting human subjects must approve the project. That probably won't be necessary for your ethnographic essay, but there are still ethical guidelines you should follow:

1. Let your research subjects know what you're doing and why you're doing it.
2. Obtain their permission to be included in your research. While a written "informed consent" may not be necessary, there should at least be a clear-cut verbal understanding between you and the people you're studying.
3. Protect their anonymity. You have an obligation to make certain that your subjects' identities are protected. It's often a wise practice to use pseudonyms in your research.

For the American Anthropological Association's ethical guidelines, visit http://ethics.aaanet.org/ethics-statement-0-preamble/.

▶ **Field Notes**

Rita Guerra hasn't bowled often in the past twenty years, but she has fond memories of holding birthday parties at the local bowling alley when she was a girl, and now her own children clamor from time to time to do some ten-pin bowling. Guerra remembers her hometown bowling alley as a social and cultural center for her small town. Wouldn't such a place be a great site to do some fieldwork for her ethnographic essay?

What follow are Guerra's field notes from her first visit to Emerald Lanes— "The Best Alley in the Valley." At this stage, she is focused on collecting data— transcribing conversations she hears, carefully describing what she sees, jotting down text from signs and notices, mapping the space, and simply watching to see what happens when. She uses double-entry field notes. On the left are her observations, and on the right are her impressions or ideas about what she sees, hears, smells, or feels. Notice that she gets a dialogue going between the two columns— speculating, interpreting, and raising questions on the right in response to specific information she collects on the left.

The success of your ethnographic essay depends on the success of your field notes. Always collect more information than you can use—which probably means multiple visits to your field sites—and push yourself to reflect on what you've found as you collect the information. Rita Guerra's field notes are a good model.

Field Notes on Friday Afternoon at Emerald Lanes
Rita Guerra

OBSERVATIONS OF	**IDEAS ABOUT**
4/9/04	
4:32 Sounds of balls hitting maple lanes, thundering toward pins. There is a constant hum of noise—rolling balls, lane chatter, country music, clanking of pins. Smells like cigarettes and beer. Smoking is allowed throughout the alley.	A Friday afternoon at Emerald Lanes appears to be more family oriented, no league play. But I was impressed by how many strong bowlers, mostly young couples played. Emerald Lanes seems a family-friendly place though I was surprised that the entire place allowed smoking. This might be indicative of the bowling culture—smoking is still okay.

(continued)

(continued)

"That will be a triple," says a woman in shorts and green tank top. She is bowling with two other young couples and they all bowl well, alternating between strikes and spares. Successful frame usually produces a kind of dance, clenched fists, "yessss!" Poor frame—silence, stone faced.

Scores are tallied electronically on monitors above each lane. Large number of families on Friday afternoon, including birthday party in far lanes.

"Got it right where I wanted to," says young player with girlfriend. He cups the ball underneath before his swing and when releasing it gives it a spin. Ball breaks from left to right. Wears own bowling shoes, no rentals, and black wrist band. Spends very little time preparing but picks up his ball, sights the pins, and goes into motion within 15 seconds.

"The Best Alley in the Valley"
"The Bowling Guy's Pro Shop" Ball polisher
Tropical theme—three plastic palm trees between lanes.
Budweiser sign: Welcome to Emerald Lanes.
Good Family Fun?
Movement

Need to check for "bowling lingo" on the Internet. What is a "triple"? Three strikes in a row? I was really interested in watching the preparation and releases of bowlers. Seems like you could tell the experienced bowlers from inexperienced ones by the smoothness of their release and especially the velocity of the ball. But maybe more than anything, I began to interpret their reactions to a good frame and bad frame. Strike produces a "yesss!" and clenched fist but not extended celebration. Bad frame a stony face. No anger, no laughter. Seemed to be no difference in this between men and women. Less experienced bowlers would react with more exaggeration.

I need to learn more about the theories behind introducing spin in releasing the ball. The ability to do this seems to distinguish the more skilled from the less skilled bowlers. This player consistently produced a left-to-right break by cupping the ball and obviously spinning it right before he releases it.

Might be interesting to actually time how long it takes for bowlers to prepare to bowl when it is their turn. My impression is that more experienced bowlers waste very little time; novices diddle and dawdle.

Like a lot of bowling alleys I've seen this one seems a bit tacky from the outside, and inside seems friendly but with an atmosphere of Budweiser beer and smoke. On a Friday afternoon, though, it seemed family friendly. Need to plan next visit for a Saturday night during league play. I have a sense that it's an entirely different culture.

Writing the Sketch

Write a sketch that provides a verbal snapshot of the culture you're studying. Using the ethnographers' questions (presented earlier) as guides for your field observation, go to a place where you can observe your culture in action. Collect observations and interviews that will allow you to create a snapshot of your group in action. For example, if you're interested in gender relations among young skateboarders, go to the skateboard park and carefully observe how the boys and girls interact. If possible, talk to some of them. Take lots of notes, and consider taking photographs as visual records, too.

Try working through the following three steps in your journal in preparation for drafting your sketch.

1. **Narrative of thought.** In your journal, tell the story of how your thinking has evolved. When you first chose your subject, what did you think about that culture? What assumptions did you make, and what did you expect to find? And then? And then? And then? And how about now?

2. **Look at strands in the web.** Which of the following features of a culture apply to the one you're studying?

   - *Shared language* (for instance, are there insider phrases and words that have significance to group members?)
   - *Shared artifacts* (for instance, are there objects that have particular significance to group members?)
   - *Common rituals and traditions* (for instance, are there patterns of behavior that surround certain activities, or are there historical understandings of how something must be done?)
   - *Shared beliefs and attitudes* (for instance, are there common attitudes toward other insiders, toward outsiders, toward new initiates; do group members share beliefs in the significance of the group and its activities?)
   - *Common motivations* (for instance, do members participate for some of the same reasons?)

3. **Examine one strand.** Choose *one* of the preceding features. In your notebook/journal, generate specific evidence from your research or fieldwork that supports your finding.

After you complete the preceding steps, write a sketch that describes what you saw and heard during one or more of your field experiences. The key is not to simply *explain* what you noticed, but to *show* it, too. In addition:

- Choose a title for your sketch.
- Whenever possible, *show* what you observed or heard using description, scene, dialogue, and similar literary devices.
- Offer a tentative theory about a belief or attitude that group members seem to share, based on your initial field observations and interviews.

Moving from Sketch to Draft

If it was successful, your sketch provided an initial snapshot of the group you're studying. The draft, of course, will provide a fuller picture. But what should that picture focus on? What kind of information should you try to gather now? Your sketch can provide some useful clues.

Evaluating Your Own Sketch. To read your sketch for these clues, focus on your strongest impressions, working through the following questions in your journal:

1. *What is my strongest impression of the group so far? What kinds of things did I see, hear, or read that gave me that impression?*
2. *What is another impression I have?*
3. *Which one of these two impressions might be a focus for the next draft?*
4. *What do I most want to know now about the culture I'm observing? What questions do I have?*

Reflecting on What You've Learned. Make a schedule that describes your plan for additional research and field observations over the next few weeks. For example:

Sunday	Monday	Tuesday	Wednesday	Thursday	Friday	Saturday
2–4 Field observations at the park		3 PM print photos		7 PM Library research		10–12 Field observations, Interview w/ Karen

Developing

The most important thing you can do to improve the next draft of your ethnography is return to the field for more observations and interviews. This project doesn't permit the kind of immersion in a culture that most ethnographic researchers enjoy, so it's essential that you focus on gathering as much data as you can in the time you have. This will take careful planning and scheduling, and your schedule will help. (In fact, your instructor may ask you to hand in your schedule.)

Sources of Data. Your field notes will be the richest source of information for your project. *You should plan to make repeated visits to places where members of the group frequent.* It's hard to overstate the importance of your firsthand observations. But there are other sources of information you might consider as well.

Photographs. Visual ethnography uses photographs, film, or video to document local culture. These can be enormously rich records, because pictures extend our perception and preserve information for later study and analysis. In addition, sharing the photographs we take with our study subjects can yield valuable insight about the significance of the images. A twelve-year-old skateboarder, for example, might look at the picture of someone attempting a trick and offer a commentary about the rider's motives and techniques, and the meanings of his moves. Digital photography has made it possible to instantaneously share this material.

Bring your camera (or smartphone) along on your site visits and record what you see. When you print the pictures, attempt to place them in a meaningful order. Try to establish relationships among the pictures. Do they fall into certain categories of activity or significance? In addition, study the photographs for information that you might have missed when taking your field notes. What do you notice about artifacts, clothing, or the context in which the action is taking place?

Interviews.   There is only so much we can see. Simply observing people won't tell us what they think or feel; we have to ask them. Your earlier practice with interviews will have prepared you for this method of collecting information; see Chapter 4 and Chapter 11 for more information on interview methods and techniques.

Artifacts.   If you can, collect or describe objects from the site or objects that people in this culture routinely make, talk about, or use. For example, if you're studying a truck stop, collect menus, placemats, and so on. If you're studying people in a bowling league, describe the differences among bowling balls or collect score sheets. Photographs can also be helpful in identifying artifacts that you can't haul away. Collecting such things can help you to determine what meaning, if any, is assigned to them by group members. For example, do members of a male bowling league see the weight of a bowling ball as a measure of not only a bowler's strength but also his manhood?

Maps.   One way to analyze a group's social relationships and the context in which activities take place is to observe where and how members occupy space. Imagine, for example, your own family dinner table as you were growing up. Did everyone sit in the same chair every night? Was there any logic to that arrangement? Does it say anything about the social role of each family member? If you were to draw a map of your family's seating arrangement, and then add arrows that follow the movement of each member of your family during a typical meal, what would that suggest about social roles and relationships? In my family, my mother's chair was always nearest the kitchen, and she moved far more than the rest of us, mostly back and forth, to and from the oven, table, and sink. Consider making similar maps of your study site, noting the arrangement of things and people, as well as their movements.

Reading Research.   Because you have weeks rather than months to write your ethnographic essay, you will probably need to rely somewhat on the work of others who have formally or informally studied the culture in which you're interested. This may include reading the hobby or specialty magazines that group members read; visiting websites, newsgroups, chat rooms, and electronic mailing lists that group members frequent online; and searching the library databases for any academic

Inquiring into the Details

Useful Library Databases for Ethnography

Don't forget to research existing ethnographies that may be published about the culture you're studying. If your library has them, the following specialized databases are worth checking:

- Anthropological Index Online
- EHRAF Collection of Ethnography
- Sociological Abstracts
- Ethnographic Bibliography of North America
- Abstracts in Anthropology
- Abstracts of Folklore Studies
- International Bibliography of the Social Sciences

research that scholars may have published on the culture you're studying (see the box "Inquiring into the Details: Useful Library Databases for Ethnography"). You'll be surprised at how much work has been done on local culture in the United States.

9.4
Analyze and interpret qualitative information.

Analyzing the Data. Analyze the data that you're gathering as you collect it. In particular, look at two kinds of patterns: recurrences and categories. As you look at your data, what things seem to recur? Do your subjects keep telling you the same stories? Are there certain ways that they describe or say something that you often hear? What themes keep coming up?

Categories will help you to organize your data. In the table below, I suggest some categories that *may* apply to your project. Come up with your own, too.

Type of analysis	What to look for
Recurrences	What ideas, themes, stories, phrases, behaviors keep coming up in your field notes and interviews?
Categories	• Social relationships • Interactions • Use of space • Key locations of activity • Rules of behavior • Authority and power • Beliefs • Rituals and customs • Language and expressions • History

Finally, don't forget to continue library and Internet research. Consult specialized indexes and databases you might have skipped earlier (see "Inquiring into the Details: Useful Library Databases for Ethnography"). What can you learn from what others have observed and said about the culture you're studying?

Drafting

Academic ethnographies often take months or even years to complete. Field notes, video, photographs, and artifacts might fill a stack of storage boxes and gigabytes of space on a researcher's hard drive. This project, obviously, is much more modest. But if you're going to write a strong essay that uses ethnographic methods, the one thing you can't have is too much information. Collect, describe, observe, record, read, photograph, and listen as much as you can in the timeframe you have for the assignment. If you have enough information, and you've analyzed it (see the previous subsection), your draft must *interpret* what you've found. What does it mean? In particular, you're trying to answer this inquiry question:

> *What do I understand about how the people in this culture see things?*

Like much research, ethnography is *inductive*. You make inferences from the data. What did people say, do, or use, and what does this indicate about how that culture seems to see things? You might start to answer this question by focusing on one of the categories you used to analyze your data. For example, what patterns did you see in social relationships within the culture you observed? Can you offer a theory about what those patterns might mean?

The practical problem is this: You're not writing a book. You can't give a very thorough picture of the group you studied; it will be necessarily limited. So how might you organize your draft with this in mind?

Methods of Development. As an extended form of inquiry, the ethnographic essay will probably combine some of the methods of development described here.

Narrative Structures. Because ethnography often involves scene or setting, character, dialogue, and action, it's a form that naturally accommodates storytelling. Try one or more of these narrative techniques.

1. *A typical day.* One way to capture your culture is to describe, in some detail, what happened on a single day that seems representative. This focus on a particular time, place, and people gives your ethnographic essay a dramatic and limited focus.

2. *Collage.* Sometimes it's effective to generate a series of significant snapshots of your subjects in their natural setting. For example, an ethnography of eighth-grade cheerleaders might feature a collage of scenes with titles like "Making the Team" or "The Squad's Social Hierarchy."

3. *Narrative of thought.* Tell the story of your initial presumptions about the culture and how your observations and research influenced those

presumptions. Or state an initial theory and then tell the story of whether the evidence supported it.

Question to Answer.   The inquiry question driving your project—*How do members of the group I studied see themselves and their world?*—will need to be more focused in your essay or project. You'll look at *some aspect* of how they see things.

Begin by establishing your focusing question (e.g., "What is the social hierarchy of dog handlers, and how is it maintained?"). Then consider including some or all of the following:

- Provide some background from research about other studies (if any) that have directly or indirectly addressed the question.

- Explain your interest in the question. What observations, interviews, or readings suggest that the social hierarchy of dog handlers might be interesting or significant to look at?

- Explain the methods you used to focus on the question.

- Offer a theory, a possible answer to the question. For example: *Based on my initial impressions, handlers and trainers who have established reputations as successful breeders tend to get the most respect.*

Compare and Contrast.   When I teach graduate workshops in creative nonfiction, I often wonder how gender shapes my students' responses to each other and the work being discussed. If I conducted a study that focused on such a question, I probably would find a range of ways in which men and women interact with each other. One useful way of exploring these interactions would be to look for similarities and differences, to compare and contrast. In fact, it's hard to imagine any ethnography not exploiting this method of development in at least a small way, and it's easy to imagine that comparisons might form the backbone of some essays.

Formal Academic Structure.   While narrative, question to answer, and comparison might all be elements of a more formally structured ethnography, academic ethnographies also often include the following sections: Abstract, Introduction, Methods, Discussion, and Conclusion. Study published ethnographies for more insight on how each of these sections work together.

Using Evidence. We've already talked a lot about the kinds of evidence an ethnographic essay draws on. This is largely *primary* research. It will draw heavily on your field notes, photographs, videos, maps, and artifacts. But don't forget to search for *secondary* sources as well. What has been published in journals, in magazines, and online about the culture you're studying?

Workshopping

If your draft is subject to peer review, see "Models for Writing Workshops" (p. 554) in Appendix A for details on how to organize workshop groups, and consult "Useful Responses" (p. 556) to help you decide on how your group can help you.

Peer review of ethnography projects is almost always fun. The diversity of the topics, the interesting findings from fieldwork, and the interest we all have in the lives of others make this workshop pretty fascinating for everyone. But there are often problems in these first drafts, and the most common one is that there simply isn't enough information to draw enough interesting inferences. Focus the workshop, as always, on whether the purpose and meaning of your project are clear. The box below might help.

Questions for Peer Reviewers	
1. Purpose	If my topic (e.g., library use on campus) is the landscape, is it clear what *part* of that landscape I'm focused on (e.g., how students use study areas)?
2. Meaning	If you had assumptions about the culture I'm studying before you read my essay, how did reading it change those assumptions? In your own words, how would you summarize my answer to the inquiry question: *How do members of this group see themselves and their world?*

Reflecting on the Draft. Go back to the categories listed in the "Analyzing the Data" subsection on page 324. Reflect on which of these categories seem central to your project, and for those that are, think about which need to be the focus of the next draft. Write in your journal about what you plan to do to generate more data in the key categories.

Revising

Revision is a continual process—not a last step. You've been revising—"reseeing" your subject—from the first messy fastwriting in your journal. But the things that get your attention vary depending on where you are in the writing process. With your draft in hand, revision becomes your focus through what I'll call shaping and tightening your draft.

9.5 Apply revision strategies that are effective for an ethnographic essay.

Chapter 14 contains strategies that can help you revise any inquiry project, and the "Guidelines: Revising Your Work" in this chapter on page 329 can help you locate these strategies. There are also certain things to think about that are especially useful for shaping an ethnographic essay.

Shaping. In your draft, you made a tentative commitment to your topic, hoping that you could shape it into something that might have meaning for someone other than you. Fundamentally, you've been trying to figure out *what you're trying to say* and then rebuild your essay so that it is both clear and convincing. Shaping focuses first on the largest concerns of purpose and meaning—which you've already looked at if you workshopped your draft—and on the next-to-largest concerns of information and organization. It starts with knowing what your essay is about—your inquiry question and maybe your claim—and then revising to make every element of the draft focused on that question or assertion.

As you know, the inquiry question that drives ethnography is how members of a culture see themselves and their world. But your essay should have a more specific focusing question, and this will be the key to shaping your essay. For example, in Kersti Harter's ethnographic essay at the end of this chapter, she asks *Is it true that homosexual men have finely tuned "gaydar," or the ability to recognize other gay men based on location, behavior, clothing, and taste?* This question is sufficiently focused to provide Kersti with great guidance as she shapes her essay. It tells her,

1. **Who exactly are the subjects of her study:** gay men (not all gay or transgender people)
2. **The types of information she will include (and, of course, what to exclude):** data about locations, behavior, clothing, and taste
3. **A key term and concept that need defining:** "gaydar"
4. **The theory she hopes to test:** that gay men are particularly good at recognizing other gay men whose sexual preference is unknown based on limited knowledge

If you haven't done so already, explicitly identify the question that you're focusing on in your study. Then use it to limit your essay's subject and to decide what to put in and what to take out, what terms and concepts need explaining, and what theory or idea you are exploring.

- Does the draft try to say things about the group rather than focus on a single main thesis, interpretation, or question?
- If your time for fieldwork was limited, did you make up for it by finding some useful research about the culture you studied in the library or on the web?

Polishing. When you are satisfied with the shape of your draft, focus on paragraphs, sentences, and words. Are your paragraphs coherent? How do you manage transitions? Are your sentences fluent and concise? Are there any errors in spelling or syntax? The section of Chapter 14 called "Problems with Clarity and Style" on p. 542 can help you focus on these issues.

Before you finish your draft, work through the following checklist:

✓ Every paragraph is about one thing.

✓ The transitions between paragraphs aren't abrupt.

✓ The lengths of sentences vary in each paragraph.

✓ Each sentence is concise. There are no unnecessary words or phrases.

✓ You've checked grammar, particularly verb agreement, run-on sentences, unclear pronouns, and misused words (*there/their, where/were*, and so on).

✓ You've run your spellchecker and proofed your paper for misspelled words.

Guidelines: Revising Your Work

A first effort is almost never a best effort. To make sure your essay is really your best work, check out Chapter 14 for help with these questions:

- What is my paper really about? (See p. 518.)

- What am I really trying to say? (See p. 523.)

- Do I have enough convincing evidence? (See p. 530.)

- Does this paper move logically and smoothly from paragraph to paragraph? (See p. 534.)

- Are the sentences and paragraphs in this paper too choppy or hard to follow? (See p. 542.)

▶ Student Essay

The term *gaydar* entered the American lexicon in the past decade or two, though few thought the idea that gay men and women can intuitively distinguish gay from straight was much more than urban legend. Recent research, however, seems to confirm that there just might be something to that idea. The ethnographic essay that follows asks whether gay men use means other than intuition to make judgments about the sexual orientation of strangers.

This study of four Boise gays is a fascinating look at gay culture. But it's a limited one, too. Like all qualitative research, "Beyond Gaydar" hopes to find useful insight into the many by looking at the few. This project, like most ethnographies conducted in a composition class, is based on only several weeks of fieldwork, rather than the years that most ethnographies require. Still, the essay offers a useful glimpse at the world of young gay men, and it seems to amplify some of the published research. Kersti Harter's essay is cited using APA guidelines.

Kersti Harter

Beyond "Gaydar": How Gay Males Identify Other Gay Males

A Study with Four Boise, Idaho, Men

Introduction

1   While people who do not fit into the codified norms of behavior in contemporary urban life are often marginalized by the mainstream, this very fact often serves to empower and reinforce the behavior of its members in marginalized groups. This is the case within gay male culture in United States urban society. Because gay males remain heavily stigmatized, they have formed a large "outside" group with subtle yet unmistakably designated patterns and categories of behavior, action, clothing, and taste. These patterns and behaviors may not be identifiable to the larger society, but they are well-known among gay men. One of these social rituals is the patterns through which gay men attempt to identify other gay males. I had very little prior knowledge that this pattern existed, but through interviews and observations of several gay men in Boise, Idaho, aged 18–25, I discovered how some gay males identify others who are gay.

I was able to model this pattern and the categories of behavior that exist within it.

Background

2   Several studies suggest that so-called "gaydar," the use of intuition to determine the sexual orientation of someone without asking the person outright whether he or she is gay, might have a basis in fact. A recent study (Lawson, 2005) demonstrated that when provided with "neck-up" photographs of strangers who weren't wearing jewelry or makeup, homosexuals were better than heterosexuals in making the correct identification of the stranger's sexual orientation, making

BEYOND GAYDAR   2

this judgment in 2 seconds or less (p. 30). Martins et al. (2005) also reported that "gay men were found to be particularly good at detecting the scent of other gay men" (p. 694). In addition, another study argued that "eye gaze," with distinct variations, is "crucial to forces that either trigger or reinforce one gay's perception of another gay's identity during social encounters" (Nicholas, 2004).

Identifying Other Gay Males: Place

There are, however, other methods of gay identification used by male homosexuals that don't rely on "gaydar" or intuition. One such method, depicted in Figure 1, relies on contextual cues or markers. The number one identifier among the four contextual cues is place: if he's in the gay bar, he's likely gay. But

3

Figure 1. The sequence of judgments used by gay men to identify other gay men

BEYOND GAYDAR   3

this does not mean for sure that any man in a gay club is gay. Julian recounted a

story in which he accidentally "hit on" a straight male who was in a gay club:

> It was at a gay club, so I'm not entirely at fault. This guy was just sitting there,
> kind of like, I don't know, just sitting there at the bar, looking kind of, well,
> sitting there sulking I guess. And I thought he was pretty good looking, so
> I thought I'd go talk to him, I wasn't going to pick him up or anything. And
> so I went up and was talking to him, and he would answer me in one-syllable
> replies. And I just walked off and I found out that he was actually the bouncer
> that worked there and he had the night off.

4   Julian's story suggests that "gaydar" isn't always reliable. Sexual orientation

signaling is based on more than intuition. It also means that place is not the only

identifier of gay males, although it is often accurate. So what happens when the

identifier of place fails to confirm sexual orientation?

Action

5   Then we must move onto appearance. I use "appearance" here because my

participants claimed that movement as well as personal style played into identify-

ing whether a man is gay. I have subdivided appearance into action, or movements

and other behaviors, and clothing, which I discuss below. During my group inter-

view, both Aaron and Steven claimed that movement is the more important part of

appearance in determining a man's orientation:

> Me: Does clothing or movement clue you in more to whether or not a person
> is gay? Aaron: Movement . . . You can tell by the way a person gesticulates,
> by how they walk. I can tell how I walk . . . I'm like God, everyone knows I'm a
> homo [laughs]! Like I like it, but yeah, it's definitely how they move.

6   It seems that certain movements are ingrained qualities that help gay males

identify other gay males. So, in Figure 1, I've identified the next step my subjects

BEYOND GAYDAR   4

might use to identify another gay male as "Action." Some of these movements are evident even to straight observers, and occasionally the actions have to do with associations with other gay men. For example, another participant, Jeff, pointed out, "Well, if they are with a guy, then yeah, they're gay."

If action is not enough to identify the man's orientation, an observer might   7
move on to more subtle parts of clothing style or even personal tastes. But this would probably not happen in such a situation, and actions are likely telling enough.

Clothing and Personal Style

There are times, however, when gay men are in places less exclusively gay, or   8
in places not defined as gay at all. Then one must skip to the latter steps, identify-ing the less obvious markers of sexual orientation such as personal style.

When I began my research, I sat with my friend Steven in a popular downtown   9
Boise coffee shop, The Flying M. While being widely known as the "gay" coffee shop, it is not exclusively so. Wednesday, according to Steven, has become known to some in the gay community as "Gay Night." This Wednesday was the first time that I met his friend Aaron, who later helped me in the group interview. I would ask Steven, "Is that guy over there gay?" and so on, and he would answer yes, because the man was simply at this coffee shop on Gay Night, or because he acted a certain way, or dressed a certain way.

When he would identify them as gay because of the way they looked, David   10
would often cite things like button-down Abercrombie and Fitch shirts or spiky hair. There was a definite gay look that he was able to identify. Steven was able to identify gay males, even though we were in a setting that was not necessarily exclusively gay. Clothing, though it is used less than place and action, still can provide clues

about sexual orientation. There are also categories of gay male dress style that the men that I interviewed identified.

Stylistic Stereotypes Among Gay Males

11   To outsiders, clothing and personal style would be one of the easiest identifiers of gay males. But it is actually, according to my subjects, a less obvious marker than place or action. Personal style also comes in many shapes and forms in the gay community. It's as if there is a set of emic values (distinctions that members of a group recognize that may not be apparent to outsiders) that are stereotypical of the gay male. This is an instance where the pattern of behavior in the group is broken down into diverse categories.

12   For example, Green and Ashmore, in "Taking and Developing Pictures in the Head: Assessing the Physical Stereotypes of Eight Gender Types" (1998), asked college students to picture various stereotypes in their heads and describe what they saw. They asked them to picture both "nerd" and "homosexual," and they found that:

> Perceivers have similar pictures of the homosexual and the nerd in their heads. Both were frequently described as being slender and of average height, wearing glasses, and wearing the "uniform" of the male college student (e.g., button-down shirt, pants or jeans, sneakers or casual shoes). (p. 1627)

13   Though these college students pictured "the nerd" and "the homosexual" together, the men I talked with identified a picture of the homosexual that was quite different from the one these college students identified. The men also emphasized that there were many different types of gay male style, not just one. They all identified several emic stereotypes, and disagreed with the "nerd" and "homosexual" being lumped together in similar stylistic categories.

BEYOND GAYDAR   6

When I mentioned this article to Julian, he explained to me why people might   14
lump the "nerd" with the "homosexual":

> In Europe they used to associate Jews and homosexuals, they were kind of
> lumped together. And so maybe whoever's on the outside is kind of labeled
> together ... I don't think that's a look that gay guys go for as far as trying to
> look like that ... there's sort of that geek chic that a lot of people do, pretty
> much if you see that you know they're straight.

According to Julian, though the outside sees homosexuals and nerds having   15
similar styles because of their roles as the "outsiders," homosexuals have a different
view of their styles, one that is much more rich and varied.

In the essay "Gay Masculinity in the Gay Disco," Cheseboro and Klenk (1981)   16
identify several categories of symbol-using in the gay disco. Though written more
than twenty-five years ago, it gives insight into some incipient analyses of stylistic categories that gay men employ. Cheseboro and Klenk describe "The Virility
Component":

> One concept asserted in the gay disco is an exaggerated, if not flagrant, form
> of masculinity in appearance ... an extreme case of this composite image in-
> cludes an explicitly displayed, muscularly developed body, a flannel shirt, a
> leather vest, denim or leather pants, construction or cowboy boots. (p. 95)

Though perhaps less in vogue now, the hyper-masculine male look is still   17
a symbolic type that some gay males employ. At first, I described these men as
"bears," a more masculine type of gay male, but Julian corrected me and said that
perhaps I was referring to something more like a butch. Julian thought that perhaps
butch gay males care about their appearance and attempt to look masculine while
bears don't really care about their appearance at all, and are more like the general
straight male.

BEYOND GAYDAR 7

18 Julian's uncertainty about what exactly the hyper-masculine gay man would be called perhaps reflects current fashion. With the rise of more males in high fashion, the advent of television programs such as *Queer Eye for the Straight Guy*, and the heterosexual adaptation of the homosexual stereotype, or the "metrosexual," it seems that the bear style has fallen out of favor. It seems that now, instead of taking its fashion cues from the heterosexual world, homosexuals are creating styles that are being used by the world of high fashion and by straight people, who dress more in the mainstream. Julian expressed this concern:

> Me and some of my friends were talking and we were mad because we feel that straight people are stealing our stuff, like have you noticed the guys wearing pink shirts? Yeah, I just don't think they have a right to do that. Like my friends and I were joking that we might go up to one of these guys and be like, "You better have put that in the laundry with something red," you know like it was white before.

19 There is a feeling of resentment within the gay community that symbols are being appropriated by the larger population. In *Gays, Lesbians, and Consumer Behavior* (1996), Wardlow explains the cause of this resentment:

> When the symbolism of the community becomes framed as the basis for a target market from an "outside" perspective, the styles become divorced of the meanings they once held . . . and the style takes on new or more vague meanings. Based on the perspectives expressed in our interviews, the issue is not so much that meaning has become diluted or that a symbol has been stolen, as it is that manufacturers are selling the product as "cool" or "hip" without reference to its meaning. (pp. 99–100)

BEYOND GAYDAR   8

The manufacturing world is taking symbols highly popularized in the gay com-   20
munity and making them available for the mainstream, for example, the pink shirts
that Julian cited which are becoming increasingly popular with heterosexual males.

Appealing to both a homosexual and a heterosexual (or perhaps metrosexual)   21
audience is a good strategy for a clothing manufacturer; it can target two highly
valuable markets at once. Based on my research, it's obvious that no other company
does this better than Abercrombie and Fitch, as every interviewee cited the popular
clothing company and its ubiquity among gay males. This leads me to the associated
stereotypes of "flamer" and "Abercrombie bitch." Both of these types would wear
Abercrombie and Fitch clothing, but the flamer would not wear it exclusively. These
two types would perhaps, if we could put all the different gay styles on a spectrum,
fall closer to femininity than butch or bear would.

What happens when place, action, and personal style all fail to disclose a   22
man's sexual orientation, or when one of these categories is missing or fragmen-
tary? Then clues can be found in personal taste, or habitus.

Subtle Clues in Personal Taste

Among the gay men I interviewed, I found that there is a distinct musical   23
taste that gay males recognize is characteristically gay. I focused on musical taste
because my interviewees discussed it the most when I brought up gay preferences
in things other than clothing. During the group interview, I asked them to comment
on gay musical taste. Jeff mentioned that "they all listened to techno" and expressed his exasperation over it. They cited Barbara Streisand as gay music. Steven
stressed that, "You can't be gay and not have Cher."

So how could musical taste signal sexual orientation? It's difficult to imagine   24
such a situation when place, action, and personal style would fail to show sexual

orientation. Personal taste might be a more cultivated part of the gay habitus, one which would be formed later after the other qualifications were met, and therefore would not be present without the other gay qualities. In other words, musical taste cannot be seen as only a signal to other gay men of a man's orientation. For example, a man who contradicted the other gay qualities regarding place, action, and personal style would probably not be viewed by the others as gay, if he simply expressed an affection for alternative music.

Conclusions

25   In interviewing four gay males in Boise, Idaho, over a period of a month, I saw some general patterns emerge. I discovered that the most importance in discovering sexual orientation was placed on the actual location where a man was seen. Behaviors and movements were also highly important, though being in a gay location might outweigh any straight symbolism that a certain man would possess, e.g., Julian's experience of assuming a man in a gay bar was gay, when in reality he was straight. Clothing can also be a signal to other males of sexual orientation, but it is not as telling as place and action. Personal tastes in things like music are less of a signal of sexual orientation and more of a cultivated gay taste.

26   In concluding my research, I also should point out that these things I have observed have merely scratched the surface of gay male identification. I do not even attempt to explain verbal behavior and its relation to nonverbal clues. I did not consider hearsay among the gay community or when gay males have simply identified themselves verbally. I do not assume that these are the only ways that gay males identify each other or that they are the most commonly used. I also do not want to trivialize intuition or conclude that there is absolutely nothing to "gaydar."

BEYOND GAYDAR 10

References

Cheseboro, J. W., & Klenk, K. L. (1981). Gay masculinity and the gay disco. In J. W. Cheseboro (Ed.), *Gayspeak: Gay male and lesbian communication* (pp. 87–103). New York: Pilgrim Press.

Green, R. J., & Ashmore, R. D. (1998). Taking and developing pictures in the head: Assessing the physical stereotypes of eight gender types. *Journal of Applied Social Psychology*, 28(17), 1609–1636.

Lawson, W. (November–December 2005). Gay men really do find it easier to spot other gays. *Psychology Today*, 30.

Martins, Y., Crabtree, C. R., Runyan, T., Vainius, A. A., & Wysocki, C. J. (2005). Preference for human body odors is influenced by gender and sexual orientation. *Psychological Science*, 16, 694–701.

Nicholas, C. L. (2004). Gaydar: Eye-gaze as identity recognition among gay men and lesbians. *Sexuality and Culture*, 8 (Winter), 60–86.

Wardlow, D. L. (1996). *Gays, lesbians, and consumer behavior: Theory, practice, and research issues in marketing*. New York: Harrington Park Press.

(All references to "Julian," Steven, Jeff, or Aaron come from either participant observation or interviews collected between November 3, 2004, and November 29, 2004.)

Evaluating the Essay

1. As its author admits, "Beyond Gaydar" is based on a month of interviews and observations and therefore "only scratches the surface" of how gay men identify other gay men. If you were going to redesign the study in ways to make its findings more authoritative, what would you suggest?

2. Your own feelings about homosexuality may have strongly affected your reading of this research. Part of becoming a sophisticated reader is developing an awareness of how your own biases and predispositions influence your understandings of and reactions to what you read. Reflect on this. Can you identify particular ideas in the essay that you resisted or didn't evaluate critically because of how you feel about homosexuality?

3. What are the ethical issues the student author of this essay needed to address?

Using What You Have Learned

Let's return to the learning objectives I outlined in the beginning of the chapter.

1. **Understand the idea of culture as a "web," and apply techniques of field research to describe it.** What were once relatively invisible in your everyday life—the often fine threads of culture in which we are all caught—are now something you see everywhere. But what do you do with this realization? For one thing, it gives you a powerful rhetorical tool for analyzing your audience. When we begin to see the affiliations people have with each other, we know what matters to them, what they value, and how they might be reached.

2. **Use appropriate features of an ethnographic essay in a project that interprets how a social group sees itself and its world.** In this chapter, you've not only used some of the techniques used to generate qualitative research, but you've also *applied* what you found, working inductively to draw some conclusions from the data. These are techniques that will significantly expand your skills as an academic researcher. They should also prove useful whenever you're asked to present findings to any audience.

3. **Use relevant methods of invention to identify a local culture to study.** When you started *The Curious Writer*, you generated topics mostly from memory (personal essay); then you used interviews (profile), observation (review), and reading (proposal, argument, analytical essay). Now in a single essay you've generated material from all these sources of information. To write with all four sources of information—memory, interviews, observation, and reading—is now something you might do with any essay, no matter what the genre. How far you cast your net for information depends, as you know now, on what question you are asking, not the type of writing you're doing.

4. **Analyze and interpret qualitative information.** In a small but significant way, you've done what all academic researchers do: generate data, identify patterns in it, and try to draw some inferences about what the patterns mean. This is the kind of reasoning that is at the heart of most academic work.

5. **Apply revision strategies that are effective for an ethnographic essay.** When you have a lot of information to work with, problems with organization are often the hardest to solve. In this chapter, you learned some approaches to organization that you can apply in other research projects as well: limiting your focus by refining your question, and exploiting the promise of *narrative* structures. We don't often use "narrative" and "research" in the same breath. But telling a story—about the subjects of your research and/or about your own discoveries along the way—can be a powerful way to organize many research-based projects.

10

Writing a Research Essay

Learning Objectives

In this chapter, you'll learn to

10.1 Apply what you've learned about writing shorter inquiry-based papers to an extended research project.

10.2 Identify different forms of researched writing and the purposes behind them.

10.3 Practice reading, analyzing, and writing with a limited number of sources on a single topic.

10.4 Use invention techniques for discovering a researchable question.

10.5 Refine a research question to narrow the topic focus and lead to a judgment.

10.6 Use audience and purpose to make decisions about the structure of the work and the types of information to use in it.

Writing with Research

In a way, there's no such thing as a research paper. Research is a source of information, not a form of writing, and it's a source you've been using all along in the inquiry projects here. And yet, instructors assign "research papers" all the time. So what are they talking about? Usually, a research paper is a thesis-driven, documented essay that draws on multiple sources of information relevant to a topic. It is modeled in some ways after the scholarly articles that your professors write.

Research is something writers naturally do whenever they have questions they can't answer on their own.

What isn't apparent is that much scholarship reports on the *products* of the inquiry process—what the researcher concluded from exploring a topic—and so it's easy to assume that writing a research paper means abandoning the goal of most academic inquiry: discovery. Yet that is the goal of scholarship—and it's the goal of the research paper, too—so in an effort to lift the curtain on the process of inquiry, I'll introduce you in this chapter to a variation of researched writing: the research *essay*. As you'll see, the research essay begins with the motive that drives any essay—the desire to find out something about a topic. Later, this desire may lead to argument—the intention to prove something—but essaying begins with exploration, the beating heart of inquiry.

Research Essays, Research Papers, and Research Reports

10.1

Apply what you've learned about writing shorter inquiry-based papers to an extended research project.

While any piece of writing can be researched—including things such as short stories, blogs, and personal essays—academic research assignments typically fall into one of three categories (see Figure 10.1):

- Research reports (sometimes called "white papers")
- Research (or term) papers
- Research essays

The least common of these in college is the research report. This is the traditional paper many of us wrote in high school that simply explains—Wikipedia-like—what is known about some topic. The writer of a research report isn't trying to *use* the information to make a point or investigate a question. There is, however, a version of the research report, called the *literature review*, that is sometimes a first step in the research process. A literature review summarizes how others have addressed the question you're exploring.

	Research Report	**Research Paper**	**Research Essay**
Purpose	To explain	To prove	To discover
Thesis	None	Up front	Delayed
Documentation	Yes	Yes	Usually
Organization	Summary-explanation	Thesis-support	Question-answer
Use of "I"	No	Sometimes	Usually
Inquiry	Low	High	Highest

Figure 10.1 Three genres of academic research

A far more common college writing assignment is the research paper, a term that is loosely used to describe an essay that is an extended argument on some topic. It's like the essay you might have tackled in Chapter 7—the argument— except that the research paper leans much more heavily on outside sources and is intended for a more academic audience. Its goal is to prove a thesis using the evidence the writer gathers.

10.2
Identify different forms of researched writing and the purposes behind them.

The research essay is the most obviously inquiry based of the three genres. While the research paper certainly can involve an open-ended investigation, such a paper usually reports conclusions rather than the questions that gave rise to those conclusions. Both the research paper and research essay have a thesis, but in the essay it might appear late in the work, as the writer works through questions and evidence to arrive at an understanding of the topic. While it may be a less common assignment than the argumentative research paper, the research essay is much more likely to promote the habits of mind that encourage genuine inquiry. It invites writers to begin with questions rather than answers, to suspend judgment, and to accept that ambiguity—even confusion—is a natural part of the research process.

> The research essay is likely to promote the habits of mind that encourage genuine inquiry and accepting ambiguity as a natural part of the process.

Motives for Writing a Research Essay

I was in the market for a new guitar, and for several weeks I'd been studying back issues of an acoustic guitar magazine, searching the web for guitar makers, and talking to people who play. My process was driven by particular questions I had: *What are the best tone woods for a classical guitar? What are the various models and how much do they cost? What are the sound qualities to consider when selecting an instrument?* Questions like these—factual or informational questions—are often where we naturally begin when we begin research. Everyday research, things like shopping for a guitar or investigating the museums in a new city before vacationing there, may never go beyond basic information-seeking: What is already known? While inquiry-based investigations often begin with factual questions, they rarely stop there. The motive behind writing a research essay—or term paper, for that matter—is to *do* something with the information you find. It's to make an argument, explore a hunch, or answer a more specific question. The research is always in the service of what a writer might be trying to *say* about a topic.

The Research Essay and Academic Writing

The research paper is a fixture in high school courses, usually lodged in the junior or senior English class and advertised as preparation for The College Research Paper. (Even my nine-year-old daughter wrote research papers.) Research-based writing assignments are probably among the most common in college, across the curriculum. In fact, at my own university, almost three-quarters of the faculty surveyed said they assign an "academic paper that requires research." That's one reason you're writing a research essay in your composition class—to help prepare you to write papers in other courses.

You've already had some practice with some of the genres of researched writing that you might encounter in college: proposals, reviews, analytical essays, and argumentative essays. But the researched academic paper is usually longer, with more sources, and it features some scholarly conventions such as citation of sources and, in some cases, a formal organization. You might imagine the conventional college research paper as organized in three acts:

- **Act I:** Establish the significance of the research question, review what has already been said by others about it, and introduce the thesis proposed to answer the research question.

- **Act II:** "Prove" the thesis by bringing the evidence on stage. Actors might include expert testimony from those who support your main idea, experiences and comments from those affected by the issue you're investigating, and especially your own analysis about how this information supports your thesis. All of this is set against the backdrop of relevant data, statistics, and factual findings.

- **Act III:** The last act unfolds as an inevitable conclusion. There's a summary of key findings, while the original thesis is revisited. Unanswered questions might make a brief appearance, along with thoughts about other directions for the research.

The research *essay* might roughly follow these three acts as well, but it may instead focus on the drama of discovering the answer to your research question. What is your motive for exploring the question? What's the story of the research, and why did your discoveries lead to your conclusions? This is the process of inquiry that is typically invisible when we read conventional scholarship, which often argues from conclusions stated early on.

The research essay is common in nonacademic writing, and particularly in creative nonfiction—the kinds of essays and articles you might read in a magazine. But even if documented research essays aren't usually assigned in college classes, I think they're a powerful *introduction* to academic inquiry, because they place emphasis on the process of coming to know. How did your thinking lead to the research question that drove your investigation into the topic? And how did your thinking evolve as you began to consider the evidence? Though the initial motive behind a research essay is *to find out*, it may end up being an attempt *to prove*—the purpose behind most conventional research papers. Inquiry precedes argument, and it is the best way to discover a thesis that grows from evidence rather than thin air.

Features of the Form

Feature	Conventions of the Research Essay
Inquiry questions	What does the evidence suggest is true? What is the relationship?

Feature	Conventions of the Research Essay
Motives	Academic inquiry always begins with the desire to find out something. Sometimes the researcher has a theory about what might be true—a hypothesis or hunch—that arises from an initial investigation. Sometimes the researcher merely begins with a question: What could be the cause of this? What is this like or unlike? What might explain it? While the initial motive is to *find out*, a subsequent motive may be *to prove*. In academic writing, this is usually the argument a researcher makes to convince others that an explanation, claim, or theory is true.
Subject matter	While academic fields often fence off certain territories of knowledge that they are particularly interested in, any topic is researchable if the researcher has a good question.
Structure	Research begins with questions, not answers. Later in this chapter, we'll explore what makes a good question, which may be the most important thing you can learn about writing with research. Research papers and research essays (see Figure 10.1) have some different features (e.g., the thesis may be delayed in a research essay), but they also have similar features, including: • A review of what has already been said by others about the research question. • A proposed answer to the question based on appropriate evidence. • Citations that signal which ideas and information belong to the writer and which belong to sources. • Information from multiple sources, analyzed by the writer for its relevance to the research question and/or thesis.
Sources of information	Informal research essays—those intended for an audience of nonexperts—may rely on all four sources of information: personal experience, observation, interview, and reading. In more formal forms, the writer's personal experiences may not be used at all. What's key is to understand what is meant by "appropriate" evidence. This is the information that is most likely to be viewed by a particular audience as the most reliable, relevant, and convincing information. The more knowledgeable your audience is about your topic, the more restrictive the rules of evidence.
Language	We often assume that all researched writing should sound "objective": It should scrupulously avoid the first person, use formal diction, and employ the passive voice. As you'll see in the next section, however, the language of researched writing, like the language of any other kind of writing, is determined by the answer to a rhetorical question: For whom am I writing and why?

Prose+

Research is gray: blocks of text with tables of data and long lists of sources. At least that's the way we usually see it. But digital media now allow us to take even the most somber data—say, information on the relationship between social media use and narcissism. Infographics like the one excerpted here are a powerful way to turn research into a visual story. You can learn more about how to take a research essay and build an infographic from it in Chapter 13, "Re-Genre."

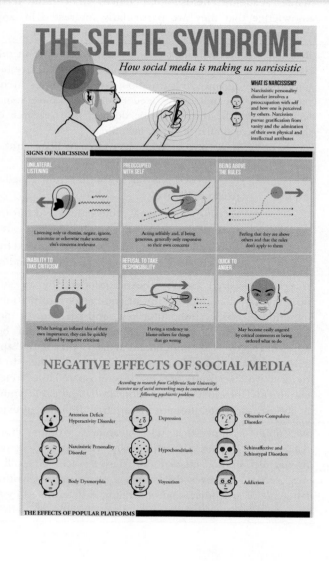

READINGS: WHY TATTOOS?

A lot of things have changed since I wrote my first research papers as an undergraduate. But one thing hasn't and never will: You still have to *do* something with the information you collect. You have to select what's relevant, understand what you've read, and use it in your writing. Experts who study student writing recently reported that when they analyzed research papers from composition classes, they found that the students seemed to struggle a lot with integrating sources. For one thing, students rarely—if ever—summarized a source. They paraphrased, copied, or "patchwrote," mixing in their own words with the words of a source in a way that sometimes crossed the line into (usually unintentional) plagiarism.

10.3

Practice reading, analyzing, and writing with a limited number of sources on a single topic.

The real problem, the experts argued, is that students have too little practice analyzing, interpreting, and evaluating the information they find. This is the essential intellectual work of researched writing. Years ago, the "controlled research paper" was all the rage. Students didn't do their own research on a topic; rather, they were given the research on a single topic—usually collected in a book—and then asked to write a paper on it. We'll try that in a much more limited way, as an exercise (a much better approach, I think) to get a conversation going about how to use sources in your writing. The readings and excerpts that follow all focus on one inquiry question that involves analyzing, interpreting, and evaluating. In Exercise 10.1, I'll encourage you, as always, to write about what you read and also to *combine* the readings into a flash (or very short) research essay.

Exercise 10.1

Flash Research on Tattoos

Attitudes towards tattoos seem generational (see infographic on page 348). My otherwise reasonable mother, now 90, told my daughter Julia that she wouldn't speak to Julia if she got a tattoo. When Julia did—a small one on her wrist—my mom gave Julia the silent treatment for three weeks. But there are other, more surprising differences between views on tattooing—some are regional, some are related to gender, some to class. In this exercise, we'll consider this initial inquiry question: *Why do people get tattoos?* Following this exercise are excerpts from four different sources on the question, and you'll draft a "flash" research essay that draws on two or more of the sources to express your view on the question.

STEP ONE: First Thoughts

To start with, what are your first thoughts about the inquiry question? What are your feelings about the tattoo trend? If you have tattoos, what might be some of the reasons you decided to get them? If you don't have tattoos, why not? Would you consider getting them? Fastwrite in your journal about this for at least four minutes.

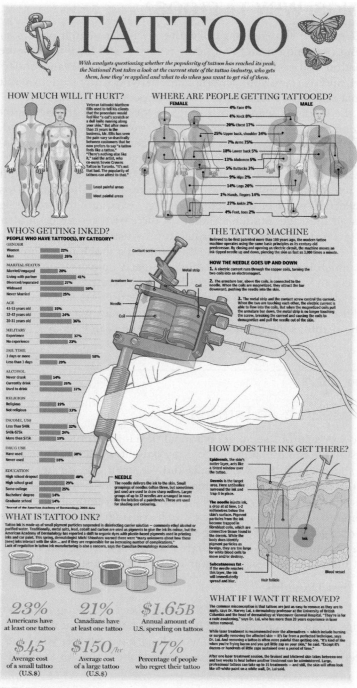

TATTOO

With analysts questioning whether the popularity of tattoos has reached its peak, the National Post takes a look at the current state of the tattoo industry, who gets them, how they're applied and what to do when you want to get rid of them.

HOW MUCH WILL IT HURT?

Veteran tattooist Matthew Ellis used to tell his clients that the procedure would feel like "a cat's scratch or a dull knife running along your skin." But after more than 15 years in the business, Mr. Ellis has seen the pain vary so drastically between customers that he now prefers to say "a tattoo feels like a tattoo." "There's nothing else like it," said the artist, who co-owns Seven Crowns Tattoo in Toronto. "It's not that bad. The popularity of tattoos can attest to that."

Least painful areas
Most painful areas

WHERE ARE PEOPLE GETTING TATTOOED?

FEMALE / MALE

4% Face 0%
4% Neck 8%
29% Chest 17%
25% Upper back, shoulder 34%
7% Arms 75%
18% Lower back 5%
13% Abdomen 5%
5% Buttocks 3%
9% Hips 2%
14% Legs 20%
1% Hands, fingers 14%
27% Ankle 2%
4% Feet, toes 2%

WHO'S GETTING INKED?

PEOPLE WHO HAVE TATTOO(S), BY CATEGORY*

GENDER
Women — 22%
Men — 26%

MARITAL STATUS
Married/engaged — 20%
Living with partner — 41%
Divorced/separated — 27%
Widowed — 50%
Never Married — 25%

AGE
43-53 years old — 15%
32-42 years old — 24%
20-31 years old — 36%

MILITARY
Experience — 37%
No experience — 23%

JAIL TIME
3 days or more — 58%
Less than 3 days — 20%

ALCOHOL
Never drank — 14%
Currently drink — 26%
Used to drink — 37%

RELIGION
Religious — 19%
Not religious — 13%

INCOME‡
Less than $40k — 32%
$40k-$75k — 24%
More than $75k — 19%

DRUG USE
Have used — 38%
Never used — 18%

EDUCATION
High school dropout — 40%
High school grad — 29%
Some college — 25%
Bachelors' degree — 14%
Graduate school — 14%

Journal of the American Academy of Dermatology, 2006 data

THE TATTOO MACHINE

Believed to be first patented more than 100 years ago, the modern tattoo machine operates using the same basic principles as its century-old predecessor. By closing and opening an electric circuit, the machine moves an ink-tipped needle up and down, piercing the skin as fast as 3,000 times a minute.

HOW THE NEEDLE GOES UP AND DOWN

1. A electric current runs through the copper coils, turning the two coils into an electromagnet.

2. The armature bar, above the coils, is connected to the needle. When the coils are magnetized, they attract the bar downward, pushing the needle into the skin.

3. The metal strip and the contact screw control the current. When the two are touching each other, the electric current is able to flow into the coils. But when the magnetized coils pull the armature bar down, the metal strip is no longer touching the screw, breaking the current and causing the coils to deomagnetize and pull the needle out of the skin.

Contact screw
Metal strip
Armature bar
Coil
Needle
Coil

NEEDLE
The needle delivers the ink to the skin. Small groupings of needles (often three, but sometimes just one) are used to draw sharp outlines. Larger groups of up to 32 needles are arranged in rows like the bristles of a paintbrush. These are used for shading and colouring.

HOW DOES THE INK GET THERE?

Epidermis, the skin's outer layer, acts like a tinted window over the tattoo.

Dermis is the target area. Here antibodies surround the ink and trap it in place.

The needle injects ink, a drop at a time, 1-2 millimetres below the skin's surface. Pigment particles from the ink become trapped in fibroblast cells, which are connective tissue found in the dermis. While the body does identify pigment particles as foreign, they are too large for white blood cells to move and/or destroy.

Subcutaneous fat - If the needle reaches this layer, the ink will immediately spread and blur.

Ink
Hair follicle
Blood vessel

WHAT IS TATTOO INK?

Tattoo ink is made up of small pigment particles suspended in disinfecting carrier solution – commonly ethyl alcohol or purified water. Traditionally, metal salts, lead and carbon are used as pigments to give the ink its colour, but the American Academy of Dermatology has reported a shift to organic dyes with plastic-based pigments used in printing inks and car paint. This spring, dermatologist Michi Shinohara warned there were "many unknowns about how these [new] inks interact with the skin ... and if they are responsible for an increasing number of complications." Lack of regulation in tattoo ink manufacturing is also a concern, says the Canadian Dermatology Association.

WHAT IF I WANT IT REMOVED?

The common misconception is that tattoos are just as easy to remove as they are to apply, says Dr. Harvey Lui, a dermatology professor at the University of British Columbia and the head of dermatology at Vancouver General Hospital. "They're in for a rude awakening," says Dr. Lui, who has more than 20 years experience in laser tattoo removal.

While laser treatment is recommended over the alternatives – which include burning or surgically removing the affected skin – it's far from a perfected technique, says Dr. Lui. And removing a tattoo is often more painful than getting one. "It's kind of like when you're frying bacon and you get little zap on your skin," he said. "Except it's dozens or hundreds of little zaps sustained over a period of time."

After one laser treatment session, the bruised and blistered skin takes between one and two weeks to heal before another treatment can be administered. Large, professional tattoos can take up to 15 treatments – and still, the skin will often look like off-white paint on a white wall, Dr. Lui said.

23%
Americans have at least one tattoo

21%
Canadians have at least one tattoo

$1.65B
Annual amount of U.S. spending on tattoos

$45
Average cost of a small tattoo (U.S.$)

$150/hr
Average cost of a large tattoo (U.S.$)

17%
Percentage of people who regret their tattoo

SOURCES: JOURNAL OF THE AMERICAN ACADEMY OF DERMATOLOGY, CANADIAN DERMATOLOGY ASSOCIATION, DR. HARVEY LUI, BASIC FUNDAMENTALS OF MODERN TATTOO, DISCOVERY, MATTHEW ELLIS, SEVEN CROWNS TATTOO, WASHINGTON POST, TATTOO-EDU.COM

MIKE FAILLE, JAKE EDMISTON, ALEX SNOW / NATIONAL POST

STEP TWO: **Conversation with Sources**

After you're done fastwriting, read all four of the selections that follow. With one exception (the book excerpt), these are all excerpts from longer academic articles that are relevant to the inquiry question. Keeping that question in mind—Why do people get tattoos?—*respond in writing in your notebook to each reading immediately after you read it.* Fastwrite for as long as you can, imagining that you are conversing informally with the author(s) of the selection. These prompts might keep you writing:

- What are my first thoughts in response to what I just read? Second thoughts?
- What does this selection seem to be saying? What do I think of that?
- Suppose I assume that what this selection is saying is true. What are the implications? Why might the selection's claims be significant? How does it change the way I think?
- What does this selection help me to understand that I didn't fully understand before?
- How is this connected to what I've already read?
- What does this understanding add to how I'm considering why people get tattoos?

▶ Excerpt 1: Journal Article

In his academic study of the cultural significance of tattoos, Derek Roberts observes that the tattoo might be a way to maintain one's "true self" in an ever-changing world. He also suggests that tattoos, once taboo, have been culturally mainstreamed by the media.

Secret Ink: Tattoo's Place in Contemporary American Culture
Derek J. Roberts

Given this history of negative attitudes, it is somewhat surprising that the number of people with tattoos has been on the rise, and it is the middle class that is at the heart of the "mainstreaming of tattoo" (Kosut 1045). There are numerous explanations for the recent embracing of tattoos among this group. For some, tattoos are merely a fashion accessory (Sweetman 51; Turner 47). Others have argued that tattoos can be viewed as tools of self-completion and permanent reminders of one's true identity in an ever changing world (Carroll and Anderson 627; Langman 242–43; Rosenblatt 308). According to Shannon Bell (57), to get a tattoo is "to live in truth for eternity." In an era when one's professional or marital identity might readily change with the ebbs and flows of life, the

1

(*continued*)

(continued)

ability of tattoos to serve as an unchangeable reminder of the true self makes them highly desirable.

2   Still other scholars have focused upon the media, suggesting they have played the pivotal role in the spread of tattoos. According to Mary Kosut, one explanation for the recent rise in the acceptability of tattoos is that current media portrayals often separate the art of tattoo from its working class roots: "popular print discourses have contributed to the erasure of early images and meanings of tattoo by recreating tattoo as a middle-class cultural practice with inherent aesthetic value" (1043). DeMello echoed this sentiment when she argued that the media has made tattoos more acceptable by first focusing their articles around a select group of middle-class individuals, most of whom have relatively small, inoffensive tattoos; by second, denying all of those who do not fit this category the right to be represented, except as the absent unit of comparison; and third, by centering the discussion around ideas which are very popular outside of the tattoo community. (42)

3   According to DeMello, the media often purposefully ignore those who were tattooed for what are deemed the old reasons, such as those who were drunk or spontaneous. Instead, she has argued that the media now focus on things such as the amount of preparation or financial resources needed for a good tattoo. By portraying tattoos as a serious investment as opposed to an intoxicated spur of the moment waste of money, the media have made it so that tattoos "can be appreciated and understood even by the non-tattoo wearing, middle-class public" (42).

▶ Excerpt 2: Journal Article

Why do people get tattoos removed? The authors of this excerpt suggest that the reasons may be different for women and men. The following excerpt reports on a 2006 study that repeated a study done ten years earlier.

Motivation for Contemporary Tattoo Removal

Myrna L. Armstrong, Alden E. Roberts, Jerome R. Koch, Jana C. Saunders, Donna C. Owen, and R. Rox Anderson

1   Historically, getting a tattoo has been a male-dominant activity, but now women have more than half of the tattoos. For women, their tattoo procurement may be a way to break out of the gender norms and take some social risk by visually displaying their assertive identity. Yet, there still may be many members of society who consider tattoos on women to be a "transgression of gender boundaries."

In the 2006 study, a shift in gender presentation for tattoo removal was observed; in the 1996 study, more men than women requested tattoo removal, but in the 2006 study, more women (including Hispanics) did. While men also reported some of these same tattoo problems leading to removal, there seemed to be more societal fallout for women with tattoos, as the tattoos began to cause embarrassment, negative comments, and clothes problems and no longer satisfied the need for uniqueness. These negative internal and external outcomes contributed to the possession risks and to the subsequent identity shift for tattoo removal.

Negative responses were also documented among career-oriented women with tattoos. Strong tattoo support from their significant others and friends was counterbalanced by negative remarks about the tattoos from their fathers, physicians, and the public. It is evident, then, that negative societal connotations still exist for women with tattoos. Therefore, for women to avoid the possession risks of their tattoos, as in the past, they may still need to deliberately think about controlling the body placement of their tattoos to reduce cognitive dissonance and to increase their psychological comfort.

In summary, tattooing is ancient, but popularity, social acceptance, tattoo inks, and laser technology are rapidly changing. How these changes will affect tattooing and tattoo removal is unknown. In the 2006 study, there was a prevalence of women seeking tattoo removal; their motivations for obtaining tattoos were often a desire for uniqueness, whereas self-reported embarrassment, negative comments, and clothes problems were motivations for tattoo removal, diminishing their feelings of uniqueness associated with the tattoo.

▶ Excerpt 3: Book

The following journal excerpt looks at why women get tattoos. Read with the other excerpts in this chapter, Kang and Jones's scholarship adds to an emerging picture of gender and tattooing.

Why Do People Get Tattoos?
Miliann Kang and Katherine Jones

Tattooing offers many women control over their own bodies. Some have used the tattoo to challenge the limited roles of wife and mother and to explore other ways to define themselves. Around the turn of the last century, aristocratic women in England, France, and the United States, including Winston Churchill's mother and members of the Vanderbilt family, sported tattoos. Margo DeMello asserts that

(continued)

(continued)

many Victorian women were drawn to tattoos as a way of demonstrating that they were "less likely to accept the idea of the quiet, pale, and bounded female body." In addition, she says, "Tattoos have long been a sign of that resistance within the working class."

2   Perceptions of tattooed women as sexually promiscuous and lower class have a long history. Albert Parry describes a rape case in late-1920s Boston in which the prosecutor, upon realizing that the young woman he was defending had a tattoo, requested that the case be dropped. The judge and jury released the two men who raped her on the grounds that they had been misled by the butterfly on her leg. As with many women in rape cases, the defendant herself was put on trial, and her tattoo was seen as evidence of her guilt, overriding whatever meaning she herself hoped to assert through it.

3   While men and women both get tattoos, men are more likely to use tattoos to reinforce traditional notions of masculinity, whereas women often both defy and reproduce conventional standards of femininity. In interviews with Atkinson, Caroline states, "Women nowadays believe that whatever men can do women can do better, and that includes tattooing." Zeta explains that tattoos provide a concrete way of challenging traditional gender norms: "I could talk and talk and talk about wearing grungy clothes and not dyeing my hair to look like a Barbie doll, and no one would care since all of that is superficial." While Zeta believes the permanence of a tattoo demonstrates a deep and tangible commitment to alternative gender definitions, other women use tattoos to conform to mainstream standards of femininity.

4   As tattoos become more common, they are less able to express subversive definitions of women and their bodies. Atkinson argues that many of the young women he interviewed used their tattoos to enforce rather than challenge traditional femininity. Their tattoos were placed in either easily hidden or sexualized areas of the body such as the shoulder, hip, or lower back. The images were also traditionally feminine, such as animals, flowers, and hearts. Stephanie Farinelli, a regular participant in tattoo contests, describes to Mifflin how mainstream expectations for feminine beauty shape these competitions: "I felt that I was not feminine looking enough and scantily clad enough to win. I got a wardrobe change, went on a diet, and won first place the following year." DeMello argues that while feminist scholars have rushed to embrace tattooing's liberatory potential for women, "people aren't interested in the women who get men's names on them, or who get what their men want on them because it's sexy and feminine rather than 'empowering.'"

▶ Excerpt 4: Journal Article

Scholars love to research students (a captive audience?), and naturally there are studies on the tattooing attitudes and behaviors of college undergraduates. Here's an excerpt from one of the more interesting of these projects.

Tattoos and Piercings: Attitudes, Behaviors, and Interpretations of College Students

Jenn Horne, David Knox, Jane Zusman, and Marty E. Zusman

Over a quarter (27.5%) of the respondents reported that they had a tattoo—25.8% of men and 28.3% of women (the gender difference was not significant). Most (63.4% = men; 57.9% = women) reported having just one tattoo but once men began getting tattooed, they were more likely to get additional tattoos as 42% had two or more compared to only 36.6% of women who had two or more. Not all tattoos were visible to others. When asked if any of the tattoos that they had on their body were "usually visible?" 54% of the men and 45% of the women answered "yes." While not statistically significant, the finding supports the argument that men wore their tattoos for reasons of group identity (e.g. they wanted others to know they were a Marine or a member of Hell's Angels). Hence, women were more likely to have a tattoo, to have fewer, and to hide them.   1

When asked whether they got a tattoo "for my own pleasure" or to "impress others" over 90 percent of the respondents reported the former (90.3% [=] men; 94.6% = women). But the respondents provided numerous motivations for their getting a tattoo. Men and women agreed that high on their list of reasons were "decorative statement[,]" "self-identity," and "symbol of their relationship."   2

As noted in Table 1, significant differences in regard to getting a tattoo occurred where women sought a tattoo as a decorative statement for enhancing personal beauty (64.3% of women compared to 32.4% of men, $p < .002$) and where men sought a tattoo as part of one's group identity (21.6% of men compared to 4.3% of women, $p < .006$). Other significant gender differences are discussed below: 3

1. Women, compared to men, were more likely to report that they "sometimes["] found "openly visible tattoos (e.g. arms) on the opposite sex attractive." Almost three-fourths (71.1%) of the undergraduate women reported that they "sometimes" viewed openly visible tattoos as attractive when on a man. Women may view men with tattoos as the "bad boy" or view such tattoos as macho reflecting masculine role behavior with either scenario increasing his attractiveness to her. In addition, historically, male tattoos have been more visible (e.g. pirates, military insignias, Hell's Ang[el]s, Harley Davidson tattoos) and presumably more normative.

In contrast, 58.8% of the undergraduate men viewed such visible tattoos as attractive when on a woman. Indeed, over 40 percent of the undergraduate men reported that they "seldom/never" viewed tattoos on a woman as attractive ($p < .007$).   4

(continued)

(*continued*)

Men		
Reason for Tattoo	Rank	% Selected
Decorative Statement (beauty …) **	1	32.4
Self Identity (birth sign, etc)	2	29.7
Symbol of an interpersonal rel.	3	27.0
Act of beauty (I feel more….)	5	10.8
Key interest … (scuba …)	5	10.8
Sign of an event (marriage …)	5	10.8
Sexual enhancement (better lover)	6	8.1
A group identity (marines etc) **	4	21.6

Women			
Reason for Tattoo	Rank	% Selected	
Decorative Statement (beauty …) **	1	64.3	p < 002
Self Identity (birth sign, etc)	2	35.7	NS
Symbol of an interpersonal rel.	3	25.7	NS
Act of beauty (I feel more….)	3	25.7	NS
Key interest … (scuba …)	4	14.3	NS
Sign of an event (marriage …)	5	10.0	NS
Sexual enhancement (better lover)	6	5.7	NS
A group identity (marines etc) **	7	4.3	p < .006

Table 1 Rank Order Difference Between Men and Women for Why They Have a Tattoo (1 = Most Important Selected)

Historically tattoos on women have been less normative. They are, as Goffman called them, a stigma. Tattoos make the wearer less normal and more of a deviant. While the occasional biker woman had tattoos, until recently, they were not part of a woman's physical persona. Nevertheless, it is important to point out that most (almost 60 percent [of]) men in our sample viewed women with tattoos as attractive.

Exercise 10.1

(Continued from p. 347)

STEP THREE: **Flash Research**

Now *do* something with all that journal writing that you generated in response to the excerpts in this section. Write a 250-word argument that somehow addresses the inquiry question *Why do people get tattoos?* Don't hesitate to refine this question. This flash research essay should:

- Make a claim (have a thesis)
- Incorporate *at least* two of the excerpts through summary, paraphrase, and/or quotation (see Chapter 12 for more on how to use each)
- For now, use a simplified citation. For example, put a parenthetical citation after borrowed material with the last name(s) of the excerpt's author(s) and the paragraph number of the relevant passage, such as (Kang, para. 3).

STEP FOUR: **Synthesizing Sources**

Share the drafts of your flash research essays in class or online. Talk about the range of responses people in class had to the excerpts, and which seemed most interesting or persuasive. The flash research step challenged you to make some moves that you'll need to make when you write a longer research essay, and one of the most important of these moves is incorporating sources into your own writing. Analyze how you did this.

1. Take two highlighters—each a different color—and use one to highlight every line, passage, or paragraph in your draft where you used an idea, phrase, or quotation from one of the excerpts. Use the other color to highlight lines and passages that represent your own thinking—analysis, commentary, evaluation, personal observation, and so on.

2. What do you notice about the patterns of color? Typically, you want your own thinking to swarm around the sources you bring into your writing. Remember, you're the narrator and guide of your essays, and sources are in service to your explorations and arguments.

3. We join the work of others with our own in several ways.

    a. **Support:** evidence for a claim (e.g., illustration, example, idea, etc.)

    b. **Explanation:** clarification or summary of a concept or idea

    c. **Complication:** detours into other ways of seeing things; ideas that make things more complicated and therefore more interesting

    d. **Dramatization:** establishing what's at stake (pathos)

Go through your flash research draft and place an "S," "E," "C," or "D" next to each instance of source use to signal your purpose in using it. What do you notice about the frequency of each letter (and motive)?

THE WRITING PROCESS

Inquiry Project **Writing a Research Essay**

Inquiry questions: What does the evidence suggest is true? What is the relationship?

Write a research essay on a topic of your choice. Choose a subject because you want to find out something about it; avoid things you *already* have a strong opinion about. This essay should

- Be based on a "researchable" inquiry question.
- Have a S.O.F.T. or a central thesis that represents your best answer to your research question. This thesis may be delayed rather than parked in the introduction.
- Use appropriate and relevant sources based on your own experiences, observations, interviews, and reading, or all four sources of information.
- Be cited using the conventions recommended by your instructor.
- Be written for an audience of peers rather than experts on the topic.

Prose+

- Make the data beautiful by creating an infographic. (See page 490 in Chapter 13, "Re-Genre," for more on how to design an infographic.)
- If your research topic has a local angle—it affects people in your community or there are local experts—then consider creating a radio documentary styled after those on NPR's *This American Life*. (See page 499 in Chapter 13 for how to create a podcast.)
- Slide software such as PowerPoint and Keynote can supplement your research essay by reimagining your findings for a public presentation. (See page 488 in Chapter 13 for more on how to create effective presentations.)

What Are You Going to Write About?

10.4

Use invention techniques for discovering a researchable question.

This choice may be wide open, or your instructor might ask you to focus on a broad theme, perhaps one on which your class is focused. Either way, the same principle applies:

There are no boring topics, only poor questions.

There is no topic—dust mites, fruit cake, Elvis, nuclear fusion, or basketballs—that won't yield to the right question. (We'll take up the characteristics of a good question later.) But there's another condition upon which the success of your research project depends: your curiosity. Whatever the question that eventually becomes a focus for inquiry, it must be one that you find interesting. Typically, this means that you choose a topic because it holds the promise of discovery.

Ask yourself this: *What have I seen, read, experienced, or heard about that raises interesting questions that research might help answer?*

Approaching your research project this way is exactly the impulse that might have motivated you to write a personal essay on growing up with an autistic sibling or a persuasive essay on the downside of recruiting NCAA athletes at your school. It's the same motive that inspires all genuine inquiry: *How do I feel about this? What do I think about this? What do I want to know?*

> While inquiry-based investigations often begin with factual questions, they rarely stop there.

Opening Up

Use your notebook to generate some material. As in previous inquiry projects, at this stage don't prejudge anything you come up with. Let yourself play around with possibilities.

Listing Prompts. Lists can be rich sources of triggering topics. Let them grow freely, and when you're ready, use a list item as the focus of another list or an episode of fastwriting. The following prompts should get you started.

1. Inventory your interests by creating five separate lists on a page of your notebook. Choose among the following words as a general category for each of the five lists you will create: Places, Trends, Objects, Technologies, People, Controversies, History, Jobs, Habits, Hobbies. In each of the five categories you choose, brainstorm a list of words or phrases that come to mind when you think about *what you know and what you might want to know.* For example, under Places, I would put "pigeons in Florence," because I want to know more about their impact on Renaissance buildings. Under Hobbies, I would put "fly fishing," because that's something I know about. Spend about fifteen minutes building these lists.

2. Look over your lists and ask yourself, *Are there research topics implied by a few of the items on these lists?* In other words, what item raises questions that more research might answer? What is it about this item that I wonder about?

3. Finally, choose a promising item from one of the lists and generate questions about it that you'd love to have answered. Perhaps you already know something about the topic but would like to learn more. Don't worry yet about whether all the questions are good.

Fastwriting Prompts. Remember, fastwriting is a great way to stimulate creative thinking. Turn off your critical side and let yourself write "badly."

1. Choose an item from your lists and use it as a prompt for a seven-minute fastwrite. Begin by telling yourself the story of when, where, and why you first got interested in the subject. When the writing stalls, write the following phrase, and follow it for as long as you can: *Among the things I most want to learn about this are....*

2. Interesting research questions can emerge from the most ordinary experiences. Take eating, for instance, or friendship, running, dreaming, depression, texting, infatuation, insomnia, listening to music, body language, butterflies, intelligence, addiction, etc. The key is to figure out what you might want to know about an ordinary experience that research might help answer. Take one of the subjects above—or another that you think of—and begin a fastwrite with this phrase: *The thing that I've always found interesting about* _____ *is* _____. *For example,* _____ . . . . Follow this writing until it stalls, and then pick another ordinary experience and fastwrite again.

Visual Prompts. Sometimes the best way to generate material is to see what we think represented in something other than sentences. Boxes, lines, webs, clusters, arrows, charts, and even sketches can help us to see more of the landscape of a subject, especially connections among fragments of information that aren't as apparent in prose.

Do an image search using Google on some person, place, thing, or event that interests you. Might one of the pictures you find be the focus of an investigation? Who was that guy? What *was* going on when this happened? Why did it happen?

Research Prompts. Should you do some research before you begin your research? Absolutely. By exploring what others have said or done or wondered about, you might discover an interest in something you wouldn't have otherwise considered.

1. Surf the Net, perhaps beginning with a subject directory like "Voice of the Shuttle" (http://vos.ucsb.edu). Start by clicking on a subject area that

One Student's Response

Julian's Journal

TOPIC: JAZZ

My dad was into jazz. Would listen to it all night long after working all day long. He listened to all kinds of jazz—Bird, Miles Davis, Billy Holiday, Monk. It took me years to really appreciate the music but now it's my favorite kind. **Among the things I most want to learn about jazz** is its connection to African music and slave songs. It makes me wonder whether the uniqueness of jazz, its spontaneity especially, has something to do with the hymns and spirituals of the slaves. **Among the other things I want to learn** is whether jazz was accepted in the early days. I seem to remember my dad saying that the. . . .

interests you. Keep following the links as you branch more deeply into the subcategories and subdisciplines of that area of knowledge. Look for specific subject areas that intrigue you. For example, you might have begun in the broad subject area of history, clicked the link for medieval history (maybe you've always wondered what was dark about the Dark Ages), and ended up reading some fascinating articles on the home life of medieval women. Does this raise some questions you'd like to explore?

2. Study the local newspaper, which may be available online. Devote some time to reading the paper to discover a local controversy that intrigues you. Say there was an article on the impact of Title IX on the university's athletic department, and you wonder, *Is the elimination of the men's wrestling team really the result of shifts in funding to women's sports?* Or perhaps there's a letter to the editor about the condition of housing for migrant workers in the valley. *Are things really that bad?*

3. Use Google Scholar. Type in a topic or a phrase that reflects an interest of yours. For example, I've been interested in peoples' beliefs in alien abduction. What might explain the persistence of these beliefs? Google Scholar will often surprise you and serve up results on even less-academic-seeming topics. For example, there's some fascinating stuff on alien abduction, as you'll see in the next section.

Narrowing Down

The great thing about simply generating material is that you can turn off your critical mind and simply muck about in all sorts of possible topics for your essay. But, as always, the process depends on taking a more analytical look at whether you've discovered anything genuinely useful. Remember your goal at this stage: You want to identify a possible topic—and maybe, if you're lucky, a research question—that will move your investigation forward in the next few days. All writing projects need to be focused, and this is especially important with a project such as the research essay, in which you're dealing with a lot of information. Focusing your project on an initial question that is narrow enough has enormous practical value:

10.5
Refine a research question to narrow the topic focus and lead to a judgment.

It helps you control the floodgates. The more specific your question, the easier it is to manage the information you find and to decide what information you can ignore. Having a focused question is a huge advantage when you're dealing with a flood of information. For example, using the topic I mentioned earlier—belief in alien abduction—there's a big difference between this question

Why do people believe in alien abduction?

and this question

What's the relationship between belief in alien abduction and the creation of "false memories"?

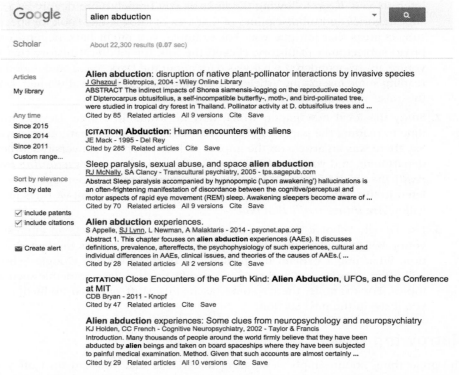

In case you doubted that there are scholarly articles on nearly any subject, you can see here that Google Scholar generated over 20,000 results from the keyword search "alien abduction."

Source: Google, Inc.

On the other hand, if you're exploring a topic about which you know little, it will be hard to come up with a focused research question until you learn more about the topic. (I got my question about the relationship between belief in alien abduction and false memory from a quick Google Scholar search.) Start by developing a "working knowledge" of your tentative topic, exploring questions of fact and definition first: *What is known about this? What is it?* When you know something about your topic, it's infinitely easier to find a focus.

What's Promising Material and What Isn't?   The most promising subject is one you're curious about. But that's not enough. Consider the following:

- **Has something already been said about it?** Is there information on your topic and is it accessible?

- **Does it raise more questions?** It shouldn't have a simple answer.

- **Does it matter to someone other than you?** Other people should have a stake in the question you're exploring.

- **Do you already know what you think?** Why inquire into a topic you've already got figured out?

- **Is it appropriate for the assignment?** Will you be able to find enough images for an infographic, enough scholarly sources for an academic paper, or enough people to interview for an audio documentary?

Questions about Audience and Purpose. When you imagine an audience for your research project, ask yourself this:

Am I writing up? Am I writing down? Am I writing across?

When you "write up," you're imagining readers who are experts on your topic, people who already know *more* than you do. When you "write down," you're imagining an audience that knows *less* than you, at least after you've done some research. Scholarly research, the kind you find in academic journals and books, is "written across," to fellow experts. Unless you're an expert writing to others with considerable knowledge about your topic, then the scholarly article isn't a model you should try to emulate in your research essay. On the other hand, there might be situations in which you're writing up for a professor, presenting research in his or her field, perhaps in a class on the subject. But for this assignment, you're likely writing down— to peers—trying to make your discoveries relevant and interesting to nonexperts.

Which audience it is makes a huge difference (as always) in how you write your essay, including:

1. The tone and formality of the language.
2. How much background on the topic you need to provide.
3. What kinds of evidence you can use.
4. The need to present an "original" finding.
5. The methods you use to come up with a finding.

A research essay is written "down" for an audience of nonexperts. A conventional research paper may be written "up" or "across." Some of the implications of these differing rhetorical situations are summarized in Figure 10.2.

10.6

Use audience and purpose to make decisions about the structure of the work and the types of information to use in it.

Trying Out

You've got a tentative topic. The next step is to develop a "working knowledge" of the topic so you can come up with a focused research question. What's a working knowledge? It's a basic factual understanding: What is known about _____? OR How is _____ defined? This understanding is hardly comprehensive, but it's enough to be able to tell someone about your topic for five minutes without stopping. Steps for developing working knowledge—and, later, focused knowledge— are covered on pages 390 through 397 in Chapter 11.

Refining the Question. Once you've got at least a working knowledge of your topic, try developing a more-focused research question. You might try fitting

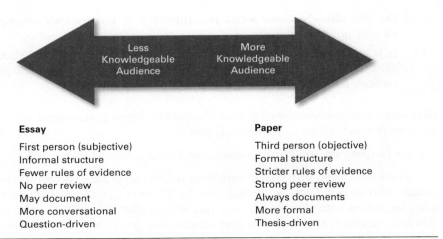

Figure 10.2 The importance of audience

your topic into one of the two inquiry questions that are often explored in research essays:

1. What does the evidence suggest that might explain _____?
2. What might be the relationship between _____ and _____? Does _____ cause _____? Is _____ similar (or dissimilar) to _____?

Focus Like a Journalist. Another way to find a narrower focus for your project is to try anchoring your subject to a particular story, person, place, event, or time period. This is something journalists do all the time. Sometimes they combine particular stories, in particular places, with particular people, at particular times, to focus on a large, complex problem. For example, if journalists want to cover the issue of climate change, they might tell the story of what's happening on one small island in the Pacific. If they want to explore a problem such as the costs of college tuition, they tell the story of a single student at Lane Community College in Oregon. If they want to show the dangers of coal mining, they write about a day in a Kentucky mine. Think about which of these—a **story**, a **person**, a **place**, or a **time period**—might focus your larger topic.

Writing a Proposal. Rather than writing a sketch, draft a proposal on your research topic, with the following elements:

1. **What's known?** What controversies, questions, or schools of thought are there on your topic? Who is involved, and what do they say? What do you find most interesting and significant?
2. **What's at stake?** Provide some background on why your research question is relevant to others. You may be curious about the topic, but why should the rest of us care about it? How does it affect us? What might we learn that we will find useful or interesting?

3. **What's the question, and what's your hunch?** What's your opening question for the inquiry project? What do you want to know? Based on what you know now, what are your assumptions about answers to the question you pose? What do you think you'll find and why?

4. **Bibliography.** Provide a list of references you've consulted so far. You can find information about how to format these citations in Chapter 12. Your instructor may ask you to annotate this bibliography as well, providing short summaries of what each source says that's relevant to your question.

▶ Sample Research Proposal

Research Essay Proposal: What is the relationship between Facebook use and depression?

1. What's known?

Most observers believe that the number of users of Facebook is nearly 1 billion worldwide, with particularly heavy use by people who are between the ages of 18 and 29 (Dugan et al.). Coincidentally, the National Institute of Mental Health notes that this is also the age group that is particularly vulnerable to depression ("Major Depressive Disorder"). Depression rates among college students, a group who are heavy Facebook users, has also increased significantly (Moreno et. al 447). Though there is some dispute about the term "Facebook depression," a recent "clinical report" claims that teenagers who turn to social networks to overcome feelings of social isolation may find "triggers" for their depression online (O'Keefe, Clarke-Pearson 802). I know from my own experience, for example, that people compare themselves to others on Facebook, often feeling badly about themselves when friends post announcements about achievements (Pappas). I've also observed that certain people are more likely to share Facebook posts about their personal struggles, challenging the boundaries between what's personal and what's private. Depending on the responses that depressed posters get from others, they may find comfort or more distress. A number of researchers are also looking at whether Facebook can be used to predict clinical depression. One study said that about 27% of the Facebook users profiled showed symptoms of depression (Moreno 447).

2. What's at stake?

I think this is an issue that obviously affects a lot of people, particularly people from teen to college age. If the research I've read so far is right, then the number of depressed college-age students is increasing, and most of these have a presence on Facebook. Does social networking help or hurt? Facebook can be a way to detect symptoms, a way to make them worse, or a way to destigmatize the problem. But which is it? The answer could make a significant difference in whether Facebook use should be encouraged for people with symptoms of depression.

3. What's the question? What's my hunch?

In general, I'm interested in the relationship between depression and Facebook use. More specifically, I'm wondering whether users who are already depressed might be particularly vulnerable. Will Facebook make their depression worse? My hunch is that it depends. I suspect I'll find that Facebook helps some depressed users and hurts others. What might be interesting is to look at the online conditions that *do* make people more depressed.

4. Working Bibliography

Baker, Levi R. and Debra L. Oswald. "Shyness and Online Networking Services." *Journal of Social and Personal Relationships* 27.7 (2010): 873–889. Print.

Grohol, John. "Pediatrics Gets It Wrong About 'Facebook Depression.'" Pyschcentral .com. No date. Web. 20 April 2012.

Duggan, Maeve, Nicole B. Ellison, Cliff Lampe, Amanda Lenhart, and Mary Madden. "Demographics of Key Social Networking Platforms." Pew Research Center. 9 January 2015. Web. 27 August 2015.

"Major Depressive Disorder Among Adults." National Institute of Mental Health. No date. Web. 4 April 2012.

Moreno, Megan A., Lauren Jelenchick, Katie Egan, Elizabeth Cox, Henry Young, Kerry Gannon, and Tara Becker. "Feeling Bad on Facebook: Depression Disclosures by College Students on Social Networking Site." *Depression and Anxiety* 28 (2011): 447–455. Print.

O'Keefe, Gwen Schurgin, and Kathleen Clarke-Pearson. "The Impact of Social Media on Children, Adolescents, and Families." *Pediatrics* (2011): 800–804. 28 March 2011. Web. 4 April 2012.

Pappas, Stephanie. "Facebook with Care: Social Networking Site Can Hurt Self-Esteem." *LiveScience*. 6 February 2012. Web. 15 April 2012.

Tandoc, Edson C., Jr., Patrick Ferrucci, and Margaret Duffy. "Facebook Use, Envy, and Depression Among College Students." *Computers in Human Behavior* 43 (Feb. 2015): 139-146. Print.

Moving from Proposal to Draft

If you developed a proposal, then you've got a tentative destination for your research essay; you know what it is you might want to know about your topic. Obviously, the next step is to continue your research, developing what I call "focused knowledge" on your topic. Take a look at the strategies for developing focused knowledge in Chapter 11, on pages 393 through 397.

Remember that the proposal is just your first stab at pinning down your project. As you learn more about the topic, your research question will evolve, and how successful you are at revising the question will most determine the success of your project. Remember that your initial questions are often questions of fact (What is known about _____?) or definition (What *is* _____?). These questions are necessary for developing a working knowledge, but they don't produce essays. They produce reports. In your proposal, you've posed a question that will hopefully guide you to some kind of judgment about your topic. Does it?

Evaluating Your Proposal. Let's look at the inquiry question in the sample research proposal, on pages 363–364.

What is the relationship between Facebook use and depression?

This is a pretty good question, and here are a few reasons:

- ✓ It isn't a question of fact or definition.
- ✓ It is likely to lead to some kind of judgment (e.g., Does Facebook use *cause* users to get depressed?).
- ✓ The question narrows the writer's sights, at least some (e.g., it isn't asking about *all* social networks, but Facebook; it isn't speculating about *all* emotional responses, but depression).

Now examine your own research question. Does it do similar things?

Reflecting on What You've Learned. Though you haven't been working on your project for long, you've been at it long enough that you can start to tell yourself the story of how your thinking about the topic has evolved. In your journal, spend a few minutes telling yourself this story: *When I first chose this topic, I thought....And then I thought....And then....And now I'm thinking....* Do this "narrative of thought" on your topic periodically, because it will help you to figure out what you think and, ultimately, what you might be trying to say in your draft.

Developing

Discovery is what drives inquiry-based research. This is why having a good question matters so much, and finding a good question for your project depends on knowing something about your topic. "Working knowledge" seeds this effort. A working knowledge will give you an encyclopedia-like view of your topic—what is the terrain, what are the controversies or the questions, who is influential—and from this you can frame a question that interests you.

But this is just the beginning. As you explore your research question in the coming weeks, you'll go beyond working knowledge to "focused knowledge," finding information that drills down more deeply into your topic's terrain. Good questions are sharper drills. However, this is an open-ended process, and your goal at this stage is to use what you discover to continually shape what you want to see. As you become more informed, you'll revise your approach, refining your question, developing ideas about what you think, and always searching for the answers to this simple question: *So what?*

Writing *while you research* will help you figure this all out and even help you get a start on drafting your essay. I'm not talking about simply taking notes on the information that you find in the coming weeks. Writing about what you *think* about what you're reading or hearing is the best incubator of insight. The double-entry journal, which was introduced to you earlier in *The Curious Writer*, is one method that encourages this kind of writing.

Inquiring into the Details

Scheduling Your Time

If you listen very, very carefully when you begin a research writing project, you will hear a sucking sound—the sound of all those things that may make your life miserable the night before your assignment is due. These include things like settling on too broad a question (which makes it hard to know *what to ignore*); getting pulled into an Internet research hole (spending too much time on tangential research—or on a single site that seems to speak directly to you); and not knowing when to stop (always assuming there is a slightly better source just one more click away). But the biggest time suck of all is procrastination. To make sure you get each assignment in on time, make a plan and stick to it.

Typically, research assignments of eight to ten pages have due dates five weeks out, so I'll use that timeframe to designate a hypothetical schedule. For briefer, shorter assignments, cut back on the time proportionally.

Task	Time
Decide on a topic.	3 days
Develop "working knowledge" (see p. 390) and draft a tentative research question.	1 week
Write a research proposal.	
Develop "focused knowledge" (see p. 393).	2 weeks
Draft an annotated bibliography (if required).	
Develop extensive notes.	
Refine your research question.	
Draft your essay.	1 week
Do additional research as needed.	1 week
Revise, polish, and edit.	

Tools for Developing The Research Essay Draft. Chapters 11 and 12 are full of tools for developing your research draft. Here's a summary of some of those helpful topics.

Quick Guide to Research Techniques

Topic	Purpose	Pages
Search terms	How to focus and improve the quality of search results	383–389
Working knowledge	Strategies for collecting information on questions of fact and definition	390–392
Developing "focused knowledge"	Strategies for searching more narrowly and deeply into a limited topic	393–397
Evaluating sources	Methods for determining the reliability and authority of sources	397–400
Interviews and surveys	How to gather information from people	401–410
Note taking	Using double-entry journals, research logs, and other techniques for "writing in the middle"	412–415
Citing sources	How to know when to cite a source and how to do so	MLA, 429–455 APA, 455–472

Drafting

Sara was a compulsive collector of information. She researched and researched, collecting more books and articles and web sources until the desk in her apartment looked like a miniature version of downtown Chicago—towering piles of paper and books everywhere. She never felt as if she knew enough to begin writing her essay, and would only begin drafting when forced to—the day before the paper was due. Neal figured he could find most of what he needed pretty quickly on the Internet. He printed out a few articles and web pages and felt confident he could write his paper using those sources. He didn't feel pressured to begin writing until the due date loomed. When Neal started writing and realized that he probably wouldn't be able to get the required page length, he widened the margins.

Sara and Neal obviously use different strategies for getting to the draft. Sara relies on accumulating great quantities of information, trusting that aggressively collecting sources will make the writing easier—the main source of her anxiety— although she doesn't really believe that it will. On the other hand, Neal suffers from overconfidence. He figures he can make do with a few sources and doesn't bother to search for more. Both Neal and Sara do what research paper writers have done forever: wait until the last minute. Neither of these writers will be happy with the result.

It's easy to avoid this situation if you begin the draft after you've accomplished the following:

- **You've done some writing before you start writing.** In other words, have you exploited the double-entry journal or an alternative note-taking method to both collect useful information and to explore your reaction to what it says?

- **You are working from abundance (but not overabundance).** Neal is much more typical than Sara. He is trying to compose his draft by drawing from a nearly empty well. Almost any writing—and particularly research writing—depends on working from abundance. You need to collect more information than you can use. But not too much. Don't let endless collecting become an avoidance tactic.

- **Your research question has helped you exclude information.** A good question is a guide. It will help you see the relevance of certain portions of the sources you've collected and give you reason to ignore the rest. If you sense that this is happening consistently as you review your sources, you're probably ready to write.

- **You have a tentative idea about what you think.** By now, you know enough about your topic to have some feelings or ideas about a possible answer to the question behind your investigation. Remember that the draft may make you change your mind—which is fine—but begin composing with at least a tentative point of view.

Methods of Development. How you decide to organize your draft begins with the question of motive. Is your purpose to *find out* (to explore) or *to prove* (to argue)? The first motive is often the purpose of a research essay, the latter the motive when we write a conventional research paper. Though both forms share a considerable number of qualities, the structure of each may differ. For example, an essay frequently has a delayed thesis appearing somewhere towards the end of the piece as the writer reports what he or she has discovered. The research paper typically has a thesis that is stated somewhere in the beginning, as a claim or assertion that the paper will prove. You might imagine it as shown in Figure 10.3.

As you can see, a research essay might have the qualities of a narrative: What did I want to know initially, what's the story of what I found out, and what do I understand now? The argumentative paper is a bit more linear, working from claim to proof. Let's look a little more closely at the microstructures that could be present in either form.

Narrative.   We don't usually associate narrative structure with research papers, but research-based writing tells stories all the time. Perhaps one of the most common techniques to do so is using a case study, which can be an excellent way to begin your paper. Case studies or anecdotes about people involved or affected by a topic often bring that topic to life by moving it closer to the everyday *lives* of people. But as I already mentioned, narrative might also be used as the backbone of a research essay. Sometimes an essay tells the story of what the writer wanted to know and what she found out—a kind of narrative of thought.

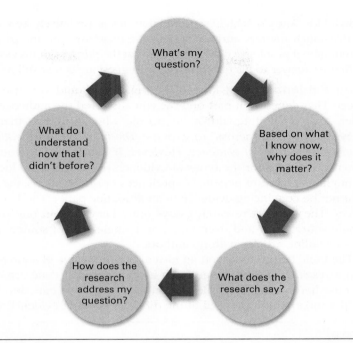

Figure 10.3a The Development of an Exploratory Research Essay

Figure 10.3b The Development of an Argumentative Research Paper

Question to Answer. Because much of the research process is devoted to developing a good question to drive the inquiry, it makes sense to consider organizing your essay around what that question is, where it came from, and what has already been said about it, and then reporting what you've discovered about possible answers to the question that triggered the investigation. A lot of formal academic research is organized this way, although there might be an added section about the methods the investigator chose to try to find the answers.

Known to Unknown. This is a variation on the question-to-answer structure that might be particularly useful if you're writing about a complex topic about which much remains unknown. Your research might have led to the discovery that the question you're interested in has very speculative or limited answers. For example, Andy was writing about the use of psychiatric medicine such as antidepressants and antipsychotics to treat children, because his family physician had recommended them for one of his own kids. Andy quickly discovered that this is a relatively new use for such drugs and that much mystery surrounds both the diagnosis and the treatment of children with emotional problems. It became clear that the purpose of his essay was not to offer a definitive answer to his question, but to suggest areas that still need further study.

Using Evidence. What kind of information should you use in your research project? That depends in part on how you answered the audience question I posed earlier. Are you writing "down" to people who know less than you do? Or are you writing "up" or "across" to experts? *The more knowledgeable your audience, the stricter the rules of evidence.* However, if you're writing your paper for peers ("down"), the rules for the types of evidence you can use are looser. For example, you might use relevant personal experiences or observations, the kind of thing that might not be convincing evidence in an academic paper. The key is this: *Vary your sources.* The weakest research essays draw heavily from one well—maybe using a single source over and over again, or a single *type* of source: e.g., popular web pages or online articles with no authors.

The table below gives you an idea about the *range* of sources you might draw on in a research project. Some, such as experimental data, are evidence that you won't use here, as you aren't doing a study. But as you begin developing your essay, consider incorporating several of the different types of evidence you see here.

Type of Evidence	Source	Description	Examples
Anecdotal	From personal experience, a story someone told you or reported from a published source.	Examples drawn from limited number of sources, usually involving stories.	Case studies, personal experiences and observations, profiles, interviews with people affected.
Statistical	From expert or research institution directly, or reported in secondary source.	Relevant facts and findings, often quantitative.	Tables, statistics in government reports, size comparisons, growth data, numbers affected, etc.
Expert testimony	From transcript, scholarly article or book, personal interview, or secondary source.	Quotes, claims, and ideas from individuals or institutions with expertise in the topic.	An argument by an influential scholar, a quote from a personal interview, a quoted passage from a book, etc.
Experimental	Data generated by the researcher to test a hypothesis.	Studies conducted with an approved methodology that often produces quantitative results.	A lab experiment, survey, transcript analysis, etc.

Type of Evidence	Source	Description	Examples
Textual	Interpretation and analysis of writing, images, and other kinds of texts.	Close "reading" of a text to interpret its meaning, test a theory, analyze its structure, or evaluate its effectiveness.	Interpretation of a poem or short story, analysis of an advertisement or photograph, rhetorical analysis of a speech.
Observation	Close observation in a controlled setting or in the field.	Methodological descriptions of what subjects do in response to a task, problem, question, or event. Or "deep descriptions" of people in natural settings to interpret behaviors, status, social roles, etc.	Analyzing video to determine usability of software, field observations of bowling-league members or an Alcoholics Anonymous meeting. Detailed description of study site, or description of the scene of a significant event.

Workshopping

If your draft is subject to peer review, see Appendix B for details on how to organize workshop groups and decide on how your group can help you. See "Models for Writing Workshops" (p. 554) for details on how to organize workshop groups. Each workshop type is described more fully in that section.

There are a couple of key things to consider as you prepare for this workshop.

- **Is it boring?** There's no reason to write an extended essay, such as the one for this project, that bores everybody to death. Why would you want to do that? You might identify passages or pages in the draft that you think seem to drag and see if your group agrees and can suggest how you might liven things up.

- **Is the question clear?** The organizing force of the research essay is the writer's research question. What is it she wants to know? This must be obvious at the beginning of the essay. If it isn't, in a page or two readers *will* get bored because they don't know where the essay is headed.

- **Does it suggest an answer?** If you're going to ask readers to peddle your bike for more than a few pages, then they not only need to know in what direction you're steering, but also that you'll have something worthwhile to say when you get there. We often call this the thesis. Whatever you call it, your draft must ultimately make a judgment, and make it clearly.

Questions for Peer Reviewers	
1. Purpose	What is the research question that is driving this project? Is it clear? Is it interesting? Is there another question that might be better?
2. Meaning	In your own words, what do you think I'm trying to say? Did the draft hint at another idea that I might develop in the next draft?

Reflecting on the Draft. A draft is a thing the wind blows through. That might be especially true of the first full draft of your research essay. After all, this project involves juggling a lot more than most other inquiry projects do: controlling information and the ideas from a wide variety of sources, trying to surround that outside material with your own ideas, worrying about following citation conventions, and struggling not to let the whole project get away from your own purposes and questions. Spend a little time reflecting on how all this went.

In your notebook or on a separate piece of paper you'll include with the draft when you hand it in, answer the following questions:

- What's the most important thing you learned about your topic after the research and writing you just completed? Is this important understanding obvious in the draft?

- Choose two paragraphs that incorporate outside sources—one that you think is written pretty well, and another that is written less well. What differences do you notice between the two? Can you identify at least one problem you need to work on in the next draft that will help you improve the way you integrate sources?

Revising

Revision is a continual process—not a last step. You've been revising—"reseeing" your subject—from the first messy fastwriting in your journal. But the things that get your attention vary depending on where you are in the writing process. With your draft in hand, revision becomes your focus through what I'll call shaping and tightening your draft.

Chapter 14 contains strategies that can help you revise any inquiry project, and the "Guidelines: Revising Your Work" in this chapter on page 373 can help you locate these strategies. There are also certain things to think about that are especially useful for shaping a research essay.

Shaping. When we shape a draft, the focus is on design—the order of information, the chain of reasoning, the coherence of paragraphs, and their contribution to the whole composition. The architecture of a research essay is particularly important, because it's longer and carries a heavy load of information. Earlier in the chapter, we discussed in general terms the different ways an exploratory research essay and an argumentative research paper might be organized. Now you've got some material to work with, and one of the best ways to consider how to shape the material is through literally cutting it apart.

One of the most effective revision exercises for a research essay is what I call the "Frankenstein Draft." This is modeled after a cut-and-paste revision exercise by writing theorist Peter Elbow. Cut up your draft with scissors, dividing it into the different elements (description, judgments, criteria, evidence), and then play with the order. What seems to be most effective? Worry about transitions later. You'll find instructions for this revision activity in Chapter 14 on page 540. Try it and play with the design of your essay.

Polishing. Shaping focuses on things such as purpose, meaning, and design. No less important is looking more closely at paragraphs, sentences, and words. But for this project, you also need to make sure that you cite sources correctly. You'll get plenty of help with that in Chapter 12, "Using and Citing Sources." Refer to it for help with how to properly quote, paraphrase, summarize, and control information. You will also find guidelines for citation using MLA and APA styles.

Before you finish your draft, work through the following checklist:

✓ Every paragraph is about one thing.

✓ The transitions between paragraphs aren't abrupt.

✓ The lengths of sentences vary in each paragraph.

✓ Each sentence is concise. There are no unnecessary words or phrases.

✓ You've checked grammar, particularly verb agreement, run-on sentences, unclear pronouns, and misused words (*there/their, where/were,* and so on).

✓ You've run your spellchecker and proofed your paper for misspelled words.

✓ You've double-checked your citations and Works Cited or References page to ensure that the formatting is correct.

Guidelines: Revising Your Work

A first effort is almost never a best effort. To make sure your essay is really your best work, check out Chapter 14 for help with these questions:

- What is my paper really about? (See p. 518.)

- What am I really trying to say? (See p. 523.)

- Do I have enough convincing evidence? (See p. 530.)

- Does this paper move logically and smoothly from paragraph to paragraph? (See p. 534.)

- Are the sentences and paragraphs in this paper too choppy or hard to follow? (See p. 542.)

▶ **Student Essay**

Some of the best research essays emerge from our personal experiences. Something happens and we wonder, "What's with that?" The research essay that follows, "The 'Unreal Dream': True Crime in the Justice System," began when Laura Burns—an avid watcher of crime shows like *CSI*—wondered how her feelings of satisfaction when the bad guys get locked up on TV could be squared with recent headlines about wrongful convictions. How could this happen, especially since the science of criminal evidence has seemed so advanced in recent years? Her research essay explores that question, and she discovers some things that will surprise you about why the justice system sometimes fails to convict the right person. Laura Burns's essay is cited using MLA guidelines.

The "Unreal Dream": True Crime in the Justice System

Laura Burns
Professor Ballenger
English 101
15 January 2015

1   I love true crime shows. The formula for these shows is simple: learn about the crime itself, investigate a few leads, find a suspect, prove the suspect is guilty, and go home, congratulating ourselves on a job well-done. Not only are these stories entertaining and chock-full of good guys, bad guys, cliff hangers, red herrings, and constant danger, but we are also granted the release of knowing that we are safe and snuggled into the couch, with the bad guys in jail and the good guys always on the right side. But the neat, pat conclusions of most of these cases masks a frightening reality. According to a recent study from the National Academy of Sciences, 4.1% of all those who are sentenced to death in the United States are innocent (Gross et al. 7230). In 1923, Judge Learned Hand said, "Our [justice system] has always been haunted by the ghost of the innocent man convicted. It is an unreal dream (7230)." However, Hand's "unreal dream" is a reality for many. How does wrongful conviction occur, and why does it occur so frequently? And even more importantly, how can we prevent it?

2   First, we need to examine what "wrongful conviction" really means. According to legal scholar Michael Risinger, there are three categories. The first is "Conviction Despite Serious Legal Error." In this case, a conviction is wrongful because a legal error was made (for example, the suspect's home was [searched] without a warrant). The second category is "Conviction Despite Lack of Legal Culpability." According to this definition, a conviction is wrongful because the convicted party was not legally culpable (for example, a crime was committed by someone with severe mental illness). The third definition is the most problematic: "Conviction Despite Factual Innocence." In these cases, one of two things occurs: either no crime was committed, so there is no offender, or, more commonly, a crime was committed, but not by the convicted party (Risinger 762).

How can this happen? Although there are countless ways an investigation and trial can veer off course, most wrongful convictions occur for one or more of the following reasons: eyewitness misidentification, false confessions, jailhouse snitches, poor forensic science, government and prosecutorial misconduct, and ineffective counsel. If I've learned anything from TV crime shows, it's that DNA is a powerful tool for convicting the guilty and exonerating the innocent. However, according to the National Registry of Exonerations, only 18 of the 91 exonerations in 2013 occurred due to DNA evidence, and the number of DNA exonerations decline annually ("Exonerations by Year"). So, although DNA evidence is an excellent tool for uncovering and proving wrongful convictions, its most effective use is uncovering the underlying causes of those wrongful convictions. It['s] only through understanding the issues and mending the fissures in the criminal justice system that allow for them, that we can slow the rate of wrongful convictions in the United States.

The most common cause of wrongful conviction is mistaken eyewitness identification. Nearly three-quarters of wrongful convictions overturned through DNA testing were caused in part by incorrect eyewitness testimony (*Innocence Project*). In order to truly understand why this is the case, we need to look at how memory works. There are two kinds of human memory: short-term and long-term. Long-term memory involves the storage of memory which can later be retrieved (Green). This is the type of memory most often accessed in eyewitness identifications, and also the type that is most easily distorted.

Take the case of Ronald Cotton. In July 1984, a young woman named Jennifer Thompson was attacked and raped in her home. Thompson made a point to try and get a good look at her rapist. She turned on lights, making sure to see his face, and immediately reported the crime to the police. Thompson was shown a photo array and informed that her assailant "may" be in the array. She identified Ronald Cotton, and the officer with her responded, "We thought this might be the one["] (*Innocence Project*). Thompson was then shown a live lineup of seven men, including Cotton. Thompson struggled with the selection, but eventually picked out Cotton—the only man who appeared in both the photo array and live lineup. The police informed Thompson that she'd selected the same person as she had in the photo array. Based on these identifications and other circumstantial evidence, Cotton was convicted and sentenced to life in prison. Ten years later, in 1994, DNA evidence from the case exonerated Cotton. Now, Thompson and Cotton travel the country to speak about eyewitness misidentification (Thompson-Cannino et al.).

So, what happened here? Jennifer Thompson did everything in her power to be an excellent eyewitness, and she still misidentified Cotton. Eyewitness identification occurs because of two variables: *system* variables, which involve the criminal justice system, and *estimator* variables, which affect eyewitness accuracy but are not under the purview of the criminal justice system (Wells et al.). Both variables were at play in the Ronald Cotton case. Some systemic factors included:

1. The second lineup. Ronald Cotton was the only person in both the photo array and the live lineup, which encouraged Thompson to identify him twice.
2. The officer's feedback. According to Thompson herself, her confidence in her identification grew after the officers provided positive feedback.

(*continued*)

(*continued*)

Some of the estimator factors included:

1. <u>Weapon presence</u>. Because her assailant had a weapon, Thompson was more inclined to focus on the weapon than on the assailant himself.

2. <u>Own-race bias</u>. Thompson is white, and her assailant was black (as is Ronald Cotton). Eyewitnesses are less accurate in their identifications when the person they are identifying is a race other than their own.

3. <u>Passage of time</u>. Memories decline in accuracy very quickly at first, then slower over time (Green).

7   Although many estimator variables cannot be controlled, system variables can be, and one of the most important systemic shifts to prevent misidentification is to ensure that the person who administers the lineup or photo array does not know the identity of the suspect. Frequently, body language cues or even (in the case of Thompson and Cotton) verbal clues from the administrator can influence a witness to identify the suspect.

8   Systemic issues in the criminal justice system cause wrongful convictions in other ways, too. While the vast majority of wrongful convictions occur due to honest mistakes or errors in judgment, there are also cases of police misconduct and government negligence. One of the most notorious of these took place in Chicago between the 1970s and 1990s under the supervision of Police Commander Jon Burge. In 1973, Anthony Holmes was arrested by Burge and brought to a police station. There, Holmes was tortured: beaten, verbally brutalized, suffocated with a bag, and subjected to a contraption of electro-shock torture, which Burge called the "nigger box" (Taylor). Eventually, under extreme duress, Holmes confessed to murder. Later, Holmes's interrogation was cited by the police department in one of Burge's commendations as demonstrating "skillful questioning" (Conroy). Journalist James Conroy wrote a series of exposes on these offenses in the *Chicago Reader* beginning in 1990, detailing the horrifying torture and the victims' failed attempts to seek justice. Burge was later fired in 1993 and retired with pension to his boat in Florida. In 2003, Governor George Ryan commuted the sentences of all 167 men on death row in Illinois, out of concern that some of their confessions were coerced through torture. Burge was not arrested until 2008, when he was charged not for the torture, but for his involvement in covering it up (Shelton). Although the Burge case is an extreme example of government and police misconduct, it is a clear example of the importance of the public holding officers and government accountable for their actions.

9   Prosecutors, who represent the government in court, also occasionally exhibit misconduct. This can range from the malicious (such as the destruction of evidence) to the subtle (such as overstating the value of evidence). The most common form of prosecutorial misconduct is a Brady violation, which is defined as: "Suppression by the prosecution of evidence favorable to an accused who has requested it violates due process where the evidence is material either to guilt or to punishment, irrespective of the good faith or bad faith of the prosecution" (Brady vs. Maryland). Consider the case of Dewey Bozella, who was convicted of murder in 1983. In 2009, Bozella's lawyers conducted an independent investigation in which they uncovered testimony from multiple witnesses that would exonerate Bozella—all of which was withheld by the prosecution. The case was overturned (Denzel). Ineffective counsel can also

be a cause of wrongful conviction. For example, an ineffective defense lawyer may fail to call witnesses who might support the defense, fail to obtain and submit DNA evidence for testing, fail to conduct independent investigations on behalf of their client, and more ("Ineffective Assistance").

While these examples demonstrate willful negligence, other causes of wrongful conviction are perfectly legal. Eighteen percent of wrongful convictions involve the testimony of a jailhouse snitch (*The Path to Justice*): a prisoner who allegedly learns information from another prisoner about an event that occurred outside the institution. So, why snitch? The main reason is that snitching is incentivized. According to *USA Today*, 48,895 federal convicts received reduced sentences for their testimony against other convicts between 2006 and 2011; that is one in every eight convicts (Heath). You could argue that jailhouse snitches should not be permitted to testify at all, but occasionally, they do help expose a wrongful conviction, such as Ronald Cotton's. While incarcerated for another crime, the actual perpetrator of the crimes Cotton was convicted of bragged about his activities to other inmates. A snitch told a prosecutor what he heard, and Cotton was granted a new trial—the one that exonerated him (*Innocence Project*).

The final element in many wrongful convictions (around 30% of DNA exonerations) is also the most misunderstood: false confessions (*Innocence Project*). How could someone confess to a crime they didn't commit, and why would they? First, we should understand the three different errors that can lead to false confessions:

1. Misclassification error: This occurs when investigators wrongly decide a suspect is guilty, and the interrogation turns into an effort not to determine a suspect's guilt, but to convince the suspect to confess.

2. Coercion error: This occurs when the interrogator uses coercive techniques (isolation, deception, sleep deprivation, etc.) to elicit a confession.

3. Contamination error: This is the error that most often leads to false confessions. In a contamination error, the interrogator influences the suspect's narrative by filling in certain details that an innocent person would not know (Leo and Drizen 13-20).

Of course, while not all interrogations end in false confessions, there are a number of indicators for interrogations that may lead to them. For example, the length of interrogations can affect the rate of false confessions. Though typical interrogations last around two hours, 84% of interrogations leading to false confessions lasted over six hours (and averaged around 16 hours) (Drizen and Leo 946). Additionally, all suspects are read their Miranda rights prior to interrogation, which is familiar to any of us who love "Law & Order":

> You have the right to remain silent. Anything you say can and will be used against you in a court of law. You have the right to an attorney. If you cannot afford an attorney, one will be provided for you. Do you understand these rights?

The delivery and exact content of this statement varies from state to state, with some states making a point to emphasize a benefit to waiving one's rights or make the statement sound like an afterthought. Also, due to the impression many people have that "the truth will

(*continued*)

(*continued*)

set me free," innocent people are significantly more likely to waive their rights and speak to police (Kassin 253).

14   Certain populations are more vulnerable to making false confessions. Juveniles are considered the most vulnerable: 42% of juvenile exonerees confessed to crimes they did not commit (Kassin 252). Minors tend to have more difficulty understanding legal wording (such as in the Miranda warning), are more susceptible to suggestion from interrogators, and have a less clear understanding of the consequences of their actions. Similarly, those with intellectual difficulties and mental illness are more vulnerable to false confessions. The case of Eddie Joe Lloyd is a clear example of this. While Lloyd was hospitalized for a mental illness, he wrote a series of letters to police, trying to help them solve local crimes. Officers selected one of Lloyd's letters and told him that if he confessed to that crime, it would help them find the real perpetrator. He did so, and was convicted and sent to prison for 17 years before his exoneration (*Innocence Project*). At least 22% of the false confessions currently known were made by those with a mental illness or intellectual disability (Drizen and Leo 918).

15   As I explored the many reasons why wrongful convictions occur, I began to wonder about the influence of the true crime shows I, and so many others, love so much. We love the drama and the human interest, but we also love seeing justice done. Does our obsession with these stories and our easy comfort with the way they end somehow add to the problem of wrongful convictions? My investigation into this issue led me to what is known in legal circles as the "CSI Effect," named for the famous TV crime show. According to the 2006 Nielsen ratings, five of the top ten television shows that year were related to forensics and criminal investigations. That's about 100 million viewers (Shelton). The "CSI effect" generally holds that due to these forensic science-focused shows, juries have excessively high expectations of the accuracy, quality, and utility of scientific evidence in the courtroom. They also tend to expect more certainty from scientific evidence, despite the fact that in most cases, there is no such thing as 100% forensic certainty. Despite how alarmist all of this sounds, no scientists can seem to agree on the extent of this effect, and many even argue that shows like this may help improve juries' understanding of the justice system.

16   There's no easy solution to stymying wrongful convictions. Stopping them entirely would require a complete overhaul in our criminal justice system, down to the very words officers use in their day-to-day interactions. I concede that it is probably impossible to accomplish a goal of that magnitude, but there are small changes we can make that might help. One change that was recently implemented in some states is the requirement that all interrogations be videotaped. According to the Illinois Public Act 93-0517, a confession resulting from interrogation will be allowed *only* if: "(1) an electronic recording is made of the custodial interrogation; and (2) the recording is substantially accurate and not intentionally altered." Remember that Illinois is the state where Jon Burge committed so many atrocities in interrogation rooms. This requirement makes torture on that scale very close to impossible.

17   Finally, considering the "CSI effect" and juries' lack of understanding about the inner workings of the justice system, an improved set of jury instructions would be useful. Juries with a clearer understanding of eyewitness misidentification, incentivized snitching, and false confessions may help them make a more informed ruling. In other words, *more information*. That is the only overarching conclusion I can make: more information not only for juries, but

for law enforcement officers, for lawyers, for government officials, and for the public. Navigating the process of the justice system requires far more than just to "learn about the crime itself, investigate a few leads, find a suspect, prove the suspect is guilty, and go home." We must navigate numerous uncertainties, take time to verify everything we learn, and most of all, understand the grey areas in a system that prefers the black and white, the right and wrong, the guilty and not guilty. Only once we understand why wrongful convictions occur can we begin to work on how to stop them.

Works Cited

Brady v. Maryland. 373 US. 83. Supreme Court of the US. 1963. *Justia*. Web. 17 Jan. 2015.

Conroy, John. "House of Screams." *ChicagoReader.com*. The Chicago Reader. 25 Jan. 1990. Web. 17 Jan. 2015.

Denzel, Stephanie. "Dewey Bozella." *The National Registry of Exonerations*. University of Michigan Law School, 16 Nov. 2014. Web. 17 Jan. 2015.

Drizin, Steven A. and Richard A. Leo. "The Problem of False Confessions in the Post-DNA World." *North Carolina Law Review*. 82 (March 2004): 891-1004. Print.

"Exonerations by Year: DNA and Non-DNA." Chart. *The National Registry of Exonerations*. University of Michigan Law School, 15 Jan. 2015. Web. 17 Jan. 2015.

Green, Marc. "Eyewitness Memory Is Unreliable." *Visual Expert*. 2013. Web. 17 Jan. 2015.

Gross, Samuel R., Barbara O'Brien, Chen Hu, and Edward H. Kennedy. "Rate of False Conviction of Criminal Defendants Who Are Sentenced to Death." *PNAS*. 111.20 (2014): 7230-7235. Print.

Heath, Brad. "Federal Prisoners Use Snitching for Personal Gain." *USAToday.com*. USA Today, 14 Dec. 2012. Web. 17 Jan. 2015.

Illinois Compiled Statutes Code of Criminal Procedure. 725 ILCS 5/103-2.1. n.d. Web. 17 Jan. 2015.

"Ineffective Assistance of Counsel." *California Innocence Project*. California Western School of Law, 2014. Web. 17 Jan. 2015.

Innocence Project. The Benjamin N. Cardozo School of Law at Yeshiva University, 2015. Web. 17 Jan. 2015.

Kassin, S. M. "False Confessions: Causes, Consequences, and Implications for Reform. *Current Directions in Psychological Science* 17 (2008): 249-253. Print.

Leo, Richard A. and Steven A. Drizin. "The Three Errors: Pathways to False Confession and Wrongful Conviction." *Interrogation and Confessions: Research, Policy and Practice*. Eds. G.D. Lassiter and C.A. Meissner. Washington, DC: American Psychological Association, 2010. 9-30. Print.

Illinois Public Act 93-0517.725 ILCS 5/103-2.1. 6 Aug. 2003. Web. 17 Jan. 2015.

Public Prosecution Service of Canada. *The Path to Justice: Preventing Wrongful Convictions*. Federal/Provincial/Territorial Heads of Prosecutions Subcommittee on the Prevention of Wrongful Convictions. 16 Sept. 2011. Web. 17 Jan. 2015.

Risinger, D. Michael. "Innocents Convicted: An Empirically Justified Factual Wrongful Conviction Rate." *Journal of Criminal Law and Criminology* 97.3 (2007): 761-806. Print.

Shelton, Donald. "The 'CSI Effect': Does It Really Exist?" *National Institute of Justice Journal* 259 (Mar. 2008). Web. 17 Jan. 2015.

(continued)

(*continued*)

Taylor, Flint. "Racism, Torture and Impunity in Chicago." *The Nation.com*. The Nation, 20 Feb. 2013. Web. 17 Jan. 2015.

Thompson-Cannino, Jennifer, Ronald Cotton, and Erin Torneo. *Picking Cotton: Our Memoir of Injustice and Redemption*. New York: St. Martin's, 2010. Print.

Wells, Gary L., Mark Small, Steven Penrod, Roy S. Malpass, Solomon M. Fulero, and C.A.E. Brimacombe. "Eyewitness Identification Procedures." *Law and Human Behavior* 22.6 (1998). Web. 17 Jan. 2015.

Evaluating the Essay

1. "The 'Unreal Dream'" is a variation of the proposal genre: What's the problem and what can be done about it? (See Chapter 6.) When you write a proposal, you typically make a choice about how much you'll emphasize the problem and how much you'll emphasize the solution. What choice do you see Burns making about that balance in this essay? Is there a rhetorical explanation for that?

2. Research essays are driven by questions, and conventional research papers are thesis-driven. What are the implications of a question-driven essay like "The 'Unreal Dream'" in terms of how it is structured, especially when compared with a thesis-driven essay?

3. Do you see elements of narrative in the essay? Where? How do these elements affect your reading of the essay?

Using What You Have Learned

Let's return to the learning goals I identified in the beginning of the chapter.

1. **Apply what you've learned about writing shorter inquiry-based papers to an extended research project.** In some ways, the research essay is the culmination of a long journey from kinds of writing that use fewer sources of information to one that uses multiple sources. Researched writing is also most likely to use conventions of academic scholarship such as citation. But in some ways, writing a research paper is simply a longer version of something you've been doing all along: identifying a question that interests you and then exploring possible answers. Discovery is the "heart of the enterprise." I hope you take that fundamental concept into any writing assignment you get in the future, no matter how formal.

2. **Identify different forms of researched writing and the purposes behind them.** You might have begun this project assuming that *all* research papers have certain qualities in common: They are formally structured, you should

know your thesis before you begin, never use "I," etc. By now, you should know that the rhetorical considerations—especially purpose and audience—provide the best guidance for your approach in any writing situation, including The College Research Paper.

3. **Practice reading, analyzing, and writing with a limited number of sources on a single topic.** I've become convinced that practice working with a limited number of sources in collaboration with others can be a useful way to learn some strategies for working with sources. Was that true for you?

4. **Use invention techniques for discovering a researchable question.** By now, you know the drill. Before you make a judgment about what to write about, open up the possibilities. This may be especially important with researched essays, because it's essential that you are *curious* about the topic you're exploring. Whenever you receive a research assignment, take time to use some of these invention strategies. Doing so may have a greater impact on the success of your project than anything else you do.

5. **Refine a research question to narrow the topic focus and lead to a judgment.** There's some scholarly evidence that the thing that students struggle most with in an inquiry-based investigation is coming up with a good question. Whenever you're working with a lot of information—as you often are in a research project—the quality of the question has huge practical implications. Having a good question will help you decide what to ignore.

6. **Use audience and purpose to make decisions about the structure of the work and the types of information to use in it.** From the first assignment chapter to this final one, you've gone from seeing that all writing uses information to recognizing that in academic writing, we evaluate this information as evidence. The quality of evidence differs, and those differences matter more when you're writing for an audience that knows something about your topic. When you get writing assignments in other classes, clarify to whom you are writing so that you know what kinds of evidence you should use.

11

Research Techniques

Learning Objectives

In this chapter, you'll learn to

11.1 Identify the "research routines" you've typically used, and practice new ones appropriate to college-level research.

11.2 Refine and improve the effectiveness of search terms.

11.3 Apply research strategies for developing "working knowledge" and "focused knowledge" on your topic.

11.4 Use a method to analyze and evaluate research sources.

11.5 Understand and apply new note-taking strategies that will help you analyze sources while you're researching.

Methods of Collecting

This chapter should tell you everything you need to know about finding what you need in the university library and on the web. It is particularly useful for collecting information for research essays, but research is a source of information that can make *any* essay stronger. Every assignment in *The Curious Writer*, therefore, includes suggestions for research as you're searching for a topic and writing your draft. Research also can be an especially useful revision strategy for any essay.

Use this chapter much as you would a toolbox—a handy collection of tips and research tools that you can use for all assignments. Refer to it whenever you discover a topic that raises questions that research can help answer, or whenever it would be helpful to hear what other people say

Topic	Pages
Crafting effective search terms	383–389
Developing "working knowledge" of a topic	390–392
Developing "focused knowledge" of a topic	393–397
Evaluating sources	397–400
Conducting and using interviews	401–406
Conducting and using surveys	406–410
Note-taking strategies	412–415

Figure 11.1   Quick Guide to Research Tools

about the things you're thinking about. Figure 11.1 is a quick reference guide for finding information on to key topics covered in this chapter.

Research in the Electronic Age

The digital revolution has profoundly changed the way we do research, and it's mostly a wonderful thing. It's extraordinary, for example, how much information I can access on any topic from right here at my desk. But research in the electronic age has also created some new challenges. For example,

There's strong evidence that college undergraduates use some pretty standard "research routines" when given a paper assignment, no matter what the assignment says.

- An extraordinary amount of information, while more accessible than ever, is really, really bad, at least for academic research.
- The information that is accessible online is as disorganized as a hoarder's closet.

What this means is (1) that you need to spend more time critically evaluating what you find when searching online, (2) that the quality of the search terms you use will make a big difference in how easy it is to find reliable and relevant information, (3) that the library, which exists in part to *organize* information so it's easier to find, is more important than ever. In this chapter, I'll cover each of these points and offer some advice about how to develop your research skills.

Research Routines

You've probably written research papers before. (My daughter Julia started writing them in the seventh grade.) And like anything you've done before, you have certain routines that you invoke when faced with a familiar task, often without thinking about them. For most of us, one of these research routines is to simply Google your topic. Another is to harvest the results from only the first page or so that appears. But as a college researcher, you need to be much more flexible and sophisticated

11.1

Identify the
"research
routines" you've
typically used,
and practice new
ones appropriate
to college-level
research.

than this. You need to look wider and deeper for information. Unlearning old routines begins with identifying what those routines are. Start this process by reflecting on what kind of researcher you are: "fast surfer," "broad scanner," or "deep diver."[1]

Fast Surfer

- I prefer to read only the sources that are written at a level that I can understand.
- If I don't find much on my topic when I search, I usually assume that there isn't much written about it.
- I always feel I'm under a lot of time pressure when I do research.
- I pretty much limit myself to searching in the kinds of sources that I'm familiar with.
- I just look for what I need and little more.

Broad Scanner

- I search for a range of sources on my topic, a process that I don't necessarily plan but that develops slowly as I work.
- I often find my best sources accidentally.
- I'm pretty careful about evaluating the reliability of the relevant sources I do find.

Deep Diver

- I'm more interested in getting the highest-quality sources than in finding a lot of sources.
- I'm very open to changing my mind about what I think about my topic.
- I spend some time planning my research because I want my search to be thorough.

Depending on the research task, "fast surfing" might be just fine. But typically, academic researchers are "deep divers," whose habits of mind you should strive to emulate. "But wait," you might say. "I'm already pretty good at doing research. I did okay in high school." Researchers use the term "information literacy" to describe people's skills at finding and evaluating information, and one of the things researchers find over and over about the information literacy of college students is that college students are overconfident about their research abilities.

There's strong evidence that college undergraduates use some pretty standard "research routines" when given a paper assignment, no matter what the assignment says. One of these routines, according to the study group Project Information Literacy, is writing a thesis and making an outline early on in the process. In some cases, this isn't a bad approach. But if your goal is discovery—and that, after all, is the motive behind academic inquiry—then dreaming up a thesis before you've done much research defeats the purpose of doing research in the first place. You might have other routines as well, such as consulting Wikipedia, waiting until the

[1]See Heinstrom, Jannica. "Fast Surfing, Broad Scanning, and Deep Diving: The Influence of Personality and Study Approach on Students' Information-Seeking Behavior." *Journal of Documentation* 60.2 (2005): 228–247.

night before the paper is due to begin doing any writing, or relying exclusively on Google and skimming only the first few sources that appear.

I'm a lousy dancer. I pretty much do the same moves over and over again and try not to be self-conscious. Similarly, writers who keep using the same routines never discover new moves that will help them adapt to new demands. In Chapter 1 and Chapter 2, you thought about your writing and reading habits, some of which you may have developed in high school, or simply by accident. To be conscious of your process is to get control over it and to see the *choices* you might make in particular writing or reading situations. Research is a process, too. And you'll find that many of the research routines you brought with you to college may not serve you well. But how can you know what you need to *unlearn* if you don't think about your process? Reflect often on what you're noticing about your ways of doing research. You'll then learn more dance moves, whatever the music.

Power Searching Using Google

Say I'm researching why people believe in alien abduction. For better or worse, most of us start our research at Google. So I type the following in the search window:

11.2

Refine and improve the effectiveness of search terms.

I get 5.87 million hits. Okay, that's a lot of stuff to scroll through. If you're like most people, you'll harvest just the first few relevant results on the opening page or two. But that would squander the power of the search engine and ignore lots of even better potential sources. But how do you find those sources?

Add a word or two:

That's a little better: Now I get less than a million results. I might refine the search further by adding some words and putting a few terms in quotation marks. The quotes tell Google that I want documents with that exact phrase. Still, I'd like fewer and better results, from sources I am likely to trust. Here's where some of the more advanced commands can help. Suppose I want to get information from a particular site—say, NASA. What does the federal government's space agency have to say about belief in alien abduction? To do this, I begin with the word *site* and the name of the website:

Ninety-seven hits! This more focused search produced more reliable sources.

Search windows from Google, Inc.

Say I stumbled on a really great article on the website *Psychology Today* about the belief in alien abduction and I'd like to see if the website has any other articles on the topic. Or perhaps I'm interested in sources that cite the original article. The operator *related: (URL of site and search terms)* will help me do this.

Google | related: www.psychologytoday.com/ belief in alien abduction | ▾ | Q |

You can also search for particular kinds of documents such as the formats pdf, jpg, doc, etc., by beginning your query with *filetype: (jpg, doc, pdf, etc., and search terms)*. To summarize, then: To use Google efficiently, play with terms, including searching for an exact phrase using quotation marks; and focus your search by using the *site, filetype,* and *related* operations.

For more on how to make the most of Google searches, see "Inquiring into the Details: Google Tips and Tricks" below.

Inquiring into the Details

Google Tips and Tricks

If You Want To ...	Use ...	For Example ...
Find related pages	**related:** followed by website address	**related:** www.epicurious.com
Automatically search within a specific site or type of site	**site:** followed by website type	microbiology **site: edu** or crime **site:** www.nytimes.com
Search for words or phrases in an open web document	**Control-F (Windows)** or **Command-F (Mac)** and a search window opens	Search for the term "revision" in an article about writing
Search by file type	**file type:** followed by 3-letter abbreviation	Obamacare **file type: PDF**
Ignore words in your search	**minus sign (–)** followed by word to ignore	pet training **– cats**

Search window from Google, Inc.

If You Want To ...	Use ...	For Example ...
Include words in your search	**quotation marks (" ")** around word to include	"the" borrowers
Include results with synonyms	**tilde sign (~)** before word	eggplant ~roasting
Retain stop words in phrases without quotes	**plus sign (+)** in front of stop word to retain	fish +and chips
Search for two options	capitalized **OR** between two options	yellow OR black Labradors
Match any single word in a search	**asterisk (*)** to find matching word or words	"four score and * years ago" or "undergrad program pre*"
Search number range	**two dots (..)** between values	used laptops **$50..$1000**
Log and search your own search history	**Web history:** www .google.com/ history	

Google Scholar. Perhaps the most useful thing you can do is to try Google Scholar, to see if there is any scholarly work published on your topic. You will be amazed at the things that academics research, including belief in alien abduction, and the results you get will produce sources with the highest quality for an academic essay. *To use Google Scholar, the first thing you should do is link with your university library using a setting in Preferences.* Once you do this, the results will allow you to retrieve documents from your campus library without having to pay for them. To do this, open Google Scholar, open "scholar preferences," and scroll down to "library links." Enter the name of your university or college. Click on your school, and then you may have to enter your login credentials. Now you will see links to your own library on your results pages when a document is available (see the screenshot in Figure 11.2).

Notice, too, that if you do find a relevant article, you can quickly discover who has cited it (leading you to other potentially useful sources) and "related" work. It's hard to overstate how useful this site is for college research.

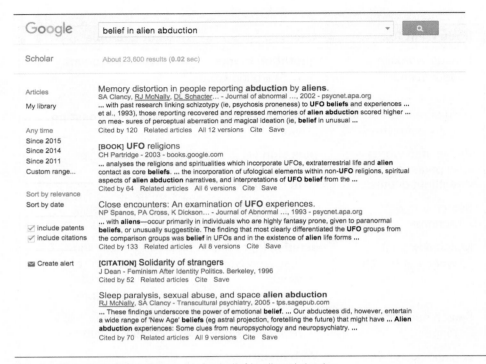

Figure 11.2 Google Scholar search for *belief in alien abduction*
Source: Google, Inc.

Power Searching in the Library

Many of us just search electronic card catalogs and library databases using our web-searching routines. And to some extent, that is sufficient. But you're going to search far more efficiently if you understand things called "controlled language searches" and "Boolean operators." Library databases often use both, so they're good to know, and they are less complicated than they sound.

Combining Terms Using Boolean Searching. George Boole, an eighteenth-century mathematician, came up with a system for using words like AND, OR, and NOT to help researchers craft logical search queries. Searches still use these words, though it isn't always obvious. Remember that I did a keyword search on *alien abduction* using Google in the previous section? What wasn't obvious is that Google assumes there is an AND between the two terms even if I don't type it; in other words, Google searches for online documents that contain *all* the terms I type in the search window. On the other hand, if I typed *alien OR abduction*, I would be telling Google to find materials that contain *either* term. In that case, by using the operator *OR*, I would be *telling* Google to broaden the search (see Figure 11.3a). Another Boolean convention you might want to try using is NOT, which excludes a term (e.g., *alien* AND *abduction* NOT *ufos*). Many databases also allow you to

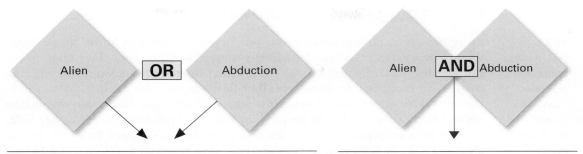

Figure 11.3a Using the *OR* operator in a keyword search yields results that contain one keyword or the other.

Figure 11.3b Using the *AND* operator (which is often implied) yields results that include all the keywords.

use quotation marks around exact phrases. What you end up with is a way to join a bunch of keywords using the operators to get better results. For example, you might search using the following string:

>   *alien* AND *abduction* AND *stories* NOT *ufos*

When I did that search on my university library's websites, I ended up with fifty-nine hits—both books and articles—and the great majority were relevant. (See Figure 11.3b.)

Using Controlled Language Searches. Mostly, we search using keywords—terms that we come up with, usually through trial and error, that we think will give us the best results. But in libraries there's another option: controlled language searches. These are the preferred words that librarians use to organize and find information. But how would you know what those authorized terms are? There are two ways to find out:

1. *Consult the Library of Congress Subject Headings.* This is the standard that reference librarians use to identify which terms to search with to yield the best results on any topic. You can search the LCSH online (authorities.loc .gov). Enter in your keywords, and voilà, there's a list of preferred headings you might use to search library databases. I found out that *alien abduction* is the favored search term, but I also discovered twenty variations, some of which I hadn't thought to use in a database search. For example,

    - Alien abduction in literature
    - Alien abduction-prevention-case studies
    - Alien abduction-psychological aspects

2. *Do a keyword search.* Sometimes you can also find the authorized terms by doing a keyword search in your library's database and looking at the results to see if the *LCSH* or other preferred vocabulary is listed in one of the relevant results.

Developing Working Knowledge

11.3

Apply research strategies for developing "working knowledge" and "focused knowledge" on your topic.

Every day we make decisions about how much we need to know about something. Twenty-five years ago, I decided I wanted to know enough to tune up my car, which I did badly. Later, I decided I wasn't interested in keeping up with the changes in electronic ignitions and fuel injection, so now I leave car repair to Davey at State Street Auto. A scholar is someone who, like Davey, has committed his or her professional life to keeping up with the knowledge in his or her field. College professors possess *expert knowledge* of their disciplines. In a way, we are all experts on at least one thing: ourselves. Five hundred years ago, the French philosopher Michel de Montaigne argued that it is most important to be a "scholar of the self." Having this expertise can help us in writing insightful personal essays. But if our research projects lead us into unfamiliar territory—and inquiry projects almost always do—then we need to know something about our subjects. But how much?

How much we need to know about a subject is, in part, a personal choice, but a college education does at least two things: It challenges you to develop new knowledge about things that will make you a better citizen and a more productive professional; and it teaches you *how* to better acquire the new knowledge that you might seek by choice. A research project is driven by both goals—you'll be challenged to go beyond superficial knowledge about a meaningful topic, and you'll learn some of the methods for doing that.

You will not end up a scholar on anorexia, college dating, the medical effects of music, or whatever topic you're researching. But you will go way beyond superficial knowledge of your subject; and when you do, it will be like opening a door and entering a crowded room of intelligent strangers, all deep in conversation about your topic. At first, you simply listen in before you speak, and that process begins with a *working knowledge*.

All of us know how to develop a working knowledge of something, especially when we need to. For example, I recently developed a working knowledge of podcasting software for a course I was teaching. Now I can knowledgeably talk, for a few minutes without repeating myself, about how to use Audacity to edit digital recordings. An audio expert would be unimpressed, but someone unfamiliar with the software might find it informative. As a researcher, you've got to know enough about your topic in order to come up with a strong research question, and this begins with two simple questions:

1. What is known about my topic? (Question of fact)

2. What *is* it? (Question of definition)

Exploring the answers to these questions will give you some essential background on your topic (see Figure 11.4), and this background will help you develop a more focused and interesting research question.

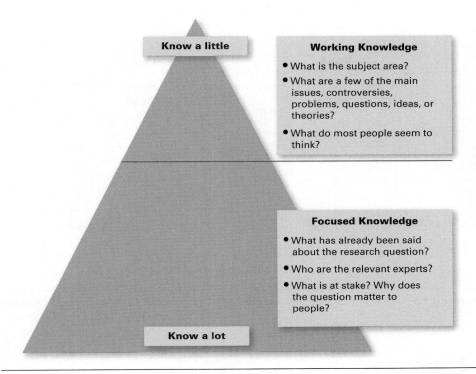

Know a little

Working Knowledge

- What is the subject area?
- What are a few of the main issues, controversies, problems, questions, ideas, or theories?
- What do most people seem to think?

Focused Knowledge

- What has already been said about the research question?
- Who are the relevant experts?
- What is at stake? Why does the question matter to people?

Know a lot

Figure 11.4 Working and focused knowledge. Inquiry projects often encourage you to choose a research topic you don't know much about. But you must quickly develop at least a *working knowledge* in order to come up with a good question. Guided by that question, you'll later develop a more *focused knowledge* of your topic and then discover what you have to say about it.

A Strategy for Developing Working Knowledge

It's hard to beat using the Internet as a quick-and-dirty way to develop working knowledge about nearly any topic. But the library can play an important role, too. Combine the two to develop a good working knowledge of your topic, efficiently. There are many ways to do this, but Figure 11.5 shows a sequence of research steps I recommend, and Figure 11.6 includes examples of specific sources.

Refine the Research Question. With a working knowledge of your topic, you're now ready to craft a stronger research question, which will guide your investigation over time and lead to some kind of judgment. It's hard to overstate how important this step is; a good question is the difference between a successful research project and one that flounders. (See pages 361–363 in Chapter 10 for advice on how to use your working knowledge to refine your research question.)

General Google Search

- Try out a range of search terms until you start getting relevant results.

Encyclopedias

- Not just Wikipedia, but also other general encyclopedias such as *Britannica*. Then check specialized encyclopedias (see list below).

Google Scholar

- Check to see what academic experts are saying about your topic.

Figure 11.5   A recommended sequence of research steps for developing working knowledge

Source	Examples
General Encyclopedias	Encyclopedia.com, Columbia Encyclopedia, Wikipedia, Oxford Reference, Encyclopedia Britannica
Specialized Encyclopedias	Encyclopedia of Psychology, Encyclopedia of World Art, Encyclopedia of Sociology, Encyclopedia of the Environment, Encyclopedia of Women and Sports, Encyclopedia of African American Culture and History, Encyclopedia of Democracy, Encyclopedia of Science and Technology, Encyclopedia of Children, Adolescents, and the Media
Google (or other search engines)	Google, Mamma, Dogpile
Google Scholar	Google Scholar

Figure 11.6   Examples of sources that will help you develop a working knowledge of your topic

Now is also a good time to begin building a "working bibliography." (See the "Inquiring into the Details: The Working Bibliography" feature on page 398 for tips on how to do that.)

Developing Focused Knowledge

If working knowledge equips you to sustain a one-minute monologue on your topic, then focused knowledge is enough for you to make a fifteen-minute presentation to your class and to answer most of their questions. Knowing this much doesn't make you an expert, but it does make you far more informed than most people on your topic. Focused knowledge grows from a well-crafted research question, one that isn't too general and allows you to *ignore* information that isn't relevant. With focused knowledge, you should be able to answer some of the following questions about your topic.

- Who are key people who have influenced the published conversation on your topic? (Example: *Among the key advocates for the current playoff system in college football were longtime Penn State coach Joe Paterno and President Barack Obama.*)

- What has already been said about the topic? Up until now, what were the major themes of the conversation? (Example: *Among the original arguments against a playoff system was that student-athletes would miss too much class. Others added that such a system would lead to the "NFL-ization" of college football, extending the season and compounding the academic problems of student-athletes, who already spend as many as forty hours a week on football.*)

- What is at stake for people? Why is the research question significant? (Example: *Thousands of student-athletes in the United States are wedged between two conflicting goals for college football: the public hunger for big-time entertainment and the athletes' desire to complete a degree.*)

Library Research: A Strategy for Developing Focused Knowledge

While the web is an intoxicating source of information, academic research still fundamentally depends on library work. Much of this work you can do online. Libraries offer database indexes to magazines, journals, and books that are accessible from your computer at home or at school, and in some cases you can retrieve and print out full-text articles.

But there are still reasons to walk into the university library. Here are six:

1. That's where the books are.
2. Some of the best articles on your topic aren't available as full-text PDFs.
3. Browsing the stacks in your topic's subject area will lead you to books you won't find any other way.
4. You can read current periodicals not yet online.
5. The reference room has books and other resources that aren't available anywhere else.
6. Reference librarians are irreplaceable.

So, you'll want to go to the library—online and on foot—but you won't want to waste your time there. The two best ways to avoid wasting time are to have a good research question, one that will allow you to focus your efforts, and to have a handful of good search terms to try. Don't forget to use "controlled language searches," or searches that use the terms librarians have chosen to organize access to materials on every subject (see pp. 388–389). As you recall, you discover these terms in the *Library of Congress Subject Headings*. Find this online (search for "Library of Congress Authorities") or look for bound copies in the library, which librarians often call the "big red books."

Where should you begin? When you developed working knowledge, you started with more-general sources such as encyclopedias and then shifted to more-specialized sources such as Google Scholar, trying to dive down a little ways into your subject. Now it's time to dive more deeply. For focused knowledge, you can start anywhere—really—especially because you've already got some background knowledge on your research question. The key is to cover a lot of ground.

Searching For Books. Every library has an online index for books (also available at computers in the library, naturally), and by using the right search terms, you'll get an instantaneous list of relevant books on your topic and their "call numbers," which will help you find them in the stacks. Your results will also tell you if the book is checked out, missing, or unavailable at your college library. If any of these apply to a book you're really hankering for, don't despair. You've got several options:

- *Recall.* Make an online request that the book be returned (usually in a few weeks) by the person who has checked it out.

- *Interlibrary loan.* This is a wonderful, underutilized service, often provided by campus libraries at no charge to students. You can request, usually online, a call-out to a large network of university libraries for the book (or article) you need. It is then delivered to you, sometimes within days.

- *Check another library.* If your campus library doesn't have it, check the community library's index online.

The book search form on your university's website, like most search portals, has simple and advanced options. The advanced page is pretty cool because it makes it easy to do a Boolean search on your topic. You can also put "limiters" on the terms, allowing you to control the results for things such as author, title, date, and so on. Learning to use the Advanced Search will really pay off after enduring the initial, brief learning curve.

Searching For Periodicals and Newspapers. It's hard to imagine a research question or topic that isn't covered by periodicals. You'll also want to check those databases, which are organized into four broad categories:

1. General subject databases, or indexes to periodicals across disciplines.
2. Specialized databases, or indexes that are discipline-specific.
3. Genre-specific databases such as Newspaper Source.
4. Government document databases.

Quite often, general subject databases include periodicals that may not be considered scholarly, including magazines such as *Discover, Newsweek*, and *Psychology Today*. These databases are a good place to start. To drill down further, use specialized databases, which are much more likely to produce the most interesting results on your research question because they are written by specialists in the fields of interest. They will also produce articles that can be a chore to understand if you don't know the jargon. That's when your working knowledge of your topic will really pay off. Also consider databases that warehouse certain types of content—plays, government documents, dissertations, and so on. You can see examples of all of these databases in Figure 11.7.

Database Type	Examples
Interdisciplinary/general subject databases	Academic Search Premier, Academic One File, JSTOR, ArticleFirst, Project Muse, MasterFILE Premier, WorldCat, Web of Science, ProQuest Central
Discipline-specific databases	ABI/INFORM (business), AnthroSource, America: History and Life, ArtSTOR, Applied Science and Technology, Biography Index, BioOne, Communication and Mass Media, ERIC (education), Health Reference Center, MLA Bibliography (languages and literature), Philosopher's Index, PsycINFO, Sociological Abstracts, Worldwide Political Science Abstracts
Genre-specific databases	National Newspaper Index, Newspaper Source, New York Times Index, Dissertation Abstracts International, Book Review Digest, Literature Criticism Online, Play Index
Government documents	Fed in Print, GPO Monthly Catalog, LexisNexis Government Periodicals Index

Search Type	Examples
General search engines	Google, Ask, Yahoo!, Bing
Metasearch engines	Dogpile, Clusty, SurfWax, Mamma
Subject directories	Yahoo!, About.com, Google, botw.org
Academic search engines or directories	Google Scholar, www.academicindex.net
Search engines for particular content	Yahoo Video Search, Google Books, Google Blogs, Google Images, www.newslink.org, www.internetarchive.org (audio, video, education, etc.), www.usa.org (federal government)

Figure 11.7   Database types and search types

Web Research: A Strategy for Developing Focused Knowledge

Web research for inquiry projects should be motivated by the following principles:

1. Maximize coverage.
2. Maximize relevant results.
3. Find stable sources.
4. Find quality sources.

Later in this chapter, I'll elaborate on what I mean by stable, quality sources, but examples would include: web pages and documents with .edu, .gov, or .org domains; those that are routinely updated; and those that might include a bibliography of references that document claims.

On the other hand, depending on your topic, you might seek a range of types of sources. For instance, suppose you're writing about green design and a blog from an architect in Texas has an interesting proposal for using turbines powered by passing cars on a highway in Austin. The proposal is interesting, and other sites refer to the blogger's idea. While this isn't a conventional academic source, the architect's blog is certainly a relevant and useful one for your essay.

Consider other types of online content as well: images, video, podcasts, discussion boards, and so on. For example, iTunes includes iTunesU, a remarkable collection of lectures, interviews, and video clips on a range of subjects, uploaded from universities around the United States.

The challenge is to find this stuff. Though Google is the dominant player in everyday research, Google is just the beginning, and good academic researchers shouldn't limit themselves to a single search service. Try some of the alternative search portals or directories listed in Figure 11.7.

Advanced Internet Research Techniques. In a previous section, you saw how to use some advanced search techniques on Google. Don't forget to use these techniques as you probe more deeply for sources relating to your research question. There are also a few other things you should try, and one of the most productive might be to use multiple search tools. Google is only one of many search portals, and there's evidence that using several search engines *will* produce unique results. In addition, there are "metasearch" tools that search multiple services at once. It's worth your time to try some of these tools. Here are a few suggestions:

Search Engines	**Metasearch Engines**
▪ Ask	▪ Dogpile
▪ Bing	▪ Mamma
▪ Hotbot	▪ SurfWax
▪ Lycos	
▪ Yahoo! Search	

Finally, you might also try using some specialized search tools (sometimes called "vertical" search engines) that focus on particular topics and kinds of content. Google Scholar is one of these tools. To find more, visit Noodletools and click on "Choose the Best Search."

Evaluating Library Sources

One of the huge advantages of finding what you need at the campus library is that nearly everything there was chosen by librarians whose job it is to make good information available to academic researchers. Now that many of the university library's databases are available online, including those of full-text articles, there really is no excuse for deciding to exclusively use the web pages you downloaded from the Internet as sources for your essays.

11.4

Use a method to analyze and evaluate research sources.

In general, the more specialized the audience for a publication, the more authoritatively scholars view the publication's content. Academic journals are at the bottom of this inverted pyramid because they represent the latest thinking and knowledge in a discipline, and most of the articles are reviewed by specialists in the field before they are published. At the top of the inverted pyramid are general encyclopedias and general-interest magazines such as *Newsweek* and *Time*. These have broader audiences and feature articles that are written by nonspecialists. They are rarely peer-reviewed. As a rule, then, the lower you draw from the inverted pyramid, the more authoritative the sources are from an academic point of view. Here are some other guidelines to consider:

- *Choose more-recent sources over older ones.* This is particularly good advice, obviously, if your subject is topical; the social and natural sciences also put much more emphasis on the currency of sources than do humanities disciplines.

- *Look for often-cited authors.* Once you've developed a working knowledge of your topic, you'll start noticing that certain authors seem to be mentioned or cited fairly frequently. These are likely to be the most listened-to authors, and may also be considered the most authoritative on your topic.

- *If possible, use primary sources over secondary sources.* In literary research, primary sources are the original words of writers—their speeches, stories, novels, poems, memoirs, letters, interviews, and eyewitness accounts. Secondary sources are articles that discuss those works. Primary sources in other fields might be original studies or experiments, firsthand newspaper accounts, marketing information, and so on.

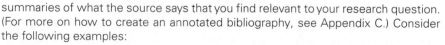

Inquiring into the Details

The Working Bibliography

A working bibliography lists sources you've collected that you think will be helpful when you draft your essay. These may include annotations or brief summaries of what the source says that you find relevant to your research question. (For more on how to create an annotated bibliography, see Appendix C.) Consider the following examples:

TOPIC: RELATIONAL AGGRESSION

PRINT SOURCES

Simmons, Rachel. *Odd Girl Out: The Hidden Culture of Aggression in Girls*. New York: Harcourt, 2002.

　　Simmons argues that the "secret world of girls' aggression"—the backstabbing, the silent treatment, the bartering of friendship for compliance to a group's "rules"—can be just as bad as the less subtle aggression of boys. Her basic thesis is that girls in American culture are supposed to be "nice" and therefore have no outlet for their anger except for exploiting the one thing they do covet: relationships. Because my essay focuses on the popularity phenomenon in high school—How does it affect girls when they become adults?—Simmons's chapter on parents of these girls seems particularly useful because it shows how the parents' responses are often shaped by their own experiences in school.

WEB SOURCES

"What Is Relational Aggression?" *The Ophelia Project*. 22 Sept. 2003 http://www.opheliaproject.org/issues/issuesRA.shtml.

　　The page defines relational aggression by contrasting it with physical aggression. It argues that most research, naturally, has focused on the latter because of the need to limit physical injury between children. But girls tend to avoid physical aggression and instead indulge in actions that harm others by disrupting their social relationships, like giving someone the silent treatment. The Ophelia Project is a nonprofit group created in 1997 by parents who wanted to address the problem.

Evaluating Web Sources

One of the more amusing sites on the web is titled "Feline Reactions to Bearded Men." At first glance, the site appears to be a serious academic study of the physiological responses of cats—heartbeat, respiration, and pupil dilation—to a series of photographs of men with beards (see Figure 11.8). The researchers are listed with their affiliations to respected universities. The article also includes an abstract, a methodology, and a results section, as well as a lengthy list of works cited.

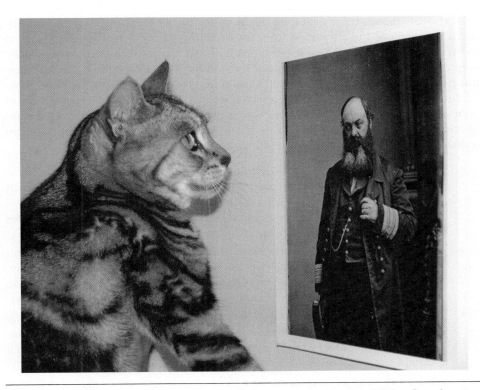

Figure 11.8   A cat reacts to a picture of a bearded man from the study "Feline Reactions to Bearded Men."

The conclusions seem genuine and include the following:

1. Cats do not like men with long beards, especially long dark beards.
2. Cats are indifferent to men with shorter beards.
3. Cats are confused and/or disturbed by men with beards that are incomplete and, to a lesser degree, by men whose beards have missing parts.

In reality, the study is a hoax, a fact that is pretty obvious to anyone who critically examines it. For one thing, it was "published" in the *Annals of Improbable Research*, but I can usually fool about a third of my class into believing it's legitimate for five to ten minutes as I discuss the conventions of academic research, some of which are accurately reproduced in the "study."

Everyone knows to be skeptical of what's on the web. But skepticism is even more crucial when using web sources for college writing. Because it's dominated by commercial sites, much of the World Wide Web has limited usefulness to the academic researcher; and although very few online authors are out to fool researchers with fake scholarship, many have a persuasive purpose. Despite its "educational" mission, for example, the purpose of the Consumer Freedom website is to promote industry views on laws relating to food and beverages. That doesn't make the information it offers useless, but a careful researcher would be wary of the site's claims and critical of its studies. At the very least, the information provided by Consumer Freedom should be attributed as a proindustry view.

Imagine, as you're researching on the web, that you've been dropped off at night in an unfamiliar neighborhood. You're alert. You're vigilant. And you're careful about whom you ask for directions. You can also be systematic about how you evaluate online sources. In general, follow these principles:

- *Favor governmental and educational sources over commercial ones.* These sites are more likely to have unbiased information. How can you tell which sites are institutional when it's not obvious? Sometimes the domain name—the abbreviation *.edu, .org,* or *.gov* at the end of an Internet address—provides a strong clue, as does the absence of ads on the site.

- *Favor authored documents over those without authors.* There's a simple reason for this: You can check the credentials of authors if you know who they are. Sometimes sites provide e-mail links so you can write to authors, or you can do a search on the Internet or in the library for other materials they've published.

- *Favor documents that are also available in print over those available only online.* Material that is published in both forms generally undergoes more scrutiny. An obvious example is newspaper articles, but some articles from journals and magazines are also available electronically and in print.

- *Favor web sources that document their claims over those that don't.* This well-known academic convention is strong evidence that the claims an online author is making are supported and verifiable.

- *Favor web pages that have been recently updated over those that haven't changed in a year or more.* Frequently at the bottom of a web page there is a line indicating when the information was posted to the Internet and/or when it was last updated. Look for that line.

An Evaluation Checklist for Web Sources

1. **Relevance.** Is this web source relevant to my research question?
2. **Authors.** Are there any? If so, can I trust them? Are they recognized experts on the subject? Do they have a bias? Do they say sensible things? If there aren't authors, are there other things about the source that make it credible?
3. **Source.** What's the domain: .edu, .gov, .org? If it's a commercial site, is it still useful because of its author, content, or relevance?
4. **Verifiability.** Can you contact the authors? Is there a bibliography of references? Do other, credible sites refer to this one?
5. **Stability.** How long has the website been around, and how often is it updated?

Research with Living Sources:
Interviews, Surveys, and Fieldwork

Sometimes the best way to get information about something is to ask someone. Sometimes the best way to see what happens is to go out and look. And sometimes the best way to find out what people think or believe is to invite them to tell you. While we often assume that research means reading, much research also involves interviews, observations, and surveys. Consider whether your research project can benefit from collecting information from these sources (see Figure 11.9).

Interviews

Tethered as we are these days to the electronic world of the web and the increasingly digital university library, it's easy to forget an old-fashioned source for research: a living, breathing human being. People are often the best sources of information because you can have a real conversation rather than the imagined one simulated by the double-entry notebook. Some kinds of writing, such as the profile, fundamentally depend on interviews; with other genres, such as the personal essay or the research paper, interviews are one of several sources of information. But interviews can be central to bringing writing to life, because when we put people on the page, abstract ideas or arguments suddenly have a face and a voice. People on the page make ideas matter.

> Tethered as we are these days to the electronic world of the web and the increasingly digital university library, it's easy to forget an old-fashioned source for research: a living, breathing human being.

The face-to-face interview often yields much better material than the online interview, so we'll look at face-to-face interviews first. But we'll also consider the convenience and usefulness of online interviews.

Interviews
- Find a local expert
- Interview people affected by the problem

Field observations
- Photograph, record, and collect
- Observe and describe

Surveys
- Determine attitudes
- Collect comments
- Describe a population

Figure 11.9   Selecting a research method

Arranging Interviews. Whom do you interview? Basically, there are two kinds of interviews: (1) the kind in which the interviewee is the main subject of your piece, as in a profile; (2) the kind in which the interviewee is a source of information about another subject.

The interviewee as a source of information is the far more common type of interview, and it usually involves finding people who either are experts on the topic you're writing about or have been touched or influenced in some way by it. For example, Tina is writing a research essay on the day-care crisis in her community. Among those affected by this crisis are the parents of small children, their day-care teachers, and even the kids themselves; all are good candidates for interviews about the problem. The appropriate experts were a little more difficult to think of immediately. The day-care teachers might qualify—after all, they're professionals in the area—but Tina also learned of a faculty member in the College of Health and Social Sciences who specializes in policies related to child care. Interviewing both types of people—experts and those affected by the crisis—gives Tina a much richer perspective on the problem.

How do you find experts on your topic? Here are a few strategies for locating potential interviewees:

- *Check the faculty directory on your campus.* Many universities publish an annual directory, which may be online, of faculty and their research interests. In addition, your university's public information office might have a similar list of faculty and their areas of expertise.

- *Cull a name from an online discussion group.* Use a specialized search engine such as Google Groups to search by topic and find someone appropriate who might be willing to do an e-mail interview.

- *Ask your friends and instructors.* They might know faculty who have a research interest in your topic or someone in the community who is an expert on that topic.

- *Check the phone book.* The familiar *Yellow Pages* can be a gold mine. For example, want to find a biologist who might have something to say about the effort to bring back migrating salmon? Look in the phone book for the number of the regional office of the U.S. Fish and Wildlife Service and ask to speak to the public information officer. He or she may be able to help you find the right expert.

- *Check your sources.* As you begin to collect books, articles, and Internet documents, note their authors and affiliations. I get calls or e-mails from time to time from writers who came across my book on lobsters, posing questions I love to try to answer because no one else in Idaho gives a hoot about lobsters. Google searches of authors who are mentioned in your sources may produce e-mail addresses or websites with e-mail links that you might query.

- *Check the Encyclopedia of Associations.* This resource—another underused book and database in your university's reference room—lists organizations in the United States with concerns as varied as promoting tofu and saving salmon.

Conducting The Interview. The kinds of questions you ask fundamentally depend on what type of interview you're conducting. In a profile, your questions will focus on the interview subject (see Chapter 4). To some extent, this is also the focus of your questions when you interview nonexperts who are *affected* by the topic you're writing about. For example, Tina is certainly interested in what the parents of preschoolers *know* about the day-care crisis in her town, but she's also interested in the feelings and *experiences* of these people. Wanting to gather this kind of information leads to some of the questions you may have used in a profile, but with more focus on the subject's experience with your topic:

- What was your first experience with _____? What has most surprised you about it?
- How does _____ make you feel?
- Tell me about a moment that you consider most typical of your experience with _____.

More often, however, your motive in an interview will be to gather information. Obviously, this motive will prompt you to ask specific questions about your topic as you try to fill in gaps in your knowledge. But some more general, open-ended questions may also be useful to ask. For example:

- What is the most difficult aspect of your work?
- What do you think is the most significant popular misconception about _____?
- What are the significant current trends in _____?
- If you had to summarize the most important thing you've learned about _____, what would that be?
- What is the most important thing other people should know or understand?
- What do you consider the biggest problem with _____?
- Who has the power to do something about that problem?
- What is your prediction about the future? Ten years from now, what will this problem look like?

Once you have a list of questions in mind, be prepared to ignore them. Good interviews often take turns that you can't predict, and these journeys may lead you to information and understandings you didn't expect. After all, a good interview is like a good conversation: It may meander, speed up or slow down, and reveal things about your topic and your interview subject that you didn't expect to discover. But good interviewers also attempt to control an interview when the turns it's taking aren't useful. You do this through questions, of course, but also with more-subtle tactics. For example, if you stop taking notes, most interview subjects notice, and the astute ones quickly understand that what they're saying has less interest to you. A quick glance at your watch can have the same effect.

E-mail interviews produce a ready-made text with both your questions and the subject's answers. This is pretty wonderful. Live interviews, on the other hand, require more skill. It's thus usually a good idea to use a tape recorder (with your subject's permission), but not to rely exclusively on it, especially because machines can fail and batteries can expire unexpectedly. *Always take notes.* If nothing else, your notes will help you know where on the tape you should concentrate later, transcribing direct quotations or gathering information. Note taking during interviews is an acquired skill; the more you do it, the better you get, along the way inventing all sorts of shorthand for commonly occurring words. Practice taking notes while watching the evening news.

Most of all, try to enjoy your interview. After all, you and your interview subject have something important in common—an interest in your topic—and this usually produces an immediate bond that transforms an interview into an enjoyable conversation.

Using The Interview In Your Writing. Putting people on the page is one of the best ways to bring writing to life. This is exactly what information from interviews can do—give otherwise abstract questions or problems a voice and a face. One of the most common ways to use interview material is to integrate it into the lead or first paragraph of your essay. By focusing on someone involved in the research question or problem you're exploring, you immediately capture reader interest. For example, here's the beginning of a *Chronicle of Higher Education* essay titled "What Makes Teachers Great?"[2] Quite naturally, the writer chose to begin by profiling someone who happened to be a great teacher, using evidence from the interviews he conducted.

> When Ralph Lynn retired as a professor of history at Baylor University in 1974, dozens of his former students paid him tribute. One student, Ann Richards, who became the governor of Texas in 1991, wrote that Lynn's classes were like "magical tours into the great minds and movements of history." Another student, Hal Wingo, the editor of *People* magazine, concluded that Lynn offered the best argument he knew for human cloning. "Nothing would give me more hope for the future," the editor explained, "than to think that Ralph Lynn, in all his wisdom and wit, will be around educating new generations from here to eternity."

This is a strong way to begin an essay, because the larger idea—the qualities that make a great teacher—is then grounded in a name and a face. But information from interviews can be used anywhere in an essay—not just at the beginning—to make an idea come to life.

Information from interviews can also provide strong evidence for a point you're trying to make, especially if your interview subject has expertise on the topic. But interviews can also be a *source* of ideas about what you might want to say in your essay. The essay on great teaching, for instance, offers seven qualities that great teachers embrace in their classrooms—things such as "create a natural critical learning environment" and "help students learn outside of class." All of these claims grew from interviews with sixty professors in a range of disciplines.

---

[2]Ken Bain, "What Makes Teachers Great?" *Chronicle of Higher Education* (April 9, 2004): B7–B9.

The principal advantage of doing interviews is that you ask the questions that you're most interested in learning the answers to. Rather than sifting through other sources that may address your research questions briefly or indirectly, interviews generate information that is often relevant to and focused on the information needs of your essay. In other words, interviews are a source of data that can also be sources of theories or ideas on your topic. And this is often the best way to use interview material in your essay.

The Online Interview

My phone doesn't ring much anymore, but I hear the "ding" of incoming messages on my computer all day long. I hear from people by e-mail, text, and Facebook, and I mostly like staying in touch with people that way, at least until I get compulsive about checking for messages. Obviously, online contact with people is convenient, and it also opens up new possibilities for researchers who want to contact people for interviews.

Finding People Online. There are lots of ways to find people online, including these:

- *Through organizational affiliation.* If in your research you discover that a key researcher works at a particular university, agency, or business, then you can search the institution online and sometimes find an e-mail address for that researcher.
- *Through a web document.* It isn't unusual for a web document or page you're using in your research to include a contact link or even the e-mail addresses of the authors or other institutional contacts.
- *Through a search function.* This is the most obvious move. Google the name and institution of the person you want to interview, or search on Facebook.
- *Through discussion groups and listservs.* It's great if you have identified in your reading the name of someone you'd like to interview, but what about *locating* people who are involved in the topic you're researching? One way to do this is to find online discussion groups that focus on your topic. Say you were researching campus sustainability. A quick search on Yahoo! Groups will yield a list of online groups around the world that are interested in the same thing you are, and often people with the expertise or experiences you're looking for. Search online discussion groups by topic using one or more of the following portals:

  BoardReader (http://boardreader.com)
  BoardTracker (http://www.boardtracker.com)
  Google Groups (http://groups.google.com)
  Yahoo! Groups (http://groups.yahoo.com)

Contacting Someone for an Online Interview. Once you find the e-mail address of someone who seems like a good interview subject, proceed courteously and cautiously. One of the Internet's haunting issues is its potential to violate privacy. Be especially careful if you've gone to great lengths in hunting down the e-mail address of someone involved with your research topic; she may not be keen on receiving unsolicited e-mail messages from strangers. It would be courteous to approach any potential interview subject with a short message that asks permission to conduct an online interview. In this message, briefly describe your project and why you think she might be a good source. You will be much more likely to get an enthusiastic response to your request if you can demonstrate your knowledge of her work on or experience with your topic.

Let's assume your initial contact has been successful and your subject has agreed to answer your questions. Your follow-up message should ask a limited number of questions—say, four or five—that are thoughtful and, if possible, specific. Keep in mind that while the e-mail interview is conducted in writing rather than through talking, many of the methods for handling oral interviews still apply.

Surveys

The survey is a fixture in American life. We love surveys. What's the best economical laptop? Should the president be reelected? Who is the sexiest man alive? What movie should win Best Picture? Some of these are scientific surveys with carefully crafted questions, statistically significant sample sizes, and carefully chosen target audiences. In your writing class, you likely won't be conducting such formal research. More likely it will be like Mike's—fairly simple—and although not necessarily statistically reliable, your informal survey will likely be more convincing than anecdotal evidence or your personal observation, particularly if your survey is thoughtfully developed.

Defining a Survey's Goals and Audience. A survey is a useful source of information when you're making some kind of claim regarding "what people think" about something. Mike observed that his friends all seem to hate pennies, and he wanted to generalize from this anecdotal evidence to suggest that most people probably share that view. But do they? And which people are we really talking about? As we discussed this in his writing group, Mike pointed out that his grandfather grew up during the Great Depression and has a very different perspective on money than Mike does. "So your grandfather would probably pick up a penny in the parking lot, right?" I asked. "Probably," Mike said.

Quickly, Mike not only had a survey question but also began to think about qualifying his claim. Maybe younger adults—Mike's generation—in particular share this attitude about the lowly penny. To confirm this, Mike's survey had both a purpose (to collect information about how people view pennies) and an audience (students on his campus). If he had the time or inclination, Mike could conduct a broader survey that included older Americans, but for his purposes the quad survey would be enough.

Two Types of Survey Questions. There are typically two broad categories of survey questions: open ended and structured. Figure 11.10 shows the advantages and disadvantages of each for your survey.

Question Type	Examples	Advantage(s)	Disadvantage(s)
Open ended	Brief response, essay question	May get surprising answers. More insight into respondents' thoughts and ideas.	Take more time. Can't easily be measured.
Structured	Multiple choice, true/false, Likert, ranking	Easier to analyze responses. Don't take much time.	Must know enough to provide appropriate choices.

Figure 11.10   Question Types: Advantages and Disadvantages

Generally speaking, you should limit the number of open-ended questions you use since they are more demanding on the respondents. But don't hesitate to use them if you hope to open a window on the thinking of your survey audience. These responses might not reveal a pattern, but they often provide interesting anecdotal evidence you can use in your essay.

Crafting Survey Questions. To begin, you want to ask questions that your target audience can answer. Don't ask a question about a campus alcohol policy that most students in your target audience have never heard of. Second, keep the questions simple and easy to understand. This is crucial because most respondents resist overly long survey questions and won't answer confusing ones. Third, make sure the questions will produce the information you want. This is a particular hazard of open-ended questions. For example, a broad open-ended question such as "What do you think of the use of animals in the testing of cosmetics?" will probably produce a verbal shrug or an answer of "I don't know." A better question is more focused: "What do you think about the U.S. Food and Drug Administration's claim that animal testing by cosmetic companies is 'often necessary to provide product safety'?"

Such a question could be an open-ended or structured question, depending on the kind of responses you're seeking. Focusing the question also makes it more likely to generate information that will help you compose your essay on the adequacy of current regulations governing animal testing. Also note that the question doesn't necessarily betray the writer's position on the issue, which is essential—a good survey question isn't biased or "loaded." Imagine how a less neutral question might skew the results: "What do you think of the federal bureaucrats' position that animal testing for cosmetics is 'often necessary to provide product safety'?" An even more subtle bias might be introduced by using the term *federal government* rather than *Food and Drug Administration* in the original question. In my part of the world, the Rocky Mountain West, the federal government is generally not viewed favorably, no matter what the issue.

Keep the number of survey questions to a minimum. It shouldn't take respondents long—no more than a few minutes at most—to complete your survey, unless you're lucky enough to have as your respondents a captive audience such as a class.

Inquiring into the Details

Types of Survey Questions

These are a few of your options when deciding what type of questions to ask in a survey.

1. **Limited choice**

   Do you believe student fees should be used to support campus religious organizations?

   ____ Yes

   ____ No

   ____ I'm not sure

   At what point in the writing process do you usually get stuck?

   ____ Getting started

   ____ In the middle

   ____ Finishing

   ____ I never get stuck

   ____ Other: _____

2. **Scaled response (Likert)**

   The Student Film Board should show more foreign films.

   ____ Strongly agree

   ____ Agree

   ____ Neither agree nor disagree

   ____ Disagree

   ____ Strongly disagree

3. **Ranking**

   Which of the following do you consider important in designing a classroom to be conducive to learning? Rank them from 1 to 5, with the most important a 1 and the least important a 5.

Comfortable seating	
Natural light from windows	
Carpeting	
Effective soundproofing	
Dimmable lighting	

4. **Open ended**

   Describe three things you learned in this course.

   What steps do you think the university should take to increase attendance at women's soccer games?

Finally, consider beginning your survey with background questions that establish the identity of each respondent. Typical information you might collect includes the gender and age or, with student-oriented surveys, the class ranking of the respondent. Depending on your topic, you might be interested in particular demographic facts, such as whether someone has children or comes from a particular part of the state. All of these questions can help you sort and analyze your results.

Conducting a Survey: Paper or Electronic?   After you mull over the purpose of your survey, you need to decide whether you'll distribute it electronically or on paper. These days, free online software like the popular SurveyMonkey allows users to easily create basic digital surveys. You can distribute the survey to a targeted list of recipients by e-mail or by posting it on a blog, website, or even social media like Facebook and Twitter. In addition, a program like SurveyMonkey helps you analyze the results and filter, compare, and summarize the data with charts and graphs. Web-based surveys are also cheaper than paper surveys. Why wouldn't you want to go digital instead of using old-fashioned paper surveys? A couple of reasons:

- With paper, you can target an audience much more easily, particularly if you can locate those potential respondents in a specific time or place. For example, if you want to survey your school's football fans, distributing your survey on game day at the tailgate party will give you direct access to your survey audience.
- Not everyone has easy Internet access.
- The free versions of the online software may limit the number of responses you can gather.
- Response rates to electronic surveys can be lower than response rates to paper surveys.

Despite these drawbacks, a web-based survey is often the best choice for an undergraduate research project, particularly if you can find ways to target your audience, make a personal appeal for a response, and send out a reminder or two.

Testing the Survey.   Whether you're using an online or a paper survey, *if you can, test it first.* Invariably, this testing turns up problems: A survey is too long, a question is poorly worded, the response rate to a particular question is low, and so on. You won't be able to test your draft survey nearly as thoroughly as the experts do, but you also shouldn't put your faith in an untested survey. Instead, ask as many people as you can to try it out and describe their experience answering your questions. Was there any confusion? How long did it take? Don't forget to also ask yourself whether the survey is generating relevant information.

Finding the Target Audience.   Once you're confident in the design of your survey, plan how you'll distribute it. There are several options:

1. *If paper, distribute it in an appropriate location.* Begin by asking yourself whether your target audience tends to gather in a particular location. For example, if you're surveying sports fans, then surveying people by the main gate at the football stadium on Saturday might work. If your target audience is first-year

college students and your university requires freshman English composition, then surveying one or more of those classes would be a convenient way to reach that audience. In some situations, you can leave your survey forms in a location that might garner responses from your target audience. For example, a student at my university wanted to survey people about which foothill's hiking trails they liked best, so she left an envelope with the forms and a pencil at several trailheads.

2. *If online, find appropriate sites.* You can reach respondents online in the following ways:
   - E-mail
   - Social media like Facebook or Twitter
   - Listservs, discussion groups
   - Posting a survey link on a blog or web page

Using Survey Results in Your Writing. The best thing about conducting an informal survey is that you're producing original and interesting information about your topic's local relevance. This kind of information can be an impressive element of your essay and will certainly make it more interesting.

Because analysis of open-ended questions can be time consuming and complicated, consider the simplest approach: As you go through the surveys, note which responses are worth quoting in your essay because they seem representative. Perhaps the responses are among the most commonly voiced in the entire sample, or perhaps they are expressed in significant numbers by a particular group of respondents.

In a more detailed analysis, you might try to nail down more specifically the *patterns* of responses. For example, perhaps you initially can divide the survey results into two categories: people who disagree with the university's general education requirements and those who agree with them, Group 1 and Group 2. The next step might be to further analyze each of these groups, looking for patterns. In particular, pay attention to responses you didn't expect, responses that might enlarge your perspective about what people think about your topic.

Your analysis of the responses to direct questions will usually be pretty simple—probably a breakdown of percentages. In a more sophisticated analysis, you might try to break the sample down, if it's large enough, into certain categories of respondents—men and women, class ranking, those with high or low test scores, and so on—and then see if any response patterns correlate to these categories. For example, perhaps a much higher percentage of sampled freshmen than seniors agreed that a good job is the most important reason to go to college.

What might this difference mean? Is it important? How does it influence your thinking about your topic, or how does it affect your argument? Each of these questions involves interpretation of the results, and sample size is the factor that most influences the credibility of survey evidence.

Fieldwork: Research on What You See and Hear

In many disciplines, field observations are at the heart of research. You might remember, for example, that the ethnographic essay in Chapter 9 is focused on describing how human cultures operate in natural settings. Field research is essential for this kind of essay. There are a lot of inquiry projects that might benefit from direct observation and description, especially if you're researching something that has a local angle and there might be something relevant to learn. Would your essay on farmer's markets, for instance, benefit from listening to and observing people at the Saturday market downtown?

There are two kinds of fieldwork:

1. *Participant observation.* You are involved as an active participant in the thing you're researching.

2. *Direct observation.* You unobtrusively observe the settings or phenomena.

Because you're not doing formal scholarship for this project, whichever method you use as your approach will probably be informal rather than carefully planned and methodologically strict. What you *are* trying to do that is common to all fieldwork is look for patterns in what you see. In particular, you might want to describe what is either *typical* (e.g., a common behavior, complaint, attitude, problem, etc.) or *exceptional* (e.g., significant differences, nonconformance, unusual circumstances, etc.). Remember, too, that you're not limited to recording these observations with a notebook and pen alone. You might also digitally record, videotape, and photograph the things you see for analysis later.

The Ethics of Fieldwork.   Because fieldwork often involves research on people, you should always be careful to protect the privacy and wishes of your subjects. For a relatively informal project such as this one—something that isn't likely to be published—there are fewer ethical concerns, but there are some principles that should guide you. The least complicated ethical situation is direct observation in a public setting. In this case, you don't need an invitation from anyone to observe unless you directly approach the people you're observing. Sometimes, though, especially when you're a participant-observer, you'll be actively seeking permission to watch, record, and interview. How should you handle those situations?

- Make your study subjects aware of the purpose of your project.
- Preserve the anonymity of the people you observe unless they give you permission to use their names.

Note-Taking Strategies.   Write down and document in detail what you see and hear. This includes descriptions of behaviors, activities, settings, conversations, and people's movements, etc. This is the raw data you'll analyze for patterns. In addition to looking for things that seem "typical" and "exceptional," consider the following frames for analysis:

- What evidence confirms, contradicts, or qualifies the theories and claims you've read about in your research?
- What do people do or say during moments of particular significance?
- What "artifacts" seem important? What things do people use?
- *How* do the people you observe talk about themselves or the activity they are participating in?

Using Field Research in Your Writing. The observations and descriptions you gather from the field can be powerful additions to your research project. For example,

- *Give your topic a face.* Use a description of an individual who is affected by the problem you're writing about, as a way to dramatize the problem's impact.
- *Make a scene.* Help your readers *see* what you're writing about.
- *Incorporate images.* Even a written research essay can benefit from pictures, which can be included in the text and analyzed.
- *Develop a multimodal essay.* Might your research project be transformed into an audio documentary or a video podcast? Could you create an online slide show?

Writing in the Middle: Note-Taking Techniques

11.5

Understand and apply new note-taking strategies that will help you analyze sources while you're researching.

Like most students, when I wrote undergraduate research papers I never did any writing until the end—usually late at night with all of my sources fanned out across my desk like cards at a blackjack table. I'm going to propose an alternative scenario that will work much better, and it looks something like this: It's not the night before but *weeks* before the paper is due, and I'm writing like mad in my notebook *as* I'm reading an article. I'm not exactly writing my paper—instead, I'm using writing to think about what I'm reading, to understand the source, and to *converse* with it.

Throughout *The Curious Writer*, I've promoted what's termed "dialectical thinking"—moving back and forth between suspending judgments and making judgments—and this method is particularly useful when writing about what you read. One way to do this as you research is to use the "double-entry journal."

Whatever method you use for "writing in the middle," these actions are key:

1. You write as—or immediately after—you read something that's relevant to your project.

2. You use the writing to talk to yourself and *to the source* about what you understand it to be saying, what you find particularly interesting, how you might agree or disagree, and what questions the source raises.

3. You carefully jot down bibliographic information so you can build your list of references as you research.

The double-entry journal makes a great research notebook. On the left-facing page, you collect passages, ideas, statistics, summaries, and so on from the source, and on the right-facing page, you explore what you make of what you've collected. You can do this in a paper notebook or in a Word document using columns. In the section that follows, you can see how the double-entry journal might work for you.

Double-Entry Journal

In the sample double-entry journal in Figure 11.11, notice how the writer collects material in the left column and then explores in the right column, looking left whenever the writing stalls to find traction on something else in from the source.

Page	Source Notes	First Thoughts
140	"Carl Sagan suggested that the 'pay dirt' of space alien abduction accounts is not in what they might tell us about alien visitation but in what they might tell us about ourselves."	Really interesting article that summarizes the research, as of 1996, on alien abduction memories. Point seems to be the ways in which these don't necessarily tell us anything about aliens but a lot about ourselves. But what? I think the evidence here suggests that it isn't necessarily some kind of psychiatric problem, but how vulnerable we are to suggestion. The stop sign case, for example. Even when the visual clearly has a yield not a stop sign, the mere suggestion it's a stop sign made people confidently believe it. But maybe the most interesting thing here to me is the dynamic of having a memory of something that is challenged, which is a kind of threat, and as a result we believe even a false memory more strongly. We believe what we want to believe and then actively seek out information that reinforces it, particularly in the face of challenge.
141	"the misinformation effect" Describes "classic experiment" to demonstrate this: a pedestrian accident in which slide shows yield sign but respondents "subtly" told was stop sign. Majority claimed stop sign was there with "high degree of confidence."	
142	"... humans can cook up false memories ..." But why aliens? ✓ variety of sources in popular culture of "true" abduction stories ✓ most reported under hypnosis, and this makes it seem more "real" to the abductee because it evokes "strong visual imagery" ✓ when belief is challenged, holder of belief clings to it more strongly ✓ reinforced by other "support groups" of believers	The thing about hypnosis being the source of most abduction reports, and how this might deepen an abductee's belief in it, is also something I need to look into more.
	Clark, Steven E. and Elizabeth F. Loftus. "The Construction of Alien Abduction Memories." *Psychological Inquiry* 7.2 (1996): 140–143. Print.	

Figure 11.11 A sample double-entry journal

Research Log

Another method of note taking that exploits dialectical thinking is the research log. Rather than using opposing pages, you'll layer your notes and responses, one after another. This is a particularly useful method for those who prefer to compose with a keyboard rather than a pencil. Here's how it works:

1. Begin by taking down the full bibliographic information on the source, something you may already have in your working bibliography.

2. Read the article, book chapter, or web page, marking up your personal copy as you typically do, perhaps underlining key facts or ideas or information relevant to your research question.

3. Your first entry in your notebook or on the computer will be a fastwrite, an open-ended response to the reading under the heading What Strikes Me Most. As the title implies, you're dealing with first thoughts here.

4. Next, take notes on the source, jotting down summaries, paraphrases, quotations, and key facts. Title this section Source Notes.

5. Finally, follow up with another episode of fastwriting. Title this The Source Reconsidered. This is a *more focused* look at the source; fastwrite about what stands out in the notes you took. Which facts, findings, claims, or arguments shape your thinking now?

One Student's Response

Claude's Research Log

SOURCE

Letawsky, Nicole R., et al. "Factors Influencing the College Selection Process of Student Athletes." *College Student Journal* 37.4 (2003): 604–11. *Academic Search Premier.* EBSCOhost Databases. Albertson's Lib. 5 Apr. 2004.

WHAT STRIKES ME MOST

Really interesting article that studied about 130 student-athletes at a large 1-A university. Noted that there have been a lot of research studies on why students choose a particular school but not so much on why student-athletes choose a school. Everyone assumes, of course, that student-athletes go somewhere because they're wined and dined and promised national TV exposure. In other words, it all has to do with the glamour of playing 1-A, particularly the so-called revenue sports like basketball and football. But this study had some surprising findings. They found that the number one reason that student-athletes chose a school was the degree options it offers. In other words, the reasons student-athletes choose a school aren't that much different than the reason regular students choose one. The study also found that the glamour stuff—getting awards, getting on TV, and future professional

One Student's Response (*continued*)

possibilities—mattered the least to the student-athletes. This study challenges some of the myths about student recruiting, and should be read by recruiters especially. If you want to get a blue-ribbon player at your school, tell him or her about the academic opportunities there.

SOURCE NOTES (CUT AND PASTED FROM ELECTRONIC VERSION)

"This study found that the most important factor for student-athletes was the degree program options offered by the University. Other important factors were the head coach, academic support services, type of community in which the campus is located, and the school's sports traditions. Two of the top three factors were specifically related to the academic rather than athletic environment. This is a key finding and should be understood as recruiting efforts should be broad based, balancing academics and athletics if they are to be effective."

"A somewhat surprising result of the study concerned relatively low ratings associated with factors considered essential to 'Big-Time College Sports.' Television exposure, perceived opportunity to play immediately, and perceived future professional sporting opportunities were among the lowest-ranked factors. Furthermore, the participants rated athletic rewards (a 5-item survey scale containing these and other reward items) consistently lower than both the campus and athletic environment. These results may be due to the fact that respondents were from each of the sports offered by the University. Many of the sports (e.g., swimming, track), although funded and supported similar to the other sports, do not receive the national attention, large crowds, and television exposure."

THE SOURCE RECONSIDERED

This article did more than anything I've read so far to make me question my thesis that big-time college sports recruiting is way out of control. It's pretty convincing on the point that athletes care about the academic programs when they're choosing a school. But then the second quotation has an interesting part that I just noticed. This study surveyed athletes in all sports, not just the big-time sports like football and basketball at the university where the study was conducted. It seems to me that that would really skew the findings because someone participating in a sport like tennis that doesn't get a lot of attention and doesn't necessarily lead to professional opportunities after school *would* be more interested in academics. They're not dreaming of making a name for themselves, but getting a scholarship to pay for school. Seems like a better study would focus on the big-time sports....

Using What You Have Learned

Let's return briefly to the learning outcomes listed at the beginning of the chapter.

1. **Identify the "research routines" you've typically used, and practice new ones appropriate to college-level research.** Since the beginning of *The Curious Writer*, I've encouraged you to look at the habits you use, often without thinking, to read and write. You have "research routines," too, often learned in high school; while some of these routines might still serve you well, many may not, particularly in college. This "unlearning" is an essential part of developing your abilities, not just in academic tasks, but also in anything you want to do that is guided by habits you rarely examine.

2. **Refine and improve the effectiveness of search terms.** This is a skill that will not only help make your academic research more efficient, but will aid you with everyday research as well. And the ability to refine search terms will become even more important as the amount of information continues to expand on the web and in library databases.

3. **Apply research strategies for developing "working knowledge" and "focused knowledge" on your topic.** I've tried to encourage you to look at any research project as a developmental process, one in which how much knowledge you have about a topic will determine how effectively you can write about it. If you don't know much about it, which is often the case in an inquiry-based class, then you need to quickly learn enough to come up with a strong research question. From there, you can mine more deeply into your topic, developing "focused" knowledge with more-advanced research strategies. This is a process you can use for nearly any research project.

4. **Use a method to analyze and evaluate research sources.** There are a lot of methods for doing this, and in this chapter you learned just one. But the key is that you actually *use* a method, one that will consistently help you to find credible sources. As we do more and more research online, it's hard to overstate what an essential skill such a method is.

5. **Understand and apply new note-taking strategies that will help you analyze sources while you're researching.** The double-entry journal and research log are two systems for note taking that I recommend here, but the important thing is that you do some writing *as* you do your research. This is likely a major break with your research routine, but it will make a huge difference because it will help you to think about what you're reading and begin to build your essay. This is yet another application of the "bad" writing—exploratory, open-ended fastwriting—that you learned to use in previous assignments.

12

Using and Citing Sources

Learning Objectives

In this chapter, you'll learn to

12.1 Use sources effectively and control sources so they don't control you.

12.2 Practice summarizing, paraphrasing, and quoting and apply these to your own work.

12.3 Understand and identify plagiarism to avoid it in your own work.

12.4 Cite sources using MLA and APA documentation styles.

Controlling Information

The first college paper that really meant something to me was an essay on whaling industry practices and their impacts on populations of humpback and sperm whales. Writing from the place of itchy curiosity and strong feelings is a wonderful thing. It will motivate you to read and learn about your topic, and when it comes to writing the draft, you might find that you have little trouble enlisting the voices of your sources to make your point. More often, however, you've chosen a topic because you don't know what you think or feel about it—the inquiry-based approach—or you've been assigned a general topic that reflects the content of a course you're taking. In these cases, writing with sources is like crashing a party of strangers that has been going on for a long time. You shyly listen in, trying to figure out what everyone is talking about, and look for an opening to enter the conversation. Mostly you just feel intimidated, so you hang back feeling foolish.

This kind of writing situation is really a matter of control. Will you control the outside sources in your research essay, or will they control you? Will you enter the conversation and make a contribution to it, or will you let others do all the talking? The easiest way to lose control is simply to turn long stretches of your paper over to a source, usually one with long quotations. I've seen a quotation from a single source run more than a full page in some drafts. Another way to lose control is to do what one of my colleagues calls a "data dump." Fill the truck with a heavy load of information, back it up to the paper, and dump in as much as you can, without analysis, without carefully selecting what is relevant and what isn't, without much thought at all. The writer in this situation sees his or her essay as a hole that must be filled with information.

> When you introduce a voice other than your own, make it clear what this new voice adds to the conversation you have going about your topic.

Using and Synthesizing Sources

The appropriate use of sources is also a matter of control. Writers who put research information to work for them see outside sources as serving a clear purpose. There are at least five of these purposes:

12.1
Use sources effectively and control sources so they don't control you.

Purpose	Description
Support a claim or idea	The motive we usually imagine for using information in academic writing.
Provide background	What does your audience need to know about your topic to understand why your inquiry question is significant?
Answer a question	Periodically asking relevant questions—and answering them with information from research—creates a structure built on reasoning.
Complicate things	This is the most counterintuitive use of information. Why would you use information that might *not* support your thesis? Because things are *always* complicated, and that's what makes them interesting.

Let's see how this works in an actual passage. In an essay that asks, "Why Did God Make Flies?", writer Richard Conniff argues that the answer might be as a punishment for human arrogance. In the middle of the essay, he draws on research to provide some background for this claim by establishing the long and sometimes unhappy relationship between the housefly and human beings.

The true housefly, *Musca domestica*, does not bite. (You may think this is something to like about it, until you find out what it does instead.) *M. domestica*, a drab fellow of salt-and-pepper complexion, is the world's most widely distribut-ed insect species and probably the most familiar, a status achieved through its pro-nounced fondness for breeding in pig, horse, and human excrement. In choosing at some point in the immemorial past to concentrate on the wastes around human habitations, *M. domestica* made a major career move. Bernard Greenberg of the University of Illinois at Chicago has traced human representations of the housefly back to a Mesopotamian cylinder seal from 3000 B.C. But houseflies were probably with us even before we had houses, and they spread with human culture.*

Here Conniff demonstrates exquisite control over outside sources, marshal-ling them in the service of his larger point. But he does this by not simply quot-ing extensively or going on and on explaining the relevant information, but also by *finding his own way of saying things*. For example, rather than writing that the housefly's fondness for associating with people had significant ecological implications for the insect, Conniff writes that it was "a major career move." We usually think that a *narrator* is something we only encounter in storytelling. But there is always a narrator, even in the most formal academic writing. There is always a guiding hand that leads readers through information, and though that presence may not be explicit (there is no "I"), readers always know when it's missing. We sense narrators when, as Conniff did in the excerpt, they find their own way of saying things. But we also sense them in the questions they ask and when they ask them. You need to be the narrator of your own work, whether it's a personal essay or a research paper. But how do you take on that role?

The Research Writer as Narrator

The narrator in literature is often a commanding presence, particularly when it's apparent in the point of view of a character. In research writing, the narrator's presence may be more subtle. Sometimes the genre exerts some control over how present the narrator is. For example, much academic writing discourages the use of the first person, or the use of personal experience as evidence. But that doesn't mean there is no narrator in academic writing; a guiding hand in writing is always necessary. If you don't use first person or talk about yourself, how else can you be that guiding hand in your writing? Here's how:

- **Control of research question.** You are drawn to particular questions for particular reasons, often because they are related in some way to something you've learned, experienced, or observed.

- **Control of sources.** The research question is like the bouncer at the club door. Based on what you're interested in, some people get in and some get turned away. Depending on your purpose for writing, some sources are in-vited into the conversation you're creating and others are not; among those who are invited, some talk a lot and some talk a little.

---

*Conniff, Richard, "Why God Created Flies," Audubon v. 91 (July 1989) p. 82–5.

■ **Control of context.** One of the most important choices you will make is whether stories will be any part of your examination of a research topic. Will you use case studies and other evidence to show how the topic affects certain people in certain times and places? Genre may influence this decision, of course. But typically, one of the reasons we're interested in researching a topic is its impact on people.

■ **Control of voice.** While first person or self-disclosure may not be an option for a research assignment, finding your own way of saying things (as Conniff did in the excerpt above) gives your writing your signature and your voice.

The Narrator as Synthesizer

Effective narrators in research writing don't just dump information into their writing. They *synthesize* it—put it to work to accomplish some purpose. This begins with deciding what outside information to use and what not to use, a decision that begins by considering its relevance, the authority of the source, and the usefulness of the information. (See Figure 12.1.)

Once the narrator of a research essay identifies a source as a strong candidate to include, the synthesis begins by swarming (think angry bees) that information, circling around it to establish its relevance, significance, and meaning to the research question (see Figure 12.2). You can begin this synthesizing in your research notebook and later export it to the draft. What this means, ultimately, is that whenever you invite a source into your own writing, the invitation is always on your terms. *Your* voice is always there to direct readers' attention.

Figure 12.1 Why Choose This Source Rather Than That One?

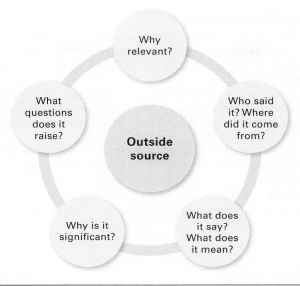

Figure 12.2   Swarming a Source

The Note Taker's Triad: Summary, Paraphrase, and Quotation

Swarming around information with your own thinking is essential when you import that information into your own writing. But so is getting your facts straight. Are you fairly and accurately describing or representing what someone else said? Are the data accurate? Is the context clear? Typically, there are three note-taking strategies we use when borrowing information: summarizing, paraphrasing, and the ever-popular quoting. We'll look at each strategy a little more closely in the following sections.

Summarizing

A summary is usually much shorter than the original. For example, consider the following summary of the earlier paragraph about the relationship between house-flies and human beings:

> The common housefly is among the "most familiar" insects because it found its long partnership with human beings, one that goes back thousands of years, extremely beneficial.

Can you see how the summary captures the main idea of the longer paragraph? Also note that when the summary uses language from the original—the phrase "most familiar"—the writer is careful to use quotation marks. Finally, the summary uses original language that breaks from the source, describing the relationship between people and flies as a "long partnership."

12.2

Practice summarizing, paraphrasing, and quoting and apply these to your own work.

Tips for Crafting a Summary

1. Academic articles in the social sciences often include abstracts, or ready-made summaries of a study. Books frequently explain their purpose in a preface or introduction. Start there. Then check the concluding chapter.
2. If your aim is to summarize a passage of a longer work, remember to look for the author's most important ideas where he or she is most likely to put them: in the first and last sentences of paragraphs or in a concluding paragraph.
3. Summary has little to do with your opinion. Try, as best you can, to capture your understanding of the *source's* meaning or argument.
4. Typically, a summary includes the name(s) of the author(s) or the title of the work, usually attached to a verb that characterizes its nature: So-and-so *argues, finds, explains, speculates, questions*, and so on.

Paraphrasing

Of the three forms of note taking, paraphrasing requires the most attention and the greatest care. Your goal is to craft a restatement, in your own words, of what an original source is saying, in roughly the same length as the original.

Here's a paraphrase of the earlier paragraph on houseflies.

Houseflies, according to Richard Conniff, have had a long partnership with human beings. They are also among "the world's most widely distributed insect species," two factors that explain our familiarity with *Musca domestica*, the housefly's Latin name. This partnership may have been cultivated for thousands of years, or certainly as long as humans—and their animal companions—have produced sufficient excrement in which the flies could breed. Ironically, these pests have benefited enormously from their "fondness" for human and animal wastes, and unwittingly we have contributed to their success at our own expense.

Tips for Crafting a Paraphrase

1. Make sure to find your own way of saying things, quoting phrases that you borrow from the source.
2. Try the "look away" strategy. Carefully read the passage several times, then set it aside. Compose your paraphrase without looking at the passage, trusting that you'll remember what's important. Then check your paraphrase against the passage, changing or quoting any borrowed language and refining your prose.
3. Like summary, introduce paraphrased material in your essay by attributing the author or the work.

Quoting

When should you turn to quotation in your essay? There are two main situations:

1. When the source says something in a distinctive way that would be lost by putting it in your own words.
2. When you want to analyze or emphasize a particular passage in the source, in which case the exact words of the author are necessary to do so.

For instance, the excerpt from "Why Did God Make Flies?" is eminently quotable because Richard Conniff, its author, writes with such a lively voice. Consider this sentence:

> The true housefly ... is the world's most widely distributed insect species and probably the most familiar, a status achieved through its pronounced fondness for breeding in pig, horse, and human excrement.

What is it about this sentence that seems so quotable? Maybe the way it goes along with fairly straightforward exposition until the second half of the sentence, when suddenly the fly seeks status and feels fondness for you know what.

When you bring someone else's voice into your own writing, it's usually a good idea to introduce the source and provide some justification for making such a move. For instance, you might introduce the preceding quote by saying something like this:

> Richard Conniff, whose popular studies of invertebrate animals have made even leeches lovable, observes that the familiarity of the housefly is no accident. He writes....

It's even more important in academic writing to follow up quoted text with your own commentary. What would you like the reader to notice about what the quotation says? What seems most relevant to your own research question or point? How does the quotation extend an important idea you've been discussing or raise an important question? What does it imply? What do you agree with? What do you disagree with? In other words, when you introduce a voice other than your own, make it clear what this new voice adds to the conversation you have going about your topic.

Tips for Handling Quotations

Integrate quoted material into your essay in the following ways:

1. **Separate it.** There are two ways to do this. Provide an introductory tag that ends in a comma or a colon. *According to Carl Elliott (82), the new drug pushers "are officially known as 'pharmaceutical sales representatives' but everyone calls them 'sales reps.'"* Or, *Carl Elliott (82) observes that drug salespeople are easy to spot: "Drug reps today are often young, well groomed, and strikingly good looking. Many are women...."*

2. **Embed it.** Integrate quoted material into your own sentence similar to this:

Carl Elliott calls drug reps "the best dressed people in the hospital."

3. **Block it.** Extended quotations (40 or more words in APA style and more than four lines in MLA) should be indented five spaces in APA style and ten spaces in MLA style in a block. Quotation marks, except those used in the source, are omitted. For instance:

Carl Elliott, in "The Drug Pushers," highlights the perks doctors have historically received:

> *Gifts from the drug industry are nothing new, of course. William Helfand, who worked in marketing for Merck for thirty-three years, told me that company representatives were giving doctors books and pamphlets as early as the late nineteenth century. "There is nothing new under the sun," Helfand says, "There is just more of it." The question is: Why is there so much more of it just now? And what changes occurred during the past decade to bring about such a dramatic increase in reps bearing gifts? (86)**

Citing Sources and Avoiding Plagiarism

Of all the rules some of my students believe were invented to torture composition students, requirements that they carefully cite their sources in research papers may cause the most anguish. They rarely question these requirements; they seem like divine and universal law. But as a matter of fact, these aren't rules at all but conventions, hardly as old as the Greeks, and historically quite new. For many centuries, writers freely borrowed from others, often without attribution, and the appropriation of someone else's words and ideas was considered quite normal and acceptable. This is still the attitude of some non-Western cultures; some students, for example, are quite puzzled in their English as a Second Language classes when they have to cite a source in their research essays.

This convention of explicitly acknowledging the source of an idea, quotation, piece of data, or information with a footnote or parenthetical citation and a bibliography entry arose in the past 150 years. It began when mostly German universities began promoting the idea that the purpose of research is not simply to demonstrate an understanding of what already is known, but to *make a contribution of new knowledge*. Further, researchers are to look for gaps in existing scholarship—questions that haven't yet been asked—or to offer extensions of what has already been posed by someone else. Knowledge making became the business of the research writer, and, like gardeners, scholars should see themselves as tending a living thing, a kind of tree that grows larger as new branches are grafted onto existing limbs.

Just as a child clambering up a tree in the park is grateful for the sturdy limbs under his or her feet, research writers acknowledge the limbs they are standing on that have helped them to see a little more of their subjects. That's why they cite their

---

*Elliott, Carl, "The Drug Pushers," Atlantic, April 2006.

sources. This is an act of gratitude, of course, but it also signals to readers on whose authority the writer's claims, conclusions, or ideas are based. Citation helps readers locate the writer's work on a specific part of the tree of knowledge in a discipline; it also gives a useful context of *what has already been said* about a question or a topic.

Student writers cite for exactly the same reasons: not because it's required in most college research writing, but because it makes their research writing more relevant and more convincing to the people who read it.

There are quite a few conventions for citing, and these conventions often vary by discipline. Humanities disciplines such as English often use the Modern Language Association (MLA) conventions, while the social sciences use the American Psychological Association (APA) methods. Both of these documentation styles are detailed later in this chapter. Although there are differences between the two styles, the purpose of each is the same: to provide a way to acknowledge those from whom you have borrowed ideas and information.

> Citation helps readers locate the writer's work on a specific part of the tree of knowledge in a discipline; it also gives a useful context of *what has already been said* about a question or a topic.

Avoiding Plagiarism

Modern authors get testy when someone uses their work without giving them credit. This is where the concept of intellectual property comes from, an idea that emerged with the invention of the printing press and the distribution of multiple copies of an author's work. In its most basic form, plagiarism is stealing someone else's words, ideas, or information. Academic plagiarism, the kind that gets a lot of ink these days, especially with the rise of the Internet, usually refers to more-specific misdeeds. Your university probably has an academic honesty or plagiarism policy posted on its website or in a student handbook. You need to look at it. But it probably includes most or all of the following forms of plagiarism:

> Intentional plagiarism stems from an intellectual laziness and dishonesty that, sooner or later, are bound to catch up with the person doing it.

1. Handing in someone else's work—a downloaded paper from the Internet or borrowed from a friend—and claiming that it's your own.

2. Using information or ideas from any source that are not common knowledge and failing to acknowledge that source.

3. Handing in the same paper for two different classes.

4. Using the exact language or expressions of a source and not indicating through quotation marks and citation that the language is borrowed.

5. Rewriting a passage from a source using substitutions of different words but retaining the same syntax and structure of the original.

Most plagiarism is unintentional. The writer simply didn't know or pay attention to course or university plagiarism policies. Equally common is simple carelessness. How can you avoid this trap? Check out the "Tips for Avoiding Plagiarism" box.

12.3

Understand and
identify plagiarism
to avoid it in your
own work.

Intentional plagiarism, of course, is a different matter. Many websites offer papers on thousands of topics to anyone willing to pay for them. College instructors, however, have tools for identifying these downloaded papers. The consequences of handing in papers bought online are often severe, including flunking the course and even expulsion—an academic Hades of sorts. Moreover, even if a person is not caught committing this academic crime, intentional plagiarism stems from an intellectual laziness and dishonesty that, sooner or later, are bound to catch up with the person doing it. So, just don't go there.

Inquiring into the Details

A Taxonomy of Copying

My colleague Casey Keck, a linguist, has studied how students paraphrase sources and ways to describe students' brushes with plagiarism. Casey notes that there are four kinds of borrowing. The **bolded** words and phrases in each of the following examples are copied from the original source:

1. *Near copy:* About half of the borrowed material is copied from the source, usually in a string of phrases. The bolded phrases are lifted verbatim from an essay titled "What Is College For?"

   Example: Students shouldn't necessarily go to college just to focus on a particular job but also to prepare for **the complexities of a world that needs rigorous analyses** and **to create joy for ourselves and others.**

2. *Minimal revision:* Less than half but more than 20 percent is copied from the original. Notice that the quotation marks appropriately signal at least one borrowed phrase from the original.

   Example: Martin says David Foster Wallace **defined** what it means to go to college as learning to avoid being "a slave to your head" and being **brave enough** to **risk what they think they know.**

3. *Moderate revision:* Less than 20 percent is copied from the original, and mostly individual words are mentioned only once in the paraphrase.

   Example: Martin says that college is the search for a **calling**, but this isn't necessarily a professional one. It includes a willingness to try new things and risk both **failure** and **growth**.

4. *Substantial revision:* Though the paraphrase might include a few general words that are used a few times in the original text, there are no copies of phrases or unique words that appear in the source.

   Example: According to Martin, college is an opportunity to reimagine ourselves—to break with old ways of thinking, and find delight in something other than the usual "distraction" and "entertainment."

Tips for Avoiding Plagiarism

■ **Don't procrastinate.** Many careless mistakes in citation or handling of source material occur in the rush to finish the draft in the wee hours of the morning.

■ **Be an active note taker.** Work in the middle of the process to take possession of the material you read, particularly by exploring your responses to sources *in your own words* and *for your own purposes*.

■ **Collect bibliographic information first.** Before you do anything else, take down complete publication information for each source, including the page numbers from which you will borrow material.

■ **Mark quoted material clearly.** Whenever you quote a source directly, make sure that it's obvious in your notes.

■ **Be vigilant whenever you cut and paste.** The great usefulness of cutting and pasting passages in electronic documents is also the downfall of many research writers. Is the copied material directly borrowed, and if so, is it properly cited?

Exercise 12.1

The Accidental Plagiarist

Most instances of plagiarism are accidental. The writer simply isn't aware that he or she has plagiarized. Here's a low-stakes exercise that can test your understanding of how to avoid the simplest—and most common—types of accidental plagiarism. If you get this wrong, the grammar police won't accost you in the middle of the night, throw you against the wall, and make you spell difficult words. You'll just learn something.

Using the words and ideas of others in your own writing is essential to most research essays and papers. Doing this without plagiarizing isn't exactly like walking through a minefield, but you do have to step carefully. For example, Beth is exploring the question "What might explain the high rate of divorce in the early years of marriage?" She's interested in divorce because she just went through one. In her research, Beth encounters Diane Ackerman's book *The Natural History of Love* and finds the following paragraph:

"Philandering," we call it, "fooling around," "hanky-panky," "skirt chasing," "man chasing," or something equally picturesque. Monogamy and adultery are both hallmarks of being human. Anthropologist Helen Fisher proposes a chemical basis for adultery, what she calls "The Four-Year Itch." Studying the United Nations survey of marriage and divorce around the world, she noticed that divorce usually occurs early in marriage, during the couple's first reproductive and parenting years. Also, that this peak time for divorce coincides with the period in which infatuation normally ends, and a couple has to decide if they're going to call it quits or stay together as companions. Some couples do stay together and have other children, but even more don't. "The human animal," she concludes, "seems built to court, to fall in love, and to marry one person at a time; then, at the height of our reproductive years, often with a single child, we divorce them; then, a few years after, we remarry once again."*

---

*Ackerman, Diane, "A Natural History of Love," Random House.

Beth thought this was pretty interesting stuff, and in her draft she summarized the paragraph in the following way:

> According to Diane Ackerman, a hallmark of being human is "monogamy and adultery," and she cites the period right after infatuation subsides—about four years for most couples—as the time when they call it quits.

STEP ONE: In small groups, analyze Beth's summary. Does Beth plagiarize the original passage, and if so, do you have ideas about how she could fix it? Revise the summary on a piece of newsprint and post it on the wall.

STEP TWO: Discuss the proposed revisions. How well do they address any plagiarism you see in Beth's summary?

STEP THREE: Now compare the following paraphrases of the same Ackerman passage. Which has plagiarism and which seems okay?

PARAPHRASE 1	PARAPHRASE 2
Divorce may have a "chemical basis," something that may kick in after four years of marriage and ironically when partners are reaching their highest potential for having children. Researcher Helen Fisher calls it "The Four-Year Itch," the time that often signals a shift from infatuation into a more sober assessment of the relationship's future: Are they going to stay together or "call it quits"? Most end up deciding to end the relationship.	When infatuation fades and couples are faced with the future of their relationship, biochemistry may help them decide. According to researcher Helen Fisher, "divorce usually occurs early in marriage, during the couple's first reproductive and parenting years" (Ackerman 165). She suggests that this is often about four years into the relationship, and argues that humans may be designed to behave this way because the pattern seems so entrenched (Ackerman 166).

STEP FOUR: In class, discuss which paraphrase seems acceptable and which does not. Note that the problems are pretty subtle.

STEP FIVE: Now practice your own *summary* of the following passage, applying what you've learned so far in the exercise about ways to avoid plagiarism when using the words and ideas of other people. This passage from Ackerman's book follows the passage you worked with earlier.

> Our chemistry makes it easy to follow that plan, and painful to avoid it. After the seductive fireworks of first attraction, which may last a few weeks or a few years, the body gets bored with easy ecstasy. The nerves no longer quiver with excitement. Nothing new has been happening for ages, why bother to rouse oneself? Love is exhausting. Then the attachment chemicals roll in their thick cozy carpets of marital serenity. Might as well relax and enjoy the calm and security some feel. Separated even for a short while, the partners crave the cradle of the other's embrace. Is it a chemical craving? Possibly so, a hunger for the soothing endorphins that flow when they're together. It is a deep, sweet river, just right for dangling one's feet in while the world waits.

MLA Documentation Guidelines

The professional organization in charge of academic writing in literature and languages, the Modern Language Association (MLA), promotes one of the two common methods of citing sources that you should be familiar with. The second method, the American Psychological Association (APA) system, is described in the next section. Your English class will most likely use the MLA system.

12.4
Cite sources using MLA and APA documentation styles.

The guidelines presented in this section are based on the seventh edition of the *MLA Handbook for Writers of Research Papers*.

You must cite a source in your paper in the following situations:

1. Whenever you quote from an original source.

2. Whenever you borrow ideas from an original source, even when you express those ideas in your own words by paraphrasing or summarizing them.

3. Whenever you borrow from an original source factual information that is not common knowledge (see the "Inquiring into the Details: The Common Knowledge Exception" box).

Inquiring into the Details

The Common Knowledge Exception

The business about common knowledge causes much confusion. Just what does this term mean? Basically, *common knowledge* means facts that are widely known and about which there is no controversy. One measure of common knowledge, one scholar argues, is if you find the exact same information in four or more different sources.

On the other hand sometimes it's really obvious whether something is common knowledge. The fact that the Super Bowl occurs in late January and pits the winning teams from the American and National Football Conferences against each other is common knowledge. The fact that former president Ronald Reagan was once an actor and starred in a movie with a chimpanzee is common knowledge, too. And the fact that most Americans get most of their news from television is also common knowledge, although this fact is getting close to leaving the domain of common knowledge.

But what about a writer's assertion that most dreaming occurs during rapid eye movement (REM) sleep? This is an idea about which all sources seem to agree. Does that make it common knowledge?

It's useful to ask next, *How common to whom? Experts in the topic at hand or the rest of us?* As a rule, consider the knowledge of your readers. What information will not be familiar to most of your readers or may surprise them? Which ideas might even raise skepticism? In this case, the fact about REM sleep and dreaming goes slightly beyond the knowledge of most readers, so to be safe, it should be cited. Use common sense, but when in doubt, cite.

Citing Sources

The foundation of the MLA method of citing sources *in your paper* is putting the last name of the author and the page number of the source material in parentheses as closely as possible to the borrowed material. For example,

> Researchers believe that there is an "infatuation chemical" that may account for that almost desperate attraction we feel when we're near someone special (Ackerman 164).

The parenthetical citation tells a reader two things: the source of the information (for example, the author's name) and where in the work to find the borrowed idea or material. A really interested reader—perhaps an infatuated one—who wanted to follow up on this citation would then refer to the Works Cited at the end of the paper, which would list the work by the author's last name and include all the pertinent information about the source:

> Ackerman, Diane. *A Natural History of Love*. New York: Vintage, 1994. Print.

Here's another example of a parenthetical author/page citation in another research paper. Note the differences from the previous example:

> "One thing is clear," writes Thomas Mallon, "plagiarism didn't become a truly sore point with writers until they thought of writing as their trade. . . . Suddenly his capital and identity were at stake" (3–4).

The first thing you may have noticed is that the author's last name—Mallon—was omitted from the parenthetical citation. It didn't need to be included because it had already been mentioned in the text. *If you mention the author's name in the text of your paper, then you only need to parenthetically cite the relevant page number(s).* This citation also tells us that the quoted passage comes from two pages rather than one.

Where To Put Citations. Place the citation as close as you can to the borrowed material, trying to avoid breaking the flow of the sentences, if possible. To avoid confusion about what's borrowed and what's not—particularly in passages longer than a sentence—mention the name of the original author *in your paper*. Note that in the next example, the writer simply cites the source at the end of the paragraph, not naming the source within the text. Doing so makes it hard for the reader to figure out whether Blager is the source of the information in the entire paragraph or just part of the paragraph:

> Though children who have been sexually abused seem to be disadvantaged in many areas, including the inability to forge lasting relationships, low self-esteem, and crippling shame, they seem advantaged in other areas. Sexually abused children seem to be more socially mature than other children of their same age group. It's a distinctly mixed blessing (Blager 994).

In the following example, notice how the ambiguity about what's borrowed and what's not is resolved by careful placement of the author's name and parenthetical citation in the text:

> Though children who have been sexually abused seem to be disadvantaged in many areas, including the inability to forge lasting relationships, low self-esteem, and crippling shame, they seem advantaged in other areas. According to Blager, sexually abused children seem to be more socially mature than other children of their same age group (994). It's a distinctly mixed blessing.

In this latter version, it's clear that Blager is the source for one sentence in the paragraph, and the writer is responsible for the rest. Generally, use an authority's last name, rather than a formal title or first name, when mentioning him or her in your text. Also note that the parenthetical citation is placed *inside* the period of the sentence (or last sentence) that it documents. That's almost always the case, except at the end of a block quotation, where the parenthetical reference is placed after the period of the last sentence.

Inquiring into the Details

Citations That Go with the Flow

There's no getting around it—parenthetical citations can be like stones on the sidewalk. Readers stride through a sentence in your essay and then have to step around the citation at the end before they resume their walk. Yet citations are important in academic writing because they help readers know whom you read or heard that shaped your thinking.

(*continued*)

Inquiring into the Details (*continued*)

However, you can minimize including citations that trip up readers and make your essay more readable by doing the following:

- Avoid lengthy parenthetical citations by mentioning the name of the author in your essay. That way, you usually have to include only a page number in the citation.
- Try to place citations where readers are likely to pause anyway—for example, at the end of a sentence or right before a comma.
- Remember that you *don't* need a citation when you're citing common knowledge or referring to an entire work by an author.
- If you're borrowing from only one source in a paragraph of your essay and all of the borrowed material comes from a single page of that source, don't bother repeating the citation over and over again with each new bit of information. Just put the citation at the end of the paragraph.

The citation can also be placed near the author's name, rather than at the end of the sentence, if it doesn't unnecessarily break the flow of the sentence. For example:

> Blager (994) observes that sexually abused children tend to be more socially mature than other children of their same age group.

When You Mention the Author's Name. It's generally good practice in research writing to identify who said what. The familiar convention of using attribution tags such as "According to Fletcher,…" or "Fletcher argues that…" and so on helps readers attach a name to a voice, or an individual to certain claims or findings. When you mention the author of a source, you can drop his or her name from the parenthetical citation and just include the page number. For example,

> Robert Harris believes that there is "widespread uncertainty" among students about what constitutes plagiarism (2).

You may also list the page number directly after the author's name.

> Robert Harris (2) believes that there is "widespread uncertainty" among students about what constitutes plagiarism.

When There Is No Author. Occasionally, you may encounter a source for which the author is anonymous—where the article doesn't have a byline or for some reason the author hasn't been identified. This isn't unusual with pamphlets, editorials, government documents, some newspaper articles, online sources, and short filler articles in magazines. If you can't parenthetically name the author, what do you cite?

Most often, cite the title (or an abbreviated version, if the title is long) and the page number. If you choose to abbreviate the title, begin with the word under which it is alphabetized in the Works Cited. For example:

> According to the *Undergraduate Catalog*, "the athletic program is an integral part of
>
> the university and its total educational purpose" (7).

Here is how this publication would be listed at the back of the paper:

Works Cited

Undergraduate Catalog, Boise State University 2014–2015.

   Boise: BSU, 2014. Print.

For clarity, it's helpful to mention the original source of the borrowed material in the text of your paper. When there is no author's name, refer to the publication (or institution) you're citing or make a more general reference to the source. For example:

> An article in *Cuisine* magazine argues that the best way to kill a lobster is to plunge
>
> a knife between its eyes ("How to Kill" 56).

or

> According to one government report, with the current minimum size limit, most
>
> lobsters end up on dinner plates before they've had a chance to reproduce ("Size
>
> at Sexual Maturity" 3–4).

Works By the Same Author. Suppose you end up using several books or articles by the same author. Obviously, a parenthetical citation that merely includes the author's name and page number won't do, because it won't be clear *which* of several works the citation refers to. In this case, include the author's name, an abbreviated title (if the original is too long), and the page number. For example:

> One essayist who suffers from multiple sclerosis writes that "there is a subtle
>
> taxonomy of crippleness" (Mairs, *Carnal Acts* 69).

The Works Cited list would show multiple works by one author as follows:

Works Cited

Mairs, Nancy. *Carnal Acts*. Boston: Beacon, 1996. Print.

   - - -. *Voice Lessons*. Boston: Beacon, 1994. Print.

It's obvious from the parenthetical citation which of the two Mairs books is the source of the information. Note that in the parenthetical reference, no punctuation separates the title and the page number, but a comma follows the author's name. If Mairs had been mentioned in the text of the paper, her name could have been dropped from the citation.

Also notice that the three hyphens used in the second bibliographic entry are meant to signal that the author's name in this source is the same as in the preceding entry.

When One Source Quotes Another. Whenever you can, cite the original source of material you use. For example, if an article on television violence quotes the author of a book and you want to use the quote, try to hunt down the book. That way, you'll be certain of the accuracy of the quote, and you may also find other usable information.

Sometimes, however, finding the original source is not possible. In those cases, use the term *qtd. in* to signal that you've quoted or paraphrased a quotation from a book or article that you found elsewhere. In the following example, the citation signals that Bacon's quote was culled from an article by Guibroy, not Bacon's original work:

Francis Bacon also weighed in on the dangers of imitation, observing that "it is hardly possible at once to admire an author and to go beyond him" (qtd. in Guibroy 113).

Personal Interviews. If you mention the name of your interview subject in your text, no parenthetical citation is necessary. On the other hand, if you don't mention the subject's name, cite it in parentheses after the quote:

Instead, the recognizable environment gave something to kids they could relate to. "And it had a lot more real quality to it than, say, *Mister Rogers* . . . ," says one educator. "Kids say the reason they don't like *Mister Rogers* is that it's unbelievable" (Diamonti).

Regardless of whether you mention your subject's name, you should include a reference to the interview in the Works Cited. In this case, the reference would look like this:

Works Cited

Diamonti, Nancy. Personal interview. 5 Nov. 1999.

Several Sources In a Single Citation. Suppose two sources contributed the same information in a paragraph of your essay. Or perhaps even more common is when you're summarizing the findings of several authors on a certain topic—a fairly common move when you're trying to establish a context for your own research question. You cite multiple authors in a single citation in the usual fashion, using author name and page number, but separating each with a semicolon. For example,

> A whole range of studies have looked closely at the intellectual development of
>
> college students, finding that they generally assume "stages" or "perspectives" that
>
> differ from subject to subject (Perry 122; Belenky et al. 12).

If you can, however, avoid long citations, because they can be cumbersome for readers to get through.

Sample Parenthetical References for Other Sources. MLA format is pretty simple, and we've already covered some of the basic variations. You should also know five additional variations, as follow:

AN ENTIRE WORK
   If you mention the author's name in the text, no citation is necessary. The work should, however, be listed in the Works Cited.

> Leon Edel's *Henry James* is considered by many to be a model biography.

A VOLUME OF A MULTIVOLUME WORK
   If you're working with one volume of a multivolume work, it's a good idea to mention which volume in the parenthetical reference. The following citation attributes the passage to volume 2, page 3, of a work by Baym and more than three other authors. The volume number always precedes the colon, which is followed by the page number:

> By the turn of the century, three authors dominated American literature: Mark
>
> Twain, Henry James, and William Dean Howells (Baym et al. 2: 3).

A LITERARY WORK
   Because so many literary works, particularly classics, have been reprinted in so many editions, it's useful to give readers more information about where a passage can be found in one of these editions. List the page number and then the chapter number (and any other relevant information, such as the section or volume), separated by a semicolon. Use arabic rather than roman numerals, unless your teacher instructs you otherwise:

> Izaak Walton warns that "no direction can be given to make a man of a dull capacity
>
> able to make a Flie well" (130; ch. 5).

When citing classic poems or plays, instead of page numbers, cite line numbers and other appropriate divisions (book, section, act, scene, part, etc.). Separate the information with periods. For example, (*Othello* 2.3.286) indicates act 2, scene 3, line 286 of Shakespeare's work.

AN ONLINE SOURCE

Online sources frequently don't have page numbers. So how can you cite them parenthetically in your essay? Most of the time, you won't include page numbers, particularly when you're citing web pages.

Rarely, digital documents include paragraph numbers. If so, use the abbreviation *par.* or *pars.*, followed by the paragraph number or numbers you're borrowing material from. For example:

> In most psychotherapeutic approaches, the personality of the therapist can have a
>
> big impact on the outcome of the therapy ("Psychotherapy," par. 1).

Sometimes the material has an internal structure, such as sections, parts, chapters, or volumes. If so, use the abbreviation *sec., pt., ch.,* or *vol.* (respectively), followed by the appropriate number.

In many cases, a parenthetical citation can be avoided entirely by simply naming the source in the text of your essay. A curious reader will then find the full citation to the article in the Works Cited page at the back of your paper. For example:

> According to Charles Petit, the worldwide effort to determine whether frogs are
>
> disappearing will take somewhere between three and five years.

Finally, if you don't want to mention the source within your text, parenthetically cite the author's last name (if any) or article title:

> The worldwide effort to determine whether frogs are disappearing will take
>
> somewhere between three and five years (Petit).

Format

The Layout. A certain fussiness is associated with the look of academic papers. The reason for it is quite simple—academic disciplines generally aim for consistency in format so that readers of scholarship know exactly where to look to find what they want to know. It's a matter of efficiency. How closely you must follow the MLA's requirements for the layout of your essay is up to your instructor, but it's really not that complicated. A lot of what you need to know is featured in Figure 12.3.

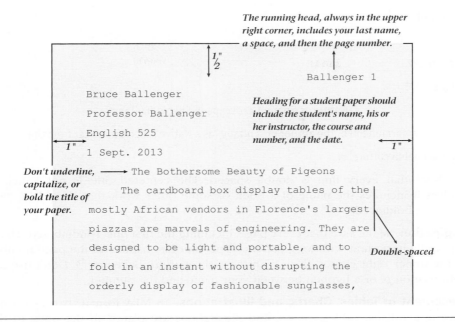

The running head, always in the upper right corner, includes your last name, a space, and then the page number.

½"

Ballenger 1

Bruce Ballenger

Professor Ballenger

English 525

1 Sept. 2013

Heading for a student paper should include the student's name, his or her instructor, the course and number, and the date.

1"   1"

Don't underline, → The Bothersome Beauty of Pigeons
capitalize, or
bold the title of   The cardboard box display tables of the
your paper.   mostly African vendors in Florence's largest

piazzas are marvels of engineering. They are

designed to be light and portable, and to   *Double-spaced*

fold in an instant without disrupting the

orderly display of fashionable sunglasses,

Figure 12.3 The basic look of an MLA-style paper

Printing. Compose your paper on white, $8^{1}/2$" × 11" printer paper. Make sure the printer has sufficient ink or toner.

Margins and Spacing. The old high school trick is to use big margins. That way, you can meet your page length requirements with less material. Don't try that with this paper. Create one-inch margins for every side. The running heads for page numbers (e.g. Ballenger 1) are a half inch from the top and always flush right. Indent the first line of each paragraph five spaces, and blocked quotes ten spaces. *Double-space all of the text, including blocked quotes and Works Cited.*

Title Page. Your paper doesn't need a separate title page. Instead, begin your paper with the first page of text. One inch below the top of the page, type your name, your instructor's name, the course number, and the date (see Figure 12.3). Below that, type the title, centered on the page. Begin the text of the paper below the title.

Julie Bird

Professor Ballenger

English 102

1 June 2013

Nature as Being: Landscape in Silko's "Lullaby"

Leslie Marmon Silko, the author of "Lullaby," is a Native American writer from the

Laguna Pueblo culture. . . .

Note that every line is double-spaced. The centered title is not italicized (unless it includes the name of a book or some other work that should be italicized) or boldfaced.

Pagination. Make sure that every page, including the first one, is numbered. That's especially important with long papers. Type your last name and the page number in the upper right corner, flush with the right margin: Ballenger 3. Don't use the abbreviation *p.* or a hyphen between your name and the number.

Placement of Tables, Charts, and Illustrations. In MLA format, papers do not have appendixes. Tables, charts, and illustrations are placed in the body of the paper, close to the text that refers to them. Number illustrations consecutively (Table 1 or Figure 3), and indicate sources below them (see Figure 12.4). If you use a chart or illustration from another text, give the full citation. Place any table caption above the table, flush left. Captions for illustrations or diagrams are usually placed below them.

Handling Titles. The MLA guidelines about the style of titles are, as the most recent *Handbook* observes, "strict." The general rule is that the writer should capitalize the first letters of all principal words in a title, including any that follow dashes. The exceptions are articles (*a, an*, and *the*), prepositions (*for, of, in, to*), and coordinating conjunctions (*and, or, but, for*). These exceptions apply *only if*

Table 1 Percentage of Students Who Self-Report Acts of Plagiarism

Acts of Plagiarism	Never/Rarely	Sometimes	Often/Very Freq.
Copy text without citation	71	19	10
Copy paper without citation	91	5	3
Request paper to hand in	90	5	2
Purchase paper to hand in	91	6	3

Source: Scanlon, Patrick M., and David R. Neumann. "Internet Plagiarism Among College Students." *Journal of College Student Development* 43.3 (2002): 379.

Figure 12.4 Example of format for a table

the words appear in the middle of a title; capitalize them if they appear at the beginning or end.

The rules for italicizing a title or putting it in quotation marks are as follows:

1. *Italicize the Title* if it is a book, play, pamphlet, film, magazine, TV program, CD, audiocassette, newspaper, or work of art.

2. "Put the Title in Quotes" if it is an article in a newspaper, magazine, or encyclopedia; a short story; a poem; an episode of a TV program; a song; a lecture; or a chapter or essay in a book.

Here are some examples:

> *The Curious Researcher* (Book)
>
> *English Online: The Student's Guide to the Internet* (CD-ROM)
>
> "Once More to the Lake" (Essay)
>
> *Historic Boise: An Introduction into the Architecture of Boise, Idaho* (Book)
>
> "Psychotherapy" (Encyclopedia article)
>
> *Idaho Statesman* (Newspaper)
>
> "One Percent Initiative Panned" (Newspaper article)

Under the most recent guidelines (the *MLA Handbook*, seventh edition), the underlining of titles is out and the use of italics is in. Now, for instance, your Works Cited page would list the book title <u>Bombproof Your Horse</u> as *Bombproof Your Horse*. (And yes, that's "horse" not "house.")

Language and Style

Names. Though it may seem by the end of your research project as if you're on familiar terms with some of the authors you cite, it's not a good idea to refer to them by their first names. Typically, initially give the full names of people you cite, and then only their last names if you mention them again in your essay.

Ellipsis Dots. Those are the three (always three unless you're omitting material that comes at the end of a sentence, where they join a period) dots that indicate you've left out a word, phrase, or even whole section of a quoted passage. It's often wise to use them because you want to emphasize only certain parts of a quotation rather than burden your reader with unnecessary information, but be careful that you preserve the basic intention and idea of the author's original statement. The ellipsis dots can come at the beginning of a quotation, in the middle, or at the end, depending where it is you've omitted material. For example,

> "After the publication of a controversial picture that shows, for example, either
>
> dead or grieving victims . . . , readers, in telephone calls and in letters to the editor,
>
> often attack the photographer for being tasteless. . . . "

Quotations. Quotations that run more than four lines long should be blocked, or indented ten spaces from the left margin. The quotation should be double-spaced and quotation marks should be omitted. In an exception from the usual convention, the parenthetical citation is placed *after* the period at the end of the quotation. A colon is a customary way to introduce a blocked quotation. For example,

> Chris Sherman and Gary Price, in *The Invisible Web*, contend that much of the
>
> Internet, possibly most, is beyond the reach of researchers who use conventional
>
> search engines:
>
>> The problem is that vast expanses of the Web are completely invisible to
>>
>> general-purpose search engines like AltaVista, HotBot, and Google. Even
>>
>> worse, this "Invisible Web" is in all likelihood growing significantly faster
>>
>> than the visible Web that you're familiar with. It's not that search engines
>>
>> and Web directories are "stupid" or even badly engineered. Rather, they
>>
>> simply can't "see" millions of high quality resources that are available
>>
>> exclusively on the Invisible Web. So what is this Invisible Web and why
>>
>> aren't search engines doing anything about it to make it visible? (xxi)*

Preparing the Works Cited Page

The Works Cited page ends the paper. Several other lists of sources may also appear at the end of a research paper, though these are much less common in college research essays. An Annotated List of Works Cited not only lists the sources used in the paper, but also includes a brief description of each. A Works Consulted list includes sources that may or may not have been cited in the paper but shaped the writer's thinking. A Content Notes page, keyed to superscript numbers in the text of the paper, lists short commentaries or asides that are significant but not central enough to the discussion to be included in the text of the paper.

The Works Cited page is the workhorse of most college papers. The other source lists are used less often. Works Cited is essentially an alphabetical listing of all the sources you quoted, paraphrased, or summarized in your paper. If you have used the MLA format for citing sources, your paper has numerous parenthetical references to authors and page numbers. The Works Cited page provides complete information on each source cited in the text for the reader who wants more details. (In APA format, this page is called References and is only slightly different in how items are listed.)

If you've been careful about collecting complete bibliographic information—author, title, editor, edition, volume, place, publisher, date, page numbers—then preparing your Works Cited page will be easy. If you've recorded that information

---

*Price, Gary, Chris Sherman, and Gary Sullivan, "The Invisible Web." Information Today, 2001.

on notecards, all you have to do is put them in alphabetical order and then transcribe them into your paper. If you've been careless about collecting that information, you may need to take a hike back to the library.

Format

Alphabetizing the List. Works Cited follows the text of your paper on a separate page. After you've assembled complete information about each source you've cited, put the sources in alphabetical order by the last name of each author. If a work has multiple authors, alphabetize by the last name of the first author listed. If a source has no author, then alphabetize it by the first key word of the title. If you're citing more than one source by the same author, you don't need to repeat the name for each source; simply use three hyphens followed by a period (—.) in place of the author's name in subsequent listings.

Indenting and Spacing. Type the first line of each entry flush left, and indent subsequent lines of that entry (if any) five spaces. Double-space between each line and each entry. For example:

Works Cited

Bianchi, William. "Education by Radio: America's Schools of the Air." *TechTrends: Linking Research & Practice to Improve Learning* 52.2 (2008): 36–44. Print.

Campbell, Gardener. "There's Something in the Air: Podcasting and Education." *EDUCAUSE Review* 40.6 (Nov.–Dec. 2005): 32–47. Print.

Checho, Colleen. "The Effects of Podcasting on Learning and Motivation: A Mixed Method Study of At-Risk High School Students." Diss. U of Nevada, Reno. Ann Arbor: UMI, 2007. Print.

Davis, Anne, and Ewa McGrail. "'Proof-Revising' With Podcasting: Keeping Readers in Mind as Students Listen to and Rethink Their Writing." *The Reading Teacher* 62.6 (2009): 522–29. Print.

Grisham, Dana L., and Thomas Devere Wolsey. "Writing Instruction for Teacher Candidates: Strengthening a Weak Curricular Area." *Literacy Research and Instruction* 50.4 (2011): 348–64. Print.

Klaus, Carl H. *The Made-Up Self: Impersonation in the Personal Essay*. Iowa City: U of Iowa P, 2010. Print.

"What Is Educational Podcasting?" *Educate*. Russell Educational Consultancy and Productions, n.d. Web. 7 July 2012.

Citing Books. You usually need three pieces of information to cite a book: the name of the author or authors, the title, and the publication information. If you're citing an e-book, however, some additional information may be required. See below.

CITING A BOOK IN PRINT	CITING AN E-BOOK
1. Author(s)	1. Author(s)
2. *Title*	2. *Title*
3. Edition and/or volume (if relevant)	3. Edition and/or volume (if relevant)
4. Where published, by whom, and date	4. If also in print, where published, by whom, and date; in any case, sponsoring organization, date of electronic publication
5. Medium: Print	5. Medium: Web
	6. Date of access
SAMPLE CITATION: BOOK IN PRINT	**SAMPLE CITATION: E-BOOK (WEB ONLY)**
Donald, David H. *Lincoln*. New York: Simon, 1995. Print.	Lincoln, Abraham. *The Writings of Abraham Lincoln*. B & R Samisdat Express. 2009. Web. 28 Jan. 2011.

Title. Titles of books are italicized, with the first letters of all principal words capitalized, including those in any subtitles. Titles that are not italicized are usually those of works found within larger works, such as poems and short stories in anthologies. These titles are set off by quotation marks. Titles of religious works (the Bible, the Qur'an, etc.) are neither italicized nor enclosed within quotation marks. (See the guidelines in the earlier "Handling Titles" subsection.)

Edition. If a book doesn't indicate an edition number, then it's probably a first edition, a fact you don't need to cite. Look on the title page. Signal an edition like this: *2nd ed., 3rd ed.*, and so on.

Publication Place, Publisher, and Date. Look on the title page to find out who published the book. Publishers' names are usually shortened in the Works Cited list: for example, *St. Martin's Press Inc.* is shortened to *St. Martin's*.

It's sometimes difficult to figure out what to cite about the publication place, because several cities are often listed on the title page. Cite the first.

The date a book is published is usually indicated on the copyright page. If several dates or several printings by the same publisher are listed, cite the original publication date. However, if the book is a revised edition, give the date of that edition. One final variation: If you're citing a book that's a reprint of an original edition, give both dates. For example:

> Stegner, Wallace. *Recapitulation*. 1979. Lincoln: U of Nebraska P, 1986. Print.

This book was first published in 1979 and then republished in 1986 by the University of Nebraska Press.

Page Numbers. You don't usually list the page numbers of the part of a book you used as a source. The parenthetical reference in your paper specifies those page numbers. But if you use only part of a book—an introduction or an essay—list the appropriate page numbers following the publication date. Use periods to set off the page numbers. If the author or editor of the entire work is also the author of the introduction or essay you're citing, list her by last name only the second time you give her name. For example:

> Lee, L. L., and Merrill Lewis. Preface. *Women, Women Writers, and the West*. By Lee
>
> and Lewis. Troy: Whitston, 1980. v–ix. Print.

Publication Medium. A recent update to the MLA's guidelines now requires that you include the type of source. In most cases, a book citation will end with the word "Print." An online book citation should end with "Web."

Sample Book Citations

A BOOK BY ONE AUTHOR

> Keen, Sam. *Fire in the Belly*. New York: Bantam, 1991. Print.
>
> *In-Text Citation:* (Keen 101)

A BOOK BY TWO AUTHORS

> Ballenger, Bruce, and Barry Lane. *Discovering the Writer Within*. Cincinnati:
>
> Writer's Digest, 1996. Print.
>
> *In-Text Citation:* (Ballenger and Lane 14)

A BOOK WITH MORE THAN THREE AUTHORS

If a book has more than three authors, list the first and substitute the term *et al.* for the others.

> Belenky, Mary Field, et al. *Women's Ways of Knowing*. New York: Basic Books,
>
> 1973. Print.
>
> *In-Text Citation:* (Belenky et al. 21–30)

SEVERAL BOOKS BY THE SAME AUTHOR

>Baldwin, James. *Going to Meet the Man*. New York: Dial, 1965. Print.
>
>- - - . *Tell Me How Long the Train's Been Gone*. Dial, 1968. Print.
>
>*In-Text Citation:* (Baldwin, *Going* 34)

A COLLECTION OR ANTHOLOGY

>Crane, R. S., ed. *Critics and Criticism: Ancient and Modern*. Chicago: U of Chicago
>
>   P, 1952. Print.
>
>*In-Text Citation:* (Crane xx)

A WORK IN A COLLECTION OR ANTHOLOGY

The title of a work that is part of a collection but was originally published as a book should be italicized. Otherwise, the title of a work in a collection should be enclosed in quotation marks.

>Bahktin, Mikhail. "Marxism and the Philosophy of Language." *The Rhetorical*
>
>   *Tradition*. Ed. Patricia Bizzell and Bruce Herzberg. New York: St. Martin's,
>
>   1990. 928–44. Print.
>
>*In-Text Citation:* (Bahktin 929–31)
>
>Jones, Robert F. "Welcome to Muskie Country." *The Ultimate Fishing Book*. Ed. Lee
>
>   Eisenberg and DeCourcy Taylor. Boston: Houghton, 1981. 122–34. Print.
>
>*In-Text Citation:* (Jones 131)

AN INTRODUCTION, PREFACE, FOREWORD, OR PROLOGUE

>Scott, Jerie Cobb. Foreword. *Writing Groups: History, Theory, and Implications*. By
>
>   Ann Ruggles Gere. Carbondale: Southern Illinois UP, 1987. ix–xi. Print.
>
>*In-Text Citation:* (Scott ix–xi)
>
>Rich, Adrienne. Introduction. *On Lies, Secrets, and Silence*. By Rich. New York:
>
>   Norton, 1979. 9–18. Print.
>
>*In-Text Citation:* (Rich 12)

A BOOK WITH NO AUTHOR

>*American Heritage Dictionary*. 3rd ed. Boston: Houghton, 1994. Print.
>
>*In-Text Citation:* (*American Heritage Dictionary* 444)

AN ENCYCLOPEDIA

"Passenger Pigeon." *Encyclopedia Britannica Online*. Encyclopedia Britannica, Inc.,

2012. Web. 26 June 2012.

In-Text Citation: ("Passenger Pigeon")

"City of Chicago." *Encyclopaedia Britannica*. 1999 ed. Print.

In-Text Citation: ("City of Chicago" 397)

A BOOK WITH AN INSTITUTIONAL AUTHOR

Hospital Corporation of America. *Employee Benefits Handbook*. Nashville: HCA,

2015. Print.

In-Text Citation: (Hospital Corporation of America 5–7)

A BOOK WITH MULTIPLE VOLUMES
Include the number of volumes in the work between the title and publication information.

Baym, Nina, et al., eds. *The Norton Anthology of American Literature*. 5th ed. 2 vols.

New York: Norton, 1998. Print.

In-Text Citation: (Baym et al. 2: 3)

If you use one volume of a multivolume work, indicate which one, along with the page numbers, followed by the total number of volumes in the work.

Anderson, Sherwood. "Mother." *The Norton Anthology of American Literature*. Ed.

Nina Baym et al. 5th ed. Vol. 2. New York: Norton, 1998. 1115–31. 2 vols. Print.

In-Text Citation: (Anderson 1115)

A BOOK THAT IS NOT A FIRST EDITION
Check the title page to determine whether the book is *not* a first edition (2nd, 3rd, 4th, etc.); if no edition number is mentioned, assume it's the first. Put the edition number right after the title.

Ballenger, Bruce. *The Curious Researcher*. 8th ed. Boston: Longman, 2014. Print.

In-Text Citation: (Ballenger 194)

Citing the edition is necessary only for books that are *not* first editions. Note that citing the edition is also necessary for revised editions (*Rev. ed.*) and abridged editions (*Abr. ed.*).

A BOOK PUBLISHED BEFORE 1900

For a book this old, it's usually unnecessary to list the publisher.

Hitchcock, Edward. *Religion of Geology*. Glasgow, 1851. Print.

In-Text Citation: (Hitchcock 48)

A TRANSLATION

Montaigne, Michel de. *Essays*. Trans. J. M. Cohen. Middlesex: Penguin,

1958. Print.

In-Text Citation: (Montaigne 638)

GOVERNMENT DOCUMENTS

Because of the enormous variety of government documents, citing them properly can be a challenge. Because most government documents do not name authors, begin an entry for such a source with the level of government (U.S. Government, State of Illinois, etc.)—unless it is obvious from the title—followed by the sponsoring agency, the title of the work, and the publication information. Look on the title page to determine the publisher. If it's a federal document, then the *Government Printing Office* (abbreviated GPO) is usually the publisher.

United States. Bureau of the Census. *Statistical Abstract of the United States.*

Washington: GPO, 2005. Print.

In-Text Citation: (United States, Bureau of the Census 79–83)

A BOOK THAT WAS REPUBLISHED

A fairly common occurrence, particularly in literary study, is to find a book that was republished, sometimes many years after the original publication date. In addition, some books first appear in hardcover, and then are republished in paperback. To cite, put the original date of publication immediately after the book's title, and then include the more current publication date, as usual, at the end of the citation. Do it like so:

Didion, Joan. *Slouching Towards Bethlehem*. 1968. New York: Farrar, 1992. Print.

In-Text Citation: (Didion 31)

Badke, William. *Research Strategies: Finding Your Way through the Information Fog.*

Lincoln: Writers Club P, 2000. Web. 12 July 2009.

In-Text Citation: (Badke)

Citing Periodicals. These days, you're more likely to find an article through a library database or on the web than in a print journal or magazine. Citation of each type of source is quite similar, with the differences listed in the table below.

PRINT ARTICLE	ARTICLE FROM A DATABASE OF THE WEB
1. Author(s)	1. Author(s)
2. "Article Title"	2. "Article Title"
3. *Periodical Title*	3. *Periodical Title*
4. Volume and issue	4. Volume and issue
5. Date published	5. Date published
6. Page numbers	6. Page numbers, if any (usually present in versions also in print)
7. Medium: Print	7. *Website, Database*, or Sponsor
	8. Medium: Web
	9. Date of access
SAMPLE CITATION: PRINT ARTICLE	**SAMPLE CITATION: DATABASE ARTICLE**
Newcomb, Matthew. "Sustainability as a Design Principle for Composition." *College Composition and Communication* 63.4 (2012): 593–614. Print.	Pereira, Tony. "The Transition to a Sustainable Society: A New Social Contract." *Environment, Development and Sustainability* 14.2 (2012): 273–81. *Crossref.* Web. 26 June 2012.

Format. Citations for magazines, journals, newspapers, and the like aren't much different from citations for books. MLA's seventh edition, however, introduced some significant changes in how you handle online periodicals (see the table).

Author's Name. List the author(s) as you would for a book citation.

Article Title. Unlike book titles, article titles are usually enclosed in quotation marks.

Periodical Title. Italicize periodical titles, dropping introductory articles (*Aegis*, not *The Aegis*). If you're citing a newspaper your readers may not be familiar with, include with the title—enclosed in brackets but not italicized—the city in which it is published. For example:

> Barber, Rocky. "DEQ Responds to Concerns About Weiser Feedlot." *Idaho Statesman*
>
>   [Boise] 23 Apr. 2014: B1. Print.

Volume and Issue Numbers. Most scholarly journals have both. The latest MLA guidelines require that you include both in your citation. These will appear as weird decimals after the journal title. For example, the sixth volume and third issue of the journal *Diseases of the Dairy Cow* would be 6.3. Popular periodicals frequently don't have issue numbers, and you're not required to use them.

Name of Website, Database, or Sponsor. If the name of the site is different from the title of the piece you're citing, include that name in italics. In addition, if the website's name is different from the name of the organization that hosts it, include the sponsor's name as well. The name of the site's sponsor isn't always obvious. Try looking at the bottom of the page or click on the "About Us" link if there is one. If the publisher is unclear, include *N.p.* (for "no publisher") in your citation. If you do include a publisher's name, don't italicize it. Finally, if you found your source in a library database, identify the database (e.g., *ProQuest, JSTOR, Google Scholar,* etc.).

Date. When citing popular periodicals, include the day, month, and year of the issue you're citing—in that order—following the periodical name. Academic journals are a little different. Because the volume number indicates when the journal was published within a given year, just include the year. Put it in parentheses following the volume number and before the page numbers (see the examples in the "A Journal Article" subsection).

Page Numbers. Include the page numbers of the article at the end of the citation, followed by a period. Just list the pages of the entire article, omitting abbreviations such as *p.* or *pp.* It's common for articles in newspapers and popular magazines *not* to run on consecutive pages. In that case, indicate the page on which the article begins, followed by a "+" (*12+*).

Newspaper pagination can be peculiar. Some papers wed the section (usually a letter) with the page number (*A4*); other papers simply begin numbering anew in each section. Most, however, paginate continuously. See the following sample citations for newspapers for how to deal with these peculiarities.

Online sources, which often have no pagination at all, present special problems. For guidance on how to handle them, see the "Citing Online and Other Sources" subsection.

Publication Medium. Indicate the form in which you found the periodical, usually either "Print" or "Web."

Date of Access. If you did find the journal or magazine online, end your citation with the date you first accessed it.

Sample Periodical Citations
A MAGAZINE ARTICLE

Elliott, Carl. "The New Drug Pushers." *Atlantic Monthly* Apr. 2006: 82–93. Print.

In-Text Citation: (Elliott 92)

Williams, Patricia J. "Unimagined Communities." *Nation* 3 May 2004: 14. Print.

In-Text Citation: (Williams 14)

Citations for magazines that you find online should also include the publication medium ("Web") and the date you accessed the material. For example,

Kaufman, Ken. "Stopover Country." *Audubon Magazine* May–June 2009. Web. 1

July 2009.

In-Text Citation: (Kaufman)

Notice that both the website's name and its publisher are included in the online article below.

Schoen, John W. "Jobless Consumers Will Hold Up Recovery." *Msnbc.com*.

NBC Universal, 2 July 2009. Web. 3 July 2009.

In-Text Citation: (Schoen)

A JOURNAL ARTICLE

There's a good chance that you found a journal article using your library's online database. If so, include the database name, italicized, in your citation. Remember to also include the volume and issue number whenever you cite a journal.

Here's an article from a library database.

Niservich, P. M. "Training Tips for Vegetarian Athletes." *IDEA Fitness Journal* 6.4

(2009). *Physical Education Index.* Web. 2 July 2009.

In-Text Citation: (Niservich)

Here is sample citation for an article in print:

Allen, Rebecca E., and J. M. Oliver. "The Effects of Child Maltreatment on

Language Development." *Child Abuse and Neglect* 6.1 (1982): 299–305. Print.

In-Text Citation: (Allen and Oliver 299–300)

A NEWSPAPER ARTICLE

Some newspapers have several editions (morning edition, late edition, national edition), and each may feature different articles. If an edition is listed on the masthead, include it in the citation.

Mendels, Pamela. "Internet Access Spreads to More Classrooms." *New York Times*

1 Dec. 1999, morning ed.: C1+. Print.

In-Text Citation: (Mendels C1)

Some papers begin numbering pages anew in each section. In that case, include the section number if it's not part of pagination.

Brooks, James. "Lobsters on the Brink." *Portland Press* 29 Nov. 2005, sec. 2: 4.

Print.

In-Text Citation: (Brooks 4)

The decline of print newspapers means you are more likely to find an article online. Because online articles often lack page numbers, you don't need to worry about including page numbers in the citation; but don't forget to include the website's name, publisher, and the date you accessed the article.

Wald, Matthew. "Court Backs EPA on Emissions Rulings." *New York Times*. New

York Times, 26 June 2012. Web. 26 July 2012.

In-Text Citation: (Wald)

AN ARTICLE WITH NO AUTHOR

"The Understanding." *New Yorker* 2 Dec. 1991: 34–35. Print.

In-Text Citation: ("Understanding" 35)

AN EDITORIAL

"Downward Mobility." Editorial. *New York Times* 27 Aug. 2006: 31. Print.

In-Text Citation: ("Downward" 31)

AN OPINION PIECE

Vanden Heuvel, Katrina. "Women Who Don't Have Anything Close to 'It All.'"

Washingtonpost.com. The Washington Post, 26 June 2012. Web. 4 July

2012.

In-Text Citation: (Vanden Heuvel)

A LETTER TO THE EDITOR

Boulay, Harvey. Letter. *Boston Globe* 30 Aug. 2006: 14. Print.

In-Text Citation: (Boulay 14)

A letter to the editor you find online would be cited like this:

Willett, Catherine. "Go Ahead and Test but Spare the Animals." *NYTimes.com*.

New York Times, 2 July 2009. Web. 2 July 2009.

In-Text Citation: (Willett)

A REVIEW

Page, Barbara. Rev. of "Allegories of Cinema: American Film in the Sixties," by David

E. James. *College English* 54 (1992): 945–54. Print.

In-Text Citation: (Page 945–46)

AN ABSTRACT

Edwards, Rob. "Air-Raid Warning." *New Scientist* 14 Aug. 1999: 48–49. Abstract.

MasterFILE Premier. Web. 1 May 2002.

In-Text Citation: (Edwards)

The following citation is from another useful source of abstracts, the *Dissertation Abstracts International*. In this case, the citation is from the print version of the index.

McDonald, James C. "Imitation of Models in the History of Rhetoric: Classical,

Belletristic, and Current-Traditional." U of Texas, Austin. *DAI* 48 (1988): 2613A.

Print.

In-Text Citation: (McDonald 2613A)

Citing Online and Other Sources
AN INTERVIEW

If you conducted the interview yourself, list your subject's name first, indicate what kind of interview it was (telephone, e-mail, or personal interview), and provide the date.

Kelley, Karen. Personal interview. 1 Sept. 2015.

In-Text Citation: (Kelley)

Or avoid parenthetical reference altogether by mentioning the subject's name in the text: According to Lonny Hall,...

If you're citing an interview done by someone else (perhaps in a book or article) and the title does not indicate that it was an interview, you should, after the subject's name, include *Interview*. Always begin the citation with the subject's name.

Stegner, Wallace. Interview. *Conversations with Wallace Stegner.* By Richard Eutlain

and Wallace Stegner. Salt Lake: U of Utah P, 1990. Print.

In-Text Citation: (Stegner 22)

If there are other works by Stegner on the Works Cited page:

(Stegner, *Conversations* 22)

As radio and TV interview programs are increasingly archived on the web, these can be a great source of material for a research essay. In the following example, the interview was on a transcript I ordered from the Fresh Air website. Note that the national network, National Public Radio, *and* the local affiliate that produced the program, WHYY, are included in the citation along with the airdate.

Mairs, Nancy. Interview by Terry Gross. *Fresh Air*. NPR. WHYY, Philadelphia.

7 June 1993. Radio.

In-Text Citation: (Mairs)

The following citation is for an interview published on the web. The second date listed is the date of access.

> Messner, Tammy Faye Bakker. Interview. *The Well Rounded Interview*. Well
>
>> Rounded Entertainment. Aug. 2000. Web. 14 July 2002.
>
> *In-Text Citation:* (Messner)

SURVEYS, QUESTIONNAIRES, AND CASE STUDIES
If you conducted the survey or case study, list it under your name and give it an appropriate title.

> Ball, Helen. "Internet Survey." Boise State U, 2012.
>
> *In-Text Citation:* (Ball)

RECORDINGS
Generally, cite a recording using the name of the performer and italicize the title. Also include the recording company, catalog number, and year. (If you don't know the year, use the abbreviation *n.d.*)

> Orff, Carl. *Carmina Burana*. Cond. Seiji Ozawa. Boston Symphony. RCA, 6533–2-RG,
>
>> n.d. CD.
>
> *In-Text Citation:* (Orff)

TELEVISION AND RADIO PROGRAMS
Include the title of the program (italicized), the station, and the broadcast date. If the episode has a title, list that first in quotation marks. You may also want to include the name of the narrator or producer after the title.

> "Congress Takes Student Loans, Highway Bill to the Wire." *All Things Considered*.
>
>> Natl. Public Radio, Washington, DC, 26 June 2012. Radio.
>
> *In-Text Citation:* ("Congress Takes Student Loans")

ONLINE AUDIO OR VIDEO

> *Sarah Palin 20/20 Interview with Charlie Gibson, Part 2/4*. *YouTube*. YouTube, 12 Sept.
>
>> 2008. Web. 3 July 2009.
>
> *In-Text Citation:* (*Sarah Palin 20/20 Interview*)

> "Bad Bank." *This American Life*. Prod. Ira Glass. NPR. Chicago Public Radio, 27 Feb.
>
>> 2009. Web. 3 July 2009.
>
> *In-Text Citation:* ("Bad Bank")

ONLINE IMAGES

"Passenger Pigeon." Online image. 26 June 2012. *Sarroffillustration.com*. Web. 2

July 2012.

In-Text Citation: ("Passenger Pigeon")

BLOG

O'Brien, Terence. "EPA May Have Suppressed Global Warming Study." *Switched*.

AOL News, 2 July 2009. Web. 3 July 2009.

In-Text Citation: (O'Brien)

PODCAST

Kermode, Mark. "Drag Me to Hell." *5 Live*. BBC Radio, 12 May 2009. Web.

3 July 2009.

In-Text Citation: (Kermode)

WIKI

"Emily Dickinson." *Wikipedia*. Wikipedia Foundation, 2009. Web. 3 July 2009.

In-Text Citation: ("Emily Dickinson")

FILMS, VIDEOTAPES, AND DVDS

Begin with the title (italicized), followed by the director, the distributor, and the year. You may also include names of writers, performers, and producers. End with the date and any other specifics about the characteristics of the film or video-tape that may be relevant (such as length and size).

Saving Private Ryan. Dir. Steven Spielberg. Perf. Tom Hanks, Tom Sizemore, and Matt

Damon. Paramount, 1998. DVD.

In-Text Citation: (*Saving*)

You can also cite a video or film by the name of a contributor you'd like to draw attention to.

Capra, Frank, dir. *It's a Wonderful Life*. Perf. Jimmy Stewart and Donna Reed. RKO

Pictures, 1946. Film.

In-Text Citation: (Capra)

ARTWORK

List each work by artist. Then cite the title of the work (italicized) and where it's located (institution and city). If you've reproduced the work from a published source, include that information as well.

Homer, Winslow. *Casting for a Rise*. N.d. Hirschl and Adler Galleries, New York.

Ultimate Fishing Book. Ed. Lee Eisenberg and DeCourcy Taylor. Boston:

Houghton, 1981. Print.

In-Text Citation: (Homer 113)

LECTURES AND SPEECHES

List by the name of the speaker, followed by the title of the address (if any) in quotation marks, the name of the sponsoring organization, the location, and the date. Be sure to indicate what kind of address it was (Lecture, Speech, etc.).

Naynaha, Siskanna. "Emily Dickinson's Last Poems." Sigma Tau Delta, Boise. 15 Nov.

2014. Lecture.

Avoid the need for parenthetical citation by mentioning the speaker's name in your text.

PAMPHLETS

Cite a pamphlet as you would a book.

New Challenges for Wilderness Conservationists. Washington, DC: Wilderness Society,

2006. Print.

In-Text Citation: (*New Challenges*)

A Sample Paper in MLA Style. Most of the student essays in *The Curious Writer* use MLA style. For a fully documented research paper, see Laura Burns's essay "The 'Unreal Dream': True Crime in the Justice System" in Chapter 10.

MLA VERSUS APA: SOME BASIC DIFFERENCES

MLA Approach	APA Approach
(Author page #)—Example:	**(Author, year)—Example:**
According to Ackerman, there is an infatuation chemical (164).	According to Ackerman (1994), there is an infatuation chemical.
Usually no title page.	Usually title page and abstract. An abstract is a short summary of the paper's content, always less than 250 words in APA style.

MLA Approach	APA Approach
Pagination uses writer's last name and page number. For example:	Pagination uses running head and page number. The "running head" includes the paper's abbreviated title. For example:
Smith 5	EXPORTING JOBS 5
Figures and tables included within the paper.	Figures and tables included in section at the end of the paper.
Bibliography called Works Cited page.	Bibliography called References page.

APA Documentation Guidelines

The American Psychological Association's (APA) citation conventions are the other dominant approach to acknowledging sources. If you're headed for courses in the social sciences, then this is the system you'll use. It's no harder than the MLA system; in fact, the two systems are quite similar. Both use parenthetical citations. Their bibliography (or References page) formats are organized in very similar ways. But there are a few significant differences, some of which are summarized in the table. Detailed descriptions of the APA system are in the following sections.

How the Essay Should Look

Page Format. Papers should be double-spaced, with at least one-inch margins on all sides. Number all pages consecutively, beginning with the title page; put the page number in the upper right corner. Place an abbreviated title of the paper (fifty characters or less, including spaces), flush left and in all capital letters, on every page. As a rule, the first line of all paragraphs of text should be indented five to seven spaces.

Title Page. Unlike a paper in MLA style, an APA-style paper has a separate title page, containing the following information: the title of the paper, the author, and the author's affiliation (e.g., what university she is from). Each line of information should be centered and double-spaced. (See Figure 12.5.) At the top of the title page, flush left and in uppercase letters, you should include the *running head*, or the abbreviation of the title. (Note that "Running head:" should precede the paper's running head only on the title page.) The page number should appear in the upper right corner.

Abstract. Although it's not always required, many APA-style papers include an abstract (no longer than 250 words) following the title page. (See Figure 12.6.) An abstract is essentially a short summary of the paper's contents.

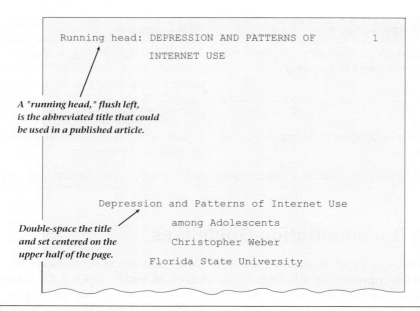

```
Running head: DEPRESSION AND PATTERNS OF          1
                     INTERNET USE
```

A "running head," flush left,
is the abbreviated title that could
be used in a published article.

```
        Depression and Patterns of Internet Use
                     among Adolescents
                     Christopher Weber
                 Florida State University
```

Double-space the title
and set centered on the
upper half of the page.

Figure 12.5 Title page in APA style

An abstract usually follows the title page.
This is a concise (no longer than 120 words)
summary of the article and its thesis,
purpose, or findings.

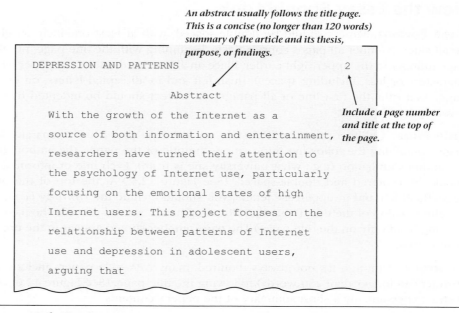

```
DEPRESSION AND PATTERNS                           2

                    Abstract

With the growth of the Internet as a

source of both information and entertainment,

researchers have turned their attention to

the psychology of Internet use, particularly

focusing on the emotional states of high

Internet users. This project focuses on the

relationship between patterns of Internet

use and depression in adolescent users,

arguing that
```

Include a page number
and title at the top of
the page.

Figure 12.6 The abstract page

This is a key feature, because it's usually the first thing a reader encounters. The abstract should include statements about what problem or question the paper examines and what approach it follows; the abstract should also cite the thesis and significant findings. Type *Abstract* at the top of the page, and type the abstract's text in a single block, without indenting the first line.

Body of the Paper. The body of the paper begins with the centered title, followed by a double space and then the text. The running head should appear flush left, and the page number ("3" if the paper has a title page and an abstract) should appear in the upper right corner. (See Figure 12.7.)

You may want to use headings within your paper. If your paper is fairly formal, some headings might be prescribed, such as *Introduction, Method, Results*, and *Discussion*. Or create your own heads to clarify the organization of your paper.

If you use headings, the APA recommends the following hierarchy:

Centered, Boldfaced, Uppercase and Lowercase Letters

Flush Left, Boldfaced, Uppercase and Lowercase Letters

    Indented, boldfaced, lowercase except first letter of first word, end in period.

    Indented, boldfaced, italicized, lowercase except first letter of first word, end in period.

    Indented, italicized, lowercase except first letter of first word, end in period.

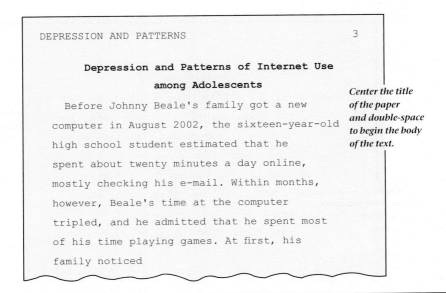

Figure 12.7 The body of the paper in APA style

Papers rarely use all five levels of headings; two or three is probably most common, particularly in student papers. When you use multiple levels, always use them consecutively. In other words, a level 1 heading would always be followed by a level 2 heading (if there is one).

For example,

The Intelligence of Crows

Current Understandings of Crow Intelligence

References Page. All sources cited in the body of the paper are listed alphabetically by author (or by title, if there is no author) on a page titled *References*. See Figure 12.8. This list should begin a new page. Each entry is double-spaced; begin each entry flush left, and indent subsequent lines five to seven spaces. Explanations of how to cite various sources in the References are in the "Preparing the References List" section.

Appendix. This is a seldom-used feature of an APA-style paper, although you might find it helpful if you want to include detailed material or material that isn't central to the discussion in the body of your paper, such as a detailed description of a device mentioned in the paper, a copy of a survey, or the like. Each appendix should begin on a separate page and be labeled *Appendix*, followed by *A*, *B*, and so on, consecutively, if there is more than one appendix.

Notes. Several kinds of notes might be included in an APA-style paper. The most common is *content notes*, or brief commentaries by the writer keyed to superscript numbers in the body of the text. These notes are useful for discussing key points

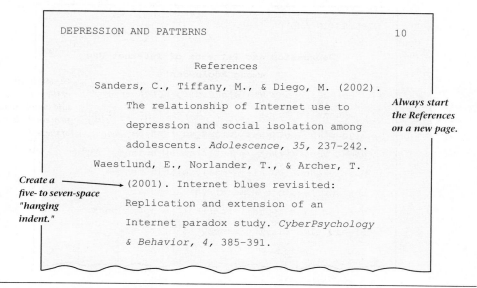

Figure 12.8 The References page

that are relevant but might be distracting if explored in the text of your paper. Present all notes, numbered consecutively, on a page titled *Footnotes*. Each note should be double-spaced. Begin each note with the appropriate superscript number. Indent each first line five to seven spaces; consecutive lines run the full page measure.

Tables and Figures. The final section of an APA-style paper includes the tables and figures that were mentioned in the text. All table text should be double-spaced. Type the table number at the top of the page, flush left. Number tables Table 1, Table 2, and so on, corresponding to the order in which they are mentioned in the text. A table may also include a title. Each table should begin on a separate page.

Figures (illustrations, graphs, charts, photographs, and drawings) are handled similarly to tables. Each should be titled *Figure* and numbered consecutively. Captions may be included, and should appear below each figure.

Language and Style. The APA is comfortable with the italicizing and boldfacing functions of word processors, and underlining is a thing of the past. The guidelines for *italicizing* call for its use when writing the following:

- The titles of books, periodicals, and publications that appear on microfilm.

- When using new or specialized terms, but only the first time you use them (e.g., "the authors' *paradox study* of Internet users...").

- When citing a phrase, letter, or word as an example (e.g., "the second *a* in *separate* can be remembered by noticing the word *rat*").

The APA calls for quotation marks around the title of an article or book chapter when mentioned in your essay.

Been nagged all your life by the question of whether to spell out numbers or use numerals in APA style? Here, finally, is the answer: Numbers less than 10 that aren't precise measurements should be spelled out, and numbers 10 or more should be digits.

Citing Sources in Your Essay

When the Author is Mentioned in the Text. The author/date system is pretty uncomplicated. If you mention the name of the author in text, simply place the year his work was published in parentheses immediately after his name. For example:

Herrick (1999) argued that college testing was biased against minorities.

When the Author Isn't Mentioned in the Text. If you don't mention the author's name in the text, then include the name parenthetically. For example:

A New Hampshire political scientist (Sundberg, 2012) recently studied the state's

presidential primary.

Note that the author's name and the year of her work are separated by a comma.

When to Cite Page Numbers. If the information you're citing came from specific pages, chapters, or sections of a source, those specific elements may also be included in the parenthetical citation. Including page numbers is essential when quoting a source. For example:

The first stage of language acquisition is called "caretaker speech" (Moskowitz,

1985, pp. 50–51), in which children model their parents' language.

The same passage might also be cited this way if the author's name is mentioned in the text:

Moskowitz (1985) observed that the first stage of language acquisition is called

"caretaker speech" (pp. 50–51), in which children model their parents' language.

A Single Work By Two or More Authors. When a work has two authors, always mention them both whenever you cite their work in your paper. For example:

Allen and Oliver (1998) observed many cases of child abuse and concluded that

maltreatment inhibited language development.

If a source has more than two authors but fewer than six, mention them all the first time you refer to their work. However, any subsequent in-text references should include the surname of the first author followed by the abbreviation *et al*. When citing works with six or more authors, *always* use the first author's surname and *et al*.

A Work With No Author. When a work has no author, cite an abbreviated title and the year. Place article or chapter titles in quotation marks, and *italicize* book titles. For example:

The editorial ("Sinking," 2012) concluded that the EPA was mired in bureaucratic

muck.

Two or More Works By the Same Author. Works by the same author are usually distinguished by the date; one author's works are rarely published the same year. But if they are, distinguish among such works by adding an *a* or *b* immediately following the year in the parenthetical citation. The References list entries will also have these suffixes. For example:

> Douglas's studies (1986a) on the mating habits of lobsters revealed that the
>
> females are dominant. He also found that the female lobsters have the uncanny
>
> ability to smell a loser (1986b).

This citation alerts readers that the information came from two different studies by Douglas, both published in 1986.

An Institutional Author. When citing a corporation or agency as a source, simply list the year of the study in parentheses if you mention the institution in the text:

> The Environmental Protection Agency (2012) issued an alarming report on ozone
>
> pollution.

If you don't mention the institutional source in the text, spell it out in its entirety, along with the year. In subsequent parenthetical citations, you can abbreviate the name as long as the abbreviation will be understandable. For example:

> A study (Environmental Protection Agency [EPA], 2012) predicted dire consequenc-
>
> es from continued ozone depletion.

And later in the text:

> Continued ozone depletion may result in widespread skin cancers (EPA, 2012).

Multiple Works in the Same Parentheses. Occasionally, you'll want to cite several works at once that speak to a topic you're writing about in your essay. Probably the most common instance is when you refer to the findings of several relevant studies, something that is a good idea as you establish a context for what has already been said about your research topic. For example,

> A number of researchers have explored the connection between Internet use and
>
> depression (Sanders, Field, & Diego, 2000; Waestlund, Norlander, & Archer, 2001).

When listing multiple authors within the same parentheses, order them as they appear in the References. Semicolons separate each entry.

Interviews, E-Mail, and Letters. Interviews and other personal communications are not listed in the References at the back of the paper because they are not *recoverable data*, but they should be parenthetically cited in the text. Provide the initials and surname of the subject (if not mentioned in the text), the nature of the communication, and the complete date, if possible.

Nancy Diamonti (personal communication, November 12, 2012) disagrees with the critics of *Sesame Street*.

In a recent e-mail, Michelle Payne (personal communication, January 4, 2012) complained that....

New Editions of Old Works. For reprints of older works, include both the year of the original publication and that of the reprint edition (or the translation).

Pragmatism as a philosophy sought connection between scientific study and real people's lives (James, 1906/1978).

A Website. When referring to an *entire* website (see the following example), cite the address parenthetically in your essay. As for e-mail, it isn't necessary to include a citation for an entire website in your References list. However, you should cite online documents that contribute information to your paper (see the "Sample References: Other" subsection).

One of the best sites for searching the so-called Invisible Web is the Librarians Index to the Internet (http://www.lii.org).

Preparing the References List

All parenthetical citations in the body of the paper correspond to a complete listing of sources on the References page. The format for this section was described earlier (see the "References Page" subsection).

Order of Sources. List the References entries alphabetically by author or by the first key word of the title if there is no author. The only complication is when you have several articles or books by the same author. If the sources weren't published in the same year, list them in chronological order, the earliest first. If the sources *were* published in the same year, include a lowercase letter to distinguish them. For example:

Lane, B. (1991a). Verbal medicine...

Lane, B. (1991b). Writing...

While the alphabetical principle—listing authors according to the alphabetical placement of their last names—works in most cases, there are a few variations you should be aware of.

- If you have several entries by the same author, list them by year of publication, beginning with the earliest.
- Because scholars and writers often collaborate, you may have several citations in which an author is listed with several *different* collaborators. List these entries alphabetically according to the second author's last name. For example,

Brown, M., & Nelson, A. (2002)

Brown, M., & Payne, M. (1999)

Order of Information. A citation of a periodical in APA style includes this information, in this order: author, year of publication, article title, periodical title, volume and section numbers, and page numbers. A citation of a book in APA style includes the following information, in this order: author, year of publication, book title, and publication information.

Citations of electronic sources include some additional information. If you're harvesting your books and articles online or from a library database, you need to cite in a way that makes it clear how readers can find the book or document. That seems simple, right? It isn't always. Typically, you include the URL for an online document in your citation, even if it's long and ugly. But URLs can change, and they are vulnerable to transcription mistakes. To solve this problem, the APA uses something called the Digital Object Identifier (see the description in the paragraph headed "DOI or URL"). This is a number that is a permanent link to the document. But not all documents have them, and if they don't, cite their URLs.

One other bit of information you usually include in a citation for an electronic document is the retrieval date, or exactly when you accessed the work online. This can be omitted, however, when the document you're citing is "archival." An archival copy is a final version, and it's usually the version that appeared in print.

Author. List up to seven authors using last name, comma, and then initials. Invert all authors' names. Use commas to separate authors' names and add an ampersand (&) before the last author's name. When citing eight or more authors, list the first six, and then add ellipses ("…") and the name of the last author. When citing an edited book, list the editor(s) in place of the author(s), and add the abbreviation Ed. or Eds. in parentheses following the initials. End the list of names with a period.

Date. List the year the work was published along with the date, if it's a magazine or newspaper article (see the "Sample References: Articles" subsection), in parentheses, immediately after the last author's name. Add a period after the closing parenthesis.

Article or Book Title. APA style departs from MLA here. In APA style, only the first word of the article title is capitalized, and the title appears without italics or quotation marks. Book titles are italicized, with only the first word of the title and the first word of any subtitle capitalized. End all titles with periods.

Periodical Title and Publication Information. Italicize the complete periodical title, and use both uppercase and lowercase letters. Add the volume number (if any), also italicized. Separate the title and volume number with a comma (e.g., *Journal of Mass Communication, 10*, 138–150). If each issue of the periodical starts with page 1, then also include, in roman type, the issue number in parentheses immediately after the volume number (see examples following). End the entry with the page numbers of the article. Use the abbreviation *p.* or *pp.* if you are citing a newspaper. Other APA-style abbreviations include the following:

chap.	p. (pp.)
Ed./Eds. (Editor/Editors), ed. (edition)	Vol.
Rev. ed.	No.
2nd ed.	Pt.
Trans.	Suppl.

For books, list the city and state or country of publication (use postal abbreviations) and the name of the publisher; separate the city and publisher with a colon. End the citation with a period.

Remember that the first line of each citation should begin flush left, and all subsequent lines should be indented five to seven spaces. Double-space all entries.

Retrieval Date. If you're citing an electronic document, you often indicate when you accessed the book or article. This is important because online documents can change, and the retrieval date gives readers a "snapshot" of what version you were looking at when you did your research. When a citation includes a Digital Object Identifier (DOI), no other retrieval information is needed. In the absence of a DOI, and when a URL is included, don't include retrieval dates unless it's likely that the source material will change in the future (e.g., Wikis).

DOI or URL. These are more ingredients for your alphabet soup. So that readers can locate the electronic documents you're citing, you need to tell them where you found them. You frequently do this by including the URL. But more and more documents in the social sciences include a Digital Object Identifier (DOI), a permanent link to the work. The DOI is often listed on the article's first page. It may also be hidden under the "Article" button that appears with the work on certain library databases.

Here's a summary of the similarities and differences involved in citing print and electronic journals and magazines in APA style:

Print Periodical	Electronic Periodical
• Author(s)	• Author(s)
• (Date)	• (Date)
• Article title	• Article title
• Periodical title	• Periodical title
• Issue and volume number	• Issue and volume number
• Page numbers	• Page numbers
	• Retrieval date (unless archival)
	• DOI (if available) or URL (if DOI unavailable)

Sample References: Articles

A JOURNAL ARTICLE

When citing an online article, include information about how readers can find it. Use the DOI, if available. For example,

Mori, K., Ujiie, T., Smith, A., & Howlin, P. (2009). Parental stress associated with caring for children with Asperger's syndrome. *Pediatrics International, 51*(3), 364–370. doi:10.1111/j.1442-200X-2008.0278.x

In-Text Citation: (Mori, Ujiie, Smith, & Howlin, 2009); (Mori et al., 2009) in subsequent citations. If authors are quoted, include page numbers.

If there is no DOI, include the document's URL.

Wing, L. (1981). Asperger's syndrome: A clinical account. *Psychological Medicine, 11*(1), 115–129. Retrieved from http://search.ebscohost.com/login.aspx?direct=true&db=psyh&AN=1981-30537-001&site=ehost-live

In-Text Citation: (Wing, 1981)

Cite a print journal article like this:

Blager, F. B. (1979). The effect of intervention on the speech and language of children. *Child Abuse and Neglect, 5*, 91–96.

In-Text Citation: (Blager, 1979)

If the author is mentioned in the text, just parenthetically cite the year:

Blager (1979) stated that....

If the author is quoted, include the page number(s):

(Blager, 1979, p. 92)

A MAGAZINE ARTICLE

Maya, P. (1981, December). The civilizing of Genie. *Psychology Today,* 28–34.

In-Text Citation: (Maya, 1981)

Maya (1981) observed that....

When citing a magazine article from a database, include the URL. Many databases include a "permanent link" to the article on the citation page. Use that if available. Notice also that the database name is not included.

Horowitz, A. (July, 2008). My dog is smarter than your dog. *Discover Magazine,*
219(9), 71. Retrieved from http://search.ebscohost.com.libproxy.boisestate.
edu/login.aspx?direct=true&db=aph&an=32580478&site=ehost-live

In-Text Citation: (Horowitz, 2008)

If quoting, include page numbers:

(Horowitz, 2008, p. 71)

AN ARTICLE ON A WEBSITE
This article has no author, so the citation begins with the title.

Enhancing male body image. (2006). *Nationaleatingdisorders.org*. Retrieved July 9,
2009, from http://www.nationaleatingdisorders.org/

In-Text Citation: ("Enhancing," 2006)

If quoting, include the page number(s): ("Enhancing," 2006, p. 28)

A NEWSPAPER ARTICLE

Honan, W. (2004, January 24). The war affects Broadway. *The New York Times,* pp. C15–C16.

In-Text Citation: (Honan, 2004)

Honan (2004) argued that. . . .

Honan (2004) said that "Broadway is a battleground" (p. C15).

If there is no author, a common situation with newspaper articles, alphabetize the entry using the first "significant word" in the article title. The parenthetical citation will use an abbreviation of the title in quotation marks, then the year.

There's a good chance that you'll find newspaper articles online. Here's how you cite them:

Jennings, D. (2009, July 7). With cancer, you can't hurry recovery. *The New York
Times*. Retrieved from http://www.nytimes.com

In-Text Citation: (Jennings, 2009)

Sample References: Books
A BOOK

Lukas, A. J. (1986). *Common ground: A turbulent decade in the lives of three
American families*. New York, NY: Random House.

In-Text Citation: (Lukas, 1986)

According to Lukas (1986), . . .

If quoting, include the page number(s).

AN ONLINE BOOK

If you're citing an entire book you found online, include the URL. For example,

Suzuki, D. T. (1914). *A brief history of early Chinese philosophy*. Retrieved from

http://www.archive.org/details/briefhistoryofea00suzuuoft

In-Text Citation: (Suzuki, 1914)

When citing a chapter from an online book, include a bit more information, including the name of the database (if any) from which you retrieved it.

Hollin, C. R. (2002). Criminal psychology. In C. R. Hollin (Ed.), *Oxford handbook of criminology* (pp. 144–174). Retrieved from Academic Research Premier database.

In-Text Citation: (Hollin, 2002)

A SOURCE MENTIONED BY ANOTHER SOURCE

Frequently you'll read an article that mentions another article you haven't read. Whenever possible, track down that original article and read it in its entirety. But when that's not possible, you need to make it clear that you know of the article and its findings or arguments indirectly. The APA convention for this is to use the expression *as cited in* parenthetically, followed by the author and date of the indirect source. For example, suppose you want to use some information from Eric Weiser's piece that you read about in Charlotte Jones's book. In your essay, you would write something like:

Weiser argues (as cited in Jones, 2002) that. . . .

A BOOK OR ARTICLE WITH MORE THAN ONE AUTHOR

Rosenbaum, A., & O'Leary, D. (1978). Children: The unintended victims of marital violence. *American Journal of Orthopsychiatry, 4,* 692–699.

In-Text Citation: (Rosenbaum & O'Leary, 1978)

Rosenbaum and O'Leary (1978) believed that. . . .

If quoting, include the page number(s).

A BOOK OR ARTICLE WITH AN UNKNOWN AUTHOR

The politics of war. (2004, June 1). *The New York Times*, p. 36.

In-Text Citation: ("Politics," 2004)

Or mention the source in the text:

In "The Politics of War" (2004), an editorialist compared Iraq to. . . .

If quoting, provide page number(s) as well.

The Chicago manual of style (14th ed.). (1993). Chicago, IL: University of Chicago Press.

In-Text Citation: (*Chicago Manual of Style,* 1993)

According to the *Chicago Manual of Style* (1993), . . .

If quoting, include the page number(s).

A BOOK WITH AN INSTITUTIONAL AUTHOR

American Red Cross. (1999). *Advanced first aid and emergency care.* New York, NY: Doubleday.

In-Text Citation: (American Red Cross, 1999)

The book *Advanced First Aid and Emergency Care* (American Red Cross, 1999) stated that. . . .

If quoting, include the page number(s).

A BOOK WITH AN EDITOR

Crane, R. S. (Ed.). (1952). *Critics and criticism.* Chicago, IL: University of Chicago Press.

In-Text Citation: (Crane, 1952)

In his preface, Crane (1952) observed that. . . .

If quoting, include the page number(s).

A SELECTION IN A BOOK WITH AN EDITOR

McKeon, R. (1952). Rhetoric in the Middle Ages. In R. S. Crane (Ed.), *Critics and criticism* (pp. 260–289). Chicago, IL: University of Chicago Press.

In-Text Citation: (McKeon, 1952)

McKeon (1952) argued that. . . .

If quoting, include the page number(s).

A REPUBLISHED WORK

James, W. (1978). *Pragmatism.* Cambridge, MA: Harvard University Press (Original work published 1907).

In-Text Citation: (James, 1907/1978)

According to William James (1907/1978), . . .

If quoting, include the page number(s).

AN ABSTRACT

The growth of online databases for articles has increased the availability of full-text versions and abstracts of articles. Although the full article is almost always best, sometimes an abstract alone contains some useful information. If the abstract was retrieved from a database or some other secondary source, include information about it. Aside from the name of the source, this information might involve the date, if different from the year of publication of the original article; an abstract number; or a page number. In the following example, the abstract was retrieved from an online database, Biological Abstracts.

> Garcia, R. G. (2002). Evolutionary speed of species invasions. *Evolution, 56,*
>
> 661–668. Abstract retrieved from Biological Abstracts database.

In-Text Citation: (Garcia, 2002), or Garcia (2002) argues that. . . .

A BOOK REVIEW

> Dentan, R. K. (1989). A new look at the brain [Review of the book *The dreaming*
>
> *brain*]. *Psychiatric Journal,* 13, 51.

In-Text Citation: (Dentan, 1989)

Dentan (1989) argues that. . . .

If quoting, include the page number(s).

An online book review would include the same information but with the phrase "Retrieved from" and the review's URL.

ONLINE ENCYCLOPEDIA

> Turner, B. S. (2007). Body and society. In G. Ritzer (Ed.), *Blackwell encyclopedia of*
>
> *sociology*. Retrieved July 7, 2009, from http://blackwellreference.com

In-Text Citation: (Turner, 2007)

Because they are collaboratively written, Wikipedia articles have no single author. Usually, therefore, the citation should begin with the article title. For example,

> Ticks. (n.d.). In *Wikipedia*. Retrieved July 9, 2009, from http://en.wikipedia.
>
> org<200b>/wiki/ticks

In-Text Citation: ("Ticks," n.d.)

Sample References: Other

A GOVERNMENT DOCUMENT

> U.S. Bureau of the Census. (2004). *Statistical abstract of the United States*
>
> (126th ed.). Washington, DC: U.S. Government Printing Office.

In-Text Citation: (U.S. Bureau of the Census, 2004)

According to the U.S. Census Bureau (2004), . . .

If quoting, include the page number(s).

A LETTER TO THE EDITOR

> Hill, A. C. (2006, February 19). A flawed history of blacks in Boston [Letter to the
>
> editor]. *The Boston Globe*, p. 22.

In-Text Citation: (Hill, 2006)

Hill (2006) complained that. . . .

If quoting, include page number(s).

A PUBLISHED INTERVIEW

Personal interviews are not cited in the References section of an APA-style paper, unlike published interviews. Here is a citation for a published interview:

> Cotton, P. (2004, April). [Interview with Jake Tule, psychic]. *Chronicles*
>
> *Magazine*, 24–28.

In-Text Citation: (Cotton, 2004)

Cotton (2004) noted that. . . .

If quoting, include the page number(s).

A FILM OR VIDEOTAPE

> Hitchcock, A. (Producer & Director). (1954). *Rear window* [Motion picture]. Los
>
> Angeles, CA: MGM.

In-Text Citation: (Hitchcock, 1954)

In *Rear Window*, Hitchcock (1954). . . .

PODCAST, VIDEO, AND AUDIO

Shier, J. (Producer & Director). (2005). Saving the grizzly: One hair at a time. *Terra: The nature of our world* [Podcast]. Retrieved from http://www<200b>. lifeonterra.com/episode.php?id=1

In-Text Citation: (Shier, 2005)

Uhry, A. (2009, July 6). Private education in America. *The Economist* [Podcast]. Retrieved from http://podcast.com/episode/40782102/5356/

In-Text Citation: (Uhry, 2009)

A TELEVISION PROGRAM

Burns, K. (Executive producer). (1996). *The west* [Television broadcast]. New York, NY, and Washington, DC: Public Broadcasting Service.

In-Text Citation: (Burns, 1996)

In Ken Burns's (1996) film, . . .

For an episode of a television series, use the scriptwriter as the author, and provide the director's name after the scriptwriter. List the producer's name after the episode.

Hopley, J. (Writer/Director), & Shannon, J. (Writer/Director). (2006). Buffalo burrito/Parkerina [Television series episode]. In J. Lenz (Producer), *Mr. Meaty*. New York, NY: Nickelodeon.

In-Text Citation: (Hopley & Shannon, 2006)

Fans were appalled by the second episode, when Hopley and Shannon (2006). . . .

A MUSICAL RECORDING

Wolf, K. (1986). Muddy roads [Recorded by E. Clapton]. *On Gold in California* [CD]. Santa Monica, CA: Rhino Records. (1990).

In-Text Citation: (Wolf, 1986, track 5)

In Wolf's (1986) song, . . .

A COMPUTER PROGRAM

OmniPage Pro 14 (Version 14) [Computer software]. (2003). Peabody, MA: Scansoft.

In-Text Citation: (OmniPage Pro, Version 14, 2003)

Scansoft's new software, OmniPage Pro (2003), is reputed. . . .

DISCUSSION LISTS

Discussion lists abound on the Internet. They range from groups of flirtatious teenagers to those with a serious academic purpose. Although virtually all of these discussion lists are based on e-mail, they do vary a bit. The most useful lists for academic research tend to be e-mail discussion lists. Newsgroups, or Usenet groups, are extremely popular among more-general Internet users. Various search engines can help you find discussion groups appropriate for your topic. You can join or monitor the current discussion or, in some cases, search the archives for contributions that interest you. Google is a great search tool for newsgroups and includes an archive for many of them. *If there are no archives, don't include the citation in your References list, because the information isn't recoverable.* However, you may still cite these discussion groups in your essay as personal communications.

The method of citation varies slightly if it's a newsgroup, an online forum, or an electronic mailing list. For example, a newsgroup posting would be cited like this:

Hord, J. (2002, July 11). Re: Why do pigeons lift one wing up in the air?

[Online forum comment]. Message archived at rec.pets.birds.pigeons

In-Text Citation: (Hord, 2002), or Hord asks (2002)....

Note that the citation includes the subject line of the message as the title and the message number of the "thread" (the particular discussion topic). The prefix for this newsgroup is *rec*, which indicates the list is hobby oriented.

Electronic mailing lists would be cited this way:

Cook, D. (2002, July 19). Grammar and the teaching of writing [Electronic mailing

list message]. Retrieved from http://listserv.comptalk<200b>.boisestate.edu

In-Text Citation: (Cook, 2002), or According to Cook (2002)....

E-MAIL

E-mail is not cited in the list of references. But you should cite e-mail in the text of your essay. It should look like this:

In-Text Citation: M. Payne (personal communication, January 4, 2012) argued that

responding to personal writing....

BLOG

Notice in this example that the blogger uses a screen name.

Rizaro. (2009, July 7). Anxiety and suicide [Web log post]. Retrieved from

HelptoHealth.co.cc

A Sample Paper in APA Style. To see a documented student research paper in APA style, go to Kersti Harter's ethnographic essay "Beyond 'Gaydar'" on pages 330–339 in Chapter 9.

Using What You Have Learned

1. **Use sources effectively and control sources so they don't control you.** In college you'll be writing about subjects you know little about. As a novice researcher in these domains, this is a juggling act. You need to understand what you read, evaluate its relevance, assess its credibility, and then deploy it in your own work. That's a lot. This is one reason why it's so tempting to throw up your hands and simply "dump" information into your writing without thinking much about it. But now you have some tools to avoid doing this, and one of the most important is writing *while* you collect and read information. Assert control over information before you start a draft and you'll find the draft much easier to write.

2. **Practice summarizing, paraphrasing, and quoting and apply these to your own work.** The Citation Project published a study recently that reviewed the research routines of college students writing research papers. One of their findings was that students almost never summarize their sources. What they do instead is something called "patchwriting," in which they essentially reproduce what they read, changing some words and maybe some grammatical structures. Patchwriting may not be plagiarism, but it doesn't involve much critical understanding of the source. Of the three— summary, paraphrasing, and quoting—summary may be the most academically useful because it requires a reader to understand and think about a source. When you can, always use summary as you're reading—and after you've read—something you want to use in your writing.

3. **Understand and identify plagiarism to avoid it in your own work.** It's no secret that plagiarism is a huge problem on college campuses. What is less well-known is that the vast majority of it is *unintentional*. If you ever have any questions about what constitutes plagiarism, return to this chapter and reread the definition on page 425 in the "Avoiding Plagiarism" section. And if you ever have questions, don't hesitate to ask your instructor.

4. **Cite sources using MLA and APA documentation styles.** Citation can be mind-numbing. I find it so. But remember that it's not just about following rules but about telling a story. When you cite an author, you are identifying the source of the ideas that changed the way you think. When you get these authors in conversation with each other, you are creating a scene that's probably never been staged before with these particular authors. And the best part? It's *your* scene in *your* story.

13

Re-Genre: Repurposing Your Writing for Multimedia Genres

Learning Objectives

In this chapter, you'll learn to

13.1 Analyze the rhetorical implications of repurposing a writing assignment into a different genre.

13.2 Develop rhetorical goals for a revision of an essay and use them to choose an appropriate multimodal genre.

13.3 Understand and apply the conventions of a multimodal genre.

An old professor of mine is retiring, and I was invited to write a short tribute. I did what I usually do: I sat down in front of my notebook and did some fastwriting to figure out what I might say, and then I started to craft a brief testimonial. "The best of my teachers I absorb into my own thinking in much the same way a successful transplant patient adapts to another's heart," I wrote. "They become a part of the way I think, and I find myself wondering from time to time whose idea was whose." This went on for a few paragraphs, and I was more or less pleased with it, when I received an e-mail. "We're going to do video tributes to Dr. Newkirk and show it at the conference," Barry wrote. "So send me a 30-second clip. I'll edit it as necessary." Certainly the easiest thing I could do, I initially thought, was to read my tribute in front of the camera. But this seemed off. Somehow the idea of reading my testimonial like a news anchor—a talking head—seemed inappropriate for the occasion and wouldn't adequately reflect how I feel about the man.

I don't know much about video. But I do know that it isn't a formal medium, and at the very least it demands that there is something to *see*, and watching me read a testimonial wouldn't be much to look at.

The problem I faced after Barry sent me his e-mail is exactly the challenge you'll explore in this chapter: How do you take something you've written and *re-purpose* it into another genre for a different audience and occasion? If you think about it, this is something we do all the time. Imagine, for example, that you wrote a narrative essay in English that you're really proud of, and at dinner that night you want to tell your partner the story. In the absence of the text itself, you have to somehow capture in speech what you wrote. Since we're all practiced at talking, you intuitively know that you will tell this story not just with words but also with gestures. You might move in a little closer to emphasize a particularly poignant moment in your story, and change the register of your voice. What you're attempting to do is go from one mode of communication—a written text—to another—speech— and in the process you make adjustments in both the content of the message and its delivery. You are *repurposing* your narrative essay in a different mode for a different rhetorical occasion: an informal conversation over the dinner table with someone you like and trust.

While this move might be a fairly common occurrence in our everyday lives, we rarely think much about what it demands, and this is especially true when we take something we've written and try to adapt it to other rhetorical situations. For example,

- When you shift from a written text to one that uses other modes—video, graphics, sound, and so on—how does that change the writing?

13.1

Analyze the rhetorical implications of repurposing a writing assignment into a different genre.

Students on Re-Genre

I have to say that, although it's early, I think this may turn out to be one of the most valuable assignments that we do. This is because it has application to more than just writing. One of the flaws of many general education classes is their lack of interconnectivity among other courses. English is JUST about writing, Biology is ONLY about science etc. Teaching this way is fundamentally flawed and lacks real world application. In the real world we often have to combine multiple different knowledge bases and skill sets in order to produce the kinds of works that employers search for.
Ryan

- What seems fundamentally different about writing in multimedia genres?
- If the choice of medium is yours, how do you choose the *right* form into which to repurpose your writing? What rhetorical considerations—purpose, audience, and message—might help in making that choice?

Then there's the question you might be asking yourself at this moment: Why would I want to experiment with repurposing a writing assignment in the first place?

What Writers Can Learn from Re-Genre: Knowledge Transfer

As I noted earlier, this isn't merely an academic exercise. As lifelong communicators, we repurpose written texts from time to time without thinking about the concept of re-genre at all. But you also do it in school whenever you are asked to develop a PowerPoint presentation to go along with your research paper, or to develop a poster that summarizes your project for an undergraduate research conference. However, practicing re-genre as a deep revision strategy in this class is useful to you as a writer, too. First, it builds your rhetorical muscle. Whenever you shift from one rhetorical situation to another, you have to reconsider all the elements that will make your message effective: What is my purpose in this situation, who is my audience, what do they know and what do they need to know about my topic, what do I want them to do? The rhetorical implications of this shift in situation become even more dramatic when you're remaking the *same material* for a different audience. In this case, though, you're not only shifting audiences, you're shifting genres. What does this mean?

The word "form" is often used interchangeably with "genre." That's okay, except that it implies that genre is merely a container into which your pour content, and like plaster in a mold, that content takes the shape of the form it's in. But genre isn't simply a container. It actively interacts with the content, changing the material it holds, and in turn being changed by the material. Genres are dynamic things. More important, though, is that the metaphor of form implies that genre is not only inert but opaque—and who can see through a plaster mold? The real power of genre is that it is something *through which we see* the things that interest us. It mediates our relationship to those things, shifting the way we see and what we notice. So when you're repurposing, say, a written proposal (Chapter 6) on campus sustainability to turn it into a video public service announcement, you'll return to the topic with new eyes. Suddenly, you'll see the visual possibilities of a chart in your written proposal that illustrates food waste at the campus cafeteria. Might the waste be dramatized by filming people throwing food into garbage bins, and editing the video so that this action is quickly replayed over and over again in a ten-second clip?

Shifting genres goes way beyond the usual rhetorical adjustments we make when writing for different audiences. Shifting genres means finding new ways to see what we've seen before. But rather than just talk about this shifting in the abstract, I'll tell you a re-genre story about one of my students.

Transfer From Blog Essay to Podcast: A Case Study

Andrea is a blogger, something that she describes as a form of "essaying" (see Chapter 3) that helps her to figure out what she thinks and feels, although sometimes, she says, "I don't hit the mark." In the midst of a breakup with her boyfriend, Andrea stumbled onto a box of old photographs in her garage, including some pictures of Jon, an old high school flame. This coincidental convergence of events—the abrupt end of a current relationship and the nostalgic recollection of an old one—naturally inspired a blog post that explored a familiar story: "the love that got away." But it had a contemporary twist. Andrea did what many of us do these days when we think of an old friend or lover: She looked on Facebook to see where Jon is and what he is doing now. The writing became not just a meditation on "the love that got away" theme but on how social media have turned this searching into a peculiar nostalgic exercise, one that involves sending out the hounds to pick up the scent of old lovers on Facebook. Andrea wrote the essay and posted the blog.

That might have been the end of it, but then Andrea thought that the essay might lend itself nicely to a podcast (or radio essay), a form that she had experimented with in several of my classes. In some ways, it was a logical rhetorical move. The blog is a genre, much like the personal essay, that establishes a relatively intimate relationship with its audience, and the radio essay is intimate, too. The voice of the narrator enters listeners' private worlds, much like a good friend does. But Andrea knew enough about this re-genre to know that it would change the original, written text in some basic ways. To start with, imagine the dramatic change in the rhetorical situation between a text that will be read and one that will only be heard once. With a written text, we can re-read, circling back to make sure that we understand. In an audio essay, we don't have that luxury, and this puts a special burden on the writer of an audio essay. The language has to be engaging, clear, and memorable. There are also implications for the structure of the work. Information has to be sequenced in a way that makes it easy to follow, and still coherent if listeners don't quite catch everything. In addition, this is a genre that exploits sound in ways that written texts can't—in addition to the spoken voice, with all of its emotional range and nuance, audio essays can include music tracks, ambient sound, and even interview clips.

Keeping all of this in mind, Andrea wrote a new version of her blog as a radio essay script, and when I asked her how this repurposing changed things, she told me about how the new genre changed the *structure* of her blog:

- She revised the beginning. In the original blog essay, the opening line was "My name is Andrea, and I suffer from nostalgia." She realized that this lacked tension and interest, things that are essential to catch a listener's ear, so she rewrote the opening to begin with this sentence: "Jon Berger will never be my husband."

- Andrea also realized that the structure of the original essay, which relied largely on exposition, simply wouldn't work well in an audio essay. Exposition isn't easy for listeners to retain, and it slows things down. The obvious solution, she thought, was to rewrite the original to emphasize the story, exploiting anecdotes rather than a lot of explanation.

Andrea also told me that the re-genre forced her to reconsider the *language and syntax* of the original blogged essay. Two things became obvious to her immediately: The language should be relatively simple and exclude words that we tend not to use in speech, and it must also be "punchy." "In writing, it's easy to add a long string of introductory clauses," Andrea said. "But in a radio essay you need an actor and an action, actor/action/actor/action." She offered this example:

> **Original essay:** "I don't know what it feels like for most scorned lovers when they find their boyfriends-of-the-past hiding in a box in their garage, but for me, it was fun and sad and unnerving and uncomfortable." While there is a subject in the beginning, we don't get to the meat of the sentence until "but for me, it was fun and sad and...."

> **Radio essay:** "When I think of Jon now, I get a lump in my throat."

All writing has qualities of speech, something that at times we describe as "voice," but it's also true that writing is *not* speech. An audio essay, however, encourages writers to move more towards the qualities of speech in their prose (simplicity and punchiness), *and* to exploit the sound of their voices for rhetorical effect. Here's what Andrea said about this: "I think the coolest aspect of the audio essay is the listener can hear emotion in your voice. They can hear exactly how your voice wavers and they can hear the rawness that doesn't necessarily come across in writing. They can hear the inflection and tone and pauses: that's one of the best parts. In this piece, I think you'd hear a bit of heartbreak come through, but also a good sense of embarrassment at the realization that I was stalking someone on Facebook because it was like this nostalgia infection I had contracted."

"Re-genre" is an act of imagination. You have to think imaginatively, as Andrea did, about the promise and possibilities that an alternative genre affords. But it is also a calculated move that requires an analysis of the genre's conventions, and the rhetorical implications of the shift in purpose and audience. In the sections that follow, I'll walk you through some of these calculations, beginning with a consideration of the "modes" of expression beyond written words that open new avenues for communication.

Beyond Words: Communicating in Other Modes

I've been on an eBay typewriter-buying binge in the past year. I'm old enough to remember using a Royal manual typewriter to compose all of my papers for college, and though I gratefully made the transition to computers in the early nineties, I still miss the sound of words clanking into place and the physical finger work of getting thoughts on paper. While typewriting back then was a sensory experience for me as a writer—it involved sound, sight, and gesture as well as words—it wasn't until I started seeing my writing on a computer screen that I began to see that the writing I produced had multimodal properties. I started to attend more to the look of the writing—the visual elements like font and spacing. When my writing students started handing in papers that they'd composed on early Macs, I began to see the graphic possibilities of written texts even more clearly.

It's easy to forget, especially in the text-centric world of writing papers in college, that all writing is "multimodal"; we not only compose words but we design, often by habit, how they will look on the page. But even this is merely scratching the surface of the possible ways to communicate our thoughts. The digital spaces in which we write these days make it possible to combine words with animated graphics, pictures, sound, and video. We can design brochures, posters, slide shows, and video trailers—genres that range from relatively static (little movement) to dynamic, all using a single device we can carry anywhere. The result, of course, is that there's a proliferation of multimedia everywhere we look, except perhaps in the one place we might most expect innovation: the college classroom. But that's changing. Not only are professors incorporating technology like video into classroom instruction, they're asking students to create multimedia projects as well. Writing may always be central to college assignments, but it is increasingly combined with other modes of expression.

What are these modes? In 1996, a group of international theorists convened in New London, Connecticut, to come up with language to describe the multiple literacies that students might need to develop for the twenty-first century. They came up with five basic modes in which we might communicate:

- Linguistic (i.e., writing)
- Visual (images but also things like graphic design and layout)
- Audio
- Spatial (physical spaces)
- Gestural (body language)

Most important of all, they concluded, is "multimodal" expression, or forms that combine more than one of these types of expression. It's not hard to see that human communication has always been a multimodal affair. What *is* different, however, is the range and accessibility of forms through which we can now communicate with one another; you'll experiment with these multimodal genres in this chapter.

The Problem of Definition

In the last few paragraphs, you encountered a scattering of terms—*form, genre, mode, multimodal, multimedia*—and before we go much further, let's tentatively agree on some definitions. But first, a basic problem: Some of these are contested concepts (none more than *genre*), and so whatever definitions we come up with will be necessarily inexact. I hope you'll revisit these definitions, particularly in the reflective writing you do in the course of this assignment, to explore how workable they are for you.

- **Form.** Often used interchangeably with *genre* (see the discussion of problems with that usage on page 476), form can also describe the structure of a composition.

- **Genre.** A loose category or classification of compositions that have "family resemblances"—similar aims, audiences, conventions, structures, and so on. For our purposes, however, a more rhetorical definition of genre seems best, one that is useful not just for describing the characteristics of a genre but also for describing what the genre can *do*. Theorist Carolyn Miller argues that genre is a rhetorical response to "recurrent situations." If the situation keeps coming up—say, the need to communicate using a limited number of characters about fast-breaking events to large numbers of people—then the response may become a genre, in this case a tweet. We learn to recognize both the recurring situations and the genre they demand. Keep in mind, though, that genres aren't necessarily stable; they change all the time.

- **Mode.** A particular way of communicating what we want to say. Modes include using writing, images, audio, and so on (see page 478).

- **Multimodal.** Using more than one mode to communicate meaning. This can be quite simple—combining written text with pictures—or quite complicated—a film that combines a written script, audio and visual elements, and gestures.

- **Multimedia.** This term is often used interchangeably with *multimodal*, and is more common outside of academia. The difference between multimedia and multimodal is subtle but significant.[1] When we talk about designing multimedia, we typically focus on the technical skills involved in production.

Students on Re-Genre

For so long in High school the only design experience I had was putting together text and pictures to create a newspaper layout.... I miss putting in the effort to make something look interesting, finding colors that work well together, and choosing the perfect font.

It's a little strange that the first opportunity to do something like this would be for an English class. As I was researching an infographic in class on Wednesday, words like juxtaposition and typography came up and it reminded me of my freshman graphic design class. I had forgotten how much I liked designing things, and this project will hopefully bring back the motivation to start designing again.

Kirsten

---

[1]Lauer, Claire. "Contending with Terms: 'Multimodal' and 'Multimedia' in the Academic and Public Spheres." *Computers & Composition* 26.4 (December 2009): 225–39. Print.

The term implies a product focus. In contrast, multimodal is typically used to describe the *process* of designing a communication. Though we're all about examining the process of composing in *The Curious Writer,* I've decided to rely on the more familiar term "multimedia" rather than "multimodal" in this chapter.

Re-Genre Is Deep Revision

This is a book about genres. For weeks now, you've drafted essays on some of the more common genres of writing inside school and out—personal essays, proposals, arguments, ethnographies, and so on. This is a chapter about genres, too, but this time you'll be *switching* genres as a revision strategy, one that in some ways radically shifts the way you see your topic, what you say about it, and also *how* you say it. In making this shift, there's an opportunity to learn a lot about two important things:

- **Rhetorical strategies for addressing big changes in purpose and audience.** These strategies include how to choose an appropriate genre and what that choice might mean about how you change the approach you took in the original writing assignment.
- **How genres differ.** Why does knowing that matter? Because we are all genre travelers. We do it every day, moving from e-mail to text message, from analytical essay in English to biology lab report, and from memorandum to PowerPoint presentation at work. Research on how we transfer knowledge from writing situation to writing situation suggests that genre knowledge is a particularly powerful vehicle for adapting to new types of writing and applying what we've already learned.

Genre as a Way of Knowing and Seeing

One of the things you might notice when you switch from one genre to another with the same topic is that it recalibrates your relationship to that topic. Taylor is interested in sports medicine, and last semester she wrote a research essay on the growing problem of concussions in team sports, especially their impact on women. She decided to re-genre her paper into an infographic (see later in this chapter on page 490 for more on infographics), thinking that was the best way to tell the story of what happens to a young woman's brain when she's hit repeatedly in the head by a soccer ball. Since an infographic is a genre that combines text and image, Taylor had to reimagine a ten-page research paper as a visual story. In other words, she had to turn 2,000 words into a series of graphics with only 250 words. What did she see? A brain, of course, and a ball, and the story of what a brain looks like when it violently collides with a ball. In a way, this is the drama that was at the heart of those ten pages, but with all those words it wasn't easy to see. Taylor's switch to an infographic shifted her gaze and helped her to see the topic freshly.

Switching genres is a form of *reseeing*. Each genre provides us with a particular orientation towards the world, which is a powerful thing. For example, imagine that in an English class you are asked to write a paper that analyzes a short story. You wrote a lot of these kinds of papers in high school, and the genre that you might have used was the deductive, thesis-proof paper: thesis in the introduction, then a series of paragraphs that follow, each sporting a topic sentence that supports the thesis, and finally ending with a restatement of the thesis. The thesis-proof essay orients you and your reader towards the literary text—the object of your attention, in this case—in a very particular way. Using this genre, as the theorist Keith Fort wrote, literature becomes, first and foremost, a "source of theses," a site to mine for main points. Imagine, as an alternative, writing about a literary text using a genre like the exploratory essay (see Chapter 3). Instead of beginning with the hunt for a point to prove, the essay genre urges the writer to begin with questions, to seek out what is complicated in the short story, and to use writing to sort out that complication. One genre prompts a writer to see a short story as a mine and the other to see it as a maze.

The implications of this shift in genres is even more profound when you're not going from one form of writing to another but from a form of writing that relies mostly on writing to a form of writing that uses multimedia. This is what Andrea learned when repurposing her blog as an audio essay and what Taylor learned when her research paper became an infographic.

Genre and Its Conventions

The optics of a magnifying glass and of a pair of binoculars limit their effectiveness to certain—and quite different—situations. One is for close work and the other for

Students on Re-Genre

When I switched to the infographic ... I really started to close in on a purpose to both the essay and the infographic. I started to think about why this topic should be shared and how important it was that I make my audience as wide as possible.... That's when I really started to question what needs to be done in this subject and why this essay and this topic are actually important. The genre shift reminded me that I was working with this topic in order to reach out to other people and draw them into a changing culture of sports. The infographic made that possible.

Taylor

seeing from a distance. Similarly, genres are constructed to work best in certain situations and for particular purposes. One of the most useful kinds of genre knowledge is an awareness of these different conventions, and that awareness is something you've been practicing since the beginning of *The Curious Writer*. You know, for example, that certain kinds of inquiry questions lead to certain forms of writing: Questions that explore something's value may lead to a review, questions that ask what should be done about a problem may prompt a proposal, and so on. Your particular purpose in writing about a topic points the way to an appropriate form for exploring it and sharing your conclusions with others. The genre you choose, in turn, influences both how you see your topic and what approach you take to writing about it, from what kinds of evidence you use to how (and often where) you state your conclusions. I hope that the "Features of the Form" box in each assignment chapter helped you become aware of different genres' conventions. Many of these choices are based on assumptions about audience. How much do readers know about my topic? Are they predisposed to believe certain things about my topic are true? What *ethos* (see p. 222) should I project? But there is another, more subtle force at work, and that's what an audience *expects* of a particular genre, including how it should be read and what its method of inquiry is. In other words, genres also have implicit conventions.

A few years back, Oprah chose James Frey's memoir, *A Million Little Pieces*, for her book club. This is a big deal for authors because Oprah's blessing can sell a lot of copies. The memoir was a dramatic tale of drug use and rehabilitation, and included a "true" account of Frey's girlfriend, who committed suicide by hanging. However, it turns out this suicide may have never happened, at least not in the way Frey described it in the memoir. Soon after these revelations, Oprah hauled Frey and his editor back on her television show and confronted them both. Oprah said she felt "duped," and that the author "betrayed millions of readers." It was dramatic stuff. One way of looking at the controversy is that Oprah felt duped because Frey violated an implicit convention of the memoir: What you write about must have actually happened; otherwise, the account is fiction. Readers who have experience with a genre have expectations, and when you don't satisfy those expectations, you may lose your audience. It's helpful, therefore, to know what some of those genre conventions are and how much you can adapt them to your own purposes.

For example, a podcast may begin as an essay that was intended to be read. But because a podcast is an audio genre meant to be *listened to* only once (and never read), there are conventions to consider, things like repeating key lines and ideas for clarity, and using anecdotes to break up stretches of exposition so listeners stay tuned in. The speaking voice also plays a key role in this genre. While you may read a script, an authoritative monotone will not do; listeners expect some of the same things they experience in conversation—a sense of intimacy with the speaker, and evidence of feeling in the spoken words. These are all design considerations you'll consider later in this chapter for the genre you choose, but they grow from conventions that arise, in part, from what audiences *expect* from their prior experiences with that form.

Inquiring into the Details

Re-Genre and Re-Flect

Thinking about your thinking while doing this project will both maximize your learning and help you to transfer what you learn to other situations. Here are some things to think and write about:

1. ***Your experience.*** Tell the story of what you understood when you began the project and what you're starting to understand now. Update this narrative regularly.
2. ***Rhetoric.*** How does the shift in purpose and audience change things (e.g., language, treatment of topic, ethos/pathos/logos, approach to persuasion)?
3. ***Genre.*** What do you notice about how the genre shift influences how and what you see? Can you identify how "conventions" (e.g., rules of evidence, types of questions asked, voice, structure, roles of writer/designer and audience) change?

Write regularly about these (and other) questions.

Re-Genre: The Assignment

You've considered a case study in re-genre, the modes of communication beyond writing, and some basic concepts about how genres work. But what exactly is your assignment in this chapter? (Your instructor may have other guidelines as well.)

1. You will choose a written assignment you completed earlier in the semester and revise it into a genre that uses *at least* one other mode of communication in addition to writing (audio, visual, spatial, gesture).

2. The choice of the new genre will be based on a rhetorical decision. You will define the purpose of the re-genre, and from this definition you will identify appropriate audiences for whom you can fulfill that purpose. This will in turn lead to the choice of the multimodal genre that is best for the project. In the "Planning the Re-Genre" section, we'll look more closely at how to do this rhetorical analysis, but for now, think of it this way: *What do I want a particular audience to think or do with respect to my topic? What form is best suited for accomplishing that goal?*

3. As part of the assignment, you will write about your experience with this kind of revision. (See "Inquiring into the Details: Re-Genre and Re-Flect" for questions to explore.)

Now for a reality check: There is too little time in a course like this to become an expert on any multimedia genre. (It's hard enough to develop expertise in writing in a single course, even though writing is something we've all done much of our lives.) But this assignment is a great learning opportunity—you'll develop new perspectives on revision, genre, and rhetoric—and in the process be introduced to some powerful new ways to communicate. That's why the writing you do about working on this project is as important as the multimedia project you design.

Planning the Re-Genre

This assignment begins with a plan that is built around a clear goal. In general, what do you want your re-genre *to do*? More specifically, which of the following rhetorical goals might the re-genre help you accomplish?

1. To dramatize a problem or idea for certain audiences. To encourage certain audiences *to feel* something.
2. To change behavior. To persuade certain audiences *to do* something.
3. To inform a particular audience about an aspect of a topic *in a timely way.* When and where might the information be most persuasive or most relevant?

13.2

Develop rhetorical goals for a revision of an essay and use them to choose an appropriate multimedia genre.

If you're thinking about a re-genre of earlier writing assignments that are more or less argumentative—review, proposal, argument, research essay, analysis, ethnography—it's likely that you won't have much trouble applying any of these goals. But what about the less explicitly argumentative forms like the profile and the personal essay? These writing assignments often lend themselves to dramatizing an idea or problem (goal #1) by using story to move an audience emotionally.

Tying goals to particular audiences will give any re-genre more rhetorical power. Use Table 13.1 as a way to start thinking about this.

Applying Rhetorical Goals

This semester, Rebecca wrote a research essay on the relationship between the emotional toll on nurses working in labor and delivery and professional burnout. Her essay celebrated the role of compassion and courage in good nursing practice but also identified some of the emotional costs to the practitioner. It's easy to imagine several purposes of a re-genre that involves both timely information and

Table 13.1

Goal	What?	Who?
Dramatize	What dilemma, idea, problem?	Audiences who might be most receptive to the story?
Persuade	To do what? What action or behavior?	Audiences whose action on the problem is needed?
Inform	About what? What information will be most relevant and useful?	Audiences who can *use* the information?

Inquiring into the Details

Levels of Content

Graphic designer Bill Shander argues that an essential part of design is thinking about how much information you'll include, and this depends on the main purpose of your communication. He believes there are essentially "four levels of content," and these levels should prove useful when thinking about your re-genre:

1. *Level One:* This level uses the least amount of information because it's an "attention grabber" meant to dramatize a topic (rhetorical goal #1) and help it to find an audience. A short video or photo essay might be a great genre for level one information.
2. *Level Two:* Once you've got the attention of an audience, some of them will be more interested in your topic, though not yet particularly invested in learning a lot more. They'd be game for a brief conversation, the kind that you facilitate with a blog or an infographic, something with a little more information.
3. *Level Three:* Audiences that are engaged with a topic will be actively information-seeking. You can provide information with multimedia genres like brochures or slide presentations.
4. *Level Four:* There are people who are passionate information-seekers on a topic. They're convinced it's important and relevant and would gladly dig into a web page with multiple links and documents.

behavior change. Would it be helpful to design a communication to nurses that helps them to identify the causes of burnout and how to avoid them? Alternatively, should patients be better informed about the roles that nurses play in the birthing experience, and is there a time when and place where this information might be most persuasive (birthing classes)? In another of my classes, Emery wrote a personal essay that begins, "I hate weddings." The piece goes on to explore her experiences and observations at a recent wedding in which she noted the many "contradictions" that the ritual entails. How might she re-genre this essay? I'm not sure that she would want to persuade people not to attend weddings—good luck with that—but might she use other modes to *dramatize* the idea that weddings are rich in contradictions?

A nearly irresistible temptation is to think about the appeal of doing one multimedia genre or another ("I want to do a podcast!") before defining your purpose. But this would be a mistake. Your choice of multimedia genre should be driven by your rhetorical goals. Keeping these goals in mind, make a preliminary pitch (written or verbal) about the writing assignment you'd like to re-genre and why.

Exercise 13.1

Re-Genre Pitch

If you want to sell a film idea, you make a pitch. Do the same for the choice of genre you made to repurpose your writing assignment. Here are the key parts your re-genre pitch should address:

1. What earlier writing assignment would you like to re-genre? Why? Is there something about this topic that lends itself to a multimodal approach? Explain.
2. Which of the three rhetorical goals seems most relevant? Develop brief answers to the questions for each relevant goal (see Table 13.1 on page 485).
3. Make a case for your choice of a multimodal genre that will best meet these goals. In your pitch, explain how the genre is rhetorically appropriate for your topic, your aims, and your potential audiences.

13.3

Understand and apply the conventions of a multimodal genre.

Eight Multimodal Genres

Online or off, genres abound that exploit modes beyond just writing. You know a lot of them, though you may not have actual experience working these forms. For example, you encounter web pages all the time. You may never have designed a brochure, but you've certainly read them at the doctor's office. You may have no recording experience, but you may have listened to NPR programs like *This American Life*. Of course, these encounters won't really help you with this assignment. For this project, you have to learn some of the conventions of one of these multimedia genres—what they are capable of as well as their limitations—and adapt your writing assignment to one of the forms. You know, too, that your choice should be based on your rhetorical goals. The sections that follow introduce you to eight multimedia genres you might consider: slide presentation, infographic, brochure, poster, photo essay, audio essay, web page, and video public service announcement. For each genre, I've included information about conventions, rhetorical considerations, design and production tips, and resources that will help you.

The genres are organized from the relatively simple—those that don't have a steep learning curve or have many moving parts—to the more complex. However, I selected these particular multimedia genres because they should be doable by nonexperts and involve relatively little production time.

The treatment of each genre is necessarily brief. You'll find some suggestions for resources that will help you get started with design and production, but they are hardly comprehensive. What you will need to learn in a relatively short time are the "best practices" for the genre you choose; in other words, what do expert producers and users of the genre believe are the fundamental principles of doing it well? You'll need to lean on your research skills to find this out, and Exercise 13.2, "Genre Analysis," on page 508, will help. Review the genres in the next sections, and when you've tentatively chosen one, follow up with it by using the research prompts in Exercise 13.2.

Slide Presentations

Bad slide

Inquiry-based Assignments

1. Are driven by questions, and teach what constitutes a *good* question.
2. Put students in charge of their own investigations.
3. Engage students' curiosity.
4. Initially encourage uncertainty.
5. Emphasize exploration before judgment.
6. Complicate prior beliefs about learning and knowledge.
7. Celebrate discovery and surprise.

Better slide

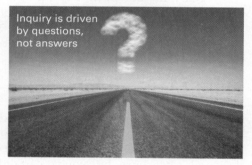

Inquiry is driven by questions, not answers

"Powerpoint is evil." So says visual storyteller Edward Tufte, who complains that too often, a slide presentation "elevates format over content" and as a result, "disrupts, dominates, and trivializes content." Worst of all, he says, bad presentations simply bore people to death. Yet a slide presentation is a genuinely multimedia genre, and one of the few here that also incorporates speech. When done well, a slide presentation can powerfully support the ideas in a talk. It's also a technology that most of have used before, and as slideware continues to evolve with software like Prezi, it's a genre that will continue to be relevant in a range of settings.

For a re-genre, a slide presentation seems a logical choice. Aside from being a familiar technology, programs like PowerPoint help us to select key points when working with a lot of information. Consider what the genre is capable of as well as a few key design and production tips culled from the vast literature on how to create good slide presentations.

Modes	Rhetorical Considerations
Writing + Visual + Spatial + Audio + Gesture	• Good for level three content (see page 486). • Can powerfully combine all five modalities. • Vulnerable to being more speaker-oriented than audience-oriented (Tufte). • Emphasizes chunks of hierarchically organized information. Good at explaining things, less good at telling stories. • Easy to target to intended audience.
Helpful Resources	
Free software	• Prezi, Google Slides, Sliderocket, PowToon
Examples	• Visit slideshare.net
Technical help	• Online: Microsoft "Tips"; PurdueOWL • Books: *Presentationzen* (Garr Reynolds); *Resonate: Present Visual Stories That Transform Audiences* (Nancy Duarte)

DESIGN TIPS FOR MAKING A SLIDE PRESENTATION

Planning
- Begin imagining rhetorical situation: How formal is the occasion? Who will the audience be? How much do they already know? What is the main thing I want them to know?
- Decide whether a linear (PowerPoint) or less-linear (Prezi) approach is best.
- Consider planning with pen and paper in a storyboard (see page 505), not in the slide program, to sketch out key ideas.
- Use handouts, not slides, to communicate information.

Content design
- Use font, background color, images, and graphics to create a consistent theme.
- Ideas in the talk should be *supplemented* by slides; slides are not a substitute for speech. The slide content is not meant to stand alone.
- Use one point, one idea per slide.

- Use graphs (to illustrate changes over time or comparisons) and pie charts (to compare parts of a whole) appropriately. Tables (for organizing information) are difficult to read in slides, so keep them simple.
- Limit use of bullets. Consider using graphic elements (pictures, graphs, etc.) instead to support your point.
- Minimize distracting animation.
- Always choose good-resolution photographs and graphics. Avoid using Microsoft clipart.

Publishing
- Save your presentation to the cloud *and* to a flash drive as backup.
- Slideshare.net is a public database of slide presentations where you can share your work.

Infographic

Infographics use factual information to tell stories visually, and they've been doing that for a long time. One of the most famous infographics was developed by British physician John Snow in the 1850s. Snow believed that cholera, which was ravaging London at the time, was a water-borne disease (in contrast, most people thought cholera was transported through the air); and as he collected data on the incidence of victims in a particularly hard-hit London neighborhood, it appeared that most lived near a water well on Broad Street. Superimposing bar graphs that represented cholera deaths on a street map of the neighborhood, Snow visually demonstrated that proximity to a certain well where residents drew water was strongly correlated to the deaths from cholera. It was a simple and dramatic visual story that ultimately saved lives.

These days, infographics are everywhere, including on television weather reports and in newspapers, magazines, and social media. Though infographics can be complicated to make, free online software exploits templates, which considerably simplifies infographic creation for novices. The key, though, is not just to come up with visually interesting graphs or tables of data but *to tell stories* with the data, and you have to figure out the stories first. Infographics are especially useful for telling stories that involve comparisons. For example, take a look at Figure 13.1, which compares how adults and teens use social media. There are lots of little stories here, some of which are unsurprising (teens use social media more than adults), but a surprising theme—that adults are more likely to be early users of new technologies than teens—also emerges. Notice, too, that part of the storytelling involves using graphics as metaphors (e.g., silhouettes of age groups).

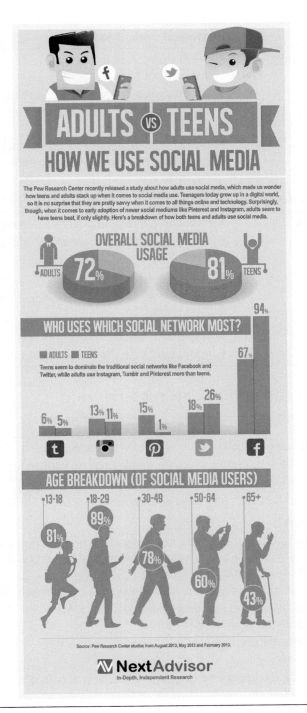

Figure 13.1   Social Media Use Among Teens And Adults

Modes	Rhetorical Considerations
Writing + Visual	• Exploits graphics to transform information into a visual story.
	• Especially useful when emphasizing comparisons.
	• Great way to dramatize quantitative data that support an argument.
	• Good for level one or two content (see page 486).
	• Combines pathos, logos, and ethos.
Helpful Resources	
Free software	• Piktochart, infogr.am, Visual.ly, easel.ly
	• Adobe Illustrator (if available on campus computers, since isn't free)
Examples	• Dailyinfographic.com
	• *The Best American Infographics 2014* (Ed. Gareth Cook)
Technical help	• *Visual Explanations* (Edward Tufte)
	• *Infographics for Dummies* (Justin Beegel)

DESIGN TIPS FOR MAKING AN INFOGRAPHIC

Planning

- Identify the key question or problem and what data will best dramatize it.
- Consider a three-part story structure: beginning, middle, and end.
- Fact-check all information you might use.
- Do a mock-up first with pen and paper (see page 507).

Content Design

- Consider using visual metaphors (e.g., a graph with beer bottles that dramatize problems with college drinking, the Monopoly game board to present data on Wall Street regulation).
- Make sure the story is apparent from the visuals by themselves.
- Use font size, color, and graphics to create a visual hierarchy of information. Don't use more than two or three fonts.
- Organize content in sections.
- Present numbers visually.
- Keep it simple, using concise language in the text and an uncluttered visual design.

- The size of your infographic will depend on where you imagine it will be viewed: Facebook? Instagram? PowerPoint? Poster?
- Cite your sources.

Publishing

- Most of the free software online allows you to post your infographic to an online link or site, or even print out a copy. (In some cases, doing this requires a subscription.)
- Post on Pinterest.
- There are multiple sites online that aggregate infographic submissions.

Brochure

Even in the digital age, the old-fashioned brochure endures. Why? The brochure is still an effective way to get information into the hands of the people who can use it and in locations where those people are most likely to be. In addition, widely available software makes brochures easier than ever to design and produce. Of course, it's still pretty easy to make a brochure that's ugly and ineffective. The following tables have some ways you can avoid doing that. The brochure might be an ideal form for a re-genre of a writing assignment. It accommodates more writing than some other multimedia forms. It is also well suited to the rhetorical goal of informing an audience about some aspect of your topic in a timely way (goal #3).

Modes	Rhetorical Considerations
Writing + Visual	• Exploits effects of combining text, image, and layout to provide "punch" and emphasis. • Relatively easy to target audiences that are looking for the information. • Good for level three content (see page 486).
Helpful Resources	
Free software	• Microsoft Word (hardly free, but most of us have it) • Adobe Illustrator, Adobe InDesign, Adobe Photoshop, and Microsoft Publisher are often used for brochure production. All cost money but might be on some campus computers.
Examples	• Search: "tri-fold brochure examples" and "brochures good and bad"
Technical help	• Creativeblog.com, YouTube

DESIGN TIPS FOR MAKING A BROCHURE

Planning
- The simplest brochure is a tri-fold.
- Use a template if available.
- Mock-up the design first with pen and paper (see page 507).

Content design
- A key principle is unity. Use consistent colors and fonts, in addition to repeating graphics
- The words in a brochure should not repeat what's in the images but *add* to them.
- Design the cover to capture readers' interest and lead them to subsequent panels.
- Develop a narrative logic for sequencing information in the panels. What information and in what order?
- Copy should be brief and punchy. Exploit simple sentences. Too much text is deadly.
- Think about arranging visual elements (including blocks of text) to create tension by varying their sizes.
- White space is an important design element.
- Layout is simplified by using a grid overlay.
- Brochure columns are narrow, so consider graphics that bleed past the edges onto other columns for visual effect.

Publishing
- Most printers will produce quality brochures. Consider heavier paper stock.

Conference Poster

The "conference poster" or "research poster" is a mainstay in the sciences, often used at events where scholars and students share information about their research. Imagine a room full of people milling about, with the walls plastered with colorful posters whose eager creators stand nearby, anxious to explain the highlights of their research. These days, poster sessions are common at colleges and universities hoping to showcase undergraduate research, and not just in the sciences but in the humanities as well.

The conference poster is an interesting genre. It should be designed to stand on its own *and* to support a talk by the speaker, who can use the poster to generate interest in his or her project. Preparation for undergraduate poster sessions usually involves preparation not only of the poster itself but also of the accompanying verbal explanation, both of which are often geared to an audience of nonexperts. In this way, the conference poster is one of the most multimodal of the eight genres discussed here. Since you'll be developing a poster for a nonexperimental project, consider a creative design, one that will likely break from the typical scientific structure of most posters (introduction, methods, results, and so on). Perhaps use the inquiry question of your original writing assignment as the title of the poster. Column sections may present information on "The Problem," "Stakeholders," "What We Know," "Solutions," "Profiles," "Case Studies," "Thesis," "Impacts," "Causes and Effects," and so on.

Modes	Rhetorical Considerations
Writing + Visual + Spatial + Gesture	• Good for level three and four content (see page 486). • Works well with speech although should be able to stand alone. • For undergraduate research, should assume an audience of nonexperts. • Meant to engage audience in conversation about topic. • Should get message across quickly. • As an academic genre, authority is tied to relevant scholarly sources, research methods, and topic's position in larger academic conversation.
Helpful Resources	
Free software	• Inkscape; Microsoft PowerPoint or Publisher (not free, but most of us have it) • Paid software for creating posters includes Adobe Photoshop, Illustrator, and InDesign.
Examples	• Search for images using "conference or research poster examples" or "poster session" • Visit F1000.com/posters
Technical help	• YouTube: Search "conference posters," "research posters"; also, Google searches using those terms will turn up .edu sites with instructional pages for students developing posters. • Visit http://colinpurrington.com/tips/poster-design

DESIGN TIPS FOR MAKING A POSTER

Planning
- Mock-up poster with pen and paper (see page 507).
- There are poster templates available online to help with formatting.
- Design poster in program at the actual size it will be printed (typically 36 × 48 inches).

Content Design
- Title should highlight either major finding or question behind project.
- Use body text minimally, no more than 300–800 words.
- Poster should be readable from five feet away (heads 48 pt. or larger, and text 24 pt. or larger).
- Use columns to structure blocks of information.
- May use scientific structure (introduction, objectives, methods, etc.) as organizing method but for less experimental projects, create a more narrative design.
- Poster should tell a story, and viewer should know how to follow the story's flow without much explicit direction.
- Use high-resolution images that can be enlarged without degradation.
- Include citations.

Publishing
- First print a small version to see how everything looks (use the "scale to fit paper" in the printer dialogue box).
- Many universities have printing services that will print the large version of your poster. There are also many companies online that will print conference posters for a fee.

Photographic Essay

The photographic essay is one of the most accessible forms of visual storytelling for nonexperts. Many of us are compulsive picture-takers, something made infinitely easier with smartphone cameras, which can now produce quality images. Of course, a photographic essay isn't a random collection of pictures but a selection of images that combine to suggest certain meanings. Visual artists who do photo essays sometimes insist that the images alone should tell the story—and that to include text is inauthentic—but for our purposes, the combination of text and images will be far more useful. The challenge, then, is to create a *sequence* of images that can be combined with some text (not very much)—a visual and verbal combination that makes an argument, emphasizes a theme, or tells a story.

Here you can see one approach to a photographic essay that makes an argument. The San Francisco Bicycle Coalition used a photo essay to dramatize the problem of insufficient space for bicycles on commuter trains. The contrast is obvious. And so is the solution: Add more space for bicycles on trains, something the transit authorities in San Francisco agreed to do. You'll be designing a photographic essay that's a little different—the images will be combined with text you draw from

No Space for Bikes:
A photo study of trains bumping cyclists out of SF.

1: Train 134: Sept 22 9:07 AM

2: Train 134: Sept 22 9:07 AM

3: Train 230: Sept 24 8:53 AM

4: Train 230: Sept 24 8:53 AM

5: Train 332: Sept 30 8:56 AM

6: Train 332: Sept 30 8:56 AM

Submitted to JBP Oct 2
by Benjamin Damm

your earlier writing assignment. Depending on your approach, you might also add some background music. For example, Rebecca repurposed her personal essay on a visit with her family to the beaches of Normandy into a photographic essay that drew on archival photographs of World War II battles at the sites she'd visited. Using PowerPoint, she juxtaposed pictures from now and then, and integrated a music track. The result was a poignant tribute to the fallen, but also an implicit theme about how war haunts places forever.

Modes	Rhetorical Considerations
Writing + Visual + Audio	• Good for level one content (see page 486). • Are images the best way to dramatize the problem, the dilemma, the question, or the idea? • The effectiveness of the genre depends on text that is *in conversation with* the image. • Arrangement of images should embody a narrative logic. • Photo essays typically exploit pathos. • Audience for photographic essays may be in-person (especially if using slideware) or online.
Helpful Resources	
Free software	• Wide range of free photo software (Picassa, iPhoto, Flickr, etc.). Microsoft Photo Story 3 turns photo essay into video with narration. • Slideware like PowerPoint is also an effective way of presenting photo essays.
Examples	• Websites include photoessay.com (journalistic examples) and williamwolff.org (a professor's site); use search term "photographic essay examples site:edu"
Technical help	• Search keywords "photography composition" and "photographic essay how to"

DESIGN TIPS FOR MAKING A PHOTOGRAPHIC ESSAY

Planning
- Identify the theme of the photo essay, and use it as a guide to select both image and text. However, be flexible. As you attempt to tell the story, it may evolve.
- You may take images and/or draw on existing photos. There are a considerable number of archival photographs online.
- Use a storyboard to plan possible images, sequences, and tentative plans for shoots (see page 505).

Content design

- If taking new shots, collect multiple pictures of important subjects, varying distance, angle, and light (time of day).
- Plan multiple shoots, returning to locations or finding new ones.
- Review images and rank them, looking for shots that are relevant to theme, idea, or argument; that are visually interesting; and especially that may invoke feeling (pathos).

- Play with the order of the images, exploiting story structures: cause/effect or effect/cause, problem/solution, change over time, movement through space and place, action/reaction, etc.
- The opening shot is crucial; it should engage the viewer and help frame the theme.
- Consider an effective combination of long shots (scene setting) or close ones (examining the details). Other images may be portraits or action shots.
- Include text when it helps dramatize an image, adds emotion, ties the image back to the theme, adds essential information, or moves the story forward.
- Consider how text will work with images. Brief captions? Superimposed over the image? Appearing after image dissolves? Voice narration?

Publishing

- For a class presentation, slideware might be the simplest way to publish your photo essay.
- Online sites like Flickr and Google+ allow photo sharing.

Radio Essays or Podcasts

The most vibrant forms of the essay these days are the radio essay and the podcast. Though it's a form that uses a relatively old technology, the radio essay has come into its own as a form of audio storytelling because of such NPR programs as *This American Life*. The podcast, a more recent version of the audio essay, emerged with the explosion of portable media players and the development of software that allows listeners to subscribe to a podcaster's "feed" and access podcasts the moment they are published online. The technology for producing podcasts and radio essays is the same; only the method of publishing the audio files might differ. Recording voice files is simpler than ever. Nearly all computers, tablets, and smartphones have internal microphones, though their quality can vary. Over the years, most of my students have relied on the free software Audacity to edit audio files, while Mac users often turn to Garage Band. These programs have a steep but small learning curve.

There are three kinds of audio essays you can try for this assignment. The simplest is a single track—just your voice narrating your essay. A great model for this kind of audio essay is "This I Believe," a program begun in the 1950s that often features average people sharing essays about a fundamental value. You can listen

Students on Re-Genre

When I originally started to think about what to do for my re-genre assignment, I was a little nervous. I didn't know what previous assignment to do and what genre to pick. I finally decided on my personal essay and to do a podcast. Once I started working on my script for the podcast, it came so easily! I was quite surprised how quickly my ideas flowed. I'm approaching the podcast as if I was just talking to a group of people, like any other conversation I might have about the topic to my friends. I think that the podcast genre is much less formal than the regular writing I originally did and that made it easier to write.
   Jessica

to these online. A second approach is to create two tracks—voice narration and music. This is fun but can get a little tricky. Finally, there is the documentary, an audio essay that might include as many as four tracks: narration, music, interview clips, and ambient sound. However, for the purposes of this assignment, consider producing a simple audio essay—with just one or two tracks and no longer than three or four minutes (which is a script of about 350–400 words).

Modes	Rhetorical Considerations
Writing + Audio	• Good for level two content (see page 486). • Exploits the power of the spoken voice for emotional effect (ethos), and when combined with music this effect is amplified. • Creates a sense of intimacy with the listener. • To sustain attention of listeners, often relies on elements of narrative. • Ethos of speaker critical.
Helpful Resources	
Free software	• Audacity for audio recording and editing (PC and Mac) • Mac users can also use Garage Band.
Examples	• Websites to listen to: This American Life, Radio Lab, This I Believe, Third Coast International Audio Festival, The Moth • Search for podcasts on iTunes. • Visit bruceballenger.com for sample student audio essays.
Technical help	• Numerous how-to sites are online. A good start is Transom.org. • On YouTube: Search for videos of Ira Glass, "Storytelling, Parts 1–4."

DESIGN TIPS FOR MAKING A RADIO ESSAY OR PODCAST

Planning

- You will narrate, so you must turn your essay into a script (see page 505). Write the way you speak.
- Consider whether you will read the script or deliver it more informally.
- Practice first with the software, learning how to record, cut and paste, insert, and shift audio files.

Content design

- Write in simple sentences.
- Exposition is difficult to listen to or remember for very long. Write a script that emphasizes *stories*: case studies, anecdotes, personal experiences, profiles, etc.
- The beginning is key. It should both capture the listener's attention and make a promise about where the piece is headed and what it's about. You have about 20 seconds to engage the listener.
- Animate your voice, exploiting the natural modulations of speech, but don't overdo it.
- Don't forget to exploit the power of pauses (which are also opportunities to bring music in and out) for emphasis after key moments or ideas.
- Repeat key ideas, particularly the one main thing you're trying to say.
- Expect interviews, if you use them, to change what you planned to do.
- Record in a quiet place. If interviewing, make sure audio levels are high enough.
- Allow considerable time for editing the audio.

Publishing

- When publishing, use the smaller MP3 files rather than WAV.
- SoundCloud is an excellent site for uploading and sharing radio essays.

Web Page

Since most of us have no experience in web page design, it's daunting to think about creating one. But the appeal is undeniable. We are experienced users of web pages—we know the genre—and for good reason. Not only is the web page a common way of communicating online, it is also a powerful way to do so, combining a wide range of modalities: writing, image, audio, and video. For this assignment, you'll be making relatively simple pages that are issue focused—pages that attempt to persuade or inform. For example, last semester Sydney wrote a research essay on the problem of dwindling water in the Colorado River system, an issue that is aggravated by drought and water mismanagement. As a southern Californian directly impacted by the problem, she saw a web page as a way to build public support for action on water waste. Sydney had no experience with web design, but fortunately online templates helped her get started.

Still, a web page has a lot of moving parts. You may have to determine the page structure. Embed images, video, or audio and incorporate hyperlinks. For this project, consider just creating a home page, one that effectively establishes the purpose of the page and might inspire users to click into pages you might develop later. And since you probably don't know how to code, for this assignment it's wise to use one of the widely available free sites that will allow you to build your web page from templates.

Modes	Rhetorical Considerations
Writing + Audio + Visual	• Good for level three and four content (see page 486). • Often has an implied author rather an explicit one. Ethos comes from the sum of the parts: reliability of information, appeal of design, and presence of implied narrator. • Can be targeted to fairly specific audiences. • Web users typically scan and extract rather than do sustained reading.
Helpful Resources	
Free software	• Many free software options are online. Consider one with templates. Popular free sites include Komodo, Sitebuilder, Wix, and Weebly, though they may charge for some services.
Examples	• Student Web Awards, The Webby Awards (Charitable/Nonprofit Organizations)
Technical help	• Writingspaces.org; WebD2 (online curriculum on design)

DESIGN TIPS FOR MAKING A WEB PAGE

Planning
- Identify the audience and purpose of your page. Put these on a Post-it to remind yourself.
- Mock-up your page (see page 507) using a grid that creates columns and sections. There are lots of variations on this, but for this assignment keep it simple.

Content design
- The most important design principles for web pages are *contrast, repetition, alignment*, and *proximity*. Contrasting elements should be visually separated; related material should be visually proximate; styles should be repeated; and everything should be aligned relative to the top, bottom, and sides of the page.
- The gaze of web page users tends to follow an "F" pattern: across the top, down the left side, and across the page from left to right. These are key locations for important information.

- Be aware of what users expect—the conventions of the genre. For example, page navigation is usually at the top or left side.
- Exploit white space. It's as important, in some ways, as space with content.
- The size of the body font should be large enough to be easily readable (typically 14–16 pixels). Keep lines of body text fairly short (about 84 characters).
- The writing should be jargon-free, with an emphasis on clarity and simplicity.

Publishing
- If your university has Google Apps for Education, you can post a web page to a folder that you make public on Google Drive.
- Free sites like Wix allow you to save your page online and publish it later if you wish.

Video PSA

The most complicated multimodal genre for a novice is the video public service announcement (PSA). Perhaps the most famous of these—and some of the earliest—were the U.S. Forest Service ads featuring Smokey the Bear and, when I was in college, an antipollution ad by the Advertising Council featuring a weeping Native American. PSAs are essentially 10- to 30-second commercials that promote a cause or raise public awareness on behalf of some nonprofit. When done effectively, PSAs can be rhetorically powerful, which of course is their appeal. But they do require some experience with video production. Fortunately, the ease of recording video on smartphones and other mobile recording devices and the availability of user-friendly editing software make it relatively easy to produce a PSA. The key here is to keep it simple. One of the most effective PSAs of all time was an anti–drug use ad that featured nothing more than a voice and a frying egg.

Modes	Rhetorical Considerations
Writing + Visual + Audio	• Good for level one and two content (see page 486). • Emphasizes pathos. • Difficult to target specific audiences.
Helpful Resources	
Free software	• Many options, including Microsoft Movie Maker, Avidemux (Mac), iMovie
Examples	• adcouncil.org, YouTube (search for "PSA," "Top 10 Public Service Announcements")
Technical help	• How to Create a PSA from the Center for Digital Education and PSA Research Center (both online); YouTube (search "how to make a PSA")

DESIGN TIPS FOR MAKING A VIDEO PSA

Planning
- A clear purpose and audience for the PSA is essential. Not just "raise awareness," but raise awareness about what, exactly? Not just "do" something, but how?
- Decide how controversial you want to be.
- Allow considerable time for production.
- This genre is most effective as a medium for storytelling.
- Develop a script and storyboard (see pages 505–507).

Content design
- It's essential to keep it simple. Begin by imagining whether the PSA might involve just one shot. Consider how you might use not just video but shots of stills and even drawings.
- Video is a genre that involves action. Action might involve subjects and movement of the camera.
- A music track can add to the emotional power of the ad. (See "The Ethics of Borrowing" section on rights issues.)
- Any text should be brief, concise, and punchy. It should appear on screen long enough to be read twice.
- When using your mobile device, hold it horizontally rather than vertically.
- Rely on fades or dissolves to transition between shots.
- Consider the purpose of each kind of shot—extreme long, long, medium, and close-up—and camera angle: overhead, high, eye level, low. Combine these for effect.
- Constantly check audio levels and be aware of background noise.

Publishing
- YouTube is an obvious choice. However, see "The Ethics of Borrowing" on page 509 for restrictions on using copyrighted content like music.

Drafting Tools: Scripts, Storyboards, and Mock-Ups

When we write an essay, we draft on the computer, usually in a word processing program like Word, or perhaps on a piece of paper with pen or pencil. Genres that involve other modes—visual, audio, and spatial—have more moving parts. Some of these parts involve the look of the thing—the layout—and some involve movement—the sequencing of images or information or story lines. This requires some different drafting tools, most of which are visual in nature. Let's look briefly at three of them:

- **Scripts.** This is a drafting tool that is especially useful for forms like the audio essay, video PSA, or perhaps even the slide presentation—anything that involves someone talking.
- **Storyboards.** As a substitute for a script, or in concert with one, storyboards are great way to plot out the presentation of information over time. They can be powerful ways to visualize the story you want to tell.
- **Mock-ups.** For less dynamic genres like brochures and web pages, mock-ups of layouts are helpful. These range from crude sketches of what something might look like to computer-based layouts—often lacking content text—that preview possible colors, fonts, and heads.

Now consider each of these drafting tools in a little more detail to determine which might be appropriate for your project.

Scripts

A script is designed to organize not only what a speaker will say but also how that speech will be coordinated with other audio, visual, and spatial elements. Naturally, when we think of scripts we think of movies and the ways each character's dialogue is keyed to physical locations on the set, camera angles, lighting, and so on. For our purposes, scripts will be considerably less complicated. In a podcast, for example, you'll likely be working with two things—narration and music. As you can see from the script Andrea developed for her audio essay, she uses a script that helps her to cue the entry and exit of music tracks, along with sound levels, in concert with her voice work.

The two-column approach in Figure 13.2 is one way to write a script for an audio or video production. You can find plenty of other templates online. But for the purposes of this project, keep it simple.

Storyboards

If you think about a storyboard as a drafting tool at all, you probably think of movies. Disney actually pioneered the storyboard approach as a method for organizing the structure of its animated films, but it is also a helpful tool for planning multimedia genres like photographic essays, web pages, and slide presentations—anything that involves visual storytelling. The most obvious corollary to storyboarding is the comic strip; however, artistic talent isn't necessary—stick figures can work just fine because you can always add written clarification about what is in each frame. Here's one version of a storyboard template for the opening shots

SOUND: *Fade in under last line:* (music here—maybe some kind of marriage march or Pachelbel's Canon in D. Maybe White Wedding by Billy Idol) *Continue for 5–7 seconds*	**INTRO:** Jon Berger will never be my husband. Twenty years ago, I wouldn't have considered Jon Berger as marriage material. Marriage wasn't a thought then; I could hardly even get a date. **(Pause)** Twenty years ago, I was an unpopular teen who didn't have many boys interested in her—except for Jon Berger—but I didn't know he was interested then. **Body:** *(no breaks):* After recently finding some pictures in a box of old boyfriends, I was reminded of Jon. When I think of Jon now, I get a lump in my throat. I miss him. He was tall and lanky and goofy. His hair looked like the end of a frayed Q-Tip after you've rummaged in your ear for a while. He had a mouth full of braces, a Honda CRX, and he worked as a pizza delivery boy. **(Pause)**
SOUND: *Play under last line:* (*Insert Ambient typing noise and maybe grumbling about searching or sounds of what it would be like if someone were brainstorming searches?*) **SOUND:** *Continue Ambient Noise throughout next section*	I have searched for Jon countless times on Facebook. No results found every time.

Figure 13.2 Andrea's Script for a Podcast

of a video PSA on homelessness that I worked up. Rather than sketch the visual, I decided to shoot images with my iPhone:

Shot #1: Extreme close-up of older person's hand against a neutral background.

Narration: This hand…

Shot #2: Dissolve slowly to extreme close-up of two hands, one holding the other.

Narration: …needs a hand.
Music: Instrumental guitar up and under

You can explore other templates online for storyboards, or go to a site like storyboardthat.com, which provides not only templates but also an image library that you can use to build a visual story. But whatever approach you take—crude or relatively polished—your storyboard should provide information about the following:

- Who or what is in each frame?
- If there are characters in the frame, where are they going?
- How much time, if any, has passed between frames and how might the transitions be handled?
- If a video, where is the camera and what is the angle and shot? Typical shots include close-up, long, and point-of-view shots and zooms; transitions might be fades, dissolves, and jump cuts; camera angles might include high-, level-, or low-angle shots, pans, or tilts.

Mock-Ups

If you're designing the layout of a brochure, web page, slide presentation, or infographic, you might work out the layout with a mock-up. While this is the kind of thing you can do pretty slickly in a program like Adobe Photoshop or Microsoft Publisher, pen and paper often work just fine. A mock-up may not include a lot of content (that will go in later) but should show the size and location of key headings and navigation menus, the placement of images and text, and perhaps sample fonts and font sizes, color schemes, and so on. One preliminary version of a web page mock-up (or an alternative to one) is called a "wireframe." A wireframe sketches the skeleton of a web page and doesn't include color, font, or images, much the way you might mock-up the content of a brochure with pencil and paper. There are some free online tools that can help you create wireframes for web pages (search "free wireframe tools"), but in the absence of software there's still a lot you can do with a pencil and a piece of graph paper.

Exercise 13.2

Genre Analysis: Conventions and Best Practices

The preceding sections gave you a very brief overview of eight multimodal genres. In a relatively short time, you will need to acquire enough knowledge about your chosen genre to plan, design, and produce it. This exercise should help. Unless your instructor tells you otherwise, this is a class presentation. Begin by searching online (or elsewhere) to find at least **three** examples of the genre you've chosen for this project. Try to find extremes—for example, a bad slide presentation and a really good one—because the comparison can be instructive. (For some of the genres, these aren't hard to find. Just search for "best" and "worst" or "reviews of.")

STEP ONE: Draw comparisons.

1. **Purpose and audience.** Do the purposes and audiences of each example differ? What are the implications of those differences in terms of design?

2. **Conventions.** Ignoring the differences between the examples for a moment, what features do they seem to have *in common*? Be specific.

3. **Rhetorical effectiveness.** Keeping audience and purpose in mind, which of the examples do you think is most rhetorically effective and why?

Analyzing Your Examples

- **Movement.** How is the example designed to guide the audience through the material?

- **Modes.** What is the balance between different modes of communication? Which does the example seem to emphasize?

- **Ethos, pathos, logos.** Which does the example emphasize?

- **Content.** What level of content (1–4) does the example emphasize?

- **Usability.** How well does the example encourage users to interact with the content?

- **Best practices.** Based on what you've learned about the genre, how well does the example reflect the techniques considered by experts to be the prevailing "standard"?

Inquiring into the Details

Citing Multimodal Content

How you cite multimodal content depends on the genre you chose. If you developed a conference poster—a more academic genre—then you might list citations of content in a fairly conventional way, placing references at the bottom of the poster. Other genres like the audio essay don't include citations at all. However, your instructor may ask you to submit a bibliography separately, whatever genre you chose.

The challenge with citing multimedia content is that sometimes the information you need is missing or hard to find. To find out how to cite images, music, audio, and video, go to the APA or MLA sections in Chapter 12.

STEP TWO: Which example seems best? Make the case in a class presentation using the examples you chose.

The Ethics of Borrowing

If you take the picture, write the essay, compose the song, or shoot the video, then the stuff is yours—it's "original" work, and the copyright belongs to you. You can use the material any way you want. However, when borrowing images, music, and film clips from other sources for your multimodal projects, you *may* confront permissions problems. I say "may" because the doctrine of "fair use" often exempts educational projects like these since they are noncommercial, and unlikely to affect the "market for and value of" the borrowed material. If you don't have plans to publish your project except in your end-of-semester portfolio for the class, then the fair use exemption likely applies, and you can use copyrighted materials without much legal risk.

However, if you try to upload your video PSA to YouTube with a soundtrack you got from your iTunes library, you may find that the song is disabled. In other words, if you want to share your project with the world, then you probably need permission to use copyrighted material. What to do?

Creative Commons Licenses

One way to tackle the copyright issue is to search the databases of a nonprofit group called Creative Commons, which was established to help artists both share their work widely and retain some control over how it's used. Artists upload images, songs, video, and other creative work and specify how it can be used. Many works are available with few restrictions at all. All you need to do is search on the Creative Commons site (search.creativecommons.org), choose an appropriate database (e.g., SoundCloud for music), and type in keywords (e.g., "acoustic Spanish guitar"). Then check the results to see if a work you're interested in is licensed through Creative Commons and what restrictions, if any, the artist imposed on the work's use. As I write, Creative Commons has licensed 882 million works, so there's quite a lot to choose from.

Public Domain

I'm a huge fan of the Library of Congress photographic collection—a rich database of historical photographs including some famous ones like Dorothea Lange's iconic image of the Depression, "Migrant Mother." Since Lange took pictures for the federal Farm Security Administration, many of her images are in the public domain, and thus free to use. Other material finds its way into the public domain when the rights lapse, which is one reason you can download Shakespeare for free. Sometimes, public domain images, films, music, and texts that would be great for your project are available, but how do you find them? A keyword search for "finding public domain music" or "finding public domain pictures" will yield a host of search engines that will help you find what you need.

Reflecting on Re-Genre

One of the reasons you're taking this course is that it will help you to use what you've learned in other writing situations, and you're likely to have plenty of those both in college and after. You've done a lot of reflective writing in *The Curious Writer*, and one reason is this: There's growing research that suggests that we *transfer* knowledge from one situation to another, related situation if we pause to consider what we're learning and how we're learning it. As I noted in the beginning of the chapter, we're all genre travelers, so what you learn by repurposing an earlier writing assignment should prove helpful if you take the time to reflect on the experience. End your experiment in re-genre by writing about how your thinking has changed, what you've learned, and how you might apply that learning in the future. Return to "Inquiring into the Details: Re-Genre and Re-Flect" on page 484 for some ideas about how to do this metacognitive work.

You can reflect on what you've done narratively—the story of your experience—but look for opportunities in telling your story to do what narrative essayists often do: Look back from time to time when remembering what happened to talk about what you know *now* that wasn't apparent to you *then*. You might also consider reflecting on what you've learned by returning to some key concepts we've touched on again and again, including genre, rhetoric, and revision. If the theories of transfer are true, then all of this thinking about your thinking in this assignment—and all the others in this book—will make you not only a curious writer, but a flexible and imaginative one, too.

Using What You Have Learned

1. **Analyze the rhetorical implications of repurposing a writing assignment into a different genre.** We are all genre travelers, often communicating the same information in different ways to different audiences. In this chapter, you were encouraged to do this consciously, with an awareness of how a shift like this changes the message, the messenger, and the messenger's purpose. This is knowledge that you can apply often. For instance, in other classes you might be asked to develop an oral presentation for a written assignment; at work you might be asked to take an annual report and rewrite it as web content; and in life, you might turn a late-night conversation into a podcast.

2. **Develop rhetorical goals for a revision of an essay and use them to choose an appropriate multimodal genre.** Throughout *The Curious Writer* I've challenged you to build a writing assignment around a specific purpose, one that in an inquiry-based project you often *discover as you write*. In this chapter, I asked you to do this up front—to define your rhetorical goals first and then to use them to make choices about what you will write and in what form. A lifetime of school writing that is less focused on discovery than on reporting what you already know has prepared you well for this. But I hope what you learned here is how powerful a change in rhetorical goals can be as "deep" revision, transforming your work and making it available to new audiences by exploiting new modes of communication and new genres.

3. **Understand and apply the conventions of a multimodal genre.** In a way, this chapter works from a crazy premise: In a few weeks' time, you will take something you've written and transform it into a multimedia genre with which you may have no experience. Not only do you have to try to revise your writing, you also have to engage in a crash course on design. While the result often isn't polished (how could it be?), what you learn in the process is powerful: new revision strategies and something about how genres work. But most important, you flex your rhetorical muscles, and these muscles will make you a better communicator, one who can slide from one rhetorical situation to the next appropriately and effectively.

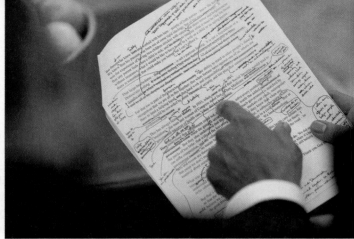

14

Revision Strategies

Learning Objectives

In this chapter, you'll learn to

14.1 Understand the meaning—and value—of revision and apply it to your own work when appropriate.

14.2 Recognize five types of revision and apply the most relevant strategies to a particular draft.

Why Revise?

The motive for revision is like a photographer's inclination to take more than one shot—both writer and photographer know not to trust their first look at something.

One draft and done. That was Shauna's motto about revision, and when she said it nearly everyone in the class nodded. "I know I should revise but usually I write papers at the last minute, so I don't really have the time," she added.

Surprisingly, one of the least discussed topics in writing classes is *time*. Perhaps no other factor influences a writer's success more than having the time to do the work, and the academic culture doesn't provide a lot of time to write. You may have multiple writing assignments at the same time in different classes, with deadlines that may fall on the same day. Getting a single draft done by the due date, much less a revision, seems like a major accomplishment. And in some classes (though not this one), it isn't even clear that instructors expect students to revise their work before they hand it in. So why bother revising?

Before I make a pitch for revision, let's be clear on a few things. Revision isn't a virtue, nor is it always a necessary step in the writing

Figure 14.1   Four levels of rewriting

process; it also doesn't always occur at the end of the process. In addition, revision is more than "fixing" things. In Figure 14.1, you can see that "proofreading" and "editing," while very important parts of rewriting, may not involve revision. They are, instead, activities that help burnish the surface of prose and make it easier to see the subject underneath it.

Revision involves "reseeing." You started with a certain idea about what you were writing and now you realize, no, that's not it at all. Or perhaps when you began writing, you had one inquiry question, but the draft now tells you that another, better question is lurking there. "Deep revision" might lead you to start all over, or shift subjects entirely, or even switch genres. Sometimes revision helps you to resee not just the subject but the draft itself: It's apparent that the beginning is all wrong, or that essential information is missing, or that the strongest part of the paper is something you can build on in the next draft.

One of the most powerful analogies for revision comes from photography, a word from Greek that means "light writing." Typically, most of us take only one picture of a subject, even in the digital age, when it's cheap and easy to shoot multiple images. In other words: one draft and done. But what would happen if you took ten pictures of the same subject—say, an old wagon in a field—varying angle, distance, and time of day? Your first shot would likely be the most obvious image, the one everyone takes of the wagon. But by the fourth or fifth image, you have to strain a bit to find a fresh shot. Maybe you lie on the ground and shoot upwards, or you try a close-up of the wooden wheel in the evening when the light is thick. The more shots you take, the more likely it is that you start seeing your subject in a way that you hadn't initially seen it. The wagon becomes infinitely more interesting. That's the payoff for reseeing, for what we call *revision* when we talk about writing. The motive for revision is like a photographer's inclination to take more than one shot—both writer and photographer know not to trust their first look at something. They also know that the longer they look, the more likely it is that they will see something interesting.

Why revise? Not because it's necessary, or it's good for you, or someone expects you to. Revise because there's more to learn and think about. Revise because you really care about what you're saying and you want to say it well. Revise because it yields the unexpected—new insights, new perspectives, new ways of seeing.

Divorcing the Draft

Sometimes I ask my students to generalize about how they approach the writing process for most papers by having them divide a continuum into three parts

> Revision, as the name implies, is a *reseeing* of the paper's topic and the writer's initial approach to it in the draft.

corresponding to how much time, roughly, they devote to prewriting, drafting, and rewriting. Then I play "writing doctor" and diagnose their problems, particularly their resistance to revision. Figure 14.2 depicts a typical example of the writing processes of most of my first-year students.

The writing process shown in Figure 14.2 obviously invests lots of time in the drafting stage and very little time in prewriting or rewriting. For most of my students, this means toiling over the first draft, starting and then starting over, carefully hammering every word into place. Strong resistance to revision is a typical symptom of students who use this process. It's easy to imagine why. If you invest all that time in the first draft, trying to make it as good as you can, you'll be too exhausted to consider a revision, delusional about the paper's quality, or, most likely, so invested in the draft's approach to the topic that revision seems impossible or a waste of time.

There also is another pattern among resistant revisers. Students who tend to spend a relatively long time on the prewriting stage also struggle with revision. My theory is that some of these writers resist revision as a final stage in the process

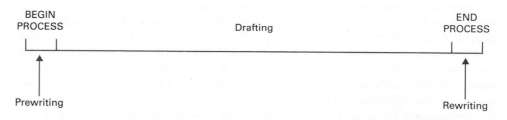

Figure 14.2 How some writers who resist revision typically divide their time among the three elements of the writing process: prewriting, drafting, and rewriting. The most time is devoted to writing the first draft, but not much time is given to prewriting or rewriting.

because *they already practiced some revision at the beginning of the process*. We often talk about revision as occurring only after you've written a draft, which of course is a quite sensible idea. But the process of revision is an effort to *resee* a subject, to circle it with questions, to view it from fresh angles; and many of the open-ended writing methods we've discussed in *The Curious Writer* certainly involve revision. Fastwriting, clustering, listing, and similar invention techniques all invite the writer to resee. Armed with these discoveries, some writers may be able to write fairly strong first drafts.

What is essential, however—whether you revise at the beginning of the writing process or, as most writers do, after you craft the draft—is achieving some separation from what you initially thought, what you initially said, and how you said it. To revise well, writers must divorce the draft.

Strategies for Divorcing the Draft

You can do some things to make separation from your work easier, and spending less time on the first draft and more time on the revision process is one of them. But aside from writing fast drafts, what are other strategies for reseeing a draft that already has a hold on you?

14.1
Understand the meaning—and value—of revision and apply it to your own work when appropriate.

1. **Take some time.** Absolutely the best remedy for overcoming revision resistance is setting the draft aside for a week or more. Professional writers, in fact, may set a piece aside for several years and then return to it with a fresh, more critical perspective. Students simply don't have that luxury. But if you can take a week or a month—or even a day—the break from looking at the work is almost always worth it.

2. **Attack the draft physically.** A cut-and-paste revision that reduces a draft to pieces is often enormously helpful, because you're no longer confronted with the familiar full draft, a version that may have cast a spell on you. By dismembering the draft, you can examine the smaller fragments more critically. How does each piece relate to the whole? Might there be alternative structures? What about gaps in information? (See Revision Strategy 14.18 later in this chapter for a useful cut-and-paste exercise.)

3. **Put it away.** Years ago I wrote a magazine article about alcoholism. It was about twenty-five pages long and it wasn't very good. I read and reread that draft, completely puzzled about how to rewrite it. One morning, I woke up and vowed I would read the draft just once more, then put it away in a drawer and start all over again, trusting that I would remember what was important. The result was much shorter and much better. In fact, I think it's the best essay I've ever written. Getting a troublesome draft out of sight—literally—may be the best way to find new ways to see it.

4. **Ask readers to respond.** Bringing other people's eyes and minds to your work allows you to see your drafts through perspectives other than your own. Other people have a completely different relationship with your writing

than you do. They will see what you don't. They easily achieve the critical distance that you are trying to cultivate when you revise.

5. **Write different leads.** The nonfiction writer John McPhee once talked about beginnings as the hardest thing to write. He described a lead as a "flashlight that shines down into the story," illuminating where the draft is headed. Imagine, then, the value of writing a new beginning, or even several new beginnings; each may point the next draft in a slightly different direction, perhaps one that you hadn't considered in your first draft.

6. **Conduct research.** One of the central themes of *The Curious Writer* is that research isn't a separate activity, but rather a source of information that can enrich almost any kind of writing. Particularly in genres such as the personal essay, in which the writer's voice, perspective, and experience dominate the draft, listening to the voices and knowledge of others can deepen and shift the writer's thinking and perspectives.

7. **Read aloud.** I always ask students in workshop groups to read their drafts aloud to each other. I do this for several reasons, but the most important is the effect that *hearing* a draft has on the writer's relationship to it. In a sense, we often hear a draft in our heads as we compose it or reread it, but when we read the words aloud, the draft comes alive as something separate from the writer. As the writer listens to herself—or listens to someone else read her prose—she may cringe at an awkward sentence, suddenly notice a leap in logic, or recognize the need for an example. Try reading your draft aloud to yourself, and the same thing may happen.

8. **Write in your journal.** One of the strategies you can use to divorce the draft is to return to your notebook and fastwrite about what you might do to improve the piece. You can do this by asking yourself questions about the draft and then—through fastwriting—attempt to answer them. The method can help you see a new idea, which may become key to the structure of your next draft. Too often we see the journal exclusively as a prewriting tool, but it can be useful throughout the writing process, particularly when you need to think about ways to solve a problem as you revise.

Later in this chapter, we'll build on some of these basic strategies by using specific revision methods that may work with particular kinds of writing and with drafts that have particular problems. All of these methods encourage a separation between the writer and his or her draft and rely on that critical distance to be effective.

14.2

Recognize five types of revision and apply the most relevant strategies to a particular draft.

Five Categories of Revision

The following kinds of writers are typically the ones who most need to revise:

1. Writers of fast drafts
2. Writers who compose short drafts
3. Writers who indulge in creative, but not critical, thinking

4. Writers who rarely go past their initial way of seeing things

5. Writers who have a hard time imagining a reader other than themselves

6. Writers who rely on limited sources of information

7. Writers who still aren't sure what they're trying to say

8. Writers who haven't found their own way of saying what they want to say

9. Writers who haven't delivered on their promises

10. Writers who think their draft is already "perfect"

These are the usual suspects whose drafts need revision, but there are many others. In general, if you think there's more to think about, more to learn, more to say, and better ways to say it, then revision is your route to surprise and discovery. Most writers agree that rewriting is a good idea but don't know where to start.

Problems in drafts vary enormously but tend to involve concerns in five general areas: purpose, meaning, information, structure, and clarity and style. Here are some typical reader responses to drafts with each kind of problem:

1. **Problems with Purpose**
   - "I don't know why the writer is writing this paper."
   - "The beginning of the essay seems to be about one thing, and the rest of it is about several others."
   - "I think there are about three different topics in the draft. Which one do you want to write about?"
   - "So what?"

2. **Problems with Meaning**
   - "I can't tell what the writer is trying to say in the draft."
   - "There doesn't seem to be a point behind all of this."
   - "I think there's a main idea, but there isn't much information on it."
   - "I thought the thesis was saying something that's already pretty obvious."

3. **Problems with Information**
   - "Parts of the draft seemed pretty vague or general."
   - "I couldn't really *see* what you were talking about."
   - "That could use more explanation."
   - "It seemed like you needed some more facts to back up your point."
   - "It needs more detail."

4. **Problems with Structure**
   - "I couldn't quite follow your thinking in the last few pages."
   - "I was confused about when this happened."
   - "I understood your point, but I couldn't figure out what this part had to do with it."
   - "The draft doesn't really flow very well."

5. **Problems with Clarity and Style**
   - "This seems a little choppy."

- "You need to explain this better. I couldn't quite follow what you were saying in this paragraph."
- "This sentence seems really awkward to me."
- "This doesn't have a strong voice."

Problems with Purpose

A draft that answers the *So what?* question is a draft with a purpose. Often enough, however, writers' intentions aren't all that clear to readers, who then don't have a strong incentive to keep reading.

It's a little like riding a tandem bike. The writer sits up front and steers while the reader occupies the seat behind, obligated to pedal but with no control over where the bike goes. As soon as the reader senses that the writer isn't steering anywhere in particular, the reader will get off the bike; why do all that work if the bike seems to be going nowhere?

Frequently when you begin writing about something, you don't have any idea where you're headed; that's exactly *why* you're writing about the subject in the first place. When you write such discovery drafts, revision often begins by looking for clues about your purpose. What you learn then becomes a key organizing principle for the next draft and for trying to clarify this purpose for your readers. The first question, therefore, is one writers must answer for themselves: "Why am I writing this?" Of course, if it's an assignment, it may be hard to get past the easy answer—"Because I have to"—but if the work is going to be any good, there must be a better answer than that. Whether your topic is your choice or your instructor's, you have to find your own reason to write about it, and what you discover will become an answer to your bike partner's nagging question, yelled into the wind from the seat behind you: "If I'm going to pedal this hard, you'd better let me know where we're going."

When we write, we may begin with wide-ranging motives: to explore, to argue, to analyze, to explain, or to reflect. Each of these motives is often associated with a particular genre (see "Inquiring into the Details: Explore or Argue?" on page 519). But in each draft, no matter what the genre, we also have narrower purposes. For example, you might want to explore the idea of gender roles in video gaming, or make a claim about the reasons behind climate change denial. In your first draft, you might be able to identify your wide-ranging motive behind writing, but you need to make your narrower purposes clear when you revise your draft.

Revision Strategy 14.1: Dialogue with Dave

Dave is a good sort. He's curious about the world and a pretty good listener. But his patience isn't endless. Imagine that you're in a conversation with Dave about the topic of your essay. Naturally, one of the first things he wants know is why

Inquiring into the Details

Explore or Argue?

We want to explore, evaluate, explain, or reflect on a topic. These are some of the primary motives for writing about something, and they're often associated with particular genres. ____

Genre	Primary Motive
Personal essay	Explore
Profile	Explore or explain
Review	Evaluate
Proposal	Evaluate
Argument	Evaluate
Analytical essay	Evaluate
Ethnographic essay	Explore or evaluate
Research essay	Explore or evaluate
Reflective essay	Reflect

Of course, any one essay may involve several motives, but as you begin revising your draft, identify the main reason you're writing about this topic. In particular, do you want to *explore* the topic, hoping to discover what you think? Or have you already figured out what you think, and you're now ready to make an *argument* by offering an evaluation or making a claim? Your primary motive has significant implications for how you approach the revision of your draft.

you're writing about this topic in the first place. Write your half of the following dialogue in a Word document or in your notebook:

Dave	You
Alrighty then, what exactly is this draft on? What were you writing about?	
Hmmm…. That's interesting. What surprised you most when you wrote about that topic?	

(*continued*)

Dave	You	
Okay. Cool. But what I really want to know is why I should care about this as much as you do. Why is it important? Why does it matter? What does it have to do with someone like me?		

This exercise has helped you to think through your answer to that vital question that all writing must answer: So what? Examine your answers to Dave's questions, particularly the questions in the third box. Somewhere in your answers, do you see a clear statement of your purpose? Can you include that purpose somewhere near the beginning of your draft so that readers like Dave know where you're headed and why?

Revision Strategy 14.2: What Do You Want to Know About What You've Learned?

Because inquiry-based writing is usually driven by questions rather than answers, one way to discover your purpose in a sketch or draft is to generate a list of questions your topic raises for you. Of course, you hope that one of those questions might lead to your purpose in the next draft. Try the following steps with a draft that needs a stronger sense of purpose.

One Student's Response

Julia's Draft

What do I understand about this topic now that I didn't understand before I started writing about it?

   After writing this essay, I understand more clearly that there's a relationship between a girl's eating disorders and how her father treated her as a child.

LIST OF QUESTIONS

- Why the father and not the mother?
- What is it about father/daughter relationships that makes daughters so vulnerable to believing in so-called "ideal" feminine body types?
- Is a father's influence on a girl's body image greater at certain ages or stages in her life?
- How can a father be more informed about his impact on his daughter's body image?

1. Choose a draft or sketch you'd like to revise, and reread it.

2. On the back of the manuscript, craft an answer to the following question: *What do I understand about this topic now that I didn't understand before I started writing about it?*

3. Next, if you can, build a list of questions—perhaps new ones—that this topic raises for you. Make this list as long as you can, and don't censor yourself (see "One Student's Response").

4. Use one or more of the questions as a prompt for a fastwrite. Follow your writing to see where it leads and what it might suggest about new directions for the revision.

5. If you can't think of any questions, or find that you didn't learn much from writing about the topic (step 2), you still have several options. One is to abandon the draft altogether. Is it possible that this topic simply doesn't interest you anymore? If abandoning the draft isn't possible, then you need to find a new angle from which to write about it. Try Revision Strategy 14.3.

Revision Strategy 14.3: Finding the Focusing Question

The best topics, and the most difficult to write about, are those that raise questions for you. In a sketch or first draft, you may not know what those questions are. But if your subsequent drafts are going to be purposeful and focused, then discovering the main question behind your essay is essential. This discovery is particularly important in essays that are research based, because the drafts are longer and you're often trying to manage a lot of information. This revision strategy works best when it's a class activity.

1. Begin by putting your essay topic at the top of a large piece of paper such as newsprint or butcher paper. If yours is a research topic—say, Alzheimer's disease—jot that down. Post your paper on the classroom wall.

2. Spend a few minutes writing a few sentences explaining why you originally chose to write about this topic.

3. Make a quick list of everything you *already know* (if anything) about your topic—for instance, facts or statistics, the extent of the problem, important people or institutions involved, key schools of thought, common misconceptions, familiar clichés that apply to the topic, observations you've made, important trends, and typical perspectives. Spend about five minutes on this.

4. Now spend fifteen to twenty minutes brainstorming a list of questions about your topic that you'd love to learn the answers to. Make this list as long as possible.

5. As you look around the room, you'll see a gallery of topics and questions on the walls. You can help your fellow students. Circulate around the room

and do two things: Add a question that you're interested in about a particular topic, and put a checkmark next to the question (yours or someone else's) that seems most interesting.

When you return to your own newsprint or butcher paper, it should be covered with questions. How will you decide which of them might provide the best focus for the next draft? Generally, there are two kinds of questions: factual questions and questions that attempt to *do* something with information. What you're mostly going to see are factual questions. When we know little about a topic, it's natural to begin with fact or definition questions: What is known about this? What *is* it? Look at your piece of paper and identify which factual questions you might want to pursue. Ultimately, though, for a research essay you'll need to use what you're learning about your topic to frame a *doing* question, a question that will purposefully *use* the factual information you've gathered. These questions include the following:

- What should be done about this? (policy question)
- What is the value of this? (value question)
- What might this mean? (interpretation question)
- What is the relationship? (relationship question)
- Might this be true? (hypothesis question)

Try to draft a question about your topic that might fit into one of these doing question categories. Because relationship questions are particularly powerful guides to research, the next exercise looks more closely at how your topic might use cause and effect or comparison and contrast to analyze your topic.

Revision Strategy 14.4: What's the Relationship?

One of the more common purposes for all kinds of essays is to explore a relationship between two or more things. We see this purpose in research all the time: What's the relationship between AIDS and IV drug use in China? What's the relationship between gender and styles of collaboration in the workplace? What's the social class relationship between Huck and Tom in *The Adventures of Huckleberry Finn*?

One way, then, to clarify your purpose in revision is to try to identify the relationship that may be at the heart of your inquiry. Relationships between things can be described in a couple different ways.

- **Cause and effect.** What is the relationship between my father's comments about my looks and my eating disorder when I was a teenager? What is the relationship between the second Iraqi war and destabilization in Saudi Arabia? What is the relationship between the decline of the Brazilian rain forest and the extinction of the native eagles? What is the relationship between my moving to Idaho and the failure of my relationship with Kevin?

- **Compare and contrast.** How is jealousy distinguished from envy? How might writing instruction in high school be distinguished from writing instruction in college? What are the differences and similarities between my experiences at the Rolling Stones concert last month and my experiences at the Stones concert fifteen years ago?

Review your sketch or draft to determine whether what you're really trying to write about is the relationship between two (or more) things. In your journal, try to state this relationship in sentences similar to those listed here. With this knowledge, return to the draft and revise from beginning to end with this purpose in mind. What do you need to add to the next draft to both clarify and develop the relationship you're focusing on? What should you cut that is irrelevant to that focus?

Problems with Meaning

Fundamentally, most of us write something in an attempt to say something to someone else. The note my wife, Karen, left for me yesterday said it in a sentence: "Bruce—could you pick up some virgin olive oil and a loaf of bread?" I had no trouble deciphering the meaning of this note. But it isn't always that easy. Certain poems, for example, may be incredibly ambiguous, and readers may puzzle over them for hours, coming up with a range of plausible interpretations of meaning. (See Figure 14.3.)

Figure 14.3 Depending on the genre, writers say it straight or tell it slant. In short stories, for example, the writers' ideas may be ambiguous, inviting interpretation. Nonfiction genres— the kind you will most often write in college and beyond—usually avoid ambiguity. Writers say what they mean as clearly and as persuasively as they can.

Where Does Meaning Come From?

Depending on the writing situation, you may know from the start what you want to say, or you may *discover* what you think as you write and research. Inquiry-based projects usually emphasize discovery, while more-conventional argument papers may rely on arriving at a thesis earlier in the process. It's something like the difference between sledding with a saucer or a flexible flyer. The saucer is likely to veer off course, and you might find yourself somewhere unexpected, yet interesting.

Terms to Describe Dominant Meaning

- Thesis
- Main point
- Theme
- Controlling idea
- Central claim or assertion

No matter what you think about a topic when you start writing—even when you begin with a thesis to which you're committed—you can still change your mind. You *should* change your mind if the evidence you've gathered leads you away from your original idea. Unfortunately, writers of thesis-driven papers and other deductive forms are far more resistant than other writers to any change in their thinking. In some writing situations—say, essay exams—this isn't a problem. But it's often important in academic writing, including arguments, to continuously be open to new insight.

Ideas about what we want to say on a writing topic grow from the following:

1. **Thesis.** This is a term most of us know from high school writing, and it's most often associated with types of writing that work deductively from a main idea. Here's a sample thesis:

   The U.S. Securities and Exchange Commission is incapable of regulating an increasingly complex banking system.

2. **Theory.** We have strong hunches all the time about how things work, but we're not certain we're right. We test our theories and report on the accuracy of our hunches. Here's an example of a theory:

   Certain people just "don't have a head" for math.

3. **Question.** In a question-driven process, the emphasis is on discovery, and you might work more inductively. You see or experience something that makes you wonder. Here's a question that led a writer to ideas about girls, advertising, and sexuality.

   Why does my ten-year-old want to dress like a hooker?

The revision strategies that follow assume either that you've got a tentative thesis and want to refine it or that you're still working on discovering what you want to say.

Methods for Discovering Your Thesis

Use the following strategies if you're not quite sure whether you know what you're trying to say in a sketch or draft. How can you discover clues about your main point or meaning in what you've already written?

Revision Strategy 14.5: Harvest Meanings from the Draft

Sometimes when you're uncertain about what you're trying to say, the draft holds clues. But where do you look for them?

1. **Look in the end.** Discovery drafts—those you write to explore a topic—are end-weighted with meaning. It's in the final paragraphs, after you've worked your way through the material, that you often feel obligated to somehow reflect on what things might mean. Frequently there will be two or three ideas, all of which surface as you move to summarize. Choose the idea that is most important, and rebuild the revision *from the beginning* around that idea.

2. **Find the "instructive line."** Every draft is made up of many sentences. But which is *the most important sentence or passage*? Which line or passage points to an idea, theme, or feeling that seems to rise above much of the draft and illuminate the significance or relevance of everything else? Go through your draft and underline the one sentence or passage that you think is the most important in the entire piece. You must underline only one. In your journal, explain why you chose it, and answer this question: *In the end, what might this mean? What does it indicate about what I think is important to say?*

3. **Highlight the road signs.** In any draft there are two kinds of language: concrete, specific language and the language of abstraction. It is the language of abstraction—the words we use when we summarize, generalize, reflect, and comment—that holds the seeds of thought. On your computer, highlight every passage in your draft that involves abstraction. Then cut and paste each passage into a new document. Examine the list of passages and move them around so that similar ideas are grouped together. What do you see? Which ideas seem most important? Which are secondary?

Revision Strategy 14.6: Looping Toward a Thesis

I've argued throughout *The Curious Writer* for a dialectical approach to writing: moving back and forth between creative and critical modes of thinking, between your observations of and your ideas about, between generating and judging, between specifics and generalities. This is how writers can make meaning. This approach can also be used as a revision strategy, in a technique called *loop writing*. When you loop write, you move back and forth dialectically between two modes of thought—opening things up and then trying to pin them down. I imagine that this way of thinking looks like an hourglass. (See Revision Strategy 14.7 for a variation on loop writing.)

1. **First steps.** Reread the draft quickly, and then turn it upside down on your desk. You won't look at it again but should trust that you'll remember what's important.

2. **Narrative of thought.** Begin a three-minute fastwrite on the draft in which you tell yourself the story of your thinking about the essay. When you first started writing it, what did you think you were writing about, and then what, and then…? Try to focus on your ideas about what you were trying to say and how those ideas evolved.

3. **Summary.** Sum up what you said in your fastwrite by answering the following question in a sentence: *What seems to be the most important thing I've finally come to understand about my topic?*

4. **Examples.** Begin another three-minute fastwrite. Focus on scenes, situations, case studies, moments, people, conversations, observations, and so on that stand out for you as you think about the draft. Think especially of the details that led to your understanding of the topic, which you stated in the preceding step. Some of these details may be in the draft, but some may *not* yet be in the draft.

5. **Summary.** Finish by restating the main point you want to make in the next draft. Begin the revision by thinking about a lead or introduction that dramatizes this point. Consider using an evocative scene, case study, finding, profile, description, comparison, anecdote, conversation, situation, or observation that points the essay toward your main idea (see the "Inquiring into the Details: Types of Leads" box later in this chapter on page 439). For example, if your point is that your university's program to help second-language learners is inadequate, you could begin the next draft by telling the story of Maria, an immigrant from Guatemala who was a victim of poor placement into a composition course that she was virtually guaranteed to fail. Follow this lead into the draft, always keeping your main point or thesis in mind.

Revision Strategy 14.7: Reclaiming Your Topic

When you do a lot of research on your topic, you may reach a point where you feel awash in information. It's easy at such moments to feel as if you're losing control of your topic—besieged by the voices of experts, a torrent of statistics and facts, and competing perspectives. Your success in writing the paper depends on your making it your own again, regaining control over the information for your own purposes, in the service of your own questions or arguments. This revision strategy, a variation of Revision Strategy 14.6, should help you regain control of the material you collected for a research-based inquiry project.

1. Spend ten to fifteen minutes reviewing all of the notes you've taken and skimming key articles or passages from books. Glance at your most important sources. If you have a rough draft, reread it. Let the information swim in your head.

2. Now clear your desk of everything but your journal. Remove all your notes and materials. If you have a rough draft, put it away.

3. Fastwrite about your topic for seven full minutes. Tell the story of how your thinking about the topic has evolved. When you began, what did you think? What were your initial assumptions or preconceptions? Then what happened, and what happened after that? Keep your pen moving.

4. Skip a few lines in your notebook, and write *Moments, Stories, People, and Scenes*. Now fastwrite for another seven minutes, this time focusing on specific case studies, situations, people, experiences, observations, facts, and so on that stand out in your mind from the research you've done so far, or perhaps from your own experience with the topic.

5. Skip a few more lines. For another seven minutes, write a dialogue between you and someone else about your topic. Choose someone who you think is typical of the audience you're writing for. (You might resurrect "Dave" from Revision Strategy 14.1.) Don't plan the dialogue. Just begin with the question most commonly asked about your topic, and take the conversation from there, writing both parts of the dialogue.

6. Finally, skip a few more lines and write this two-word question in your notebook: *So what?* Now spend a few minutes trying to summarize the most important thing you think your readers should understand about your topic, based on what you've learned so far. Distill this summary into a sentence or two.

As you work your way to the last step, you're reviewing what you've learned about your topic without being tyrannized by the many voices, perspectives, and facts in the research you've collected. The final step, step 6, leads you toward a thesis statement. In the revision, keep this statement in mind as you reopen your notes, reread your sources, and check on facts. Remember in the rewrite to put all of this information in the service of this main idea—as examples or illustrations, necessary background, evidence or support, counterexamples, and ways of qualifying or extending your main point.

Revision Strategy 14.8: The Believing Game

In school, we're often told that doubt is at the heart of critical thinking. But what this emphasis on doubting can lead to is the assumption that we have to pick sides, and that once we do, we have to suppress the impulse to consider any virtues in the ideas of those with whom we disagree. Compositionist Peter Elbow suggested that we can develop a richer understanding of a subject when we at least entertain other points of view. He called this "the believing game." *This exercise is particularly helpful when revising drafts that make an argument.*

Set aside seven minutes for an episode of fastwriting in your journal or on the computer. The "believing game" involves quieting your doubting mind to "try on" the ways of thinking of people with whom you might disagree.

- Quickly jot down some of the claims or ideas on your topic with which you disagree or have questions about.

- Begin your fastwrite by choosing one of these ideas and responding in writing to the following two questions:

  - Why might someone see things this way?

  - If I assume there might be some truth to this idea, how does that change the way I think about the topic?

Many things might emerge from this writing that will help you revise. Start with the following:

1. Take another look at your thesis. Should it be revised? Should you qualify your claim or idea to reflect a more nuanced understanding of the arguments on your topic?

2. Should you import some of this material into a section of the draft where you examine points of view you don't share, or that don't fit neatly in your argument?

Methods for Refining Your Thesis

You may emerge from writing a draft with a pretty clear sense of what you want to say in the next one. But does this idea seem a little obvious or perhaps too general? Does it fail to adequately express what you really feel and think? Use one or more of the following revision strategies to refine a thesis, theme, or controlling idea.

Revision Strategy 14.9: Questions as Knives

Imagine that your initial feeling, thesis, or main point is like an onion (see Figure 14.4). Ideas, like onions, have layers, and to get closer to their hearts you need to cut through the most obvious outer layers to reveal what is less obvious, probably more specific, and almost certainly more interesting. Questions are to ideas as knives are to onions: They help you slice past your initial impressions. The most important question—the sharpest knife in the drawer—is simply *Why? Why* was the Orwell essay interesting? *Why* do you hate foreign films? *Why* should the university do more for second-language speakers? *Why* did you feel a sense of loss when the old cornfield was paved over for the mall?

Why may be the sharpest knife in the drawer, but there are other W questions with keen blades, too, including *What?, Where?, When?*, and *Who?* In Figure 14.4 you can see how these questions can cut a broad thesis down to size. The result is a much more specific, more interesting controlling idea for the next draft.

1. Subject your tentative thesis to the same kind of narrowing. Write your theme, thesis, or main point as a single sentence in your notebook.

2. Slice it with questions and restate it each time.

3. Continue this process until your point is appropriately sliced—that is, when you feel that you've gone beyond the obvious and stated what you think or feel in a more specific and interesting way.

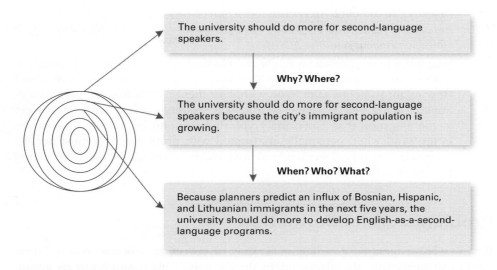

The university should do more for second-language speakers.

Why? Where?

The university should do more for second-language speakers because the city's immigrant population is growing.

When? Who? What?

Because planners predict an influx of Bosnian, Hispanic, and Lithuanian immigrants in the next five years, the university should do more to develop English-as-a-second-language programs.

Figure 14.4   Why? Where? When? Who? and What? Using questions to narrow the focus of a thesis is like using a knife to cut into the heart of an onion.

As before, rewrite the next draft with this new thesis in mind, reorganizing the essay around it from beginning to end. Add new information that supports the thesis, provides the necessary background, offers opposing views, or extends it. Cut information that isn't relevant to the new thesis.

Revision Strategy 14.10: Qualifying Your Claim

In your research you discovered that, while 90 percent of Americans think that their fellow citizens are too "fat," only 39 percent would describe themselves that way. This evidence leads you to make the following claim: *Although Americans agree that obesity is a national problem, their response is typical: It's somebody else's problem—an attitude that will cripple efforts to promote healthier lifestyles.* This seems like a logical assertion to make, if the evidence is reliable. But if you're going to try to build an argument around that assertion, it should be rigorously examined. Toulmin's approach to analyzing arguments provides a method for doing this rigorous examination.

1. Toulmin observes that sometimes a claim should be *qualified* so that it is more accurate and persuasive. The initial question is simple: *Is what you're asserting always or universally true?* Essentially, you're being challenged to examine your certainty about what you're saying. This might lead you to add "hedging" words or phrases that acknowledge your degree of certainty: *sometimes, always, mostly, in this case, based on available evidence*, and so on. In this example, the claim is already qualified because of its specification that it is limited to Americans, but the claim is also based on evidence from a single source. The claim, therefore, might be further qualified by saying this: *One survey*

suggests that although Americans agree that obesity is a national problem, their response is typical: It's somebody else's problem—an attitude that will cripple efforts to promote healthier lifestyles.

2. Imagining how your claim might be rebutted is another way to strengthen it. (Revision Strategy 14.8, "The Believing Game," can help you with this.) How might someone take issue with your thesis? What might be the exceptions to what you're saying is true? For example, might someone object to the assertion that Americans "typically" respond by putting their heads in the sand when personally confronted with problems? You must decide, then, whether this clever aside in your claim is something you're prepared to support. If you're not, cut it.

Problems with Information

Writers who've spent a lot of time generating or collecting information about their topics can work from abundance rather than scarcity. This is an enormous advantage, because the ability to throw stuff away means you can be selective about what you use, and the result will be a more focused draft. But as you revise, your purpose and assertion might shift, and you may find yourself in the unhappy position of working from scarcity again. Most of your research, observation, or fastwriting was relevant to the triggering subject in your initial sketch or draft, not to the generated subject you decide is the better direction for the next draft. In some cases, you may need to research the new topic or return to the generating activities of listing, fastwriting, clustering, and so on that will help provide information for the next draft.

More often, however, writers don't have to begin from scratch in revision. Frequently, shifting the focus of or refining the thesis in the first draft just means emphasizing different information or perhaps filling in gaps in later drafts. The strategies that follow will help you solve this problem.

Revision Strategy 14.11: Explode a Moment

The success of essays that rely on stories, observations, or case studies frequently depends on how well the writer renders an important scene, situation, moment, or description. In an ethnography on women in rodeo, for example, "deep" descriptions of these women interacting with men in the arena might help illuminate gender differences. This takes efficient observation (and note-taking) skills but also requires the appropriate treatment: building a scene with concrete details. To create such a scene, you need to "explode the moment."

1. Choose a draft that relies on description, scene, or stories.
2. Make a list in your journal of the moments (for example, scenes, situations, and turning points) that stand out in the draft.
3. Circle one moment that you think is the most important to your purpose in the essay. It could be the situation that is most telling, a dramatic turning

point, the moment of a key discovery that is central to what you're trying
to say, or a scene that illustrates the dilemma or raises the question you're
exploring in the draft.

4. Write that moment at the top of a blank journal page (for example, the rodeo
    riders prepare).

5. Now put yourself back into that moment and fastwrite about it for seven
    full minutes. Make sure that you use as much detail as possible, *drawing on
    all your senses*. Write in the present tense if it helps.

6. Use this same method with other moments in the draft that might deserve
    more emphasis in the next draft. Remember that real time means little in
    writing. An experience that lasted seven seconds can easily take up three
    pages of writing if it's described in enough detail. Rewrite and incorporate
    the best of the new information in the next draft.

Revision Strategy 14.12: Beyond Examples

When we decide to add information to a draft, we normally think of adding examples. If you're writing a research essay on living with a sibling who suffers from
Down syndrome, you might mention that your brother typically tries to avoid certain cognitive challenges. Members of your workshop group wonder, "Well, what
kind of cognitive challenges?" In revision, you add an example or two from your
own experience to clarify what you mean. This is, of course, a helpful strategy;
examples of what you mean by your assertion are a kind of evidence that helps
readers more fully understand your work. But also consider adding other types of
information to the next draft. Some of the following additions present opportunities for new research.

- **Presenting counterarguments.** Typically, persuasive essays include information that represents an opposing view. (See Revision Strategy 14.8, "The
  Believing Game," for help in generating material on other points of view.)
  Say you're arguing that except for "avoidance" behaviors, there really aren't
  personality traits that can be attributed to most people with Down syndrome. You include a summary of a study that says otherwise. Why? Because
  it provides readers with a better understanding of the debate, and enhances
  your ethos because you appear fair.

- **Providing background.** When you drop in on a conversation between two
  of your friends, you initially may be clueless about the subject. Naturally,
  you ask questions: "Who are you guys talking about? When did this happen? What did she say?" Answers to these questions provide a context that
  allows you to understand what your friends are saying and to participate in
  their conversation. Such background information is often essential in written
  communication, too. In a personal essay, readers may want to know when
  and where the event occurred or the relationship between the narrator and a
  character. In an analytical essay, it might be necessary to provide background

information on the short story because readers may not have read it. In a research essay, it's often useful to provide background information about what has already been said on the topic and the research question.

- **Establishing significance.** Let's say you're writing about the problem of obesity in America, something that most of us are generally aware of these days. But the significance of the problem really strikes home when you add information from research suggesting that 30 percent of American adults are overweight, up from 23 percent just six years ago. It is even more important to establish the significance of a problem about which there is little awareness or consensus. For example, most people don't know that America's national park system is crumbling and in disrepair. Your essay needs to provide readers with information that establishes the significance of the problem. In a profile, readers need to have a reason to be interested in the profile subject—perhaps he or she represents a particular group of people of interest or concern.

- **Giving it a face.** One of the best ways to make an otherwise abstract issue or problem come to life is to show how it affects someone. We can't fully appreciate the social impact of deforestation in Brazil unless we are introduced to someone such as Chico Mendes, a forest defender who was murdered for his activism. Obesity might be an abstract problem until we meet Carl, a 500-pound 22-year-old who is "suffocating in his own fat." To make your essay more interesting and persuasive, add case studies, anecdotes, profiles, and descriptions that put people on the page.

- **Defining it.** If your essay is on a subject your readers know little about, you'll likely use concepts or terms that readers will need you to define. What exactly do you mean, for example, when you say that the Internet is vulnerable to cyberterror? What exactly is cyberterror anyway? In your personal essay on your troubled relationship with your mother, what do you mean when you call her a narcissist? Frequently, your workshop group will alert you to terms and concepts in the draft that need defining, but also go through your draft and ask yourself, *Will my readers know what I mean?*

Revision Strategy 14.13: Research the Conversation

Your draft opens a door to a room in which there is an "unending conversation" about your topic, one that you've just dropped into. This is Kenneth Burke's "parlor metaphor" for how knowledge about the world is made: Imagine that all the people who share an interest in your question are in one room and are engaged in a lively debate and dialogue that has been going on for a long time. Drafts help us to figure out what parlor we've stumbled into, and when we know this, we also know what conversations to listen in on.

An example: You're writing about the campus's sustainability projects. This is a door into a conversation where a range of people are talking: college administrators who have implemented recycling programs, scholars who have researched ways of calculating carbon footprints, editorialists who opine about why it's a good idea—or not—to invest student funds in such projects. You may have already found some of this in your research, but there are always more voices to hear. In fact, this is the research that will have the biggest impact in strengthening your draft.

Research the conversation about your topic in the following ways:

1. **Mine bibliographies.** Often there is a scholarly article or book that is spot on and speaks directly to your research question. Look at its bibliography and scan the titles. Search for relevant articles or books among those that your favorite source cited. Pursue the promising titles. Can you use any of this new information somewhere in your draft?

2. **Gather names.** Who has said the most on your topic? Whose work is most influential? Collect these names, and using your library's database or Google Scholar, find the original works by these experts that caused the stir. Skim the articles and books that get cited most by others.

3. **Drill down from Wikipedia.** Wikipedia has its faults, but it's also a portal to relevant articles, websites, and organizations. Search for your topic on Wikipedia, hunting for relevant links in the text and bibliography. Use the links to find other voices who have shaped the conversation on your topic.

Revision Strategy 14.14: Backing Up Your Assumptions

Targeted research is particularly important when you're making an argument. In addition to providing evidence that is relevant to your thesis, an argument frequently is based on the assumptions behind that thesis. Stephen Toulmin calls these assumptions *warrants*. A warrant bridges the evidence with a related claim that reveals the assumptions on which the argument rests. A warrant essentially answers this question: What do you have to believe is true to believe a claim? For example, suppose your claim is the following: *Reading a lot makes people better writers.* And here's the evidence supporting the claim: *English majors read a lot and they are also strong writers.* What do you need to assume is true to believe this assertion? Lots. One particularly key warrant is that what's true of English majors is true of all "people." Warrants are often implicit, so it can be really helpful to bring them out into the open and see if they're sound.

1. Write your claim at the top of a journal page, and then list the assumptions or warrants on which it seems to rest. For example, consider this claim: *Teacher salary increases should be tied to student performances on tests.*

2. Now list the warrants behind your claim. In other words, what does one have to believe is true to buy the argument? In our example about teacher salaries and test scores, one warrant would be that *the quality of teaching is reflected in how students perform on tests.* Is there backing for that assumption?

3. Review your list of warrants. Which of them are assumptions that need supporting evidence? Focus your research on finding that evidence.

Problems with Structure

When it's effective, the structure of a piece of writing is nearly invisible. Readers don't notice how the writer is guiding them from one piece of information to the next. When structure is a problem, though, the writer asks readers to walk out on a shaky bridge and trust that it will help them get to the other side—but the walkers can think of little else but the shakiness of the bridge. Some professional writers, such as John McPhee, obsess about structure, and for good reason; when you're working with a tremendous amount of information, as McPhee often does in his research-based essays, it's important to have a clear idea about how you'll use that information.

It's helpful to distinguish between two basic structures for writing. One typically organizes the information of our experiences, and the other organizes our thinking so that it's clear and convincing. Typically, we use narrative, and especially chronology, to organize our experiences, though how we handle time can vary considerably. Writing that presents information based on the writer's reasoning—perhaps making an argument or reporting on an experiment—is logically structured. The most common example is the thesis-example or the thesis-proof paper. Much formal academic writing relies on logical structures that use deduction or induction.

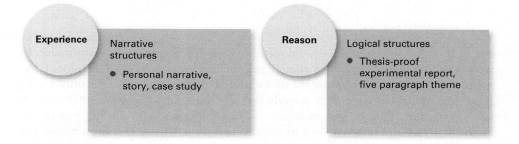

And yet some kinds of writing, such as the researched essay or ethnography, may *combine* both patterns, showing how the writer reasoned through to the meaning of an experience, observation, reading, and so on. These essays tell a "narrative of thought."

Formal Academic Structures

In some academic writing, the structure is prescribed. Scientific papers often have particular sections—Introduction, Methodology, Results, Discussion—but within those sections, writers must organize their material. Certain writing assignments may also require you to organize your information in a certain way. The most common of these arrangements is the thesis/support structure. In such essays, you typically establish your thesis in the first paragraph, spend the body of the paper presenting evidence that supports the thesis, and conclude the essay with a summary that restates the thesis in light of what you've presented.

Thesis/support is a persuasive form, so it lends itself to arguments, analytical essays, reviews, proposals, and similar pieces. In fact, you may have already structured your draft using this approach. If so, the following revision strategy may help you tighten and clarify the draft.

Beginning

- Establishes purpose (answers So what? question)
- Introduces question, dilemma, problem, theory, thesis, claim (sometimes dramatically)
- Helps readers understand—and feel—what's at stake for them

Middle

- Tests theory, claim, thesis against the evidence
- Develops reasons, with evidence, for writer's thesis or claim
- Tells story of writer's inquiry into question, problem, or dilemma

End

- Proposes answer, even if tentative, for writer's key question
- Revisits thesis or claim, extending, qualifying, contradicting, or reconfirming initial idea
- Raises new questions, poses new problems, or offers new understanding of what is at stake for readers

Revision Strategy 14.15: Beginnings, Middles, Ends, and the Work They Do

Stories, we are often told, are structured in three acts: They always have a beginning, middle, and end. This may be the most fundamental structure of all, and it doesn't just apply to narratives. The illustration with the butterfly explains what a beginning, middle, and end might contribute to making nearly any piece of writing coherent and convincing. Apply some of these ideas to your draft.

1. Draw a line in the draft where you think Act 1 ends and another line where you think Act 2 ends. Where you decide to divide the draft is entirely up to you; there's no formula to this. But you may change your mind as you go along.

2. Now use the illustration with the butterfly to analyze your beginning, middle, and end. Does each section do at least *one* of the listed tasks? If not, revise the section so that it does. This may involve adding a sentence or two—or possibly a couple paragraphs—of new information, perhaps moving some from elsewhere in the draft.

3. Generally speaking, Act 2 does the most work, and so proportionally it should have the most information. For example, many essays look like this:

If you find, for example, that your beginning takes three pages of a five-page essay, then you might want to remove material from the first few pages and concentrate on developing the body of your essay.

Revision Strategy 14.16: Reorganizing Around Thesis and Support

Because the thesis/support structure is fairly common, it's useful to master. Most drafts, even if they weren't initially organized in that form, can be revised into a thesis/support essay (personal essays would be an exception). The order of information in such an essay generally follows this design:

- **Lead paragraph:** This paragraph introduces the topic and explicitly states the thesis, usually as the last sentence in the paragraph. For example, a thesis/support paper on the deterioration of America's national parks system might begin this way:

    Yellowstone National Park, which shares territory with Idaho, Montana, and

    Wyoming, is the nation's oldest park and, to some, its most revered. Established on

March 1, 1872, the park features the Old Faithful geyser, which spouts reliably every 76 minutes on average. What isn't nearly as reliable these days is whether school groups will get to see it. Last year 60% of them were turned away because the park simply didn't have the staff. <u>This essay will argue that poor funding of our national park system is a disgrace that threatens to undermine the Park Service's mission to preserve the areas "as cumulative expressions of a single national heritage" ("Famous Quotes")</u>.

The thesis (underlined) is the final sentence in the paragraph, for emphasis.

Body: Each succeeding paragraph until the final one attempts to prove or develop the thesis. Often, each paragraph is devoted to a single *reason* why the thesis is true, frequently stated as the topic sentence of the paragraph. Specific information then explains, clarifies, and supports the reason. For example, here's a typical paragraph from the body of the national parks essay:

<u>One aspect of the important national heritage at risk because of poor funding for national parks is the pride many Americans feel about these national treasures.</u> *Newsweek* writer Arthur Frommer says the national park system is among the "crowning glories of our democracy." He adds, "Not to have seen them is to have missed something unique and precious in American life" (12). To see the crumbling roads in Glacier National Park, or the incursion of development in Great Smoky Mountains National Park, or the slow strangulation of the Everglades is not just an ecological issue; it's a sorry statement about a democratic nation's commitment to some of the places that define its identity.

The underlined sentence is the topic sentence of the paragraph and is an assertion that supports and develops the thesis in the lead paragraph of the essay. The rest of the paragraph offers supporting evidence of the assertion, in this case a quotation from a *Newsweek* writer who recently visited several parks.

Concluding paragraph: This paragraph reminds the reader of the central argument, not simply by restating the original thesis from the first paragraph, but also by reemphasizing some of the most important points. This reemphasis may lead to an elaboration or restatement of the thesis. One common technique is to find a way at the end of the essay to return to the beginning. Here's the concluding paragraph of the essay on national park funding:

We would never risk our national heritage by allowing the White House to deteriorate or the Liberty Bell to rust away. <u>As the National Park Service's own mission</u>

states, the parks are also "expressions" of our "single national heritage," one this paper contends is about preserving not only trees, animals, and habitats, but also our national identity. The Old Faithful geyser reminds Americans of their constancy and their enduring spirit. What will it say about us if vandals finally end the regular eruptions of the geyser because Americans didn't support a park ranger to guard it? What will we call Old Faithful then? Old Faithless?

Note that the underlined sentence returns to the original thesis but doesn't simply repeat it word for word. Instead, it amplifies the original thesis, adding a definition of "national heritage" that includes national identity. It returns to the opening paragraph by finding a new way to discuss Old Faithful. Revise your draft to conform to this structure, beginning with a strong opening paragraph that explicitly states your thesis and concluding with an ending that somehow returns to the beginning without simply repeating what you've already said.

Revision Strategy 14.17: Multiple Leads

The element that may affect a draft more than any other is the beginning. There are many ways into the material, and of course you want to choose a beginning, or lead, that a reader would find interesting. You also want to choose a beginning that makes some kind of promise and provides readers with a sense of where you intend to take them. But a lead also has a less-obvious influence on both readers and writers. How you begin often establishes the voice of the essay; signals the writer's emotional relationship to the material (the writer's ethos); and might suggest the form the essay will take.

This is, of course, why beginnings are so hard to write. But the critical importance of where and how to begin suggests that examining alternative leads can give writers more choices and more control over their essays. To borrow John McPhee's metaphor, if a lead is a "flashlight that shines down into the story," then pointing that flashlight in four different directions might reveal four different ways to write about the same subject. This can be a powerful revision strategy.

1. Choose a draft that has a weak opening, doesn't have a strong sense of purpose, or needs to be reorganized.

2. Compose four *different* openings to the *same* draft. One way to generate ideas for this is to cluster your topic and write leads from four different branches. Also consider varying the type of lead you write (see the "Inquiring into the Details: Types of Leads" box).

3. Bring a typed copy of these four leads (or five, if you want to include the original lead from the first draft) to class and share them with a small group. First, simply ask your classmates to choose the lead they like best.

4. Choose the lead *you* prefer. It may or may not be the one your classmates chose. Find a partner who was not in your small group and ask him or her the following questions after sharing the lead you chose:

    ▪ Based on this lead, what do you predict that this paper is about?

    ▪ Can you guess the question, problem, or idea I'm writing about in the rest of the essay?

    ▪ Do you have a sense of what my thesis is?

    ▪ What is the ethos of this beginning? In other words, how do I come across as the narrator or author of the essay?

If the reader's predictions, using the lead you preferred, were fairly accurate, this lead might be a good opening of the next draft. Follow it in a fastwrite in your notebook to see where it leads you. Go ahead and use the other leads elsewhere in the revision, if you like.

Inquiring into the Details

Types of Leads

Writer John McPhee says beginnings—or leads— are "like flashlights that shine down into the story." If you imagine that information about your topic is collected in a darkened room, then where and how you choose to begin an essay will, like a flashlight, illuminate some aspect of that room and that information. Different beginnings will point the flashlight in different directions and imply the different directions in which the essay might go. Consider a few types of leads:

1. ***Announcement.*** Typical of a thesis/support essay, among others. Explicitly states the purpose and thesis of the essay.
2. ***Anecdote.*** A brief story that nicely frames the question, dilemma, problem, or idea behind the essay.
3. ***Scene.*** Describes a situation, place, or image that highlights the question, problem, or idea behind the essay.
4. ***Profile.*** Begins with a case study or description of a person who is involved with the question, problem, or idea.
5. ***Background.*** Provides a context through information that establishes the significance of the question, problem, or idea.
6. ***Quotation or Dialogue.*** Begins with the voice of someone (or several people) involved or whose words are relevant.
7. ***Comparison.*** Presents two or more things that, when compared or contrasted, point to the question, problem, or idea.
8. ***Question.*** Frames the question the essay addresses.

If your reader's predictions were off, the lead may not be the best choice for the revision. However, should you consider this new direction an appealing alternative for the next draft? Or should you choose another lead that better reflects your current intentions rather than strike off in new directions? Either way, follow a new lead to see where it goes.

Revision Strategy 14.18: The Frankenstein Draft

One way to divorce a draft that has you in its clutches is to dismember it; that is, cut it into pieces and play with the parts, looking for new arrangements of information or new gaps to fill. Writing teacher Peter Elbow's cut-and-paste revision strategy can be a useful method, particularly for drafts that don't rely on narrative structures (although sometimes playing with alternatives, particularly if the draft is strictly chronological, can be helpful). Research essays and other pieces that attempt to corral lots of information seem to benefit the most from this strategy.

1. Choose a draft that needs help with organization. Make a one-sided copy.

2. Cut apart the copy, paragraph by paragraph. (You may cut it into smaller pieces later.) Once you have completely disassembled the draft, shuffle the paragraphs to get them wildly out of order so the original draft is just a memory.

3. Now go through the shuffled stack and find the *core paragraph*. This is the paragraph the essay really couldn't do without because it helps answer the *So what?* question. It might be the paragraph that contains your thesis or establishes your focusing question. It should be the paragraph that explains, implicitly or explicitly, what you're trying to say in the draft. Set this paragraph aside.

4. With the core paragraph directly in front of you, work your way through the remaining stack of paragraphs and make two new stacks: one of paragraphs that don't seem relevant to the core paragraph (such as unnecessary digressions or information) and those that do (they support the main idea, explain or define a key concept, illustrate or exemplify something important, or provide necessary background).

5. Put your reject pile aside for the moment. You may later decide to salvage some of those paragraphs. But for now, focus on your relevant pile, including the core paragraph. Now play with order. Try new leads, ends, and middles. Consider trying some new methods of development as a way to organize your next draft (see the "Methods of Development" box). As you spread the paragraphs out before you and consider new arrangements, don't worry about the lack of transitions; you can add those later. Also look for gaps, places where more information might be needed. Consider some of the information in the reject pile as well. Should you splice in *parts* of paragraphs that you initially discarded?

6. As a structure begins to emerge, tape together the fragments of paper. Also splice in scraps in appropriate places and jot down what you might add in the next draft that is currently missing.

Methods of Development
- Narrative
- Problem to solution
- Cause to effect, or effect to cause
- Question to answer
- Known to unknown, or unknown to known
- Simple to complex
- General to specific, or specific to general
- Comparison and contrast
- Combinations of any of these

Now you've created a Frankenstein draft. But hopefully this ugly mess of paper and tape and scribbled notes holds much more promise than the monster did. On the other hand, if you end up with basically the original organization, perhaps your first approach wasn't so bad after all. In that case, maybe you at least found places where more information is needed.

Revision Strategy 14.19: Reverse Outline

While outlines can be a useful tool for planning a formal essay, they can also help writers revise a draft. The "reverse outline" is one method for doing this.

1. Number every paragraph in the draft.
2. Put your inquiry question or thesis at the top of a separate piece of paper, and then write a one- or two-sentence summary of each paragraph's purpose. For an argumentative piece, the purpose will likely be the central point of the paragraph. For other essays, the summary might identify the category of information the paragraph represents and what work the paragraph is intended to do, such as "present definition of autism to provide background information" or "present case study of autistic child to dramatize the problem," etc.
3. Analyze the list of your summaries.
   - **Is the order of information logical?** Does it move effectively from claims to reasons to evidence? Does it have three acts (see Revision Strategy 14.15)?
   - **Are some paragraphs about more than one thing?** Should they be two paragraphs instead?

Sample PowerPoint slide outlining a plan for an essay.

- **Is every paragraph *relevant* to the research question or thesis?**   If a paragraph digresses, is it a useful digression?
- **Is the emphasis off?** Do you provide too much information on a minor purpose or idea and not enough on more central purposes or ideas?

Problems with Clarity and Style

One thing should be made clear immediately: Problems with clarity and style need not have anything to do with grammatical correctness. You can have a sentence that follows all the rules and still lumbers, sputters, and dies like a Volkswagen bug towing a heavy trailer up a steep hill. Take this sentence, for instance:

> Once upon a point in time, a small person named Little Red Riding Hood initiated plans for the preparation, delivery, and transportation of foodstuffs to her grandmother, a senior citizen residing at a place of residence in a wooded area of indeterminate dimension.

Strong writing at the sentence and paragraph levels always begins with clarity.

This beastly sentence opens Russell Baker's essay "Little Red Riding Hood Revisited," a satire about the gassiness of contemporary writing. It's grammatically correct, of course, but it's also pretentious and unnecessarily wordy, and would be annoying to read if it wasn't pretty amusing. This section of the chapter focuses on revision strategies that will improve the clarity of your writing and help you consider the effects you want to create through word choice and arrangement.

Because we often think that revision work with paragraphs, sentences, and words always involves problems of correctness, it may be hard to believe at first that writers can actually manage readers' responses and feelings by using different words or by rearranging the parts of a sentence or paragraph. Once you begin to play around with style, however, you will realize that style is much more than cosmetic. In fact, style in writing is a lot like music in movies. Chris Douridas, a Hollywood music supervisor who picked music for *Shrek* and *American Beauty*, said recently that he sees "music as an integral ingredient to the pie. I see it as helping to flavor the pie and not as whipped cream on top." Certainly, people don't decide to see a movie because of its music, but we know that music is central to our experience of a film. Similarly, *how* you say things in a piece of writing powerfully shapes the reader's experience of *what* you say.

But style is a secondary concern. Strong writing at the sentence and paragraph levels always begins with clarity. Do you say what you mean as directly and economically as you can? This can be a real problem, particularly with academic writing, in which it's easy to get the impression that a long word is always better than a short word and that the absence of anything interesting to say can be remedied by sounding smart. Nothing could be further from the truth.

Solving Problems of Clarity

Begin revising your draft for clarity by using one or more of the following revision strategies, any of which will make your writing more direct and clear.

Revision Strategy 14.20: The Three Most Important Sentences

Writers, like car dealers, organize their lots to take advantage of where customers are most likely to look and what they're most likely to remember. In many essays and papers, there are three places to park important information and to craft your very best sentences. These are:

- the very first sentence
- the last line of the first paragraph
- the very last line of the essay

The Very First Sentence. Obviously, there are many important places in a piece of writing—and longer essays, especially, have more and different locations—for your strongest sentences. But in an informal piece of modest length, the first sentence not only should engage the reader, it should, through strong language and voice, introduce the writer as well. For example, here's the first line of Richard

Conniff's researched essay "Why Did God Make Flies?": "Though I've been killing them for years now, I have never tested the folklore that, with a little cream and sugar, flies taste very much like black raspberries." In more formal writing, the first line is less about introducing the writer's persona than about introducing the subject. Here's the first line of an academic piece I'm reading at the moment: "Much of the international debate about the relationship between research and teaching is characterized by difference." This raises an obvious question—"What is this difference?"—which is exactly what the author proposes to explore.

The Last Line of the First Paragraph. The so-called "lead" (or "lede" in journalism speak) of an essay or article does three things: It establishes the purpose of the work, raises interesting questions, and creates a register or tone. A lead paragraph in a shorter essay is just that—the first paragraph—while a lead in a longer work may run for paragraphs, even pages. Whatever the length, the last sentence of the lead launches the work and gets it going in a particular direction. In conventional, thesis-proof essays, then, this sentence might be where you state your main claim. In inquiry-based forms such as the essay, this sentence might be where you post the key question you're exploring or illuminate the aspect of the problem you're looking at.

The Very Last Line of the Essay. If it's good, this is the sentence readers are most likely to remember.

Try this revision strategy:

1. Highlight or underline each of the three key sentences in your draft.
2. Ask yourself these questions about the first line and, depending on your answers, revise the sentence:
   - Is the language lively?
   - Does it immediately raise questions the reader might want to learn the answers to?
   - Will readers want to read the second sentence, and why?
3. Analyze the last sentence of your "lead" paragraph for ideas about revision. Ask yourself this:
   - Is the sentence well crafted?
   - Does it hint at or explicitly state your motive for asking readers to follow along with you in the paragraphs and pages that follow?
4. Finally, scrutinize your last sentence:
   - Is it one of the best-written sentences in the piece?
   - Does it add something to the piece?

Revision Strategy 14.21: Untangling Paragraphs

One of the things I admire most in my friends David and Margaret is that they both have individual integrity—a deep understanding of who they are and who they want to be—and yet they remain just as profoundly connected to the people close to them. They manage to exude both individuality and connection. I hope my friends will forgive the comparison, but good paragraphs have the same qualities: Alone, they have their own identities, yet they are also strongly hitched to the paragraphs that precede and that follow them. This connection happens quite naturally when you're telling a story, but in expository writing the relationship between paragraphs is related more to content than to time.

The following passage is the first three paragraphs of Paul de Palma's essay on computers, with the clever title "http://www.when_is_enough_enough?.com." Notice the integrity of each paragraph—each is a kind of mini-essay—as well as the way each one is linked to the paragraph that precedes it.

> In the misty past, before Bill Gates joined the company of the world's richest men, before the mass-marketed personal computer, before the metaphor of an information superhighway had been worn down to a cliché, I heard Roger Schank interviewed on National Public Radio. Then a computer science professor at Yale, Schank was already well known in artificial intelligence circles. Because those circles did not include me, a new programmer at Sperry Univac, I hadn't heard of him. Though I've forgotten details of the conversation, I have never forgotten Schank's insistence that most people do not need to own computers.
>
> That view, of course, has not prevailed. Either we own a personal computer and fret about upgrades, or we are scheming to own one and fret about the technical marvel yet to come that will render our purchase obsolete. Well, there are worse ways to spend money, I suppose. For all I know, even Schank owns a personal computer. They're fiendishly clever machines, after all, and they've helped keep the wolf from my door for a long time.
>
> It is not the personal computer itself that I object to. What reasonable person would voluntarily go back to a typewriter? The mischief is not in the computer itself, but in the ideology that surrounds it. If we hope to employ computers for tasks more interesting than word processing, we must devote some attention to how they are actually being used, and beyond that, to the remarkable grip that the idol of computing continues to exert.

A paragraph should be unified, focusing on a single topic, idea, or thing. It's like a mini-essay in that sense.

Note how the first sentence in the new paragraph links with the last sentence in the preceding paragraph.

As before, the first sentence links with the last sentence in the previous paragraph.

The final sentence is the most important one in a paragraph. Craft it carefully.

Well-crafted paragraphs such as these create a fluent progression, all linked together like train cars; they make readers feel confident that this train is going somewhere. Paragraphs might do this by including information that clarifies, extends, proves, explains, or even contradicts. Do the paragraphs in your draft work well on their own *and* together?

1. Check the length of every paragraph in your draft. Are any too long, going on and on for a full page or more? Can you create smaller paragraphs by breaking out separate ideas, topics, discussions, or claims?

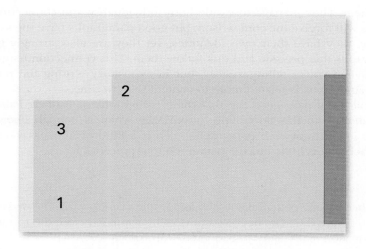

Figure 14.5   Order of important sentences in a paragraph. Often the first sentence is the second-most-important sentence in a paragraph. The third-most-important sentence follows immediately thereafter. The most important sentence usually comes at the end of the paragraph.

2. Now examine each paragraph in your draft for integrity. Is it relatively focused and unified? Should it be broken down into two or more paragraphs because it covers too much territory?

3. In Figure 14.5, note the order of the most important information in a typical paragraph. Is each of your paragraphs arranged with that order in mind? In particular, how strong is the final sentence in each paragraph? Does it prepare readers to move into the next paragraph? In general, each paragraph should add some kind of new information to the old information in the paragraphs preceding it. This new information may clarify, explain, prove, elaborate on, contrast, summarize, contradict, or alter time. Sometimes you should signal the nature of this addition using transition words and phrases (see the "Inquiring into the Details: Transition Flags" box). Are there any awkward transitions? Should you smooth them using transition flags?

Revision Strategy 14.22: Cutting Clutter

> *"Once upon a point in time—at coordinates as yet too sensitive to disclose—a small person named Little Red Riding Hood initiated an operation involving the preparation, transportation, and delivery of foodstuffs to her grandmother, a senior citizen residing in a forest of indeterminate dimension."*

Russell Baker's overinflated version of "Little Red Riding Hood," repeated above, suffers from what writer and professor William Zinsser called "clutter." This disease afflicts much writing, particularly in academic settings. Clutter, simply put, is

Inquiring into the Details

Transition Flags

One way to connect paragraphs is to use words that signal to a reader what the relationship is between them.

- ■ *Clarifying:* for example, furthermore, specifically, also, to illustrate, similarly
- ■ *Proving:* in fact, for example, indeed
- ■ *Time:* first . . . second . . . finally, subsequently, following, now, recently
- ■ *Cause or effect:* therefore, consequently, so, accordingly
- ■ *Contrast or contradiction:* on the other hand, in contrast, however, on the contrary, despite, in comparison
- ■ *Summarizing:* finally, in the end, in conclusion, summing up, to conclude

saying in three or four words what you might say in two, or choosing a long word when a short one will do just as well. It grows from the assumption that simplicity means simplemindedness. This assumption is misguided. Simplicity is a great virtue in writing. It's respectful of the readers, for one thing, who are mostly interested in understanding what you mean without having to deal with unnecessary detours or obstacles.

In case Russell Baker's tongue-and-cheek example of cluttered writing isn't convincing because it's an invention, here's a brief passage from a memo I received from a fellow faculty member some years ago. I won't make you endure more than a sentence of it.

> While those of us in the administration are supporting general excellence and consideration of the long-range future of the University, and while the Faculty Senate and Caucus are dealing with more immediate problems, the Executive Committee feels that an ongoing dialogue concerning the particular concerns of faculty is needed to maintain the quality of personal and educational life necessary for continued educational improvement.

That's a sixty-three-word sentence, and while there is nothing inherently wrong with long sentences, I'm pretty sure that at least half of the words are unnecessary. For the fun of it, see if you can cut at least thirty words from the sentence without compromising the writer's intent. Look for ways to say the same things in fewer words, and look for short words that might replace long ones. What kinds of choices did you make to improve the clarity of the sentence?

Now shift your attention to one of your own drafts and see if you can be as ruthless with your own clutter as you were with the memo writer's:

1. One of the most common kinds of clutter is stock phrases, things we mindlessly say because we've simply gotten in the habit of saying them.

Stock Phrase	Simpler Version
Due to the fact that...	Because
At the present time...	Now
Until such time as...	Until
I am of the opinion that...	I think
In the event of...	When *or* If
Referred to as...	Called
Totally lacked the ability to...	Couldn't
A number of...	Many
There is a need for...	We must

2. Another thing to consider is choosing a shorter, simpler word rather than a long, complicated word. For example, why not say *many* rather than *numerous*, or *ease* rather than *facilitate*, or *do* rather than *implement*, or *found* rather than *identified?* Go through your draft and look for opportunities such as these to use simpler, more direct words.

3. In his book *Style: Ten Lessons in Clarity and Grace*, Joseph Williams cleverly calls the habit of using meaningless words "verbal tics." My favorite verbal tic is the phrase *in fact*, which I park at the front of a sentence when I feel I'm about to clarify something. Williams mentions a few other common ones, including *kind of, actually, basically, generally, given, various*, and *certain*. Go through your draft and search for words and phrases that you use out of habit, and cut them if they don't add meaning.

Revision Strategy 14.23: The Actor and the Action Next Door

I live in a relatively urban neighborhood, and so I can hear Kate play her music across the street and Gray powering up his chainsaw to cut wooden pallets next door. I have mixed feelings about this. Kate and I have different tastes in music, and Gray runs the chainsaw at dusk. But I am never confused about who is doing what. That's less obvious in the following passage:

> A conflict that was greeted at first with much ambivalence by the American public, the war in Iraq, which caused a tentativeness that some experts call the "Vietnam syndrome," sparked protests among Vietnam veterans.

The subject, or actor, of the sentence (*the war in Iraq*) and the action (*sparked protests*) are separated by a few city blocks. In addition, the subject is buried behind a long introductory clause. As a result, it's a bit hard to remember who is doing what. Putting actor and action next door to each other makes writing livelier, and bringing the subject up front helps clarify who is doing what.

> The war in Iraq sparked protests among Vietnam veterans even though the conflict was initially greeted with public ambivalence. Some experts call this tentativeness the "Vietnam syndrome."

Review your draft to determine whether the subjects in your sentences are buried or are in the same neighborhood as the verbs that modify them. If they're too far away from each other, rewrite to bring the actors up front in your sentences and to close the distance between actors and actions.

Improving Style

The revision strategies in this section will improve the style of your writing. Writers adopt a style because it serves a purpose, perhaps encouraging a certain feeling that makes a story more powerful; enhancing the writer's ethos and making an essay more convincing; or simply giving certain information particular emphasis. For example, here's the beginning of an article about Douglas Berry, a Marine drill sergeant.

> He is seething, he is rabid, he is wound up tight as a golf ball, with more adrenalin surging through his hypothalamus than a cornered slum rat, he is everything these Marine recruits with their heads shaved to dirty nubs have ever feared or ever hoped a drill sergeant might be.

The style of this opening is calculated to have an obvious effect—the reader is pelted with words, one after another, in a breathless sentence that almost simulates the experience of having Sgt. Douglas Berry in your face. There's no magic to this. It is all about using words that evoke action and feeling, usually verbs or words based on or derived from verbs.

Revision Strategy 14.24: Actors and Actions

Academic writing sometimes lacks strong verbs and relies instead on old, passive standbys such as *it was concluded by the study* or *it is believed*. Not only are the verbs weak, but the actors—the people or things engaged in the action—are often missing completely from the sentences. *Who* or *what* did the study? *Who* believes?

This is called *passive voice*, and while it's not grammatically incorrect, it can suck the air out of a room. One of the easiest ways to locate passive voice in your drafts is to conduct a *to be* search. Most forms of the verb *to be* signal passive voice.

1. Conduct a *to be* search of your own draft. Whenever you find passive construction, try to put the actor into the sentence.
2. Try to use lively verbs as well. Can you replace weak verbs with stronger ones? How about *discovered* instead of *found*, or *seized* instead of *took*, *shattered* instead of *broke*? Review every sentence in your draft and, when appropriate, revise with a stronger verb.

Revision Strategy 14.25: Smoothing the Choppiness

Consider the following sentences, each labeled with the number of syllables it contains:

> When the sun finally rose the next day I felt young again.(15) It was a strange feeling because I wasn't young anymore.(15) I was fifty years old and felt like it.(10) It was the smell of the lake at dawn that thrust me back into adolescence.(19) I remembered the hiss of the waves.(9) They erased my footprints in the sand.(9)

The cause of the plodding rhythm is the unvarying length of the pauses. The last two sentences in the passage each have nine syllables, and the first two sentences are nearly identical in length as well (fifteen syllables each).

Now notice how this choppiness disappears by varying the lengths of the pauses through combining sentences, inserting other punctuation, and dropping a few unnecessary words.

> When the sun finally rose the next day I felt young again,(15) and it was a strange feeling because I wasn't young.(13) I was fifty years old.(6) It was the smell of the lake at dawn that thrust me back into adolescence and remembering the hiss of the waves as they erased my footprints in the sand.(39)

The revision is much more fluent, and the reason is simple: The writer varies the pauses and the number of syllables within each sentence—15, 13, 6, 39.

1. Choose a draft of your own that doesn't seem to flow or seems choppy in places.
2. Mark the pauses in the problem areas. Put slash marks next to periods, commas, semicolons, dashes, and so on—any punctuation that prompts a reader to pause briefly.
3. If the intervals between the pauses seem similar in length, revise to vary them, combining sentences, adding punctuation, dropping unnecessary words, or varying long and short words.

Revision Strategy 14.26: Fresh Ways to Say Things

It goes without saying that a tried-and-true method of getting to the heart of revision problems is to just do or die. Do you know what I mean? Of course you don't, because the opening sentence is laden with clichés and figures of speech that obscure meaning.

Removing clichés and shopworn expressions from your writing will make it sound as if you are writing with your own voice rather than someone else's.

1. Reread your draft and circle clichés and hand-me-down expressions. If you're not sure whether a phrase qualifies for either category, share your circled items with a partner and ask: Have you heard these things before?

2. Cut the clichés and overused expressions and rewrite your sentences by finding your own way to say things. In your own words, what do you really mean by "do or die" or "striking while the iron is hot" or becoming a "true believer"?

Using What You Have Learned

Take a few moments to reflect on what you have learned in this chapter and how you can apply it to your writing.

1. **Understand the meaning—and value—of revision and apply it to your own work when appropriate.** Even if an instructor doesn't explicitly require a revision for a writing assignment, you now have experience with what a difference revision can make in the quality of your work.

2. **Recognize five types of revision and apply the most relevant strategies to a particular draft.** As you continue to develop as a writer, you'll become a more critical reader of your own work, and assessing the quality of your writing will get easier. Learn to recognize your weaknesses—maybe you're not great at organizing drafts or you're wordy—and find strategies that help you address those problems.

Appendix A
THE WRITER'S WORKSHOP

Making the Most of Peer Review

Sharing your writing with strangers can be both frightening and gratifying; it can be a key to the success of the next draft or a complete waste of time. But one thing sharing your writing can't be in most composition courses these days is avoided. This is a good thing, I think, for three reasons:

1. *Being read* by others is a useful experience.
2. Workshops can be among the most effective ways for writers to *divorce the draft*.
3. The talk about writing in workshops can be enormously *instructive*.

Being Read

As we share our writing, sometimes reading our own work aloud to a group, we are sharing ourselves in a very real way. This is most evident with a personal essay, but virtually any piece of writing bears our authorship—our particular ways of seeing and saying things—and included in this sense of authorship are our feelings about ourselves as writers. While you might take personally group members' comments about your writing, workshops offer the really rare and unusual opportunity to actually hear the murmurs, the sighs, and the laughter of your readers responding to your work. You can also see their smiles, puzzled expressions, nodding heads, and even tears. You can experience your readers' experiences of your writing in ways that most published authors never can.

What is so valuable about this process is that audience is no longer an abstraction. After your first workshop, it's no stretch to imagine the transaction that most writing involves—a writer's words being received by a reader, who thinks and feels something in response. And when you take this back to the many solitary hours of writing, you may feel you have company—that members of your workshop group are interested in what you have to say. This is a powerful feeling.

Divorcing the Draft

Our writing relationships include our emotional connections to drafts, and these connections often have to do with the time we spent writing the drafts. In Chapter 14, I described the ways we get entangled in first drafts that can blind us to other ways of seeing a topic. Sometimes we need to divorce a draft, and the best way to do so is to spend time away from it. But students rarely have that luxury.

Workshops provide an alternative to time away from a draft, and they are effective for the same reason some people see therapists—group members offer an "outsider's" perspective on your work that may give it new meanings and raise new possibilities. If nothing else, readers offer a preview of whether your current meanings are clear and whether what you *assume* is apparent actually *is* apparent to someone other than yourself. It's rare when a workshop doesn't jerk writers away from at least a few of their assumptions about a draft, and the best of these experiences inspire writers to want to write again. This is the outcome writers should always hope to attain.

Instructive Talk

The talk in workshops is not always about writing. Rather than listen to lectures or study a textbook, writing courses ask you to make your own meanings. Whenever we are asked to assume new roles, some resistance can set in, and workshops can become an occasion to talk about the class, often out of earshot of the instructor—an opportunity to complain, but also to share understandings of, or approaches to, or experiences with assignments. Workshops can also be a chance for students to try out new identities—"I really liked writing this. Maybe I'm an okay writer after all."

This kind of talk can help you negotiate the new roles you're being asked to assume in your writing class; this is part of becoming a better, more confident writer. But the main purpose of workshop groups is to help students revise their drafts. So why seek advice from writers who are clearly less experienced than the instructor?

1. By talking with other students about writing, you get practice using the language you're learning in the writing classroom—language that helps you describe important features of your own work.
2. Because writing is about making choices in a draft, workshop groups are likely to bring to the surface possibilities that never occurred to you (and perhaps wouldn't occur to the instructor, either).
3. Your peers are also student writers, and because they come from similar circumstances—demands of other classes, part-time jobs, and perhaps minimal experiences with college writing—they are in a position to offer practical and realistic revision suggestions.

4. Finally, in most writing courses, the students in the class are an important audience for your work. Getting firsthand responses makes the rhetorical situation real rather than imagined.

Will you get bad advice in a peer workshop? Of course. Your group members will vary in their experiences and abilities to identify the problems and possibilities in a draft. But in the best writing workshops, you learn together, and as time goes by, the feedback gets better and better. Paradoxically, it pays off in your own writing to be generous in your responses to the work of others.

Models for Writing Workshops

The idea of peer-review workshops in writing classes has been around for years. Because collaboration in the writing classroom fits in perfectly with the class's aim of generating knowledge about the many ways to solve writing problems, peer review of drafts in small groups is now fairly common; you'll find workshops in writing classes ranging from first-year composition to advanced fiction writing. Workshop groups will likely reflect one of three models: full-class groups, small peer groups, or one-on-one reviews. (Full-class workshops are typical in creative writing courses; smaller groups are more common in composition.)

Group Workshops. In both full-class and small group sessions, you will probably be asked to provide copies of your draft for the group, either in advance of or at the beginning of the meeting. And you will be asked to read your draft aloud. You may feel hesitant about reading your draft aloud to your workshop group, but the usefulness of reading aloud will soon become apparent. Literally giving voice to your words is an entirely different experience from reading your work silently to yourself. You'll stumble over passages in your draft that seemed fine, and you may notice gaps you glossed over during your silent reading. You'll hear what your writing voice sounds like, and whether it works for you and your readers.

There may be guidelines or ground rules for responses from your classmates or fellow group members. You may be asked simply to listen to their responses, or to present the group with questions to consider. Sharing your work with up to twenty-five people can be scary—and probably the bigger the group, the scarier—but imagine the range of perspectives you'll get!

More typical than a full-class workshop is the smaller group, usually consisting of between three and seven members, either chosen randomly by your instructor or self-selected. These groups may stay together all semester or part of the semester, or you may find yourself working with fresh faces every workshop session. (Each of these alternatives has advantages and disadvantages.)

Ideally, your workshop group will meet in a circle, because facing each other encourages conversation rather than monologues.

One-on-One Peer Review. Your instructor also may ask you to work with a partner, exchanging drafts and discussing them with each other. What you lose in range and quantity of feedback you may gain in quality, because each of you is reading the other's work with particular care and attention, and you'll have more time to focus on your own work.

The Writer's and Reader's Responsibilities

No matter what model your instructor chooses, the success of the workshop depends largely on its participants. As a writer, you will get more useful feedback if you prepare appropriately: Reflect before the workshop on what questions you have about your work, and what responses would be most helpful; make sure everyone gets a copy of your draft; and in the workshop itself, avoid getting defensive. Listen to comments with an open mind; remember, you don't need to follow all the suggestions offered. And take notes, both to be sure you remember the comments, and also to assure your peers that you are taking their comments seriously.

As a reader, the most important rule to follow is this: Be generous with your responses to others' work, because in the end, you will learn more about your own work. Your comments will be particularly valuable if you keep the following in mind:

- **Be specific.** Focus your responses on particular parts or passages of the draft, but (except in an editorial workshop), avoid talking about grammar or mechanics.

- **Identify strengths.** This is often a good place to begin because it sets writers at ease, but, more importantly, writers often build on strengths in revision.

- **Offer suggestions, not directives.** The word *could* is usually better than *should*. Remember that the purpose of the workshop is to help identify the range of choices a writer might make to improve a draft. There is almost always more than one option.

- **Think about the role you play in the group.** It's easy to fall into a rut in group work, saying the same kinds of things or developing certain patterns of responses. Stay vigilant about *not* doing this, and try deliberately shifting the role you play in the workshop group.

Things can go wrong in workshops, of course. Typically, unsuccessful workshop groups suffer from two major problems: lack of commitment of group members and lack of clarity about the process of giving feedback. Lack of commitment is obvious to see: Writers fail to distribute drafts; members fail to offer written comments when requested; responders give comments that are general and perfunctory ("Really good. I wouldn't change a thing"). Instructors may evaluate or even grade workshop participation, but a group can evaluate itself, too. Ask yourselves: How effectively does this group work together? Do we all participate, or do some dominate the sessions? How useful are the comments we make?

Groups that work together over a period of time should always monitor how things are going. Remember, the best workshops have a simple but powerful effect on writers who share their work: *It makes them want to write again.*

Useful Responses

The *kinds* of responses to our writing we seek in workshops depend on at least two things: where we are in the writing process, and how we feel about the work in progress. Different kinds of problems arise during different stages of the writing process. Sometimes what we really need from readers of our work is more emotional than practical—we need to be motivated, encouraged, or validated—and sometimes we need straightforward suggestions about what works and what doesn't work. These responses can be labeled, respectively, *experiential* ("This is how I experienced your draft") and *directive* ("This is what you can do to make it better").

Depending on who you are and how you write, it may be most helpful to get less-directive responses to your work early on, when some people feel that specific suggestions undermine their sense of ownership. They don't want to know what readers think they should do in the revision, but rather how readers experienced their draft. What parts were interesting? What parts were confusing? On the other hand, other writers feel particularly lost in the early stages of the writing process; they can use all the direction they can get. Your group can decide (or your instructor will make suggestions) on the appropriate workshop response format, choosing from the following format types.

Response Formats

The following writing workshop formats move from the most experiential methods to more directive methods. While many of these formats feature particular ways of responding to drafts, remember that your responsibilities as reader apply to all of them: Respect the work; participate equally; say "could" rather than "should"; and use "I" statements rather than "you" statements ("This part confused me," rather than "You really need to clear this part up").

The No-Response Workshop. You may not be ready for comments because your work is unformed and you're confident that'll you discover the direction you want to go in with the next draft. Comments may confuse or distract you. However, it's always helpful to read your work aloud to an audience even if you don't invite a response. You will read with more attention and awareness. If you don't want comments—if you just want to hear yourself read your work—say so.

The Initial-Response Workshop. You might be interested only in first reactions to what you have written. Robert Brooke, Ruth Mirtz, and Rick Evans[1] suggest that you invite the following three kinds of initial responses to your work:

- **A relating response.** Group members share any personal associations your topic inspires. They may have had a similar or a contradictory experience, or read or seen something that is relevant to what you are trying to say.

- **A listening response.** Participants try to summarize what they hear you saying in the draft. This is much like the "say back" method some therapists use with patients.

- **A positive response.** Group members articulate what parts of the draft really work well and why, and suggest how you might build on these parts in the next draft.

The Narrative-of-Thought Workshop. Sometimes, seeing how readers experienced each section of a draft is helpful. To enable this experience, prepare copies of your draft for the group that leave a couple of inches of white space in three places: after the "lead," or opening paragraph; in the middle; and at the end. Then read the draft section by section, allowing ample time between sections for group members to write their comments, and then to share them.

- **After hearing the lead:** What do you feel about the topic or the writer so far? Can you predict what the essay is about? What questions does the lead raise for you that you expect might be answered later?

- **After hearing half:** What do you think or feel about what you've heard so far? Has the draft fulfilled your expectations from the lead? What do you expect will happen next?

- **After hearing it all:** What is the draft about? What does it seem to be saying (or not quite saying)? How well does it deliver on its promises? What part of your experience of the draft was most memorable? What part seemed least clear?

The conversation, along with the written comments you receive when you collect the group's copies of your draft, should give you strong clues about how well you've established a clear purpose in your essay and sustained that purpose from beginning to end. The responses also might give you ideas about new directions in which to take the next draft.

The Instructive-Lines Workshop. Most essays balance on a thesis, theme, question, or idea. Like the point of a spinning top, these claims, ideas, or questions are the things around which everything else revolves. In discovery drafts especially, a writer may be seeking the piece's center or centers of gravity.

---

[1]Robert Brooke, Ruth Mirtz, and Rick Evans, *Small Groups in Writing Workshops* (Urbana, IL: NCTE, 1994).

In this workshop format, members try to identify the draft's *most important lines and passages* and clearly mark them with underlining or highlighting. These are places where writers explicitly or implicitly seem to suggest what they're trying to say, and may include a line or passage that clearly states a thesis, a section where the writer adopts a critical stance or poses a question about meaning, a section where the writer seems to make an important claim—or even a digression that doesn't seem important but just might be.

Participants might discuss why a particular line or passage seems important, what it implies about the meaning of the essay as a whole, and whether the highlighted passages "speak" to each other—whether they might be revised or combined into an organizing principle or controlling idea for the next draft.

The Purpose Workshop. Sometimes writers know their purpose in a draft: "I'm proposing that having vegetarian fast-food restaurants would reduce American obesity," or "This essay explores why I felt relieved when my father died." What these writers may need most from their workshop groups is feedback on how well the draft accomplishes that particular purpose.

With this goal in mind, the writer crafts a statement of purpose that clearly states what she is trying to do in the draft. This statement should include a verb that implies what action she is trying to take—for example, *explore, argue, persuade, propose, review, explain*, or *analyze* (as you probably guessed, these verbs are usually associated with a particular form of inquiry or genre). The statement should appear at the *end* of the draft. Group members might then focus on questions like these:

- Were you surprised by the stated purpose, or did the essay prepare you for it?

- If you were surprised, what did you think the writer was trying to do in the draft instead?

- What parts or paragraphs of the draft seemed clearly relevant to the stated purpose, and which seemed to point in another direction?

The Graphing-Reader-Interest Workshop. Knowing what commands readers' attention in a draft and what doesn't is useful, because our overall aim is to engage readers from beginning to end—not an easy task, especially in longer drafts. But if long sections of your draft drone on, then the piece isn't working well, and you need to do something about it in revision. One way to uncover what parts of your essay are interesting and what parts are less so is to ask your workshop group members to graph their response to your essay, paragraph by paragraph.

For this format, consecutively number all the paragraphs in your draft, and provide your group with a "reader-interest chart" that has paragraph numbers along the top and reader-interest numbers, from 5 (high-interest) down to 1 (low-interest), along the side. Ask your listeners to graph their reactions to your draft, paragraph by paragraph, as you read aloud. When you're finished, the graphs will provide a visual representation of how the essay worked, paragraph by paragraph, and the discussion that follows, based on these responses, will tell you what and how you need to revise.

The Sum-of-the-Parts Workshop. A well-written essay moves fluently forward because all of its parts work together. Workshops do not provide enough time to talk about each of these parts, but you can use a checklist to make sure the most important parts—including purpose, theme, structure, information, and style—are discussed. Try to cover as much territory as possible. The responses you get will necessarily have breadth but not depth and may be fairly directive, identifying specific areas of confusion as well as interpretations of your purpose and theme.

A worksheet, ideally distributed along with your draft, might include the following:

- **Purpose:** What is the writer's motive in the draft? Use one of the following verbs to describe this motive: *explore, explain, argue, analyze, review, report, propose, persuade, reflect.*
- **Theme:** What is the thesis, main point, or central issue in this draft? What question does this idea or issue raise for you?
- **Information:** Where specifically do you feel the need for more information to support the main thesis? What kind of information do you need (anecdote, story, fact, detail, background, example, interview, dialogue, opposing perspective, description, case study, etc.)?
- **Design:** What paragraphs or passages, if any, seem out of place? Do you have suggestions about where they belong instead?
- **Style:** Do any sentences or passages seem awkward or confusing to read? Use brackets to identify them in the draft.

The Thesis Workshop. An essay without an implicit theme or explicit thesis is an essay without meaning. A thesis workshop helps you make sure there is a controlling idea or question behind your draft and helps you think more deeply about what you're trying to say. Your workshop members bring a range of perspectives and experiences to a conversation about your theme that might make your theme richer and more informative.

In this format, group members need to receive the draft ahead of time and should arrive having underlined the thesis, main idea, theme, or question that seems to underlie the draft. This isn't difficult to do in essays with explicit thesis statements, such as arguments or proposals, but in personal essays and other more literary pieces, the theme may be harder to find—it might be a reflective passage, a scene, or a moment that seems central to the meaning of the essay. In their own words, readers should restate the thesis in a sentence or two at the top of the paper. Finally, readers should fastwrite for five minutes about their own thoughts and experiences with the writer's thesis or theme, continually hunting for questions that it raises for them. Keep the fastwrite focused on the thesis; if you get stuck, stop and reread it.

The workshop session that follows will be a conversation largely focused on what people thought was the point of the draft, and their own thoughts and feelings about it. Do readers agree on what the main thesis is? Is the thesis clear? How do the readers' experiences and observations relate to the writer's main point or question? And especially, what questions should the writer consider in the next draft?

You may discover that several of your group members either failed to understand what you were trying to say or raised completely new ideas—things you hadn't thought about. At its best, the thesis workshop will inspire you to think more deeply about your main idea as you consider the range of experiences and questions that other people have about it. Take lots of notes during this workshop.

The Editing Workshop. In workshopping a later version of a draft, the larger issues—having a clear purpose and appropriate information to support it—may be resolved to your satisfaction. What you may need instead is editorial advice: responses to your work at the sentence and paragraph levels. Editing workshops focus on style and clarity, even grammar and mechanics. Group members can bracket sections that exhibit problems such as:

- Awkward passages that interrupt the fluency of the writing
- Sentences or passages that they had to read a few times to understand
- Long paragraphs that might be broken down into smaller ones, or that seem to be about more than one thing
- Poorly crafted and weak first and last lines of the essay, and of paragraphs
- Abrupt transitions between paragraphs
- Inconsistent voice or tone
- Patterns of grammatical problems, including run-on sentences, unclear pronoun references, or lack of subject–verb agreement

Because style can be very personal, group members should be especially respectful of the writer's feelings in an editing workshop. Don't argue about editorial judgments; offer comments on style as suggestions and then move on (although don't hesitate to offer a differing opinion). As always, identify places in the draft where the writing is working just fine; identifying sentences, paragraphs, or passages that work well stylistically can often help the writer see how to revise the less effective parts.

Reflecting on the Workshop

Your real work as a writer follows the workshop, when you mull over the things you've heard and decide how you're going to rewrite. This process calls for a way of inquiring—reflection—that you've already practiced. As soon as possible after your workshop session, reread your notes and your readers' comments, and then go to your journal and fastwrite for five minutes, responding to the following prompts.

- What did I hear that seemed most useful? What did I hear that I'm not sure about?

- What responses to my draft do I remember most? Why do these responses stand out?

- Before the workshop, what did I think I needed to do to revise the draft? Did my peer-review experience change my mind? Did it reinforce my initial plans?

- What do I plan to do to revise this draft to make it stronger?

Appendix B
THE WRITING PORTFOLIO
Dr. Michelle Payne, Boise State University

What Is a Portfolio?

A writing portfolio, like an investment portfolio, is a collection of items that are owned or produced by a particular individual. Portfolios can provide information about that individual—an investment portfolio that consists of 75% stocks (fairly high risk) and 25% bonds (very low risk), for example, suggests that the owner is a risk-taker. A writing portfolio, in which you collect the work you have done for a writing course, also tells a story about you.

It can demonstrate how you've developed as a writer, reflect specific writing principles you've learned, or illustrate the range of genres you have worked with, for example. In additional to assembling (and perhaps revising) your work, you may be asked to reflect on what you have accomplished. In fact, the whole idea of using a portfolio to evaluate your work emphasizes the principles of inquiry and reflection at the heart of this book.

Instructors use portfolios in different ways: Some require certain essays and assignments to be included, some allow *you* to choose what to include, and others ask that you choose according to particular guidelines (for example, pieces that demonstrate your ability to conduct research, to put a lesson plan together if it's a teaching portfolio, or to revise). It's important that you understand what kind of portfolio your instructor is requiring and why.

Types of Portfolios

It's important here to distinguish between *unevaluated* and *evaluated* portfolios. An unevaluated portfolio is one in which you collect all your work for the course—including, possibly, notes, drafts, exercises, and journal entries—but your instructor does not evaluate the material. From that portfolio, you might be asked to *choose specific assignments*, and perhaps continue working on them, for your final portfolio. The work is "final" in that you have revised it, done your best to make it as effective as possible, and are ready to have it graded. Unevaluated portfolios, then, are places in which you experiment with, collect, and play around with your ideas and your writing, not worrying about evaluation as much as you would when you assemble an evaluated portfolio. All the activities in this book, for example, might be part of a writing journal or working folder that your instructor might not evaluate. Then, as you develop essays from those exercises, you might revise them into final products that your instructor can grade.

Unevaluated Portfolios

The unevaluated portfolios you are most likely to encounter in your college writing are the following:

- *A journal or working folder.* This is a portfolio in which you keep all your work for your writing course—everything that you do in and out of class, all your assignments and drafts. It's a place where you can track your progress as a writer throughout the course. Some instructors do grade working folders, based on criteria that are different from the criteria used for evaluating a portfolio of final drafts. For example, your instructor might consider whether you've completed all the assignments, taken risks in your writing, and experimented, rather than consider the quality of the writing itself.

- *A learning portfolio.* For this type of unevaluated portfolio, you collect materials from your course as well as from other places that reflect something about your learning process. Let's say your writing instructor wants you to keep a record of your learning in another course, such as sociology. You might include class notes that changed the way you understood a concept, restaurant napkins scribbled with conversations you've overheard, a paper you've been assigned to write, and some reflections on how the theories you've been learning affect how you perceive your world. You can include both print and nonprint materials, such as photos or music. Learning portfolios often allow for free choice, so you have to carefully select what you will include and why. This type of portfolio may be helpful as you apply the concepts you learn in this course—about inquiry, essay writing, and reflection—to another course.

Evaluated Portfolios

Evaluated portfolios are generally collected and evaluated either midcourse or for final grades.

- *A midterm portfolio.* As the name suggests, you assemble this portfolio at midterm. Your instructor might ask you to include particular assignments—such as your two best reading responses and a revised essay—and write a cover letter that explains, for example, what you've learned about writing that is reflected in these pieces. You might also be asked to evaluate the portfolio yourself and discuss your goals for the rest of the course. A midterm portfolio might be evaluated, but it might also be used as a practice run for the final portfolio at the end of the course.

■ ***A final portfolio—limited choice.*** Your instructor may require you to include specific assignments and essays in a portfolio that you turn in at the end of the course. Let's say your university's writing program requires all students to write a research essay and to demonstrate that they can use documentation effectively, support their claims with evidence, and do more than simply string information together. Your instructor, then, would ask you to include one or more research essays in the final portfolio to check that you have learned what is required. Or you might be required to include an example of another genre—a profile, an argument, or an ethnographic essay. And you might be asked to include a reflective essay about the pieces included. In general, a final portfolio emphasizes the final products of the course, the revised and polished work that shows what you've learned over the entire term.

■ ***A final portfolio—open choice.*** Your instructor may ask you to choose what you consider your best writing for the course, rather than require particular essays. He or she may require a certain number of pages, or a certain number of assignments, or she may leave the length and number of assignments open. If you feel your research essay is better than your ethnographic essay, then you might revise the research essay for the final portfolio and not work any further on your ethnographic essay. Or you might include your personal essay, an argument, and your response to particular writing exercises. You would select these pieces because you believe they are your best work—but be sure you can talk specifically about *why* they are the best and *what* they show your instructor about what you've learned. For instance, do you want to show your growth, your success in using writing as inquiry, or what you've learned about crafting paragraphs?

Why Require a Portfolio?

If you are asked to keep an unevaluated portfolio, your instructor probably wants you to focus on your learning process at least as much as you focus on your final product. We rarely take the time to reflect on how we learn, but doing so can help us learn better in other courses. Are you a visual learner? Do you learn best when you have a relationship with your teacher or when the teacher is more removed? If you learn more outside the classroom—at work, for example—why? Learning portfolios, writing journals, and working folders allow you to develop even better learning strategies and understand why you might struggle with certain learning situations. Collecting your work allows you to pause periodically and reflect on which writing strategies seem to sabotage your efforts, which seem to work well, how you might work through writer's block, or what principles about writing you've been learning. Many of the exercises in this book prompt you to reflect on your writing process, your reading strategies, and your learning and thinking, so if you've been doing them, you have already seen the benefits of reflecting on your process.

In unevaluated portfolios, the *process* of whatever you're doing is being emphasized and valued. You don't have to worry about writing beautifully styled sentences the first time around or having a complicated reading all figured out the first time through. An unevaluated portfolio allows for—in fact, encourages—the messiness of writing and thinking instead of focusing only on polished work. These portfolios emphasize risk, experimentation, and reflection on the process of writing and learning—exactly as this book (and no doubt the course you are taking) does.

Evaluated portfolios are important for similar reasons: To get your drafts ready to be evaluated, you will experiment, rewrite, and critique them. Most of the term, you will be making entries in your writing journal, exploring ideas, commenting on peers' drafts in workshops, and revising your own drafts, all in an effort to learn more about writing and make your essays more effective. Portfolios allow you to do all that over a long period and in a relatively "evaluation-free" zone. You are graded on your final product at the end—not in the middle—of the process.

If you've completed the reflection exercises in this book, then you have been thinking about your own learning throughout the term. You will be more conscious of the writing and reading strategies that work best for you, and so will be better prepared to write the reflective essay that your instructor may require in the portfolio.

Of course, the final product is what is evaluated in a final portfolio—and what often comprises a major part of your final grade. So while this kind of portfolio reinforces the processes of inquiry and reflection, it also emphasizes the way a writer crafts a sentence, organizes an essay, and explores an idea. Why do instructors require portfolios? Because a portfolio allows an instructor to evaluate *both* the process of writing *and* the quality of the final product.

Organizing Portfolios

A writing portfolio emphasizes the *process* of writing and learning as much as the final product, so the way you organize its contents should demonstrate that process. Whether or not your instructor assigns a journal or working folder, it's a good idea to keep one, either on computer or in a notebook. You can organize your writing journal or working folder in a number of ways. Here are some options.

1. *By chronological order.* Keep everything that you do in the course in the order you complete it.
2. *By assignment.* Include all the writing you've done (fastwriting, drafts, exercises), peer and teacher responses, notes, research materials, and so on for each course assignment. Your portfolio might include sections on personal writing, argument, analytical writing, and so on.
3. *By subjects or themes.* Have you written several pieces about the same topic during the course? You might find that you have written both a profile and a research essay touching on racism, for example, or several pieces about a trip to Italy you took before your freshman year of college. With this

approach, you have a better sense of how you've explored a topic using different genres, and can compare what you've learned about the subject as well as about the different forms.

4. *By stage of process.* Categorize your writing based on where it falls in the writing process. Group together all your fastwriting and journal writing, then your drafts, and end with your final, revised pieces.

You can also create your own categories to organize your class work. However you choose to organize your writing, be sure to *keep everything* you write for the course; don't throw anything away. If you are using a computer, save all of your writing files, and keep a separate backup copy.

If your instructor asks you to include a reflective letter or essay as a preface to your portfolio, you may want to create a separate section in your journal or folder for all the reflective writing you've done in the class. Keeping your reflective writing in one place will make it easier to compose your reflective letter or essay.

Writing a Reflective Letter or Essay

You may be asked to preface your final portfolio with a letter or essay that introduces the pieces you've included and reflects on what you've learned about writing, reading, and inquiry. For some instructors, this letter or essay is crucial to evaluating the whole portfolio because it gives coherence and purpose to the material and articulates what you've learned. As always, clarify with your instructor what is expected in the reflective letter or essay and how it will be weighed in the portfolio grade. Different instructors may require different things: a five- to seven-page essay or letter that begins the portfolio, a prefatory letter for *each piece* included in the portfolio, a reflection on the writing process for each essay, a narrative of how your thinking changed about each subject you wrote about. Regardless of the assignment, you'll want to spend some time going through your writing journal or folder and reflecting on what you notice. Here are some questions that might help:

- *Patterns.* As you flip through the pages of your writing journal or folder, what patterns do you notice? What seems to happen frequently or stand out? For example, you might notice that you always began your essays the same way, or you ended up writing about the same subject the whole semester without realizing it, or you got better at organizing your essays and using significant details.

- *Reflective writing.* As you look only at the reflective writing you've done throughout the course (and the reflective exercises in this book), what do you notice? What five things have you learned about writing, reading, and inquiry based on that reflective writing?

- *Change over time.* How did you describe your writing process (and/or reading process) at the beginning of the course? How would you describe it now? If it has changed, why and how?

- *Writing principles.* What are the five to seven most important things you have learned about writing, reading, and inquiry in this course? What strategies for writing and reading have you learned that you will take with you into other writing situations?

- *Revision.* For each of the essays included in your portfolio, what would you do differently if you had more time?

- *Writing processes.* Can you describe the writing and thinking processes that led to the final product for each piece included in your portfolio? What were the most important changes you made? Why did you make them?

- *Most and least effective writing.* Which essay in the portfolio is your strongest? Your weakest? Why?

- *Effect of peer response.* How have your peers and other readers of your work affected the revisions you've made?

- *Showing what you've learned.* What does your portfolio demonstrate about you as a writer, a student, a reader, a researcher? How? Be as specific as possible.

- *What's missing.* What is *not* reflected in your portfolio that you believe is important for your instructor to know?

- *Expectations.* How does your portfolio meet the expectations for effective writing defined in your class?

- *Applying the textbook.* How have you applied the principles about each essay form that are outlined in this textbook?

- *Personal challenge.* In what ways did you challenge yourself in this course?

Your instructor might ask you to address only three or four of these questions in the letter or essay itself, but it's a good idea to do some fastwriting on all of them. Doing so will help your essay or letter be more specific, thoughtful, and persuasive.

As with any essay, you'll want to take this one through several revisions and get feedback from readers before you include it in the portfolio. Your instructor might even ask you to workshop a draft of this essay with your group. If you've done some fastwriting on the preceding questions, you are in good shape to compose a first draft of your reflective letter or essay. Keep in mind who your audience is—your teacher, teachers unknown to you, and/or your peers—and address what that audience expects. Be as specific as possible, citing examples from your work and drawing on the terms and principles you've discussed in class and read about in this book.

If you've been doing reflective writing all term, you will have plenty of material to draw from to make your reflective essay or letter concrete, substantive, and as honest as it can be (given the circumstances). You'll probably surprise yourself with all that you've learned.

CHECKLIST FOR REFLECTIVE ESSAYS/LETTERS

- Be specific. Beware of using overly general and vague comments. Include details and examples.
- Write what you believe is true, not what you think the instructor wants to read.
- Avoid criticism of the course or the instructor. Save this for the course and professor evaluations most students are asked for at the end of each course.
- Take the assignment seriously. Avoid comments that sound flip or thoughtless.

Final Preparations

Before you turn your portfolio in, take time to proofread it carefully. You may even want to ask a classmate or friend to look it over as well. Check again to be sure you've included everything that is required, assembled the content appropriately, and formatted it as requested. Because this is work that you are proud of, the way you present it should reflect that pride, which means it should meet high standards for presentation and quality.

Appendix C
THE ANNOTATED BIBLIOGRAPHY

Dr. Michelle Payne, Boise State University

What Is an Annotated Bibliography?

An annotated bibliography, unlike a Works Cited or References page, includes descriptions and comments about each of your sources. It is a list in which each citation is followed by a short descriptive and sometimes evaluative paragraph or annotation. Many scholars use published annotated bibliographies during their research to help them narrow down the material that seems most relevant to their work, but you might be asked to write one as part of a larger project for a class, sometimes in preparation for a literature review or a research proposal. Annotated bibliographies, then, can serve many different purposes, so if you are assigned one, be sure you understand your role as a researcher and writer.

This appendix examines four types of annotated bibliographies: those that indicate content and coverage; those that describe thesis and argument; those that offer evaluations; and those that combine these three functions.[1] When you are assigned to write an annotated bibliography, you'll need to decide which of these forms is the most appropriate—but you may also consider using any one of them to aid your own research process.

Indicative Bibliography. Are you being asked *to indicate* what the source contains or simply to identify the topic of the source, but *not to evaluate or discuss the argument and evidence?* If so, explain what the source is about (e.g., "This article explores gender in Shakespeare's tragedies"). List the main ideas it discusses—this list may include chapter titles, names of authors included in an anthology, or the main ideas covered in the subsections if it's an article (e.g., "Topics covered include male homosocial desire, women as witches, and conceptions of romantic love"). Usually, in a descriptive annotation, you don't evaluate the source's argument or relevance, nor do you describe its overall thesis.

Informative Bibliography. Are you being asked *to summarize the argument* for each source? If so, briefly state each work's thesis, the primary assertions and

---

[1]The four forms discussed are found on the Writing Center website for the University of Wisconsin–Madison (http://www.wisc.edu/writing/Handbook/AnnBib_content.html).

WHY WRITE AN ANNOTATED BIBLIOGRAPHY?

■ To help you compile a list of sources that you can sort through later.
■ To help you decide if you want to return to a source later in your process.
■ To help you develop your own thesis.
■ To help you create a literature review.

evidence that support the main argument, and any conclusions the author makes. You are not evaluating the effectiveness of the argument, nor are you delineating the content of the source (as you would in an indicative form); instead, you are informing your audience about the work's arguments and conclusions.

Evaluative Bibliography. Are you being asked *to evaluate the sources* you find? If so, your annotations will include a brief summary of the arguments and conclusions and then critically evaluate them: How useful is the source to your particular project? What are the limitations of the study or argument? What are its strengths? How reliable are its conclusions? How effective are its research methods? The criteria you use for evaluating each source depend on the purpose of the bibliography— whether you are compiling it to help focus your research project and sort out the most important articles or writing it to help others decide what is most relevant in the subject area. Be sure you understand the evaluation criteria.

Combination of Types. Are you being asked *to be both informative and evaluative*? Many annotated bibliographies have multiple purposes, so you will be combining the preceding forms. Because most annotations can be up to 150 words, you need to devote only a sentence or two to each purpose—in other words, a few lines to summarize and describe, a few to evaluate and comment. However, you may be told exactly what to include in the annotations and how many words or sentences to use. Your instructor might, for example, ask that you write one sentence summarizing each work's argument and then another sentence describing how the work relates to your own developing thesis.

Writing an Annotated Bibliography

Choose a Subject. Before you can begin writing an annotated bibliography, you must choose a subject on which to focus. From there, you will move to gathering materials, applying reading strategies, and finally, writing the annotated bibliography.

Gather Materials. See Chapter 11, "Research Techniques," to help you find material relevant to your subject. Are you supposed to find a wide range of materials, such as reviews, scholarly articles, and books? Are you to focus only on materials from the last five years? What are the parameters of your research? Be sure to clarify these issues with your instructor.

Because annotations are so brief, it's tempting to think that they are easy to write. But as in any writing project, you need to have a lot of material to draw from—in this case, substantive notes and reflective writing about each work. It is better to work from abundance than from scarcity—remember, you need material to work with if you are going to identify what's worth keeping and what should be dropped.

Read Strategically. You'll use the critical reading strategies you've learned as you read the sources you've decided to include in your bibliography. If the materials you've gathered will become part of a research essay, then you will be taking notes and writing about them, as discussed in Chapter 11. But to create your annotated bibliography, you'll have an additional purpose for reading your sources. If you simply need to describe the content of the sources (indicative form), you will do little critical evaluation; instead, you'll focus on explanation. Once you determine the focus for your annotations, use the following questions (which apply primarily to evaluative forms of annotation, but also can help with informative and indicative forms) to guide your reading.

- Who is the intended audience for this article, review, or book?
- What central research question or claim does the material address? Write it out in one or two sentences.
- What kind of evidence is used to support the conclusions, argument, and thesis? How valid is the evidence, given what the intended audience values? For example, literary examples wouldn't be taken seriously as evidence in a biology paper, nor would anecdotal evidence about an experiment.
- How effectively has the author addressed the central question or claim?
- What are the main ideas or topics covered? Sketch them out in a brief outline.
- How credible is this author(s)? Have you seen her name appear in other works on this subject? Is she publishing in her area of expertise?
- Is the material current? Does it need to be? Is this a revised edition? (Note the dates on the copyright page of a book.)
- Are the ideas in this source similar enough to those in other sources to suggest that this author is working with accepted knowledge? If not, do you find the ideas valid, significant, or well researched? Does the source build on the ideas of others, critique them, and add new knowledge?
- How effectively is the source written?
- Can you find reviews of the material or commentaries from other scholars in the area? How was the work received? What (if any) controversy has it generated? What praise has it drawn?

Length. Depending on the requirements for and purposes of the annotations, each entry could be one paragraph or only a few sentences long, so choose your words carefully and use specific details judiciously. Clarify with your instructor the kind of writing style he expects; that is, does he want brief phrases, almost like a bulleted list of main points, or full sentences and paragraphs?

Content. Begin with the proper citation form for the source, following the guidelines for the specific documentation style your instructor requires (APA or MLA). Organize this list alphabetically. After each source, compose a paragraph or two that addresses your purpose for the bibliography. That purpose, again, will depend on the requirements your instructor has given you. If you are describing the content of the source, for example, begin with an overview of the work and its thesis; then select the specific points you want to highlight about it (such as chapter titles, subjects covered, authors included). If you are explaining the main argument of the work, begin with the central thesis and then include the main claims, evidence, research methods, and conclusions. Finally, if you are evaluating the source, add comments that summarize your critique.

Sample Student Annotated Bibliography

In the example that follows, Lauren Tussing wanted to apply what she's learned about feminist theory to the film *Lost in Translation,* and her annotated bibliography helped her focus her research question and decide which of the sources would be most useful in composing her essay. Notice that she has written an annotated bibliography that combines the informative and evaluative forms—she primarily summarizes the main argument of each source and then discusses its relevance to her research project.

Lauren Tussing

Instructor Michelle Payne

Engl 497

18 April 2004

Annotated Bibliography

Doane, Mary Ann. "Film and the Masquerade: Theorising the Female Spectator."

    Feminism and Film. Ed. E. Ann Kaplan. Oxford: Oxford UP, 2000. 418–36. Print.

    This is an article in a collection of articles on feminist film theory. In the essay, Doane works to create a theory for the female spectator, moving away from prior focus on the male spectator. Doane does, however, reintroduce the idea of Laura Mulvey's binary opposition of passive/female and active/male that she introduced in her essay "Visual Pleasure and Narrative Cinema." Doane applies the notion of distance to Mulvey's binary opposition.

    This essay, written for an academic audience, is esoteric and sometimes difficult to understand, but it might be helpful for my paper if I decide to talk about the female spectator. Despite my difficulty with this essay, Doane did give me some ideas about how to think about *Lost in Translation,* the film that I discuss in my essay. A woman directs this film, so I wonder how her direction affects the gaze. Is there a uniquely female gaze for this film? Or does the film conform to the male gaze? How might viewers, both male and female, gaze upon this film?

Gaines, Jane. "White Privilege and Looking Relations: Race and Gender." *Feminism*

    and Film. Ed. E. Ann Kaplan. Oxford: Oxford UP, 2000. 336–55. Print.

    This essay, also included in the same collection as the above essay, argues that psychoanalysis isn't a good way to critique films, particularly because it overlooks racial and sexuality issues. Even when theorists use psychoanalysis to describe black family interaction, they impose "an erroneous universalisation and inadvertently reaffirm white middle-class norms" (337). When feminist theory uses gender first and foremost in discussing oppressions, it "helps to reinforce white middle-class values" (337). Also, Gaines argues, because feminist theory universalizes white middle-class values, it ideologically hides other forms of oppression from women.

This essay has given me new ideas about how to read *Lost in Translation*. Although I wasn't initially going to talk about issues of race, I might want to. Race actually plays a big role in the movie because it is about white people in an Asian country. Also, I think this essay is helpful in its critique of psychoanalysis. In my research of feminist film theory, I have found that you can't escape psychoanalysis. I don't particularly like psychoanalysis, but I realize that it is an important theory to understand. It is at the basis of many articles on feminist film theory. However, I don't think I will be discussing psychoanalysis in my essay.

Jayamanne, Laleen, ed. *Kiss Me Deadly: Feminism and Cinema for the Moment*. Sydney: Power Institute of Fine Arts, 1995. Print.

This is a collection of articles about feminism and film. The articles in this book focus mostly on directors, such as Kathryn Bigelow, Rainer Werner Fassbinder, Alexander Kluge, and Nicolas Roeg. Before looking at this book, I had never heard of any of these directors. I didn't find this book particularly helpful, especially because, as Jayamanne notes in the introduction, some of the directors and films discussed are "foreign to the semi-official canons of feminist film theory" (14).

Johnston, Claire. "Dorothy Arzner: Critical Strategies." *Feminism and Film*. Ed. E. Ann Kaplan. Oxford: Oxford UP, 2000. 139–50. Print.

In this essay, Johnston discusses Dorothy Arzner, a director from the 1920s to the 1940s who was nearly the only woman during her time to create a lucid bulk of work in Hollywood. Because not many studies have been written about Arzner—especially in male-dominated film studies—Johnston's purpose is to explore various approaches to Arzner's work and to discuss how her films are important for contemporary feminists.

This essay also gave me a new idea about how to look at the film I will be discussing in my paper. I'd like to discuss the director of *Lost in Translation*. Are her films, particularly *Lost in Translation*, important for contemporary feminists?

Kaplan, E. Ann, ed. *Women in Film Noir*. London: British Film Institute, 1978. Print.

This book is a collection of articles about film noir. Because the book is aimed at scholars who are educated in feminist film theory, it does not actually give a definition of film noir, and I didn't know what film noir was, so I looked it up in the *Oxford English Dictionary*. According to the *Oxford English Dictionary*, film noir is "a cinematographic film of a gloomy or fatalistic character." I don't think the film I will be discussing falls into this category, so I don't think I will be using this source for my essay.

Kuhn, Annette. *Women's Pictures: Feminism and Cinema*. London: Verso, 1994. Print.

In this book, Kuhn argues that "feminism and film, taken together, could provide the basis for new forms of expression, providing the opportunity for a truly feminist alternative cinema in terms of film language, of reading that language and of representing the world." The book provides a systematic view of film. First, Kuhn discusses the dominant cinema. Then, she explores "rereading dominant cinema" from a feminist stance. Finally, she discusses "replacing dominant cinema" with feminist film.

I think this book will be helpful when I attempt to understand where *Lost in Translation* fits into film culture. Is the film part of dominant cinema? How can it be read from a feminist viewpoint? How is it a feminist film? How isn't it a feminist film?

Handbook

1. Sentence Boundaries (578):
 1A Fragments, (578)
 1B Comma Splices, (582)
 1C Fused Sentences, (585)

2. Sentence Inconsistencies, (586):
 2A Parallelism, (587)
 2B Coordination and Subordination, (588)
 2C Mixed Sentences, (589)
 2D Shifts, (590)

3. Problems with Modification, (591):
 3A Dangling and Misplaced Modifiers, (592)
 3B Restrictive and Nonrestrictive Modifiers, (593)
 3C Adjectives and Adverbs, (594)

4. Verbs, (595):
 4A Tense, (596)
 4B Voice, (597)
 4C Mood, (598)
 4D Subject–Verb Agreement, (599)

5. Pronouns, (601):
 5A Pronoun Case, (601)
 5B Pronoun Reference, (603)
 5C Pronoun Agreement, (604)
 5D Relative Pronouns, (605)

6. Style, (606):
 6A Conciseness, (606)
 6B Appropriate Language, (608)

7. Punctuation, (610):
 7A End Punctuation, (611)
 7B Semicolon, (612)
 7C Comma, (612)

7D Colon, (*616*)

7E Dash, (*616*)

7F Quotation Marks, (*617*)

7G Other Marks, (*617*)

8. Mechanics and Spelling, (*619*):

8A Capitalization, (*619*)

8B Abbreviation, (*620*)

8C Apostrophe, (*621*)

8D Hyphens, (*622*)

8E Italics (Underlining), (*623*)

8F Numbers, (*624*)

8G Spelling, (*625*)

9. Review of Basic Grammar, (*628*):

9A Parts of Speech, (*628*)

9B Subjects and Predicates, (*639*)

9C Objects and Complements, (*640*)

9D Phrases, (*641*)

9E Clauses, (*643*)

9F Basic Sentence Patterns, (*644*)

9G Types of Sentences, (*645*)

10. Tips for ESL Writers, (*646*):

10A Articles, (*646*)

10B Verbs, (*647*)

10C Adjectives and Adverbs, (*651*)

10D Prepositions, (*653*)

10E Participles, (*653*)

1 Sentence Boundaries

Learning Objectives

H1.A   Recognize and correct sentence fragments.

H1.B   Recognize and correct comma splices.

H1.C   Recognize and correct fused sentences.

Sentence boundaries are marked by end punctuation (see 7A End Punctuation): periods, question marks, or occasionally exclamation points. Because they mark the ends of sentences, each mark of end punctuation must be preceded by at least one independent clause (a complete statement containing a subject and a verb). Using inappropriate punctuation—a period where a comma should go, or a comma where a period should go—creates errors in sentence boundaries and confuses your readers.

1A Fragments

H1.A

Recognize and correct sentence fragments.

Sentence fragments result from treating a partial sentence—a phrase or a clause— as if it were a whole sentence. The fragment may be a *subordinate clause*, a *phrase*, or a *combination of subordinate elements*. A fragment lacks a subject or a verb, or has a subject and a verb but begins with a subordinating word. **Only an independent clause can make an independent statement.**

Subordinate Clause Fragment

Recognition. A subordinate clause has a subject and a verb but cannot make an independent statement because of the connector, which implies it is only part of a sentence. Here are two lists of the most common subordinating connectors.

Subordinating conjunctions, arranged by function

Time	Place
after	where
before	wherever
once	
since	Cause
until	as
when	because
whenever	since
while	

Contrast	Condition
although	even if
even though	if
though	
while	Result
	in order that
Alternative	so
than	so that
whether	that

Relative pronouns	
who (whom, whose)	whoever (whomever, whosever)
which	whichever
that	
what	whatever
where	wherever
when	whenever
why	
unless	
whereas	

Any clause beginning with one of these words is *subordinate* and should not be written as a sentence. Here are examples of clause fragments (italicized):

The Vikings revolutionized shipbuilding with the keel. *Which allowed their ships to go faster and farther without stopping for supplies.*

Norway's Lapps are believed to be a nomadic people of Asian heritage. *Who follow reindeer herds through Norway's cold, rugged land.*

Because the northern part of Norway is so far north. It has long periods during the summer when the sun shines 24 hours a day.

Correction. There are mainly two ways of correcting clause fragments: (1) attaching them to the preceding or following sentence and (2) removing or changing the subordinating connector. These sentences illustrate both types of correction:

The Vikings revolutionized shipbuilding with the keel. *This innovation* allowed their ships to go faster and farther without stopping for supplies. The subordinating word of the fragment is changed.

Norway's Lapps are believed to be of Asian heritage—nomadic people who follow reindeer herds through Norway's cold, rugged land. The fragment is connected to the preceding sentence with a dash.

Because the northern part of Norway is so far north, it has long periods during the summer when the sun shines 24 hours a day. The fragment is connected to the following sentence with a comma.

Phrase Fragment

Phrase fragments lack a subject, a verb, or both. The most common phrases written as fragments are *verbal phrases* and *prepositional phrases*.

Recognition. A *verbal phrase* is a word group made up of a verb form and related modifiers and other words. As opposed to *verb phrases*, which are made up of verb parts (such as *has been gone*), a verbal phrase is constituted with a *verbal*, a word formed from a verb but not functioning as a verb. *Going*, for example, is a verbal, as is *gone*. You probably wouldn't write, "Charles going to St. Louis" or "Charles gone to St. Louis." Instead, you would add helping verbs: "Charles *is going* to St. Louis" and "Charles *has gone* to St. Louis."

There are three kinds of verbals: gerunds, participles, and infinitives. Gerunds end in *-ing*; participles end in either *-ing* (present) or *-ed* (regular past); infinitives have no ending but are usually introduced by *to*. Here are a few examples of how verbals are formed from verbs:

Verb	Present participle and gerund	Past participle	Infinitive
snap	snapping	snapped	to snap
look	looking	looked	to look
want	wanting	wanted	to want
go	going	gone	to go
has	having	had	to have

Verbals function primarily as adjectives and nouns, most often in verbal phrases.

In the following examples, the italicized verbal phrases are fragments because they are written as sentences:

Eero Saarinen designed the 630-foot Gateway Arch for the St. Louis riverfront. *Imagining a giant stainless steel arch.* Participial phrase modifying Eero Saarinen.

Critics said that cranes could not reach high enough. *To lift the steel sections into place.* Infinitive phrase modifying high.

Under Saarinen's plan, a derrick would creep up the side of each leg of the arch. *Lifting each plate into position.* Participial phrase modifying derrick.

Saarinen knew that precision was of utmost importance. *In building the arch.* Gerund phrase as object of preposition In.

Correction. Verbal phrase fragments can be corrected in one of two ways: (1) by connecting them to a related sentence or (2) by expanding them to a sentence. Both ways are illustrated next.

Eero Saarinen designed the 630-foot Gateway Arch for the St. Louis riverfront. *He imagined a giant stainless steel arch.* The verbal fragment is expanded to a sentence.

Critics said that cranes could not reach high enough *to lift the steel sections into place.* The verbal fragment is connected to a related sentence.

Under Saarinen's plan, a derrick would creep up the side of each leg of the arch, *lifting each plate into position.* The verbal fragment is connected to a related sentence.

1. Separate the independent clauses using a comma and a *coordinating conjunction*. The list of coordinating conjunctions is short:

and	or	for	yet
but	nor	so	

   To correct a comma splice, begin the second independent clause with one of these conjunctions, preceded by a comma. For example:

   > The economy of Algeria is in trouble, *and* many citizens blame the government.

2. Separate the independent clauses using a semicolon (with or without a transitional adverb). Semicolons are often interchangeable with periods and therefore can be used to separate independent clauses. For example:

   > The economy of Algeria is in trouble; many citizens blame the government.

   > The death of any soldier is tragic; *however*, death by friendly fire is particularly disturbing.

In the second example, *however* is a transitional adverb. Unlike coordinating conjunctions, *transitional adverbs* are not conjunctions and so do not join sentence elements. They do, however, connect ideas by showing how they relate to one another. Like conjunctions, they can show addition, contrast, result, and other relationships. Here are some of the common transitional adverbs, arranged by function:

Addition	Examples
in addition	for example
also	for instance
moreover	in fact
next	specifically
then	
finally	

Comparison	Contrast
likewise	however
similarly	nevertheless
in comparison	on the contrary
	on the other hand
	otherwise

Result	Time
therefore	
consequently	meanwhile
then	subsequently
as a result	finally
	then

A semicolon should always precede the transitional adverb that begins the second independent clause. A comma usually follows the transitional adverb, although in some instances, the comma is omitted:

> Air bags deflate within one second after inflation; *therefore*, they do not interfere with control of the car.

Some comma splices result when writers use transitional adverbs as if they were coordinating conjunctions. If you have trouble distinguishing transitional adverbs from coordinating conjunctions, remember that none of the coordinating conjunctions is longer than three letters, and all of the transitional adverbs are four letters or longer. Also, keep in mind that transitional adverbs are movable within the sentence, while coordinating conjunctions are not; for instance, the preceding example could be rewritten as:

> Air bags deflate within one second after inflation; they do not *therefore* interfere with control of the car.

3. Make one of the independent clauses subordinate to the other by inserting a subordinating conjunction. When one of the clauses explains or elaborates on the other, use an appropriate subordinating conjunction to make the relationship between the two clauses more explicit (see 1A Fragments for a list of subordinating conjunctions). Consider the following comma splice and its revision:

> Henry forgot to fill in his time card on Friday, he is going to have a hard time getting paid for the overtime he put in last week.

> *Because* Henry forgot to fill in his time card on Friday, he is going to have a hard time getting paid for the overtime he put in last week.

4. Rewrite one of the independent clauses as a modifying phrase. A *modifying phrase* serves as an adjective or adverb within a sentence. By rewriting one of the independent clauses as a phrase, you can eliminate unneeded words. For example, consider the following comma splice and its revision:

> The celebrity couple smiled for the cameras, they were glowing of wealth and fame.

> The celebrity couple smiled for the cameras, glowing of wealth and fame. Here, *glowing of wealth and fame* acts as an adjective modifying the noun *couple*.

5. Punctuate each independent clause as a separate sentence. No law of grammar, punctuation, or style says you must present the two independent clauses together within one sentence, so you won't be cheating if you write them as two separate sentences. The example from before is perfectly acceptable written as follows:

> The economy of Algeria is in trouble. Many citizens blame the government.

It may be to your advantage to divide long and/or complex independent clauses into separate sentences; doing so may help convey your meaning to readers more clearly.

1C Fused Sentences

Fused sentences, sometimes called *run-on sentences*, are similar to comma splices. However, instead of a comma between the two independent clauses, there is no punctuation—the two independent clauses simply run together. For example:

H1.C
Recognize and correct fused sentences.

> The United States has 281 lawyers per 100,000 people Japan has only 11 attorneys per 100,000.

> The World Cup is the most popular sporting event in the world you would never know it based on the indifferent response of the average American.

Recognition. Unlike the comma splice, there is no punctuation in the fused sentence to indicate the end of the first independent clause and the beginning of the second. As a result, it can be more challenging to identify independent clauses within fused sentences, particularly if the sentence also contains modifying phrases or dependent clauses set off by commas. The best way to identify them is to read from the beginning of the sentence (reading aloud may help) until you have found the end of the first independent clause. Consider the following example:

> Even though I was still sick with the flu, I attended the awards banquet as my family watched, the coach presented me with the trophy for most valuable player.

This fused sentence contains two subordinate clauses (*Even though I was still sick with the flu* and *as my family watched*), each one attached to one of the two independent clauses (*I attended the awards banquet* and *the coach presented me with the trophy*).

Correction. Revise fused sentences using any one of the same five strategies employed for correcting comma splices (see 1B Comma Splices for more information on each strategy).

1. Separate the independent clauses using a comma and a coordinating conjunction. For example:

   > The United States has 281 lawyers per 100,000 people, *but* Japan has only 11 attorneys per 100,000.

2. Separate the independent clauses using a semicolon (with or without a transitional adverb). For example:

   > The United States has 281 lawyers per 100,000 people; Japan has only 11 attorneys per 100,000.

   > The World Cup is the most popular sporting event in the world; *however*, you would never know it based on the indifferent response of the average American.

3. Make one of the independent clauses subordinate to the other by inserting a subordinating conjunction. The newly formed dependent clause should explain the remaining independent clause. For example, consider the following fused sentence and its revision:

> I run a marathon my feet get sore.
>
> *Whenever* I run a marathon, my feet get sore.

4. Rewrite one of the independent clauses as a modifying phrase. Remember, modifying phrases act as adjectives or adverbs. Consider the following fused sentence and its revision:

> Last night the tomcats fought outside my window they were crying and hissing for what seemed like hours.
>
> Last night the tomcats fought outside my window, crying and hissing for what seemed like hours. Here, *crying and hissing* acts as an adjective modifying the noun *tomcats*.

5. Punctuate each independent clause as a separate sentence. As with comma splices, you can write the independent clauses (and their related phrases and dependent clauses) as separate sentences. Indeed, this is often the easiest way to handle fused sentences. For example:

> I attended the awards banquet even though I was still sick with the flu. As my family watched, the coach presented me with the trophy for most valuable player. Here, the subordinate clause attached to the first independent clause *even though I was still sick with the flu* was also moved to the back of the first sentence for the sake of greater readability.

2 Sentence Inconsistencies

Learning Objectives

H2.A   Recognize and correct faulty parallelism.

H2.B   Use coordination and subordination effectively.

H2.C   Revise mixed sentences to make sentences consistent.

H2.D   Recognize and revise unintended shifts in sentence elements.

Sentences pose difficulties for readers when the grammar is confused or inconsistent. Such problems happen when writers pay attention to what they are saying and not to how they are saying it. Such attention is a natural condition of writing, and careful revision usually takes care of any problems.

2A Parallelism

Parallelism results when two or more grammatically equivalent sentence elements are joined. The sentence elements can be nouns, verbs, phrases, or clauses. (See 2B Coordination and Subordination.) Here is a sentence with parallel elements:

> In a country where college education becomes increasingly everybody's chance, where executives and refrigerator salesmen and farmers play golf together, where a college professor may drive a cab in the summertime to keep his family alive, it becomes harder and harder to guess a person's education, income, and social status by the way he talks. —Paul Roberts

Here is the same sentence with the parallel elements arranged to be more visually accessible:

> In a country
> > {where college education becomes increasingly everybody's chance,
> >
> > {where {executives
> >
> > > and {refrigerator salesmen
> > >
> > > and {farmers play golf together,
> >
> > {where a college professor may drive a cab in the summertime to keep
> >
> > > his family alive,
> >
> > it becomes {harder
> >
> > > and {harder to guess a person's {education
> > >
> > > > > > {income,
> > > >
> > > > and {social status
> >
> > by the way he talks.

This sentence has parallel clauses (each beginning with *where*), parallel subjects (*executives, refrigerator salesmen*, and *farmers*), parallel adverbs (*harder* and *harder*), and parallel direct objects (*education, income*, and *social status*). As this sentence illustrates, the principle of parallelism does not require that elements be alike in every way. Some of these nouns have modifiers, for example, and the clauses have different structural patterns.

Parallelism becomes a problem when dissimilar elements are joined in pairs, in series, in comparisons using *than* or *as*, or in comparisons linked by correlative conjunctions. Consider the following examples of faulty parallelism:

> She did not like rude customers or taking orders from her boss. The two elements in the pair are not parallel.

> We were having a hard time deciding what to do in the afternoon: go snorkeling, go fishing, or swim out to the sand bar. The last of the three elements in the series is not parallel.

> Michael decided to complete his degree next semester rather than studying abroad for another year. The two elements compared using *than* are not parallel.

My sister not only lost the race but also her leg got hurt. The two elements compared by the correlative conjunction *not only...but also* are not parallel. Other correlative conjunctions include *both...and, either...or, neither...nor, whether...or*, and *just as...so*.

Faulty parallelism can be corrected in various ways:

She did not like *dealing with* rude customers or taking orders from her boss. Words were added to the first element to make it parallel to the second.

We were having a hard time deciding what to do in the afternoon: go snorkeling, go fishing, or *go swimming*. The last element was rewritten to make it parallel with the others in the series.

Michael decided to complete his degree next semester rather than *to study* abroad for another year. The verb form of the second element is changed from a participle to an infinitive to make it parallel with the verb form in the first element.

My sister not only lost the race but also *hurt her leg*. The second element was rewritten to make it parallel with the first element.

Revision of faulty parallelism is usually fairly easy to achieve. What is difficult is recognizing it, and unfortunately there are no tricks to easy recognition. Even experienced writers find that in their own writing, they need to make an editing trip through their drafts looking just at their parallel structures. The absence of faulty parallels is a sign of careful writing.

2B Coordination and Subordination

H2.B

Use coordination and subordination effectively.

Most sentence relationships embody either coordination or subordination. That is, sentence elements are either grammatically equal to other elements (coordination) or grammatically dependent on other parts (subordination). For example, two independent clauses in a sentence are coordinate; but in a sentence containing an independent clause and a dependent clause, the dependent clause is subordinate (indeed, dependent clauses are also called subordinate clauses).

Coordination

When two or more equivalent sentence elements appear in one sentence, they are coordinate. These elements can be words, phrases, or clauses. Only parallel elements can be coordinated: verbs linked with verbs, nouns with nouns, phrases with phrases, and clauses with clauses. (See 2A Parallelism.) For example:

Broccoli and *related vegetables* contain beta-carotene, a substance that may reduce the risk of heart attack. Two nouns are joined by a coordinating conjunction.

We *ran, swam*, and *cycled* every day while we were at the fitness camp. Three parallel verbs are joined in a series with commas and a coordinating conjunction.

American medical devices are equally remarkable, *giving life to those with terminally diseased organs, giving mobility to those crippled with arthritic joints and deadened nerves*, and even, miraculously, *restoring the sense of hearing to those deprived of it. —Atlantic.* The participial (verbal) phrases are joined by commas and a final coordinating conjunction. Also, embedded in the second participial phrase, two coordinate noun phrases are joined by a coordinating conjunction: *arthritic joints and deadened nerves.*

The term "Big Bang" is common usage now with scientists, but it originated as a sarcastic rejection of the theory. Two independent clauses are joined by a comma and a coordinating conjunction.

Subordination

Subordination is an essential aspect of sentence relations. If all sentence elements were grammatically equivalent, the sameness would be tedious. Subordinate elements show where the emphasis lies in sentences and modify elements with independent clauses. A subordinate element—be it a phrase or a clause—is dependent for its meaning on the element it modifies. At the same time, it often provides a fuller meaning than could be achieved exclusively through the use of independent elements.

For example:

For walking and jogging, the calorie expenditure is greater for people of greater body weight. The subordinate element is a prepositional phrase, modifying *is greater.*

Increasing both speed and effort in aerobic activities, the exerciser burns more calories. The subordinate element is a verbal phrase, modifying *exerciser.*

Because sedentary people are more likely to burn sugar than fat, they tend to become hungry sooner and to overeat. The subordinate clause modifies the verb *tend.*

People *who exercise on a regular basis* change certain enzyme systems *so that they are more likely to burn fat than sugar.* There are two subordinate clauses, one beginning with *who* and modifying *People*, and the other beginning with *so that* and modifying the verb *change.*

Effective writing has both coordination and subordination—coordination sets equivalent elements side by side, and subordination makes some elements dependent on others. Both are useful writing tools.

2C Mixed Sentences

In mixed sentences, called faulty predications when they involve the mismatching of subject and predicate, two or more parts of a sentence do not make sense together. Like other inconsistencies, this kind of problem usually occurs when writers concentrate harder on meaning than on grammar.

The following mixed sentences are common in everyday speech and may not seem inconsistent to you. Indeed, in casual speech they are usually accepted as consistent. In standard written English, however, they qualify as grammatical errors.

H2.C
Revise mixed sentences to make sentences consistent.

By driving to the movie was how we saw the accident happen. The prepositional phrase *By driving to the movie* is treated as the subject for the verb *was*. Prepositional phrases cannot serve as subjects.

Just because the candidate once had a drinking problem doesn't mean he won't be a good mayor now. The adverb clause *because the candidate once had a drinking problem* is treated as the subject of the verb *doesn't mean*. Adverbs modify verbs and adjectives and cannot function as subjects.

A CAT scan is when medical technicians take a cross-sectional X-ray of the body. The adverb clause *when medical technicians take a cross-sectional X-ray of the body* is treated as a complement of the subject *CAT scan*—another function adverbs cannot serve.

The reason I was late today is because my alarm clock broke. The subject, *reason*, is illogically linked with the predicate, *is because*. *Reason* suggests an explanation, so the predicate, *is because*, is redundant.

Revise mixed sentences by ensuring that grammatical patterns are used consistently throughout each sentence. For cases of faulty predication, either revise the subject so it can perform the action expressed in the predicate or revise the predicate so it accurately depicts an action performed by the subject. Also avoid using the constructions *is when* and *is where* to explain an idea and *The reason...is because* in your writing.

There are often many ways to revise mixed sentences. In each of the following revisions, the grammatical patterns are consistent and the subjects and predicates fit together logically:

While driving to the movie, we saw the accident happen.

Just because the candidate once had a drinking problem, we can't conclude that he won't be a good mayor.

A CAT scan is a cross-sectional X-ray of the body.

The reason I was late today is that my alarm clock broke.

2D Shifts

H2.D
Recognize and revise unintended shifts in sentence elements.

Shifts occur when writers lose track of their sentence elements. Shifts occur in a variety of ways:

In person

In music, where left-handed people seem to be talented, the right-handed world puts *you* at a disadvantage. Shift from *people*, third person, to *you*, second person.

In tense

Even though many musicians *are* left-handed, instruments *had been designed for right-handers*. Shift from present tense to past perfect.

In number

A left-handed *violinist* has to pay extra to buy *their* left-handed violin. Shift from singular to plural.

In mood

Every time the *violinist played, she could always know* when her instrument was out of tune. Shift from the indicative mood, *violinist played*, to the subjunctive mood, *she could always know.*

In voice

The sonata *was being practiced* by the violinists in one room while the cellists *played* the concerto in the other room. Shift from the passive voice, *was being practiced*, to active voice, *played.*

In discourse type

She said, "*Your violin is out of tune*," and that *I was playing the wrong note.* Shift from the direct quotation, *Your violin is out of tune*, to indirect quotation, that *I was playing the wrong note.*

Once you recognize shifts, revise them by ensuring that the same grammatical structures are used consistently throughout the sentence:

In music, where left-handed *people* seem talented, the right-handed world puts *them* at a disadvantage.

Even though many musicians *are* left-handed, instruments *have been designed* for right-handers.

Left-handed *violinists* have to pay extra to buy *their* left-handed violins.

Every time the violinist *played*, she *knew* when her instrument was out of tune.

The violinists *practiced* the sonata in one room while the cellists *played* the concerto in the other room.

She said, "*Your violin is out of tune and you are playing the wrong note.*"

3 Problems with Modification

Learning Objectives

H3.A Recognize and correct dangling and misplaced modifiers.

H3.B Distinguish between restrictive and nonrestrictive modifiers.

H3.C Recognize and revise sentences to correct common errors with adverbs and adjectives.

One part of a sentence can be *modified* by another part. A part that is modified is changed in some way: limited or broadened, perhaps, or described, defined, identified, or explained. Adjectives and adverbs always serve modifying functions, but phrases and subordinate clauses also can be modifiers. This section deals with problems in modification. (See 2B Coordination and Subordination.)

3A Dangling and Misplaced Modifiers

Dangling and misplaced modifiers are words and word groups that, because of their position or the way they are phrased, make the meaning of a sentence unclear and sometimes even ludicrous. These troublesome modifiers are most commonly verbal phrases, prepositional phrases, and adverbs. Here are examples:

Reaching to pick up the saddle, the obnoxious horse may shake off the blanket. The dangling verbal phrase appears to relate to *horse.*

To extend lead out of the ever-sharp pencil, the eraser cap is depressed. The dangling verbal phrase implies that *the eraser cap* does something.

The ever-sharp pencil is designed to be used permanently, *only periodically replacing the lead*. The dangling verbal phrase implies that the pencil replaces the lead.

Dick *only* had to pay ten dollars for his parking ticket. The misplaced adverb should immediately precede *ten.*

Theodore caught a giant fish in the very same spot where he had lost the ring *two years later*. The misplaced adverb phrase confusingly appears to modify the last part of the sentence instead of, correctly, the first part.

Errors of this type are difficult for writers to recognize, because, to the writers, they are not ambiguous.

Recognition. Verbal phrases always have implied subjects; in other words, somebody is performing the action. For clarity, that implied subject should be the same as the subject of the sentence or clause. To recognize your own dangling verbal modifiers, make sure that the implied subject of the verbal phrase is the same as the subject of the sentence. In the first example above, the implied subject of *Reaching* is not *the horse*. In the second example, the implied subject of *To extend* is not *the eraser cap*. And in the third example, the implied subject of *replacing* is not *the pencil*. Also check passive voice, because in a passive sentence, the subject is not the doer of the action. In the second example, the dangler can be corrected when the verb, changed from passive to active voice, tells who should depress the eraser (see correction that follows).

Correction. Correcting dangling and misplaced modifiers depends on the type of error. Misplaced modifiers can often be moved to a more appropriate position:

Dick had to pay *only* ten dollars for his parking ticket.

Two years later, Theodore caught a giant fish in the very same spot where he had lost the ring.

Dangling modifiers usually require some rewording:

As you reach to pick up the saddle, the obnoxious horse may shake off the blanket. The dangling verbal phrase is converted to a clause.

To extend lead out of the ever-sharp pencil, *depress the eraser cap*. The main clause is revised so that *you* is the implied subject of *depress* (as it is for *To extend*).

The ever-sharp pencil is designed to be used permanently, *only periodically needing the lead replaced*. The dangling verbal phrase is revised so that the implied subject of *needing* is *pencil*.

3B Restrictive and Nonrestrictive Modifiers

Some modifiers are essential to a sentence because they *restrict*, or limit, the meaning of the words they modify; other modifiers, while adding important information, are not essential to the meaning of a sentence. The first type is called restrictive and the second nonrestrictive. The terms usually refer to subordinate clauses and phrases. Here are examples of restrictive and nonrestrictive modifiers:

H3.B
Distinguish between restrictive and nonrestrictive modifiers.

Restrictive

People *who plan to visit Europe* should take time to see Belgium. Relative clause modifying and identifying *People*.

The industrialized country *between the Netherlands and France on the North Sea* is constitutionally a kingdom. Prepositional phrases modifying and identifying *country*.

The Kempenland was thinly populated *before coal was discovered there*. Subordinate clause modifying *was populated* and giving meaning to the sentence.

Language and cultural differences have created friction *that has existed for centuries*. Relative clause modifying and identifying *friction*.

Nonrestrictive

Belgium has two major populations: the Flemings, *who live in the north and speak Flemish*, and the Walloons, *who live in the south and speak French*. Two relative clauses, the first modifying *Flemings* and the second modifying *Walloons*.

With Brussels in the middle of the country, both groups inhabit the city. Prepositional phrases, together modifying *inhabit*.

NATO's headquarters is in Brussels, *where it has been since its beginning in 1950*. Subordinate clause modifying *Brussels*.

Covering southeastern Belgium, the sandstone Ardennes Mountains follow the Sambre and Meuse rivers. Participial (verbal) phrase modifying *Ardennes Mountains*.

These examples illustrate several aspects of restrictive and nonrestrictive modifiers:

1. They *modify* a word in the clause or sentence; they therefore function as adjectives or adverbs.
2. They can appear at the beginning, somewhere in the middle, or at the end of a sentence or clause.
3. Most types of subordinate elements can be restrictive and nonrestrictive.
4. Whether a clause or phrase is restrictive or nonrestrictive depends on its function in the sentence.

5. Restrictive elements are not set off with punctuation; nonrestrictive elements are set off with commas (and sometimes dashes).

If you think the distinction between restrictive and nonrestrictive is not worth making, consider the following sentences, the first restrictive and the second nonrestrictive:

People who wear braces on their teeth should not eat caramel apples.

People, who wear braces on their teeth, should not eat caramel apples.

Set off with commas, the nonrestrictive *who* clause implies that all people wear braces on their teeth and should not eat caramel apples, which is clearly not the case. It does not *restrict*, or limit, the meaning of *people*. In the first sentence, however, the *who* clause does restrict, or limit, the meaning of *people* to only those who wear braces on their teeth. Often, only the writer knows the intended meaning and therefore needs to make the distinction by setting off, or not setting off, the modifier.

Here are a few guidelines that might help you in making this subtle distinction:

1. A modifier that modifies a proper noun (one that names a person or thing) is usually nonrestrictive, because the name is sufficient identification. Notice *Flemings* and *Walloons* in the previous example.

2. A *that* clause is almost always restrictive.

3. Adverbial subordinate clauses (those beginning with subordinating conjunctions such as *because* and *when*; see list on pages 621–622) are almost always restrictive and usually not set off with commas when they appear at the end of their sentences. If they appear at the beginning of sentences, they are almost always set off with commas.

4. A nonrestrictive modifier at the beginning of a sentence is followed by a comma, one at the end is preceded by a comma, and one in the middle is enclosed with two commas.

3C Adjectives and Adverbs

Adjectives and adverbs, often called *modifiers*, describe nouns and verbs (see 9A Parts of Speech). Adjectives modify nouns; that is, they describe, limit, explain, or alter them in some way. By modifying, they *limit* the meaning of the nouns: *red car* is narrower in meaning than *car*, and *fast red car* is narrower than *red car*. Adverbs modify verbs, adjectives, and other adverbs, telling more than the words by themselves could tell: drive *carefully* (adverb modifying a verb), *unexpectedly* early (adverb modifying an adjective), drive *very* carefully (adverb modifying an adverb). Adverbs usually tell how, where, when, and how much.

Adjectives and adverbs occasionally present some problems for writers. Be careful not to use adjectives when adverbs are needed, as in this sentence:

The governor suspected that the legislators were not taking him *serious*. The sentence element receiving modification is the verb *were not taking*, yet the modifier *serious* is an adjective, which can only modify nouns. The correct modifier for this sentence is the adverb *seriously*. (If you are not sure whether a word is an adjective or an adverb, check your dictionary, which should identify parts of speech.)

Another problem in form concerns the *comparative* and *superlative* degrees. The comparative form of adjectives and adverbs shows a greater degree between two things:

> Your luggage is *stronger* than mine. Adjective comparing *your luggage* and *mine*.

> Your luggage survives airport baggage handling *better* than mine does. Adverb comparing how the two *survive* handling.

The comparative degree is formed by adding *-er* to shorter adjectives and adverbs (*strong, stronger; hard, harder*); longer words are preceded by *more* (*beautiful, more beautiful; seriously, more seriously*). Do not use *-er* with *more* (not *more harder*).

The superlative form shows a greater degree among three or more things:

> This is the *strongest* luggage I have ever seen. Adjective comparing the present luggage to all other luggage the writer has seen.

> Your luggage survives airport baggage handling *best* of all luggage I've seen. Adverb comparing how all luggage the writer has seen survives handling.

The superlative degree is formed by adding *-est* to shorter adjectives and adverbs (*strong, strongest; hard, hardest*); longer words are preceded by *most* (*beautiful, most beautiful; seriously, most seriously*). Do not use *-est* with *most* (not *most strongest*).

Do not use adjectives and adverbs gratuitously, just to fill space or because you think you ought to. They are effective only when they add meaning to a sentence.

4 Verbs

Learning Objectives

H4.A Recognize common verb tenses and forms.

H4.B Revise sentences to avoid overusing passive voice.

H4.C Use correct verb forms to express indicative, imperative, and subjunctive moods.

H4.D Recognize and correct common errors in subject–verb agreement.

Verbs are the central core of a sentence; together with subjects, they make statements. Verbs often tell what the subject is doing:

> The company *agreed* to plead guilty to criminal charges.

> Nearly every miner *can name* a casualty of black lung disease.

Another common function of verbs is to link subjects to complements:

Logan *is* an isolated county in the corner of the state.

Sometimes the verb tells something about the subject, as the following passive verb does:

Casualties of mining *cannot be measured* only by injuries.

Through changes in form, verbs can indicate the time of the action (past, present, future); the number of the subject (singular or plural); and the person of the subject (first person, *I, we*; second person, *you*; third person, *he, she, it, they*).

4A Tense

The problems that writers sometimes encounter when using verbs result from the fact that verbs, unlike most other words in English, have many forms, and a slight shift in form can alter sentences' meanings. Notice how the meanings of the following pairs of sentences change as their verbs change:

The fish *has jumped* into the boat.
The fish *have jumped* into the boat.

The concert *starts* at 8:15 p.m.
The concert *started* at 8:15 p.m.

In the first pair, the meaning changes from one fish to more than one fish jumping into the boat. In the second pair, the first verb implies that the concert has not yet begun; the second, that it had already begun. It is important, therefore, to use the verb form that conveys the intended meaning. Observe how the verb *vanish* changes in the following sentences to indicate differences in time, or *tense*:

Present:	Many agricultural jobs *vanish*.
Past:	Many agricultural jobs *vanished*.
Future:	Many agricultural jobs *will vanish*.
Perfect:	Many agricultural jobs *have vanished*.
Past Perfect:	Many agricultural jobs *had vanished*.
Future Perfect:	Many agricultural jobs *will have vanished*.

To omit an -*ed* ending or to use the wrong helping verb gives readers a false message.

Helping (Auxiliary) Verbs. It is also important to use a form that is a *finite*, or an actual, verb. In the following example, the word that appears to be a verb (italicized) is not a finite verb:

The fish *jumping* into the boat.

The word *jumping* does not have one of the primary functions of verbs—telling the time of the action, called *tense*. The time of the occurrence could have been the past (*the fish were jumping*), present (*the fish are jumping*), or the future (*the fish will be jumping*). We also don't know whether the writer meant one fish or many. The *-ing* form is a *verbal* and requires a helping, or auxiliary, verb to make it finite, or able to tell time: words such as *am, is, are, was, were* (forms of *be*). Other helping verbs are *do* (*Do* you *want* the paper? She *doesn't want* the paper) and *have* (I *haven't seen* the paper; *has* she *seen* it?).

Irregular Verbs. Most verbs change forms in a regular way: *want* in the present becomes *wanted* in the past, *wanting* is used with the auxiliary *be* (i.e., *is wanting*), and *wanted* is used with the auxiliary *have* (i.e., *have wanted*). Many verbs change irregularly, however—internally rather than at their ends. Here are a few of the most common irregular verbs:

Base form	Past tense	Present participle	Past participle
be (is, am, are)	was, were	being	been
come	came	coming	come
do	did	doing	done
drink	drank	drinking	drunk
give	gave	giving	given
go	went	going	gone
grow	grew	growing	grown
lie	laid	lying	lain
see	saw	seeing	seen
take	took	taking	taken
teach	taught	teaching	taught
throw	threw	throwing	thrown
wear	wore	wearing	worn
write	wrote	writing	written

Check your dictionary for the forms of other verbs you suspect may be irregular.

The verb form that is perhaps the most troublesome is the *-s* form in the present tense. This form is used for all singular nouns and the pronouns *he, she,* and *it.* (See 4D Subject–Verb Agreement.)

4B Voice

English sentences are usually written in the active voice, in which the subject of the sentence is the doer of the action of the verb:

> Scott misplaced the file folder. *Scott*, the subject of the sentence, performed the action, *misplaced*.

With the passive voice, the doer of the action is the object of a preposition or is omitted entirely:

> The file folder was misplaced by Scott. *File folder* is now the subject of the sentence.

> The file folder was misplaced. The person doing the action is not named.

H4.B
Revise sentences to avoid over-using passive voice.

At best, the passive voice is wordier than the active voice; at worst, it fails to acknowledge who performs the action of the verb. Use the passive voice when you do not know or do not want to name the doer or when you want to keep the subjects consistent within a paragraph.

To avoid using the passive voice, look for *by* phrases near the ends of your sentences; if you find any, see if the subject of your sentence performs the action of your verb. If not, revise the sentence so that it does. Another way to find occurrences of the passive voice is to look for forms of *be: am, is, are, was, were, been, being*. Not all these verbs will be passive, but if they function as part of an action verb, see if the subject performs the action. If it does not, and if your sentence would be clearer with the subject performing the action, revise to the active voice.

4C Mood

H4.C

Use correct verb forms to express indicative, imperative, and subjunctive moods.

Mood refers to the writer's attitude toward the action of the verb. There are three forms: indicative, imperative, and subjunctive. Verbs in the *indicative mood* are used to make statements, to ask questions, and to declare opinions. For example:

Not many people today *think* the world *is* flat. Makes a statement.

Does anybody today *think* the world is flat? Asks a question.

Members of the Flat Earth Society *should reevaluate* their thinking. Declares an opinion.

Verbs in the *imperative mood* issue commands, requests, or directions. Imperative verbs never change form. When the subject of an imperative verb is not explicitly identified, it is understood to be *you*.

Julia, *stop* teasing your baby brother. Issues command.

Please *complete* this report by tomorrow morning. Issues request.

Turn right at the light and *drive* for another two blocks. Issues directions.

Verbs in the *subjunctive mood* communicate wishes, make statements contrary to fact, list requirements and demands, and imply skepticism or doubt. They usually appear in clauses introduced by *if, that, as if*, and *as though*. Use the base form of the verb for the present-tense subjunctive. For the past-tense subjunctive of the verb *be*, use *were* for all subjects.

She wishes that her son's best friend *were* more responsible. Communicates wish.

If the world *were* to end tomorrow, we would not have to pay taxes anymore. Makes statement contrary to fact.

The jury summons requires that your cousin *arrive* punctually at 8:00 a.m. and *sign* in with the court clerk. Lists requirements.

His girlfriend talks as if she *were* a pop music diva. Implies skepticism.

Be sure to select the correct verb forms to express indicative, imperative, and subjunctive moods.

4D Subject–Verb Agreement

Clauses are made of subjects and verbs plus their modifiers and other related words. A fundamental principle of usage is that verbs agree with their subjects. In most cases, this principle presents no problem: You say, "Birds *have* feathers," not "Birds *has* feathers." But not all sentences are this simple. Before getting into the problem areas, consider first that errors in subject–verb agreement occur only with present-tense verbs and the verb tenses that use present-tense forms of helping verbs (such as *have* and *be*). And, except for the irregular verb *be* (with its forms *am, is, are, was, were*), the problem centers on third-person singular verbs with their *-s* ending. Here is the problem illustrated. Notice that only the verbs in the third-person singular are different. The unfortunate thing is that all nouns are in the third person and, when singular, require this form in the present tense.

H4.D

Recognize and correct common errors in subject–verb agreement.

	Present singular	plural	Present Perfect singular	plural
first person	I work	we work	I have worked	we have worked
second person	you work	you work	you have worked	you have worked
third person	he works (she, it)	they work	he has worked (she, it)	they have worked

It is the *-s* form, then, that you need to watch for to avoid errors in subject–verb agreement. Here are some situations that may cause problems.

Intervening Subordinate Element

When a subject and a verb are side by side, they usually do not present a problem. Often, however, writers separate them with subordinate elements, such as clauses, prepositional or verbal phrases, and other elements. The result may be a verb error. The following sentence illustrates this problem:

The realization that life is a series of compromises never occur to some people. The subject is *realization*, a singular noun, and should be followed by the singular verb *occurs*. The corrected sentence would read "The realization that life is a series of compromises never occurs to some people."

Subject Complement

Subject complements follow some verbs and rename the subject, although they are not always in the same number as the subject. Because a singular subject may have a plural complement, and vice versa, confused writers might make the verb agree with the complement instead of the subject. Here's an example:

The result of this mistake are guilt, low self-esteem, and depression. The subject is *result*, not *guilt, low self-esteem, and depression*; the singular subject should be followed by the singular verb *is*. The corrected sentence would read "The result of this mistake is guilt, low self-esteem, and depression."

Compound Subject

Two or more words may be compounded to make a subject. Whether they are singular or plural depends on their connector. Subjects connected by *and* and *but* are plural, but those connected by *or* and *nor* are singular or plural depending on whether the item closer to the verb is singular or plural. Here are examples:

The young mother and the superior student *are* both candidates for compulsive perfectionism. Two subjects, *mother* and *student*, are joined by *and* and take a plural verb.

Promotions or an employee award *tells* the perfectionist he or she is achieving personal goals. When two subjects, *promotions* and *award*, are joined by *or*, the verb agrees with the nearer one; in this sentence, a singular verb is required.

An employee award or promotions *tell* the perfectionist he or she is achieving personal goals. Here, the plural verb, *tell*, agrees with *promotions*, the closer of the two subjects.

Indefinite Pronoun as Subject

Indefinite pronouns are defined and listed under 5C Pronoun Agreement. Although these words often seem plural in meaning, most of them are singular grammatically. When indefinite pronouns are the subjects of sentences or clauses, their verbs are usually singular. Here are examples:

Everyone *has* at some time worried about achieving goals. The singular indefinite pronoun *Everyone* takes a singular verb, *has*.

Each car and truck on the highway *was* creeping along on the icy pavement. The singular indefinite pronoun *Each* requires a singular verb, *was*.

Neither of us *is* going to worry about being late. The singular indefinite pronoun *Neither* takes a singular verb, *is*.

Nevertheless, some of us *are* going to be very late. The indefinite pronoun *some* (like *all*, *any*, and *none*) is singular or plural, depending on context; compare with "Some of the book *is* boring."

Inverted Sentence Order

Inverted sentence order can confuse your natural inclination to use subject–verb agreement. Examples of inverted order are questions, plus sentences beginning with *there*. Sentences like these demand closer attention to agreement.

Have the results of the test come back yet? The plural subject, *results*, takes a plural verb, *have*.

There *are* many special services provided just for kids at hotels, ski lodges, and restaurants. The plural subject, *services*, takes a plural verb, *are*. *There* is never a subject; it only holds the place for the subject in an inverted sentence.

Intervening Relative Clause

Subordinate clauses that begin with the relative pronouns *who*, *which*, or *that* present special problems in subject–verb agreement. Their verbs must agree with their own subjects, not with a word in another clause. These subordinate clauses demand special attention, because whether the pronouns are singular or plural depends on their antecedents. These sentences illustrate agreement within relative clauses:

> Every person who *attends* the baseball game will receive a free cap. *Who*, the subject of *attends*, means "person," a singular noun.

> John is one of the few people I know who *care* about frogs. *Who*, the subject of *care*, means "people," a plural noun.

> John is the only one of all the people I know who *cares* about frogs. *Who* in this sentence means "one."

5 Pronouns

Learning Objectives

H5.A   Recognize and correct common errors with pronoun case.

H5.B   Recognize and correct unclear pronoun reference.

H5.C   Recognize and correct faulty pronoun agreement.

H5.D   Recognize and correct common errors with relative pronouns.

Pronouns can have all the same sentence functions as nouns; the difference is that pronouns do not have the meanings that nouns have. Nouns name things; a noun stands for the thing itself. Pronouns, however, refer only to nouns. Whenever that reference is ambiguous or inconsistent, there is a problem in clarity.

5A Pronoun Case

Case is a grammatical term for the way nouns and pronouns show their relationships to other parts of a sentence. In English, nouns have only two case forms: the regular form (the one listed in a dictionary, such as *year*) and the possessive form (used to show ownership or connection, such as *year's*; possessive nouns are discussed in 8C Apostrophe).

H5.A

Recognize and correct common errors with pronoun case.

Pronouns, however, retain their case forms. Here are the forms for personal and relative pronouns:

	Subjective	Objective	Possessive
Personal	I	me	my, mine
	you	you	your, yours
	he	him	his
	she	her	her, hers
	it	it	its
	we	us	our, ours
	they	them	their, theirs
Relative	who	whom	whose
	whoever	whomever	whosever

Notice, first, that possessive pronouns, unlike possessive nouns, do not take apostrophes—none of them. Sometimes writers confuse possessive pronouns with contractions, which do have apostrophes (such as *it's*, meaning *it is* or *it has*; and *who's*, meaning *who is*; for further discussion, see 8C Apostrophe).

Another problem writers sometimes have with pronoun case is using a subjective form when they need the objective or using an objective form when they need the subjective.

Subjective Case. Use the subjective forms for subjects and for words referring to subjects, as in these examples:

Among the patients a nutritionist sees are the grossly overweight people *who* have tried all kinds of diets. *Who* is the subject of the verb *have tried* in its own clause.

They have a life history of obesity and diets. *They* is the subject of *have*.

He and *the patient* work out a plan for permanent weight control. *He* and *the patient* are the compound subjects of *work*.

The patient understands that the ones who work out the diet plan are *he* and *the nutritionist*. *He* and *the nutritionist* refer to *ones*, the subject of the clause.

Notice that pronoun case is determined by the function of the pronoun in its own clause and that compounding (*he and the patient*) has no effect on case.

Objective Case. Use the objective forms for objects of all kinds:

"Between *you* and *me*," said the patient to his nutritionist, "I'm ready for something that works." *You* and *me* are objects of the preposition *Between*.

An exercise program is usually assigned to the patient for *whom* the diet is prescribed. *Whom* is the object of the preposition *for*.

The nutritionist gives *her* a suitable alternative to couch sitting. *Her* is the indirect object of *gives*.

Modest exercise combined with modest dieting can affect *him or her* dramatically. *Him or her* is the direct object of *can affect*.

Having advised *them* about diet and exercise, the nutritionist instructs dieters about behavioral change. *Them* is the object of the participle *Having advised*.

Notice again that the case of a pronoun is determined by its function in its own clause and is not affected by compounding (*you and me*).

Possessive Case. Use the possessive forms to indicate ownership. Possessive pronouns have two forms: adjective forms (*my, your, his, her, its, our, their*) and possessive forms (*mine, yours, his, hers, its, ours, theirs*). The adjective forms appear before nouns or gerunds; the possessive forms replace possessive nouns.

The patient purchased *his* supplements from the drugstore *his* nutritionist recommended. Adjective form before nouns.

His swimming every day produced results faster than he anticipated. Adjective form before gerund.

His was a difficult task to accomplish, but the rewards of weight loss were great. Possessive form replacing possessive noun.

5B Pronoun Reference

Personal and relative pronouns (see the list in section 5A Pronoun Case) must **H5.B** refer to specific nouns or antecedents. By themselves they have no meaning. As Recognize and a result, they can cause problems in clarity for readers. If you were to read, "She correct unclear teaches technical writing at her local technical college," you would know only that pronoun *someone*, a woman, teaches technical writing at the college. But if the sentence reference. were preceded by one like this, "After getting her master's degree, my mother has achieved one of her life goals," the pronoun *she* would have meaning. In this case, *mother* is the antecedent of *she*. The antecedent gives meaning to the pronoun. For this reason, it is essential that pronouns refer unambiguously to their antecedents and that pronouns and antecedents agree.

Ambiguous pronoun reference may occur in various ways:

- More than one possible antecedent.
- Adjective used as intended antecedent.
- Implied antecedent.
- Too great of a separation between antecedent and pronoun.

Here are sentences in which the pronouns do not clearly refer to their antecedents:

The immunologist refused to admit the fraudulence of the data reported by a former colleague in a paper *he* had cosigned. More than one possible antecedent. *He* could refer to *immunologist* or to *colleague.*

In Carolyn Chute's book *The Beans of Egypt, Maine*, she treats poverty with concern and understanding. Adjective used as intended antecedent (possessive nouns function as adjectives). In this case, *Carolyn Chute's* modifies *book* and cannot serve as an antecedent of the pronoun *she.*

It says in the newspaper that the economy will not improve soon. Implied antecedent. There is no antecedent for *It.*

At Ajax *they* have tires on sale til the end of the month. Implied antecedent. There is no antecedent for *they.*

This only reinforces the public skepticism about the credibility of scientists. Implied antecedent. There is no antecedent for *This.*

One of the primary rules for using humor in advertising is often broken, *which* is that the ad doesn't make fun of the product. Too great a separation between antecedent and pronoun. The antecedent of *which* is *rules*, but its distance from the pronoun makes reference difficult.

Faulty pronoun reference is corrected by clarifying the relationship between the pronoun and its intended antecedent. Observe how the example sentences have been revised:

The immunologist refused to admit the fraudulence of the data reported by a former colleague in a paper *the immunologist* had cosigned. *The immunologist* replaces the unclear pronoun *he.*

In her book *The Beans of Egypt, Maine*, Carolyn Chute treats poverty with concern and understanding. The possessive pronoun *her* replaces the possessive noun and refers to the noun subject, *Carolyn Chute*.

The newspaper reports that the economy will not improve soon. The unclear pronoun *It* is replaced by its implied antecedent, *The newspaper*.

Ajax has tires on sale til the end of the month. The unclear pronoun *they* is replaced by *Ajax*.

This *kind of waffling* only reinforces public skepticism about the credibility of scientists. The unclear pronoun *This* is replaced by the adjective *This* modifying the intended antecedent *kind of waffling*.

That the ad doesn't make fun of the product is an often-broken primary rule for using humor in advertising. Parts of the sentence are moved around until they are clear.

Revising unclear pronoun reference is sometimes like working a jigsaw puzzle: finding and adding a missing piece or moving parts around to achieve the best fit. Often, only the writer can make the right connections.

5C Pronoun Agreement

H5.C
Recognize and correct faulty pronoun agreement.

Some pronoun errors result because the pronoun and its antecedent do not agree. In the sentence "When a student is late for this class, they find the door locked," the plural pronoun *they* refers to a singular antecedent, *a student*. There is no agreement in *number*. In the sentence "When a student is late for this class, you find the door locked," again the pronoun, this time *you*, does not agree with the antecedent. Here the problem is *person*. Pronouns must agree with their antecedents in number, person, and gender. (See the list of pronouns in 5A Pronoun Case.)

Compound Antecedents
Problems sometimes occur with compound antecedents. If the antecedents are joined by *and*, the pronoun is plural; if joined by *or*, the pronoun agrees with the nearer antecedent. Here are examples of correct usage:

In the pediatric trauma center, the head doctor and head nurse direct *their* medical team. The pronoun *their* refers to both *doctor* and *nurse*.

The head doctor or the head nurse directs *his or her* team. The pronouns *his or her* refer to the closer antecedent, *nurse* (because the gender of the nurse is not known, the neutral alternatives are used).

The head doctor or the other doctors give *their* help when it is needed. The pronoun *their* agrees with the closer antecedent, *doctors*.

Indefinite Pronouns as Antecedents
A particularly troublesome kind of agreement is that between personal or relative pronouns and *indefinite pronouns*. As their name implies, indefinites do not refer

to particular people or things; grammatically they are usually singular but are often intended as plural. Here are the common indefinite pronouns:

all	every	none
any	everybody	nothing
anybody	everyone	one
anyone	everything	some
anything	neither	somebody
each	no one	someone
either	nobody	something

Like nouns, these pronouns can serve as antecedents of personal and relative pronouns. But because most of them are grammatically singular, they can be troublesome in sentences. Here are examples of correct usage:

> Everyone in the trauma center has *his or her* specific job to do. **or** *All* the personnel in the trauma center have *their* specific jobs to do. The neutral, though wordy, alternative *his or her* agrees with the singular indefinite *Everyone*. The second sentence illustrates the use of plural when gender is unknown.

> *Each* of them does *his or her* job efficiently and competently. **or** *All* of them do *their* jobs efficiently and competently. *Each* is singular, but *all* is either singular or plural, depending on context (compare "*All* literature has *its* place").

Shifts in Person

Agreement errors in *person* are shifts between *I* or *we* (first person), *you* (second person), and *he, she, it*, and *they* (third person). These errors are probably more often a result of carelessness than of imperfect knowledge. Being more familiar with casual speech than formal writing, writers sometimes shift from *I* to *you*—for example, when only one of them is meant, as in these sentences:

> Last summer *I* went on a canoeing trip to northern Manitoba. It was *my* first trip that far north, and it was so peaceful *you* could forget all the problems back home. The person represented by *you* was not present. The writer means *I*.

See also 2D Shifts.

5D Relative Pronouns

Use relative pronouns to introduce clauses that modify nouns or pronouns. Personal relative pronouns refer to people. They include *who, whom, whoever, whomever*, and *whose*. Nonpersonal relative pronouns refer to things. They include *which, whichever, whatever*, and *whose*.

H5.D
Recognize and correct common errors with relative pronouns.

Most college writers know to use *who* when referring to people and *which* or *that* when referring to things, but sometimes carelessness or confusion can lead to errors. Many writers assume that *which* and *that* are interchangeable, when they are not. Use *which* to introduce nonrestrictive clauses and *that* to introduce restrictive clauses (see 3B Restrictive and Nonrestrictive Modifiers). Another problem area concerns the correct use of *who* and *whom*. Use *who* to refer to the subject of the sentence and *whom* to refer to an object of the verb or preposition. Following are examples of common errors:

The lawyer *that* lost the case today went to law school with my sister. Uses impersonal relative pronoun *that*.

Conflict between the two parties led to the lawsuit *that* was finally settled today. The relative pronoun *that* introduces a nonrestrictive clause that modifies *lawsuit*. Nonrestrictive clauses supply extra information to the sentence, not defining information.

The case resulted in a ruling, *which* favored the plaintiff. The relative pronoun *which* introduces a restrictive clause that modifies *ruling*. Restrictive clauses supply defining information.

Later, the lawyer *whom* lost the case spoke with the jurors *who* we had interviewed. The first relative pronoun, *whom*, refers to the subject, *lawyer*, while the second relative pronoun, *who*, refers to the object of the verb *had interviewed*.

Once you recognize relative-pronoun errors, it is usually easy to fix them:

The lawyer *who* lost the case today went to law school with my sister.

Conflict between the two parties led to the lawsuit, *which* was finally settled today.

The case resulted in a ruling *that* favored the plaintiff.

Later, the lawyer *who* lost the case spoke with the jurors *whom* we had interviewed.

6 Style

Learning Objectives

H6.A   Use editing strategies to achieve conciseness.

H6.B   Use appropriate language that is suitable for your audience and free of sexism and other forms of bias.

Style in writing—like style in clothes, art, or anything else—is individual and develops with use and awareness. But even individual writers vary their style, depending on the situation. At school and work, the preferred style tends to be more formal and objective. The readings in this book provide abundant examples of this style. It is not stuffy, patronizing, or coldly analytical. It is simply clean, direct, and clear. This Handbook section treats a few of the obstacles to a good writing style.

6A Conciseness

H6.A

Use editing strategies to achieve conciseness.

Nobody wants to read more words than necessary. When you write concisely, therefore, you are considerate of your readers. To achieve conciseness, you do not need to eliminate details and other content; rather, you cut empty words, repetition, and unnecessary details.

In the following passage, all the italicized words could be omitted without altering the meaning.

> *In the final analysis, I feel that* the United States should have converted to the *use of the* metric system *of measurement* a long time ago. *In the present day and age,* the United States is the *one and* only country in the *entire* world except for Borneo and Liberia that has not yet adopted this measurement system.

Repetition of keywords is an effective technique for achieving emphasis and coherence, but pointless repetition serves only to bore the reader.

Follow these guidelines to achieve conciseness in your writing:

1. **Avoid redundancy.** Redundant words and expressions needlessly repeat what has already been said. Delete them when they appear in your writing.

2. **Avoid wordy expressions.** Phrases such as *In the final analysis* and *In the present day and age* in the preceding example add no important information to sentences and should be removed and/or replaced with less-wordy constructions.

3. **Avoid unnecessary intensifiers.** Intensifiers such as *really, very, clearly, quite,* and *of course* usually fail to add meaning to the words they modify and therefore are often unnecessary. Deleting them does not change the meaning of the sentence.

4. **Avoid excess use of prepositional phrases.** The use of too many prepositional phrases within a sentence makes for wordy writing. Always use constructions that require the fewest words.

5. **Avoid negating constructions.** Negating constructions using words such as *no* and *not* often add unneeded words to sentences. Use shorter alternatives when they are available.

6. **Avoid the passive voice.** Passive constructions require more words than active constructions (see 4B Voice). They can also obscure meaning by concealing the sentence's subject. Write in the active voice whenever possible.

Following are more examples of wordy sentences that violate these guidelines:

If the two groups *cooperate together*, there will be *positive benefits* for both. Uses redundancy.

There are some people *who* think the metric system is un-American. Uses wordy expression.

The climb up the mountain was *very* hard on my legs and *really* taxed my lungs and heart. Uses unnecessary modifiers.

On the day of his birth, we walked *to the park down the block from the house of his mother.* Uses too many prepositional phrases.

She *did not like* hospitals. Uses negating construction when a shorter alternative is available.

The door *was closed* by that man over there. Uses passive voice when active voice is preferable.

Corrections to the previous wordy sentences result in concise sentences:

If the two groups cooperate, both will benefit. This correction also replaces the wordy construction *there will be...for both* with a shorter, more forceful alternative.

Some people think the metric system is un-American.

The climb up the mountain was hard on my legs and taxed my lungs and heart.

On his birthday, we walked to the park near his mother's house.

She hated hospitals.

That man over there closed the door.

6B Appropriate Language

H6.B

Use appropriate language that is suitable for your audience and free of sexism and other forms of bias.

Effective writers communicate using appropriate language; that is, language that:

1. Suits its subject and audience.
2. Avoids sexist usage.
3. Avoids bias and stereotype.

Suitability

The style and tone of your writing should be suitable to your subject and audience. Most academic and business contexts require the use of *formal language*. Formal language communicates clearly and directly, with a minimum of stylistic flourish. Its tone is serious, objective, and detached. Formal language avoids slang, pretentious words, and unnecessary jargon. *Informal language*, on the other hand, is particular to the writer's personality and also assumes a closer and more familiar relationship between the writer and the reader. Its tone is casual, subjective, and intimate. Informal language can also employ slang and other words that would be inappropriate in formal language.

As informal language is rarely used within an academic setting, the following examples show errors in the use of formal language:

The director told the board members to *push off*. Uses informal language.

Professor Oyo *dissed* Marta when she arrived late to his class for the third time in a row. Uses slang.

The *aromatic essence* of the gardenia was intoxicating. Uses pretentious words.

The doctor told him to take *salicylate* to ease the symptoms of *viral rhinorrhea*. Uses unnecessary jargon.

Employing formal language correctly, these examples could be revised as follows:

The director told the board members to leave.

Professor Oyo spoke disrespectfully to Marta when she arrived late to his class for the third time in a row.

The scent of the gardenia was intoxicating.

The doctor told him to take aspirin to ease his cold symptoms.

Sexist Usage

Gender-exclusive terms such as *policeman* and *chairman* are offensive to many readers today. Writers who are sensitive to their audience, therefore, avoid using such terms, replacing them with expressions such as *police officer* and *chairperson* or *chair*. Most sexist usage in language involves masculine nouns, masculine pronouns, and patronizing terms.

Masculine Nouns. Do not use *man* and its compounds generically. For many people, these words are specific to men and do not account for women as separate and equal people. Here are some examples of masculine nouns and appropriate gender-neutral substitutions:

Masculine Noun	Gender-Neutral Substitution
mailman	mail carrier
businessman	businessperson, executive, manager
fireman	firefighter
man-hours	work hours
mankind	humanity, people
manmade	manufactured, synthetic
salesman	salesperson, sales representative, sales agent
congressman	member of Congress, representative

Using gender-neutral substitutions often entails using a more specific word for a generalized term, which adds more precision to writing.

Masculine Pronouns. Avoid using the masculine pronouns *he, him*, and *his* in a generic sense when meaning both male and female. This can pose some challenges, however, because English does not have a generic singular pronoun that can be used instead. Consider the following options:

1. Eliminate the pronoun.

   Every writer has an individual style. Instead of Every writer has his own style.

2. Use plural forms.

   Writers have their own styles. Instead of A writer has his own style.

3. Use *he or she, one*, or *you* as alternates only sparingly.

   Each writer has his or her own style. Instead of Each writer has his own style.

   One has an individual writing style. Instead of He has his own individual writing style.

   You have your own writing style. Instead of A writer has his own style.

Patronizing Terms. Avoid terms that cast men or women in gender-exclusive roles or that imply that women are subordinate to men. Here are some examples of biased or stereotypical terms and their gender-neutral substitutions:

Biased/Stereotypical Term	Gender-Neutral Substitution
lady lawyer	lawyer
male nurse	nurse
career girl	professional, attorney, manager
coed	student
housewife	homemaker
stewardess	flight attendant
cleaning lady	housecleaner

Biases and Stereotypes

Biased and stereotypical language can be hurtful and can perpetuate discrimination. Most writers are sensitive to racial and ethnic biases or stereotypes but should also avoid language that shows insensitivity to age, class, religion, and sexual orientation. The accepted terms for identifying groups and group members have changed over the years and continue to change today. Avoid using terms that have fallen into disuse, such as *Indian* or *Oriental*; instead, use accepted terms such as *Native American* or *Asian*.

7 Punctuation

Learning Objectives

H7.A   Use periods, question marks, and exclamation points correctly to end sentences.

H7.B   Use semicolons correctly to connect independent clauses.

H7.C   Use commas correctly to punctuate sentences.

H7.D   Use colons correctly to punctuate sentences.

H7.E   Use dashes correctly to separate sentence elements.

H7.F   Use quotation marks correctly to set off direct quotations.

H7.G   Use parentheses, brackets, and ellipses correctly to punctuate sentences.

Punctuation is a system of signals telling readers how the parts of written discourse relate to one another. They are similar to road signs that tell the driver what to expect: A sign with an arrow curving left means that the road makes a left curve, a "stop ahead" sign means that a stop sign is imminent, a speed-limit sign indicates what the legal speed is, etc. Drivers trust that the signs mean what they say. Readers, too, expect punctuation marks to mean what they say: A period means the end of a sentence, a colon that an explanation will follow, a comma that the sentence is not finished. Punctuation is a way for writers to help readers understand their words in the intended way.

Punctuation corresponds roughly to intonations and other physical signals in speech. When you speak, you use pitch levels, pauses, hand signals, head movements, and facial expressions to make sure your audience understands you. At the end of a sentence, you unconsciously let your voice drop—not just pause, but decidedly drop in pitch. With some questions, your voice rises at the end, as in "Do you want to go?" With other questions, the pitch drops, as in "Do you want to go or not?" You can have brief pauses, or you can lengthen them to increase the drama of what you are saying. You can increase or decrease the sound (volume) of your words. None of these signals are available to writers. To make their situation even more difficult, writers do not have their audience right in front of them to look puzzled or to question them when meaning is unclear. So writers use punctuation.

Ends of sentences are punctuated with periods, question marks, or exclamation points. Semicolons function as "soft" periods, usually marking the end of independent clauses (as periods do) but not of complete thoughts. Commas show relationships within sentences, as do colons, dashes, quotation marks, parentheses, brackets, and ellipsis dots. These marks are explained in the sections that follow. Other marks—those used within words (apostrophes, hyphens, italics, and slashes)—are explained in Section 8, Mechanics and Spelling.

7A End Punctuation

A period is the normal mark for ending sentences. A question mark ends a sentence that asks a direct question, and an exclamation point ends forceful assertions.

H7.A
Use periods, question marks, and exclamation points correctly to end sentences.

Period

Sentences normally end with a period.

> Studies suggest that eating fish two or three times a week may reduce the risk of heart attack. Statement.

> Eat two or three servings of fish a week. Mild command.

> The patient asked whether eating fish would reduce the risk of heart attack. Indirect question.

Avoid inserting a period before the end of a sentence; the result will be a fragment (see 1A Fragments). Sentences can be long or short; their length does not determine their completion. Both of the following examples are complete sentences.

> Eat fish. Mild command; the subject, *you*, is understood.

> In a two-year study of 1,000 survivors of heart attack, researchers found a 29 percent reduction in mortality among those who regularly ate fish or took a fish-oil supplement. Statement; one sentence.

Question Mark

A sentence that asks a direct question ends in a question mark:

> How does decaffeinated coffee differ from regular coffee?

Do not use a question mark to end an indirect question:

> The customer asked how decaffeinated coffee differs from regular coffee.

With quoted questions, place the question mark inside the final quotation marks:

> The customer asked, "How does decaffeinated coffee differ from regular coffee?"

Exclamation Point

The exclamation point ends forceful assertions:

> Fire!
>
> Shut that door immediately!

Because they give the impression of shouting, exclamation points are rarely used in formal business and academic writing.

7B Semicolon

H7.B

Use semicolons correctly to connect independent clauses.

The main use for a semicolon is to connect two closely related independent clauses:

> Dengue hemorrhagic fever is a viral infection common to Southeast Asia; it kills about 5,000 children a year.

Sometimes the second clause contains a transitional adverb (see 1B Comma Splices):

> Dengue has existed in Asia for centuries; *however*, it grew more virulent in the 1950s.

Do not use a comma where a semicolon or period is required; the result is a comma splice (see 1B Comma Splices). In contrast, a semicolon used in place of a comma may result in a type of fragment (see 1A Fragments):

> In populations where people have been stricken by an infectious virus, survivors have antibodies in their bloodstreams; *which prevent or reduce the severity of subsequent infections*. The semicolon makes a fragment of the *which* clause.

Do not confuse the semicolon with the colon (see 7D Colon). While the semicolon connects independent clauses, a colon ordinarily does not. The semicolon is also used to separate items in a series when the items contain internal commas:

> Scientists are researching the effects of staphylococcus bacteria, which cause infections in deep wounds; influenza A virus, which causes respiratory flu; and conjunctivitis bacteria, which have at times caused fatal purpuric fever.

7C Comma

H7.C

Use commas correctly to punctuate sentences.

The comma is probably the most troublesome mark of punctuation because it has so many uses. It is a real punctuation workhorse within a sentence. Its main uses are explained here.

Compound Sentences. A comma joins two independent clauses connected with a coordinating conjunction (see 1B Comma Splices):

> Martinique is a tropical island in the West Indies, *and* it attracts flocks of tourists annually.

Do not use a comma between independent clauses without a conjunction, even if the second clause begins with a transitional adverb:

> Faulty: Martinique is a tropical island in the West Indies, it attracts flocks of tourists annually. Two independent clauses with no conjunction; it is a comma splice.

> Faulty: Martinique is a tropical island in the West Indies, consequently it attracts flocks of tourists annually. Two independent clauses with transitional adverb; it is a comma splice.

Introductory Sentence Elements. Commas set off a variety of introductory sentence elements, as illustrated here:

> *When the French colonized Martinique in 1635,* they eliminated the native Caribs. Introductory subordinate clause.

> *Choosing death over subservience,* the Caribs leaped into the sea. Introductory participial (verbal) phrase.

> *Before their death,* they warned of a "mountain of fire" on the island. Introductory prepositional phrase.

> *Subsequently,* the island's volcano erupted. Introductory transitional adverb.

Short prepositional phrases sometimes are not set off:

> *In 1658* the Caribs leaped to their death.

Sometimes, however, a comma must be used after a short prepositional phrase, so that it is not misread:

> *Before,* they had predicted retribution. Comma is required to prevent misreading.

Nonrestrictive and Parenthetical Elements. Words that interrupt the flow of a sentence are set off with commas before and after. If they come at the end of a sentence, they are set off with one comma.

In this class are nonrestrictive modifiers (see 3B Restrictive and Nonrestrictive Modifiers), transitional adverbs (see 1B Comma Splices), and a few other types of interrupters. Here are examples:

> This rugged island, *which Columbus discovered in 1502,* exports sugar and rum. Nonrestrictive *which* clause; commas before and after.

> A major part of the economy, *however,* is tourism. Interrupting transitional adverb; commas before and after.

> Tourists, *attracted to the island by its climate,* enjoy discovering its culture. Interrupting participial (verbal) phrase (see 1A Fragments); commas before and after.

> A popular tradition in Martinique is the Carnival, *which occurs just before Lent each year.* Nonrestrictive *which* clause; one comma.

> Martinique is an overseas department of France, *a status conferred in 1946.* An absolute, ending the sentence (participial phrase plus the noun it modifies).

Series

Commas separate items in a series:

Martiniquans dance to *steel drums, clarinets, empty bottles, and banjos.* Four nouns.

Dressing in colorful costumes, dancing through the streets, and thoroughly enjoying the celebration, Martiniquans celebrate Carnival with enthusiasm. Three participial (verbal) phrases.

Martinique has a population of over 300,000, its main religion is Roman Catholicism, and its languages are French and Creole. Three independent clauses.

Various sentence elements can make up a series, but the elements joined should be equivalent grammatically (see 2A Parallelism, which discusses faulty parallelism). Common practice calls for a comma before the conjunction joining the last item in the series.

Quotations

Commas set off quoted sentences from the words that introduce them:

"A wise man," says David Hume, "proportions his belief to the evidence."

According to Plato, "Writing will produce forgetfulness" in writers because "they will not need to exercise their memories." The second clause is not set off with a comma.

"X on beer casks indicates beer which paid ten shillings duty, and hence it came to mean beer of a given quality," reports *The Dictionary of Phrase and Fable.*

Quotations introduced with *that* and other connectors (such as *because* in the second sentence here) are not set off with commas. Commas at the end of quotations go inside the quotation marks.

Coordinate Adjectives

Commas separate adjectives that equally modify a noun:

The "food pyramid" was designed as a *meaningful, memorable* way to represent the ideal daily diet. Two adjectives modify equally the noun *way.*

When you're not sure about using a comma, try inserting the coordinating conjunction *and* between the two adjectives to see if they are truly coordinate (*meaningful and memorable*). Another test is to reverse the order of the adjectives (*memorable, meaningful*). Do not use a comma between adjectives that are not coordinate or between the last adjective and the noun being modified. (See also 3C Adjectives and Adverbs.)

Addresses and Dates

Use a comma to separate city and state in an address, but do not set off the zip code:

Glen Ridge, New Jersey 07028 *or* Glen Ridge, NJ 07028

In a sentence, a state name is enclosed in commas:

The letter from Glen Ridge, New Jersey, arrived by express mail.

Dates are treated similarly:

> January 5, 1886, *but* 5 January 1886
>
> The events of January 5, 1886, are no longer remembered. When other punctuation is not required, the year is followed by a comma.

Commas to Avoid

Some people mistakenly believe that commas should be used wherever they might pause in speech. A comma does mean pause, but not all pauses are marked by commas. Use a comma only when you know you need one. Avoid the following comma uses:

1. To set off restrictive sentence elements:

   > People, *who want a balanced diet*, can use the food pyramid as a guide. The restrictive *who* clause is necessary to identify *people* and should not be set off with commas.

2. To separate a subject from its verb and a preposition from its object:

   > People who want a balanced diet, can use the food pyramid as a guide. The comma following the *who* clause separates the subject, *people,* from its verb, *can use.*

   > The bottom level of the food pyramid contains food from grains, *such as*, bread, cereals, rice, and pasta. The preposition *such as* should not be followed by a comma.

3. To follow a coordinating conjunction (see 1B Comma Splices):

   > The food pyramid describes a new approach to a balanced diet. But, the meat and dairy industries opposed it. The coordinating conjunction *but* should not be set off with a comma.

4. To separate two independent clauses (see 1B Comma Splices) not joined with a coordinating conjunction:

   > The pyramid shows fewer servings of dairy and meat products, therefore, consumers would buy less of these higher-priced foods. The comma should be replaced with a semicolon (see 7B Semicolon).

5. To set off coordinate elements joined with a coordinating conjunction:

   > Vegetables and fruits are near the bottom of the pyramid, *and should be eaten several times a day*. The coordinating conjunction *and* joins a second verb, *should be eaten,* not a second independent clause; therefore, no comma is needed.

7D Colon

The colon is used most often to introduce an explanatory element, often in the form of a list:

> The space shuttle *Challenger* lifted off on January 28, 1986, with a seven-member crew: Francis R. Scobee, Michael J. Smith, Ronald E. McNair, Ellison S. Onizuka, Judith A. Resnik, Gregory B. Jarvis, and Christa McAuliffe. The list explains *crew.*

> A twelve-member investigating team discovered the cause of the disaster: a leak in one of the shuttle's two solid-fuel booster rockets. The phrase explains *the cause of the disaster.*

Do not use colons interchangeably with semicolons (see 7B Semicolon). Semicolons separate two independent clauses (see 1B Comma Splices); colons ordinarily are followed by a phrase or phrases. Also avoid using colons after verbs and prepositions (see 1A Fragments):

> The two causes of the O-ring failure were cold temperatures and design deficiencies. No colon after *were.*

> The commission investigating the disaster noted a number of failures in communication, such as one within the National Aeronautics and Space Administration. No colon after *such as.*

Colons have a few other set uses:

Time:	10:15 a.m.
Salutation in a business letter:	Dear Patricia Morton:
Biblical reference:	Genesis 2:3

7E Dash

The dash separates sentence elements with greater emphasis than a comma does:

> In *The War of the Worlds* (1898), science fiction writer H. G. Wells described an intense beam of light that destroyed objects on contact—the laser.

It is also used to set off a nonrestrictive sentence element (see 3B Restrictive and Nonrestrictive Modifiers) that might be confusing if set off with commas:

> A number of medical uses—performing eye surgery, removing tumors, and unclogging coronary arteries—make the laser more than a destructive weapon. The three explanatory items separated by commas are set off from the rest of the sentence with dashes.

Like commas that set off nonrestrictive elements within a sentence, dashes often are used in pairs—at the beginning of the interruption and at the end.

A dash is sometimes used in place of a colon when a colon might seem too formal:

> Besides its medical uses, the laser serves many other functions—reading price codes, playing compact audio disks, and sending telephone messages.

Use the dash with caution, however; overuse gives the impression that you aren't familiar with alternative means of punctuation.

7F Quotation Marks

The main use for quotation marks is to set off direct quotations:

> Professor Charlotte Johnson announced, "Interdisciplinary science is combining fields of scientific knowledge to make up new disciplines."

> "Biochemistry," she went on to say, "combines biology and chemistry."

Quotations within quotations are marked with single quotation marks:

> "The term 'interdisciplinary science' thus describes a change in how processes are investigated," she concluded.

Use quotation marks correctly with other punctuation marks. Periods and commas (see 7C Comma) always go inside the end quotation marks; colons and semicolons almost always go outside the quotation. Dashes, question marks, and exclamation points go inside or outside depending on meaning—inside if the mark applies to the quotation and outside if it applies to the surrounding sentence:

> "Do you know the various branches of the physical sciences?" asked Professor Johnson. Question mark goes inside quotation marks because it applies to the quotation.

> Did the professor say, "Histology deals with tissues and cytology with the fine structures of individual cells"? Question mark goes outside quotation marks because it applies to the surrounding sentence, not the quotation.

Do not use quotation marks to set off indirect quotations:

> The professor said that histology and cytology are different branches of study.

Another use for quotation marks is to enclose titles of works that are not published separately, including short stories, poems, and essays:

> "You Are a Man" by Richard Rodriguez

> "The Incident" by Countee Cullen

Do not enclose titles of your own essays in quotation marks when they are in title position. (See 8E Italics (Underlining) for treatment of titles of works that are published separately.)

Quotation marks are sometimes used to enclose words used in a special sense, but be careful not to abuse this function:

> The "right" way to do something is not always the best way.

See Chapter 12 for more details on using quoted material in your writing.

H7.F
Use quotation marks correctly to set off direct quotations.

7G Other Marks

Parentheses

Parentheses enclose interrupting elements, setting them off from the rest of the sentence or discourse with a greater separation than provided by other enclosing

H7.G
Use parentheses, brackets, and ellipses correctly to punctuate sentences.

marks such as commas and dashes. They usually add explanatory information that might seem digressive to the topic.

> The Particle Beam Fusion Accelerator *(PBFA II)* is a device designed to produce energy by fusion. Parentheses set off an abbreviation that will henceforth be used in place of the full term.

> The PBFA II stores up to 3.5 million joules of energy. *(One joule is the amount of energy expended by a one-watt device in one second.)* Parentheses set off an explanation framed as a complete sentence.

Parentheses are always used in pairs. They might have internal punctuation (as in the second example), but punctuation related to the sentence as a whole goes outside the parentheses. Parentheses are almost never preceded by a comma. Note the following example:

> During fusion *(joining of two atomic nuclei to form a larger nucleus)*, mass is converted to energy. Parenthetical element is followed by a comma, showing that it relates to *fusion*. If it had been preceded by a comma, it would appear, illogically, to relate to *mass*.

Brackets

Square brackets have limited uses and are not interchangeable with parentheses. Their most common use is to indicate insertions in quoted material:

> Describing the Great Depression, Frederick Lewis Allen says, "The total amount of money paid out in wages *[in 1932]* was 60 percent less than in 1929." The words *in 1932* were not part of the original text.

Some writers use brackets to enclose brief parenthetical material within parentheses:

> Jules Verne (*Journey to the Center of the Earth [1864]*) described giant apes and a vast subterranean sea at the core of the earth. The date of publication is parenthetical to the title of the book.

Ellipses

Ellipses (spaced periods) are used in quotations to indicate where words have been omitted. Three spaced periods mark omissions within a sentence. If the omission comes at the end of your sentence but not at the end of the original sentence, use four spaced periods.

> One of the legacies of the Great Depression, says Frederick Lewis Allen, is that "if individual Americans are in deep trouble,…their government [should] come to their aid." Words following a comma in the original sentence are omitted within the sentence. The brackets enclose an inserted word.

> This idea, adds Allen, "was fiercely contested for years…." Allen's sentence did not end at *years*, where the quoted sentence ends.

When using ellipses, be careful not to distort the meaning of the original by your selection of what to include and what to omit (see also Chapter 12).

8 Mechanics and Spelling

Learning Objectives

H8.A   Follow conventions for correct capitalization.

H8.B   Follow guidelines for abbreviating names, dates, and other sentence elements.

H8.C   Use apostrophes correctly to indicate possessions or contractions.

H8.D   Use hyphens correctly to divide words and form compounds.

H8.E   Use italics correctly for titles and emphasis.

H8.F   Use numbers correctly.

H8.G   Use strategies to correct common spelling errors.

Some "rules" of writing are flexible and allow choices, but this is not the case with spelling. With the invention of the printing press in the fifteenth century and the publication of dictionaries in the eighteenth century, flexibility in spelling all but vanished. Dictionaries spell almost all their words in exactly the same ways as other dictionaries do, and readers expect writers to do likewise. We have expectations about the way hyphens are used in compound words, the way apostrophes show possession or contraction, the way suffixes are added to root words, and so on. This section covers the treatment of words: capitalizing, abbreviating, punctuating (apostrophes and hyphens), italics, and spelling.

8A Capitalization

The rules for capitalization are relatively fixed. Following are examples of situations calling for capitalization.

H8.A
Follow conventions for correct capitalization.

Beginning of a sentence

In 1929, the whole credit structure of the American economy was shaken.

Proper names or nouns

With the onset of the *Great Depression, President Hoover* at first tried to organize national optimism. Historical period or event; person.

Bankers on *Wall Street*, manufacturers in *Detroit*, and legislators in *Washington* all had an effect on the economy. Place.

The Great Depression was part of a worldwide collapse, ending only with *World War II*. Historical period or event.

President Hoover set up the *Reconstruction Finance Corporation* to aid banks and businesses. Person; institution.

In 1900, most of the *African Americans* in this country lived in the *South*. Race and nationality; geographical region.

Jell-O, Pepsi, Rice Krispies Trade names.

Aunt Beatrice, Grandmother Dietz, Dad Relationships when they are part of the name; but not *my dad* and *my aunt and uncle.*

Titles

Death at an Early Age by Jonathan Kozol; *The Dancing Wu Li Masters: An Overview of the New Physics* by Gary Zukav. Capitalize first and last words, words following colons, and all other words except articles (*a, an,* and *the*) and conjunctions and prepositions of fewer than five letters (*and, but, in, by,* etc.).

Avoid capitalizing common nouns; for example:

For many people, the *winter* of 1902 was bleak. Seasons.

Many people moved *south* to a warmer climate. Compass directions.

My *great-grandparents* were among those who moved. Relationships.

Simon Waterson was a *professor of history* at the time. Titles that are not part of proper names.

8B Abbreviation

H8.B
Follow guidelines for abbreviating names, dates, and other sentence elements.

While abbreviations are part of the language, not all are acceptable in all circumstances. A general guideline is that they are less common in formal prose than in less-formal circumstances.

Titles with proper names
Dr. Paul Gordon   Paul Gordon, Ph.D.
George Grossman, Jr.

Times and dates
11:15 A.M. *or* 11:15 a.m.   53 B.C.   A.D. 371

Names of organizations and countries
NATO   CIA   NBC

Use U.S. as an adjective (*in a U.S. city*) and *United States* as a noun (*a city in the United States*).

Latin abbreviations (write out except in source citations and parenthetical comments)

etc.	and so forth (*et cetera*—applies to things)
i.e.	that is (*id est*)
e.g.	for example (*exempli gratia*)
cf.	compare (*confer*)
et al.	and others (*et alii*—applies to people)
N.B.	note well (*nota bene*)

Abbreviations to be avoided in most prose

The school board not bd. met on Tuesday, not Tues. February not Feb. 3.

William not Wm. Townsend was a guest lecturer in the economics not econ. class.

Townsend arrived from Pittsburgh, Pennsylvania, not PA or Penn. late last night. For letters and envelopes, use the U.S. Postal zip codes, such as PA for *Pennsylvania* and IL for *Illinois.* Note that both letters are capitalized and are not followed by periods.

Consult your dictionary when you have questions about specific abbreviations.

8C Apostrophe

The apostrophe has two main uses in English—to mark possessive nouns and to show contractions—plus a few specialized uses. Avoid all other uses.

H8.C Use apostrophes correctly to indicate possession or contractions.

Possessive Nouns

Ownership or connection is indicated with apostrophes:

Norton's resume is short and concise. The resume belongs to Norton.

This *week's* newsletter will be a little late. The newsletter of this week.

The *article's* title is confusing. The title of the article.

To make nouns possessive, follow one of these steps:

1. For singular nouns, add *'s* (*nature* + *'s* = *nature's; Tess* + *'s* = *Tess's*).
2. For plural nouns ending in *s*, add *'* (*strangers* + *'* = *strangers'*).
3. For plural nouns not ending in *s*, add *'s* (*men* + *'s* = *men's*).

Do not use apostrophes to make nouns plural. (See 8G Spelling.) And do not use apostrophes with possessive and relative pronouns. (See 5A Pronoun Case and the Contractions section that follows.)

For example:

The *Harris's* are in Florida. Incorrectly uses apostrophe to make the noun *Harris* plural.

The family lost *it's* home in the fire. Incorrectly uses apostrophe with the pronoun *it* to make it possessive.

Contractions

Apostrophes stand in place of omitted letters in contractions:

doesn't	does not
isn't	is not
I'd	I would
you've	you have
it's	it is *or* it has

who's	who is *or* who has
let's	let us
we'll	we will

Because contractions reflect a casual style, they are usually not acceptable in formal writing. Do not confuse the contracted *it is* (*it's*) and *who is* (*who's*) with the possessive pronouns *its* and *whose*. (See 5A Pronoun Case.)

Special Uses

Plurals of letters, numbers, and words used as terms

I am hoping to get all A's this year.

The memo had four misspelled *there*'s. See 8E Italics (Underlining), which discusses underlining words used as terms.

All the *7*'s are upside down in the 1990s catalog. The plural for years is usually formed without apostrophes.

Omitted letters or numbers

We'll never forget the summer of '*78*. Restrict to informal writing.

"Be *seein'* ya," Charlie said. Dialect in quoted speech.

8D Hyphens

H8.D
Use hyphens correctly to divide words and form compounds.

Hyphens have three main uses: to divide words at the ends of lines, to form compound words, and to connect spelled-out numbers.

Dividing Words

There are three general rules to remember when using hyphens to divide words at the ends of lines: (1) Always divide between syllables, (2) don't divide one-syllable words, and (3) don't divide words so that only two letters carry over to the second line. Consider the following examples:

After the results came back, the doctor sat me down and explained my *condi-tion*. Correctly divides a word between syllables.

While they could not cure the condition, at least they could alleviate its *symp-toms*. Correctly divides a word between syllables.

In the end, after months of waiting and mountains of legal fees, the court *ru-led* against him. Incorrectly divides the one-syllable word *ruled*.

Needless to say, when the court ruled against him, he was not *particular-ly* pleased. Incorrectly divides the word *particularly* so that only its last two letters carry over to the second line.

Forming Compound Words

Knowing when to hyphenate compound words can be tricky. This is because some compound words are written as single words (for example, *graveyard* and *postmaster*), while others are written as two separate words (for example, *place kick* and *executive secretary*). Complicating matters further, compound adjectives take hyphens when they precede nouns but not when they follow nouns. Here are some examples of the correct and incorrect uses of hyphens:

My *ex-husband* is a *pro-Communist* crackpot. Use hyphens after the prefix *ex-* and any prefix placed before a proper name, in this case, *pro-* before *Communist*. In general, though, most words formed with prefixes are written as one word; for example, *antisocial* and *multicultural*.

The *post-mortem* revealed that her *brother in law* died of natural causes. This sentence contains two hyphenation errors. First, the compound word *post-mortem* should be written as a single word, *postmortem* (see the comment on prefixes in the preceding example). Second, the compound noun *brother in law* should be hyphenated as *brother-in-law*.

Twentieth-century fiction is notable for its experimentation. **or** The fiction of the *twentieth century* is notable for its experimentation. In the first sentence, *Twentieth-century* functions as a compound adjective modifying the noun *fiction* and so requires a hyphen. In the second sentence, *twentieth century* functions as a compound noun (specifically, the object of the preposition *of*) and does not require a hyphen.

The *secretary treasurer* discouraged the group from making *highly-risky* investments. This sentence contains two hyphenation errors. First, the compound noun *secretary treasurer* requires a hyphen. Second, *-ly* adverbs such as *highly* are written as separate words when they precede adjectives such as *risky*.

Connecting Spelled-Out Numbers

Use hyphens to link compounds of spelled-out numbers and to link numbers to nouns. For example:

twenty-fifth time

nine-page letter

132-page report

six-year-old

35-year-old

Whenever you have a question about dividing words and hyphenating compound words, consult your dictionary. Dots usually indicate syllables, and hyphens indicate hyphenated compounds.

8E Italics (Underlining)

Italic type slants to the right and is used in printed material in the same way that underlining is used in handwritten or typed copy.

H8.E
Use italics correctly for titles and emphasis.

Titles of works published independently

The Atlantic Monthly (magazine)

A Farewell to Arms (book)

The Wall Street Journal (newspaper)

Desperate Housewives (television program)

Cats (play)

Ships, aircraft, spacecraft, and trains

Challenger (spacecraft)

Leasat 3 (communications satellite)

San Francisco *Zephyr* (train)

Words, letters, and numbers used as themselves

The process of heat transfer is called *conduction*.

The Latin words *et cetera* mean "and other things."

The letter *e* is the most commonly used vowel.

Many people consider *13* to be an unlucky number.

Emphasis

"I said, '*Did* you buy the tickets?' not '*Would* you buy the tickets?' "

Most people writing with computers use italics instead of underlining. If you are writing a documented paper for class, find out if your teacher approves of italics for titles.

8F Numbers

H8.F
Use numbers correctly.

Numbers can be spelled out or written as numerals. When to employ one style or the other depends on the writing context. In most academic writing in the humanities, and indeed in most writing geared for a general audience, numbers are usually spelled out as discussed next. In the sciences, however, numbers are usually written as numerals.

Unless you are asked to follow different conventions, use the following guidelines to handle numbers in your writing:

1. Spell out numbers requiring two words or fewer, and write numerals for numbers requiring three or more words. In practice, this means you will write out numbers *one* to *ninety-nine* and write numerals for *100* and above.

2. Spell out numbers that begin sentences. For long numbers, this can lead to awkward sentences. In such instances, you should consider revising the sentence to move the number away from the beginning of the sentence so it can be written in numerals.

3. Make exceptions for numbers used in certain figures and contexts. In these instances, numbers are usually written as numerals. For example, use numbers for dates and years; pages, chapters, and volumes; acts, scenes, and lines; decimals, fractions, ratios, and percentages; temperatures; addresses; statistics; and amounts of money.

Consider the following examples:

The company mailed *twenty-one* parcels yesterday.

She bought *2,200* acres of ranch land with her lottery winnings.

One hundred and fifty-two cows drowned in the flood.

The Japanese attacked Pearl Harbor on December *7, 1941*.

You will find the answer on page *87* in Chapter *5*.

The famous "To be, or not to be" soliloquy appears in act *3*, scene *1* of *Hamlet*.

The temperature reached *105°*F yesterday.

The suspect resided at *221* Dolores Street, apartment *3*B.

The winning margin was *2* to *1*.

With tax, the umbrella cost $*15.73*.

8G Spelling

One of the unfair facts of life is that the ability to spell is not equally distributed: Some people can spell easily and some can't. If you're one of the latter, you'll need to put extra time into making sure your words are spelled correctly. A spellchecker is helpful because it flags most misspelled words and suggests alternatives. If you are using this aid, however, be especially careful to look for misspelled homonyms. Rules of spelling sometimes help, though too many of them can be a hindrance. Therefore, only the most useful and dependable ones are included here.

H8.G
Use strategies to correct common spelling errors.

Doubling a Final Consonant

When adding a suffix such as *-ing* or *-ed* to a word that ends in a consonant, double the final consonant to keep the internal vowel short; for example, *permit, permitted; stop, stopped*. Double the final consonant when all three of the following are true:

1. The word ends in a consonant preceded by a vowel.

2. The word is one syllable or the stress is on the final syllable.

3. The suffix begins with a vowel.

Here are some other examples:

hop	hopped	begin	beginning
sit	sitting	prefer	preferred
put	putting	occur	occurrence
win	winner	recap	recapped

Words Containing *ie* or *ei*

The familiar rhyme about when to use *ie* or *ei* is true most of the time—enough times that it is worth remembering: *i* before *e* except after *c* when the sound is long *e*. Thus, words such as these follow the rule:

receive	believe	weight
ceiling	chief	beige
conceited	siege	eight

There are a few common exceptions: *caffeine, either, neither, seize,* and *weird.* Another common word that the rule does not address is *friend* (spelled *i* before *e*, but the sound is not long *e*).

Final *e*

To add an ending to a word that ends in a silent *e*, drop the *e* when the ending begins with a vowel:

believe + able = believable	believe + ed = believed
move + able = movable	move + ment = movement
hope + ing = hoping	hope + ful = hopeful

When the consonant preceding the final *e* is a soft *c* or *g*, the *e* is dropped only when the ending begins with *e* or *i*:

change + ing = changing	change + able = changeable
notice + ing = noticing	notice + able = noticeable
manage + er = manager	manage + ment = management
nice + er = nicer	nice + ly = nicely

Final *y*

To add an ending to a word with a final *y* preceded by a consonant, change the *y* to *i* except when the ending is *-ing*:

happy + ly = happily	study + ing = studying
apply + s = applies	apply + ing = applying
vary + ous = various	vary + ing = varying
try + ed = tried	try + ing = trying

When the final *y* is preceded by a vowel, keep the *y*:

play + ed = played	play + ful = playful
employ + ed = employed	employ + ment = employment

but

say + s = says	say + d = said
pay + ment = payment	pay + d = paid

Never change the *y* when adding an ending to a proper noun: *the Barrys.*

Plurals

Plural nouns ordinarily have an *s* ending:

    boy + s = boys   car + s = cars

Words that end in *ch, s, sh, x,* or *z* require *-es*:

    box + es = boxes   church + es = churches

Words ending in *o* are a little more troublesome. If the *o* is preceded by a vowel, add *s*:

    radio + s = radios   video + s = videos

If the *o* is preceded by a consonant, you ordinarily add *-es*:

    hero + es = heroes   potato + es = potatoes

A few common words take either *s* or *-es*:

    tornados, tornadoes   zeros, zeroes   volcanos, volcanoes

Some words form their plurals internally or do not have a plural form. Do not add an *s* to these words:

    child, children   deer, deer
    man, men   fish, fish
    mouse, mice   moose, moose

Compound words ordinarily have an *s* at the end of the compound:

    textbook, textbooks   snowshoe, snowshoes
    text edition, text editions

But when the first word of the compound is the main word, add the *s* to it:

    sisters-in-law   attorneys-general

Whenever you are in doubt about the correct plural ending, consult your dictionary.

Homonyms

Some of the most troublesome words to spell are homonyms—words that sound alike but are spelled differently. Here is a partial list of the most common ones:

    accept, except   maybe, may be
    affect, effect   of, 've (have)
    already, all ready   passed, past
    cite, sight, site   than, then
    forth, fourth   their, there, they're
    it's, its   to, too, two
    know, no   whose, who's
    lead, led   your, you're

A few other words, not exactly homonyms, are sometimes confused:

breath, breathe	lightning, lightening
choose, chose	loose, lose
clothes, cloths	precede, proceed
dominant, dominate	quiet, quite

Check your dictionary for the meanings of any sound-alike words you are unsure of.

9 Review of Basic Grammar

Learning Objectives

H9.A   Recognize the nine parts of speech.

H9.B   Identify subjects and predicates in sentences.

H9.C   Recognize objects and complements in sentences.

H9.D   Recognize the six types of phrases.

H9.E   Recognize the primary types of clauses.

H9.F   Identify the five basic sentence patterns.

H9.G   Distinguish simple, compound, complex, and compound-complex sentences.

Grammar is the set of rules used for communicating in a language. Words are the basic units of grammar, which classifies them by their functions into the *parts of speech*. In English, grammar determines the form words take and the order in which they can be combined into *phrases, clauses*, and *sentences*. Sentences, un-like phrases and clauses, must represent complete thoughts; and to do so, each must contain at least one *subject* and one *predicate*. Sentences can also include *objects* and *complements*.

9A Parts of Speech

H9.A
Recognize the
nine parts of
speech.

This section examines nine parts of speech: verbs, nouns, pronouns, adjectives, adverbs, prepositions, conjunctions, articles, and interjections. Some words can function as more than one part of speech. For example, the word "crow" can function as a noun (The *crow* stole food from our table) and a verb (The fans *crow* insults at the referee). For such words, determining the function the word plays within a sentence will help you identify the part of speech it constitutes.

Verbs
Verbs express action (She *ran* for the senate) or a state of being (I *am* sick). Through changes in *form*, verbs can indicate the following: *tense* (present, past, future, etc.); *person* (first person, second person, or third person); *number*

(singular or plural); *voice* (active or passive); and *mood* (indicative, imperative, and subjunctive). Other classifications of verbs include *linking verbs, transitive and intransitive verbs, helping verbs*, and *verbals*.

Form. Verbs have five primary forms:

Base	Present + s	Present Participle	Past	Past Participle
ask	asks	asking	asked	asked
climb	climbs	climbing	climbed	climbed
jump	jumps	jumping	jumped	jumped
move	moves	moving	moved	moved
reach	reaches	reaching	reached	reached
vanish	vanishes	vanishing	vanished	vanished
walk	walks	walking	walked	walked

The *base form* is used to indicate present-tense action in the first-person singular (*I*) and plural (*we*), the second person (*you*), and the third-person plural (*they* or a plural noun).

> We *hope* that you *drive* safely.

> The hikers *vanish* into the fog.

The *present + s form* is made by adding an *-s* or *-es* to the base form and is used only to indicate present-tense action in the third-person singular (*he, she, it*, or a singular noun).

> She *walks* up the stairs.

> The voter *reaches* for the ballot.

The *present participle form* is created by adding *-ing* to the base form. When used as a participle, this form functions as an adjective.

> The *dripping* faucet kept him up all night.

When used as a *gerund*, the form functions as a noun.

> *Dancing* was her favorite activity.

When joined with the verb *be* and helping verbs, the present participle form indicates the ongoing action of the progressive tense.

> He *is studying* at the moment. Present progressive tense.

> They *have been listening* to music. Past perfect progressive tense.

The *past form* is made by adding a *-d* or *-ed* to the base form. This form is used to indicate past action.

> The committee *waited* for our answer.

> He *moved* with the beat.

Verbs that express past action without adding a -*d* or -*ed* to the base form are known as *irregular verbs* (see the list below).

The *past participle form* is also made by adding a -*d* or -*ed* to the base form. In fact, for regular verbs, the past participle form and the past form are identical. When used as a participle, this form functions as an adjective.

The *wilted* flowers lay on the table.

When joined with the helping verbs *have* and *will*, the past participle form indicates the perfect tenses.

We *have waited* for a long time. Present perfect tense.

She *will have finished* her paper by noon. Future perfect tense.

When joined with the verb *be*, the past participle form is used to indicate *passive voice*.

The guests *were escorted* to their table.

The plan *was approved* unanimously.

Just as in the past form, irregular verbs do not add -*d* or -*ed* to make the past participle form. Irregular verbs often change internally to indicate their past and past participle forms. Common irregular verbs and their past and past participle forms include the following:

Base	Past	Past Participle
be (is, am, are)	was, were	been
come	came	come
do	did	done
drink	drank	drunk
eat	ate	eaten
give	gave	given
go	went	gone
grow	grew	grown
see	saw	seen
take	took	taken
throw	threw	thrown
write	wrote	written

Tense. A verb's tense indicates when its action occurred. The *simple tenses* are used the most frequently. They depict action in a straightforward manner in the present, past, and future.

Present	The children *kiss* their grandmother.
Past	The children *kissed* their grandmother.
Future	The children *will kiss* their grandmother.

The *perfect tenses* express action that has been completed by a specific time or action that has already been completed before another action begins.

Present Perfect	The children *have kissed* their grandmother.
Past Perfect	The children *had kissed* their grandmother.
Future Perfect	The children *will have kissed* their grandmother.

The *progressive tenses* express ongoing actions.

Present Progressive	The children *are kissing* their grandmother.
Past Progressive	The children *were kissing* their grandmother.
Future Progressive	The children *will be kissing* their grandmother.
Present Perfect Progressive	The children *have been kissing* their grandmother.
Past Perfect Progressive	The children *had been kissing* their grandmother.
Future Perfect Progressive	The children *will have been kissing* their grandmother.

Person and Number. The relationship between person and number is intertwined, so the two need to be discussed together. The subject's connection *as a speaker* to the verb is expressed through person. In the first person, the subject does the speaking (*I, we*); in the second person, the subject is spoken to (*you*); and in the third person, the subject is spoken about (*he, she, it, they*).

A verb's number can be either singular or plural and is determined by its subject. Singular verbs show the action of an individual subject (*I, you, he, she, it*), while plural verbs show the action of a collective subject (*we, you, they*). The verb form is the same for the singular and the plural in all of the tenses, with the exception of present tense in the third-person singular, which adds an *-s* or *-es* to the base form (see *present + s* form on p. 674).

	Singular	Plural
first person	*I forgive* the debt.	*We forgive* the debt.
second person	*You forgive* the debt.	(All of) *You forgive* the debt.
third person	*He (she, it) forgives* the debt.	*They forgive* the debt.

Voice. In a sentence written in the *active voice*, the subject is the doer of the verb's action. In a sentence written in the *passive voice*, the subject is not the doer of the verb's action. Instead, the doer of the verb's action is the object of a preposition or is not stated at all. Because the active voice is clearer, more direct, and less wordy than the passive voice, you should strive to write in the active voice whenever possible. Reserve use of the passive voice for instances in which you do not know or do not want to name the doer of the verb's action.

Susan lost the car keys. Active voice: Here, the subject, *Susan*, performs the action of the verb *lost*.

The car keys were lost by Susan. Passive voice: The information communicated in this example is the same as that expressed in the previous example, but now *car keys* has become the subject, and the doer of the verb's action, *Susan*, is the object of the preposition *by*.

The car keys were lost. Passive voice: Here, the subject remains *car keys*, but the doer of the verb's action is not stated.

Mood. Mood expresses the writer's attitude toward the action of the verb. There are three forms of mood: indicative, imperative, and subjunctive. Verbs in the *indicative mood* make statements, ask questions, and declare opinions. For example:

He *said* that your argument *is* wrong. Makes a statement.

Did he really *say* that? Asks a question.

He *should rethink* his objection to my argument. Declares an opinion.

Verbs in the *imperative mood* issue commands, requests, or directions. When the subject of an imperative verb is not explicitly identified, it is understood to be *you*.

Don't touch the hot plate. Issues a command.

Class, please *read* the essays tonight. Issues a request.

Turn right at the next intersection. Issues directions.

Verbs in the *subjunctive mood* communicate wishes, make statements contrary to fact, list requirements and demands, and imply skepticism or doubt. They usually appear in clauses introduced by *if, that, as if*, and *as though*. Use the base form of the verb for the present-tense subjunctive. For the past-tense subjunctive of the verb *be*, use *were* for all subjects.

He wishes that he *were* a movie star. Communicates wish.

If I *were* to live for a thousand years, think of all that I would see. Makes statement contrary to fact.

The day-care center requires that your sister *sign* a consent form and *provide* proof of immunization for her daughter. Lists requirements.

The lawyer acts as if his client *were* a saint. Implies skepticism.

Linking Verbs. Verbs that link the subject to a subject complement (see 9C Objects and Complements) are called linking verbs. These verbs commonly express states of being rather than action. Common linking verbs include *be, look, sound, taste, smell, feel, grow, appear, seem, become, remain*, and *get*.

I *am* tired.

You *look* thirsty.

Things *sound* grim over there.

She *felt* happy.

Your neighbors *seem* angry.

Helping Verbs. Some verbs require the addition of helping verbs (or auxiliary verbs) to communicate their meanings. The combination of a main verb and a helping verb forms a *verb phrase*. The most frequently used helping verbs are *be*, *do*, and *have*. These three helping verbs can also stand alone as main verbs: I *am* hungry; She *did* her chores; You *have* won. Other helping verbs, however, cannot stand alone as main verbs and can only be used in verb phrases. These helping verbs include *can, could, may, might, should, will*, and *would*. Helping verbs are often required to indicate tense, voice, and mood.

> Mr. Nguyen *will* call you tomorrow. Future tense.
>
> The students *have* completed the test. Present perfect tense.
>
> Next month I *will have been* living here for three years. Future perfect progressive tense.
>
> The report *was* delivered early. Passive voice.
>
> We *can* help you. Indicative mood.
>
> *Did* you leave the door open? Indicative mood.

Transitive and Intransitive Verbs. Transitive verbs express action at objects, which receive that action (see 9C Objects and Complements). Intransitive verbs do not express action at objects.

> She *mailed* the letter to me. Transitive: The direct object *letter* receives the action of the transitive verb *mailed*.
>
> The children *slept* peacefully. Intransitive: The verb *slept* does not express its action at an object—the adverb *peacefully* functions only to modify the verb.

Many verbs can function as both transitive and intransitive verbs.

> The athlete *ate* the roast turkey. Transitive: The direct object *roast turkey* receives the action of the transitive verb *ate*.
>
> The athlete *ate* like a pig. Intransitive: The verb *ate* does not express its action at an object—the adverbial phrase *like a pig* only modifies the verb.

Verbals. Verb forms that function as nouns, adjectives, or adverbs in sentences are known as *verbals*. There are three kinds of verbals: participles, gerunds, and infinitives. *Participles* function as adjectives. The present participle form adds *-ing* to the base form. The past participle form adds a *-d* or *-ed* to the base form of regular verbs (irregular verbs are often conjugated internally).

> The *howling* wolf startled the hunters. The present participle *howling* modifies the subject *wolf*.
>
> She threw the *chipped* vase into the trash. The past participle *chipped* modifies the direct object *vase*.

Gerunds function as nouns and use the present participle form—that is, *-ing* added to the base form of the verb.

> *Fishing* takes patience.
>
> The consequences of *drinking* and *driving* are often tragic.

Infinitives can function as nouns, adjectives, or adverbs. Infinitives begin with the word *to*, followed by the base form of the verb.

> Everyone wants *to fall in love*. The infinitive *to fall in love* acts as a direct object and so functions as a noun.

> They had nothing *to eat* today. The infinitive *to eat* modifies the noun *nothing* and so acts as an adjective.

> You must persevere *to succeed* in life. The infinitive *to succeed* modifies the verb phrase *must persevere* and so acts as an adverb.

Nouns

Nouns include people (ice skater, Malcolm X), places (playground, Grand Canyon), things (bicycle, Empire State Building), and concepts (happiness, liberty). *Common nouns* refer to people, places, things, or concepts that are representative of groups or classes (mechanics, colleges, keys, hardness). *Proper nouns* refer to specific people, places, things, or concepts (President Chirac, Tokyo, the *Titanic*, Marxism). Common nouns may be either concrete or abstract in character. *Concrete nouns* refer to things that have a tangible existence in the world (tears, lawyer, roast beef). *Abstract nouns*, on the other hand, refer to ideas and feelings that do not exist outside of our thoughts or emotions (sadness, justice, hunger). *Count nouns* can be counted and have singular (cat, cookie, bike) and plural forms (cats, cookies, bikes). *Noncount nouns* (or mass nouns) cannot be counted and do not possess plural forms (violence, copper, stability). *Collective nouns* refer to groups; although they are frequently used in the singular, they also possess plural forms (people, family, crowd, party, horde). Nouns may indicate possession by the addition of an apostrophe and *-s* to singular forms (Michael's car, cat's meow) and an apostrophe to plural forms (dancers' clothes, birds' feathers). Nouns are often preceded by articles (a, an, the) or quantifiers (one, many, some, a few, several). They may also be modified by adjectives (*black* cat), adjective phrases (keys *on the table*), or adjective clauses (car *that was stolen last night*).

Pronouns

Pronouns act as substitutes for nouns. They perform the same functions as nouns, but whereas nouns actually name people, places, things, and concepts, pronouns only stand in for nouns. The noun to which a pronoun refers is known as the pronoun's *antecedent*.

> *Mrs. Ghatta* had a nightmare while *she* slept on the couch. The subject *Mrs. Ghatta* is the antecedent of the pronoun *she*.

> While *she* slept on the couch, *Mrs. Ghatta* had a nightmare. The subject *Mrs. Ghatta* remains the antecedent of the pronoun *she* even though the pronoun now precedes the subject in the sentence.

Pronouns are classified by function into the following groups: personal, relative, interrogative, reflexive/intensive, indefinite, and demonstrative. Personal, relative, and interrogative pronouns possess subjective, objective, and possessive case forms.

Personal Pronouns. These replace nouns that name people or things and possess subjective, objective, and possessive case forms.

Subjective	Objective	Possessive
I	me	my, mine
you	you	your, yours
he	him	his
she	her	hers
it	it	its
we	us	our, ours
they	them	their, theirs

The *subjective case form* stands in for nouns that function as subjects or subject complements.

> *They* crossed the street. The pronoun *They* serves as the sentence's subject.

> The fool is *he* who turns his back on wisdom. The pronoun *he* serves as the subject complement.

The *objective case form* stands in for nouns that function as objects of verbs or prepositions.

> Ms. Lin paid *us* in cash. The pronoun *us* serves as an indirect object.

> Their grievances seemed petty to *me*. The pronoun *me* serves as an object of the preposition *to*.

The *possessive case form* shows ownership. This form can function as a possessive adjective (*my, your, his, her, its, our, their*) or as both a possessive adjective and the noun or gerund it modifies (*mine, yours, his, hers, its, ours, theirs*).

> *Your* cat ate *my* canary. The pronouns *Your* and *my* function as adjectives indicating ownership.

> *Theirs* was an unhappy fate. The pronoun *Theirs* functions as both the possessive adjective *their* and the noun *fate*.

Relative Pronouns. These pronouns introduce adjective clauses. Relative pronouns that refer to people possess subjective, objective, and possessive case forms.

Subjective	Objective	Possessive
who	whom	whose
whoever	whomever	whosever

Relative pronouns that do not refer to people (*that, what, whatever, which, whichever, whose*) do not possess subjective, objective, and possessive case forms.

> Ahmed, *who* lives next door, was promoted today. The pronoun *who* is the subject of *lives*.

> She hung up on her boyfriend, *whom* she despised. The pronoun *whom* is the object of *despised*.

We greeted our friends, *whose* home we had watched for the last two weeks. The pronoun *whose* indicates ownership.

They bought a car *that* was within their price range. The pronoun *that* indicates ownership.

Interrogative Pronouns. These pronouns take the same forms as relative pronouns, including subjective, objective, and possessive case forms when they refer to people.

Interrogative pronouns, however, do not introduce adjective clauses. Instead, they introduce questions.

Who lost the argument?

To *whom* did the prize go?

Whose car is that?

What questions did he ask you?

Whatever happened to her?

Reflexive/Intensive Pronouns. Reflexive pronouns refer to subjects or objects introduced earlier in the same clause. Their function is to show action directed by the antecedent at itself. Reflexive pronouns include *myself, yourself, himself, herself, itself, oneself, ourselves, yourselves,* and *themselves.*

She asked me how I managed to keep cutting *myself* while shaving.

Please make *yourself* at home. The unstated subject of this sentence is understood to be *you.*

We tell *ourselves* the same stories over and over again.

The campers washed *themselves* in the river.

Intensive pronouns take the same forms as reflexive pronouns but are used only to emphasize the action of the antecedent, not to show action directed by the antecedent at itself.

She fixed the flat tire by *herself.*

It is surprising the resources one finds inside *oneself.*

Indefinite Pronouns. These pronouns refer to quantities or unspecified people and things. Indefinite pronouns include *a few, a lot, all, another, any, anybody, anyone, anything, anywhere, both, each, either, enough, everybody, everyone, everything, everywhere, few, many, more, most, much, neither, nobody, none, no one, nothing, one, several, some, somebody, someone, something,* and *somewhere.*

Anybody caught shoplifting will be prosecuted.

Few have sacrificed as much as we have.

One good deed deserves *another.*

I have called *everyone* together today to say *a few* words about *something* very important.

Demonstrative Pronouns. These pronouns (*this, that, these, those*) point to antecedents in such a way as to hold them up for special scrutiny or discussion.

> *That* was a spectacular meal.
>
> I will take *these* shoes, please.

Adjectives

Adjectives modify nouns and pronouns. They answer questions such as *How many? What kind? Which?* and *Whose?*

> She bought *five jumbo-sized* platters of appetizers for *tomorrow's* party at *Ken's* house. How many platters? *Five.* What kind of platters? *Jumbo-sized.* Which party? *Tomorrow's.* Whose house? *Ken's.*

Adjectives usually precede the words they modify, but they can come after words or, as subject complements, even come after the verb.

> The ocean, *cool* and *inviting*, lapped at our feet.
>
> The movie was *boring*.

Nouns and pronouns often function as adjectives, in both their subjective case forms and their possessive forms. Indeed, a word may function as a noun in one part of a sentence and as an adjective elsewhere in the same sentence.

> *Some* children attend *summer* school; *some* do not. The word *some* functions as an adjective in its first instance and as a noun in its second instance. The word *summer*, frequently used as a noun, functions here as an adjective modifying *school.*

Adjectives have positive, comparative, and superlative forms.

> Their house is *big*. Positive form.
>
> Their house is *bigger* than mine. Comparative form.
>
> Theirs is the *biggest* house on the block. Superlative form.

Adverbs

Adverbs modify verbs, adjectives, and other adverbs. They answer questions such as *How? How often? When?* and *Where?*

> *Yesterday*, we *narrowly* won the championship game. How did we win? *Narrowly.* When did we win? *Yesterday.* Both adverbs modify verbs.
>
> Our rivals play *nearby* and had beaten us *frequently*. Where do the rivals play? *Nearby.* How often had they beaten us? *Frequently.* Both adverbs modify verbs.
>
> It was a *desperately* needed victory. The adverb *desperately* modifies the adjective *needed.*
>
> The losing team left the field *very* quietly. The adverb *very* modifies the adverb *quietly.*

Adverbs can come before or after the words they modify. Sometimes, for the sake of rhythm or emphasis, adverbs can be placed at the beginning or end of the sentence.

> The detective *slowly* opened the door.
>
> *Slowly*, the detective opened the door.
>
> The detective opened the door *slowly*.

Adverbs, like adjectives, have positive, comparative, and superlative forms. For adverbs that end in *-ly*, the comparative adds the word *more* to the positive form, while the superlative adds the word *most*.

> She sings *beautifully*. Positive form.
>
> She sings *more beautifully* than I do. Comparative form.
>
> She sings *most beautifully* of us all. Superlative form.

Prepositions

Prepositions introduce *prepositional phrases* and show the relationship (place, destination, possession, time, cause, movement, purpose, etc.) between the *object of the preposition*, which is always a noun or pronoun, and another word or group of words. Common prepositions include *about, above, after, around, at, before, behind, below, beneath, between, beyond, by, down, for, from, in, inside, into, like, of, off, on, onto, out, over, past, since, through, to, toward, under, until, up, with*, and *without*.

> The police car parked *in* our driveway. Place.
>
> The protestors marched *toward* city hall. Destination.
>
> This is the home *of* a World War II veteran. Possession.
>
> We will arrive *at* 8:00 p.m. Time.
>
> The water is dripping *from* the leak. Cause.
>
> She walked *into* the theater. Movement.
>
> The students studied *for* the final exam. Purpose.

Conjunctions

Conjunctions link one or more words, phrases, or clauses within a sentence. There are three types of conjunctions: coordinating, subordinating, and correlative.

Coordinating Conjunctions. These conjunctions join parallel words, phrases, and clauses (see 2A Parallelism). Coordinating conjunctions include *and, but, for, nor, or, so*, and *yet*.

> The pitcher *and* the hitter confronted each other.
>
> She wanted to go to the beach, *but* she had to stay home instead.
>
> You can have orange juice *or* lemonade.

Subordinating Conjunctions. These conjunctions introduce subordinate (dependent) clauses. Subordinating conjunctions include *after, although, as, because, before, even if, even though, if, once, since, so, so that, than, that, unless, until, when, whenever, where, whereas, wherever, whether*, and *while*.

> *After* she won the race, Robin celebrated with her family and friends.
>
> We will not leave *until* Jim returns.
>
> I was on the phone *when* the earthquake struck.

Correlative Conjunctions. Like coordinating conjunctions, correlative conjunctions join parallel words, phrases, and clauses. Correlative conjunctions, however, occur only in pairs. They include *both...and, either...or, just as...so, neither...nor, not only...but also*, and *whether...or*.

> She wanted *both* to have a career *and* to start a family.
>
> We will visit *either* the museum *or* the park this afternoon.

Articles

Articles introduce nouns. The word *the* is a *definite article* and it introduces nouns whose specific character is known (*The* cat walked down *the* path). The words *a* and *an* are *indefinite articles* and they introduce nouns whose specific character is not known (*A* cat walked down *a* path). *A* precedes words that begin with consonants; *an* precedes words that begin with vowels or a silent *h* (*an* hour).

Interjections

Interjections are words that express strong feelings, alarm, or surprise. They are common in speech and may be used in personal or informal writing, but are generally inappropriate for formal and academic writing. When they do appear in writing, they typically stand alone as fragments. Common interjections include *boo, cool, oh, oh no, ouch, shhh, uh-oh, wow, yea*, and *yikes*. Profanity is often used as an interjection, particularly in speech, but it is considered offensive in most academic and professional settings.

9B Subjects and Predicates

The *subject* of a sentence is its main topic. The subject is always a noun, pronoun, noun phrase, or noun clause. The *predicate* makes a statement or asks a question about the subject. The predicate must always contain a verb, but it can also contain adjectives, adverbs, nouns, pronouns, and other words.

H9.B
Identify subjects and predicates in sentences.

Subjects

The simple subject is the noun or pronoun that represents the sentence's main topic. It is usually a single word, although proper nouns can run to two or more words (*General George Washington*). The complete subject contains the simple subject and any words or phrases that modify it.

Subject	Predicate
He	slept.
The man	had terrible nightmares that night.
The wearied, defeated prime minister	tossed fitfully in his bed.

Most of us at dinner that evening got sick the next day. The pronoun *Most* is the sentence's simple subject, and *Most of us at dinner that evening* is the complete subject.

Compound subjects are two or more parallel nouns or pronouns linked by commas and coordinating conjunctions or correlative conjunctions.

Mishal, Zanab, and Amir swam out to the sailboat.

Playing to win and playing fair are not mutually exclusive concepts.

Neither you nor I will win the lottery.

Predicates

The simple predicate is the sentence's main verb. The complete predicate contains the simple predicate and any words or phrases that modify it.

The strikers *picketed outside the factory's main gate despite the wind and rain*. The verb *picketed* is the sentence's simple predicate; the simple predicate and all of the words that follow it represent the complete predicate.

Compound predicates represent two or more main verbs linked by commas and coordinating conjunctions or correlative conjunctions.

We *laughed, ate, and drank* our way through the evening.

He *tiptoed* to the door *and pressed* his ear up against its cold, hard wood.

That afternoon she *not only aced* the exam, *but* she *also submitted* her final paper to her instructor.

9C Objects and Complements

H9.C
Recognize objects and complements in sentences.

Objects are nouns or pronouns that appear within a sentence's predicate and complete its meaning. *Complements* are nouns or adjectives that rename or describe the sentence's subject or direct object.

Objects

There are three types of objects: direct objects, indirect objects, and objects of prepositions.

Direct Objects. These are nouns or pronouns that accept the action of *transitive verbs* (see 9A Parts of Speech). Direct objects answer questions such as *What?* or *Whom?* about their verbs.

She kissed *her children* good night. Kissed whom? *Her children.*

He wrote *the essay* on sustainable growth. Wrote what? *The essay.*

The teacher gave *them* to us. Gave what? *Them.*

Indirect Objects. These are nouns or pronouns for which the action of the transitive verb is performed. Indirect objects answer questions such as *For what? To what? For whom?* or *To whom?* about their verbs. Because indirect objects never appear without direct objects, one way to avoid confusing the two is to identify the direct object (DO) first and then identify the indirect object (IO).

> We mailed *them* the invitations. Mailed what? The invitations (DO). To whom? *Them* (IO).

> The county clerk issued *Michael and Caitlin* a marriage license. Issued what? A marriage license (DO). To whom? *Michael and Caitlin* (IO).

> Her father gave *their union* his blessing. Gave what? His blessing (DO). To what? *Their union* (IO).

Objects of Prepositions. These are nouns or pronouns that complete the meaning of *prepositional phrases* (see 9A Parts of Speech). When they appear in sentences with direct objects, objects of prepositions convey the same meaning as indirect objects. Objects of prepositions, however, can also appear in sentences that do not contain direct objects.

> We mailed the invitations to *them*.

> I left the keys in *the ignition*.

> For *the older couple*, the hike would be long and hard.

Complements

There are two types of complements: subject complements and object complements.

Subject Complements. These are nouns or adjectives that follow a *linking verb* (see 9A Parts of Speech) and rename or describe the subject. Subject complements that are nouns rename their subjects, and those that are adjectives describe their subjects.

> Margaret is *a lawyer*. The subject complement *a lawyer* is a noun.

> My grandfather is *ill*. The subject complement *ill* is an adjective.

Object Complements. These are nouns or adjectives that rename or describe the direct object. Object complements that are nouns rename their direct objects, and those that are adjectives describe their direct objects.

> The panel voted Sagiko *the winner*. The object complement *the winner* is a noun.

> Many people consider travel *pleasurable*. The object complement *pleasurable* is an adjective.

9D Phrases

A *phrase* is a group of related words that lack a subject or a predicate or both. A phrase, then, can never express a complete thought as a sentence and independent clause can. Phrases modify words, groups of words, or the entire sentence.

H9.D
Recognize the six types of phrases.

There are six types of phrases: prepositional phrases, participial phrases, gerund phrases, absolute phrases, infinitive phrases, and appositive phrases.

Prepositional Phrases

Prepositional phrases begin with a *preposition* (see 9A Parts of Speech) and contain a noun or pronoun and its modifiers, if any. Prepositional phrases act as adjectives and adverbs.

> The neighbors *across the street* own a speedboat. The prepositional phrase functions as an adjective modifying the noun *neighbors.*

> The satellite burned up *in the upper atmosphere.* The prepositional phrase functions as an adverb modifying the verb *burned up.*

Participial Phrases

Participial phrases contain *present* or *past participles* (see 9A Parts of Speech) and their modifiers or complements. Participial phrases act as adjectives.

> The man *arrested yesterday* was an industrial spy. The participial phrase modifies the noun *man.*

> The dancers *demonstrating the tango right now* are my friends. The participial phrase modifies the noun *dancers.*

Gerund Phrases

Gerund phrases contain *gerunds* (see 9A Parts of Speech) and their modifiers, objects, and complements. Gerund phrases function as nouns and therefore can serve as a subject, direct object, object of the preposition, object complement, and subject complement.

> *Dating over the Internet* has become popular. The gerund phrase serves as the subject.

> The children love *playing computer games.* The gerund phrase serves as the direct object.

> He was exhausted from *running under the hot sun.* The gerund phrase serves as the object of the preposition.

> We wished them luck *climbing the mountain.* The gerund phrase serves as an object complement.

> Her favorite pastime is *knitting wool sweaters.* The gerund phrase serves as the subject complement.

Absolute Phrases

Absolute phrases contain a noun or pronoun, a present or past participle, and any modifiers. Absolute phrases modify an entire sentence, not just one word or group of words within a sentence. Whether they appear at the beginning, middle, or end of a sentence, absolute phrases are always set off with a comma.

> *Its whistle blowing,* the ferry pulled away from the dock.

> The patient, *his body convulsed with fever,* slipped into unconsciousness.

> He stepped on the gas, *his heart racing with adrenaline.*

Infinitive Phrases

Infinitive phrases contain *infinitives* (see 9A Parts of Speech) and their modifiers, objects, or complements. Infinitive phrases function as adjectives, adverbs, and nouns.

He wanted his son *to help him fix the leak.* The infinitive phrase modifies the noun *son* and so acts as an adjective.

She studied *to pass the exam.* The infinitive phrase modifies the verb *studied* and so acts as an adverb.

Before I made a decision, I needed *to think things over thoroughly.* The infinitive phrase acts as a direct object and so functions as a noun.

Appositive Phrases

Appositive phrases are nouns and their modifiers that rename the nouns or pronouns that immediately precede them. They are often set off with commas.

My neighbor, *a doctor,* is a very kind woman.

He has an engineering degree from CalTech, *one of the most prestigious universities in the country.*

9E Clauses

A clause is a group of words containing both a subject and a predicate. An *independent clause* can function on its own as a sentence.

A *subordinate clause* (dependent clause) cannot function on its own as a sentence and must be linked to an independent clause by a subordinating conjunction or relative pronoun. There are three types of subordinate clauses: adjective clauses, adverb clauses, and noun clauses.

H9.E
Recognize the primary types of clauses.

Adjective Clauses

Adjective clauses modify nouns or pronouns in an independent clause or in another subordinate clause. Adjective clauses begin with *relative pronouns* (see 9A Parts of Speech) such as *who, whom, whose, which*, and *that*.

The doctor *who delivered our baby* is from India.

She wrote a letter *that explained how she felt*.

Adverb Clauses

Adverb clauses usually modify verbs in an independent clause or in another subordinate clause, but on occasion they may also modify adjectives and adverbs. Adverb clauses begin with *subordinating conjunctions* (see 9A Parts of Speech) such as *after, although, as, because, before, if, since, so, than, that, unless, until, when, where*, and *while*.

After the movie was over, we strolled through the mall.

They planned to travel the world *until they ran out of money*.

She left the party *when her ex-boyfriend* arrived.

Noun Clauses

Noun clauses serve as a subject, object, or complement. They can begin with relative pronouns or subordinating conjunctions.

Where the ship sank no one knows. The noun clause serves as the subject.

She asked him *when he would be leaving*. The noun clause serves as the direct object.

I will not run from *what is coming*. The noun clause serves as the object of the preposition.

Their complaint was *that the contract had not been fulfilled*. The noun clause serves as the subject complement.

9F Basic Sentence Patterns

H9.F

Identify the five basic sentence patterns.

A sentence must contain a subject and a predicate. The complexity of predicates, however, means that sentences can follow one of five basic patterns:

Subject + Intransitive verb

Subject + Transitive verb + Direct object

Subject + Linking verb + Subject complement

Subject + Transitive verb + Indirect object + Direct object

Subject + Transitive verb + Direct object + Object complement

These five patterns form the foundation on which all sentences in the English language are constructed. The following examples show only the simplest uses of these patterns. Because all of the elements that make up these patterns can be modified by other words, phrases, and clauses, these sentence patterns can assume much more complicated forms in everyday writing.

Subject	Predicate
She	wept.
The woman who lives next door	personally delivered the letter to me today.

Subject	Intransitive verb
We	won.

Subject	Transitive verb	Direct object
Our team	defeated	our rivals.

Subject	Linking verb	Subject complement
My teammates	were	ecstatic.

Subject	Transitive verb	Indirect object	Direct object
They	gave	us	the trophy.

Subject	Transitive verb	Direct object	Object complement
Our coach	declared	the game	a milestone.

9G Types of Sentences

Sentences are also classified by the way in which they use *clauses* (see 9E Clauses), into four categories: simple sentences, compound sentences, complex sentences, and compound-complex sentences.

H9.G
Distinguish simple, compound, complex, and compound-complex sentences.

Simple Sentences

A simple sentence is made up of one *independent clause*. The independent clause may contain compound *subjects*, compound *predicates*, and modifying *phrases*, but must not be linked with other clauses.

> Some professional athletes are poor role models for children. Single subject and single predicate.

> Some professional athletes and movie stars are poor role models for children. Compound subject and single predicate.

> Some professional athletes lack social responsibility and are poor role models for children. Single subject and compound predicate.

> Some professional athletes, *their interests focused exclusively on themselves*, lack social responsibility. Single subject, with modifying phrase (in italics) and single predicate.

Compound Sentences

A compound sentence is made up of two or more independent clauses (IC) linked by a semicolon or a comma and a *coordinating conjunction*. Each clause may contain compound subjects, compound predicates, and modifying phrases, but must not be linked with a subordinate clause.

> John was uneasy, but he didn't believe in werewolves. The two independent clauses are linked by a comma and the coordinating conjunction *but*.

> He checked the lock and stood motionless; there was someone or something growling on the other side of the door. The two independent clauses are linked with a semicolon.

Complex Sentences

A complex sentence is made up of one independent clause (IC) and one or more *subordinate clauses* (SC). Both the independent and subordinate clause(s) may contain compound subjects, compound predicates, and modifying phrases. Subordinate clauses always begin with *subordinating conjunctions* or *relative pronouns* (see 9A Parts of Speech).

> The lawyer laughed when my wife told the joke. The subordinate clause begins with the subordinating conjunction *when*.

> I reluctantly shook the hand of the lawyer who was representing my wife in the divorce. The subordinate clause begins with the relative pronoun *who*.

Compound-Complex Sentences

A compound-complex sentence contains two or more independent clauses (IC) and at least one subordinate clause (SC). The independent clauses must be linked by a semicolon or a comma and a coordinating conjunction. Each clause may contain compound subjects, compound predicates, and modifying phrases.

> They won't believe me until they see you, for you have completely changed. The first independent clause and its subordinate clause are linked to the second independent clause with a comma and the coordinating conjunction *for*.

10 Tips for ESL Writers

Learning Objectives

H10.A Use definite and indefinite articles correctly.

H10.B Recognize and correct common verb challenges for ESL writers.

H10.C Use conventional placement and word order for adjectives and adverbs.

H10.D Use prepositions properly to show relationships of place and time.

H10.E Correct common errors with participles.

Many non-native writers of English find it challenging to master the language's complicated grammatical rules. This section offers advice in traditional problem areas for writers of English as a second language (ESL).

10A Articles

H10.A

Use definite and indefinite articles correctly.

Articles introduce nouns, but the rules for determining how they do so are complex. *The* is the *definite article* that introduces nouns whose specific character is known (*The* cat), while *a* and *an* are *indefinite articles* that introduce nouns whose specific character is not known (*A* cat). To use definite and indefinite articles correctly, however, you also need to know whether the noun under consideration is a *count noun*, a *noncount noun*, or a *proper noun*.

Count Nouns

Count nouns can be counted and have singular forms (*cat, cookie, bike*) and plural forms (*cats, cookies, bikes*). Singular count nouns whose specific character is not known take the indefinite articles *a* and *an*; those whose specific character is known take the definite article *the*. Plural count nouns whose specific character is not known—that is, nouns that are referred to in general—do not take articles. Plural count nouns whose specific character is known take the definite article *the*.

> *An aardvark* turned up in my backyard. Singular count noun of unknown specific character—use the appropriate indefinite article *a* or *an*.

The aardvark befriended us. Singular count noun of known specific character—use the definite article *the*.

Aardvarks are interesting animals. Plural count noun of unknown specific character—do not use an article.

The aardvarks moved to our neighbor's backyard. Plural count noun of known specific character—use the definite article *the*.

Noncount Nouns

Noncount nouns (or mass nouns) cannot be counted and do not possess plural forms (*violence, copper, stability*). Noncount nouns whose specific character is not known—that is, nouns that are referred to in general—do not take articles. Noncount nouns whose specific character is known take the definite article *the*.

Peace is universally valued around the world. Noncount noun of unknown specific character—do not use an article.

The peace held while the negotiations dragged on. Noncount noun of known specific character—use the definite article *the*.

Proper Nouns

Proper nouns refer to specific people, places, things, or concepts (President Chirac, Tokyo, the *Titanic*, Marxism). Singular proper nouns generally do not take definite articles, with the exception of the following: noun phrases (*the* Man in the Moon); geographic features (*the* Himalayas); architectural landmarks (*the* Brooklyn Bridge); titles of ships, aircraft, spacecraft, and vehicles (*the Challenger*); titles of political and religious institutions (*the* Senate, *the* Episcopalian Church); titles of political and religious leaders (*the* prime minister, *the* pope); titles of documents (*the* Emancipation Proclamation); and titles of periods and events (*the* Middle Ages, *the* Great Depression). Plural proper nouns take definite articles, with the exception of the titles of companies (General Mills).

President Obama spoke at the commencement. The singular proper noun *President Obama* does not take a definite article.

The president spoke at the commencement. The singular common noun *president* is the title of a political leader and so does take a definite article.

The De Beers are a very wealthy family. The plural proper noun *De Beers* takes a definite article.

De Beers is a very wealthy company. The plural proper noun *De Beers* is the title of a company and so does not take a definite article.

10B Verbs

H10.B

The common verb errors and the basic functions and forms of verbs are discussed elsewhere in this Handbook (see 4 Verbs and 9A Parts of Speech). Challenging areas for ESL writers can include the helping verbs *be, do*, and *have*; modal auxiliaries; phrasal verbs; and gerunds and infinitives.

Recognize and correct common verb challenges for ESL writers.

Helping Verbs *be*, *do*, and *have*

Helping verbs (or auxiliary verbs) join with main verbs to create verb phrases. The most frequently used helping verbs are *be*, *do*, and *have*, which can also stand alone as main verbs. How to use these three helping verbs with main verbs can sometimes be confusing.

The Helping Verb *be*. Use the present forms of *be* (*am, is, are*) with the present participle (base form + *-ing*) to make the present progressive tense. Use the past forms of *be* (*was, were*) with the present participle to make the past progressive tense. The other progressive tenses require the addition of the helping verbs *have* and *will* (see the following examples) along with the forms of *be* and the present participle.

> She *is working* at the moment. Present progressive.
>
> I *was calling* overseas when the doorbell rang. Past progressive.
>
> They *will be sailing* tomorrow. Future progressive.
>
> Larry *has been sulking* since last night. Present perfect progressive.
>
> We *had been skiing* for three hours when your brother showed up. Past perfect progressive.
>
> You *will have been barbecuing* chicken all day long before the party is over. Future perfect progressive.

Use the present forms of *be* (*am, is, are*) with the past participle (base form + *-ed*) to create the present tense in the passive voice. Other tenses in the passive voice require the addition of the helping verbs *will* and *have* along with the forms of *be* and the past participle.

> The car *is stopped* at the light.
>
> In some countries, the local elections *have been rigged* for many years.

The Helping Verb *do*. Use forms of *do* (*do, does, did*) with the base form of the verb to create a verb phrase. Use verb phrases of this sort to add emphasis or to restate a claim that provokes doubt or disbelief. Add the modal auxiliary *not* to make negative claims.

> We *do believe* in the judicial system.
>
> She *does drive* carefully.
>
> I *did mail* the letter to you.
>
> He *does not know* the answer.

The Helping Verb *have*. Use the present forms of *have* (*have, has*) with the past participle (base form + *-ed*) to make the present perfect tense. Use the past forms of *have* (*had*) with the past participle to make the past perfect tense. The future perfect tense requires the addition of the helping verb *will* along with the present form of *have* and the past participle.

> She *has purchased* a new car. Present perfect.
>
> We *had vacationed* at the Grand Canyon before we went to Monument Valley. Past perfect.
>
> They *will have painted* the house by this evening. Future perfect.

Modal Auxiliaries

Modal auxiliaries are helping verbs that cannot stand alone as main verbs. Joined with a main verb, modals express ability, intention, necessity, permission, possibility, or prohibition. Modals include *can, cannot, could, have to, may, might, must, must not, not, should,* and *would*. These modals do not change form, regardless of the main verb's tense or whether the main verb is singular or plural. They have only one form. When joining modals with main verbs, use the base form of the main verb immediately after the modal. Never use more than one modal with one main verb.

We *can* reach the stars if we try. Expresses ability.

We *cannot* get there tomorrow. Expresses prohibition.

I *have* to wash the dishes. Expresses necessity.

I *might* even clean out the refrigerator. Expresses possibility.

You *should* forget the past. Expresses advisability.

You *would* have a great time in Italy. Expresses probability.

Phrasal Verbs

A phrasal verb is an idiomatic verb phrase that contains a verb and one or two prepositions or adverbs. The meaning of the two- or three-word phrasal verb generally cannot be understood by combining the literal meanings of its words. For example, the phrasal verb *turn down* does not mean "to turn downward" but rather "to reject or refuse." Common phrasal verbs include the following:

act up	run into
break down	stay up
call on	step in
catch on	take off
cut in	throw away
figure out	turn down
hang on	turn on
look into	walk out on
look out for	watch out for

Phrasal verbs are informal and often are inappropriate for academic and professional writing. If you do choose to use them in your writing, be sure you understand their correct meanings.

Gerunds and Infinitives

Gerunds function as nouns and use the present participle form (base form + *-ing*). Infinitives usually function as nouns but can also function as adjectives or adverbs. They begin with the word *to* followed by the base form of the verb. Gerunds and infinitives that follow after main verbs function as objects.

Keep the following guidelines in mind when using gerunds and infinitives with main verbs.

1. **Verbs that do not change meaning whether followed by gerunds or infinitives:**

attempt	like
begin	love
can't stand	omit
continue	prefer
hate	start

   In the following examples, the meaning of the verb *hated* and the gerund *losing* is the same as that of the verb *hated* and the infinitive *to lose*.

   > We hated *losing* the game.

   > We hated *to lose* the game.

2. **Verbs that change meaning when followed by gerunds or infinitives:**

forget	stop
remember	try

   In the following examples, notice how the meaning of the first sentence differs from that of the second.

   > I forgot *practicing* the piano yesterday. Forgot while *practicing* yesterday.

   > I forgot *to practice* the piano yesterday. Forgot actually *to practice* yesterday.

3. **Verbs that can precede gerunds but not infinitives:**

admit	keep
appreciate	miss
avoid	postpone
cannot help	practice
consider	put off
delay	quit
deny	recall
discuss	resist
enjoy	risk
finish	suggest
imagine	tolerate

   In the following examples, the gerund in the first sentence is correct and the infinitive in the second sentence represents an error.

   > She enjoys *painting* watercolors. Gerunds may be used after the verb *enjoy*.

   > She enjoys *to paint* watercolors. Infinitives may not be used after the verb *enjoy*.

4. **Verbs that can precede infinitives but not gerunds:**

agree	mean
ask	need
beg	offer
choose	plan
claim	pretend
decide	promise
expect	refuse
fail	venture
have	wait
hope	want
manage	wish

In the following examples, the infinitive in the first sentence is correct and the gerund in the second sentence represents an error.

> They decided *to climb* the mountain. Infinitive may be used after the verb *decided*.

> They decided *climbing* the mountain. Gerund may not be used after the verb *decided*.

10C Adjectives and Adverbs

The correct use of adjectives and adverbs can present challenges for all writers; however, for ESL writers in particular, the placement and word order of these modifiers can be troublesome.

H10.C
Use conventional placement and word order for adjectives and adverbs.

Adjectives

Adjectives modify nouns and pronouns (see 9A Parts of Speech). Other words such as articles and pronouns can also act as adjectives and modify nouns and pronouns. When using multiple adjectives to modify one or more words in the sentence, use the word order listed here:

1. **Article, pronoun, and possessive noun:** *a, an, the, his, my, our, your, a lot, many, some, that, their, those, Steve's, the neighbor's*, etc.

2. **Adjectives indicating number or order:** *one, two, three, one hundred, one thousand, first, second, third, last, final*, etc.

3. **Adjectives indicating judgment, opinion, or evaluation:** *awful, astonishing, beautiful, excellent, evil, good, faithful, ugly, wicked*, etc.

4. **Adjectives indicating size:** *big, diminutive, giant, large, little, long, massive, minuscule, short*, etc.

5. **Adjectives indicating shape:** *boxy, circular, loose, rectangular, round, snug, square, tight, triangular, wide*, etc.

6. **Adjectives indicating condition:** *broken, damaged, fixed, functional, operating, repaired, reconditioned, running, undamaged, whole, working*, etc.

7. **Adjectives indicating age:** *aged, ancient, antique, fresh, immature, mature, new, old, young,* etc.

8. **Adjectives indicating color:** *black, blue, green, mauve, orange, purple, violet, white, yellow,* etc.

9. **Adjectives indicating nationality, ethnicity, and religion:** *African American, Anglo, Arabic, Armenian, Brazilian, Canadian, Chinese, Kenyan, Latin American, Mandarin, Buddhist, Catholic, Hindu, Presbyterian,* etc.

10. **Adjectives indicating material:** *aluminum, birch, copper, cotton, gold, iron, oak, metal, pine, plastic, platinum, polyester, silk, steel, wood,* etc.

11. **Nouns used as adjectives:** *bird* (brain), *dog* (house), *car* (park), *floor* (mat), *mosquito* (net), etc.

12. **The noun being modified.** Examples:

    His last undamaged birch-bark canoe sank yesterday.

    She found *some beautiful little green turquoise* beads at the flea market.

    My grandmother gave *that antique black Chinese silk* dress to my sister as a birthday gift.

Adverbs

Adverbs modify verbs, adjectives, and other adverbs (see 9A Parts of Speech). Adverbs can come before or after the words they modify. Sometimes, for the sake of rhythm or emphasis, adverbs can be placed at the beginning or end of the sentence. Although there is considerable flexibility in where you can place most adverbs, there are also some limitations. Use the following guidelines:

1. **Place adverbs indicating the author's or speaker's *perspective* at the front of the sentence:**

   Thankfully, I had recovered from the flu by then.

   Unfortunately, we won't be able to make your party tonight.

2. **Place adverbs indicating *order* at the front or end of the sentence:**

   First, we will consider the results of our fund-raising efforts.

   Proposals for overhauling the department will be discussed *last.*

3. **Place adverbs indicating *manner* immediately before the words they modify or at the end of the sentence:**

   They *softly* entered the room.

   She answered my questions *sheepishly.*

4. **Place adverbs indicating *time* immediately after any adverbs indicating *manner* or *place* or, if none exist, at the front or end of the sentence:**

   The earth shook *ferociously here yesterday.*

   Tomorrow, I am leaving for California.

   He writes reports *slowly.*

10D Prepositions

Prepositions introduce *prepositional phrases* and show the relationship (place, destination, possession, time, cause, movement, purpose, etc.) between the *object of the preposition*, which is always a noun or pronoun, and another word or group of words. The prepositions used to show place and time can be troublesome for non-native speakers of English.

H10.D
Use prepositions properly to show relationships of place and time.

Place

The prepositions showing place include *in, on*, and *at*. Use the preposition *in* to refer to an established physical, geographic, or political space (*in* the garage, *in* Egypt). Use the preposition *on* as a synonym for *on top of* (*on* the coffee table, *on* the roof) and to indicate location on mass transportation, streets, book pages, building floors, and land (*on* the bus, *on* 114th Street, *on* page 177, *on* the eleventh floor, *on* the field). Use the preposition *at* to refer to specific locations, general locations, and addresses (*at* the Museum of Modern Art, *at* my mother's house, *at* the beach, *at* 23349 Westwood Boulevard).

> The Band-Aids are *in* the medicine box.
>
> Her apartment is *on* the fourth floor.
>
> You are welcome to stay *at* my house.

Time

The prepositions showing time also include *in, on*, and *at*. Use the preposition *in* to refer to general time of day (except *noon* and *night*), months, seasons, and years (*in* the afternoon, *in* December, *in* spring, *in* 1983). Use the preposition *on* to refer to days of the week and dates (*on* Friday, *on* the 28th, *on* July 4, 1776). Use the preposition *at* to refer to specific time of day and with *night* (*at* 1:15, *at* noon, *at* night).

> I will see her *in* the evening.
>
> We will see them *on* Friday.
>
> He will see you *at* noon.

10E Participles

Present participles (base form of the verb + *-ing*) and *past participles* (base form of the verb + *-d* or *-ed*) can both function as adjectives in sentences. Their meanings are different, however, and they cannot be used interchangeably. In particular, participles that describe feelings and mental states can sometimes be troublesome for ESL writers. These participles include the following:

H10.E
Correct common errors with participles.

amazing/amazed	fascinating/fascinated
annoying/annoyed	frightening/frightened
boring/bored	interesting/interested

confusing/confused   pleasing/pleased
depressing/depressed   satisfying/satisfied
disappointing/disappointed surprising/surprised
exciting/excited   terrifying/terrified
exhausting/exhausted   tiring/tired

To avoid errors with these participles and others, use only present participles to describe nouns and pronouns that *cause* a feeling or mental state. Similarly, use only past participles to describe nouns and pronouns that *experience* a feeling or mental state.

The lecture was *fascinating*. The noun being modified, *lecture*, causes the mental state, so the present participle *fascinating* is required.

We were *fascinated* by the lecture. The pronoun being modified, *We*, experiences the mental state, so the past participle *fascinated* is required.

The news is filled with *depressing* events. The noun being modified, *events*, causes the mental state, so the present participle *depressing* is required.

Julia was *depressed* by events in the news. The noun being modified, *Julia*, experiences the mental state, so the past participle *depressed* is required.

Credits

Text

Chapter 1
Olivas, Bernice, "Bernice's Journal." Reprinted by permission of the author.

Chapter 2
Ballenger, Bruce, The Curious Writer, 5th Ed., Pearson Education, Inc., 2016.

Chapter 3
Zazulak, Laura, "Every Morning for Five Years." Reprinted by permission of the author.

Blanford, Virginia, "My Turn: The Dog That Made Us a Family," Newsweek, March 16 © 2009 IBT Media. All rights reserved. Used by permission and protected by the Copyright Laws of the United States. The printing, copying, redistribution, or retransmission of this Content without express written permission is prohibited.

Stewart, Amanda, "Learning a Sense of Place." Reprinted by permission of the author.

Marlin, Seth, "Smoke of Empire." Reprinted by permission of the author.

Chapter 4
Ballenger, Bruce, The Curious Writer, 5th Ed., Pearson Education, Inc., 2016.

Frazier, Ian, "Passengers," The New Yorker, September 12, 2011, (c) Conde Nast. Reprinted with permission.

Pang, Amelia, "This is New York: Jafari Sampson, a Violin Prodigy Inspired by Silences", Epoch Times, Jan 11, 2014. Reprinted with permission.

The Veterans History Project, "Flash Profile: Dan Akee," Library of Congress.

Fisher, Michela, "Number 6 Orchid". Reprinted by permission of the author.

Chapter 5
Ebert, Roger, "A Christmas Story." © 2000 The Ebert Company. Dist. By UNIVERSAL UCLICK. Reprinted with permission. All rights reserved.

Holstead, Carol, "The Benefits of No-Tech Note Taking," The Chronicle of Higher Education, March 4, 2015. Used with permission of The Chronicle of Higher Education Copyright© 2015. All rights reserved.

Schiesel, Seth: "Grand Theft Auto Takes on New York," The New York Times, April 28 © 2008 The New York Times. All rights reserved. Used by permission and protected by the Copyright Laws of the United States. The printing, copying, redistribution, or retransmission of this Content without express written permission is prohibited.

Burns, Laura, "Recipe for a Great Film: Unlikeable People, Poor Choices, and Little Redemption." Reprinted by permission of Becca Ballenger.

Burns, Laura, "How to Not Feel Good and Feel Good About It: A Review of Young Adult." Reprinted by permission of Becca Ballenger.

Chapter 6
Bissinger, Buzz, "Why College Football Should Be Banned," The Wall Street Journal, May 8, 2012. Reprinted with permission of the author.

Chapter 7

Chapter 8

Chapter 9

Chapter 10

Kang, M., Jones, K. (2007). "Why Do People Get Tattoos?" *Contexts* Vol. 6(1) pp. 42-47 Copyright © 2007 by American Sociological Association. Reprinted by permission of SAGE Publications, Inc.

Horne, Jenn, et al: "Tattoos and Piercings: Attitudes, Behaviors, and Interpretations of College Students," College Student Journal, 41(4), 2007. Republished with permission of Project Innovation, Inc. Publishers of College Student Journal.

Burns, Laura, "The Unreal Dream: True Crime in the Justice System." Reprinted with permission of the author.

Chapter 13
Orlando, Ryan, "Students on Re-genre."

Wingrove, Kirsten, "Students on Re-genre."

Weatherby, Taylor, "Students on Re-genre."

Oyarzabal, Andrea. "Andrea's Script."

Chapter 14
de Palma, Paul, "http://www.when_is_enough_enough?.com.," The American Scholar, Winter 1992, pp. 61-72.

Photo

Chapter 1
Zurijeta/Shutterstock

Richard Sharrocks/Alamy

Chapter 2
Balazs Kovacs Images/Shutterstock

Chapter 3
Elzbieta Sekowska/Shutterstock

Neufeld, Josh, "A Matter of Perspective," Unexpected World of Nature #3 (Thirteen/WNET, 2008). Copyright © 2008 Josh Neufeld

Lupien, Craig, Doll "Mable". Reprinted with permission.

Rebecca Benedict

Rottenman/Fotolia

Chapter 4
Almgren/Shutterstock

Jim Newberry/Alamy

Samira Bouaou/Epoch Times

Jon Freeman/REX/Newscom

Chapter 5
Christian Bertrand/Shutterstock

Dorthea Lange/Library of Congress (5 images)

Tatsuya Ishida, "One Shade of Grey: A Feminist Fantasy." Reprinted by permission of Tatsuya Ishida.

Everett Collection

Everett Collection

Stephen Trupp/Starmaxinc.com/AP Images

Chapter 6
Atm2003/Shutterstock

Used with the permission of the San Francisco Bicycle Coalition: sfbike.org (6 images)

Chapter 7

Rena Schild/Shutterstock

Joe Heller/PoliticalCartoons.com

Photo B.D.V./Corbis

Chapter 8

Rob Hyrons/Fotolia

James Steidl/Fotolia

Gift of Walter and Naomi Rosenblum/Brooklyn Museum

Motoko Ishii, "Last Flowers." Reprinted with permission of the artist.

Used by permission of Olga Mezhibovskaya

Boise State University

Boise State University

Chapter 9

Kamira/Shutterstock

McNely, Brian, Gestwicki, Paul, Gelms, Bridget, and Ann Burke. "Spaces and Surfaces of Invention: A Visual Ethnography of Game Development." Enculturation: A Journal of Rhetoric, Writing, and Culture 15. 28 Feb. 2013. Web. 29 March 2015

O'Connell, Eric: "Cowboy Squaredance." Used by permission of Eric O'Connell Photography.

Chapter 10

Vasilyev Alexandr/Shutterstock

Mike Faille, Jake Edmiston, Alex Jivov/NATIONAL POST

Chapter 11

WDG Photo/Shutterstock

Robert Bull

Brian Jackson/Fotolia

Tim/Fotolia

Xuejun li/Fotolia

Chapter 12

Veronika Mannova/Shutterstock

Chapter 13

Nicholas Pitt/Getty Images

Juice Images/Corbis

This infographic was created and provided by NextAdvisor.com

Bruce Ballenger

Chapter 14

Peter Souza/White House Photo Office

Steven Russell Smith Photos/Shutterstock

DelMonaco/Shutterstock

Rafael Ben-Ari/Fotolia

Inquiring into the Details icon. Frederick Bass/Getty Images

One Student's Response icon. Purestock/Getty Images

Writing Beyond the Classroom icon. Fuse/Getty Images

Index

A

Abbreviations, 620–621

Absolute phrases, 642

Abstracts
APA-style for, 455–457, 469
MLA-style for, 451

Abstracts in Anthropology (database), 324

Abstracts of Folklore Studies (database), 324

Academic discourse
features of, 58–60
inquiry-based reading and, 57–60

Academic journals, 397

Academic Literacies: The Public and Private Discourse of University Students (Chiseri-Strater), 303

Academic reading. *See* Reading, inquiry-based approach

Academic writing. *See also* Research essays
analytical essays, 260–266
arguments, 214–216
ethnographic essays, 299–302
personal essay, 64–68
profiles, 101–102
proposals, 178–181
public argument essay vs., 213
reviews, 140–143
revision strategies for structure of, 535–542

Active/passive voice, 549, 597–598, 631–632

Ad hominem argument, 227

Adjective clauses, 643

Adjectives, 594–595, 637

Adobe Photoshop, 507

Adverb clauses, 643

Adverbs, 594–595, 637–638

Advertising
analytical essays and, 270–272
brand logos, 278–279
rhetorical analysis of, 51–52

After-words summary, 56

Akee, Dan, 125–126

"All About That Hate" (Johnson-Waskow), 286–288

"All About That Hate: A Critical Analysis of 'All About That Bass'" (Johnson-Waskow), 293–296

all-at-once-ness, 6

Alphabetization
of References pages, APA-style, 462
of Works Cited, MLA-style, 441

al Qaeda, 232–234

Ambiguity, 523

American Anthropological Association (website), 318

American Fact Finder (website), 248

American Psychological Association (APA), 425, 455. *See also* APA documentation style

Analysis, methods of, 273–274

Analytical essays, 259–297
academic writing and, 260–266
advertising analysis, 270–272
choosing subjects, 281–286
drafts for, 289–293
evaluation of, 288
examples of, 267–269, 274–279, 293–296
features of, 264
literary analysis of poetry, 267–269
literary devices, 283–284
methods of analysis, 273–274
motives for writing, 260, 264
questions for, 280, 291
research strategies, 282
sketch writing, 286–288
student essays, 293–296
writing process and, 280–293
writing to interpret, 259–260

Analytical frame of mind (Fraser and Davidson), 260–261

Anecdotal evidence, 370

Anecdotes, as leads, 539

Angle, in reading visual text, 50

"Anna as Reader: Intimacy and Response" (Chiseri-Strater), 303–306

Annotated bibliographies, 569–575
combination of types, 570
content of, 572
evaluative, 570
examples of, 572–575
indicative, 569
informative, 569–570
length of, 571
reading strategies, 571
research strategies, 570–571
writing process for, 570–572

Annotated List of Works Cited, 440

Announcements, 539

Antecedents and pronouns, 603–605, 634

Anthropological Index Online (website), 324

APA documentation style, 455–472.
See also References pages, APA-style
abstracts, 455–457
anonymous authors, 460
appendices, 458
authors' names, 459–461
body of paper, 457–458
e-mail communications, 461–462
examples of, 329–339
format/layout, 455
institutional authors, 461
interviews, 461–462
language and style, 459
multiple sources in citation, 461
multiple works by author, 460–461
new editions of older works, 462
notes, 458–459
online sources, 462
tables/charts/illustrations, 459
title pages, 455–456

Apostrophes
contractions, 621–622
possessive nouns, 621
special uses, 622

Appeal to authority fallacy, 227

Appeal to popularity fallacy, 228

Appendices
    annotated bibliographies, 569–575
    APA-style for, 458
    portfolios, 562–568
    writer's workshops, 552–561
Apple Inc., 270–272
Appleman, Jenna
    "Avoidable Accidents: How
        to Make Reality TV Safer,"
        207–209
    "Loving and Hating Reality TV,"
        199–200
Appositive phrases, 643
Argument as therapy (Rogers),
    225–226
Argument essays, 211–258
    academic writing and, 214–216
    choosing subjects, 237–242
    claims and, 219–222
    classical (*ethos/pathos/logos*),
        222–223
    definition of, 216–219
    drafts for, 249–253
    logical fallacies, 227–228
    motives for writing, 212–214
    multiple sides to, 217
    persuasion in, 211–212
    questions for, 237, 252
    research strategies, 240,
        248–249
    rhetorical design for, 249
    Rogerian approach, 224–227
    sketch writing, 244–246
    stakeholder analysis, 218–219
    student essays, 229–232
    Toulmin's approach, 223–224
    writing for your readers,
        246–248
    writing process and, 237–253
Aristotle, rhetorical triangle of,
    222–223
Armstrong, Myrna, et al.,
    "Motivation for Contemporary
    Tattoo Removal," 350–351
Arrangement, in reading visual
    text, 50
Articles, in sentences, 639
Artifacts, 323
Artwork, 453–454. *See also*
    Photographs
Assumptions as warrants, 533
Audacity (software), 94, 122, 124,
    390, 499, 500

Audience
    for analytical essays, 286
    for argument essays, 222–223,
        241–242
    for ethnographic essays, 316–317
    for personal essays, 82
    for profiles, 119
    for proposals, 196–197
    for research essays, 361, 362
    for review essays, 158
    in rhetorical choices, 12–15
    for surveys, 406
Audio files, Library of Congress, 115
Authors
    APA-style for, 459–461, 463
    authoritative and cited, 397
    MLA-style for, 430–434, 439
    research on, 289
"Avoidable Accidents: How to Make
    Reality TV Safer" (Appleman),
    207–209

B

Background information, 531–532,
    539
Backing, in argument, 223–224
Backstory, in argument, 246–247
"Bad" writing, 9–10, 16–17, 53–55
Baker, Russell, "Little Red Riding
    Hood Revisited," 542–543,
    546–547
Ballenger, Bruce
    "The Importance of Writing
        Badly," 53–55
    "Museum Missionary," 104–107,
        128, 129, 131
Begging the question fallacy, 228
Beliefs
    in ability to learn to write well, 7
    about reading, 40–42
    about writing development, 3–7
    identifying, 3–4
    journal prompts for, 4
    unlearning unhelpful, 6
Believing, as reading perspective, 45
Believing/doubting technique,
    527–528
Benedict, Rebecca, Normandy battle
    (photo essay), 74–75, 498
"The Benefits of No-Tech Note
    Taking" (Holstead),
    147–150, 167

Berthoff, Ann E., 6
"Beyond Gaydar" (Harter), 328,
    329–339
Biases/stereotypes, in language, 610
Bibliographies
    annotated, 569–575
    research strategies and, 533
    working type of, 398
Billboards, in academic discourse,
    58–59
Bishop, Bryan, "Why Won't You
    Die?! The Art of the Jump
    Scare," 274–278
Bissinger, Buzz, "Why College
    Football Should Be Banned,"
    182–184
Blanford, Ginny, "The Dog That
    Made Us a Family," 71–74,
    83, 89
Blogs, 213, 395, 453, 477–478
Boise State University, brand logo,
    278–279
Books
    APA-style for, 466–469
    library searches for, 394
    online, 467
    reviews of, 469
    Works Cited, MLA-style, 442–446
Boole, George, 388
Boolean searches, 388–389
Boynton, Abby, 99–100
Brackets, 618
Brainstorming
    for profile titles, 128
    rules for, 10
Brand logos, 278–279
Brinkman, Bart, "On 'The Shield
    That Came Back'," 268–269
Brochures, 493–494
"From Bullets to Bottles: The Two
    Wars of Dan Akee," 125–126
Burke, Kenneth, 532–533
Burns, Laura
    "How to Not Feel Good and Feel
        Good About It, A Review of
        Young Adult," 171–173
    "Recipe for a Great Film:
        Unlikeable People,
        Poor Choices, and Little
        Redemption," 163–164
    "The 'Unreal Dream': True Crime
        in the Justice System,"
        374–380

C

Capitalization, 619–620
Case studies
    blog to podcast re-genre, 532
    MLA-style for, 452
    revision strategies and, 532
Catalist (website), 248
Categorical thinking, 65–66
Causal claims, in argument, 219,
    234–236
Cause and effect method, 250, 522
Census Bureau, U.S. (website),
    248, 315
Characters, 283
Charts
    APA-style for, 459
    MLA-style for, 438
Chiseri-Strater, Elizabeth
    *Academic Literacies: The Public
    and Private Discourse of
    University Students*, 303
    "Anna as Reader: Intimacy and
    Response," 303–306
Choppiness, revision strategies
    and, 550
A Christmas Story, film review
    (Ebert), 144–147
Chronicle of Higher Education,
    39, 404
Chronological narrative, 89, 90, 534
CIA World Factbook (website), 248
Citations, 424–428. *See also* APA
    documentation style; MLA
    documentation style
Claim questions, 29
Claims
    in argument essays, 223–224, 533
    qualifying of during revision,
    529–530
    types of, 219–222
Clarity and style, 542–551. *See also*
    Revision strategies
    actors/action, 548–549
    choppiness, 550
    important sentences, 543–544, 546
    improving style, 549–551
    problems with, 517–518
    removing clichés, 550–551
    removing clutter, 546–548
    untangling paragraphs, 544–546
Classical argument essays, 222–223
Clauses, 643–644

Clichés, revision strategies and,
    550–551
Clustering
    examples of, 79–80, 81
    as invention strategy, 23
Clutter, revision strategies and, 581
"CO₂ Paper Pie Chart" (Muresan),
    181
Cohen, Daniel, 213–214
Colons, 616
Color
    in evaluation of sketches, 86
    in reading visual text, 50
"Colorado Will Show Why
    Legalizing Marijuana is a
    Mistake" (Sabet), 234–236
Commas, 612–615
    addresses and dates, 614–615
    compound sentences, 612–613
    coordinate adjectives, 614
    introductory sentence
    elements, 613
    nonrestrictive and parenthetical
    elements, 613
    quotations, 614
    series of, 614
    when to avoid, 615
Comma splices, in sentences,
    582–585
Commercial ethnography, 313
Common knowledge exception, 429
Comparison and contrast
    in analytical essays, 290
    in ethnographic essays, 326
    as leads, 539
    in review essays, 167
    as revision strategy, 522–523
Complements. *See* Objects and
    complements
Complex sentences, 645
Compound-complex sentences, 646
Compound sentences, 645
Conference posters, 494–496
Conjunctions, in sentences,
    638–639
Connecting, as reading
    perspective, 45
Conniff, Richard, "Why Did God
    Make Flies?," 418–419, 423,
    543–544
Content analysis, 273
Contrast. *See* Comparison and
    contrast

Conversing, as invention
    strategy, 23
Coordinate elements, in sentences,
    588–589
Copying, levels of, 426
Counterargument, 531
Crank, film review excerpt, 170
Creative Commons, 509–510
Creative thinking, 24–28
Critical analysis, 274
Critical thinking, 24–28, 260–261
Culture, 298–299. *See also*
    Ethnographic essays
Cut-and-paste revision, 540–541

D

Damm, Benjamin, "No Space for
    Bikes," 191–192, 496–497
Dangling/misplaced modifiers, in
    sentences, 592–593
Dashes, 616–617
Databases. *See also specific
    databases*
    APA-style for, 463
    Boolean searches in, 388–389
    ethnographic, 324
    full-text articles in, 397
    MLA-style for, 446–448
    periodical and newspaper,
    394–395
Davidson, Chad, 260–261
Deep revision, 481–484, 513
Definitional claims, in argument,
    220, 232–234
Demonstrative pronouns, 637
Development methods
    for analytical essays, 289–290
    for argument essays, 249–250
    for ethnographic essays,
    325–326
    for personal essays, 88–89
    for profiles, 129
    for proposals, 203
    for research essays, 368–369
    for review essays, 167
    for revisions to structure, 541
Dialectical thinking
    asking "so what?," 27–28
    inquiry questions, 28–29
    observation in, 27
    writing process and, 24–28
Dialogue, 539

Dialogue journals. *See* Journals, writing
Digital Object Identifier (DOI), 463, 464
Digital profiles, 121–122. *See also* Profiles
Digital recorders, 121–122
Dillard, Annie, 91
Discourse communities, 57
Discover (magazine), 299
Discussion groups (Internet), 248, 402, 405, 472
Disney, 505
Dispositions. *See* Habits of mind
Divorcing the draft, 514–516
Documentation styles. *See* APA documentation style; MLA documentation style
Dogpile.com, 392
"The Dog That Made Us a Family" (Blanford), 71–74, 83, 89
Domain names, 400
Dominant meaning, 524
Double-entry journal writing, 49–56, 412–413
Doubting, as reading perspective, 45
Douridas, Chris, 543
Drafts. *See also* Revision strategies
  for analytical essays, 289–293
  for argument essays, 249–253
  for ethnographic essays, 325–329
  for personal essays, 86–94
  for profiles, 129–133
  for proposals, 201–207
  for research essays, 366–373
  for review essays, 167–171
  tools for re-genre of writing, 504–509
Drama of coming to know, 65
DVD content, 453

E

"Earning a Sense of Place" (Stewart), 84–85, 87
Eber, Roger, film review of *A Christmas Story*, 144–147
Editing, 513
Editorials
  MLA-style for, 450
  in public argument, 213
EHRAF Collection of Ethnography (database), 324
Either/or fallacy, 228

Elbow, Peter, 527–528, 540–541
Ellipsis points, 439, 618
E-mail communications, 403–406, 461–462, 472
Encyclopedia of Associations, 402
Encyclopedias. *See also specific encyclopedias*
  APA-style for, 469
  MLA-style for, 439, 445
  working knowledge and, 392, 394
End-weighted vs. front-weighted essays, 71, 88, 525
ESL writers, tips for, 646–654
  adjectives, 651–652
  adverbs, 652
  articles, 646
  count nouns, 646–647
  noncount nouns, 647
  participles, 653–654
  prepositions, 653
  proper nouns, 647
  verbs, 647–651
Essai (personal essay), 64
Ethical issues
  in ethnography, 318
  in field work, 411
  plagiarism, 424–428, 438
  in re-genre of writing, 509–510
Ethnographic databases, 324
Ethnographic essays, 298–340
  academic writing and, 299–302
  choosing subjects, 312–317
  drafts for, 325–329
  ethical issues in, 318
  examples of, 303–310, 329–339
  features of, 300–302
  field notes, 318, 319–320, 322
  motives for writing, 299, 300–301
  questions for, 300, 311, 317, 327
  research strategies, 314–315, 323–325
  sketch writing, 321–322
  student essays, 328
  writing about culture, 298–299
  writing process and, 311–329
Ethnography, 299
Evaluated portfolios, 563–564
Evaluation. *See also* Review essays
  of analytical essays, 288
  of library sources, 397–398
  of personal essays, 86–87
  of profiles, 118–119
  as reading question, 38, 40

Events, profiles of participants of, 119
"Every Morning for Five Years" (Zazulak), 69–71, 76, 89
Evidence
  in analytical essays, 290
  in argument essays, 220–222, 223–224, 250–251
  credibility levels of, 370
  in ethnographic essays, 326
  multiple usages of, 251
  in personal essays, 89
  in profiles, 129–130
  in proposals, 203–204
  in research essays, 370–371
  in review essays, 160–161, 168
Exclamation points, 612
Experiences
  in personal essays, 62–64
  writing structure and, 534
Experimental evidence, 370
Expert testimony evidence, 370
Explanation, as reading question, 38, 40
Explicit meaning, 523
Explode a moment technique, 88, 530–531
Exploration, as reading question, 38–39

F

Factual claims, in argument, 219, 229–230
Faculty directories, 402
Fair use doctrine, 509
Fake scholarship, 398–400
Fallacies, 227–228
False analogy fallacy, 227–228
False cause fallacy, 228
Familiar, making it strange, 8
Fastwriting. *See also specific exercises*
  after-words summary, 56
  for analytical essays, 282
  for argument essays, 239–240
  brainstorming details for, 10–11
  in double-entry journal writing, 49–50
  for ethnographic essays, 314
  as invention strategy, 23
  in loop writing, 525–526
  for personal essays, 78–79, 82–83, 87

for profiles, 116–117
for proposals, 195
for research essays, 357–358
for review essays, 156, 159
rules for, 4
Field notes, 318, 319–320, 322,
    411–412
"Field Notes on Friday Afternoon
    at Emerald Lanes" (Guerra),
    319–320
Fieldwork, 410–412
Fifty Shades of Grey, cartoon review
    of (Ishida), 143
Film analysis, 274–278
Films
    APA-style for, 470
    as ethnographic essay, 300, 302
    MLA-style for online sources, 453
    as visual ethnography, 322–323
Fisher, Michaela, "Number 6
    Orchard," 133–136
Flash profile, Veterans History
    Project, 125–126
Flexible writing process, 22
Focused knowledge, in research,
    391, 393–397
Focusing questions, 521–522
Formal/informal language, 608
Fort, Keith, 482
Fragments of sentences. *See*
    Sentence boundaries
Framing, in reading visual text, 50
Frankenstein Drafts, 132, 540–541
Fraser, Gregory, 260–261
Frazier, Ian, "Passengers," 107–109
Frey, James, *A Million Little
    Pieces*, 483
Full-text articles, 397
Fused sentences, 585–586

G

Gallup Poll (website), 315
Gender-exclusive language, 609–610
Genre analysis, 274–278
Genre/medium. *See also* Re-genre of
    writing
    definition of, 480
    form vs., 476
    motive statements for, 519
    as reading frame, 43–46
    research techniques for, 289
    in rhetorical choices, 12–15
    unfamiliar, 37

"German Cowboys" (O'Connell), 310
Gerund phrases, 642
Godwin, Gail, 9
Google (search engine), 160
Google Directory (website), 315
Google Groups, 248, 402
Google Image Search (website), 249
Google Scholar (website), 359, 360,
    387–388, 392, 533
Google search engine, 385–389, 392
Government documents
    APA-style for, 470
    for local interest topics, 202
    MLA-style for, 446
    online resources for, 395
Grammar, teaching of, 6
Grammar review, 628–646. *See also
    specific parts of speech*
    clauses, 643–644
    objects and complements,
        640–641
    parts of speech, 628–639
    phrases, 641–643
    sentence patterns, 644–645
    sentences, types of, 645–646
    subjects and predicates, 639–640
"Grand Theft Auto Takes on New
    York" (Schiesel), 150–154
Group members, profiles of, 119
Guerra, Rita, "Field Notes on Friday
    Afternoon at Emerald Lanes,"
    319–320

H

Habits of mind, 7–12
    familiar, making it strange, 8
    questions vs. answers, 7–8
    surprise, 9–12
    suspension of judgment, 8–9, 25
    willingness to write badly, 9–10,
        16–17, 53–55
Handbook guidelines, 576–654
    grammar review, 628–646
    mechanics of writing, 619–625
    modification of sentences,
        591–595
    pronouns, 601–606
    punctuation, 610–618
    sentence guidelines, 578–586
    sentence inconsistencies,
        586–591
    spelling, 625–628
    style, 606–610

tips for ESL writers, 646–654
    verbs, 595–601
Harter, Kersti, "Beyond Gaydar,"
    328, 329–339
Hasty generalization fallacy, 227
Hedges, in academic discourse, 59
Hines, Lewis, 262, 263
Holstead, Carol E., "The Benefits
    of No-Tech Note Taking,"
    147–150, 167
Homonyms, 627–628
Horne, Jenn, et al., "Tattoos and
    Piercings: Attitudes, Behaviors,
    and Interpretations of College
    Students," 353–354
Howarth, William, 121
"How to Not Feel Good and Feel
    Good About It, A Review
    of *Young Adult*" (Burns),
    171–173
Hunting and gathering, as reading
    perspective, 45
Hyphens
    connecting spelled-out numbers,
        623
    dividing words, 622
    forming compound words,
        622–623
Hypothesis questions, 29

I

Ideas, generation of, 16–17, 23. *See
    also* Subjects
Images. *See* Photo essays;
    Photographs
Images, evocation of, 284
Imagetexts, as argument, 221
Imperative mood, and verbs, 598
Implicit meaning, 523
"The Importance of Writing Badly"
    (Ballenger), 53–55
"An Inconvenient Truth" (Gore), 213
Indefinite pronouns. *See* Pronouns
Indicative mood, and verbs, 598
Infinitive phrases, 643
Infographics
    "CO$_2$ Paper Pie Chart"
        (Muresan), 181
    re-genre of writing and, 490–493
    "The Selfie Syndrome," 346
    social media use among teens/
        adults, 491
    "Tattoo," 348

Infoplease (website), 248
Information, revision strategies and, 530–533
  background, 531–532, 539
  case studies and profiles, 532
  counterargument, 531
  definitions, 532
  explode a moment technique, 530–531
  problems with, 517
  research strategies, 532–533
  significance of topic, 532
  warrants for, 533
Inquiry-based approach, 1–35. *See also* Writing
  asking "so what?," 27–28
  beliefs about writing, 3–7
  habits of mind, 7–12
  literacy narrative collage, 16–17
  motives for writing, 2–3
  nature of writing process, 21–29
  problem solving in writing process, 20–21
  questions for, 27–29
  reflection on writing process, 15–20
  rhetorical choices, 12–15
  self-evaluation survey, 17–20
  strategies for, 30–34
Insight, generation of, 26
Intellectual property, 425
Interjections, in sentences, 639
Internal critics, 4, 5, 9, 10, 24
International Bibliography of Social Sciences (database), 324
Internet. *See also* Websites
  APA-style for online sources, 461–462, 464–469, 471–472
  boolean searches, 388–389
  controlled language searches, 389
  databases online, 394–395
  discussion groups, 248, 402, 405
  domain names, 400
  essays on, 76
  imagetexts on, 221
  keyword searches, 385–387, 389
  language logic in, 386–387
  MLA-style for online sources, 436, 451–454
  public argument writing on, 213
  as research tool, 160, 197–198, 243, 315, 384–387
  surveys on, 409

Interpretation questions, 29
Interpreting, as reading perspective, 45
Interrogative pronouns, 636
Interviews
  APA-style for, 461–462, 470
  for argument essays, 243, 248
  arranging for, 402
  conducting, 403–404
  e-mail communications, 403–406
  for ethnographic essays, 323
  of experts for proposals, 202
  Internet subjects for, 248
  listening and watching, 124–125
  MLA-style for, 434, 451–452
  note taking, 124, 403–404
  online, 405–406
  open-ended questions, 123, 407, 408
  for profiles, 120–125
  recording of, 121–122, 124, 404
  structured questions, 407
  writing process and, 404–405
Invention strategies
  journal prompts for, 5
  literacy narrative collage, 16–17
  in personal essays, 65
  types of, 23
  writing badly and, 9
"Is College Worth It?" (Leonhardt), 229–232
Ishida, Tatsuya, cartoon review of *Fifty Shades of Grey*, 143
Ishii, Motoko, "Last Flowers," 265–266
Italics and underlining, 623–624
iTunesU, 396

J

Jensen, Robin, 221
Jersey Shore (tv show), 299
Johnson-Waskow, Hailie
  "All About That Hate," 286–288
  "All About That Hate: A Critical Analysis of 'All About That Bass'," 293–296
Jones, Katherine, "Why Do People Get Tattoos?," 351–352
Journals (periodicals)
  APA-style for, 464–466
  MLA-style for, 449
Journals, writing
  dialogue, 50–56

double-entry, 49–56, 412–413
  purpose of, 5
  as revision strategy, 516
Judgments
  making of, 25
  suspension of, 8–9, 25

K

Kang, Miliann, "Why Do People Get Tattoos?," 351–352
Keck, Casey, 426
Keyword searches, Internet, 385–387, 389
Kitchen knives of thought. *See* "Wh" questions
Known to unknown structure
  in profiles, 129
  in research essays, 369–370
Kress, Gunther, 50

L

Lange, Dorothea, "Migrant Mother," 140–141, 510
Language
  in analytical essays, 264
  in ethnographic essays, 301
  formal/informal language, 608
  gender-exclusive, 609–610
  in personal essays, 67
  in proposals, 180
  in research essays, 345
  in writing profiles, 102
  in writing review essays, 143
Language and style
  APA-style for, 459
  MLA-style for, 439–440
"The Language of War Is Killing" (Mohammed), 228, 232–234
"Last Flowers" wall art (Ishii), 265–266
Leads, 128, 538–540, 543–544
Lectures, 454
Leeuwen, Theo van, 50
Leonhardt, David, "Is College Worth It?," 229–232
Letters to the editor
  APA-style for, 470
  MLA-style for, 450
  as public argument, 213
  as research tool, 240
Libraries
  book searches, 394

ethnographic databases, 324
evaluation of sources in, 397–398
research in, 243, 248, 393–397
Library of Congress, 389, 394, 510
Library of Congress Subject
        Headings (LCSH), 389, 394
"The Life of a Violin Prodigy from
        South Bronx" (A. Pang),
        109–113
Light, in reading visual text, 50
Limited choice survey questions, 408
Listing, as invention strategy, 23
Listing prompts
    for analytical essays, 281
    for argument essays, 238–239
    for ethnographic essays, 312–314
    for personal essays, 78
    for profiles, 116
    for proposals, 194
    for research essays, 357
    for review essays, 156
Literacy narrative collage, 16–17
Literary analysis, 267–269
Literary devices, 283–284
"Little Red Riding Hood Revisited"
        (Baker), 542–543, 546–547
Logical fallacies, 227–228
Logical structures, 534
Loop writing, 525–526
"Loving and Hating Reality TV"
        (Appleman), 199–200

M

Magazines. *See* Periodicals and
        newspapers
Making judgments, 25
Mamma.com, 392
Mapping. *See* Clustering
Maps, 323
Margins and spacing, MLA-style
        for, 437
Marlin, Seth, "Smoke of Empire,"
        94–96
Masculine nouns and pronouns, 609
"A Matter of Perspective" (Neufeld),
        67–68
McPhee, John, 116, 120, 121–122,
        516, 534, 538
Meaning, 523–530
    believing/doubting technique,
        527–528
    problems with, 517
    qualifying claims, 529–530

questions for, 524, 528–529
reclaiming topics, 526–527
theories, 524
thesis and, 524, 525–530
Mechanics of writing, 619–625. *See
    also specific conventions*
abbreviations, 620–621
apostrophes, 621–622
capitalization, 619–620
hyphens, 622–623
italics and underlining,
        623–624
numbers, 624–625
Metasearch engines, 395, 396
Microsoft Photo Story
        (software), 122
Microsoft PowerPoint (software),
        198, 213, 488
Microsoft Publisher (software), 507
"Migrant Mother" (Lange),
        140–141, 510
Miller, Carolyn, 480
A Million Little Pieces (Frey), 483
Mills, David, 104, 128, 129, 131
Mixed sentences, 589–590
MLA documentation style, 429–455.
        See also Works Cited,
        MLA-style
abstracts, 451
anonymous authors, 432–433
authors' names, 430–434, 439
citing sources, 430–436
common knowledge
        exception, 429
ellipsis points, 439
format/layout, 436–440
language and style, 439–440
location of citation, 430–431
margins and spacing, 437
multiple sources in single
        citation, 434–435
multiple works by author,
        433–434
one source quoting another, 434
online sources, 436, 451–454
pagination, 438
parenthetical citations, 431–432,
        435–436
personal interviews, 434
quotations, 440
tables/charts/illustrations, 438
title pages, 437–438
titles of works, 438–439

variations on, 435–436
Works Cited page, 440–441
*MLA Handbook for Writers of
    Research Papers*, 429, 439
Mock-ups, 505, 507–508
Modern Language Association
        (MLA), 425. *See also* MLA
        documentation style
Modification of sentences, 591–595
adjectives and adverbs, 594–595,
        637–638
dangling/misplaced modifiers,
        592–593
restrictive/nonrestrictive
        modifiers, 593–594
Mohammed, Khalid Sheikh, "The
        Language of War is Killing,"
        228, 232–234
Momaday, N. Scott, "The Shield That
        Came Back," 267–268
Montaigne, Michel de, 64, 97
Mood, and verbs, 598, 632
Moss, Kate, imagetext of, 221
"Motivation for Contemporary
        Tattoo Removal" (Armstrong
        et al.), 350–351
Motives
    for inquiry-based writing, 2–3
    for reading, 37–40
    revision statements of, 519
    revision strategies and, 512–514
    for writing analytical
        essays, 260, 264
    for writing argument, 212–214
    for writing ethnographic essays,
        299, 300–301
    for writing personal essays, 64, 66
    for writing profiles, 100–101, 102
    for writing proposals,
        177–178, 179
    for writing research essays,
        343, 345
    for writing review essays,
        139–140, 142
Motive statements for genres, 519
Mount Desert Oceanarium, 104, 129
MP3 players, 122
Multimedia. *See* Re-genre of writing;
        specific types
Multimodal expression. *See* Re-genre
        of writing
Multivolume works, 435
Muresan, Alexandra, "CO_2 Paper Pie
        Chart," 181

Murrow, Edward R., 76
"Museum Missionary" (Ballenger), 104–107, 128, 129, 131
Musical recordings, APA-style for, 471
"My Freshman Year: Worldliness and Worldview" (Nathan), 306–310

N

Names. *See* Authors; Domain names
Nanook of the North (film), 302
Narrative
    in analytical essays, 290
    in argument essays, 250
    in ethnographic essays, 325–326
    in personal essays, 88–89
    in profiles, 129
    in research essays, 368
    in review essays, 167
    revision strategies and, 534
Narrative thinking, 65–66
Narrator, 65, 88
Narrowing down subjects
    in analytical essays, 284–286
    in argument essays, 240–242
    in ethnographic essays, 315–317
    in personal essays, 81–92
    in profiles, 118–119
    in proposals, 196–197
    in research essays, 359–361
    in review essays, 157–158
Nathan, Rebekah, "My Freshman Year: Worldliness and Worldview," 306–310
National Geographic (magazine), 299
National Institute on Alcohol Abuse and Alcoholism (NIAAA), 185–189
Neufeld, Josh, "A Matter of Perspective," 67–68
Newspapers. *See* Periodicals and newspapers
Nike, 279
9/11 attacks, 107–109
Note taking
    for ethnographic essays, 318
    field work, 411–412
    in interviews, 124, 403–404
    paraphrasing of, 422
    quotations, 423–424
    summaries, 421–422
    techniques for, 412–415
Noun clauses, 644
Nouns, 621
"Number 6 Orchard" (Fisher), 133–136
Numbers, in sentences, 624–625

O

Objective case, of pronouns, 601–602, 635
Objects and complements, 640–641
Observation, 23, 27, 62–64, 371. *See also* Ethnographic essays
O'Connell, Eric, "German Cowboys," 310
Odd Girl Out (Simmons), 398
Online sources
    APA-style for, 461–462, 464–469, 471–472
    MLA-style for, 436, 451–454
Op-ed essays, 213
Open-ended interview questions, 123
Open-ended survey questions, 407, 408
Openings. *See* Leads; Subjects
Orange County Housewives (tv show), 299
The Orphelia Project, 398

P

Page numbers
    APA-style for, 460
    in double-entry journals, 55
    MLA-style for, 438
De Palma, Paul, "When is Enough Enough?," 545–565
Pamphlets, 454
Pang, Alex Soojung-Kim, "What Does Apple's 'Misunderstood' Advertisement Mean?," 270–272
Pang, Amelia, "The Life of a Violin Prodigy from South Bronx," 109–113
Paradigmatic thinking, 65–66
Paragraphs, clarity in, 544–546, 547. *See also* Drafts; Revision strategies
Parallelism, in sentences, 587–588
Paraphrasing, 422
Parentheses, 617–618
Parenthetical citations. *See* APA documentation style; MLA documentation style
Parlor metaphor (Burke), 532–533
"Passengers" (Frazier), 107–109
Passive/active voice, 549, 597–598, 631–632
Patronizing language, 609–610
Peer review. *See* Workshopping the draft; Writer's workshops
Periodicals and newspapers
    APA-style for, 464–466
    databases for, 394–395
    in hierarchy of sources, 397
    MLA-style for, 449
    print vs. online citations, 449–450
    as research tool, 314–315, 359
Periods, 611
Personal essays, 62–98
    academic writing and, 64–68
    choosing subjects, 66, 76–92
    drafts for, 86–94
    evaluation of, 86–87
    examples of, 67–74
    features of, 66–67
    motives for writing, 64, 66
    narrative thinking, 65–66
    questions for, 66, 75, 83–84, 88, 91
    revision procedures for, 91–94
    sketch writing, 84–87
    student essays, 94–96
    writing about experiences and observations, 62–64
    writing process, 75–91
Personal letters, APA-style for, 461–462
Personal relative pronouns, 605–606, 635–636
Persuasive writing, 527–528. *See also* Review essays
Pew Internet and American Life Project (website), 315
Photo essays
    imagetexts, as argument, 221
    Normandy battle (Benedict), 74–75, 498
    "No Space for Bikes" (Damm), 191–192, 496–497
    "Power House Mechanic Working on a Steam Pump" (Lewis), 262, 263
    in public argument, 213

"Ruth's Vanity," 45–46
"Sun Boy" (Soule), 113–114
Photographs
    as essays, 213
    Google Image Search, 249
    as profiles, 113–114
    in proposals, 191–192
    reading of, 50
    re-genre of writing and, 496–499
    as revision metaphor, 513–514
    in visual ethnography, 300, 302, 310, 322–323
Phrases, 641–643
Plagiarism, 424–428, 438
Plato, 222
Pleasure seeking, as reading perspective, 45
Plot and significant events, 283
Podcasts
    APA-style for, 471
    MLA-style for, 453
    re-genre of writing and, 477–478, 499–501
Poetry
    "The Shield That Came Back" (Momaday), 267–268
Point of view, 283
Policy questions, 29
Polishing of drafts. See Revision procedures
Portfolios, 562–568
    evaluated types of, 563–564
    organization of, 565–566
    purpose of, 564–565
    reflective letter/essay, 16, 566–568
    unevaluated types of, 563
Possessive case, of pronouns, 601–602, 635
Post hoc fallacy, 228
"Power House Mechanic Working on a Steam Pump" (Lewis), 262, 263
Predicates. See Subjects and predicates
Prepositional phrases, 642
Prepositions, 638, 641
"Preventing Alcohol-Related Problems on College Campuses—Summary of the Final Report of the NIAAA Task Force on College Drinking" (Saltz), 185–191

Prewriting, 18, 23, 514–515. See also Journals, writing; Revision strategies
Prezi (software), 488
Primary sources, 290, 397
Problems and solutions. See also Proposals
    in argument essays, 250
    justifications, 202–203
    problems of consequence, 176–177
    problems of manageable scale, 177
Profiles, 99–137
    about people, 99–100
    academic writing and, 101–102
    choosing subjects, 116–119
    digital, 121–122
    drafts for, 129–133
    evaluation of, 118–119
    examples of, 104–114
    features of, 102
    interviewing techniques, 120–125
    as leads, 539
    motives for writing, 100–101, 102
    photographs as, 113–114
    questions for, 102, 115, 130
    revision procedures for, 130–133
    as revision strategy, 532
    sketch writing, 126–127
    student essays, 133–136
    writing process and, 115–133
Prompts
    fastwriting, 78–79, 116–117, 156, 159, 195, 239–240, 282, 314, 357–358
    listing, 78, 116, 156, 194, 238–239, 281, 312–314, 357
    research, 80, 117–118, 157, 195–196, 201–202, 240, 243, 248–249, 282, 314–315, 358–359
    visual, 23, 79–80, 81, 117, 156–157, 195, 240, 282, 314, 358
Pronouns, 601–606
    agreement with antecedents, 603–605, 634
    case, 601–602
    compound antecedents, 604
    demonstrative, 637
    indefinite, 636

indefinite pronoun as antecedents, 604–605
indefinite pronoun as subject, 600
interrogative, 636
masculine, 609
personal relative, 605–606, 635–636
reference to antecedents, 603–604, 634
reflexive/intensive, 636
shifts in person, 605
Proofreading, 513
Proposals, 175–210
    academic writing and, 178–181
    choosing subjects, 180, 196–197
    drafts for, 201–207
    elements of, 179
    examples of, 181–192
    features of, 179–180
    motives for writing, 177–178, 179
    problems and solutions, 175–177
    questions for, 179, 193, 205
    research strategies, 201–202
    sketch writing, 198–201
    student essays, 207–209
    writing process and, 193–199
Public argument essays, 213. See also Argument essays
Public domain, 510
Public service announcements (PSAs), 503–504
Punctuation, 610–618
    brackets, 618
    colons, 616
    commas, 612–615
    dashes, 616–617
    ellipses, 618
    exclamation points, 612
    parentheses, 617–618
    periods, 611
    question marks, 611
    quotation marks, 617
    semicolons, 612
Purpose. See also Revision strategies
    in analytical essays, 286
    in argument essays, 241–242
    cause and effect, 522
    comparison and contrast, 522–523
    in ethnographic essays, 316–317
    focusing questions, 521–522
    of inquiry-based reading, 37–40
    of journal writing, 5
    motive statements, 519

Purpose (*Continued*)
in personal essays, 82, 90
problems with, 517
in profiles, 119
in proposals, 196–197
questions for strengthening,
520–521
as reading frame, 43–46
of reflective letters, 16
in research essays, 361
in review essays, 158
of using sources, 418–419

Q

Qualitative analysis, 261
Questioning, as invention strategy, 23
Question marks, 611
Questionnaires, 452
Questions
in academic discourse, 59
for analytical essays, 280, 291
for argument essays, 237, 252
for ethnographic essays, 300, 311,
317, 327
for inquiry-based writing, 28–29
as leads, 539
open-ended, 123, 407, 408
for personal essays, 66, 75, 83–84,
88, 91
for proposals, 179, 193, 205
for reading to write, 47–49
for research essays, 344, 356, 372
for review essays, 142, 155, 167, 170
revision strategies and, 520–521,
524, 528–529
"So what?" question, 27–28
structured, 407
for surveys, 406–409
"Wh" questions, 200–201
in writing profiles, 102, 115, 130
Question to answer development
in analytical essays, 290
in argument essays, 250
in ethnographic essays, 326
in research essays, 369
in review essays, 167
Quotation marks, 617
Quotations, 423–424, 434, 440, 539

R

Radio programs
essays for, 76, 499–501
MLA-style for, 452

Ranking survey questions, 408
Readers. *See* Audience
Reading, inquiry-based approach,
36–61
academic discourse and, 57–60
aloud to others, 516
beliefs about, 40–42
four frames for, 42–46
genre/medium, 37, 43–46
motives for, 37–40
purposes of, 37–40
questions for, 47–49, 59
reading to write, 47–56
rhetorical choices and, 42–47
*Reading Images: The Grammar of
Visual Design* (Kress and van
Leeuwen), 50
Reading perspectives, 45
Reading to write, 47–56
after-words summary, 56
double-entry journal writing,
49–56
having dialogue with reading
content, 49–56
questions for, 47–49
reading creatively/critically, 53–56
reading visual text, 50
Three-Act notes, 56
Reality TV shows, 299
Reason-evidence loop, in argument,
246–247
"Recipe for a Great Film: Unlikeable
People, Poor Choices, and
Little Redemption" (Burns),
163–164
Recordings. *See also specific types*
APA-style for, 471
of interviews, 121–122, 124, 404
MLA-style for, 452
musical, 471
Recursive writing process, 22
References pages, APA-style,
462–472. *See also* APA
documentation style
authors' names, 463
DOI/URL, 463, 464
format/layout, 458
online sources, 464–469, 471–472
order of sources/information,
462–464
periodicals, 463–464
personal letters, 461–462
print vs. online citations, 464
retrieval dates, 464

title of works, 463
Reflection
in inquiry-based approach, 15–20
as reading perspective, 38, 40, 45
Reflective letters, 16, 566–568
Reflexive/intensive pronouns, 636
Re-genre of writing, 74, 75–76,
474–511
analysis of, 508–509
assignment for, 484–487
blog to podcast (case study),
477–478
brochures, 493–494
citation of multimodal
content, 509
conference posters, 494–496
content levels, 486
as deep revision, 481–484
drafting tools for, 504–509
ethical issues, 509–510
infographics, 490–493
knowledge transfer, 476
"Last Flowers" (Ishii), 265–266
multimodal expression, 478–509
photographic essays, 496–499
podcasts/radio essays, 499–501
slide presentations, 488–490
video PSAs, 503–504
web pages, 501–503
Relationship questions, 28–29
Relationships, in reading visual
text, 50
Repurposing of writing. *See*
Re-genre of writing
Research essays, 341–381
academic writing and, 343–346
choosing subjects, 345, 356–361
drafts for, 366–373
examples of, 347–355
features of, 344–345
motives for writing, 343, 345
questions for, 344, 356, 372
reports and papers, comparison
to, 342–343
research strategies, 358–359, 367
revision procedures for, 372–373
student essays, 374–380
timetables for, 366
writing process and, 356–373
writing proposal for, 362–365
Research logs, 414–415
Research papers, 342–343
Research prompts
for analytical essays, 282

for argument essays, 240, 243, 248–249
for ethnographic essays, 314–315
for personal essays, 80
for profiles, 117–118
for proposals, 195–196, 201–202
for research essays, 358–359
for review essays, 157
Research reports, 342–343
Research techniques, 382–416
  for annotated bibliographies, 570–571
  collection methods, 382–383
  electronic, 383–389
  for ethnographic essays, 323–325
  evaluation of library sources, 397–398
  evaluation of web sources, 400
  fieldwork, 410–412
  focused knowledge and, 391, 393–397
  interviews, 401–405
  as invention strategy, 23
  libraries and, 243, 248
  note taking, 403–404, 411–415
  for profiles, 127–128
  for proposals, 201–202
  for research essays, 367
  research logs, 414–415
  for review essays, 166
  for specific genres, 289
  surveys, 406–410
  working knowledge and, 390–392
Reseeing. See Re-genre of writing; Revision strategies
Resisting, as reading perspective, 45
Restrictive/nonrestrictive modifiers, in sentences, 593–594
Reverse outlines, 541–542
Review essays, 138–174. See also Evaluation
  academic writing and, 140–143
  APA-style for, 469
  choosing subjects, 142, 157–158, 160
  criteria for, 160–163
  drafts for, 167–171
  examples of, 144–154
  features of, 142–143
  MLA-style for, 450
  motives for writing, 139–140, 142
  questions for, 142, 155, 167, 170
  sketch writing, 162–165
  student essays, 171–173

writing an evaluation, 138–139
writing process and, 155–163
Reviews, in academic discourse, 58–59
Revision procedures
  for analytical essays, 291–293
  for argument drafts, 252–253
  for ethnographic essays drafts, 327–329
  for personal essay drafts, 91–94
  for profile drafts, 130–133
  for proposal drafts, 205–207
  for research essays, 372–373
  for review drafts, 169–171
Revision strategies, 512–551
  categories of, 516–518
  dialogue exercise, 518–520
  divorcing the draft, 514–516
  four levels of rewriting, 513
  motives for, 512–514
  problems of clarity and style, 517–518, 542–551
  problems of purpose, 517
  problems with information, 517, 530–533
  problems with meaning, 517, 523–530
  problems with structure, 517, 534–542
Rhetorical analysis, 51, 273
Rhetorical choices, 12–15, 42–46
Roberts, Derek J., "Secret Ink: Tattoo's Place in Contemporary American Culture," 349–350
Rogers, Carl, 224–227
"Ruth's Vanity" (photographic essay), 45–46

S

Sabet, Kevin, "Colorado Will Show Why Legalizing Marijuana is a Mistake," 234–236
Saltz, Robert F., "Preventing Alcohol-Related Problems on College Campuses—Summary of the Final Report of the NIAAA Task Force on College Drinking," 185–191
Sampson, Jafari, 109–113
San Francisco Bicycle Coalition (SFBC), 191–192, 496–497

Scaled response survey questions (Likert), 408
Scenes, 539
Schiesel, Seth "Grand Theft Auto Takes on New York," 150–154
Scripts, 505, 506
Sea and Mountain analogy, in thinking, 26–27
Search engines, 392, 395–397
Secondary sources, 290–291, 397
"Secret Ink: Tattoo's Place in Contemporary American Culture" (Roberts), 349–350
Self-evaluation survey, 17–20
"The Selfie Syndrome" (infographic), 346
Self-perception, as reading frame, 43–46
Semicolons, 612
Semiotic analysis, 273
Sentence boundaries, 578–586
  acceptable fragments, 582
  comma splices, 582–585
  fragments, 578–582
  fused sentences, 585–586
  incomplete thoughts, 582
  phrase fragments, 580–581
  subordinate clause fragments, 578–579
Sentence inconsistencies, 586–591
  coordinate elements, 588–589
  mixed sentences, 589–590
  parallelism, 587–588
  shifts in sentences, 590–591
  subordinate elements, 589
Sentence modification. See Modification of sentences
Sentence patterns, 644–645
Sentences, types of, 645–646
Settings, as literary device, 283
Sexist language, 609–610
Shakespeare, 510
Shander, Bill, 486
Shaping of drafts. See Revision procedures
"On 'The Shield That Came Back'" (Brinkman), 268–269
"The Shield That Came Back" (Momaday), 267–268
Shifts, in sentences, 590–591
Siano, Salvatore, 107–109
Signposts, in academic discourse, 59
Simmons, Rachel, *Odd Girl Out*, 398
Simple sentences, 645

Sketch writing. *See also* Student
    sketches
    for analytical essays, 286–288
    for argument essays, 244–246
    for ethnographic essays, 321–322
    for personal essays, 84–87
    for profiles, 126–127
    for proposals, 198–201
    for review essays, 162–165
Slide presentations, 488–490
Slippery slope fallacy, 228
Small, Cathy. *See* Nathan, Rebekah
"Smoke of Empire" (Marlin), 94–96
Snow, John, 490
"Social Networking Social Good?"
    (Thompson), 253–257
Sociological Abstracts
    (database), 324
Software. *See also specific software*
    APA-style for names of, 471
    for brochures, 493
    for conference posters, 495
    for creating websites/pages, 502
    for infographics, 492
    for photo essays, 498
    for podcasts/radio essays, 500
    for slide presentations, 488, 489
    for transcription, 124
    for video PSAs, 503
Soule, William, "Sun Boy," 113–114
Sources, use of, 417–473. *See also*
    APA documentation style; MLA
    documentation style
    in analytical essays, 264
    citation of, 424–428
    control of information, 417–418
    for ethnographic essays, 301
    paraphrasing, 422
    in personal essays, 67
    in proposals, 180
    purpose of, 418–419
    quotations, 423–424
    in research essays, 345
    summarizing of, 421–422
    synthesizing of, 420–421
    writer as narrator and, 419–420
    in writing profiles, 102
    in writing review essays, 142
"So what?" question, 27–28. *See also*
    specific uses
Speeches, 454
Spelling, 619, 625–628
    doubling final consonants, 625
    homonyms, 627–628

plurals, 627
suffixes, 625
words containing *ie* or *ei*, 626
words with final *e*, 626
words with final *y*, 626
Spirit of inquiry. *See* Inquiry-based
    approach
Stakeholder analysis, in argument,
    218–219
Statistical evidence, 370
Stewart, Amanda, "Earning a Sense
    of Place," 84–85, 87
Stock phrases, 548
Storyboards, 505, 507
Straw man fallacy, 227
Structure, 534–542. *See also* Revision
    strategies
    academic writing and, 535–542
    in analytical essays, 264
    beginning/middle/end, 535–536
    cut-and-paste technique, 540–541
    in ethnographic essays, 301
    multiple leads, 538–540
    in personal essays, 66, 90
    problems with, 517
    in proposals, 180
    in research essays, 345
    reverse outlines, 541–542
    thesis/support and, 536–537
    in writing profiles, 102
    in writing review essays, 142
Structured questions, 407
Student essays
    "All About That Hate: A Critical
        Analysis of 'All About That
        Bass'" (Johnson-Waskow),
        293–296
    "Avoidable Accidents: How
        to Make Reality TV Safer"
        (Appleman), 207–209
    "Beyond Gaydar" (Harter), 328,
        329–339
    "How to Not Feel Good and Feel
        Good About It, A Review of
        Young Adult" (Burns), 171–173
    "Is College Worth It?"
        (Leonhardt), 229–232
    "Number 6 Orchard" (Fisher),
        133–136
    "Smoke of Empire" (Marlin),
        94–96
    "Social Networking Social Good?"
        (Thompson), 253–257

"The 'Unreal Dream': True Crime
    in the Justice System" (Burns),
    374–380
"Why College Football Should Be
    Banned" (Bissinger), 182–184
Student sketches
    "All About That Hate" (Johnson-
        Waskow), 286–288
    "Earning a Sense of Place"
        (Stewart), 84–85, 87
    "Loving and Hating Reality TV"
        (Appleman), 199–200
    "Recipe for a Great Film:
        Unlikeable People,
        Poor Choices, and Little
        Redemption" (Burns), 163–164
    "Twitter a Profound Thought?"
        (Thompson), 244–245
Style, 606–610
    appropriate language, 608–610
    biases/stereotypes, 610
    conciseness, 606–608
    formal/informal language, 608
    gender-exclusive language,
        609–610
    patronizing terms, 609–610
    revision strategies and, 549–551
*Style: Ten Lessons in Clarity and
    Grace* (Williams), 548
Subjective case, of pronouns,
    601–602
Subject knowledge, as reading
    frame, 43–46
Subjects. *See also* Narrowing down
    subjects
    in analytical essays, 264
    in argument essays, 237–240
    in ethnographic essays, 301,
        312–317
    for interviews, 248
    in personal essays, 66, 76–80
    in profiles, 102, 116–119
    in proposals, 180
    in research essays, 345
    in review essays, 142,
        157–158, 160
    in rhetorical choices, 12–15
Subjects and predicates, 639–640
Subject-verb agreement, 599–601
Subjunctive mood, and verbs, 598
Subordinate elements, in
    sentences, 589
Summaries, 421–422

"Sun Boy" (Soule), 113–114
Surprise, 9–12
Surveys
    audience and goals of, 406,
        409–410
    MLA-style for, 452
    paper vs. electronic, 409
    questions for, 406–409
    self-evaluation, 17–20
    testing of, 409
    using results in writing, 410
Suspension of judgment, 8–9

T

Tables/charts/illustrations
    APA-style for, 459
    MLA-style for, 438
*Taking Things Seriously: 75 Objects
    with Unexpected Meanings*
    (Glenn and Hayes), 69, 71
"Tattoo" (infographic), 348
"Tattoos and Piercings: Attitudes,
    Behaviors, and Interpretations
    of College Students" (Horne
    et al.), 353–354
To be, passive voice forms of, 549
Television programs
    APA-style for, 471
    MLA-style for, 452
Tenses of verbs, 596–597, 630–631
Textual evidence, 371
Themes, as literary device, 284
Theron, Charlize, film review,
    163–164, 171–173
Thesis, 524, 525–530
    believing/doubting technique,
        527–528
    concrete vs. abstract
        language, 525
    definition of, 524
    end-weighted with meaning, 525
    instructive line and, 525
    loop writing and, 525–526
    qualifying claims, 529–530
    reclaiming topics, 526–527
    refinement of, 528–530
    structure of, 535–542
Thinking
    dialectically, 24–28
    Sea and Mountain analogy in,
        26–27
    writing process and, 22–28

This I Believe (radio program), 76,
    499–500
Thompson, Florence, 140–141
Thompson, Rebecca
    "Social Networking Social Good?,"
        253–257
    "Twitter a Profound Thought?,"
        244–245
Three-Acts writing process, 56, 344
Title pages
    APA-style for, 455–456
    MLA-style for, 437–438
Title tsunami, 128
Topics. *See also* Subjects
    inverted triangle for focusing on,
        158–159
    reclaiming in thesis writing,
        526–527
    significance of during
        revision, 532
Toulmin, Stephen, 223–224,
    529–530, 533
Transcription software, 124
Transition words, for paragraphs, 547
Tufte, Edward, 488
Tussing, Lauren, annotated
    bibliography, 572–575
"Twitter a Profound Thought?"
    (Thompson), 244–245

U

Underlining. *See* Italics and under-
    lining
Unevaluated portfolios, 563
"The 'Unreal Dream': True Crime in
    the Justice System" (Burns),
    374–380
Updating, as reading perspective, 45
URLs, in APA-style
    documentation, 463

V

Value questions, 28–29
Verbals, in sentences
    gerunds, 633
    infinitives, 634
    participles, 633
Verbs, 595–601
    compound subject, 600
    forms of, 629–630
    helping/auxiliary, 596–597, 633
    indefinite pronoun as subject, 600

intervening relative clause,
    600–601
intervening subordinate
    elements, 599
inverted sentence order, 600
irregular, 597
linking type, 632
mood, 598, 632
passive/active voice, 597–598,
    631–632
person and number
    relationship, 631
subject complements, 599
subject-verb agreement, 599–601
tense, 596–597, 630–631
transitive/intransive, 633
verbals, 633–634
voice, 631–632
Video public service
    announcements, 503–504
Videotapes
    APA-style for, 470
    MLA-style for, 453
Visual ethnography, 300, 302,
    311–312, 322–323
Visual prompts
    for analytical essays, 282
    for argument essays, 240
    clustering, 23, 79–80, 81
    for ethnographic essays, 314
    for personal essays, 79–80
    for profiles, 117
    for proposals, 195
    for research essays, 358
    for review essays, 156–157
Visual text, 50
Voice. *See* Active/passive voice

W

Warrants, in argument, 223–224, 533
Watchers at the Gates, Godwin on, 9
Web pages, 501–503
Websites. *See also* Internet
    academic search directories, 395
    American Anthropological
        Association, 318
    American Fact Finder, 248
    Anthropological Index
        Online, 324
    blogs, 213, 395
    Catalist, 248
    Census Bureau, U.S., 248, 315
    CIA World Factbook, 248

Websites (*Continued*)
Creative Commons, 509
dogpile.com, 392
encyclopedias, 392
evaluation of, 400
Gallup Poll, 315
Google Directory, 315
Google Image Search, 249
Google Scholar, 360, 387–388, 392, 533
Google search engine, 392
Infoplease, 248
Library of Congress, 389, 394
Library of Congress's Veterans History Project, 115, 125
mamma.com, 392
metasearch engines, 395, 396
Pew Internet and American Life Project, 315
search engines, 395–397
subject directories, 395
transcription software, 124
U.S. Census Bureau, 248
WebSitesThatSuck.com, 139
"What Is Relational Aggression?," 398
"When is Enough Enough?" (De Palma), 545–565
Wikipedia, 315, 533
"What Does Apple's 'Misunderstood' Advertisement Mean?" (A. S-K. Pang), 270–272
White, E. B., 100
"Wh" questions, 200–201, 242–243, 528–529
"Why College Football Should Be Banned" (Bissinger), 182–184
"Why Did God Make Flies?" (Conniff), 418–419, 423, 543–544
"Why Do People Get Tattoos?" (Kang and Jones), 351–352
"Why Won't You Die?! The Art of the Jump Scare" (Bishop), 274–278
Wikipedia (website), 315, 533
Wikis, 453
Williams, Joseph, 548
Winfrey, Oprah, 483

Working bibliographies, 398
Working knowledge, in research, 390–392
Works Cited, MLA-style, 440–455. *See also* MLA documentation style
alphabetization, 441
books, 442–446
comparison to APA-style, 454–455
indenting and spacing, 441
nonprint sources, 451–454
periodicals, 446–451
Works Consulted list, 440
Workshopping the draft
for analytical essays, 290–291
for argument essays, 251–252
for ethnographic essays, 326–327
for personal essays, 90–91
for profiles, 130
for proposals, 204–205
for research essays, 371–372
for review essays, 168–169
Workshops. *See* Writer's workshops
World Wide Web. *See* Internet
Writers, in rhetorical choices, 12–15
Writer's block, 21
Writer's workshops, 552–561
being read, 552
directive responses, 556
drafts and, 553
editing workshops, 560
experiential responses, 556
graphing reader interest workshops, 558–559
group reviews, 554–555
initial-response workshops, 557
instructive-lines workshops, 557–558
instructive talk, 553–554
narrative-of-thought workshops, 557
no-response workshops, 556–557
one-on-one reviews, 555
readers' responsibilities in, 555–556
reflection on, 560–561
response formats, 556–560

review of purpose statements, 558
sum-of-the-parts workshops, 559
thesis workshops, 559–560
worksheet, 559
writers' responsibilities in, 555–556
Writing. *See also* Writing process; *specific aspects*
beliefs about, 3–7
habits of mind, 7–12
rhetorical choices, 12–15
Writing badly, 9–10, 16–17, 53–55
Writing portfolios. *See* Portfolios
Writing process. *See also* Inquiry-based approach; *specific aspects*
all-at-once-ness, 6
analytical essays and, 280–293
argument and, 237–253
dialectical thinking and, 24–28
as driven by questions, 28–29
ethnographic essays and, 311–329
personal essays, 75–91
profiles and, 115–133
proposals and, 193–199
as recursive and flexible, 22
research essays and, 356–373
reviews essays, 155–163
that encourages thinking, 23–25
timelines for, 514–515
using interviews in, 404–405
using survey results in, 410
Writing situation, and rhetorical choices, 12–15

Y

Yahoo Groups, 248
Yellow Pages, 402
Young Adult, film review, 163–164, 171–173
YouTube, 213

Z

Zazulak, Laura, "Every Morning for Five Years," 69–71, 76, 89
Zinsser, William, 546